EXPLORING MICROSOFT® OFFICE PROFESSIONAL FOR WINDOWS® 95

Volume I

VERSION 7.0

EXPLORING MICROSOFT® OFFICE PROFESSIONAL FOR WINDOWS® 95

Volume I

VERSION 7.0

Robert T. Grauer / Maryann Barber

University of Miami

Prentice Hall, Upper Saddle River, New Jersey 07458

Acquisitions editor: Carolyn Henderson
Editorial/production supervisor: Greg Hubit Bookworks
Interior and cover design: Suzanne Behnke
Manufacturing buyer: Paul Smolenski
Managing editor: Nicholas Radhuber
Editorial assistant: Audrey Regan
Production coordinator: Renée Pelletier

©1996 by Prentice Hall, Inc.
A Simon & Schuster Company
Upper Saddle River, New Jersey 07458

All rights reserved. No part of this book may be
reproduced, in any form or by any means,
without permission in writing from the publisher.

Printed in the United States of America
10 9 8 7 6 5 4 3 2 1

ISBN 0-13-504069-8

Prentice Hall International (UK) Limited, *London*
Prentice Hall of Australia Pty. Limited, *Sydney*
Prentice Hall of Canada Inc., *Toronto*
Prentice Hall Hispanoamericano, S.A., *Mexico*
Prentice Hall of India Private Limited, *New Delhi*
Prentice Hall of Japan, Inc., *Tokyo*
Simon & Schuster Asia Pte. Ltd., *Singapore*
Editora Prentice Hall do Brasil, Ltda., *Rio de Janeiro*

Contents

PREFACE xi

Microsoft Office for Windows 95: Four Applications in One xvii

Exploring Microsoft Word for Windows 95

1

Microsoft Word 7.0: What Will Word Processing Do for Me? 1

CHAPTER OBJECTIVES 1
OVERVIEW 1
The Basics of Word Processing 2
    Word Wrap 2 The Insertion Point 2
    Toggle Switches 3 Insertion versus
    Overtype 4 Deleting Text 5
Introduction to Microsoft Word 5
The File Menu 8
Learning by Doing 8

HANDS-ON EXERCISE 1: MY FIRST DOCUMENT 10
Troubleshooting 16
The TipWizard 17
HANDS-ON EXERCISE 2: MODIFYING AN EXISTING DOCUMENT 18
The Spell Check 26
    AutoCorrect 28
Save Command 28
    Backup Options 30
HANDS-ON EXERCISE 3: THE SPELL CHECK 31
Summary 35
Key Words and Concepts 36
Multiple Choice 37
Exploring Microsoft Word 38
Practice with Microsoft Word 42
Case Studies 45

2

Gaining Proficiency: Editing and Formatting   47

CHAPTER OBJECTIVES   47
OVERVIEW   47
Select-Then-Do   48
Moving and Copying Text   49
Undo and Redo Commands   49
Find and Replace Commands   50
Scrolling   51
View Menu   53
HANDS-ON EXERCISE 1: EDITING A DOCUMENT   55
Typography   63
 Typeface   63 Type Size   65
 Format Font Command   65
Page Setup Command   67
 Page Breaks   67
An Exercise in Design   68
HANDS-ON EXERCISE 2: CHARACTER FORMATTING   69
Paragraph Formatting   76
 Alignment   76 Indents   76 Tabs   79 Line Spacing   79 Format Paragraph Command   80 Borders and Shading   82
HANDS-ON EXERCISE 3: PARAGRAPH FORMATTING   84
Summary   90
Key Words and Concepts   91
Multiple Choice   92
Exploring Microsoft Word   94
Practice with Microsoft Word   97
Case Studies   101

3

Enhancing a Document: Proofing, Wizards, ClipArt, and WordArt   103

CHAPTER OBJECTIVES   103
OVERVIEW   103
Thesaurus   104
Grammar Check   104
A Résumé and Cover Letter   107
 The Insert Date and Time Command   110
 The Insert Symbol Command   110 Creating an Envelope   111
HANDS-ON EXERCISE 1: PROOFING A DOCUMENT   111
Wizards and Templates   120
HANDS-ON EXERCISE 2: WIZARDS AND TEMPLATES   123
The Insert Object Command   129
 Microsoft ClipArt Gallery   129 Microsoft WordArt   131
HANDS-ON EXERCISE 3: THE CLIPART GALLERY AND WORDART   133
Summary   140
Key Words and Concepts   141
Multiple Choice   141
Exploring Microsoft Word   144
Practice with Microsoft Word   146
Case Studies   151

APPENDIX A: OBJECT LINKING AND EMBEDDING   153

APPENDIX B: TOOLBARS   171

Exploring Microsoft Excel for Windows 95

1

Introduction to Microsoft Excel: What Is a Spreadsheet?   1

CHAPTER OBJECTIVES   1
OVERVIEW   1
Introduction to Spreadsheets   2
   The Professor's Grade Book   3   Row and Column Headings   4   Formulas and Constants   5
Introduction to Microsoft Excel   6
   Toolbars   7   Entering Data   9
The File Menu   9
Learning by Doing   11
HANDS-ON EXERCISE 1: INTRODUCTION TO MICROSOFT EXCEL   11
Modifying the Worksheet   18
   Insert and Delete Commands   18   The Page Setup Command   20
HANDS-ON EXERCISE 2: MODIFYING A WORKSHEET   22
Summary   31
Key Words and Concepts   32
Multiple Choice   32
Exploring Excel 7.0   34
Practice with Excel 7.0   37
Case Studies   39

2

Gaining Proficiency: Copying, Formatting, and Isolating Assumptions   41

CHAPTER OBJECTIVES   41
OVERVIEW   41

A Better Grade Book   42
Cell Ranges   43
Copy Command   43
Move Operation   44
The TipWizard   46
Learning by Doing   46
HANDS-ON EXERCISE 1: CREATING A WORKSHEET   47
Formatting   53
   Column Widths   55   Row Heights   55
Format Cells Command   55
   Numeric Formats   55   Alignment   57   Fonts   58   Borders, Patterns, and Shading   59
HANDS-ON EXERCISE 2: FORMATTING A WORKSHEET   60
A Financial Forecast   69
HANDS-ON EXERCISE 3: A FINANCIAL FORECAST   71
Summary   75
Key Words and Concepts   76
Multiple Choice   76
Exploring Excel 7.0   79
Practice with Excel 7.0   82
Case Studies   85

3

Spreadsheets in Decision Making: What If?   87

CHAPTER OBJECTIVES   87
OVERVIEW   87
Analysis of a Car Loan   88
   PMT Function   89   The Goal Seek Command   90
HANDS-ON EXERCISE 1: ANALYSIS OF A CAR LOAN   90
Home Mortgages   95
   Relative versus Absolute Addresses   97
The Power of Excel   98
   The Fill Handle   98   Pointing   98
   The Function Wizard   98

HANDS-ON EXERCISE 2: MORTGAGE ANALYSIS   100
The Grade Book Revisited   106
   Statistical Functions   107   Arithmetic
   Expressions versus Functions   108
   IF Function   109   VLOOKUP
   Function   111   Scrolling   112
   Freezing Panes   112   Scenario
   Manager   114   AutoFill   114
HANDS-ON EXERCISE 3: THE EXPANDED GRADE BOOK   116
Summary   127
Key Words and Concepts   127
Multiple Choice   128
Exploring Excel 7.0   130
Practice with Excel 7.0   133
Case Studies   136

4

Graphs and Charts: Delivering a Message   139

CHAPTER OBJECTIVES   139
OVERVIEW   139
Chart Types   140
   Pie Charts   141   Column and Bar
   Charts   143

Creating a Chart   146
   The ChartWizard   148   Enhancing a
   Chart   150
HANDS-ON EXERCISE 1: THE CHARTWIZARD   150
Multiple Data Series   160
   Rows versus Columns   162   Default
   Selections   164
HANDS-ON EXERCISE 2: MULTIPLE DATA SERIES   164
Object Linking and Embedding   171
HANDS-ON EXERCISE 3: OBJECT LINKING AND EMBEDDING   172
Additional Chart Types   181
   Line Chart   182   Combination Chart   182
Use and Abuse of Charts   182
   Improper (Omitted) Labels   183   Adding
   Dissimilar Quantities   184
Summary   185
Key Words and Concepts   186
Multiple Choice   186
Exploring Excel 7.0   188
Practice with Excel 7.0   191
Case Studies   194

APPENDIX A: THE SPREADSHEET AUDIT   195
APPENDIX B: TOOLBARS   205

EXPLORING MICROSOFT ACCESS FOR WINDOWS 95

1

Introduction to Microsoft Access: What Is a Database?   1

CHAPTER OBJECTIVES   1
OVERVIEW   1
Case Study: The College Bookstore   2
Introduction to Microsoft Access   3
   The Database Window   3   Tables   4

Learning by Doing   6
HANDS-ON EXERCISE 1: INTRODUCTION TO MICROSOFT ACCESS   6
Maintaining the Database   14
   Find and Replace Commands   14   Data
   Validation   15
Forms, Queries, and Reports   15
HANDS-ON EXERCISE 2: MAINTAINING THE DATABASE   18
Looking Ahead: A Relational Database   25
Summary   28
Key Words and Concepts   29
Multiple Choice   29
Exploring Microsoft Access 7.0   31
Practice with Microsoft Access 7.0   34
Case Studies   37

2

Tables and Forms: Design, Properties, Views, and Wizards   39

CHAPTER OBJECTIVES   39
OVERVIEW   39
Case Study: A Student Database   40
    Include the Necessary Data   41   Store Data in Its Smallest Parts   41   Avoid Calculated Fields   42
Creating a Table   43
    Primary Key   43   Views   44   Properties   45
HANDS-ON EXERCISE 1: CREATING A TABLE   45
Forms   55
    Controls   55   Properties   57   The Form Wizard   57   Modifying a Form   58
HANDS-ON EXERCISE 2: CREATING A FORM   60
A More Sophisticated Form   69
HANDS-ON EXERCISE 3: A MORE SOPHISTICATED FORM   70
Summary   79
Key Words and Concepts   80
Multiple Choice   80
Exploring Microsoft Access 7.0   82
Practice with Microsoft Access 7.0   85
Case Studies   88

3

Information from the Database: Reports and Queries   91

CHAPTER OBJECTIVES   91
OVERVIEW   91
Reports   92
    Anatomy of a Report   94   The Report Wizard   94   Apply What You Know   94
HANDS-ON EXERCISE 1: THE REPORT WIZARD   97
Introduction to Queries   105
    Query Window   105   Data Type   107   Selection Criteria   108
HANDS-ON EXERCISE 2: CREATING A SELECT QUERY   110
Grouping Records   117
HANDS-ON EXERCISE 3: GROUPING RECORDS   119
Summary   130
Key Words and Concepts   131
Multiple Choice   131
Exploring Microsoft Access 7.0   134
Practice with Microsoft Access 7.0   137
Case Studies   140

APPENDIX A: TOOLBARS   141

EXPLORING MICROSOFT POWERPOINT FOR WINDOWS 95

1

Introduction to PowerPoint: Presentations Made Easy   1

CHAPTER OBJECTIVES   1
OVERVIEW   1
A PowerPoint Presentation   2
Introduction to PowerPoint   2
    Toolbars   5   The File Menu   5
Learning by Doing   8
HANDS-ON EXERCISE 1: INTRODUCTION TO POWERPOINT   8
Five Different Views   16
Adding and Deleting Slides   18
HANDS-ON EXERCISE 2: POWERPOINT VIEWS   19
Slide Show Tools   28
    Rehearse Timings   28   Action Items   28   Hidden Slides   30

HANDS-ON EXERCISE 3: SLIDE SHOW TOOLS   30
Summary   37
Key Words and Concepts   37
Multiple Choice   38
Exploring Microsoft PowerPoint 7.0   40
Practice with Microsoft PowerPoint 7.0   42
Case Studies   45

2

Creating a Presentation: Content, Formatting, and Animation   47

CHAPTER OBJECTIVES   47
OVERVIEW   47

Creating a Presentation   48
    The Outline View   48   The AutoContent Wizard   50
Templates   50
HANDS-ON EXERCISE 1: CREATING A PRESENTATION   53
Creating a Slide Show   61
AutoLayouts   61
HANDS-ON EXERCISE 2: ANIMATING THE PRESENTATION   63
Fine-Tuning   70
    The Color Scheme   70   The Background Shading   72   PowerPoint Masters   72   Style Checker   73
HANDS-ON EXERCISE 3: FINE-TUNING A PRESENTATION   74
Summary   81
Key Words and Concepts   81
Multiple Choice   81
Exploring Microsoft PowerPoint 7.0   83
Practice with Microsoft PowerPoint 7.0   87
Case Studies   90

APPENDIX A: TOOLBARS   93

Prerequisites: Essentials of Windows 95   1

A PC Buying Guide   1

The Internet and the World Wide Web   1

INDEX

Preface

Exploring Microsoft Office Professional for Windows 95—Volume I contains selected chapters from individual books in the *Exploring Windows* series. We created the combined book in response to the many instructors who found they could not cover all of the individual books in one course. Hence, instructors seeking greater coverage of specific applications should consider the stand-alone texts: *Exploring Windows 95 and Essential Computing Concepts, Exploring Microsoft Word Version 7.0, Exploring Microsoft Excel Version 7.0, Exploring Microsoft PowerPoint Version 7.0,* and *Exploring Microsoft Access Version 7.0.* Other books include *Exploring the Internet* and *Exploring Microsoft Office Professional—Volume II.* The latter contains the advanced chapters and appendices from the individual books that were not included in *Volume I.*

The *Exploring Windows* series is different from other books, both in its scope and in the way in which material is presented. Students learn by doing. Concepts are stressed and memorization is minimized. Shortcuts and other important information are consistently highlighted in the many tips that appear throughout the series. Every chapter contains an average of three guided exercises to be completed at the computer.

Each book in the *Exploring Windows* series is accompanied by a comprehensive Instructor's Resource Manual (also available on CD-ROM) with tests, transparency masters, and student/instructor resource disks. Instructors can also use the Prentice Hall Computerized Online Testing System to prepare customized tests for their courses and may obtain Interactive Multimedia courseware as a further supplement. The *Exploring Windows* series is part of the Prentice Hall custom binding program.

What's New

Exploring Microsoft Office Professional—Volume I is a revision of our existing text on Microsoft Office. In addition to updating our book to reflect changes in Windows 95, we sought to add topics that were previously omitted. Chapter 2 in Excel, for example, has been expanded to include a financial forecast that teaches the development of a spreadsheet model. Chapter 3 in Word emphasizes Object Linking and Embedding. We also added an introductory section on Microsoft Office that emphasizes the common user interface and shows how knowledge of one Office application helps in learning another. We added a supplement on Windows 95 and a brief introduction to the Internet. And finally, we created *Exploring Microsoft Office Professional—Volume II,* which is intended for an intermediate course in microcomputer applications, as it continues where this book ends.

We believe, however, that our most important improvement is the expanded end-of-chapter material, which provides a wide variety of student assignments. Every chapter contains 15 *multiple-choice questions* (with answers) so that students can test themselves quickly and objectively. Every chapter has *four conceptual problems* that do not require participation at the computer. Every chapter also has *four computer-based practice exercises* to build student proficiency. And finally, every chapter ends with *four case studies* in which the student is given little guidance in the means of solution.

FEATURES AND BENEFITS

Exploring Microsoft Office Professional is written for the computer novice and assumes no previous knowledge about Windows 95. Each application (Word, Excel, Access, and PowerPoint) begins with an introductory chapter.

An introductory section on the Microsoft Office emphasizes the benefits of the common user interface. Although the text assumes no previous knowledge, some users may already be acquainted with another Office application, in which case they can take advantage of what they already know.

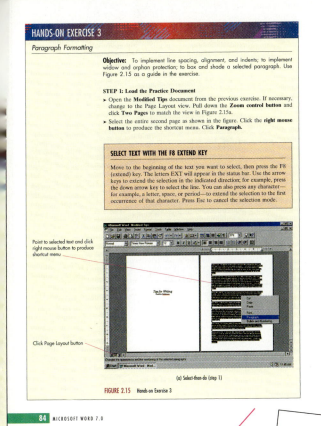

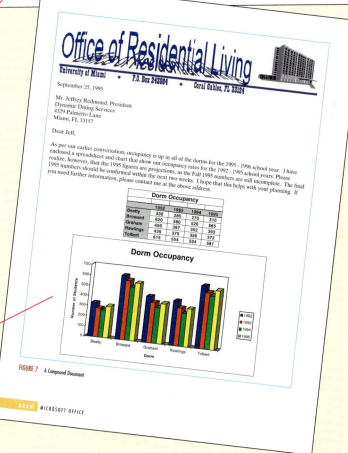

FIGURE 7 A Compound Document

A total of 34 in-depth tutorials (hands-on exercises) guide the reader at the computer. Each tutorial is illustrated with large, full-color, screen captures that are clear and easy to read. Each tutorial is accompanied by numerous tips that present different ways to accomplish a given task, but in a logical and relaxed fashion.

Object Linking and Embedding is stressed throughout the series, beginning in the introductory section on Microsoft Office, where the reader is shown the power of this all-important technology. Examples of OLE appear throughout the book and are distinguished by an OLE icon. Appendix A in Word, on pages 153–170, provides additional information.

PRACTICE WITH EXCEL 7.0

1. Figure 2.14 contains a worksheet that was used to calculate the difference between the Asking Price and Selling Price on various real estate listings that were sold during June, as well as the commission paid to the real estate agency as a result of selling those listings. Complete the worksheet, following the steps outlined below:

   a. Open the partially completed *Chapter 2 Practice 1* workbook on the data disk, then save the workbook as *Finished Chapter 2 Practice 1*.
   b. Click cell E5 and enter the formula to calculate the difference between the asking price and the selling price for the property belonging to Mr. Landry.
   c. Click cell F5 and enter the formula to calculate the commission paid to the agency as a result of selling the property. (Pay close attention to the difference between relative and absolute cell references.)
   d. Select cells E5:F5 and copy the formulas to E6:F11 to calculate the difference and commission for the rest of the properties.
   e. Click cell C13 and enter the formula to calculate the total asking price, which is the sum of the asking prices for the individual listings in cells C5:C11.
   f. Copy the formula in C13 to the range D13:F13 to calculate the other totals.
   g. Select the range C5:F13 and format the numbers so that they display with dollar signs and commas, and no decimal places (e.g., $450,000).
   h. Click cell B15 and format the number as a percentage.
   i. Click cell A1 and center the title across the width of the worksheet. With the cell still selected, select cells A3:F4 as well and change the font to 12 point Arial bold italic.
   j. Select cells A4:F4 and create a bottom border to separate the headings from the data.
   k. Select cells F5:F11 and shade the commissions.
   l. Print the worksheet.

FIGURE 2.14 Spreadsheet for Practice Exercise 1

2. The Sales Invoice: Use Figure 2.15 as the basis for a sales invoice that you will create and submit to your instructor. Your spreadsheet should follow the general format shown in the figure with respect to including a uniform discount for each item. Your spreadsheet should also include the sales tax. The discount percentage and sales tax percentage should be entered in a separate area so that they can be easily modified.

   Use your imagination and sell any product at any price. You must, however, include at least four items in your invoice. Formatting is important, but you need not follow our format exactly. See how creative you can be, then submit your completed invoice to your instructor for inclusion in a class contest for the best invoice. Be sure your name appears somewhere on the worksheet as a sales associate. If you are really ambitious, you might include an object from the ClipArt Gallery.

FIGURE 2.15 Spreadsheet for Practice Exercise 2

3. The Probability Expert: How much would you bet *against* two people in your class having the same birthday? Don't be too hasty, for the odds of two classmates sharing the same birthday (month and day) are much higher than you would expect. For example, there is a fifty percent chance (.5063) in a class of 23 students that two people will have been born on the same day, as shown in the spreadsheet in Figure 2.16. The probability jumps to seventy percent (.7053) in a class of 30, and to ninety percent (.9025) in a class of 41. Don't take our word for it, but try the experiment in your class.

   You need a basic knowledge of probability to create the spreadsheet. In essence you calculate the probability of individuals not having the same birthday, then subtract this number from one, to obtain the probability of the event coming true. In a group of two people, for example, the probability of not being born on the same day is 365/366; i.e., the second person can be born on any of 365 days and still have a different birthday. The probability of two people having the same birthday becomes 1 − 365/366.

   The probability for different birthdays in a group of three is (365/366)*(364/366); the probability of not having different birthdays—that is, of two people having the same birthday, is one minus this number. Each row in the spreadsheet is calculated from the previous row. It's not as hard as it looks, and the results are quite interesting!

CASE STUDIES

The Financial Consultant

A friend of yours is in the process of buying a home and has asked you to compare the payments and total interest on a 15- and a 30-year loan. You want to do as professional a job as possible and have decided to analyze the loans in Excel, then incorporate the results into a memo written in Microsoft Word. As of now, the principal is $150,000, but it is very likely that your friend will change his mind several times, and so you want to use the OLE capability within Windows to dynamically link the worksheet to the word processing document. Your memo should include a letterhead that takes advantage of the formatting capabilities within Word; a graphic logo would be a nice touch.

Compensation Analysis

A corporation typically uses several different measures of compensation in an effort to pay its employees fairly. Most organizations closely monitor an employee's salary history, keeping both the present and previous salary in order to compute various statistics, including:

- The percent salary increase, which is computed by taking the difference between the present and previous salary, and dividing by the previous salary.
- The months between increase, which is the elapsed time between the date the present salary took effect and the date of the previous salary. (Assume 30 days per month for ease of calculation.)
- The annualized rate of increase, which is the percent salary increase divided by the months between increase; for example, a 5% raise after 6 months is equivalent to an annualized increase of 10%; a 5% raise after two years is equivalent to an annual increase of 2.5%.

Use the data in the *Compensation Analysis* workbook on the data disk to compute salary statistics for the employees who have had a salary increase; employees who have not received an increase should have a suitable indication in the cell. Compute the average, minimum, and maximum value for each measure of compensation for those employees who have received an increase.

The Automobile Dealership

The purchase of a car usually entails extensive bargaining between the dealer and the consumer. The dealer has an asking price but typically settles for less. The commission paid to a salesperson depends on how close the selling price is to the asking price. Exotic Motors has the following compensation policy for its sales staff:

- A 3% commission on the actual selling price for cars sold at 95% or more of the asking price.
- A 2% commission on the actual selling price for cars sold at 90% or more (but less than 95%) of the asking price
- A 1% commission on the actual selling price for cars sold at less than 90% of the asking price. The dealer will not go below 85% of his asking price.

Chapter 1 in each section introduces the basics of the specific application. No previous knowledge is assumed on the part of the reader.

The *Exploring Windows* series emphasizes concepts as well as keystrokes and mouse clicks. Students are provided with the rationale for what they are doing, and are able to extend the information to additional learning on their own.

INTRODUCTION TO MICROSOFT ACCESS: WHAT IS A DATABASE?

OBJECTIVES

After reading this chapter you will be able to:

1. Define the terms field, record, table, and database.
2. Start Microsoft Access; describe the Database window and the objects in an Access database.
3. Add, edit, and delete records within a table; use the Find command to locate a specific record.
4. Describe the record selector; explain when changes are saved to a database.
5. Explain the importance of data validation in table maintenance.
6. Describe a relational database; distinguish between a one-to-many and a many-to-many relationship.

OVERVIEW

All businesses and organizations maintain data of one kind or another. Companies store data about their employees. Schools and universities store data about their students and faculties. Magazines and newspapers store data about their subscribers. The list goes on and on, and while each of these examples refers to different types of data, they all operate under the same basic principles of database management.

This chapter provides a broad-based introduction to database management through the example of a college bookstore. We begin by showing how the mechanics of manual record keeping can be extended to a computerized system. We discuss the basic operations in maintaining data and stress the importance of data validation.

The chapter also introduces you to Microsoft Access, the fourth major application in the Microsoft Office Professional suite. We describe the objects within an Access database and show you how to add, edit, and delete records in an Access table. We also explain how

1

FIVE DIFFERENT VIEWS

PowerPoint offers five different views in which to create, modify, and show a presentation. Figure 1.6 shows the five views for the introductory presentation from the first exercise. Each view represents a different way of looking at the presentation, and each view has unique capabilities. Some views display only a single slide, whereas others show multiple slides, making it easy to organize the presentation. You can switch back and forth between the views by clicking the appropriate view button at the bottom of the presentation window.

The *Slide view* in Figure 1.6a displays one slide at a time and enables all operations for that slide. You can enter, delete, or format text. You can draw or add objects such as a graph, clip art, or an organization chart. The *Drawing Toolbar* is displayed by default in this view.

The *Slide Sorter view* in Figure 1.6b displays multiple slides on the screen (each slide is in miniature) and lets you see the overall flow of the presentation. You can change the order of a presentation by clicking and dragging a slide from one position to another. You can delete a slide by clicking the slide and pressing the Del key. You can also set transition (animation) effects on each slide to add interest to the presentation. The Slide Sorter view has its own toolbar, which is discussed in Chapter 2 in conjunction with creating transition effects.

The *Outline view* in Figure 1.6c shows the presentation in outline form. You can see all of the text on every slide, but you cannot see the graphic elements that may be present on the individual slides. (A different icon appears next to the slides containing a graphic element.) The Outline view is the fastest way to enter or edit text, in that you type directly into the outline. You can copy and/or move text from one slide to another. You can also rearrange the order of the slides within the presentation. The Outline view has its own toolbar and is discussed more fully in Chapter 2.

The *Notes Pages view* in Figure 1.6d lets you create speaker's notes for some or all of the slides in a presentation. These notes do not appear when you show the presentation, but can be printed for use during the presentation to help you remember what you want to say about each slide.

The *Slide Show view* displays the slides one at a time as an electronic presentation on the computer. The show may be presented manually, where you click the mouse to move from one slide to the next. The presentation can also be shown automatically, where each slide stays on the screen for a predetermined amount of time, after which the next slide appears automatically. Either way, the slide show may contain transition effects from one slide to the next as was demonstrated in the first hands-on exercise.

The easiest way to switch from one view to another is by clicking the appropriate view button. The buttons are displayed in the lower-left part of the screen (above the status bar) in all views except the Slide Show view.

POWERPOINT VIEWS

PowerPoint has five different views of a presentation, each with unique capabilities. Anything you do in one view is automatically reflected in the other views. If, for example, you rearrange the slides in the Slide Sorter view, the new arrangement is reflected in the Outline view. In similar fashion, if you add or format text in the Outline view, the changes are also made in the Slide view.

Drawing toolbar

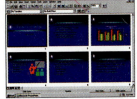
Slide Sorter toolbar

(a) Slide View

(b) Slide Sorter View

Outline toolbar

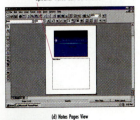
Speaker notes can be entered

(c) Outline View

(d) Notes Pages View

(e) Slide Show View

FIGURE 1.6 PowerPoint Views

PREFACE XV

Acknowledgments

We want to thank the many individuals who helped bring this project to fruition. We are especially grateful to our editors at Prentice Hall, Carolyn Henderson and P. J. Boardman, without whom the series would not have been possible. Cecil Yarbrough and Susan Hoffman did an outstanding job in checking the manuscript and proofs for technical accuracy. Suzanne Behnke developed the innovative and attractive design. Phyllis Bregman helped us to go online. Grace Walkus produced the CD-ROM for the Instructor Manuals, and Gretchen Marx of Saint Joseph College and Carlotta Eaton of Radford University wrote the text. Nicholas Radhuber was managing editor. Paul Smolenski was senior manufacturing supervisor. Greg Hubit was in charge of production and kept the project on target from beginning to end. Nancy Evans and Deborah Emry, our marketing managers at Prentice Hall, developed the innovative campaigns that made the series a success. We also want to acknowledge our reviewers who, through their comments and constructive criticism, greatly improved the *Exploring Windows* series.

Lynne Band, Middlesex Community College
Stuart P. Brian, Holy Family College
Carl M. Briggs, Indiana University School of Business
Kimberly Chambers, Scottsdale Community College
Alok Charturvedi, Purdue University
Jerry Chin, Southwest Missouri State University
Dean Combellick, Scottsdale Community College
Cody Copeland, Johnson County Community College
Larry S. Corman, Fort Lewis College
Janis Cox, Tri-County Technical College
Martin Crossland, Southwest Missouri State University
Paul E. Daurelle, Western Piedmont Community College
David Douglas, University of Arkansas
Carlotta Eaton, Radford University
Raymond Frost, Central Connecticut State University
James Gips, Boston College
Vernon Griffin, Austin Community College
Michael Hassett, Fort Hays State University
Wanda D. Heller, Seminole Community College
Bonnie Homan, San Francisco State University
Ernie Ivey, Polk Community College
Mike Kelly, Community College of Rhode Island
Jane King, Everett Community College
John Lesson, University of Central Florida
David B. Meinert, Southwest Missouri State University
Alan Moltz, Naugatuck Valley Technical Community College
Kim Montney, Kellogg Community College
Kevin Pauli, University of Nebraska
Mary McKenry Percival, University of Miami
Delores Pusins, Hillsborough Community College
Gale E. Rand, College Misericordia
Judith Rice, Santa Fe Community College
David Rinehard, Lansing Community College
Marilyn Salas, Scottsdale Community College
John Shepherd, Duquesne University
Helen Stoloff, Hudson Valley Community College
Mike Thomas, Indiana University School of Business
Suzanne Tomlinson, Iowa State University
Karen Tracey, Central Connecticut State University
Sally Visci, Lorain County Community College
David Weiner, University of San Francisco
Connie Wells, Georgia State University
Wallace John Whistance-Smith, Ryerson Polytechnic University
Jack Zeller, Kirkwood Community College

A final word of thanks to the unnamed students at the University of Miami who make it all worthwhile. And most of all, thanks to you, our readers, for choosing this book. Please feel free to contact us with any comments and suggestions.

Robert T. Grauer
RGRAUER@UMIAMI.MIAMI.EDU
http://www.bus.miami.edu/~rgrauer

Maryann Barber
MBARBER@UMIAMI.MIAMI.EDU
http://www.bus.miami.edu/~mbarber

MICROSOFT OFFICE FOR WINDOWS 95: FOUR APPLICATIONS IN ONE

OVERVIEW

Word processing, spreadsheets, and data management have always been significant microcomputer applications. The early days of the PC saw these applications emerge from different vendors with radically different user interfaces. WordPerfect, Lotus, and dBASE, for example, were dominant applications in their respective areas, and each was developed by a different company. The applications were totally dissimilar, and knowledge of one application did not help in learning another.

The widespread acceptance of Windows 3.1 promoted the concept of a common user interface, which required all applications to follow a consistent set of conventions. This meant that all applications worked essentially the same way, and it provided a sense of familiarity when you learned a new application, since every application presented the same user interface. The development of a suite of applications from a single vendor extended this concept by imposing additional similarities on all applications within the suite.

This introduction will acquaint you with the ***Microsoft Office for Windows 95*** and its four major applications—Word, Excel, PowerPoint, and Access. Our primary purpose is to emphasize the similarities between these applications and to help you extend your knowledge from one application to the next. You will find the same commands in the same menus. You will also recognize familiar toolbars and will be able to take advantage of similar keyboard shortcuts. Our goal is to show you how much you already know and to get you up and running as quickly as possible.

The introduction also introduces you to Schedule+, and to shared applications and utilities such as the ClipArt Gallery and WordArt, which are included within Microsoft Office. We discuss the Office Shortcut Bar and describe how to start an application and open a new or existing document. We also introduce you to Object Linking and Embedding, which enables you to combine data from multiple applications into a single document.

> **TRY THE COLLEGE BOOKSTORE**
>
> Any machine you buy will come with Windows 95, but that is only the beginning since you must also obtain the application software you intend to run. Many first-time buyers are surprised that they have to pay extra for software, so you had better allow for software in your budget. Some hardware vendors will bundle (at no additional cost) Microsoft Office as an inducement to buy from them. If you have already purchased your system and you need software, the best place to buy Microsoft Office is the college bookstore, where it can be obtained at a substantial educational discount.

MICROSOFT OFFICE FOR WINDOWS 95

All Office applications share the common user interface for Windows 95 with which you may already be familiar. (If you are new to Windows 95, then read the appendix on the "Essentials of Windows 95," which appears at the end of this book.) Figure 1 displays a screen from each application in the Microsoft Office—Word, Excel, PowerPoint, and Access, in Figures 1a, 1b, 1c, and 1d, respectively. Look closely at Figure 1, and realize that each screen contains both an application window and a document window, and that each document window has been maximized within the application window. The title bars of the application and document windows have been merged into a single title bar that appears at the top of the application window. The title bar displays the application (e.g., Microsoft Word in Figure 1a) as well as the name of the document (Letter to My Instructor in Figure 1a) on which you are working.

All four screens in Figure 1 are similar in appearance despite the fact that the applications accomplish very different tasks. Each application window has an identifying icon, a menu bar, a title bar, and a minimize, maximize or restore, and a close button. Each document window has its own identifying icon, and its own minimize, maximize or restore, and close button. The Windows 95 taskbar appears at the bottom of each application window and shows the open applications. The status bar appears above the taskbar and displays information relevant to the window or selected object.

Each application in Microsoft Office uses a consistent command structure in which the same basic menus are found in all applications. The File, Edit, View, Insert, Tools, Window, and Help menus are present in all four applications. The same commands are found in the same menus. The Save, Open, Print, and Exit commands, for example, are contained in the File menu. The Cut, Copy, Paste, and Undo commands are found in the Edit menu.

The means for accessing the pull-down menus are consistent from one application to the next. Click the menu name on the menu bar, or press the Alt key plus the underlined letter of the menu name; for example, press Alt+F to pull down the File menu. If you already know some keyboard shortcuts in one application, there is a good chance that the shortcuts will work in another application. Ctrl+Home and Ctrl+End, for example, move to the beginning and end of a document, respectively. Ctrl+B, Ctrl+I, and Ctrl+U boldface, italicize, and underline text. Ctrl+X (the "X" is supposed to remind you of a pair of scissors), Ctrl+C, and Ctrl+V will cut, copy, and paste, respectively. You may not know what these commands do now, but once you learn how they work in one application, you will intuitively know how they work in the others.

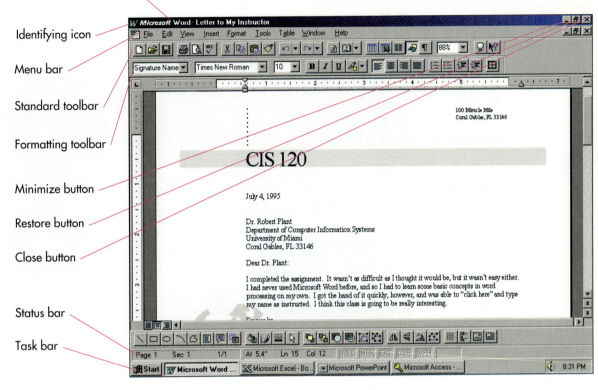

(a) Microsoft Word

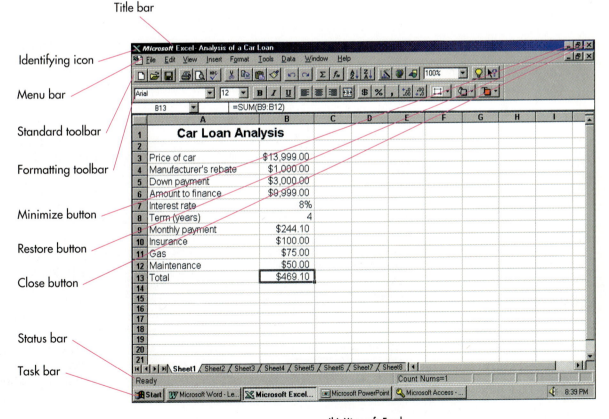

(b) Microsoft Excel

FIGURE 1   The Common User Interface

FIGURE 1 The Common User Interface (continued)

All four applications use consistent (and often identical) dialog boxes. The dialog boxes to open and close a file, for example, are identical in every application. All four applications also share a common dictionary. The AutoCorrect feature (to correct common spelling mistakes) works identically in all four applications. The help feature also functions identically.

There are, of course, differences between the applications. Each application has its own unique menus and associated toolbars. Nevertheless, the Standard and Formatting toolbars in all applications contain many of the same tools (especially the first several tools on the left of each toolbar). The ***Standard toolbar*** contains buttons for basic commands such as Open, Save, or Print. It also contains buttons to cut, copy, and paste, and all of these buttons are identical in all four applications. The ***Formatting toolbar*** provides access to common formatting operations such as boldface, italics, or underlining, or changing the font or point size, and again, these buttons are identical in all four applications. ToolTips are present in all applications. Suffice it to say, therefore, that once you know one Office application, you have a tremendous head start in learning another.

> **MICROSOFT OFFICE VERSUS OFFICE PROFESSIONAL**
>
> Microsoft distributes two versions of the Office Suite: Standard Office and Office Professional. Both versions include Word, Excel, and PowerPoint. The Office Professional also has Microsoft Access. The difference is important when you are shopping and comparing prices from different sources. Be sure to purchase the version that is appropriate for your needs.

Online Help

Each application in the Microsoft Office has the extensive ***online help*** facility as shown in Figure 2. Help is available at any time, and is accessed from the application's Help menu. (The Help screens in Figure 2 pertain to Microsoft Office, as opposed to a specific application, and were accessed through the Answer Wizard button on the Office Shortcut Bar.)

The ***Contents tab*** in Figure 2a is similar to the table of contents in an ordinary book. The major topics are represented by books, each of which can be opened to display additional topics. Each open book displays one or more topics, which may be viewed and/or printed to provide the indicated information.

The ***Index tab*** in Figure 2b is analogous to the index of an ordinary book. Type the first several letters of the topic to look up, such as "he" in Figure 2b. Help then returns all of the topics beginning with the letters you entered. Select the topic you want, then display the topic for immediate viewing, or print it for later reference.

The ***Answer Wizard*** in Figure 2c lets you ask questions in your own words, then it returns the relevant help topics. The Help screen in Figure 2d was accessed from the selections provided by the Answer Wizard, and it, in turn, will lead you to new features in the individual applications.

Office Shortcut Bar

The ***Microsoft Office Shortcut Bar*** provides immediate access to each application within Microsoft Office. It consists of a row of buttons and can be placed anywhere on the screen. The Shortcut Bar is anchored by default on the right side of the desktop, but you can position it along any edge, or have it "float" in the middle of the desktop. You can even hide it from view when it is not in use.

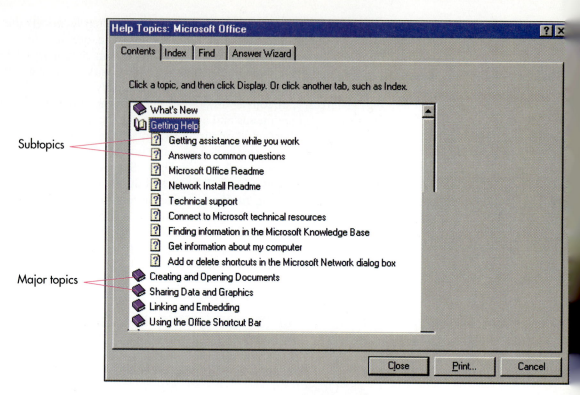

(a) Contents Tab

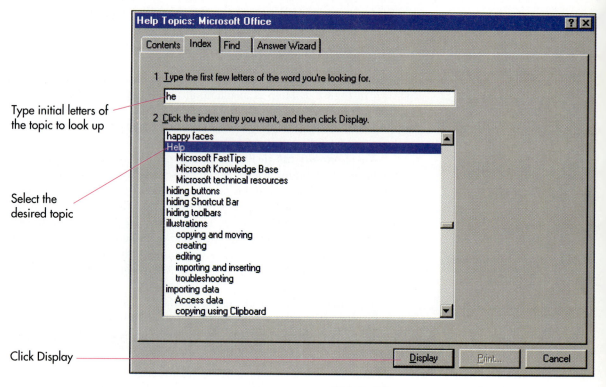

(b) Index Tab

FIGURE 2 Online Help

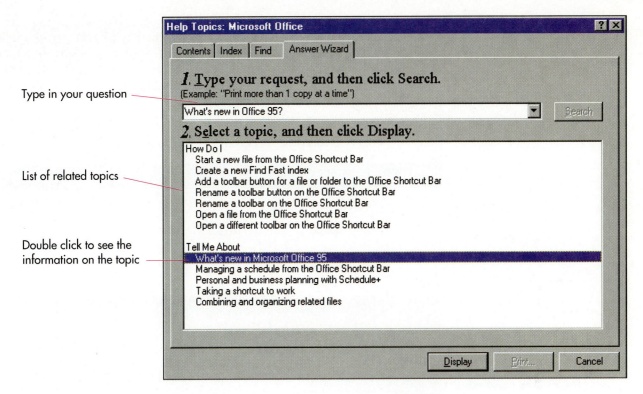

(c) Answer Wizard

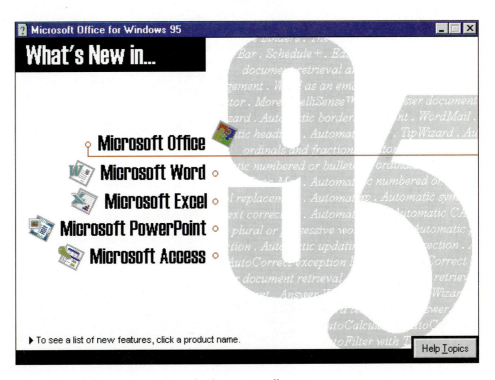

(d) What's New in Office 95?

FIGURE 2 Online Help (continued)

Figure 3a displays the Shortcut Bar as it appears on our desktop. The buttons that are displayed (and the order in which they appear) are established through the Customize dialog box in Figure 3b. (We show you how to customize the Shortcut Bar in the hands-on exercise that follows shortly.) Our Shortcut Bar contains a button for each Office application, a button for the Windows Explorer, and a button to access help.

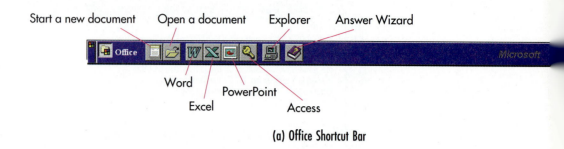

(a) Office Shortcut Bar

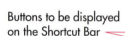

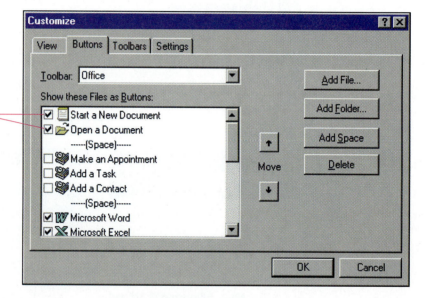

(b) Customize Dialog Box

FIGURE 3 Office Shortcut Bar

Docucentric Orientation

Our Shortcut Bar contains two additional buttons: to open an existing document and to start a new document. These buttons are very useful and take advantage of the "docucentric" orientation of Microsoft Office, which lets you think in terms of a document rather than the associated application. You can still open a document in traditional fashion, by starting the application (e.g., clicking its button on the Shortcut Bar), then using the File Open command to open the document. It's easier, however, to locate the document, then double click its icon, which automatically loads the associated program.

Consider, for example, the Open dialog box in Figure 4a, which is displayed by clicking the Open a Document button on the Shortcut Bar. The Open dialog box is common to all Office applications, and it works identically in each application. The My Documents folder is selected in Figure 4a, and it contains four documents of various file types. The documents are displayed in the Details view,

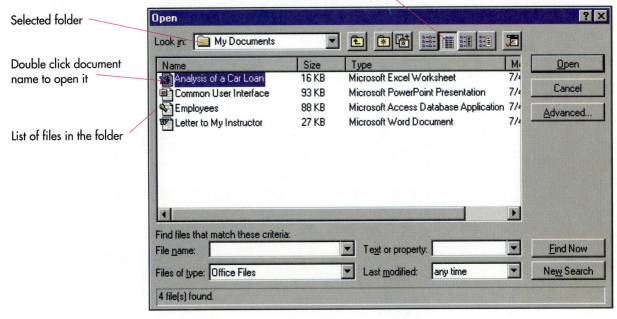

(a) Open an Existing Document

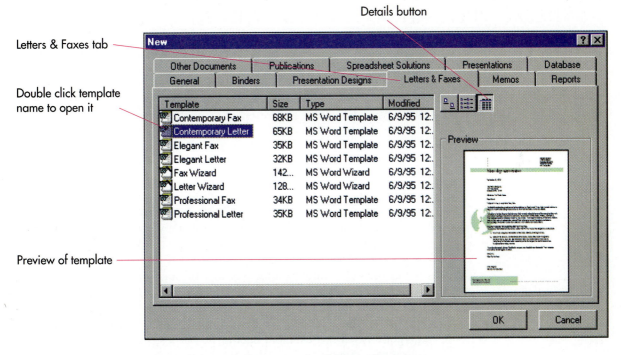

(b) Start a New Document

FIGURE 4   Document Orientation

which shows the document name, size, file type, and date and time the document was last modified. To open any document—for example, "Analysis of a Car Loan"—just double click its name or icon. The associated application (Microsoft Excel in this example) will be started automatically; and it, in turn, will open the selected workbook.

The "docucentric" orientation also applies to new documents. Click the Start a New Document button on the Office Shortcut Bar, and you display the New dialog box in Figure 4b. Click the tab corresponding to the type of document you want to create, such as Letters & Faxes in Figure 4b. Change to the Preview view then click (select) various templates so that you can choose the one most appropriate for your purpose. Double click the desired template to start the application which opens the template and enables you to create the document.

> **CHANGE THE VIEW**
>
> The toolbar in the Open dialog box displays the documents within the selected folder in one of several views. Click the Details button to switch to the Details view and see the date and time the file was last modified, as well as its size and type. Click the List button to display an icon representing the associated application, enabling you to see many more files than in the Details view. The Preview button lets you see a document before you open it. The Properties button displays information about the document, including the number of revisions.

SHARED APPLICATIONS AND UTILITIES

Microsoft Office includes a fifth application, Schedule+, as well as several smaller applications and shared utilities. ***Schedule+*** can be started from the Office Shortcut Bar or from the submenu for Microsoft Office, which is accessed through the Programs command on the Start button. Figure 6a displays one screen from Schedule+, providing some indication of what the application can do.

In essence, Schedule+ is a personal information manager that helps you schedule (and keep) appointments. It will display your schedule on a daily, weekly, or monthly basis. It will beep to remind you of appointments. It will also maintain a list of important phone numbers and contacts. Schedule+ is beyond the scope of our text, but it is an easy application to learn since it follows the common user interface and has a detailed help facility.

The other applications (or applets as they are sometimes known) are easy to miss because they do not appear as buttons on the Shortcut Bar. Nor do they appear as options on any menu. Instead, these applications are loaded from within one of the major applications, typically through the Insert Object command. Two of the more popular applications, the ***ClipArt Gallery*** and ***WordArt,*** are illustrated in Figures 6b and 6c, respectively.

The ClipArt Gallery contains more than 1,100 clip art images in 26 different categories. Select a category such as Cartoons, select an image such as the duck smashing a computer, then click the Insert command button to insert the clip art into a document. Once an object is inserted into a document (regardless of whether it is a Word document, an Excel worksheet, a PowerPoint presentation, or an Access form or report), it can be moved and sized like any other Windows object.

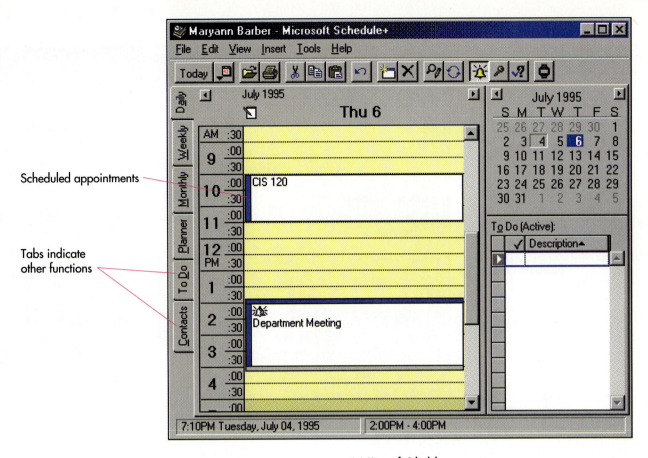

(a) Microsoft Schedule+

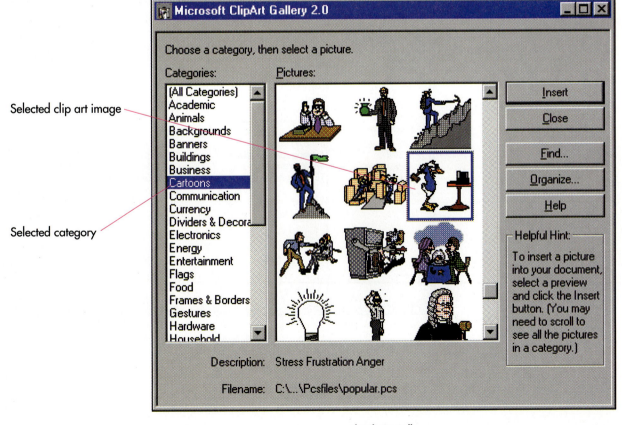

(b) ClipArt Gallery

FIGURE 6 Shared Applications

MICROSOFT OFFICE xxvii

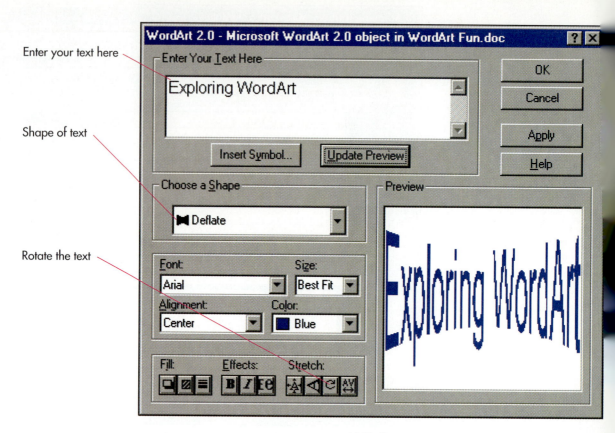

(c) WordArt

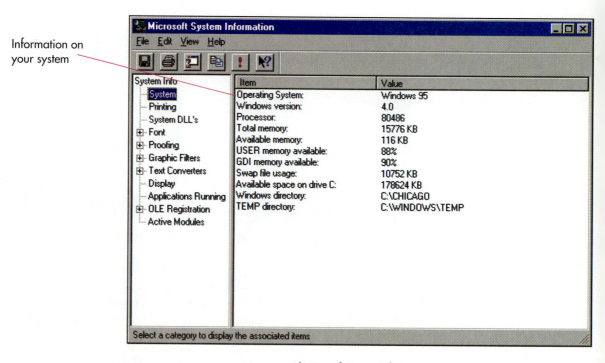

(d) Microsoft System Information

FIGURE 6 Shared Applications (continued)

WordArt enables you to create special effects with text. It lets you rotate and/or flip text, shade it, slant it, arch it, or even print it upside down. WordArt is intuitively easy to use. In essence, you enter the text in the dialog box of Figure 6c, choose a shape from the drop-down list box, then choose a font and point size. You can boldface or italicize the text or add special effects such as stretching or shadows.

The *System Information Utility* in Figure 6d is accessed from any major application by pulling down the Help menu, clicking the About button, then clicking the System Info command button. The utility provides detailed information about all aspects of your system. The information may prove to be invaluable should problems arise on your system and you need to supply technical details to support personnel.

THE OTHER SHARED APPLICATIONS

Microsoft Office includes several additional applications whose functions can be inferred from their names. The Equation Editor, Organization Chart, Data Map, and Graph utilities are accessed through the Insert Object command. All of these applications are straightforward and easy to use as they follow the common user interface and provide online help.

OBJECT LINKING AND EMBEDDING

The applications in Microsoft Office are thoroughly integrated with one another. They look alike and they work in consistent fashion. Equally important, they share information through a technology known as **Object Linking and Embedding** (OLE), which enables you to create a *compound document* containing data (objects) from multiple applications.

The compound document in Figure 7 was created in Word, and it contains objects (a worksheet and a chart) that were created in Excel. The letterhead uses a logo that was taken from the ClipArt Gallery, while the name and address of the recipient were drawn from an Access database. The various objects were inserted into the compound document through linking or embedding, which are actually two very different techniques. Both operations, however, are much more sophisticated than simply pasting an object, because with either linking or embedding, you can edit the object by using the tools of the original application.

The difference between linking and embedding depends on whether the object is stored within the compound document (*embedding*) or in its own file (*linking*). An *embedded object* is stored in the compound document, which in turn becomes the only user (client) of that object. A *linked object* is stored in its own file, and the compound document is one of many potential clients of that object. The compound document does not contain the linked object per se, but only a representation of the object as well as a pointer (link) to the file containing the object. The advantage of linking is that the document is updated automatically if the object changes.

The choice between linking and embedding depends on how the object will be used. Linking is preferable if the object is likely to change and the compound document requires the latest version. Linking should also be used when the same object is placed in many documents so that any change to the object has to be made in only one place. Embedding should be used if you need to take the object with you—for example, if you intend to edit the document on a different computer.

Office of Residential Living

University of Miami • P.O. Box 243984 • Coral Gables, FL 33124

September 25, 1995

Mr. Jeffrey Redmond, President
Dynamic Dining Services
4329 Palmetto Lane
Miami, FL 33157

Dear Jeff,

As per our earlier conversation, occupancy is up in all of the dorms for the 1995 - 1996 school year. I have enclosed a spreadsheet and chart that show our occupancy rates for the 1992 - 1995 school years. Please realize, however, that the 1995 figures are projections, as the Fall 1995 numbers are still incomplete. The final 1995 numbers should be confirmed within the next two weeks. I hope that this helps with your planning. If you need further information, please contact me at the above address.

Dorm Occupancy				
	1992	1993	1994	1995
Beatty	330	285	270	310
Broward	620	580	520	565
Graham	450	397	352	393
Rawlings	435	375	326	372
Tolbert	615	554	524	581

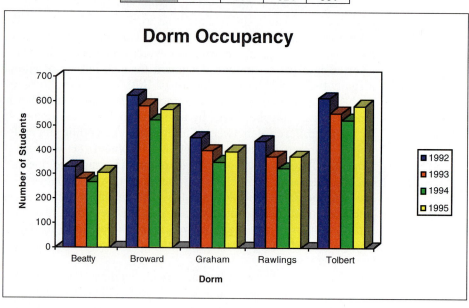

FIGURE 7   A Compound Document

OBJECT LINKING AND EMBEDDING

Object Linking and Embedding (OLE) enables you to create a compound document containing objects (data) from multiple Windows applications. OLE is one of the major benefits of working in the Windows environment, but it would be impossible to illustrate all of the techniques in a single exercise. Accordingly, we have created the icon at the left to help you identify the many examples of object linking and embedding that appear throughout the Exploring Windows series.

SUMMARY

The common user interface requires every Windows application to follow a consistent set of conventions and ensures that all applications work basically the same way. The development of a suite of applications from a single vendor extends this concept by imposing additional similarities on all applications within the suite.

Microsoft distributes two versions of the Office Suite: Standard Office and Office Professional. Both versions include Word, Excel, and PowerPoint. The Office Professional also has Microsoft Access. Both versions also include a fifth application, Schedule+, as well as several smaller applications and shared utilities.

The Microsoft Office Shortcut Bar provides immediate access to each application in Microsoft Office. The Shortcut Bar is fully customizable with respect to the buttons it displays, its appearance, and its position on the desktop. The Open a Document and Start a New Document buttons enable you to think in terms of a document rather than the associated application.

Object Linking and Embedding (OLE) enables you to create a compound document containing data (objects) from multiple applications. Linking and embedding are different operations. The difference between the two depends on whether the object is stored within the compound document (embedding) or in its own file (linking).

KEY WORDS AND CONCEPTS

Answer Wizard
ClipArt Gallery
Compound document
Common user interface
Contents tab
Embedding
Formatting toolbar
Index tab
Linking

Microsoft Access
Microsoft Excel
Microsoft Office Professional
Microsoft PowerPoint
Microsoft Standard Office
Microsoft Word
Object Linking and Embedding (OLE)

Microsoft Office Shortcut Bar
Online help
Schedule+
Standard toolbar
System Information Utility
WordArt

MICROSOFT WORD 7.0: WHAT WILL WORD PROCESSING DO FOR ME?

OBJECTIVES

After reading this chapter you will be able to:

1. Define word wrap; differentiate between a hard and a soft return.
2. Distinguish between the insert and overtype modes; explain how to switch from one mode to the other.
3. Describe the elements on the Microsoft Word screen.
4. Create, save, retrieve, edit, and print a simple document.
5. Check a document for spelling; describe the function of the custom dictionary.
6. Describe the AutoCorrect feature; explain how it can be used to create your own shorthand.
7. Differentiate between the Save and Save As commands; describe various backup options that can be selected.

OVERVIEW

Have you ever produced what you thought was the perfect term paper only to discover that you omitted a sentence or misspelled a word, or that the paper was three pages too short or one page too long? Wouldn't it be nice to make the necessary changes, and then be able to reprint the entire paper with the touch of a key? Welcome to the world of word processing, where you are no longer stuck with having to retype anything. Instead, you retrieve your work from disk, display it on the monitor and revise it as necessary, then print it at any time, in draft or final form.

This chapter provides a broad-based introduction to word processing in general and Microsoft Word in particular. We begin by presenting (or perhaps reviewing) the essential concepts of a word processor, then show you how these concepts are implemented in Word. We show you how to create a document, how to save it on disk, then retrieve the document you just created. We also introduce you to the spell check, an essential tool in any word processor.

The chapter contains three hands-on exercises that enable you to apply the material at the computer. The exercises are indispensable to the learn-by-doing philosophy we follow throughout the text. The exercises also assume a basic knowledge of Windows 95. (See the appendix on Windows essentials if you need to review this material.)

THE BASICS OF WORD PROCESSING

All word processors adhere to certain basic concepts that must be understood if you are to use the program effectively. The next several pages introduce ideas that are applicable to any word processor (and which you may already know). We follow the conceptual material with a hands-on exercise that gives you the opportunity to practice all that you have learned.

Word Wrap

A newcomer to word processing has one major transition to make from a typewriter, and it is an absolutely critical adjustment. Whereas a typist returns the carriage at the end of every line, just the opposite is true of a word processor. One types continually *without* pressing the enter key at the end of a line because the word processor automatically wraps text from one line to the next. This concept is known as ***word wrap*** and is illustrated in Figure 1.1.

The word *primitive* does not fit on the current line in Figure 1.1a, and is automatically shifted to the next line, *without* the user having to press the enter key. The user continues to enter the document, with additional words being wrapped to subsequent lines as necessary. The only time you use the enter key is at the end of a paragraph, or when you want the insertion point to move to the next line and the end of the current line doesn't reach the right margin.

Word wrap is closely associated with another concept, that of hard and soft returns. A ***hard return*** is created by the user when he or she presses the enter key at the end of a paragraph; a ***soft return*** is created by the word processor as it wraps text from one line to the next. The locations of the soft returns change automatically as a document is edited (e.g., as text is inserted or deleted, or as margins or fonts are changed). The locations of the hard returns can be changed only by the user, who must intentionally insert or delete each hard return.

There are two hard returns in Figure 1.1b, one at the end of each paragraph. There are also six soft returns in the first paragraph (one at the end of every line except the last) and four soft returns in the second paragraph. Now suppose the margins in the document are made smaller (that is, the line is made longer) as shown in Figure 1.1c. The number of soft returns drops to four and two (in the first and second paragraph, respectively) as more text fits on a line and fewer lines are needed. The revised document still contains the two original hard returns, one at the end of each paragraph.

The Insertion Point

The ***insertion point*** is a flashing vertical line that marks the place where text will be entered. The insertion point is always at the beginning of a new document, but it can be moved anywhere within an existing document. If, for example, you wanted to add text to the end of a document, you would move the insertion point to the end of the document, then begin typing.

The original IBM PC was extremely pr

primitive cannot fit on current line

The original IBM PC was extremely primitive

primitive is automatically moved to the next line

(a) Entering the Document

Hard returns are created by pressing the enter key at the end of a paragraph.

The original IBM PC was extremely primitive (not to mention expensive) by current standards. The basic machine came equipped with only 16Kb RAM and was sold without a monitor or disk (a TV and tape cassette were suggested instead). The price of this powerhouse was $1565. ¶
    You could, however, purchase an expanded business system with 256Kb RAM, two 160Kb floppy drives, monochrome monitor, and 80-cps printer for $4425. ¶

(b) Completed Document

Revised document still contains two hard returns, one at the end of each paragraph.

The original IBM PC was extremely primitive (not to mention expensive) by current standards. The basic machine came equipped with only 16Kb RAM and was sold without a monitor or disk (a TV and tape cassette were suggested instead). The price of this powerhouse was $1565. ¶
    You could, however, purchase an expanded business system with 256Kb RAM, two 160Kb floppy drives, monochrome monitor, and 80-cps printer for $4425. ¶

(c) Completed Document

FIGURE 1.1 Word Wrap

Toggle Switches

Suppose you sat down at the keyboard and typed an entire sentence without pressing the Shift key; the sentence would be in all lowercase letters. Then you pressed the Caps Lock key and retyped the sentence, again without pressing the Shift key. This time the sentence would be in all uppercase letters. You could repeat the process as often as you like. Each time you pressed the Caps Lock key, the sentence would switch from lowercase to uppercase and vice versa.

    The point of this exercise is to introduce the concept of a ***toggle switch,*** a device that causes the computer to alternate between two states. The Caps Lock key is an example of a toggle switch. Each time you press it, newly typed text will change from uppercase to lowercase and back again. We will see several other examples of toggle switches as we proceed in our discussion of word processing.

Insert versus Overtype

Microsoft Word is always in one of two modes, ***insert*** or ***overtype,*** and uses a toggle switch (the Ins key) to alternate between the two. Press the Ins key once and you switch from insert to overtype. Press the Ins key a second time and you go from overtype back to insert.

Text that is entered into a document during the insert mode moves existing text to the right to accommodate the characters being added. Text entered from the overtype mode replaces (overtypes) existing text. Text is always entered or replaced immediately to the right of the insertion point.

The insert mode is best when you enter text for the first time, but either mode can be used to make corrections. The insert mode is the better choice when the correction requires you to add new text; the overtype mode is easier when you are substituting one or more character(s) for another. The difference is illustrated in Figure 1.2.

Figure 1.2a displays the text as it was originally entered, with two misspellings. The letters *se* have been omitted from the word *insert,* whereas an *x* has been erroneously typed instead of an *r* in the word *overtype*. The insert mode is used in Figure 1.2b to add the missing letters, which in turn moves the rest of the line to the right. The overtype mode is used in Figure 1.2c to replace the *x* with an *r*.

Misspelled words

> The inrt mode is better when adding text that has been omitted; the ovextype mode is easier when you are substituting one (or more) characters for another.

(a) Text to Be Corrected

"se" has been inserted and existing text moved to the right

> The insert mode is better when adding text that has been omitted; the ovextype mode is easier when you are substituting one (or more) characters for another.

(b) Insert Mode

"r" replaces the "x"

> The insert mode is better when adding text that has been omitted; the overtype mode is easier when you are substituting one (or more) characters for another.

(c) Overtype Mode

FIGURE 1.2 Insert and Overtype Modes

Deleting Text

The backspace and Del keys delete one character immediately to the left or right of the insertion point, respectively. The choice between them depends on when you need to erase a character(s). The backspace key is easier if you want to delete a character immediately after typing it. The Del key is preferable during subsequent editing.

You can delete several characters at one time by selecting (dragging the mouse over) the characters to be deleted, then pressing the Del key. And finally, you can delete and replace text in one operation by selecting the text to be replaced and then typing the new text in its place.

LEARN TO TYPE

The ultimate limitation of any word processor is the speed at which you enter data; hence the ability to type quickly is invaluable. Learning how to type is easy, especially with the availability of computer-based typing programs. As little as a half hour a day for a couple of weeks will have you up to speed, and if you do any significant amount of writing at all, the investment will pay off many times.

INTRODUCTION TO MICROSOFT WORD

We used Microsoft Word to write this book, as can be inferred from the screen in Figure 1.3. Your screen will be different from ours in many ways. You will not have the same document nor is it likely that you will customize Word in exactly the same way. You should, however, be able to recognize the basic elements that are found in the Microsoft Word window that is open on the desktop.

There are actually two open windows in Figure 1.3—an application window for Microsoft Word and a document window for the specific document on which you are working. Each window has its own Minimize, Maximize (or Restore), and Close buttons. Both windows have been maximized, and thus the title bars have been merged into a single title bar that appears at the top of the application window and reflects the application (Microsoft Word) as well as the document name (Exploring Word Chapter 1). A menu bar appears immediately below the title bar. Vertical and horizontal scroll bars appear at the right and bottom of the document window. The Windows taskbar appears at the bottom of the screen and shows the open applications.

Microsoft Word is also part of the Microsoft Office suite of applications, and thus shares additional features with Excel, Access, and PowerPoint, that are also part of the Office suite. *Toolbars* provide immediate access to common commands and appear immediately below the menu bar. The toolbars can be displayed or hidden using the View menu as described on page 17 later in the chapter.

The *Standard toolbar* contains buttons corresponding to the most basic commands in Word—for example, opening and closing a file or printing a document. The icon on the button is intended to be indicative of its function (e.g., a printer to indicate the Print command). You can also point to the button to display a *ToolTip* showing the name of the button. The *Formatting toolbar* appears under the Standard toolbar and provides access to common formatting operations such as boldface, italics, or underlining.

The toolbars may appear overwhelming at first, but there is absolutely no need to memorize what the individual buttons do. That will come with time. We

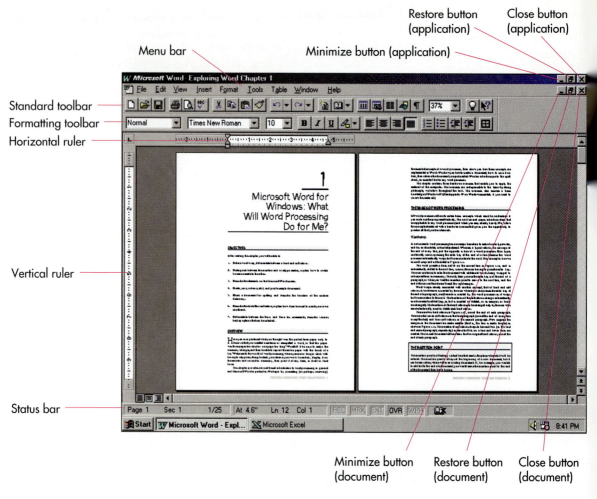

FIGURE 1.3 Microsoft Word

suggest, however, that you will have a better appreciation for the various buttons if you consider them in groups according to their general function as shown in Figure 1.4a.

The ***horizontal ruler*** is displayed underneath the toolbars and enables you to change margins, tabs, and/or indents for all or part of a document. A ***vertical ruler*** shows the vertical position of text on the page and can be used to change the top or bottom margins.

The ***status bar*** at the bottom of the document window displays the location of the insertion point (or information about the command being executed.) The status bar also shows the status (settings) of various indicators—for example, OVR to show that Word is in the overtype, as opposed to the insert, mode.

USE ONLINE HELP

The answer to almost anything you need to know about Microsoft Word is available through online help if only you take the trouble to look. The Help facility is intuitive and easy to use. The help displays are task-specific and fit in a single screen to keep you from having to scroll through large amounts of information.

Starts a new document, opens an existing document, or saves the document in memory

Prints the document or previews the document prior to printing

Checks spelling

Cuts, copies, or pastes the selected text; copies formatting of selected text

Undoes or redoes a previously executed command

AutoFormats the document or inserts an address

Creates a table, inserts an Excel spreadsheet, or creates columns; creates a drawing or chart

Shows (hides) nonprinting characters within a document

Changes the zoom percentage

Toggles the Tip Wizard on (off); displays formatting information

(a) Standard Toolbar

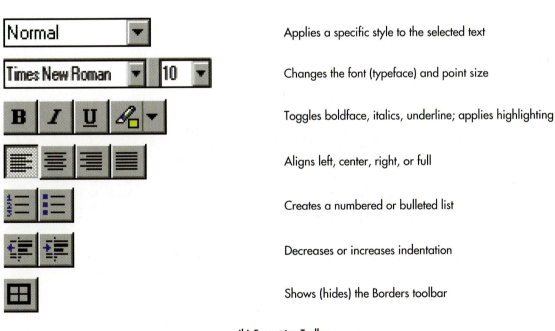

Applies a specific style to the selected text

Changes the font (typeface) and point size

Toggles boldface, italics, underline; applies highlighting

Aligns left, center, right, or full

Creates a numbered or bulleted list

Decreases or increases indentation

Shows (hides) the Borders toolbar

(b) Formatting Toolbar

FIGURE 1.4 Toolbars

THE FILE MENU

The *File menu* is a critically important menu in virtually every Windows application. It contains the Save and Open commands to save a document on disk, then subsequently retrieve (open) that document at a later time. The File menu also contains the Print command to print a document, the Close command to close the current document but continue working in the application, and the Exit command to quit the application altogether.

The *Save command* copies the document that is currently being edited (the document in memory) to disk. The Save As dialog box appears the first time that the document is saved so that you can specify the file name and other required information. All subsequent executions of the Save command save the document under the assigned name, replacing the previously saved version with the new version.

The Save As dialog box requires a file name (e.g., My First Document in Figure 1.5a), which can be up to 255 characters in length. The file name may contain spaces but cannot contain commas. (Periods are permitted, but discouraged since they are too easily confused with DOS extensions.)

The dialog box also requires the specification of the drive and folder in which the file is to be saved as well as the file type that determines which application the file is associated with. (Long-time DOS users will remember the three-character extension at the end of a file name—for example, DOC—to indicate the associated application. The extension may be hidden in Windows 95 according to options set through the View menu in My Computer. Refer to page 30 in the Windows appendix.)

The *Open command* brings a copy of a previously saved document into memory enabling you to work with that document. The Open command displays the Open dialog box in which you specify the file to retrieve. You indicate the drive (and optionally the folder) that contains the file, as well as the type of file you want to retrieve. Word will then list all files of that type on the designated drive (and folder), enabling you to open the file you want.

The Save and Open commands work in conjunction with one another. The Save As dialog box in Figure 1.5a, for example, saves the file *My First Document* onto the disk in drive A. The Open dialog box in Figure 1.5b brings that file back into memory so that you can work with the file, after which you can save the revised file for use at a later time.

A VERY USEFUL TOOLBAR

The Open and Save As dialog boxes share a common toolbar with several very useful buttons. Click the Details button to switch to the Details view and see the date and time the file was last modified as well as its size. Click the List button to display an icon for each file enabling you to see many more files than in the Details view. The Preview button lets you see a document before you open it. The Properties button displays information about the document, including the number of revisions.

LEARNING BY DOING

Every chapter contains a series of hands-on exercises that enable you to apply what you learn at the computer. The exercises in this chapter are linked to one another in that you create a simple document in exercise one, then open and edit

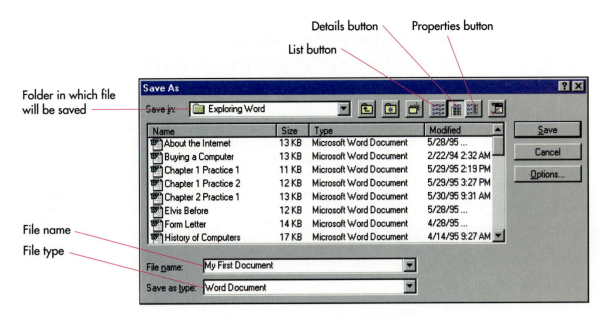

(a) Save As Dialog Box

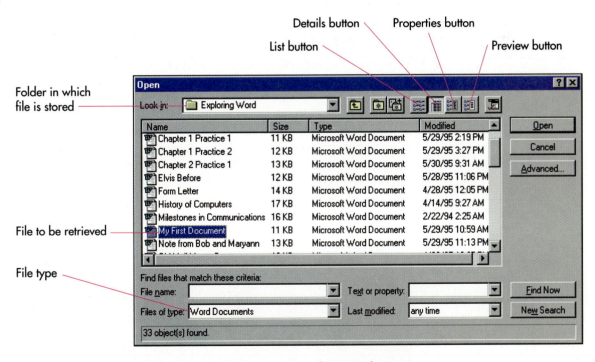

(b) Open Dialog Box

FIGURE 1.5 The Save and Open Commands

that document in exercise two. The ability to save and open a document is critical, and you do not want to spend an inordinate amount of time entering text unless you are confident in your ability to retrieve it later.

The following exercise also introduces you to the data disk that is referenced throughout this text. You can obtain a copy of the data disk from your instructor, or you can download the files on the data disk as described in step 2. The data disk contains a series of documents that are used in various exercises throughout the text. It can also be used to store the documents you create (or you can store the documents on a hard disk if you have access to your own computer).

THERE'S ALWAYS A REASON

We would love to tell you that everything will go perfectly, that you will never be frustrated, and that the computer will always perform exactly as you expect. Unfortunately, that is not going to happen, because a computer does what you tell it to do, which is not necessarily what you want it to do. There can be a tremendous difference! There is, however, a logical reason for everything the computer does or does not do; sooner or later you will discover that reason, at which point everything will fall into place.

HANDS-ON EXERCISE 1

My First Document

Objective: To start Microsoft Word in order to create, save, and print a simple document. To execute commands via the toolbar or from pull-down menus. Use Figure 1.6 as a guide in doing the exercise.

STEP 1: Welcome to Windows 95

➤ Turn on the computer and all of its peripherals. The floppy drive should be empty prior to starting your machine. This ensures that the system starts from the hard disk, which contains the Windows files, as opposed to a floppy disk, which does not.

➤ Your system will take a minute or so to get started, after which you should see the Windows desktop in Figure 1.6a. Do not be concerned if the appearance of your desktop is different from ours, or if you do not see the Welcome message.

➤ If you are new to Windows 95 and you want a quick introduction, click the **What's New** or **Windows Tour command buttons.** Follow the instructions in the boxed tip to display the Welcome window if it does not appear on your system.

➤ Click the **Close button** if you see the Welcome message in Figure 1.6a.

TAKE THE WINDOWS 95 TOUR

Windows 95 greets you with a Welcome window that contains a command button to take you on a 10-minute tour of Windows 95. Click the command button and enjoy the show. You might also try the What's New command button for a quick overview of changes from Windows 3.1. If you do not see the Welcome window when you start Windows 95, click the Start button, click Run, type C:\WINDOWS\WELCOME in the Open *text box,* and press enter.

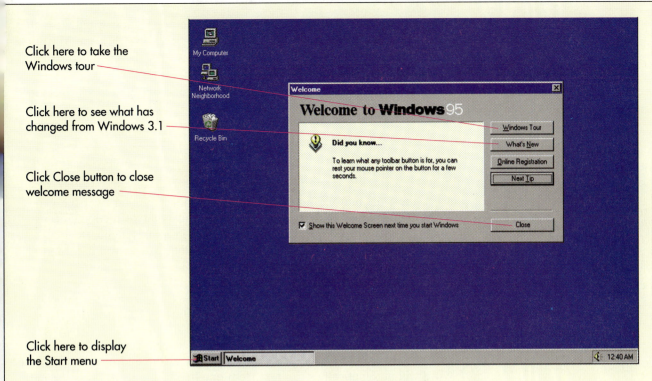

(a) Welcome to Windows 95 (step 1)

FIGURE 1.6 Hands-on Exercise 1

STEP 2: Install the Data Disk

➤ Do this step *only* if you have your own computer and you want to install (copy) the files from the data disk to the hard drive. Place the data disk in drive A.

➤ Click the **Start button** to display the Start menu. Click the **Run command** to display the Run dialog box.

➤ Type **A:\Install C** in the text box. (The drive letter, drive C in the example, is variable and indicates the drive on which to install the data disk.) Click **OK** or press the **enter key**.

DOWNLOAD THE DATA DISK

The data disk for all books in the Exploring Windows series can be downloaded from the Prentice Hall Web site (http://www.prenhall.com). Use any Web browser to log on to the site, select Business and Economics, then move to the Exploring Windows page. To download the files for a single application, go to the page for that book, then click the icon to download the data disk. To download the files for all Office applications simultaneously, go to the Exploring Microsoft Office page.

STEP 3: Start Microsoft Word

➤ Click the **Start button** to display the Start menu. Click (or point to) the **Programs menu,** then click **Microsoft Word** to open the program.

➤ If necessary, click the **Maximize button** in the application window so that Word takes the entire desktop as shown in Figure 1.6b. Click the **Maximize button** in the document window (if necessary) so that the document window is as large as possible.

➤ Do not be concerned if your screen is different from ours as we include a troubleshooting section immediately following this exercise.

> ### POINT AND SLIDE
>
> Click the Start button, then slowly slide the mouse pointer over the various menu options. Notice that each time you point to a submenu, its items are displayed. Point to (don't click) the Programs menu, then click Microsoft Word to open the application. In other words, you don't have to click a submenu—you can just point and slide!

STEP 4: Create the Document
➤ Create the document in Figure 1.6c. Type just as you would on a typewriter with one exception; do *not* press the enter key at the end of a line because Word will automatically wrap text from one line to the next. Press the **enter key** at the end of the paragraph.

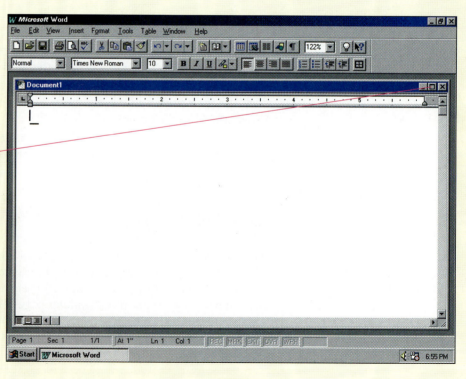

Click here to maximize the document window

(b) Load Microsoft Word (step 3)

FIGURE 1.6 Hands-on Exercise 1 (continued)

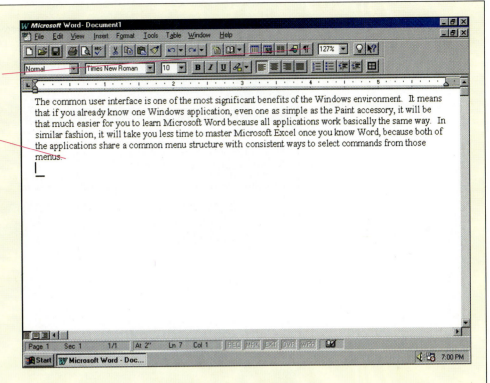

Show/Hide button (displays/hides nonprinting characters)

Press the enter key at the end of the paragraph

(c) Create the Document (step 4)

FIGURE 1.6 Hands-on Exercise 1 (continued)

➤ Proofread the document and correct any errors. Use the **Ins key** to toggle between the insert and overtype modes as appropriate.

➤ You may (or may not) see a red wavy underline beneath misspelled words, depending on whether (or not) the automatic spell check is in effect. If a misspelling is indicated, point to the misspelled word, click the right mouse button, then select (click) the correct spelling from the list of suggestions.

DISPLAY THE HARD RETURNS

Click the Show/Hide ¶ button on the Standard toolbar to display the hard returns (paragraph marks) and other nonprinting characters (such as tab characters or blank spaces) contained within a document. The Show/Hide ¶ button (denoted by the ¶ symbol indicating a hard return) functions as a toggle switch: the first time you click it, the hard returns are displayed; the second time you press it, the returns are hidden; and so on.

STEP 5: Save the Document

➤ Pull down the **File menu** and click **Save** (or click the **Save button** on the Standard toolbar). You should see the Save As dialog box in Figure 1.6d. If necessary, click the **List button** so that the display on your monitor more closely matches our figure.

MICROSOFT WORD 7.0 **13**

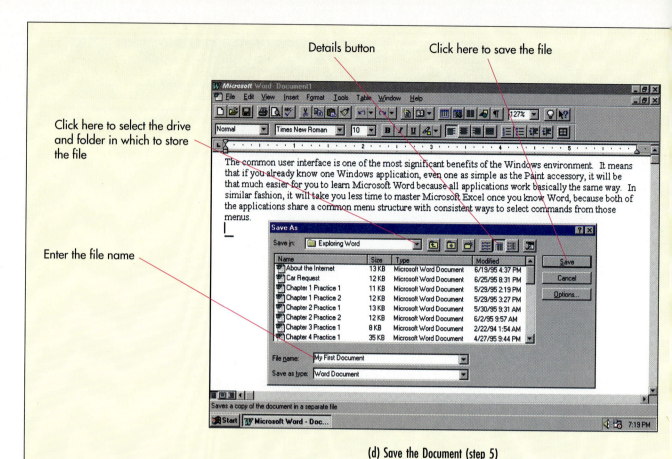

(d) Save the Document (step 5)

FIGURE 1.6 Hands-on Exercise 1 (continued)

➤ To save the file:
- Click the **drop-down arrow** on the Save In list box.
- Click the appropriate drive, drive C or drive A, depending on whether or not you installed the data disk on your hard drive.
- Double click the **Exploring Word folder,** to make it the active folder (the folder in which you will save the document).
- Click and drag over the default entry in the File name text box. Type **My First Document** as the name of your document. (A DOC extension will be added automatically when the file is saved to indicate that this is a Word document.)
- Click **Save** or press the **enter key.** The title bar changes to reflect the document name.

DOUBLE CLICKING FOR BEGINNERS

If you are having trouble double clicking, it is because you are not clicking quickly enough, or more likely, because you are moving the mouse (however slightly) between clicks. Relax, hold the mouse firmly in place, and try again.

➤ Add your name at the end of the document, then click the **Save button** on the Standard toolbar to save the document with the revision. This time the Save As dialog box does not appear, since Word already knows the name of the document.

STEP 6: Print the Document

➤ You can print the document in one of two ways:

- Pull down the **File menu.** Click **Print** to display the dialog box of Figure 1.6e. Click the **OK command button** to print the document.
- Click the **Print button** on the Standard toolbar to print the document immediately without displaying the Print dialog box.

ABOUT MICROSOFT WORD

Pull down the Help menu and click About Microsoft Word to display the specific release number and other licensing information, including the product serial number. This help screen also contains two very useful command buttons, System Information and Technical Support. The first button displays information about the hardware installed on your system, including the amount of memory and available space on the hard drive. The Technical Support button provides telephone numbers for technical assistance.

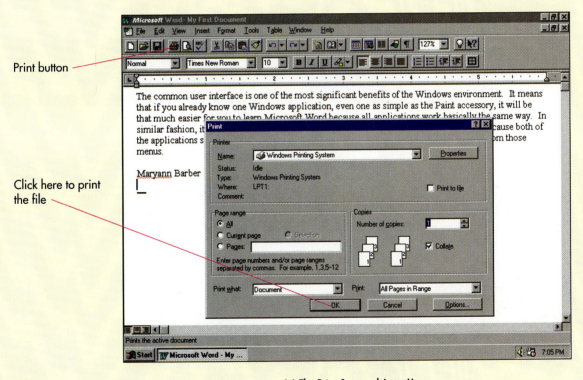

(e) The Print Command (step 6)

FIGURE 1.6 Hands-on Exercise 1 (continued)

STEP 7: Close the Document

➤ Pull down the **File menu.** Click **Close** to close this document but remain in Word. (Click **Yes** if prompted to save the document.) The document disappears from the screen, but Word is still open.

➤ Pull down the **File menu** a second time. Click **Exit** to close Word and return to Windows.

➤ Submit the printed document from step 6 to your instructor as proof that you did the exercise.

TROUBLESHOOTING

We trust that you completed the hands-on exercise without difficulty, and that you were able to create, save, and print the document in Figure 1.6. There is, however, one area of potential confusion in that Word offers different views of the same document, depending on the preferences of the individual user. Your screen will not match ours exactly, and, indeed, there is no requirement that it should. The *contents* of the document, however, should be identical to ours.

Figure 1.6 displayed the document in the **Normal view.** Figure 1.7 displays an entirely different view called the **Page Layout view.** Each view has its advantages. The Normal view is generally faster, but the Page Layout view more closely

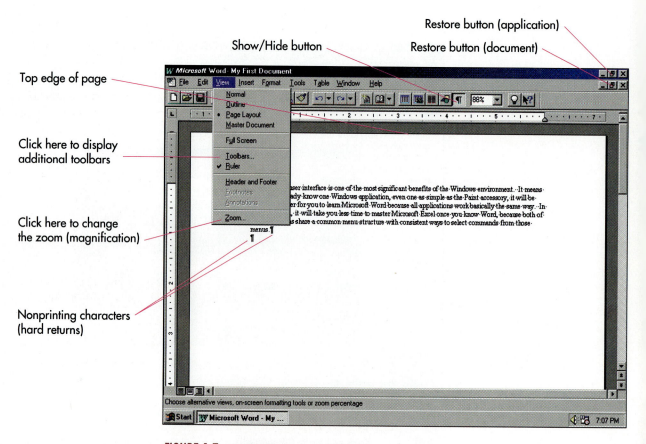

FIGURE 1.7 Troubleshooting

resembles the printed page as it displays top and bottom margins, headers and footers, graphic elements in their exact position, a vertical ruler, and other elements not seen in the Normal view. The Normal view is preferable only when entering text and editing. The Page Layout view is used to apply the finishing touches and check a document prior to printing.

Your screen may or may not match either figure, and you will undoubtedly develop preferences of your own. The following suggestions will help you match the screens of Figure 1.6:

- If the application window for Word does not take the entire screen, and/or the document does not take the entire window within Word, click the Maximize button in the application and/or the document window. There are two Restore buttons in Figure 1.6b to indicate that the application window and its associated document window have been maximized.
- If the text does not come up to the top of the screen—that is, you see the top edge of the page (as in Figure 1.7)—it means that you are in the Page Layout view instead of the Normal view. Pull down the View menu and click Normal to match the document in Figure 1.6c.
- If the text seems unusually large or small, it means that you or a previous user elected to zoom in or out to get a different perspective on the document. Pull down the View menu, click Zoom, then click Page Width so that the text takes the entire line as in Figure 1.6b.
- If you see the ¶ and other nonprinting symbols, it means that you or a previous user elected to display these characters. Click the Show/Hide ¶ button on the Standard toolbar to make the symbols disappear.
- If the Standard or Formatting toolbar is missing and/or a different toolbar is displayed, pull down the View menu, click Toolbars, then click the appropriate toolbars on or off. If the ruler is missing, pull down the View menu and click Ruler.
- The automatic spell check may (or may not) be implemented as indicated by the appearance (absence) of the open book icon on the status bar. If you do not see the icon, pull down the Tools menu, click Options, click the Spelling tab, then check the box for Automatic Spell Checking.

THE WRONG KEYBOARD

Microsoft Word facilitates conversion from WordPerfect by providing an alternative (software-controlled) keyboard that implements WordPerfect conventions. If you are sharing your machine with others, and if various keyboard shortcuts do not work as expected, it could be because someone else has implemented the WordPerfect keyboard. Pull down the Tools menu, click Options, then click the General tab in the dialog box. Clear the check box next to Navigation keys for WordPerfect users to return to the normal Word keyboard.

THE TIPWIZARD

The *TipWizard* has a different **Tip of the Day** every time you start Word, but that is only one of its capabilities. The true purpose of the TipWizard is to introduce you to new features by suggesting more efficient ways to accomplish the tasks you are doing.

The TipWizard monitors your work and offers advice throughout a session. The TipWizard button on the Standard toolbar "lights up" whenever there is a suggestion. (Click the button to display the TipWizard; click the button a second time to close it.) You can read the suggestions as they occur and/or review them at the end of a session. You needn't always follow the advice of the TipWizard (at first you may not even understand all of its suggestions), but over time it will make you much more proficient.

HANDS-ON EXERCISE 2

Modifying an Existing Document

Objective: To open an existing document, revise it, and save the revision; to demonstrate the Undo command and online help. Use Figure 1.8 as a guide in doing the exercise.

STEP 1: Open an Existing Document
- Start Microsoft Word as described in step 3 of the previous exercise.
- Pull down the **File menu** and click **Open** (or click the **Open button** on the Standard toolbar). You should see a dialog box similar to the one in Figure 1.8a. (The Exploring Word folder is not yet selected.)

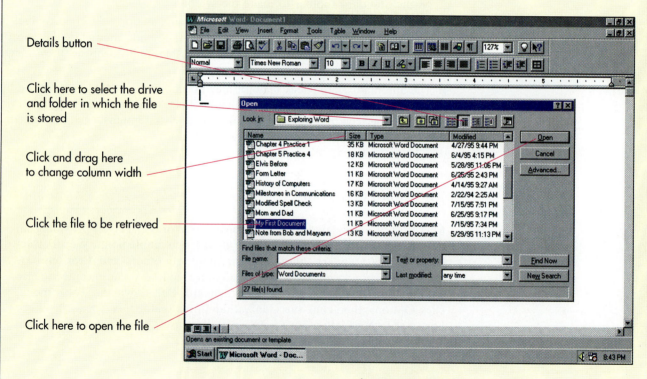

(a) The Open Command (step 1)

FIGURE 1.8 Hands-on Exercise 2

18 EXPLORING MICROSOFT WORD 7.0

➤ To open a file:
  - Click the **Details button** to change to the Details view. Click and drag the vertical border between columns to increase (or decrease) the size of a column.
  - Click the **drop-down arrow** on the Look In list box.
  - Click the appropriate drive, drive C or drive A, depending on the location of your data.
  - Double click the **Exploring Word folder** to make it the active folder (the folder in which you will save the document).
  - Click the **down arrow** in the Name list box, then scroll until you can select **My First Document** from the first exercise. Click the **Open command button** to open the file.
➤ Your document should appear on the screen.

THE MOST RECENTLY OPENED FILE LIST

The easiest way to open a recently used document is to select the document directly from the File menu. Pull down the File menu, but instead of clicking the Open command, check to see if the document appears on the list of the most recently opened documents at the bottom of the menu. If so, you can click the document name rather than having to make the appropriate selections through the Open dialog box.

STEP 2: The View Menu (Troubleshooting)
➤ Modify the settings within Word so that your settings correspond to ours.
  - To change to the Normal view, pull down the **View menu** and click **Normal** (or click the **Normal View** button at the bottom of the window).
  - To change the amount of text that is visible on the screen, click the **drop-down arrow** on the Zoom Control box on the Standard toolbar and select **Page Width.**
  - To display (hide) the ruler, pull down the **View menu** and toggle the **Ruler command** on or off. End with the ruler on.
➤ There may still be subtle differences between your screen and ours, depending on the resolution of your monitor. These variations, if any, need not concern you at all as long as you are able to complete the exercise.

DISPLAY (HIDE) TOOLBARS WITH THE RIGHT MOUSE BUTTON

Point to any visible toolbar, then click the right mouse button to display a shortcut menu listing the available toolbars. Click the individual toolbars on or off as appropriate. If no toolbars are visible, pull down the View menu, click Toolbars, then display or hide the desired toolbars.

STEP 3: The Tip of the Day

▶ Click the **TipWizard button** to display the Tip of the Day as shown in Figure 1.8b. (You will probably see a different tip than the one in the figure.)

▶ Click the **TipWizard button** a second time to close the TipWizard dialog box.

RESET THE TIPWIZARD

The TipWizard will not repeat a tip from one session to the next unless it is specifically reset each time you start Microsoft Word. Press and hold the Ctrl key as you click the TipWizard button (the light bulb) to reset the TipWizard. You will see a tip indicating that you have reset the TipWizard and that it may display tips you have already seen. This is especially important in a laboratory situation when you are sharing the same computer with other students.

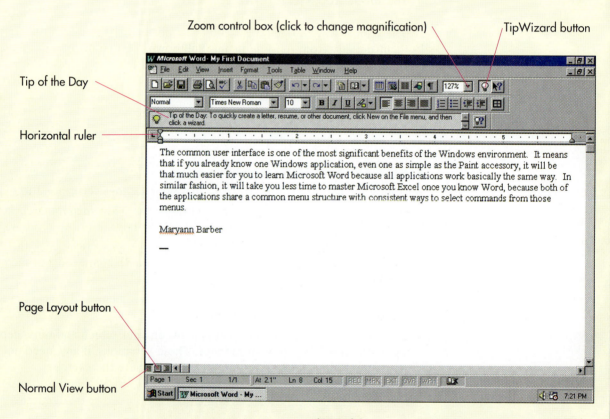

(b) Tip of the Day (step 3)

FIGURE 1.8 Hands-on Exercise 2 (continued)

STEP 4: Display the Hard Returns

▶ The **Show/Hide ¶** button on the Standard toolbar functions as a toggle switch to display (hide) the hard returns (and other nonprinting characters) in a document.

➤ Click the **Show/Hide ¶ button** to display the hard returns as in Figure 1.8c. Click the **Show/Hide ¶ button** a second time to hide the nonprinting characters.

➤ Display or hide the paragraph markers as you see fit.

TOOLTIPS

Point to any button on any toolbar and Word displays a ToolTip, containing the name of the button to indicate its function. If pointing to a button has no effect, pull down the View menu, click Toolbars, and check the box to Show ToolTips.

STEP 5: Modify the Document

➤ Press **Ctrl+End** to move to the end of the document. Press the **up arrow key** once or twice until the insertion point is on a blank line above your name. If necessary, press the **enter key** once (or twice) to add additional blank line(s).

➤ Add the sentence, **Success, I can save and retrieve a document!,** as shown in Figure 1.8c.

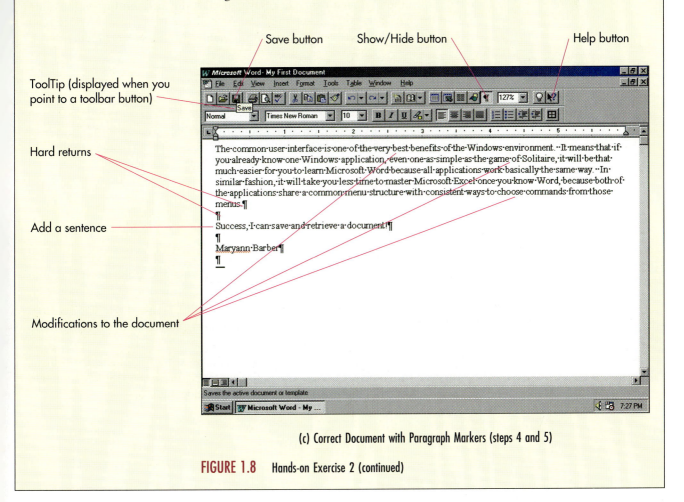

(c) Correct Document with Paragraph Markers (steps 4 and 5)

FIGURE 1.8 Hands-on Exercise 2 (continued)

- Make the following additional modifications to practice editing:
  - Change the phrase *most significant* to **very best**.
  - Change *Paint accessory* to **game of Solitaire**.
  - Change the word *select* to **choose**.
- Switch between the insert and overtype modes as necessary. Press the **Ins key** or double click the **OVR indicator** on the status bar to toggle between the insert and overtype modes.

MOVING WITHIN A DOCUMENT

Press Ctrl+Home and Ctrl+End to move to the beginning and end of a document, respectively. These shortcuts work not just in Word, but in any other Windows application, and are worth remembering as they allow your hands to remain on the keyboard as you type.

STEP 6: Save the Changes
- It is very, very important to save your work repeatedly during a session.
- Pull down the **File menu** and click **Save,** or click the **Save button** on the Standard toolbar. You will not see the Save As dialog box because the document is saved automatically under the existing name (My First Document).

THE HELP BUTTON

Click the Help button on the Standard toolbar (the mouse pointer changes to include a large question mark), then click any other toolbar button to display a help screen with information about that button. Double click the Help button as a shortcut to the help facility, then click the Answer Wizard tab to ask a question in your own words.

STEP 7: Deleting Text
- Point to the first letter in the first sentence. Press and hold the left mouse button as you drag the mouse over the first sentence. Release the mouse.
- The sentence should remain selected as shown in Figure 1.8d. The selected text is the text that will be affected by the next command. Click anywhere else in the document to deselect the text.
- Point to any word in the first sentence, then press and hold the **Ctrl key** as you click the mouse, to select the entire sentence. Press the **Del key** to delete the selected text (the first sentence) from the document.

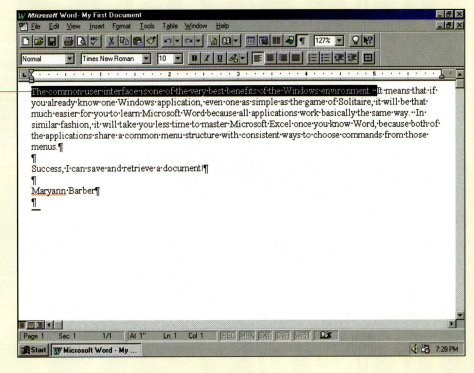

(d) Selecting Text (step 6)

FIGURE 1.8 Hands-on Exercise 2 (continued)

PICK UP THE MOUSE

It seems that you always run out of room on your real desk, just when you need to move the mouse a little further. The solution is to pick up the mouse and move it closer to you—the pointer will stay in its present position on the screen, but when you put the mouse down, you will have more room on your desk in which to work.

STEP 8: The Undo Command

➤ Pull down the **Edit menu** as shown in Figure 1.8e. Click **Undo** to reverse (undo) the last command.

100 LEVELS OF UNDO

The *Undo command* is present in Word as it is in every Windows application. Incredible as it sounds, however, Word enables you to undo the last 100 changes to a document. Click the drop-down arrow next to the Undo button to produce a list of your previous actions. (The most recent command is listed first.) Click the action you want to undo, which also undoes all of the preceding commands. Undoing the fifth command in the list, for example, will also undo the preceding four commands.

MICROSOFT WORD 7.0 **23**

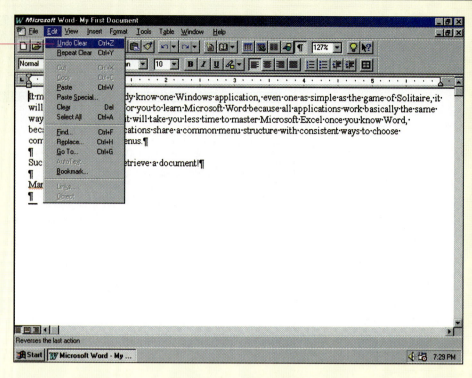

(e) The Undo Command (step 7)

FIGURE 1.8 Hands-on Exercise 2 (continued)

➤ The deleted text should be returned to your document. The Undo command is a tremendous safety net and can be used at almost any time.

➤ Click anywhere outside the selected text to deselect the sentence.

STEP 9: Online Help

➤ Pull down the **Help menu.** Click **Microsoft Word Help Topics** to display the Help topics window in Figure 1.8f.

➤ Click the **Index tab.** Type **Undo** (the topic you wish to look up). The Undoing actions topic is automatically selected. Click **Display** to show a second help screen.

➤ Click **Undo mistakes** to select this topic. Click the **Display command button** to show the detailed instructions.

➤ Click the **Close button** to close the Help window.

THE ANSWER WIZARD

The *Answer Wizard* enables you to request help by posing a question in English. Pull down the Help menu, click Microsoft Word Help Topics, then click the Answer Wizard tab. Type your question in the text box—for example, "How do I request help?"—then click the Search command button. The wizard will return a list of help topics that answer your question, together with a list of related topics that may be of interest to you.

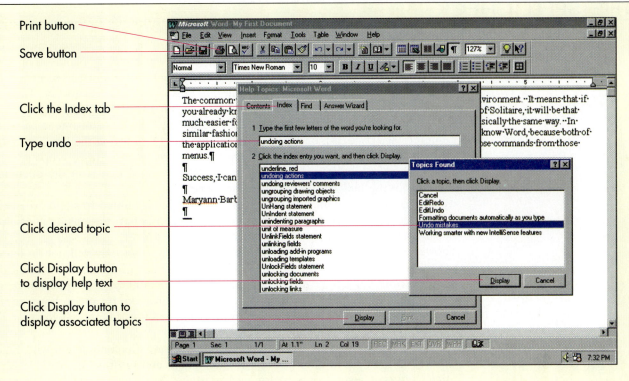

(f) Online Help (step 8)

FIGURE 1.8 Hands-on Exercise 2 (continued)

STEP 10: Print the Revised Document

➤ Click the **Save button** on the Standard toolbar to save the revised document a final time.

➤ Click the **Print button** to print the document.

➤ Pull down the **File menu.** Click **Close** to close the document and remain in Word. Click **Exit** if you do not want to continue with the next exercise at this time.

SUMMARY INFORMATION

Word maintains summary statistics about a document that include the number of pages, words, and characters; the date and time of the last revision; and the total editing time. You can view this *summary information* from both the Open and Save As dialog boxes by clicking the Properties button on the toolbar. You can also print the statistics with your document and show your instructor how much time you spent on the assignment. Pull down the Tools menu, click Options, click the Print tab, then check the box to print summary information. Click OK. The summary statistics will appear on a separate page the next time you print a document.

THE SPELL CHECK

There is simply no excuse to misspell a word, since the **spell check** is an integral part of Microsoft Word. (The spell check is also available for every other application in the Microsoft Office.) Spelling errors make your work look sloppy and discourage the reader before he or she has read what you had to say. They can cost you a job, a grade, a lucrative contract, or an award you deserve.

The spell check can be set to automatically check a document as text is entered (see page 34), or it can be called explicitly by clicking the Spelling button on the Standard toolbar. The spell check compares each word in a document to the entries in a built-in dictionary, then flags any word that is in the document but not in the built-in dictionary, as an error.

The dictionary included with Microsoft Office is limited to standard English and does not include many proper names, acronyms, abbreviations, or specialized terms, and hence, the use of any such item is considered a misspelling. You can however, add such words to a **custom dictionary** so that they will not be flagged in the future. You can also purchase specialized dictionaries containing medical or legal terminology or even a foreign language dictionary. The spell check will inform you of repeated words and irregular capitalization. It cannot, however, flag properly spelled words that are used improperly, and thus cannot tell you that *Two bee or knot too be* is not the answer.

The capabilities of the spell check are illustrated in conjunction with Figure 1.9a. The spell check goes through the document and returns the errors one at a time, offering several options for each mistake. You can change the misspelled word to one of the alternatives suggested by Word, leave the word as is, or add the word to a custom dictionary.

The first error is *embarassing* with Word's suggestion(s) for correction displayed in the list box in Figure 1.9b. To accept the highlighted suggestion, click the Change command button and the substitution will be made automatically in the document. To accept an alternative suggestion, click the desired word, then click the Change command button. Alternatively, you can click the AutoCorrect button to correct the mistake in the current document, and, in addition, automatically correct the same mistake in any future document.

The spell check detects both irregular capitalization and duplicated words as shown in Figures 1.9c and 1.9d, respectively. The error in Figure 1.9e, *Grauer,* is not a misspelling per se, but a proper noun not found in the standard dictionary. No correction is required and the appropriate action is to ignore the word (taking no further action)—or better yet, add it to the custom dictionary so that it will not be flagged in future sessions. And finally, we could not resist including the example in Figure 1.9f, which shows another use of the spell check.

HELP IN CROSSWORDS

Quick, what is a five-letter word, meaning severe or firm, with the pattern S _ _ RN? If you answered stern, you don't need our help. But if not, you might want to use the spell check to come up with the answer. Type the pattern using a question mark for each unknown character; for example, S??RN. Click anywhere within the word, then click the Spelling button on the Standard toolbar. Word will return all of the matching words in the dictionary (scorn, shorn, spurn, stern, and sworn). It's then a simple matter to pick out the word that fits.

Flagged errors

A spelling checker will catch embarassing mistakes, iRregular capitalization, and duplicate words words. It will also flag proper nouns, for example, Robert Grauer, but you can add these terms to an auxiliary dictionary so that they will not be flagged in the future. It will not, however, notice properly spelled words that are used incorrectly; for example, Two bee or knot too be is not the answer.

(a) The Text

(b) Ordinary Misspelling

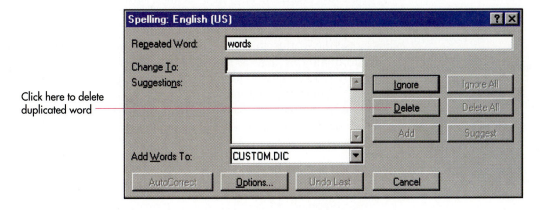

(c) Irregular Capitalization

(d) Duplicated Word

FIGURE 1.9   The Spell Check

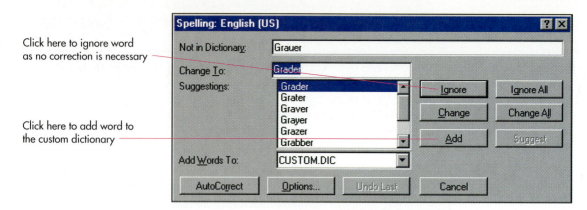

(e) Proper Noun

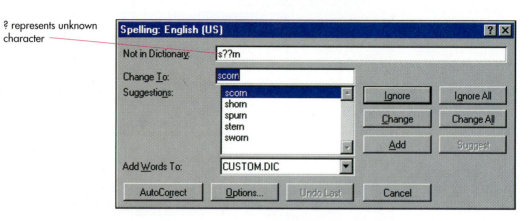

(f) Help with Crosswords

FIGURE 1.9 The Spell Check (continued)

AutoCorrect

The *AutoCorrect* feature corrects mistakes as they are made without any effort on your part. It makes you a better typist. If, for example, you typed *teh* instead of *the,* Word would change the spelling without even telling you. Word will also change *adn* to *and, i* to *I,* and *occurence* to *occurrence.*

Microsoft Word includes a predefined table of common mistakes and uses that table to make substitutions whenever it encounters an error it recognizes. You can add additional items to the table to include the frequent errors you make. You can also use the feature to define your own shorthand—for example, *cis* for Computer Information Systems as shown in Figure 1.10.

The AutoCorrect will also correct mistakes in capitalization; for example, it will capitalize the first letter in a sentence, recognize that MIami should be Miami, and capitalize the days of the week. It's even smart enough to correct the accidental use of the Caps Lock key, and it will toggle the key off!

SAVE COMMAND

The Save command was used in the first two exercises. The Save As command will be introduced in the next exercise as a very useful alternative. We also introduce you to different backup options. We believe that now, when you are first

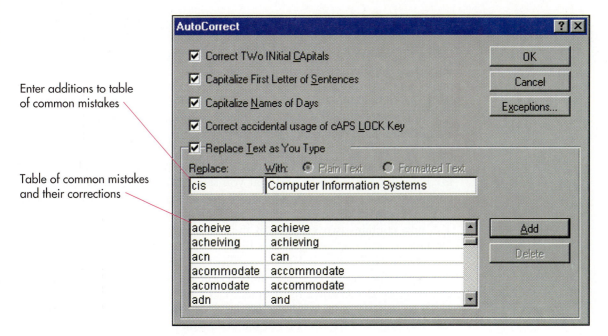

FIGURE 1.10 AutoCorrect

starting to learn about word processing, is the time to develop good working habits.

You already know that the Save command copies the document currently being edited (the document in memory) to disk. The initial execution of the command requires you to assign a file name and to specify the drive and folder in which the file is to be stored. All subsequent executions of the Save command save the document under the original name, replacing the previously saved version with the new one.

The **Save As command** saves another copy of a document under a different name, and is useful when you want to retain a copy of the original document. The Save As command provides you with two copies of a document. The original document is kept on disk under its original name. A copy of the document is saved on disk under a new name and remains in memory. All subsequent editing is done on the new document.

We cannot overemphasize the importance of periodically saving a document, so that if something does go wrong, you won't lose all of your work. Nothing is more frustrating than to lose two hours of effort, due to an unexpected problem in Windows or to a temporary loss of power. Save your work frequently, at least once every 15 minutes. Pull down the File menu and click Save, or click the Save button on the Standard toolbar. Do it!

QUIT WITHOUT SAVING

There will be times when you do not want to save the changes to a document, such as when you have edited it beyond recognition and wish you had never started. Pull down the File menu and click the Close command, then click No in response to the message asking whether you want to save the changes to the document. Pull down the File menu and reopen the file (it should be the first file in the list of most recently edited documents), then start over from the beginning.

Backup Options

Microsoft Word offers several different **backup** options. We believe the two most important options are to create a backup copy in conjunction with every save command, and to periodically (and automatically) save a document. Both options are implemented in step 3 in the next hands-on exercise.

Figure 1.11 illustrates the option to create a backup copy of the document every time a Save command is executed. Assume, for example, that you have created the simple document, *The fox jumped over the fence* and saved it under the name "Fox". Assume further that you edit the document to read, *The quick brown fox jumped over the fence,* and that you saved it a second time. The second save command changes the name of the original document from "Fox" to "Backup of Fox", then saves the current contents of memory as "Fox". In other words, the disk now contains two versions of the document: the current version "Fox" and the most recent previous version "Backup of Fox".

The cycle goes on indefinitely, with "Fox" always containing the current version, and "Backup of Fox" the most recent previous version. Thus if you revise and save the document a third time, "Fox" will contain the latest revision while "Backup of Fox" would contain the previous version alluding to the quick brown fox. The original (first) version of the document disappears entirely since only two versions are kept.

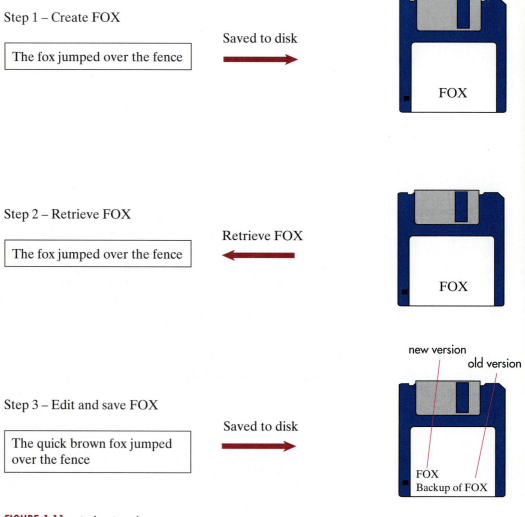

FIGURE 1.11   Backup Procedures

The contents of "Fox" and "Backup of Fox" are different, but the existence of the latter enables you to retrieve the previous version if you inadvertently edit beyond repair or accidentally erase the current "Fox" version. Should this occur (and it will), you can always retrieve its predecessor and at least salvage your work prior to the last save operation.

> **KEEP DUPLICATE COPIES OF IMPORTANT FILES**
>
> It is absolutely critical to maintain duplicate copies of important files on a separate disk stored away from the computer. In addition, you should print each new document at the end of every session, saving it before printing (power failures happen when least expected—for example, during the print operation). Hard copy is not as good as a duplicate disk, but it is better than nothing.

HANDS-ON EXERCISE 3

The Spell Check

Objective: To open an existing document, check it for spelling, then use the Save As command to save the document under a different file name. Use Figure 1.12 as a guide in the exercise.

STEP 1: Preview a Document

➤ Start Microsoft Word. Pull down the **File menu** and click **Open** (or click the **Open button** on the Standard toolbar). You should see the dialog box similar to the one in Figure 1.12a.

➤ Select the appropriate drive, drive C or drive A, depending on the location of your data. Double click the **Exploring Word folder** to make it the active folder (the folder in which you will save the document).

➤ Scroll in the Name list box until you can select (click) the **Try the Spell Check** document. Click the **Preview button** on the toolbar to preview the document as shown in Figure 1.12a.

➤ Click the **Open command button** to open the file. Your document should appear on the screen.

> **CHANGE THE DEFAULT FOLDER**
>
> The default folder is the folder where Word opens (saves) documents unless it is otherwise instructed. To change the default folder, pull down the Tools menu, click Options, click the File Locations tab, click Documents, and click the Modify command button. Enter the name of the new folder (for example, C:\Exploring Word), click OK, then click the Close button. The next time you access the File menu, the default folder will reflect these changes.

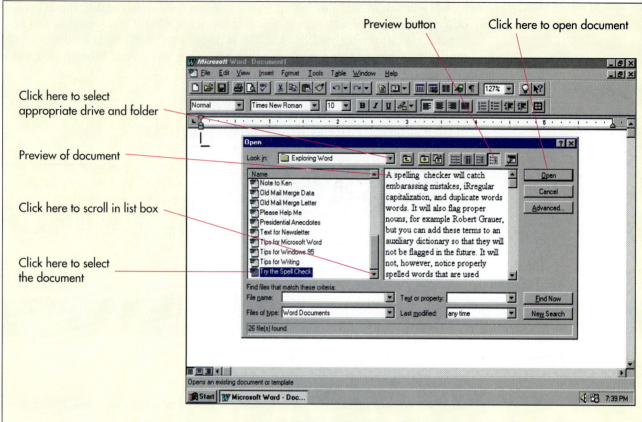

(a) Preview a Document (step 1)

FIGURE 1.12 Hands-on Exercise 3

STEP 2: The Save As Command

➤ Pull down the **File menu.** Click **Save As** to produce a dialog box in Figure 1.12b.

➤ Enter **Modified Spell Check** as the name of the new document. (A file name may contain up to 255 characters, and blanks are permitted.) Click the **Save command button.**

➤ There are now two identical copies of the file on disk: Try the Spell Check, which we supplied, and Modified Spell Check, which you just created. The title bar of the document window shows the latter name.

STEP 3: Establish Automatic Backup

➤ Pull down the **Tools menu.** Click **Options.** Click the **Save tab** to display the dialog box of Figure 1.12c.

➤ Click the first check box to choose **Always Create Backup Copy.**

➤ Set the other options as you see fit; for example, you can specify that the document be saved automatically every 10–15 minutes. Click **OK**.

STEP 4: The Spell Check

➤ If necessary, press **Ctrl+Home** to move to the beginning of the document. Click the Spelling button on the Standard toolbar to initiate the spell check.

➤ "Embarassing" is flagged as the first misspelling as shown in Figure 1.12d. Click the **Change button** to accept the suggested spelling.

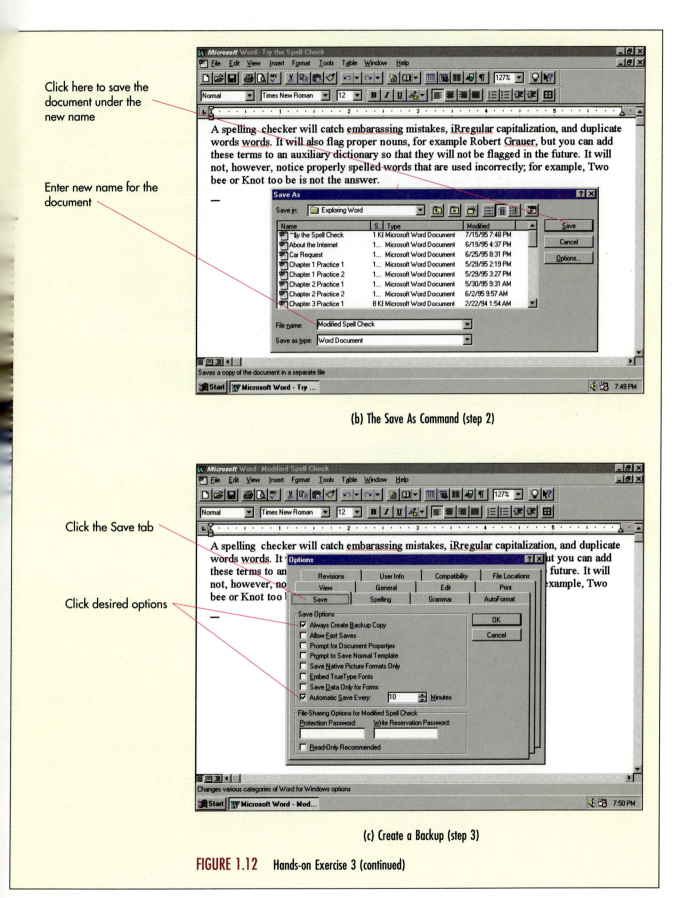

(b) The Save As Command (step 2)

(c) Create a Backup (step 3)

FIGURE 1.12 Hands-on Exercise 3 (continued)

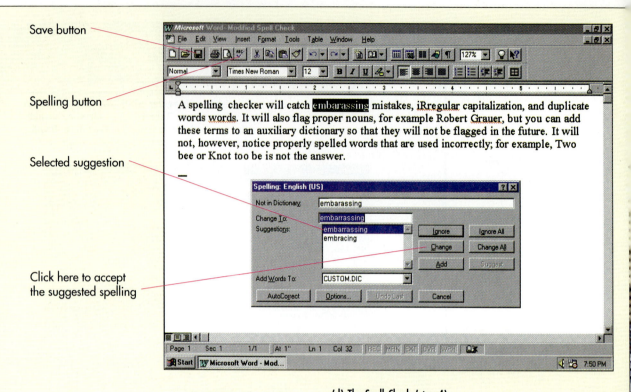

(d) The Spell Check (step 4)

FIGURE 1.12 Hands-on Exercise 3 (continued)

➤ "iRregular" is flagged as an example of irregular capitalization. Click the **Change button** to accept the suggested correction.
➤ Continue checking the document, which displays misspellings and other irregularities one at a time. Click the appropriate command button as each mistake is found.
  • Click the **Delete button** to remove the duplicated word.
  • Click the **Ignore button** to accept Grauer (or click the **Add button** to add Grauer to the supplementary dictionary).
➤ Click **OK** when the spell check has finished checking the document.

CHECK SPELLING AUTOMATICALLY

The spell check can be set to automatically check a document as text is entered, which in turn displays a red wavy line under any misspelled word. To correct a misspelling, right click the wavy line, then choose the appropriate correction from the suggested list or choose the option to add the word to the custom dictionary. To set the option, pull down the Tools menu, click Options, click the Spelling tab, then check (clear) the box for Automatic Spell Checking. An open book icon will appear on the status bar to indicate that the automatic spell check is in effect.

STEP 5: AutoCorrect

➤ Check to be sure that you are positioned at the beginning of the document and be sure you are in the Insert mode.

➤ Type the *misspelled* phrase **Teh Spelling Check will be used to check this document.** Try to look at the monitor as you type the word *Teh* to see the AutoCorrect feature in action; Word will correct the misspelling and change *Teh* to *The*.

➤ If you did not see the correction being made, click the arrow next to the Undo command on the Standard toolbar and undo the last several actions. Click the arrow next to the Redo command and redo the corrections in order to see the typing and auto correction.

➤ Save the file.

CREATE YOUR OWN SHORTHAND

Use AutoCorrect to expand abbreviations such as "usa" for United States of America. Pull down the Tools menu, click AutoCorrect, type the abbreviation in the Replace text box and the expanded entry in the With text box. Click the Add command button, then click OK to exit the dialog box and return to the document. The next time you type usa in a document, it will automatically be expanded to United States of America.

STEP 6: Exit Word

➤ Pull down the **File menu.** Click **Exit** to exit Word.

SUMMARY

The chapter provided a broad-based introduction to word processing in general and Microsoft Word in particular. Microsoft Word is always in one of two modes, insert or overtype, and uses a toggle switch (the Ins key) to alternate between the two. The insertion point marks the place within a document where text is added or replaced.

The enter key is pressed at the end of a paragraph, but not at the end of a line because Word automatically wraps text from one line to the next. A hard return is created by the user when he or she presses the enter key; a soft return is created by Word as it wraps text and begins a new line.

The Save and Open commands work in conjunction with one another. The Save command copies the document in memory to disk under its existing name. The Open command retrieves a previously saved document. The Save As command saves the document under a different name and is useful when you want to retain a copy of the current document prior to all changes.

A spell check compares the words in a document to those in a standard and/or custom dictionary and offers suggestions to correct the mistakes it finds. It will detect misspellings, duplicated phrases, and/or irregular capitalization, but will not flag properly spelled words that are used incorrectly.

The AutoCorrect feature corrects predefined spelling errors and/or mistakes in capitalization, automatically, as the words are entered. The feature can also be used to create a personal shorthand as it will expand abbreviations as they are typed.

KEY WORDS AND CONCEPTS

Answer Wizard	Open command	Text box
AutoCorrect	Overtype mode	Tip of the Day
Backup	Page Layout view	TipWizard
Custom dictionary	Save As command	Toggle switch
File menu	Save command	Toolbar
Formatting toolbar	Show/Hide ¶ button	ToolTip
Hard return	Soft return	Undo command
Horizontal ruler	Spell check	Vertical ruler
Insert mode	Standard toolbar	View menu
Insertion point	Status bar	Word wrap
Normal view	Summary Information	

MULTIPLE CHOICE

1. When entering text within a document, the enter key is normally pressed at the end of every:
   (a) Line
   (b) Sentence
   (c) Paragraph
   (d) All of the above

2. Which menu contains the commands to save the current document, or to open a previously saved document?
   (a) The Tools menu
   (b) The File menu
   (c) The View menu
   (d) The Edit menu

3. How do you execute the Print command?
   (a) Click the Print button on the standard toolbar
   (b) Pull down the File, then click the Print command
   (c) Use the appropriate keyboard shortcut
   (d) All of the above

4. The Open command:
   (a) Brings a document from disk into memory
   (b) Brings a document from disk into memory, then erases the document on disk

(c) Stores the document in memory on disk
(d) Stores the document in memory on disk, then erases the document from memory

5. The Save command:
   (a) Brings a document from disk into memory
   (b) Brings a document from disk into memory, then erases the document on disk
   (c) Stores the document in memory on disk
   (d) Stores the document in memory on disk, then erases the document from memory

6. What is the easiest way to change the phrase, *revenues, profits, gross margin*, to read *revenues, profits, and gross margin*?
   (a) Use the insert mode, position the cursor before the *g* in *gross*, then type the word *and* followed by a space
   (b) Use the insert mode, position the cursor after the *g* in *gross*, then type the word *and* followed by a space
   (c) Use the overtype mode, position the cursor before the *g* in *gross*, then type the word *and* followed by a space
   (d) Use the overtype mode, position the cursor after the *g* in *gross*, then type the word *and* followed by a space

7. What happens if you press the Ins key *twice in a row* from within Word?
   (a) You will be in the insert mode
   (b) You will be in the overtype mode
   (c) You will be in the same mode you were in before pressing the key at all
   (d) You will be in the opposite mode you were in before pressing the key at all

8. A document has been entered into Word with a given set of margins, which are subsequently changed. What can you say about the number of hard and soft returns before and after the change in margins?
   (a) The number of hard returns is the same, but the number and/or position of the soft returns is different
   (b) The number of soft returns is the same, but the number and/or position of the hard returns is different
   (c) The number and position of both hard and soft returns is unchanged
   (d) The number and position of both hard and soft returns is different

9. Which of the following is an example of a toggle switch within Word?
   (a) The Ins key
   (b) The Caps Lock key
   (c) The Show/Hide ¶ button on the Standard toolbar
   (d) All of the above

10. Which of the following will be detected by the spell check?
    (a) Duplicate words
    (b) Irregular capitalization
    (c) Both (a) and (b)
    (d) Neither (a) nor (b)

11. Which of the following is likely to be found in a custom dictionary?
    (a) Proper names
    (b) Words related to the user's particular application

(c) Acronyms created by the user for his or her application
(d) All of the above

12. Ted and Sally both use Word but on different computers. Both have written a letter to Dr. Joel Stutz and have run a spell check on their respective documents. Ted's program flags *Stutz* as a misspelling, whereas Sally's accepts it as written. Why?
    (a) The situation is impossible; that is, if they use identical word processing programs they should get identical results
    (b) Ted has added *Stutz* to his custom dictionary
    (c) Sally has added *Stutz* to her custom dictionary
    (d) All of the above reasons are equally likely as a cause of the problem

13. The spell check will do all of the following *except:*
    (a) Flag properly spelled words used incorrectly
    (b) Identify misspelled words
    (c) Accept (as correctly spelled) words found in the custom dictionary
    (d) Suggest alternatives to misspellings it identifies

14. The AutoCorrect feature will:
    (a) Correct errors in capitalization as they occur during typing
    (b) Expand user-defined abbreviations as the entries are typed
    (c) Both (a) and (b)
    (d) Neither (a) nor (b)

15. When does the Save As dialog box appear?
    (a) The first time a file is saved using either the Save or Save As commands
    (b) Every time a file is saved by clicking the Save button on the Standard toolbar
    (c) Both (a) and (b)
    (d) Neither (a) nor (b)

ANSWERS

1. c	6. a	11. d
2. b	7. c	12. c
3. d	8. a	13. a
4. a	9. d	14. c
5. c	10. c	15. a

EXPLORING MICROSOFT WORD

1. Use Figure 1.13 to match each action with its result; a given action may be used more than once or not at all.

Action		Result
a. Click at 1		____ Save the document
b. Click at 2		____ Hide the paragraph markers
c. Click at 3		____ Toggle the overtype mode off

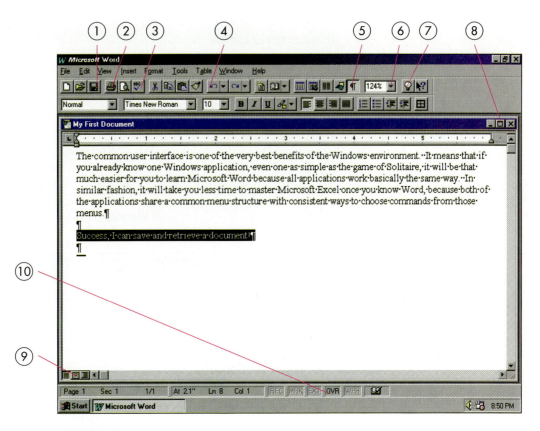

FIGURE 1.13 Screen for Problem 1

d. Click at 4   ____ Print the document
e. Click at 5   ____ Maximize the document window
f. Click at 6   ____ Display the TipWizard
g. Click at 7   ____ Change the magnification
h. Click at 8   ____ Switch to the Page Layout view
i. Click at 9   ____ Correct the spelling in the document
j. Double click at 10
     ____ Undo the previous action

2. Troubleshooting: The informational messages in Figure 1.14 appeared (or could have appeared) in response to various commands issued during the chapter.
   a. Which command produced the message in Figure 1.14a? What action is necessary to correct the indicated problem?
   b. Which command produced the message in Figure 1.14b? When would No be an appropriate response to this message?
   c. The message in Figure 1.14c appeared in response to a File Open command in which the user typed the name of the file to open. What is the most likely corrective action?
   d. What is the effect of pressing the enter key in response to any of the error messages? What is the effect of pressing the Esc key?

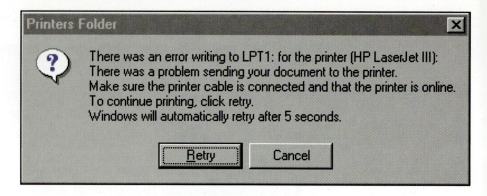

(a) Informational Message 1

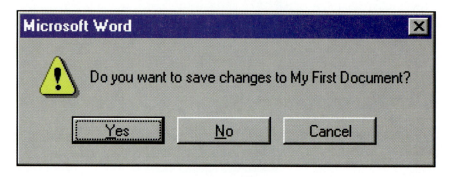

(b) Informational Message 2

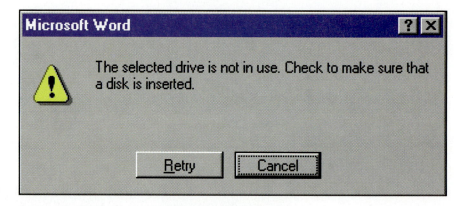

(c) Informational Message 3

FIGURE 1.14   Scrrens for Problem 2

3. Answer the following with respect to Figure 1.15:
   a. What is the name of the document currently being edited?
   b. Which view is selected, Page View or Normal?
   c. Is the ruler present? The Formatting toolbar? The Standard toolbar? How do you cause the missing elements to reappear?
   d. Which mode is active, insert or overtype? How do you switch from one mode to the other?
   e. How do you display (hide) the hard returns? Are the hard returns displayed in the figure?

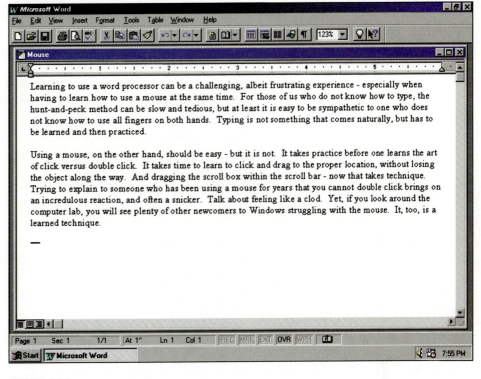

FIGURE 1.15   Screen for Problem 3

4. Answer the following with respect to Figure 1.16:
   a. Which command produced the dialog box shown in the figure?
   b. Which view is selected? How do you change to the List view?
   c. Which document is selected? In which folder is the document located?
   d. How do you preview the selected document? How do you view the properties of that document?
   e. What happens if you double click the selected document? If you right click the selected document?

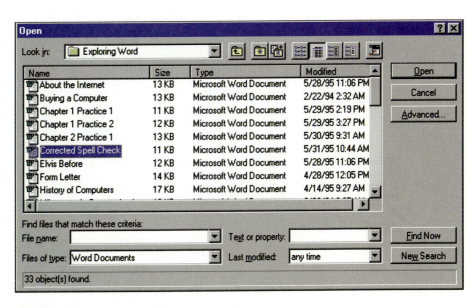

FIGURE 1.16   Screen for Problem 4

PRACTICE WITH MICROSOFT WORD

1. Retrieve the *Chapter1 Practice 1* document shown in Figure 1.17 from the Exploring Word folder, then make the following changes:
   a. Select the text *Your name* and replace it with your name.
   b. Replace *May 31, 1995* with the current date.
   c. Insert the phrase *one or* in line 2 so that the text reads . . . *one or more characters than currently exist.*
   d. Delete the word *And* from sentence four in line 5, then change the w in *when* to a capital letter to begin the sentence.
   e. Change the phrase *most efficient to best.*
   f. Place the insertion point at the end of sentence 2, make sure you are in the insert mode, then add the following sentence: *The insert mode adds characters at the insertion point while moving existing text to the right in order to make room for the new text.*
   g. Place the insertion point at the end of the last sentence, press the enter key twice in a row, then enter the following text: *There are several keys that function as toggle switches of which you should be aware. The Ins key switches between the insert and overtype modes, the Caps Lock key toggles between upper- and lowercase letters, and the Num Lock key alternates between typing numbers and using the arrow keys.*
   h. Save the revised document, then print it and submit it to your instructor.

2. Select-then-do: Formatting is not covered until Chapter 2, but we think you are ready to try your hand at basic formatting now. Most formatting operations are done in the context of select-then-do as described in the document in Figure 1.18. You select the text you want to format, then you execute the appropriate formatting command, most easily by clicking the appropriate button on the Formatting toolbar. The function of each button should be apparent from its icon, but you can simply point to a button to display a ToolTip that is indicative of the button's function.

   An unformatted version of the document in Figure 1.18 exists on the data disk as *Chapter1 Practice 2*. Open the document, then format it to match the completed version in Figure 1.18. Just select the text to format, then click the appropriate button. We changed type size in the original document to 24 points for the title and 12 points for text in the document itself. Be sure to add your name and date as shown in the figure, then submit the completed document to your instructor.

3. Your background: Write a short description of your computer background similar to the document in Figure 1.19. The document should be in the form of a note from student to instructor that describes your background and should mention any previous knowledge of computers you have, prior computer courses you have taken, your objectives for this course, and so on. Indicate whether you own a PC, whether you have access to one at work, and/or whether you are considering purchase. Include any other information about yourself and/or your computer-related background.

   Place your name somewhere in the document in boldface italics. We would also like you to use boldface and italics to emphasize the components of any computer system you describe. Use any font or point size you like. Note, too, the last paragraph, which asks you to print the summary statistics for the document when you submit the assignment to your instructor.

To: Your Name

From: Robert Grauer and Maryann Barber

Subject: Microsoft Word for Windows

Date: May 31, 1995

This is just a short note to help you get acquainted with the insertion and replacement modes in Word for Windows. When the editing to be done results in more characters than currently exist, you want to be in the insertion mode when making the change. On the other hand, when the editing to be done contains the same or fewer characters, the replacement mode is best. And when replacing characters, it is most efficient to use the mouse to select the characters to be deleted and then just type the new characters; the selected characters are automatically deleted and the new characters typed take their place.

FIGURE 1.17 Document for Practice with Word Exercise 1

Select-Then-Do

Many operations in Word are executed as select-then-do operations. You first select a block of text, then you issue a command that will affect the selected text. You may select the text in many different ways, the most basic of which is to click and drag over the desired characters. You may also take one of many shortcuts, which include double clicking on a word, pressing Ctrl as you click a sentence, and triple clicking on a paragraph.

Once text is selected, you may then delete it, **boldface** or *italicize* it, or even change its color. You may move it or copy it to another location, in the same or a different document. You can highlight it, underline, or even check its spelling. Then, depending on whether or not you like what you have done, you may undo it, redo it, and/or repeat it on subsequently selected text.

Jessica Kinzer
September 1, 1995

FIGURE 1.18 Document for Practice with Word Exercise 2

The Computer and Me

My name is Jessica Kinzer and I am a complete novice when it comes to computers. I did not take a computer course in high school and this is my first semester at the University of Miami. My family does not own a computer, nor have I had the opportunity to use one at work. So when it comes to beginners, I am a beginner's beginner. I am looking forward to taking this course, as I have heard that it will truly make me computer literate. I know that I desperately need computer skills not only when I enter the job market, but to survive my four years here as well. I am looking forward to learning Word, Excel, and PowerPoint, and I hope that I can pick up some Internet skills as well.

I did not buy a computer before I came to school as I wanted to see what type of system I would be using for my classes. After my first few weeks in class, I think that I would like to buy **100 Mz Pentium** machine with **16Mb RAM** and a **1 Gb hard drive**. I would like a **quad speed CD-ROM** and a **sound card** (with **speakers**, of course). I also would like to get a laser printer. Now, if only I had the money.

This document did not take long at all to create as you can see by the summary statistics that are printed on the next page. I think I will enjoy this class.

Jessica Kinzer
September 1, 1995

FIGURE 1.19 Document for Practice with Word Exercise 3

Exploring Word Assignment

Jessica Kinzer
CIS 120
September 1, 1995

FIGURE 1.20 Document for Practice with Word Exercise 4

4. The cover page: Create a cover page that you can use for your assignments this semester. Your cover page should be similar to the one in Figure 1.20 with respect to content and should include the title of the assignment, your name, course information, and date. The formatting is up to you. Print the completed cover page and submit it to your instructor for inclusion in a class contest to judge the most innovative design.

Case Studies

It's a Mess

Newcomers to word processing quickly learn the concept of word wrap and the distinction between hard and soft returns. This lesson was lost, however, on your friend who created the *Please Help Me* document on the data disk. The first several sentences were entered without any hard returns at all, whereas the opposite problem exists toward the end of the document. This is a good friend, and her paper is due in one hour. Please help.

Planning for Disaster

Do you have a backup strategy? Do you even know what a backup strategy is? You should learn, because sooner or later you will wish you had one. You will erase a file, be unable to read from a floppy disk, or worse yet suffer a hardware failure in which you are unable to access the hard drive. The problem always seems to occur the night before an assignment is due. The ultimate disaster is the disappearance of your computer, by theft or natural disaster (e.g., Hurricane Andrew). Describe in 250 words or less the backup strategy you plan to implement in conjunction with your work in this class.

A Letter Home

You really like this course and want very much to have your own computer, but you're strapped for cash and have decided to ask your parents for help. Write a one-page letter describing the advantages of having your own system and how it will help you in school. Tell your parents what the system will cost, and that you can save money by buying through the mail. Describe the configuration you intend to buy (don't forget to include the price of software) and then provide prices from at least three different companies. Cut out the advertisements and include them in your letter. Bring your material to class and compare your research with that of your classmates.

Computer Magazines

A subscription to a computer magazine should be given serious consideration if you intend to stay abreast in a rapidly changing field. The reviews on new products are especially helpful and you will appreciate the advertisements should you need to buy. Go to the library or a newsstand and obtain a magazine that appeals to you, then write a brief review of the magazine for class. Devote at least one paragraph to an article or other item you found useful.

GAINING PROFICIENCY: EDITING AND FORMATTING

OBJECTIVES

After reading this chapter you will be able to:

1. Define the select-then-do methodology; describe several shortcuts with the mouse and/or the keyboard to select text.
2. Use the clipboard and/or the drag-and-drop capability to move and copy text within a document.
3. Use the Find and Replace commands to substitute one character string for another.
4. Define scrolling; scroll to the beginning and end of a document.
5. Distinguish between the Normal and Page Layout views; state how to change the view and/or magnification of a document.
6. Define typography; distinguish between a serif and a sans serif typeface; use the Format Font command to change the font and/or type size.
7. Use the Format Paragraph command to change line spacing, alignment, tabs, and indents, and to control pagination.
8. Use the Borders and Shading command to box and shade text.
9. Describe the Undo and Redo commands and how they are related to one another.
10. Use the Page Setup command to change the margins and/or orientation; differentiate between a soft and a hard page break.

OVERVIEW

The previous chapter taught you the basics of Microsoft Word and enabled you to create and print a simple document. The present chapter significantly extends your capabilities, by presenting a variety of commands to change the contents and appearance of a document. These operations are known as editing and formatting, respectively.

You will learn how to move and copy text within a document and how to find and replace one character string with another. You will also learn the basics of typography and be able to switch between the different fonts included within Windows. You will be able to change alignment, indentation, line spacing, margins, and page orientation. All of these commands are used in three hands-on exercises, which require your participation at the computer, and which are the very essence of the chapter.

As you read the chapter, realize that there are many different ways to accomplish the same task and that it would be impossible to cover them all. Our approach is to present the overall concepts and suggest the ways we think are most appropriate at the time we introduce the material. We also offer numerous shortcuts in the form of boxed tips that appear throughout the chapter and urge you to explore further on your own. It is not necessary for you to memorize anything as online help is always available. Be flexible and willing to experiment.

> **WRITE NOW, EDIT LATER**
>
> You write a sentence, then change it, and change it again, and one hour later you've produced a single paragraph. It happens to every writer—you stare at a blank screen and flashing cursor and are unable to write. The best solution is to brainstorm and write down anything that pops into your head, and to keep on writing. Don't worry about typos or spelling errors because you can fix them later. Above all, resist the temptation to continually edit the few words you've written because overediting will drain the life out of what you are writing. The important thing is to get your ideas on paper.

SELECT-THEN-DO

Many operations in Word take place within the context of a **select-then-do** methodology; that is, you select a block of text, then you execute the command to operate on that text. The most basic way to select text is by dragging the mouse; that is, click at the beginning of the selection, press and hold the left mouse button as you move to the end of the selection, then release the mouse.

There are, however, a variety of shortcuts to facilitate the process; for example, double click anywhere within a word to select the word, or press the Ctrl key and click the mouse anywhere within a sentence to select the sentence. Additional shortcuts are presented in each of the hands-on exercises, at which point you will have many opportunities to practice selecting text.

Selected text is affected by any subsequent operation; for example, clicking the Bold or Italic button changes the selected text to boldface or italics, respectively. You can also drag the selected text to a new location, press the Del key to erase the selected text, or execute any other editing or formatting command. The text continues to be selected until you click elsewhere in the document.

> **THE RIGHT MOUSE BUTTON**
>
> Point anywhere within a document, then click the right mouse button to display a shortcut menu. Shortcut menus contain commands appropriate to the item you have selected. Click in the menu to execute a command, or click outside the menu to close the menu without executing a command.

MOVING AND COPYING TEXT

The ability to move and/or copy text is essential in order to develop any degree of proficiency in editing. A move operation removes the text from its current location and places it elsewhere in the same (or even a different) document; a copy operation retains the text in its present location and places a duplicate elsewhere. Either operation can be accomplished using the Windows clipboard and a combination of the **Cut, Copy,** and **Paste commands.** (A shortcut, using the mouse to ***drag-and-drop*** text from one location to another, is described in step 8 in the first hands-on exercise.)

The *clipboard* is a temporary storage area available to any Windows application. Selected text is cut or copied from a document and placed onto the clipboard from where it can be pasted to a new location(s). A move requires that you select the text and execute a Cut command to remove the text from the document and place it on the clipboard. You then move the insertion point to the new location and paste the text from the clipboard into that location. A copy operation necessitates the same steps except that a Copy command is executed rather than a cut, leaving the selected text in its original location as well as placing a copy on the clipboard.

The Cut, Copy, and Paste commands are found in the Edit menu, or alternatively, can be executed by clicking the appropriate buttons on the Standard toolbar. The contents of the clipboard are replaced by each subsequent Cut or Copy command, but are unaffected by the Paste command; that is, the contents of the clipboard can be pasted into multiple locations in the same or different documents.

> **DELETE WITH CAUTION**
>
> You work too hard developing your thoughts to see them disappear in a flash. Hence, instead of deleting large blocks of text, try moving them to the end of your document (or even a new document) from where they can be recalled later if you change your mind. A related practice is to remain in the insert mode (as opposed to overtype) to prevent the inadvertent deletion of existing text as new ideas are added.

UNDO AND REDO COMMANDS

The **Undo command** was introduced in Chapter 1, but it is repeated here because it is so valuable. The command is executed from the Edit menu or by clicking the Undo button on the Standard toolbar. Word enables you to undo up to the last 100 changes to a document. You just click the arrow next to the Undo button on the Standard toolbar to display a reverse-order list of your previous commands, then you click the command you want to undo, which also undoes all of the preceding commands. Undoing the fifth command in the list, for example, will also undo the preceding four commands.

The **Redo command** redoes (reverses) the last command that was undone. As with the Undo command, the Redo command redoes all of the previous commands prior to the command you select. Redoing the fifth command in the list, for example, will also redo the preceding four commands. The Undo and Redo commands work in conjunction with one another; that is, every time a command is undone it can be redone at a later time.

FIND AND REPLACE COMMANDS

The **Find command** enables you to locate a specific occurrence of a character string in order to perform a subsequent editing or formatting operation. The **Replace command** incorporates the Find command and allows you to locate and optionally replace (one or more occurrences of) a designated character string with a different character string.

The two strings are known as the find and replacement strings, respectively and may consist of a single letter, a word, a sentence, or any combination of text and/or formatting. The two strings do *not* have to be the same length; for example, you could replace *16* with *sixteen*. The commands are illustrated in Figure 2.1

The search may or may not be **case-sensitive.** A case-sensitive search (where Match Case is selected as in Figure 2.1a) matches not only the characters, but the use of upper- and lowercase letters. Thus, *There* is different from *there*, and a search on one will not identify the other. A **case-insensitive** search (where Match Case is *not* selected) is just the opposite and finds both *There* and *there*. The search may also specify a match on **whole words only,** which will identify *there*, but not *therefore* or *thereby*.

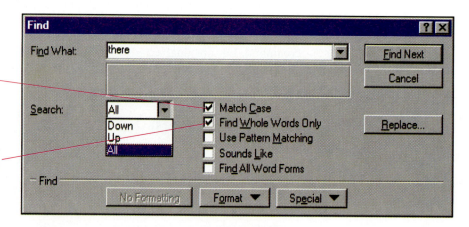

Search will be case-sensitive (will not find *There* or *THERE*)

Search will find whole words only (will not find *therefore* or *thereby*)

(a) Find Command

FIGURE 2.1 Find and Replace Commands

The Replace command in Figure 2.1b implements either **selective replacement,** which lets you examine each occurrence of the character string in context and decide whether to replace it, or **automatic replacement,** where the substitution is made automatically. The latter often produces unintended consequences and is not recommended; for example, if you substitute the word *text* for *book*, the phrase *text book* would become *text text*, which is not what you had in mind.

Selective replacement is implemented in Figure 2.1b by clicking the Find Next command button, then clicking (or not clicking) the Replace button to make the substitution. Automatic replacement (through the entire document) is implemented by clicking the Replace All button.

The Find and Replace commands can include formatting and/or special characters. You can change all italicized text to boldface, or you can change five consecutive spaces to a tab character. You can also use pattern matching to introduce a wild card into the search string. For example, to find all four-letter words that begin with "f" and end with "l" (such as fall, fill, or fail), enter f??l as the find string and select the option for pattern matching. You can even search for a word based on how it sounds. When searching for Marion, for example, check the Sounds Like check box, and the search will find both Marion and Marian.

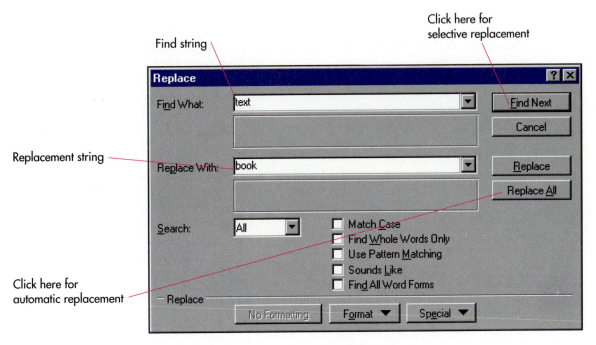

(b) Replace Command

FIGURE 2.1 Find and Replace Commands (continued)

SCROLLING

Scrolling occurs when a document is too large to be seen in its entirety. Figure 2.2a displays a large printed document, only part of which is visible on the screen as illustrated in Figure 2.2b. In order to see a different portion of the document, you need to scroll, whereby new lines will be brought into view as the old lines disappear.

Scrolling comes about automatically as you reach the bottom of the screen. Entering a new line of text, clicking on the down arrow within the scroll bar, or pressing the down arrow key brings a new line into view at the bottom of the screen and simultaneously removes a line at the top. (The process is reversed at the top of the screen.)

Scrolling can be done with either the mouse or the keyboard. Scrolling with the mouse (e.g., clicking the down arrow in the scroll bar) changes what is displayed on the screen, but does not move the insertion point, so that you must click the mouse after scrolling prior to entering the text at the new location. Scrolling with the keyboard, however (e.g., pressing Ctrl+End to move to the end of a document), changes what is displayed on the screen as well as the location of the insertion point, and you can begin typing immediately.

Scrolling occurs most often in a vertical direction as shown in Figure 2.2. It can also occur horizontally, when the length of a line in a document exceeds the number of characters that can be displayed horizontally on the screen.

To: Our Students
From: Robert Grauer and Mary Ann Barber

    Welcome to the wonderful world of word processing. Over the next several chapters we will build a foundation in the basics of Word for Windows, then teach you to format specialized documents, create professional looking tables and charts, and produce well-designed newsletters. Before you know it, you will be a word processing wizard!

    The first chapter presented the basics of Windows as they apply to Word for Windows, then showed you how to create a simple document. You learned how to insert, replace, and/or delete text. This chapter will teach you about fonts and special effects (such as boldfacing and italicizing) and how to use them effectively -- how too little is better than too much.

    You will go on to experiment with margins, tab stops, line spacing, and justification, learning first to format simple documents and then going on to longer, more complex ones. It is with the latter that we explore headers and footers, page numbering, widows and orphans (yes, we really did mean widows and orphans). It is here that we bring in graphics, working with newspaper-type columns, and the elements of a good page design. And without question, we will introduce the tools that make life so much easier (and your writing so much more impressive) -- the Speller, Grammar Checker, Thesaurus, Glossaries, and Styles.

    If you are wondering what all these things are, read on in the text and proceed with the hands-on exercises. Create a simple newsletter, then really knock their socks off by adding graphics, fonts, and WordArt. Create a simple calendar and then create more intricate forms that no one will believe were done by little old you. Create a resume with your beginner's skills, and then make it look like so much more with your intermediate (even advanced) skills. Last, but not least, run a mail merge to produce the cover letters that will accompany your resume as it is mailed to companies across the United States (and even the world).

    It is up to you to practice for it is only through working at the computer that you will learn what you need to know. Experiment and don't be afraid to make mistakes. Practice and practice some more.

    Our goal is for you to learn and to enjoy what you are learning. We have great confidence in you, and in our ability to help you discover what you can do. And to prove us right, we'd love to have you mail us copies of documents that you have created. Write to us at the following address:

        Dr. Robert Grauer/Ms. Mary Ann Barber
        University of Miami
        421 Jenkins Building
        Coral Gables, Florida 33124

    We look forward to hearing from you and hope that you will like our textbook. You are about to embark on a wonderful journey toward computer literacy. Be patient, be inquisitive, and enjoy.

(a) Printed Document

FIGURE 2.2 Scrolling

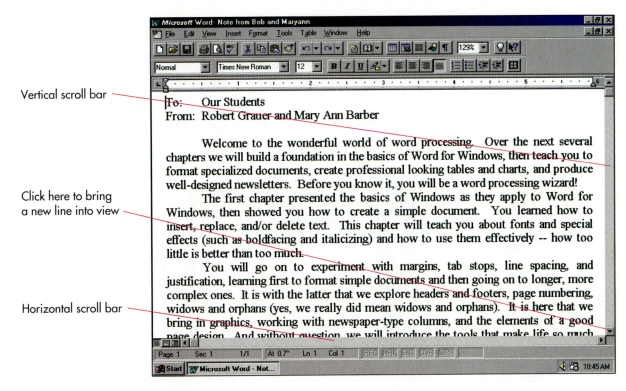

(b) Screen Display

FIGURE 2.2 Scrolling (continued)

VIEW MENU

The *View menu* provides different views of a document. Each view can be displayed at different magnifications, which in turn determine the amount of scrolling necessary to see remote parts of a document.

The *Normal view* is the default view and the one you use most of the time. The *Page Layout* view more closely resembles the printed document and displays the top and bottom margins, headers and footers, page numbers, and other features that do not appear in the Normal view. The Normal view tends to be faster because Word spends less time formatting the display.

The *Zoom command* displays the document on the screen at different magnifications; for example, 75%, 100%, or 200%. (The Zoom command does not affect the size of the text on the printed page.) A Zoom percentage (magnification) of 100% displays the document in the approximate size of the text on the printed page. You can increase the percentage to 200% to make the characters appear larger. You can also decrease the magnification to 75% to see more of the document at one time.

You can let Word determine the magnification for you, by selecting one of three additional Zoom options—Page Width, Whole Page, or Many Pages (Whole Page and Many Pages are available only in the Page Layout view). Figure 2.3a, for example, displays a two-page document in Page Layout view. Figure 2.3b shows the corresponding settings in the Zoom command. (The 37% magnification is determined automatically once you specify the number of pages as shown in the figure.)

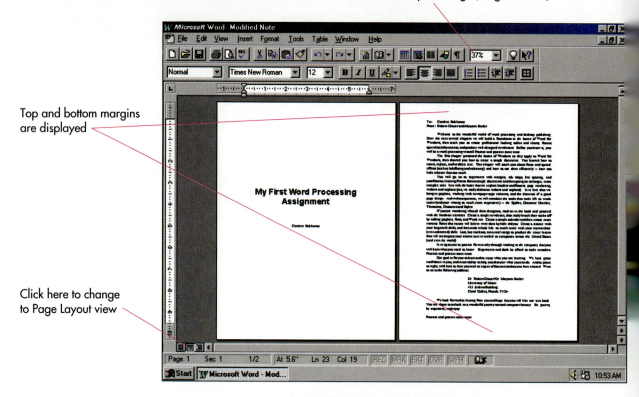

(a) Page Layout View (Zoom to Many Pages)

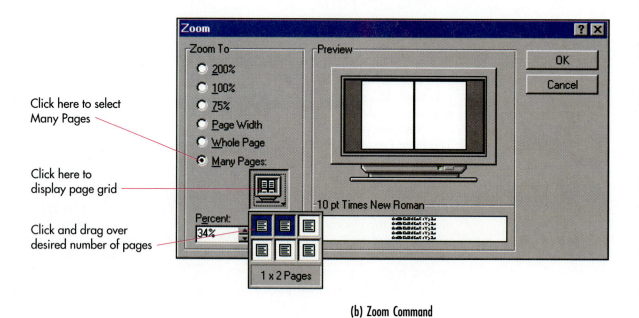

(b) Zoom Command

FIGURE 2.3 View Menu and Zoom Command

HANDS-ON EXERCISE 1

Editing a Document

Objective: To edit an existing document; to change the view and magnification of a document; to scroll through a document. To use the Find and Replace commands; to move and copy text using the clipboard and the drag-and-drop facility. Use Figure 2.4 as a guide in the exercise.

STEP 1: Open the Existing Document

➤ Start Word as described in the hands-on exercises from Chapter 1. Pull down the **File menu** and click **Open** (or click the **Open button** on the toolbar).

- Click the **drop-down arrow** on the Look In list box. Click the appropriate drive, drive C or drive A, depending on the location of your data.
- Double click the **Exploring Word folder** to make it the active folder (the folder in which you will save the document).
- Scroll in the Name list box (if necessary) until you can click the **Note from Bob and Maryann** to select this document. Double click the **document icon** or click the **Open command button** to open the file.

➤ The document should appear on the screen as shown in Figure 2.4a.

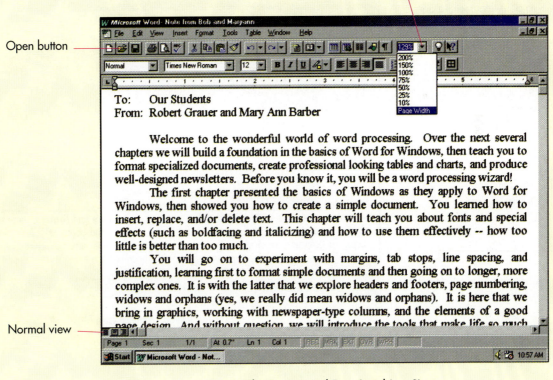

(a) The View Menu and Zoom Control (step 2)

FIGURE 2.4 Hands-on Exercise 1

STEP 2: The View Menu

➤ Change the view:
  - Pull down the **View menu.** Click **Normal.** *Or*
  - Click the **Normal view button** above the status bar.

➤ Change the zoom percentage:
  - Pull down the **View menu.** Click **Zoom.** Click **Page Width.** Click **OK.** *Or*
  - Click the **drop-down arrow** on the Zoom control box and click **Page Width.**

STEP 3: The Save As Command

➤ Pull down the **File menu.** Click the **Save As** command to produce the dialog box in Figure 2.4b.

➤ Enter **Modified Note** as the name of the new document. Click **Save.**

➤ There are now two identical copies of the file on disk: A Note from Bob and Maryann, which we supplied, and Modified Note, which you just created. The title bar of the document window shows the latter name.

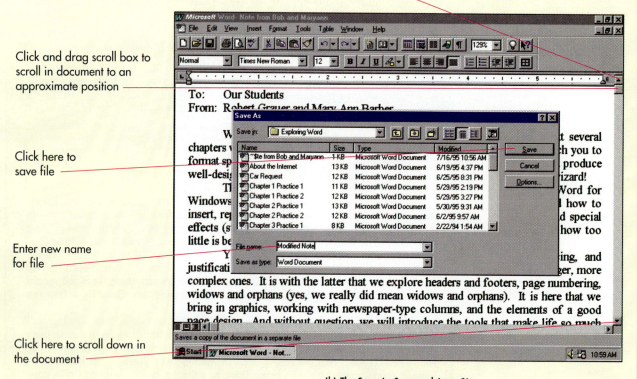

(b) The Save As Command (step 3)

FIGURE 2.4 Hands-on Exercise 1 (continued)

CREATE A BACKUP COPY

The Options button in the Save As dialog box enables you to specify the backup options in effect. Click the Options command button, then check the box to Always Create Backup Copy. The next time you save the document, the previous version on disk becomes a backup copy while the document in memory becomes the current version on disk. See the discussion on page 30 for additional information.

STEP 4: Scrolling

- Click the **down arrow** at the bottom of the vertical scroll bar to move down in the document, causing the top line to disappear and be replaced with a new line at the bottom.
- Click the **down arrow** several times to move through the document, then click the **up arrow key** to scroll in the other direction.
- Drag the **scroll box** to the bottom of the scroll bar, to the top of the scroll bar, then to the middle of the scroll bar, noting that in every instance the insertion point does *not* follow the scrolling; that is, you must click the mouse to move the insertion point to the new location after scrolling with the mouse.

THE MOUSE AND THE SCROLL BAR

Scroll quickly through a document by clicking above or below the scroll box to scroll up or down an entire screen. Move to the top, bottom, or an approximate position within a document by dragging the scroll box to the corresponding position in the scroll bar; for example, dragging the scroll box to the middle of the bar moves the mouse pointer to the middle of the document. Scrolling with the mouse does not change the location of the insertion point, however, and thus you must click the mouse at the new location prior to entering text at that location.

STEP 5: Insert versus Overtype

- Press the **Ins key** once or twice until you clearly see OVR in one of the status boxes at the bottom of the screen. Press the **Ins key** once more so that OVR becomes dim. You are now in the insert mode.
- Use the mouse to scroll to the top of the document, click immediately before the period ending the first sentence, press the **space bar,** then add the phrase **and desktop publishing.**
- Drag the **scroll box** to scroll to the bottom of the document, and click immediately before the first M in Ms. Mary Ann Barber.
- Press the **Ins key** (OVR should appear in the status bar) to toggle to the replacement mode, then type **Dr** to replace Ms. Press the **Ins key** a second time to toggle back to the insert mode.

GAINING PROFICIENCY

➤ Press **Ctrl+Home** to move to the beginning of the document. Click and drag the mouse to select the phrase **Our Students.** Type your name to replace the selected text.

➤ Pull down the **File menu** and click **Save** (or click the **Save button**) to save the changes.

> ### SCROLLING WITH THE KEYBOARD
>
> Scrolling with the mouse or keyboard changes the text that you see displayed on the screen, but only the keyboard changes the location of the insertion point in conjunction with scrolling. Press Ctrl+Home and Ctrl+End to move to the beginning and end of a document. Press Home and End to move to the beginning and end of a line. Press PgUp or PgDn to scroll one screen in the indicated direction. The advantage to scrolling via the keyboard (instead of the mouse) is that the location of the insertion point changes automatically and you can begin typing immediately.

STEP 6: Find and Replace

➤ Press **Ctrl+Home** to move to the beginning of the document. Pull down the **Edit menu.** Click **Replace** to produce the dialog box of Figure 2.4c.

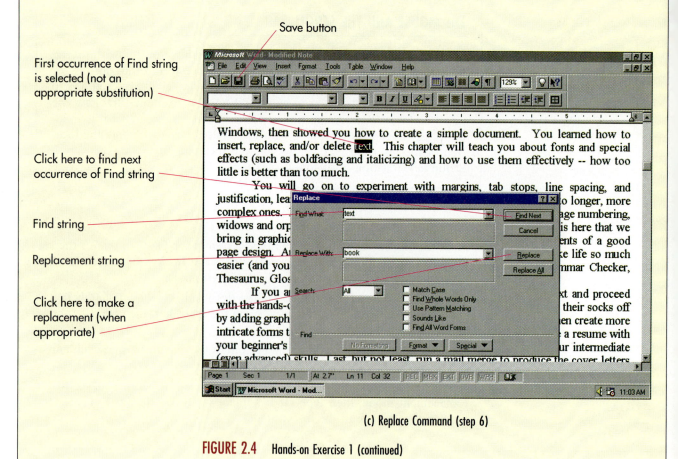

(c) Replace Command (step 6)

FIGURE 2.4 Hands-on Exercise 1 (continued)

- Type **text** in the Find What text box.
- Press the **Tab key.** Type **book** in the Replace With text box.

➤ Click the **Find Next button** to find the first occurrence of the word "text". The dialog box remains on the screen and the first occurrence of "text" is selected. This is *not* an appropriate substitution; that is, you should not substitute book for text at this point.

➤ Click the **Find Next button** to move to the next occurrence without making the replacement. This time the substitution is appropriate.

➤ Click **Replace** to make the change and automatically move to the next occurrence where the substitution is again inappropriate. Click **Find Next** a final time. Word will indicate that it has finished searching the document. Click **OK.**

➤ Change the Find and Replace strings to **Mary Ann** and **Maryann,** respectively. Click the **Replace All** button to make the substitution globally without confirmation. Word will indicate that it has finished searching and that two replacements were made. Click **OK.**

➤ Click the **Close command button** to close the dialog box. Click the **Save button** to save the document. Scroll through the document to review your changes.

SEARCH THE ENTIRE DOCUMENT

The Find command searches from the insertion point *down* to the end of the document, or *up* to the beginning of the document, then asks whether you want to continue searching from the end or beginning of the document (according to the direction you specified). To search the entire document automatically, click the down arrow in the Search list box, and select All (instead of down or up), which will search the document from the beginning to the end.

STEP 7: The Clipboard

➤ Press **PgDn** to scroll toward the end of the document until you come to the paragraph beginning **It is up to you.** Select the sentence **Practice and practice some more** by dragging the mouse over the sentence. (Be sure to include the period.) The sentence will be selected as shown in Figure 2.4d.

➤ Pull down the **Edit menu** and click the **Copy command** or click the **Copy button** on the Standard toolbar.

➤ Press **Ctrl+End** to scroll to the end of the document. Press the **enter key** twice. Pull down the **Edit menu** and click the **Paste command** (or click the **Paste button** on the Standard toolbar). The contents of the clipboard (the copied sentence) are pasted into the document.

➤ Move the insertion point to the end of the first paragraph (following the exclamation point after the word *Wizard*). Press the **space bar** twice. Click the **Paste button** on the Standard toolbar to paste the sentence a second time.

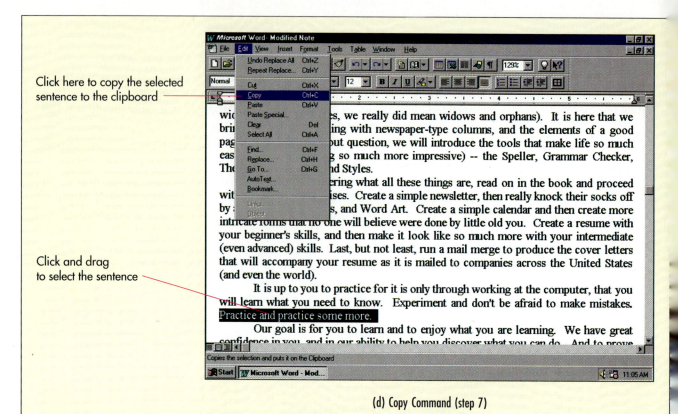

Click here to copy the selected sentence to the clipboard

Click and drag to select the sentence

(d) Copy Command (step 7)

FIGURE 2.4   Hands-on Exercise 1 (continued)

CUT, COPY, AND PASTE

Ctrl+X, Ctrl+C, and **Ctrl+V** are shortcuts to cut, copy, and paste, respectively, and apply to all applications in the Office suite as well as to Windows applications in general. (The shortcuts are easier to remember when you realize that the operative letters X, C, and V are next to each other at the bottom left side of the keyboard.) You can also use the Cut, Copy, and Paste buttons on the Standard toolbar.

STEP 8: Undo and Redo

➤ Click the **drop-down arrow** next to the Undo button to display the previously executed actions as in Figure 2.4e.

➤ The list of actions corresponds to the editing commands you have issued since the start of the exercise. (Your list will be different from ours if you deviated from any instructions in the hands-on exercise.)

➤ Click the **drop-down arrow** for the Redo command. You will hear a beep indicating that there are no actions to be redone; that is, the Undo command has not yet been issued and so there is nothing to redo.

➤ Click the **drop-down arrow** for the Undo command. Click **Paste** (the first command on the list) to undo the last editing command; the sentence, Practice and practice some more, disappears from the end of the first paragraph.

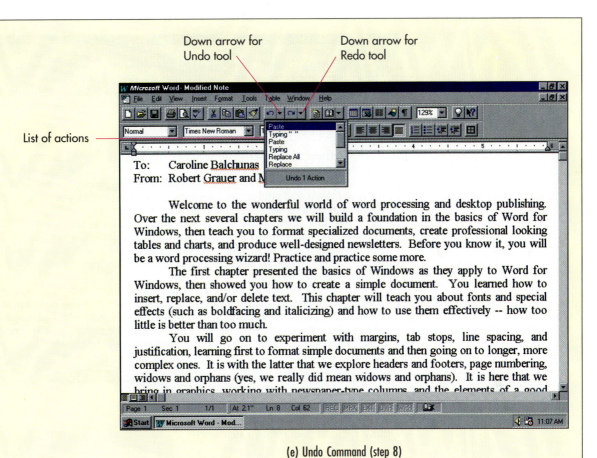

(e) Undo Command (step 8)

FIGURE 2.4 Hands-on Exercise 1 (continued)

➤ Click the remaining steps on the undo list to retrace your steps through the exercise one command at a time. Alternatively, you can scroll to the bottom of the list and click the last command, which automatically undoes all of the preceding commands. Either way, when the undo list is empty, you will have the document as it existed at the start of the exercise.

➤ Click the **down arrow** for the Redo command. This time you will see the list of commands you have undone; click each command in sequence (or click the command at the bottom of the list) and you will restore the document.

STEP 9: Drag and Drop

➤ This step takes a little practice, but it is well worth it. Use the Find command to locate and select the phrase **format specialized documents,** as shown in Figure 2.4f. (Be sure to search the entire document and to include the comma and the space after the comma in the search string.)

➤ Drag the phrase to its new location immediately before the word "and", then release the mouse button to complete the move. (A dotted vertical bar appears as you drag the text, to indicate its new location.)

➤ Click the **drop-down list box** for the Undo command; click **Move** to undo the move.

➤ To copy the selected text to the same location (instead of moving it), press and hold the **Ctrl key** as you drag the text to its new location. (A plus sign appears as you drag the text, to indicate it is being copied rather than moved.)

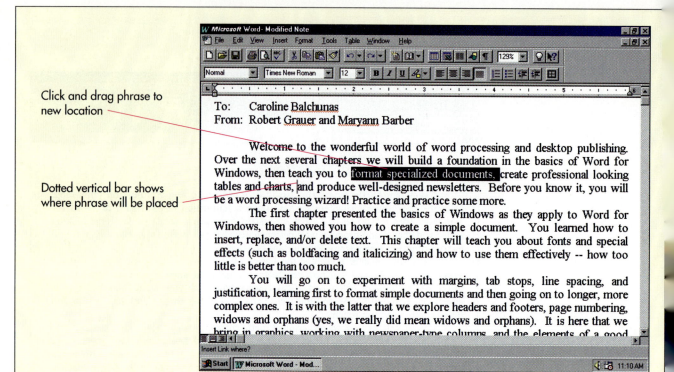

(f) Drag and Drop (step 9)

FIGURE 2.4   Hands-on Exercise 1 (continued)

- Practice the drag-and-drop procedure several times until you are confident you can move and copy with precision.
- Click anywhere in the document to deselect the text. Save the document.

STEP 10: Print the Completed Document

- Pull down the **View menu** and click the **Page Layout command** (or click the **Page Layout button** above the status bar).
- Pull down the **View menu,** click **Zoom,** select **Whole Page,** and click **OK** (or use the **Zoom control box** on the Standard toolbar). Your screen should match Figure 2.4g, which shows the completed document.
- Pull down the **File menu,** click **Print,** and click **OK** (or click the **Print button** on the Standard toolbar) to print the completed document. Submit the document to your instructor as proof you did the exercise.
- Pull down the **File menu.** Click **Close** to close the document and remain in Word.
- Pull down the **File menu** a second time. Click **Exit** if you do not want to continue with the next exercise at this time.

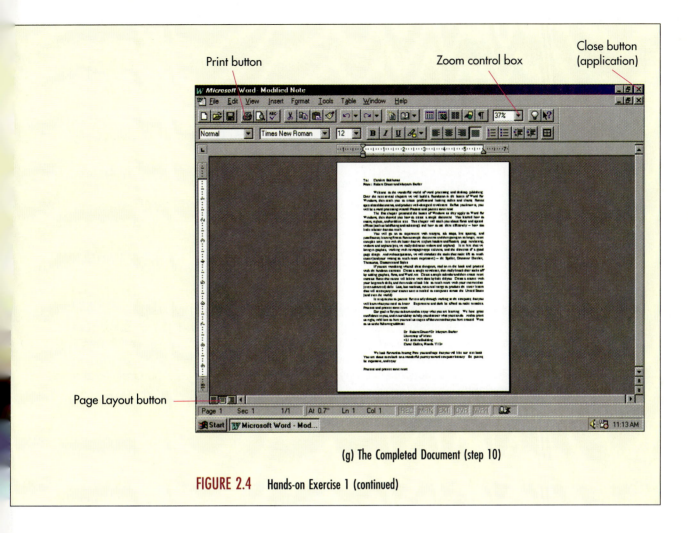

(g) The Completed Document (step 10)

FIGURE 2.4 Hands-on Exercise 1 (continued)

TYPOGRAPHY

Typography is the process of selecting typefaces, type styles, and type sizes. The importance of these decisions is obvious, for the ultimate success of any document depends greatly on its appearance. Type should reinforce the message without calling attention to itself and should be consistent with the information you want to convey.

Typeface

A ***typeface*** is a complete set of characters (upper- and lowercase letters, numbers, punctuation marks, and special symbols). Figure 2.5 illustrates three typefaces—***Times New Roman, Arial,*** and ***Courier New***—that are supplied with Windows, and which in turn are accessible from any Windows application.

One definitive characteristic of any typeface is the presence or absence of tiny cross lines that end the main strokes of each letter. A ***serif*** typeface has these lines. A ***sans serif*** typeface (*sans* from the French for *without*) does not. Times New Roman and Courier New are examples of a serif typeface. Arial is a sans serif typeface.

Serifs help the eye to connect one letter with the next and are generally used with large amounts of text. This book, for example, is set in a serif typeface. A sans serif typeface is more effective with smaller amounts of text and appears in headlines, corporate logos, airport signs, and so on.

Typography is the process of selecting typefaces, type styles, and type sizes. A serif typeface has tiny cross strokes that end the main strokes of each letter; a sans serif typeface does not. A monospaced typeface uses the same amount of space for every character. A proportional typeface allocates space in accordance with the width of the character. The ultimate success of any document depends on its appearance and underlying typography.

(a) Times New Roman (serif and proportional)

Typography is the process of selecting typefaces, type styles, and type sizes. A serif typeface has tiny cross strokes that end the main strokes of each letter; a sans serif typeface does not. A monospaced typeface uses the same amount of space for every character. A proportional typeface allocates space in accordance with the width of the character. The ultimate success of any document depends on its appearance and underlying typography.

(b) Arial (sans serif and proportional)

```
Typography  is  the  process  of  selecting  typefaces,  type  styles
and  type  sizes.   A  serif  typeface  has  tiny  cross  strokes  that  end
the  main  strokes  of  each  letter;  a  sans  serif  typeface  does  not.
A  monospaced  typeface  uses  the  same  amount  of  space  for  every
character.   A  proportional  typeface  allocates  space  in  accordance
with  the  width  of  the  character.   The  ultimate  success  of  any
document  depends  on  its  appearance  and  underlying  typography.
```

(c) Courier New (serif and monospaced)

FIGURE 2.5   Typefaces

A second characteristic of a typeface is whether it is monospaced or proportional. A *monospaced typeface* (e.g., Courier New) uses the same amount of space for every character regardless of its width. A *proportional typeface* (e.g., Times New Roman or Arial) allocates space according to the width of the character. Monospaced fonts are used in tables and financial projections where items must be precisely lined up, one beneath the other. Proportional typefaces create a more professional appearance and are appropriate for most documents.

Any typeface can be set in different *type styles* (e.g., regular, bold, or italic). A *font* (as the term is used in Windows) is a specific typeface in a specific style; for example, *Times New Roman Italic,* **Arial Bold,** or **`Courier New Bold Italic.`**

> ### TYPOGRAPHY TIP—USE RESTRAINT
>
> More is not better, especially in the case of too many typefaces and styles, which produce cluttered documents that impress no one. Try to limit yourself to a maximum of two typefaces per document, but choose multiple sizes and/or styles within those typefaces. Use boldface or italics for emphasis; but do so in moderation, because if you emphasize too many elements, the effect is lost.

Type Size

Type size is a vertical measurement and is specified in points, where one *point* is equal to 1/72 of an inch; that is, there are 72 points to the inch. The measurement is made from the top of the tallest letter in a character set (for example, an uppercase T) to the bottom of the lowest letter (for example, a lowercase y). Most documents are set in 10 or 12 point type; newspaper columns may be set as small as 8 point type. Type sizes of 14 points or higher are ineffective for large amounts of text. Figure 2.6 shows the same phrase set in varying type sizes.

Some typefaces appear larger (smaller) than others even though they may be set in the same point size. The type in Figure 2.6a, for example, looks smaller than the corresponding type in Figure 2.6b even though both are set in the same point size. This is because the letters in the Arial typeface have a taller body than the letters in the Times New Roman design.

Format Font Command

The *Format Font command* gives you complete control over the typeface, size, and style of the text in a document. Executing the command before entering text will set the format of the text you type from that point on. You can also use the command to change the font of existing text by selecting the text, then executing the command. Either way, you will see the dialog box in Figure 2.7, in which you specify the font (typeface), style, and point size.

You can choose any of the special effects (e.g., ~~strikethrough~~ or SMALL CAPS) and/or change the underline options (whether or not spaces are to be underlined). You can even change the color of the text on the monitor, but you need a color printer for the printed document. (The Character Spacing tab produces a different set of options in which you control the spacing of the characters and is beyond our discussion.)

The Preview box shows the text as it will appear in the document. The message at the bottom of the dialog box indicates that Times New Roman is a

This is Arial 8 point type

This is Arial 10 point type

This is Arial 12 point type

This is Arial 18 point type

This is Arial 24 point type

(a) Sans Serif Typeface

This is Times New Roman 8 point type

This is Times New Roman 10 point type

This is Times New Roman 12 point type

This is Times New Roman 18 point type

This is Times New Roman 24 point type

(b) Serif Typeface

FIGURE 2.6 Type Size

TrueType font and that the same font will be used on both the screen and the monitor. TrueType fonts ensure that your document is truly WYSIWYG (What You See Is What You Get) because the fonts you see on the monitor will be identical to those in the printed document. Equally important, TrueType fonts are scaleable, so that you can select any font in any (reasonable) size.

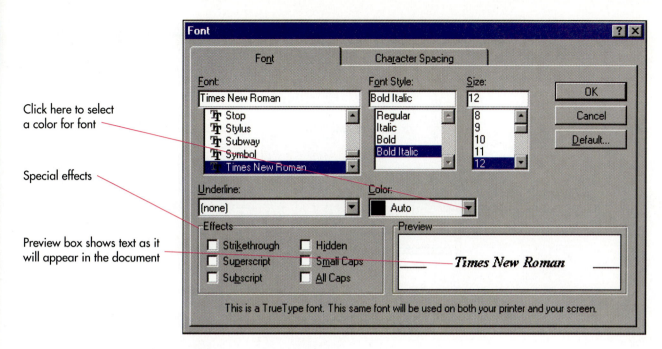

FIGURE 2.7 Format Font Command

PAGE SETUP COMMAND

The **Page Setup command** in the File menu lets you change margins, paper size, orientation, paper source, and/or layout. All parameters are accessed from the dialog box in Figure 2.8 by clicking the appropriate tab within the dialog box.

The default margins are indicated in Figure 2.8a and are one inch on the top and bottom of the page, and one and a quarter inches on the left and right. You can change any (or all) of these settings by entering a new value in the appropriate text box, either by typing it explicitly or clicking the up/down arrow. All of the settings in the Page Setup command apply to the whole document regardless of the position of the insertion point. (Different settings can be established for different parts of a document by creating sections, which is beyond the scope of our present discussion.)

The Paper Size tab within the Page Setup command enables you to change the orientation of a page as shown in Figure 2.8b. **Portrait orientation** is the default. **Landscape orientation** flips the page 90 degrees so that its dimensions are 11 × 8½ rather than the other way around. Note, too, the Preview box in the figure, which shows how the document will appear with the selected parameters.

The Paper Source tab is used to specify which tray should be used on printers with multiple trays, and is helpful when you want to load different types of paper simultaneously. The Layout tab is used to specify options for headers and footers (text that appears at the top or bottom of each page in a document).

Page Breaks

One of the first concepts you learned was that of word wrap, whereby Word inserts a soft return at the end of a line in order to begin a new line. The number and/or location of the soft returns change automatically as you add or delete text within a document. Soft returns are very different from the hard returns inserted by the user, whose number and location remain constant.

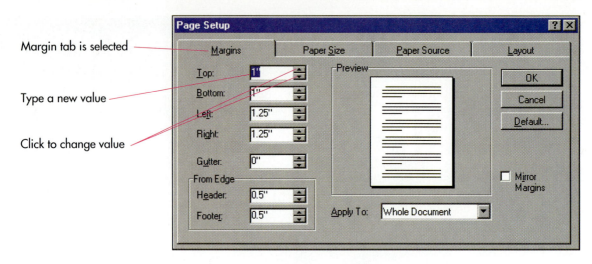

(a) Margins

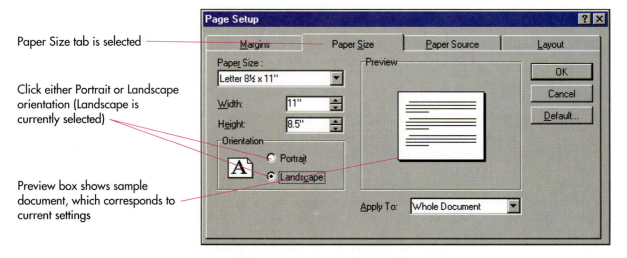

(b) Size and Orientation

FIGURE 2.8 Page Setup Command

In much the same way, Word creates a ***soft page break*** to go to the top of a new page when text no longer fits on the current page. And just as you can insert a hard return to start a new paragraph, you can insert a ***hard page break*** to force any part of a document to begin on a new page. A hard page break is inserted into a document using the Break command in the Insert menu or through the Ctrl+enter keyboard shortcut. (You can prevent the occurrence of awkward page breaks through the Format Paragraph command as described later in the chapter on page 81.)

AN EXERCISE IN DESIGN

The following exercise has you retrieve an existing document from the data disk, then experiment with various typefaces, type styles, and point sizes. The original document uses a monospaced (typewriter style) font, without boldface or italics, and you are asked to improve its appearance. The first step directs you to save the document under a new name so that you can always return to the original if necessary.

There is no right and wrong with respect to design, and you are free to choose any combination of fonts that appeals to you. The exercise takes you through various formatting options but lets you make the final decision. It does, however, ask you to print the final document and submit it to your instructor.

> **IMPOSE A TIME LIMIT**
>
> A word processor is supposed to save time and make you more productive. It will do exactly that, provided you use the word processor for its primary purpose—writing and editing. It is all too easy, however, to lose sight of that objective and spend too much time formatting the document. Concentrate on the content of your document rather than its appearance. Impose a time limit on the amount of time you will spend on formatting. End the session when the limit is reached.

HANDS-ON EXERCISE 2

Character Formatting

Objective: To experiment with character formatting; to change fonts and to use boldface and italics; to copy formatting with the format painter; to insert a page break and see different views of a document. Use Figure 2.9 as a guide in the exercise.

STEP 1: Open the Existing Document

➤ Start Word. Pull down the **File menu** and click **Open** (or click the **Open button** on the toolbar). To open a file:
- Click the **drop-down arrow** on the Look In list box. Click the appropriate drive, drive C or drive A, depending on the location of your data.
- Double click the **Exploring Word folder** to make it the active folder (the folder in which you will open and save the document).
- Scroll in the **Name list box** (if necessary) until you can click **Tips for Writing** to select this document. Double click the **document icon** or click the **Open command button** to open the file.

> **SELECTING TEXT**
>
> The *selection bar,* a blank column at the far left of the document window, makes it easy to select a line, paragraph, or the entire document. To select a line, move the mouse pointer to the selection bar, point to the line and click the left mouse button. To select a paragraph, move the mouse pointer to the selection bar, point to any line in the paragraph, and double click the mouse. To select the entire document, move the mouse pointer to the selection bar and press the Ctrl key while you click the mouse.

➤ Pull down the **File menu.** Click the **Save As command** to save the document as **Modified Tips.**
➤ Pull down the **View menu** and click **Normal** (or click the **Normal View button** above the status bar).
➤ Set the magnification (zoom) to **Page Width.**

STEP 2: The Right Mouse Button

➤ Select the first tip as shown in Figure 2.9a. Click the **right mouse button** to produce the shortcut menu shown in the figure. The shortcut menu contains selected commands from both the Edit and Format menus.
➤ Click outside the menu to close the menu without executing a command.
➤ Press the **Ctrl key** as you click the selection bar to select the entire document, then click the **right mouse button** to display the shortcut menu.
➤ Click **Font** to execute the Format Font command.

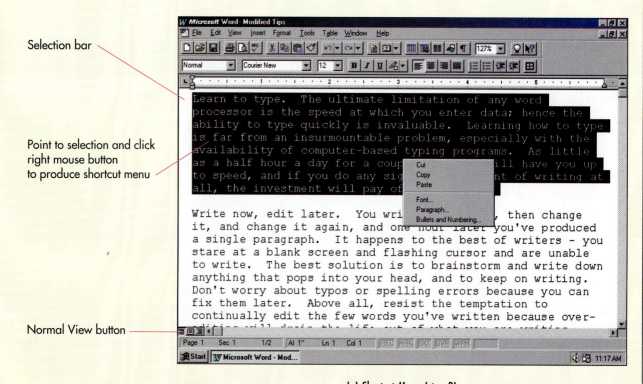

(a) Shortcut Menu (step 2)

FIGURE 2.9 Hands-on Exercise 2

STEP 3: Changing Fonts

➤ Click the **drop-down arrow** on the Font list box of Figure 2.9b to scroll through the available fonts. Select a different font, such as Times New Roman.
➤ Click the **drop-down arrow** in the Font Size list box to choose a point size.
➤ Click **OK** to change the font and point size for the selected text.
➤ Pull down the **Edit menu** and click **Undo** (or click the **Undo button** on the Standard toolbar) to return to the original font.
➤ Experiment with different fonts and/or different point sizes until you are satisfied with the selection; we chose 12 point Times New Roman.
➤ Save the document.

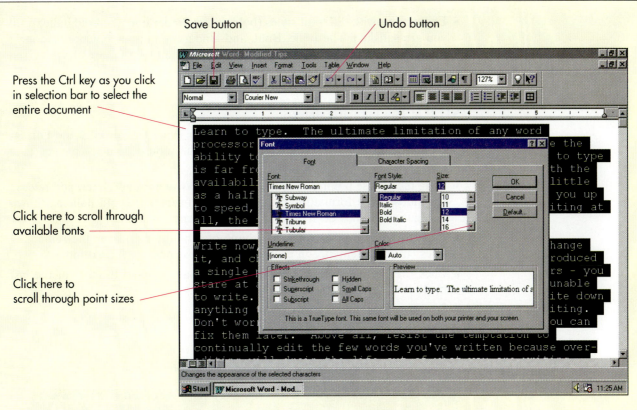

(b) Format Font Command (step 3)

FIGURE 2.9 Hands-on Exercise 2 (continued)

STEP 4: Boldface and Italics

▶ Drag the mouse over the sentence **Learn to type** at the beginning of the document.

▶ Click the **Italic button** on the Formatting toolbar to italicize the selected phrase, which will remain selected after the italics take effect.

▶ Click the **Bold button** to boldface the selected text. The text is now in bold italic.

FIND AND REPLACE FORMATTING

The Replace command enables you to replace formatting as well as text. For example, to replace any text set in bold with the same text in italics, pull down the Edit menu, and click the Replace command to display the Replace dialog box. Click the Find What text box, but do *not* enter any text. Click the Format command button, click Font, click Bold in the Font Style list, and click OK. Click the Replace With text box and again do *not* enter any text. Click the Format command button, click Font, click Italic in the Font Style list, and click OK. Click the Find Next or Replace All command button to do selective or automatic replacement. Use a similar technique to replace one font with another—for example, to replace Times New Roman with Arial.

GAINING PROFICIENCY 71

- Experiment with different styles (bold, italics, underlining, or bold italic) until you are satisfied. The Italic, Bold, and Underline buttons function as toggle switches; that is, clicking the Italic button when text is already italicized returns the text to normal.
- Save the document.

STEP 5: The Format Painter
- Click anywhere within the sentence Learn to Type. **Double click** the **Format Painter button** on the Standard toolbar. The mouse pointer changes to a paintbrush as shown in Figure 2.9c.
- Drag the mouse pointer over the next title, **Write now, edit later,** and release the mouse. The formatting from the original sentence (bold italic as shown in Figure 2.9c) has been applied to this sentence as well.
- Drag the mouse pointer (in the shape of a paintbrush) over the remaining titles (the first sentence in each paragraph) to copy the formatting.
- Click the **Format Painter button** after you have painted the title of the last tip to turn the feature off.
- Save the document.

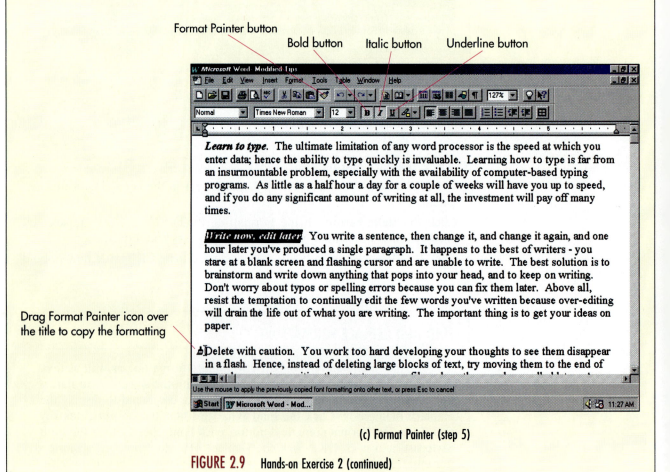

(c) Format Painter (step 5)

FIGURE 2.9 Hands-on Exercise 2 (continued)

THE FORMAT PAINTER

The *Format Painter* copies the formatting of the selected text to other places in a document. Select the text with the formatting you want to copy, then click or double click the Format Painter button on the Standard toolbar. Clicking the button will paint only one selection. Double clicking the button will paint multiple selections until the feature is turned off by again clicking the Format Painter button. Either way, the mouse pointer changes to a paintbrush to indicate that you can paint other selections in the document with the current formatting. Just drag the paintbrush over selected text, which will assume the identical formatting characteristics as the original selection.

STEP 6: Change Margins

▶ Press **Ctrl+End** to move to the end of the document as shown in Figure 2.9d. You will see a dotted line indicating a soft page break. (If you do not see the page break, it means that your document fits on one page because you used a different font and/or a smaller point size; we used 12 point Times New Roman.)

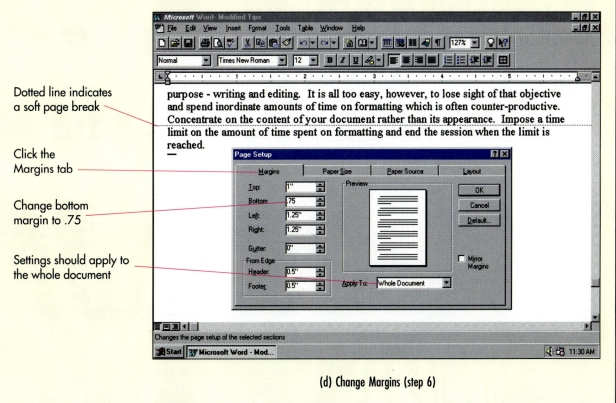

(d) Change Margins (step 6)

FIGURE 2.9   Hands-on Exercise 2 (continued)

- Pull down the **File menu.** Click **Page Setup.** Click the **Margins tab** if necessary. Change the bottom margin to **.75** inch. Check that these settings apply to the **Whole Document.** Click **OK.** The page break disappears because more text fits on the page.

DIALOG BOX SHORTCUTS

You can use the mouse to click an option button, to mark a check box on or off, or to select an option from a list. You can also use a keyboard shortcut for each of these actions. Press Tab (Shift+Tab) to move forward (backward) from one field or command button to the next. Press Alt plus the underlined letter to move directly to a field or command button. Press enter to activate the selected command button. Press Esc to exit the dialog box without taking action. Press the space bar to toggle check boxes on or off. Press the down arrow to open a drop-down list box once the list has been accessed, then press the up or down arrow to move between options in a list box

STEP 7: Create a Title Page

- Press **Ctrl+Home** to move to the beginning of the document. Press **enter** three or four times to add a few blank lines.
- Press **Ctrl+enter** to insert a hard page break. You will see the words "Page Break" in the middle of a dotted line as shown in Figure 2.9e.
- Press the **up arrow key** three times. Enter the title **Tips for Writing.** Select the title, and format it in a larger point size, such as 24 points.
- Enter your name on the next line and format it in a different point size, such as 14 points. Select both the title and your name as shown in the figure. Click the **Center button** on the Formatting toolbar. Save the document.

THE SPELL CHECK

Use the spell check prior to saving a document for the last time, even if the document is just a sentence or two. Spelling errors make your work look sloppy and discourage the reader before he or she has read what you had to say. Spelling errors can cost you a job, a grade, or a lucrative contract. The spell check requires but a single click, so why not use it?

STEP 8: The Completed Document

- Pull down the **View menu** and click **Page Layout** (or click the **Page Layout button** above the status bar).
- Click the **Zoom Control arrow** on the Standard toolbar and select **Two Pages.** Release the mouse to view the completed document in Figure 2.9f. You may want to add additional blank lines on the title page to move the title further down on the page.
- Save the document a final time. Exit Word if you do not want to continue with the next exercise at this time.

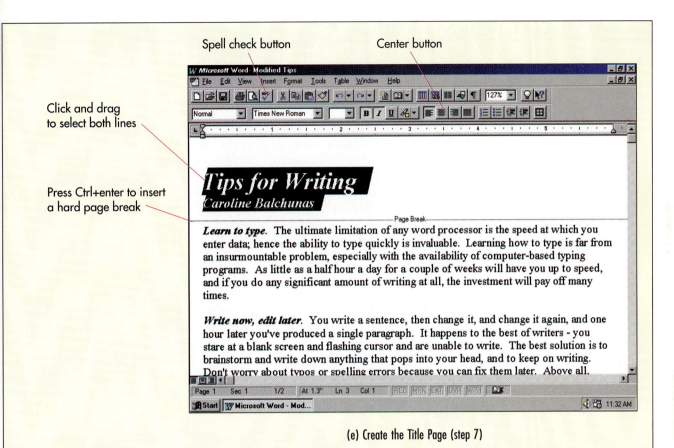

(e) Create the Title Page (step 7)

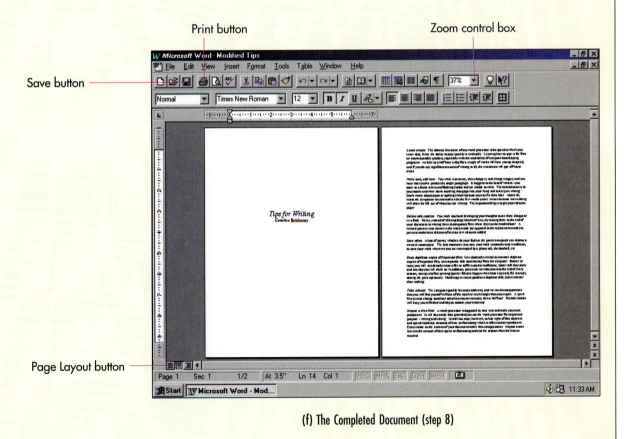

(f) The Completed Document (step 8)

FIGURE 2.9 Hands-on Exercise 2 (continued)

PARAGRAPH FORMATTING

A change in typography is only one way to alter the appearance of a document. You can also change the alignment, indentation, tab stops, or line spacing for any paragraph(s) within the document. You can control the pagination (text flow) and prevent the occurrence of awkward page breaks by specifying that an entire paragraph has to appear on the same page, or that a one-line paragraph (e.g., a heading) should appear on the same page as the next paragraph. You can include borders or shading for added emphasis around selected paragraphs.

All of these features are implemented at the paragraph level and affect all selected paragraphs. If no paragraphs are selected, the commands affect the entire current paragraph (the paragraph containing the insertion point), regardless of the position of the insertion point when the command is executed.

Alignment

Text can be aligned in four different ways as shown in Figure 2.10. It may be justified (flush left/flush right), left aligned (flush left with a ragged right margin), right aligned (flush right with a ragged left margin), or centered within the margins (ragged left and right).

Left aligned text is perhaps the easiest to read. The first letters of each line align with each other, helping the eye to find the beginning of each line. The lines themselves are of irregular length. There is uniform spacing between words, and the ragged margin on the right adds white space to the text, giving it a lighter and more informal look.

Justified text produces lines of equal length, with the spacing between words adjusted to align at the margins. It may be more difficult to read than text that is left aligned because of the uneven (sometimes excessive) word spacing and/or the greater number of hyphenated words needed to justify the lines.

Type that is centered or right aligned is restricted to limited amounts of text where the effect is more important than the ease of reading. Centered text, for example, appears frequently on wedding invitations, poems, or formal announcements. Right aligned text is used with figure captions and short headlines.

Indents

Individual paragraphs can be indented so that they appear to have different margins from the rest of a document. Indentation is established at the paragraph level; thus different indentation can be in effect for different paragraphs. One paragraph may be indented from the left margin only, another from the right margin only, and a third from both the left and right margins. The first line of any paragraph may be indented differently from the rest of the paragraph. And finally, a paragraph may be set with no indentation at all, so that it aligns on the left and right margins.

The indentation of a paragraph is determined by three settings: the ***left indent,*** the ***right indent,*** and a special indent (if any). There are two types of special indentation, first line and hanging, as will be explained shortly. The left and right indents are set to zero by default and produce a paragraph with no indentation at all as shown in Figure 2.11a. Positive values for the left and right indents offset the paragraph from both margins as shown in Figure 2.11b.

We, the people of the United States, in order to form a more perfect Union, establish justice, insure domestic tranquillity, provide for the common defense, promote the general welfare, and secure the blessings of liberty to ourselves and our posterity, do ordain and establish this Constitution for the United States of America.

(a) Justified (flush left/flush right)

We, the people of the United States, in order to form a more perfect Union, establish justice, insure domestic tranquillity, provide for the common defense, promote the general welfare, and secure the blessings of liberty to ourselves and our posterity, do ordain and establish this Constitution for the United States of America.

(b) Left Aligned (flush left/ragged right)

We, the people of the United States, in order to form a more perfect Union, establish justice, insure domestic tranquillity, provide for the common defense, promote the general welfare, and secure the blessings of liberty to ourselves and our posterity, do ordain and establish this Constitution for the United States of America.

(c) Right Aligned (ragged left/flush right)

We, the people of the United States, in order to form a more perfect Union, establish justice, insure domestic tranquillity, provide for the common defense, promote the general welfare, and secure the blessings of liberty to ourselves and our posterity, do ordain and establish this Constitution for the United States of America.

(d) Centered (ragged left/ragged right)

FIGURE 2.10 Alignment

The *first line indent* (Figure 2.11c) affects only the first line in the paragraph and is implemented by pressing the Tab key at the beginning of the paragraph. A *hanging indent* (Figure 2.11d) sets the first line of a paragraph at the left indent and indents the remaining lines according to the amount specified. Hanging indents are often used with bulleted or numbered lists.

The left and right indents are defined as the distance between the text and the left and right margins, respectively. Both parameters are set to zero in this paragraph and so the text aligns on both margins.

(a) No Indents

      Positive values for the left and right indents offset a paragraph from the rest of a document and are often used for long quotations. This paragraph has left and right indents of one-half inch each.

(b) Left and Right Indents

    A first line indent affects only the first line in the paragraph and is implemented by pressing the Tab key at the beginning of the paragraph. The remainder of the paragraph is aligned at the left margin (or the left indent if it differs from the left margin) as can be seen from this example.

(c) First Line Indent

A hanging indent sets the first line of a paragraph at the left indent and indents the remaining lines according to the amount specified. Hanging indents are often used with bulleted or numbered lists.

(d) Hanging Indent

FIGURE 2.11 Indents

> ### INDENTS VERSUS MARGINS
>
> ***Indents*** measure the distance between the text and the margins. ***Margins*** mark the distance from the text to the edge of the page. Indents are determined at the paragraph level, whereas margins are established at the section (document) level. The left and right margins are set (by default) to 1.25 inches each; the left and right indents default to zero. The first line indent is measured from the setting of the left indent.

Tabs

Anyone who has used a typewriter is familiar with the function of the Tab key; that is, press Tab and the insertion point moves to the next ***tab stop*** (a measured position to align text at a specific place.) The Tab key is much more powerful in Word as you can choose from four different types of tab stops (left, center, right, and decimal). You can also specify a ***leader character,*** typically dots or hyphens, to draw the reader's eye across the page. Tabs are often used to create tables within a document.

The default tab stops are set every ½ inch and are left aligned, but you can change the ***alignment*** and/or position with the Format Tabs command in Figure 2.12. Four types of alignment are possible:

- Left alignment, where the text *begins* at the tab stop, corresponds to the Tab key on a typewriter.
- Right alignment, where the text *ends* at the tab stop, is used to align page numbers in a table of contents or to align text at the right margin.
- Center alignment, where text centers over the tab stop, is used infrequently for special effect.
- Decimal alignment, which lines up numeric values in a column on the decimal point, is helpful with statistical text.

Figure 2.12 illustrates a dot leader in combination with a right tab to produce a Table of Contents. The default tab stops have been cleared in Figure 2.12a, in favor of a single right tab at 5.5 inches. The option button for a dot leader has also been checked. The resulting document is shown in Figure 2.12b.

Line Spacing

Line spacing determines the space between the lines in a paragraph. Word provides complete flexibility and enables you to select any multiple of line spacing (single, double, line and a half, and so on). You can also specify line spacing in terms of points (there are 72 points per inch).

Line spacing is set at the paragraph level through the Format Paragraph command, which sets the spacing within a paragraph. The command also enables you to add extra spacing before the first line in a paragraph or after the last line. (Either technique is preferable to the common practice of single spacing the paragraphs within a document, then adding a blank line between paragraphs.)

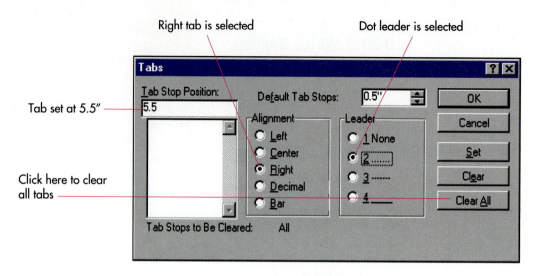

(a) Tab Stops

(b) Table of Contents

FIGURE 2.12 Tabs

FORMAT PARAGRAPH COMMAND

The **Format Paragraph command** is where you specify the alignment, indentation, line spacing, and pagination (text flow) for the selected paragraph(s). As indicated, all of these features are implemented at the paragraph level and affect all selected paragraphs. If no paragraphs are selected, the command affects the entire current paragraph (the paragraph containing the insertion point), regardless of the position of the insertion point when the command is executed.

The Format Paragraph command is illustrated in Figure 2.13. The Indents and Spacing tab in Figure 2.13a calls for a hanging indent, line spacing of 1.5 lines, and justified alignment. The preview within the dialog box enables you to see how the paragraph will appear within the document.

The Text Flow tab in Figure 2.13b illustrates an entirely different set of parameters in which you control the pagination within a document. You are

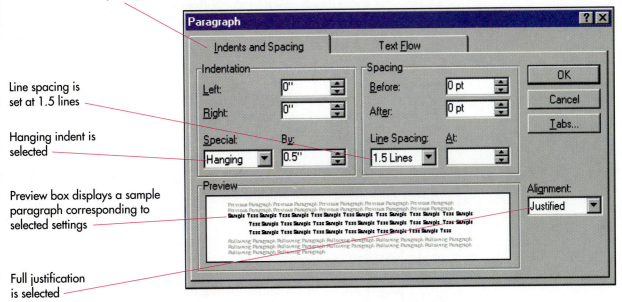

FIGURE 2.13   Format Paragraph Command

already familiar with the concept of page breaks, and the distinction between soft page breaks (inserted by Word) versus hard page breaks (inserted by the user). The check boxes in Figure 2.13b enable you to prevent the occurrence of awkward soft page breaks that detract from the appearance of a document.

You might, for example, want to prevent widows and orphans, terms used to describe isolated lines that seem out of place. A ***widow*** refers to the last line of a paragraph appearing by itself at the top of a page. An **orphan** is the first line of a paragraph appearing by itself at the bottom of a page.

You can also impose additional controls by clicking one or more check boxes Use the Keep Lines Together option to prevent a soft page break from occurring within a paragraph and ensure that the entire paragraph appears on the same page. (The paragraph is moved to the top of the next page if it doesn't fit on the bottom of the current page.) Use the Keep with Next option to prevent a soft page break between the two paragraphs. This option is typically used to keep a heading (a one-line paragraph) with its associated text in the next paragraph.

FORMATTING AND THE PARAGRAPH MARK

The paragraph mark ¶ at the end of a paragraph does more than just indicate the presence of a hard return. It also stores all of the formatting in effect for the paragraph. Hence in order to preserve the formatting when you move or copy a paragraph, you must include the paragraph mark in the selected text. Click the Show/Hide ¶ button on the toolbar to display the paragraph mark and make sure it has been selected.

Borders and Shading

The **Borders and Shading command** puts the finishing touches on a document and is illustrated in Figure 2.14. It lets you create boxed and/or shaded text as well as

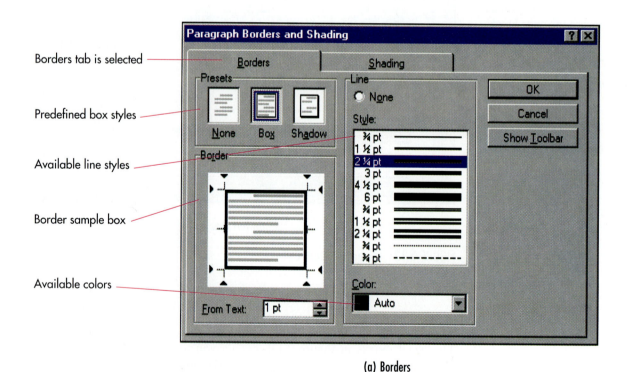

(a) Borders

FIGURE 2.14   Paragraph Borders and Shading

place horizontal or vertical lines around a paragraph. You can choose from several different line styles in any color (assuming you have a color printer). You can place a uniform border around a paragraph (choose Box), or you can create a *drop shadow* effect with thicker lines at the right and bottom. You can also apply lines to selected sides of a paragraph(s) by selecting a line style, then clicking the desired sides within the Border sample box.

Shading is implemented independently of the border. Clear (no shading) is the default. Solid (100%) shading creates a solid box where the text is turned white so you can read it. Shading of 10 or 20 percent is generally most effective to add emphasis to the selected paragraph. The Borders and Shading command is implemented on the paragraph level and affects the entire paragraph—either the current or selected paragraph(s).

PARAGRAPH FORMATTING AND THE INSERTION POINT

Indents, tab stops, line spacing, alignment, text flow, borders, and shading are all set at the paragraph level and affect all selected paragraphs and/or the current paragraph (the paragraph containing the insertion point). The position of the insertion point within the paragraph does not matter as the insertion point can be anywhere within the paragraph when the Format Paragraph command is executed. Keep the concept of paragraph formatting in mind as you do the following hands-on exercise.

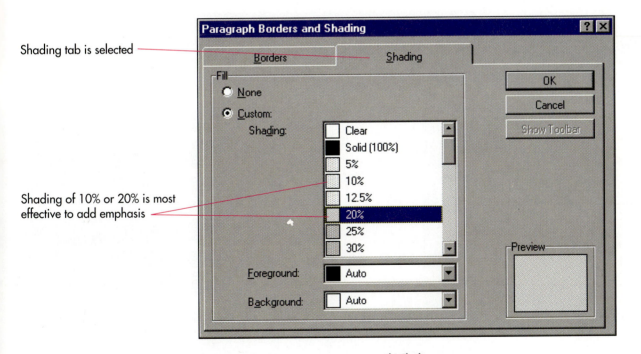

(b) Shading

FIGURE 2.14   Paragraph Borders and Shading (continued)

HANDS-ON EXERCISE 3

Paragraph Formatting

Objective: To implement line spacing, alignment, and indents; to implement widow and orphan protection; to box and shade a selected paragraph. Use Figure 2.15 as a guide in the exercise.

STEP 1: Load the Practice Document

➤ Open the **Modified Tips** document from the previous exercise. If necessary, change to the Page Layout view. Pull down the **Zoom control button** and click **Two Pages** to match the view in Figure 2.15a.

➤ Select the entire second page as shown in the figure. Click the **right mouse button** to produce the shortcut menu. Click **Paragraph.**

SELECT TEXT WITH THE F8 EXTEND KEY

Move to the beginning of the text you want to select, then press the F8 (extend) key. The letters EXT will appear in the status bar. Use the arrow keys to extend the selection in the indicated direction; for example, press the down arrow key to select the line. You can also press any character—for example, a letter, space, or period—to extend the selection to the first occurrence of that character. Press Esc to cancel the selection mode.

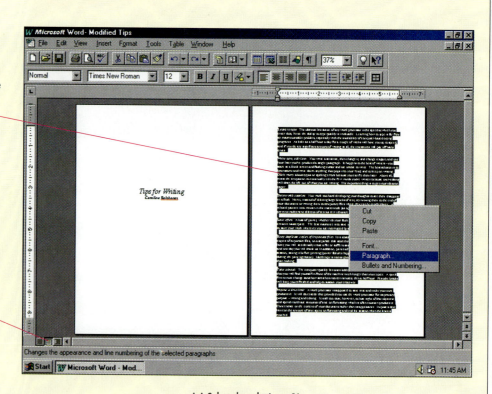

Point to selected text and click right mouse button to produce shortcut menu

Click Page Layout button

(a) Select-then-do (step 1)

FIGURE 2.15 Hands-on Exercise 3

STEP 2: Line Spacing, Justification, and Text Flow

➤ If necessary, click the **Indents and Spacing tab** to view the options in Figure 2.15b.
  • Click the **down arrow** on the list box for Line Spacing and select **1.5 Lines.**
  • Click the **down arrow** on the Alignment list box and select **Justified** as shown in Figure 2.15b.
  • Click the tab for **Text Flow.** Check the box for **Keep Lines Together.** If necessary, check the box for **Widow/Orphan Control.**

➤ Click **OK** to accept all of the settings in the dialog box; that is, you need to click OK only once to accept the settings for Indents and Spacing and Text Flow.

➤ Click anywhere in the document to deselect the text and see the effects of the formatting changes:
  • The document is justified and the line spacing has increased.
  • The document now extends to three pages, with all of the fifth paragraph appearing on the last page.
  • There is a large bottom margin on the second page as a consequence of keeping the lines together in paragraph five.

➤ Save the document.

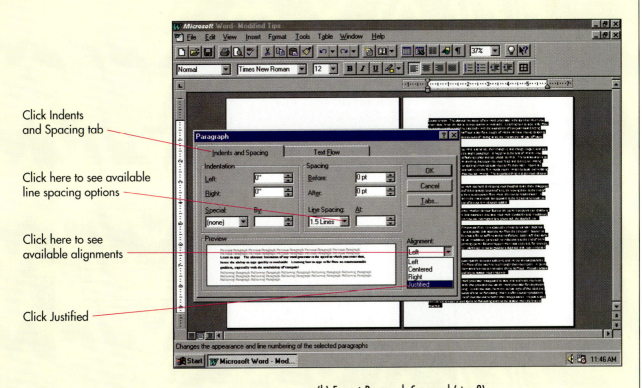

(b) Format Paragraph Command (step 2)

FIGURE 2.15 Hands-on Exercise 3 (continued)

LINE SPACING

Place the insertion point anywhere within a paragraph(s), then press Ctrl+1, Ctrl+2, or Ctrl+5 to set the line spacing at one line (single space), two lines (double space), or 1.5 lines, respectively. You can also customize the Formatting toolbar to display buttons for different line spacing. Point to any toolbar, click the right mouse button to display a shortcut menu, then click Customize to display the Customize dialog box. Select Format from the categories list box, then click and drag the line spacing buttons from the Customize dialog box to the desired position on the toolbar. Click the Close command button to close the dialog box and continue working.

STEP 3: Indents

➤ Select the second paragraph as shown in Figure 2.15c. (The second paragraph will not yet be indented.)

➤ Pull down the **Format menu** and click **Paragraph** (or press the **right mouse button** to produce the shortcut menu and click **Paragraph**).

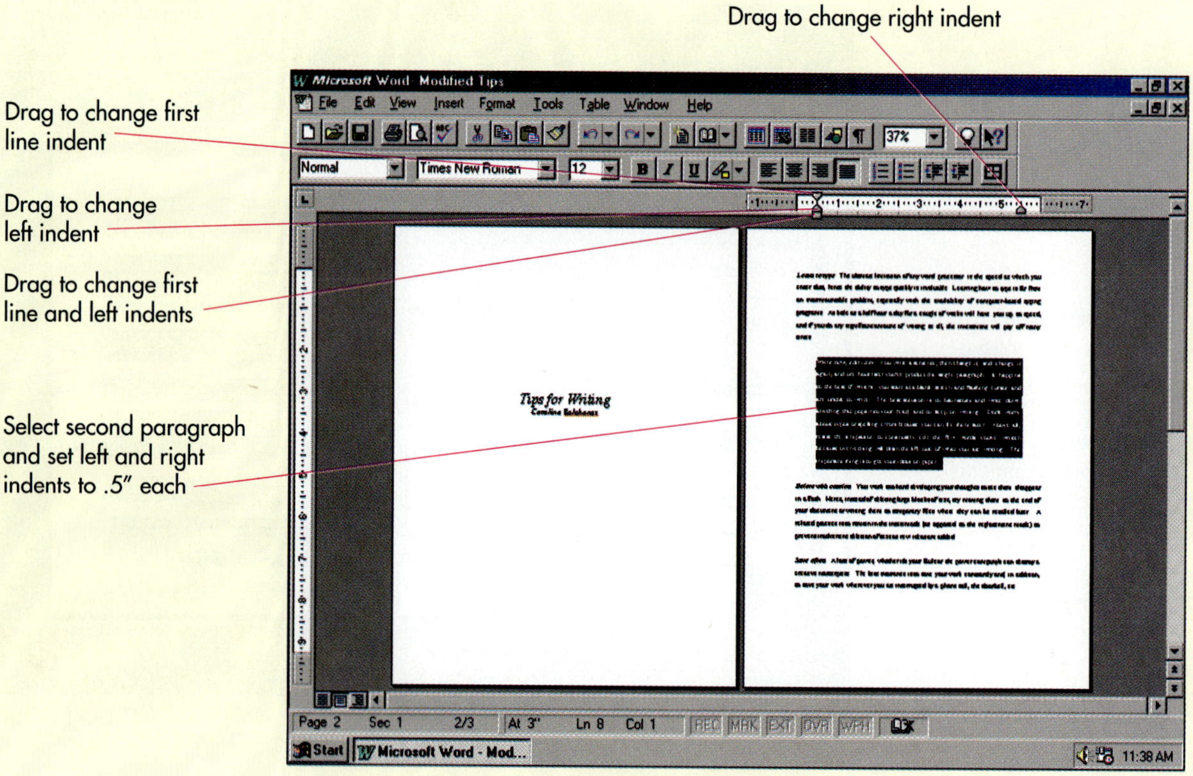

(c) Indents and the Ruler (step 3)

FIGURE 2.15 Hands-on Exercise 3 (continued)

- If necessary, click the **Indents and Spacing tab** in the Paragraph dialog box. Click the **up arrow** on the Left Indentation text box to set the **Left Indent** to **.5** inch. Set the **Right indent** to **.5** inch. Click **OK**. Your document should match Figure 2.15c.
- Save the document.

> ### INDENTS AND THE RULER
>
> Use the ruler to change the first line, left, and/or right indents. Select the paragraph (or paragraphs) in which you want to change indents, then drag the appropriate indent markers to the new location(s).
>
> | | |
> |---|---|
> | First line indent only | Drag the top triangle |
> | Left indent only | Drag the bottom triangle |
> | First line *and* left indents | Drag the box (both triangles move) |
> | Right indent | Drag the triangle at the right margin |
>
> If you get a hanging indent when you wanted to change the left indent, it means you dragged the bottom triangle instead of the box. Click the Undo button and try again. (You can always use the Format Paragraph command rather than the ruler if you continue to have difficulty.)

STEP 4: Borders and Shading

- Pull down the **Format menu**. Click **Borders and Shading** to produce the dialog box in Figure 2.15d.
- If necessary, click the **Borders tab.** Click a style for the line around the box. Click the rectangle labeled **Box** under Presets.
- Click the **Shading Tab**. Click **10%** within the Shading list box.
- Click **OK** to accept the settings for both Borders and Shading.
- Save the document.

> ### THE BORDERS TOOLBAR
>
> Click the Borders button on the Formatting toolbar to display (hide) the Borders toolbar, which contains buttons for many capabilities within the Borders and Shading command. The Borders toolbar contains a list box for the line width, buttons for the border types, and a second list box for shadings.

STEP 5: Help with Formatting

- Click outside the selected text to see the effects of the Borders and Shading command.

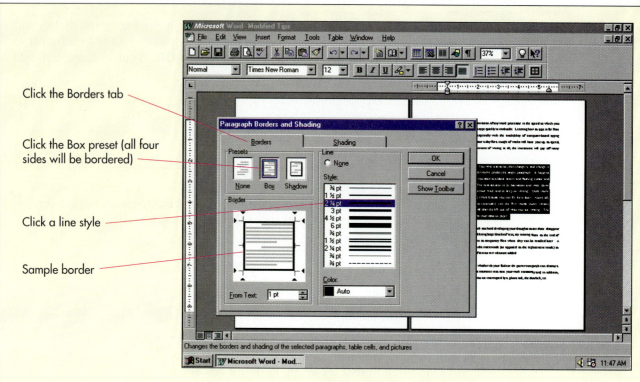

(d) Borders and Shading Command (step 4)

FIGURE 2.15 Hands-on Exercise 3 (continued)

➤ Click the **Help button** on the Standard toolbar. The mouse pointer changes to include a large question mark. Click inside the boxed paragraph to see the formatting in effect for this paragraph as shown in Figure 2.15e.

➤ Click the **Help button** a second time to exit help. The mouse pointer returns to normal.

THE INCREASE AND DECREASE INDENT BUTTONS

The Formatting toolbar provides yet another way to indent (unindent) a paragraph(s). The Increase Indent button increases the left indent, which moves the paragraph to the right; that is, it indents the paragraph to the next tab stop and wraps the text to fit the new indentation. The Decrease Indent button moves the paragraph one tab stop back (to the left).

STEP 6: The Zoom Command

➤ Pull down the **View menu.** Click **Zoom** to produce the dialog box in Figure 2.15f.

➤ Click the **Many Pages** option button. Click the **monitor icon** to display a sample selection box, then click and drag to display three pages across as shown in the figure. Release the mouse. Click **OK**.

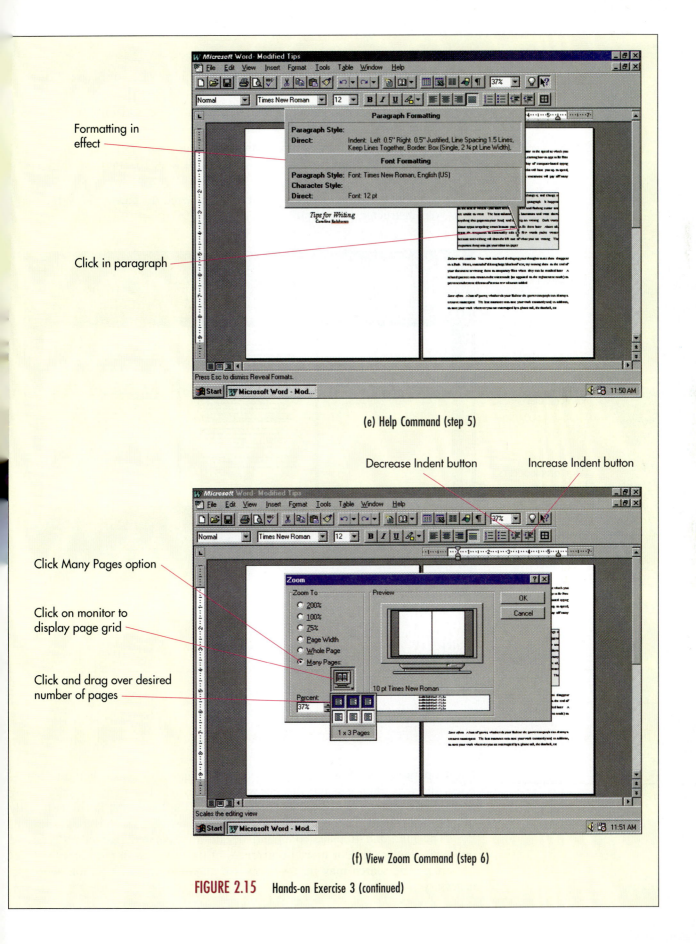

(e) Help Command (step 5)

(f) View Zoom Command (step 6)

FIGURE 2.15 Hands-on Exercise 3 (continued)

STEP 7: The Completed Document

➤ Your screen should match the one in Figure 2.15g, which displays all three pages of the document.

➤ The Page Layout view displays both a vertical and a horizontal ruler. The boxed and indented paragraph is clearly shown in the second page.

➤ The soft page break between pages two and three occurs between tips rather than within a tip; that is, the text of each tip is kept together on the same page.

➤ Save the document a final time. Print the completed document and submit it to your instructor. Exit Word.

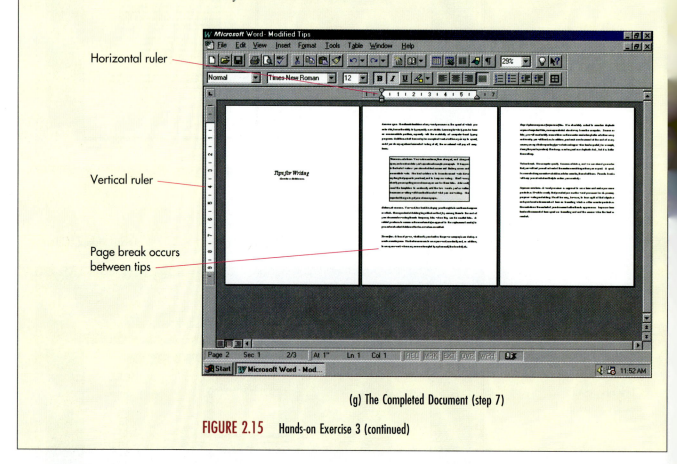

(g) The Completed Document (step 7)

FIGURE 2.15 Hands-on Exercise 3 (continued)

SUMMARY

Many operations in Word are done within the context of select-then-do; that is, select the text, then execute the necessary command. Text may be selected by dragging the mouse, by using the selection bar to the left of the document, or by using the keyboard. Text is deselected by clicking anywhere within the document.

The Find and Replace commands locate a designated character string and optionally replace one or more occurrences of that string with a different character string. The search may be case-sensitive and/or restricted to whole words as necessary.

Text is moved or copied through a combination of the Cut, Copy, and Paste commands and/or the drag-and-drop facility. The contents of the clipboard are replaced by any subsequent Cut or Copy command, but are unaffected by the Paste command; that is, the same text can be pasted into multiple locations.

The Undo command reverses the effect of previous commands. The Undo and Redo commands work in conjunction with one another; that is, every command that is undone can be redone at a later time.

Scrolling occurs when a document is too large to be seen in its entirety. Scrolling with the mouse changes what is displayed on the screen, but does not move the insertion point; that is, you must click the mouse to move the insertion point. Scrolling via the keyboard (for example, PgUp and PgDn) changes what is seen on the screen as well as the location of the insertion point.

The Page Layout view displays top and bottom margins, headers and footers, and other elements not seen in the Normal view. The Normal view is faster because Word spends less time formatting the display. Both views can be seen at different magnifications.

TrueType fonts are scaleable and accessible from any Windows application. The Format Font command enables you to choose the typeface (e.g., Times New Roman or Arial), style (e.g., bold or italic), point size, and color of text.

The Format Paragraph command determines the line spacing, alignment, indents, and text flow, all of which are set at the paragraph level. Borders and shading are also set at the paragraph level. Margins, page size, and orientation, are set in the Page Setup command and affect the entire document (or section).

KEY WORDS AND CONCEPTS

Alignment
Arial
Automatic replacement
Borders and Shading command
Case-insensitive replacement
Case-sensitive replacement
Clipboard
Copy command
Courier New
Cut command
Drag and drop
Drop shadow
Find command
First line indent
Font
Format Font command
Format Painter
Format Paragraph command

Hanging indent
Hard page break
Indents
Landscape orientation
Leader character
Left indent
Line spacing
Margins
Monospaced typeface
Normal view
Page break
Page Layout view
Page Setup command
Paste command
Point size
Portrait orientation
Proportional typeface
Redo command
Replace command
Right indent
Sans serif typeface

Scrolling
Select-then-do
Selection bar
Selective replacement
Serif typeface
Shortcut menu
Soft page break
Tab stop
Times New Roman
Typeface
Type size
Type style
Typography
Undo command
View menu
Whole word replacement
Widows and orphans
Zoom command

Multiple Choice

1. Which of the following commands does *not* place data onto the clipboard?
   (a) Cut
   (b) Copy
   (c) Paste
   (d) All of the above

2. What happens if you select a block of text, copy it, move to the beginning of the document, paste it, move to the end of the document, and paste the text again?
   (a) The selected text will appear in three places: at the original location, and at the beginning and end of the document
   (b) The selected text will appear in two places: at the beginning and end of the document
   (c) The selected text will appear in just the original location
   (d) The situation is not possible; that is, you cannot paste twice in a row without an intervening cut or copy operation

3. What happens if you select a block of text, cut it, move to the beginning of the document, paste it, move to the end of the document, and paste the text again?
   (a) The selected text will appear in three places: at the original location and at the beginning and end of the document
   (b) The selected text will appear in two places: at the beginning and end of the document
   (c) The selected text will appear in just the original location
   (d) The situation is not possible; that is, you cannot paste twice in a row without an intervening cut or copy operation

4. Which of the following are set at the paragraph level?
   (a) Borders and shading
   (b) Tabs and indents
   (c) Line spacing and alignment
   (d) All of the above

5. How do you change the font for *existing* text within a document?
   (a) Select the text, then choose the new font
   (b) Choose the new font, then select the text
   (c) Either (a) or (b)
   (d) Neither (a) nor (b)

6. The Page Setup command can be used to change:
   (a) The margins in a document
   (b) The orientation of a document
   (c) Both (a) and (b)
   (d) Neither (a) nor (b)

7. Which of the following is a true statement regarding indents?
   (a) Indents are measured from the edge of the page rather than from the margin
   (b) The left, right, and first line indents must be set to the same value
   (c) The insertion point can be anywhere in the paragraph when indents are set
   (d) Indents must be set with the Format Paragraph command

8. The spacing in an existing multipage document is changed from single spacing to double spacing throughout the document. What can you say about the number of hard and soft page breaks before and after the formatting change?
   (a) The number of soft page breaks is the same, but the number and/or position of the hard page breaks is different
   (b) The number of hard page breaks is the same, but the number and/or position of the soft page breaks is different
   (c) The number and position of both hard and soft page breaks is the same
   (d) The number and position of both hard and soft page breaks is different

9. The default tab stops are set to:
   (a) Left indents every ½ inch
   (b) Left indents every ¼ inch
   (c) Right indents every ½ inch
   (d) Right indents every ¼ inch

10. Which of the following describes the Arial and Times New Roman fonts?
    (a) Arial is a sans serif font, Times New Roman is a serif font
    (b) Arial is a serif font, Times New Roman is a sans serif font
    (c) Both are serif fonts
    (d) Both are sans serif fonts

11. The find and replacement strings must be
    (a) The same length
    (b) The same case, either upper or lower
    (c) The same length and the same case
    (d) None of the above

12. Assume that you are in the middle of a multipage document. How do you scroll to the beginning of the document and simultaneously change the insertion point?
    (a) Press Ctrl+Home
    (b) Drag the scroll bar to the top of the scroll box
    (c) Both (a) and (b)
    (d) Neither (a) nor (b)

13. Which of the following substitutions can be accomplished by the Find and Replace command?
    (a) All occurrences of the words "Times New Roman" can be replaced with the word "Arial"
    (b) All text set in the Times New Roman font can be replaced by the Arial font
    (c) Both (a) and (b)
    (d) Neither (a) nor (b)

14. Which of the following deselects a selected block of text?
    (a) Clicking anywhere outside the selected text
    (b) Clicking any alignment button on the toolbar
    (c) Clicking the Bold, Italic, or Underline button
    (d) All of the above

15. Which view, and which magnification, lets you see the whole page, including top and bottom margins?
    (a) Page Layout view at 100% magnification
    (b) Page Layout view at Whole Page magnification
    (c) Normal view at 100% magnification
    (d) Normal view at Whole Page magnification

ANSWERS

1. c	**6.** c	**11.** d
2. a	**7.** c	**12.** a
3. b	**8.** b	**13.** c
4. d	**9.** a	**14.** a
5. a	**10.** a	**15.** b

EXPLORING MICROSOFT WORD

1. Use Figure 2.16 to match each action with its result; a given action may be used more than once or not at all.

   Action
   a. Click at 1
   b. Click at 2
   c. Click at 3
   d. Click at 4
   e. Click at 5
   f. Click at 6
   g. Click at 7
   h. Click at 8
   i. Click at 9
   j. Click at 10

   Result
   ____ Undo the previous two commands
   ____ Cut the selected text from the document
   ____ Change the alignment of the current paragraph to justified
   ____ Change the font of the selected text to Arial
   ____ Change the left and right indents to .5 inch
   ____ Change the size of the selected text to 16 point
   ____ Remove the boldface from the selected text
   ____ Change to the Page Layout view
   ____ Paint another phrase with the same format as the currently selected phrase
   ____ Change the magnification to Whole Page

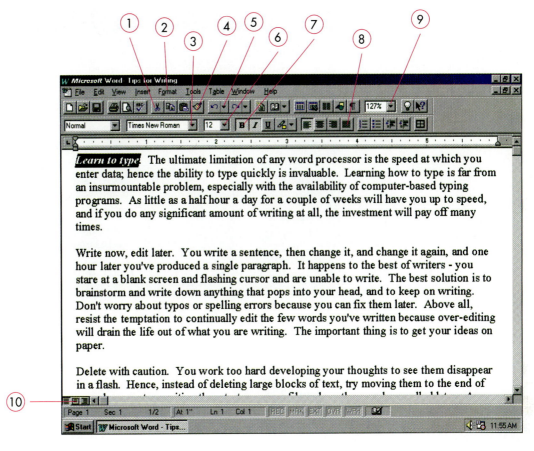

FIGURE 2.16 Screen for Problem 1

2. Describe at least one way, using the mouse or keyboard, to do each of the following. (The answers are found in the boxed tips throughout the chapter. Alternatively, you can access the online help facility to find the information.) How do you:
   a. Scroll to the beginning or end of a document? Does the action you describe also change the insertion point?
   b. Select a sentence? a paragraph? the entire document?
   c. Set the left and right indents?
   d. Insert an additional tab stop?
   e. Copy the formatting in a block of text to multiple places in the same document?
   f. Change selected text to bold, italic, or underlining?
   g. Change the line spacing and alignment for a selected paragraph?
   h. Save the document under a different name?
   i. Box and shade a selected paragraph?

3. The dialog box in Figure 2.17 is intended to replace all occurrences of IT (set in uppercase) with the words Information Technology, with the latter set in italics.
   a. Which options (if any) should be changed so that the command works as intended?
   b. What is the difference between clicking the Find Next and Replace command buttons? Between the Replace and Replace All buttons?

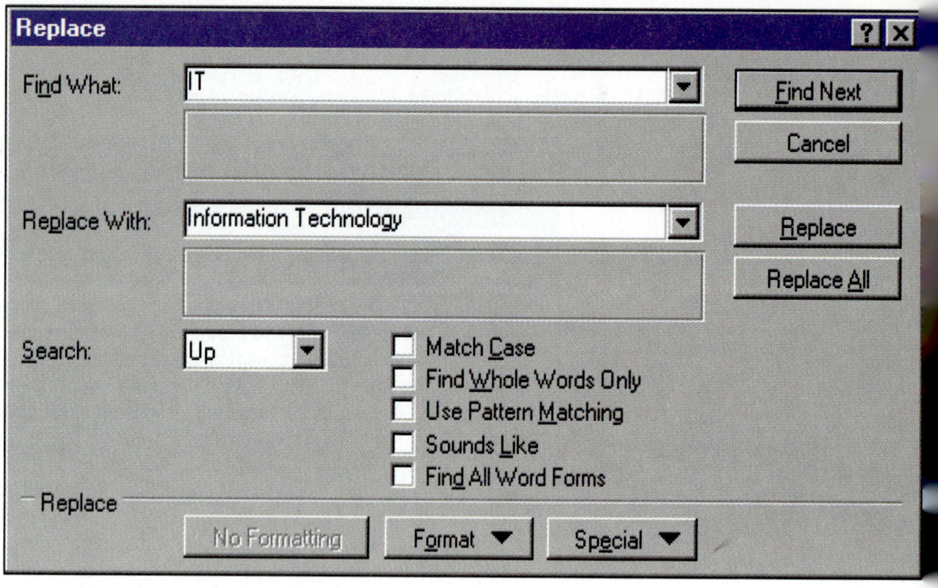

FIGURE 2.17   Screen for Problem 3

4. Exploring Fonts: The fonts available to Microsoft Word (and to every other Windows application) are located in a special Fonts folder as shown in Figure 2.18.

   a. How do you open the Fonts folder? (Hint: Look at the buttons displayed on the taskbar, which indicate the open applications and/or folders on the desktop.)

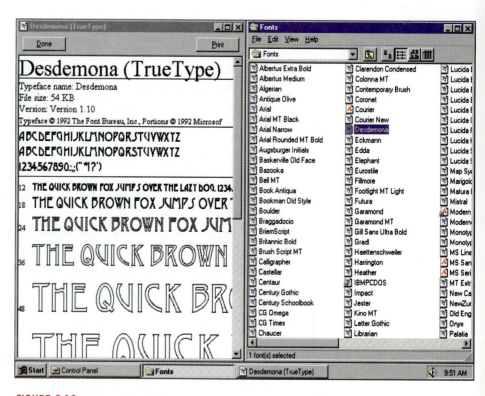

FIGURE 2.18   Screen for Problem 4

96   EXPLORING MICROSOFT WORD 7.0

b. Which view is displayed in the Fonts folder? How do you change the view?
c. Is a toolbar displayed in the window containing the Fonts folder? How do you display (hide) the toolbar?
d. How do you print a sample of the Desdemona font? How would you print a sample of a different font?
e. How do you minimize the Fonts folder? Would this action remove the Fonts folder from the taskbar?
f. How do you close the Fonts folder? Would this action remove the Fonts folder from the taskbar?

PRACTICE WITH MICROSOFT WORD

1. Open the *Chapter 2 Practice 1* document that is displayed in Figure 2.19 and make the following changes.
    a. Copy the sentence *Discretion is the better part of valor* to the beginning of the first paragraph.
    b. Move the second paragraph to the end of the document.
    c. Change the typeface of the entire document to 12 point Arial.
    d. Change all whole word occurrences of *feel* to *think*.
    e. Change the spacing of the entire document from single spacing to 1.5. Change the alignment of the entire document to justified.

It is not difficult, especially with practice, to learn to format a document. It is not long before the mouse goes automatically to the Format Font command to change the selected text to a sans-serif font, to increase the font size, or to apply a boldface or italic style. Nor is it long before you go directly to the Format Paragraph command to change the alignment or line spacing for selected paragraphs.

What is not easy, however, is to teach discretion in applying formats. Too many different formats on one page can be distracting, and in almost all cases, less is better. Be conservative and never feel that you have to demonstrate everything you know how to do in each and every document that you create. Discretion is the better part of valor. No more than two different typefaces should be used in a single document, although each can be used in a variety of different styles and sizes.

It is always a good idea to stay on the lookout for what you feel are good designs and then determine exactly what you like and don't like about each. In that way, you are constantly building ideas for your own future designs.

FIGURE 2.19 Document for Practice with Word Exercise 1

f. Set the phrases *Format Font command* and *Format Paragraph command* in italics.
g. Indent the second paragraph .25 inch on both the left and right.
h. Box and shade the last paragraph.
i. Create a title page that precedes the document. Set the title, *Discretion in Design*, in 24 point Arial bold and center it approximately two inches from the top of the page. Right align your name toward the bottom of the title page in 12 point Arial regular.
j. Print the revised document and submit it to your instructor.

2. Figure 2.20 displays a completed version of the *Chapter 2 Practice 2* document that exists on the data disk. We want you to retrieve the original document from the data disk, then change the document so that it matches Figure 2.20. No editing is required as the text in the original document is identical to the finished document. The only changes are in formatting, but you will have to compare the documents in order to determine the nature of the changes. Color is a nice touch (which depends on the availability of a color printer) and is not required. Add your name somewhere in the document, then print the revised document and submit it to your instructor.

TYPOGRAPHY

The art of formatting a document is more than just knowing definitions, but knowing the definitions is definitely a starting point. A ***typeface*** is a complete set of characters with the same general appearance, and can be *serif* (cross lines at the end of the main strokes of each letter) or *sans serif* (without the cross lines). A ***type size*** is a vertical measurement, made from the top of the tallest letter in the character set to the bottom of the lowest letter in the character set. ***Type style*** refers to variations in the typeface, such as boldface and italics.

Several typefaces are shipped with Windows, including **Times New Roman,** a serif typeface, and **Arial**, a sans serif typeface. Times New Roman should be used for large amounts of text, whereas Arial is best used for titles and subtitles. It is best not to use too many different typefaces in the same document, but rather to use only one or two and then make the document interesting by varying their size and style.

FIGURE 2.20   Document for Practice with Word Exercise 2

3. Create a simple document containing the text of the Preamble to the Constitution as shown in Figure 2.21.
    a. Set the Preamble in 12 point Times New Roman. Use single spacing and left alignment.
    b. Copy the Preamble to a new page, then change to a larger point size and more interesting typeface.
    c. Create a title page for your assignment, containing your name, course name, and appropriate title. Use a different typeface for the title page than in the rest of the document, and set the title in at least 24 points. Submit all three pages (the title page and both versions of the Preamble) to your instructor.

> We, the people of the United States, in order to form a more perfect Union, establish justice, insure domestic tranquillity, provide for the common defense, promote the general welfare, and secure the blessings of liberty to ourselves and our posterity, do ordain and establish this Constitution for the United States of America.

FIGURE 2.21 Document for Practice with Word Exercise 3

4. As indicated in the chapter, anyone who has used a typewriter is familiar with the function of the Tab key; that is, press Tab and the insertion point moves to the next tab stop (a measured position to align text at a specific place.) The Tab key is more powerful in Word because you can choose from four different types of tab stops (left, center, right, and decimal). You can also specify a leader character, typically dots or hyphens, to draw the reader's eye across the page.

    Create the document in Figure 2.22 (on the next page) and add your name in the indicated position. (Use the Help facility to discover how to work with tab stops.) Submit the completed document to your instructor as proof that you have mastered the Tab key.

EXAMPLES OF TAB STOPS

Example 1 - Right tab at 6":

CIS 120 **Maryann Barber**
FALL 1995 **September 21, 1995**

Example 2 - Right tab with a dot leader at 6":

Chapter 1 1
Chapter 2 31
Chapter 3 56

Example 3 - Right tab at 1" and left tab at 1.25":

           To: Maryann Barber
      From: Joel Stutz
Department: Computer Information Systems
   Subject: Exams

Example 4 - Left tab at 2" and a decimal tab at 3.5":

           Rent $375.38
           Utilities $125.59
           Phone $56.92
           Cable $42.45

FIGURE 2.22 Document for Practice with Word Exercise 4

Case Studies

Computers Past and Present

The ENIAC was the scientific marvel of its day and the world's first operational electronic computer. It could perform 5,000 additions per second, weighed 30 tons, and took 1,500 square feet of floor space. The price was a modest $486,000 in 1946 dollars. The story of the ENIAC and other influential computers of the author's choosing is found in the file *History of Computers,* which we forgot to format, so we are asking you to do it for us. Be sure to use appropriate emphasis for the names of the various computers. Create a title page in front of the document, then submit the completed assignment to your instructor.

Your First Consultant's Job

Go to a real installation, such as a doctor's or an attorney's office, the company where you work, or the computer lab at school. Determine the backup procedures that are in effect, then write a one-page report indicating whether the policy is adequate and, if necessary, offering suggestions for improvement. Your report should be addressed to the individual in charge of the business, and it should cover all aspects of the backup strategy—that is, which files are backed up and how often, and what software is used for the backup operation. Use appropriate emphasis (for example, bold italics) to identify any potential problems. This is a professional document (it is your first consultant's job), and its appearance must be perfect in every way.

Paper Makes a Difference

Most of us take paper for granted, but the right paper can make a significant difference in the effectiveness of the document. Reports and formal correspondence are usually printed on white paper, but you would be surprised how many different shades of white there are. Other types of documents lend themselves to colored paper for additional impact. In short, which paper you use is far from an automatic decision. Walk into a local copy store and see if they have any specialty papers available. Our favorite source for paper is a company called PAPER DIRECT (1-800-APAPERS). Ask for a catalog, then consider the use of a specialty paper the next time you have an important project.

The Invitation

Choose an event and produce the perfect invitation. The possibilities are endless and limited only by your imagination. You can invite people to your wedding or to a fraternity party. Your laser printer and abundance of fancy fonts enable you to do anything a professional printer can do. Clip art and/or special paper will add the finishing touch. Go to it—this assignment is a lot of fun.

ENHANCING A DOCUMENT: PROOFING, WIZARDS, CLIPART, AND WORDART

OBJECTIVES

After reading this chapter you will be able to:

1. Use the thesaurus to look up synonyms and antonyms.
2. Explain the objectives and limitations of the grammar check; customize the grammar check for business or casual writing.
3. Use the Insert Symbol command to insert special characters into a document.
4. Use the Insert Date command to insert a date into a document; explain the advantage of inserting the date as a field rather than as text.
5. Create an envelope.
6. Use wizards and templates to create a document; list several wizards provided with Microsoft Word.
7. Use the ClipArt Gallery to insert clip art into a document; explain how frames are used to move and size a graphic object.
8. Use WordArt to insert decorative text into a document.

OVERVIEW

This chapter describes how to add the finishing touches to a document and make it as error free as possible. In it, we review the spell check and introduce the thesaurus as a means of adding precision to your writing. We present the grammar check as a convenient way of finding a variety of errors, but remind you there is no substitute for carefully proofreading the final document. We also show you how to add the date to a document, how to insert special symbols, and how to create and print an envelope.

The second half of the chapter introduces the wizards and templates that are built into Microsoft Word to help you create professionally formatted documents quickly and easily. A template is a partially completed document that contains formatting, text, and/or graphics to which you add additional information to personalize the document. A wizard makes the process even easier as it asks you questions about the document you wish to create, then creates a custom template for you.

The last portion of the chapter introduces the Microsoft ClipArt Gallery, a collection of 1,100 clip art images that can be added to any document. It also introduces Microsoft WordArt, an application included with Microsoft Word that enables you to create decorative text. We believe this to be a very enjoyable chapter that will add significantly to your capability in Microsoft Word. As always, learning is best accomplished by doing, and the hands-on exercises are essential to master the material.

THESAURUS

Mark Twain said the difference between the right word and almost the right word is the difference between a lightning bug and lightning. The *thesaurus* is an important tool in any word processor and is both fun and educational. It helps you to avoid repetition, and it will polish your writing.

The thesaurus is called from the Tools menu. You position the cursor at the appropriate word within the document, then invoke the thesaurus and follow your instincts. The thesaurus recognizes multiple meanings and forms of a word (for example, adjective, noun, and verb) as in Figure 3.1a, and (by double clicking) allows you to look up any listed meaning to produce additional choices as in Figure 3.1b.

Substitutions in the document are made automatically by selecting the desired synonym and clicking the Replace button. You can explore further alternatives by selecting a synonym and clicking on the Look Up button. The thesaurus also provides a list of antonyms for most entries, as in Figure 3.1c.

GRAMMAR CHECK

The *grammar check* attempts to catch mistakes in punctuation, writing style, and word usage by comparing strings of text within a document to a series of predefined rules. As with the spell check, errors are brought to the screen where you can accept the suggested correction and make the replacement automatically, or more often, edit the selected text and make your own changes.

You can also ask the grammar check to explain the rule it is attempting to enforce. Unlike a spell check, the grammar check is subjective, and what seems appropriate to you may be objectionable to someone else. The English language is also too complex for the grammar check to detect every error, although it will find many errors.

CASUAL OR BUSINESS WRITING

Word enables you to change almost every aspect of its environment to suit your personal preference. One option you may want to change is the rules in effect within the grammar check—for example, whether Word should check for business or casual writing. Pull down the Tools menu, click Options, then click the Grammar tab. Choose the option(s) you want, then click OK.

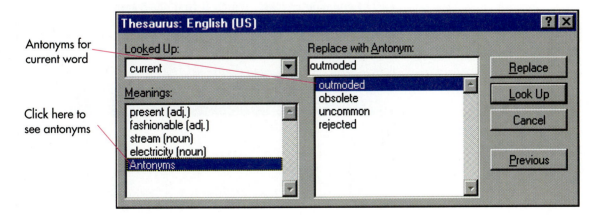

FIGURE 3.1 The Thesaurus

The grammar check caught the inconsistency between subject and verb in Figure 3.2a and suggested the appropriate correction (catch instead of catches). In Figure 3.2b, it suggested the elimination of the superfluous comma. These examples show the grammar check at its best, but much of the time it is more subjective and less capable.

It objects, for example, to the phrase *all men are created equal* in Figure 3.2c, citing excessive use of the passive voice and (in a second message) indicating that the phrase is gender specific. Whether or not you accept the suggestion is entirely up to you. Even with the most stringent options in effect, the entire paragraph in Figure 3.2d went through without error, showing that there is no substitute for carefully proofreading every document.

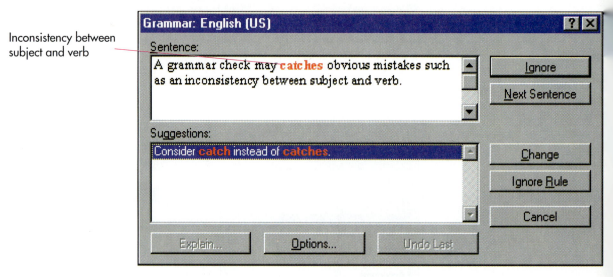

(a) Inconsistent Verb

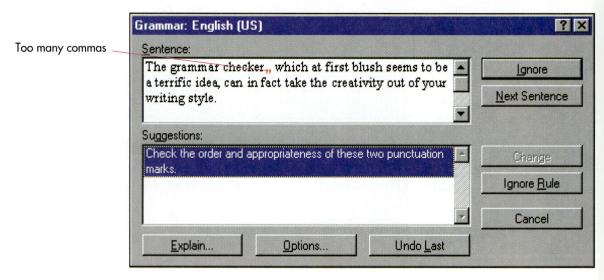

(b) Doubled Punctuation

FIGURE 3.2   The Grammar Check

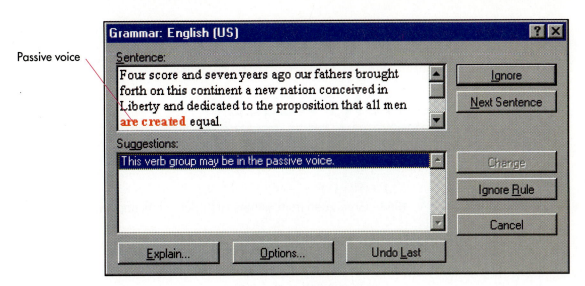

(c) Subjective Rules

> Most items are not notice because English is just to complicated. The grammar program will accept this entire paragraph even though it contains many errors and this sentence is very long and the paragraph does not make any cents. It did not find any mistakes in the previous sentences that used notice rather than noticed, to instead of too, and cents instead of sense. It does not object to misplaced tenses such as yesterday I will go to the store or tomorrow I went to the store.

(d) Limitations

FIGURE 3.2   The Grammar Check (continued)

A RÉSUMÉ AND COVER LETTER

The hands-on exercise that follows shortly is based on the cover letter and accompanying résumé shown in Figure 3.3. The résumé was created using the Résumé Wizard supplied with Microsoft Word as described later in the chapter. The cover letter includes the date and requires an envelope in which it can be mailed. The cover letter also illustrates the use of special symbols such as the accented e's in the word résumé.

THIRTY SECONDS IS ALL YOU HAVE

Thirty seconds is the average amount of time a personnel manager spends skimming your résumé and deciding whether or not to call you for an interview. It doesn't matter how much training you've had or how good you are if your résumé and cover letter fail to project a professional image. Know your audience and use the vocabulary of your targeted field. Be positive and describe your experience from an accomplishment point of view. Maintain a separate list of references and have it available on request. Be sure all information is accurate. Be conscientious about the design of your résumé and proofread the final documents very carefully.

1 Graceland Mansion
Memphis, Tennessee
(901) 332-3322

ELVIS AARON PRESLEY

Objective To emerge from hiding and perform once more before live audiences at major Las Vegas night clubs

Education 1953 - Graduated from Humes High School, Memphis, Tennessee

Employment 1954 - 1977
Featured Singer - Concert Circuit
- Traveled extensively on the concert circuit, including 22 club appearances in Las Vegas and Lake Tahoe

1956 - 1977
Recording Artist
- Recorded 72 albums, including *Loving You, Elvis' Christmas Album, Elvis Is Back, G.I. Blues, Blue Hawaii, Elvis for Everyone, How Great Thou Art, Worldwide 50 Gold Award Hits*, and *Moody Blues*

1956 - 1972
Recording Artist
- Recorded 38 Top Ten hits, 18 of which climbed to #1 on the chart, including *Heartbreak Hotel, Hound Dog, Don't Be Cruel, Love Me Tender, All Shook Up, Teddy Bear, Jailhouse Rock, Hard Headed Woman, Stuck on You, It's Now or Never, Are You Lonesome Tonight, Good Luck Charm*, and *Suspicious Minds*

1956 - 1972
Movie and Television Star
- Performed in 38 feature length movies, including *Love Me Tender, Jailhouse Rock, Blue Hawaii, Viva Las Vegas, The Trouble with Girls*, and *Elvis On Tour*
- Featured on 15 television shows, including *The Milton Berle Show, The Steve Allen Show, Ed Sullivan's Toast of the Town*, and the *Today Show*

1958 - 1960
Soldier, United States Army
- Served in the United States Army as a tank crewman with the Third Armored Division. Stationed in Germany

Awards received Picture placed on United States Postage Stamp
3 Grammy Awards
Male Entertainer of the Year

References Colonel Thomas Andrew Parker, Manager
John Q. Public, Elvis Impersonator's Association
Priscilla Presley, Actress

(a) Résumé

FIGURE 3.3 The Presley Comeback

ELVIS PRESLEY

Graceland Mansion
Memphis, TN 38116
(901) 332-3322

June 1, 1995

Mr. David Letterman
1697 Broadway
New York, NY 10019

Dear Mr. Letterman,

I am seeking an engagement at a Las Vegas night club. I have extensive experience both in private clubs and road tours throughout the United States, and have enclosed my résumé for your review.

It has been some time since I have been in the public eye, but I have never stopped singing or living my music. I am well aware of current trends and have many new songs that will, without question, catch the public's imagination. Everyone needs a gimmick in today's market and I have several extraordinary ideas in mind.

I would welcome the opportunity to meet you to discuss my ideas and audition my new act. Please contact me at the above address or call me at 1-800-HOUND-DOG. I look forward to hearing from you.

Sincerely,

Elvis

(b) Cover Letter

FIGURE 3.3   The Presley Comeback (continued)

The Insert Date and Time Command

The *Insert Date and Time command* puts the date (and/or time) into a document. The information can be inserted as either a specific value (the date and time on which the command is executed) or as a *field.* The latter is updated automatically from the computer's internal clock whenever the document is opened in the Page Layout view or when the document is printed. You can also update a field manually by selecting the appropriate command from a shortcut menu.

The date may be printed in a variety of formats as shown in Figure 3.4. Note that the Insert as Field box is checked, so that the date is inserted as a field. If the box were not checked, the date would be inserted as text and remain constant.

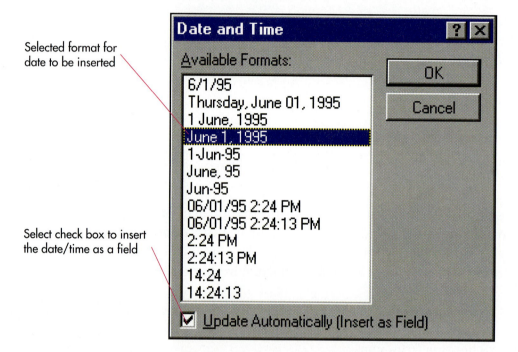

FIGURE 3.4   Insert Date and Time Command

The Insert Symbol Command

One quality that distinguishes the professional document is the use of typographic characters or foreign language symbols; for example, ™ rather than TM, © rather than (C), or ½ and ¼ rather than 1/2 and 1/4. Many of these symbols are contained within the Wingdings or Symbol fonts that are supplied with Windows.

AUTOCORRECT AND AUTOFORMAT

The AutoCorrect feature corrects mistakes as you type by substituting one character string for another—for example "the" for "teh". It will also substitute symbols for typewritten equivalents such as © for (c), provided the entries are included in the table of substitutions. The AutoFormat feature is similar in concept and replaces common fractions such as 1/2 or 1/4 with ½ or ¼. It also converts ordinal numbers such as 1st or 2nd to 1st or 2nd. See practice exercise 4 on page 147 for additional examples.

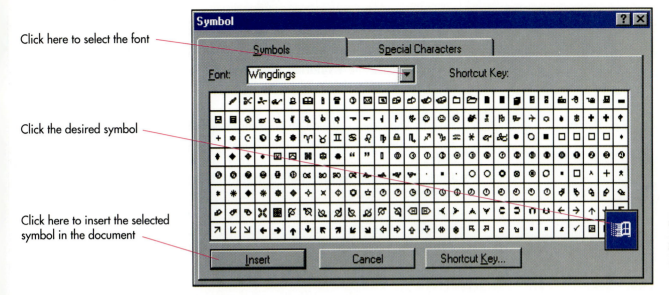

FIGURE 3.5 Insert Symbol Command

The *Insert Symbol command* provides easy access to all of the fonts installed on your system. Choose the font containing the desired symbol—for example, Wingdings in Figure 3.5—then click the Insert command button to place the character into the document. Remember, too, that TrueType fonts are scaleable, enabling you to create some truly unusual documents. (See practice exercise 3 at the end of the chapter.)

Creating an Envelope

An envelope is based on a different physical document from the letter it will contain. Microsoft Word saves you the trouble of having to change margins and orientation by providing the *Envelopes and Labels command* in the Tools menu. Execution of the command produces a dialog box where you supply or edit the necessary addresses. Word takes care of the rest.

The addressee's information can be taken directly from the cover letter as described in step 8 of the following exercise. The return address can be entered directly into the dialog box, or it can be selected from a set of previously stored return addresses. Word also lets you choose from different size envelopes; it will even supply the postal bar code if you request that option.

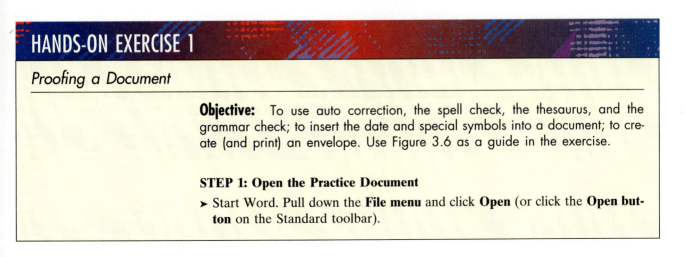

HANDS-ON EXERCISE 1

Proofing a Document

Objective: To use auto correction, the spell check, the thesaurus, and the grammar check; to insert the date and special symbols into a document; to create (and print) an envelope. Use Figure 3.6 as a guide in the exercise.

STEP 1: Open the Practice Document
▶ Start Word. Pull down the **File menu** and click **Open** (or click the **Open button** on the Standard toolbar).

- If you have not yet changed the default folder:
  - Select the appropriate drive, drive C or drive A, from the Look in list.
  - Double click the **Exploring Word folder** to make it the active folder.
  - Double click the **Elvis Before** document to open the document.
- The document opens in the Page Layout view (the view in which it was last saved). The date displayed on your monitor should reflect today's date rather than the date in our document, because the date field is updated automatically.
- Click the **Normal button** above the status bar to change to the Normal view as shown in Figure 3.6a.
- Pull down the **File menu.** Click the **Save As command** to save the document as **Elvis After.** Click **Save.** The title bar reflects the new document **Elvis After,** but you can always return to the original document if you edit the duplicated file beyond redemption.

DATES AND VIEWS

Any document that is opened in the Page Layout view will have all of its fields updated automatically. This is not true in the Normal view, however, and date fields must be updated manually. Point to the field, click the right mouse button to display a shortcut menu, then click the Update Field command.

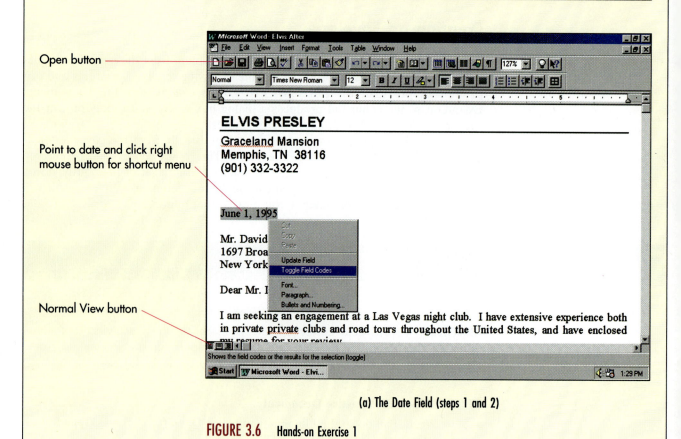

(a) The Date Field (steps 1 and 2)

FIGURE 3.6   Hands-on Exercise 1

STEP 2: The Date Field

- Click anywhere in the date, which is then displayed in gray as shown in Figure 3.6a, to indicate the date is a field rather than text.
- Press **Shift+F9** to display the date as a field (code). Press **Shift+F9** a second time to toggle back to the formatted date.
- Point to the date, then click the **right mouse button** to display the shortcut menu in Figure 3.6a, which contains commands relevant to the date field (Update Field and Toggle Field Codes). This is an alternate way to update the date and toggle between displaying a field code or field result.
- Press **Esc** to close the shortcut menu without executing a command.

FIELD CODES VERSUS FIELD RESULTS

All fields are displayed in a document in one of two formats, as a *field code* or as a *field result*. A field code appears in braces and indicates instructions to insert variable data when the document is printed; a field result displays the information as it will appear in the printed document. You can toggle the display between the field code and field result by pressing Shift+F9 during editing.

STEP 3: Customize the Spell Check

- Pull down the **Tools menu,** click **Options** to display the Options dialog box, then click the **Spelling tab** to display the dialog box in Figure 3.6b.
- Set the spelling options to match those in the figure so that the results of the spell check in step 4 will match the instructions in our exercise.
- Click **OK** to accept the settings and close the dialog box.

STEP 4: The Spell Check

- A red wavy underline appears under misspelled words because the automatic spell check is in effect according to the options set in the previous step. Regardless, it's faster to use the Spelling button to automatically go from one misspelling to another, rather than moving through the document manually.
- Press **Ctrl+Home** to move to the beginning of the document. Click the **Spelling button** on the Standard toolbar to initiate the spell check.
- Graceland is flagged as the first misspelling as shown in Figure 3.6c. Click the **Ignore command button** to accept Graceland as written (or click the **Add command button** to add Graceland to the custom dictionary).
- Continue checking the document, which returns misspellings and other irregularities one at a time.
  - Click **Delete** to delete the second occurrence of the repeated word (*private*).
  - Click **Change** to correct the irregular capitalization in *everyone.*
  - Click **Change** to accept the correct spelling for *gimmick.*
  - Click **Change** to accept the correct spelling for *Sincerely.*
- Click **OK** when the spell check is complete.
- Save the document.

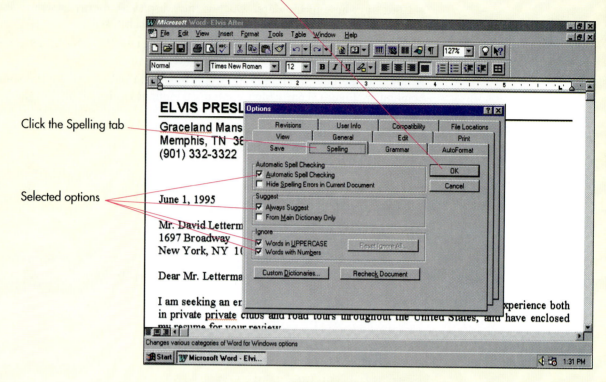

(b) Customize the Spell Check (step 3)

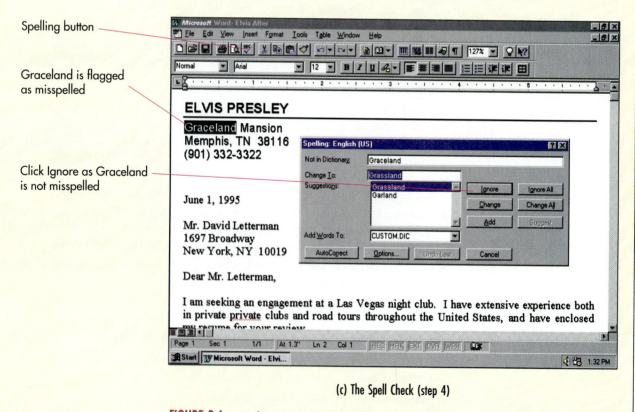

(c) The Spell Check (step 4)

FIGURE 3.6 Hands-on Exercise 1 (continued)

THE CUSTOM DICTIONARY

It's easy to add a word to the custom dictionary, but how do you delete a word if you've added it incorrectly? Word anticipates the problem and allows you to edit the custom dictionary as an ordinary Word document. Pull down the Tools menu, click Options, and select the Spelling tab. Click the Custom Dictionaries command button, select the custom dictionary (if there is more than one) and click Edit. The custom dictionary opens as a Word document. Make and save the necessary changes, close the custom dictionary, and continue working in your regular document. Editing the custom dictionary turns off the automatic spell check, which must be reset if you want the option in effect. Pull down the Tools menu, click the Spelling tab, and check the box for Automatic Spell Checking.

STEP 5: The Thesaurus

➤ Click anywhere within a word you wish to change—for example, the word **magnificent** in Figure 3.6d.

➤ Pull down the **Tools menu.** Click **Thesaurus** to display synonyms for the selected word (magnificent) as shown in the figure.

➤ Double click **grand** (in either list box) to display synonyms for this word.

➤ Click the **Previous command button** to return to the original synonyms for magnificent.

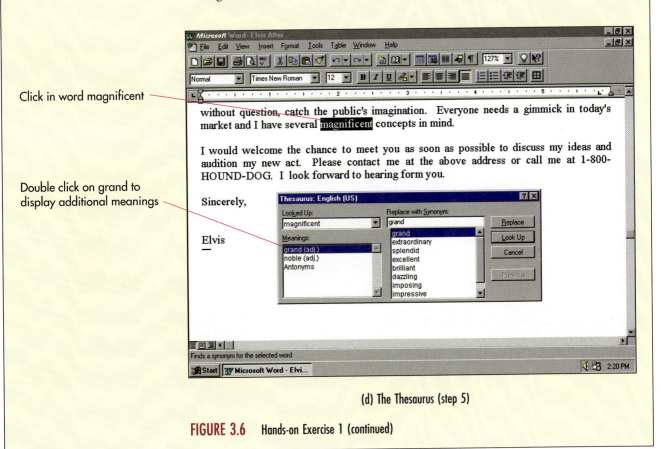

(d) The Thesaurus (step 5)

FIGURE 3.6 Hands-on Exercise 1 (continued)

ENHANCING A DOCUMENT 115

➤ Click **extraordinary** in the list of synonyms. Click **Replace**.

➤ Change other words as you see fit; for example, we changed **chance** to opportunity.

➤ Save the document.

> **TO CLICK OR DOUBLE CLICK**
>
> The thesaurus displays the different meanings and forms of the selected word. Click any meaning, and its synonyms appear in the synonym list box in the right of the window. Double click any meaning or synonym, and Word will look up the selected word and provide additional meanings and synonyms

STEP 6: Customize the Grammar Check

➤ Pull down the **Tools menu.** Click **Options** to display the Options dialog box in Figure 3.6e.

➤ Click the **Grammar tab** and select **For Business Writing** from the list box of available styles. Be sure there is a check next to the box to Show Readability Statistics.

➤ Click the **Customize Settings command button** to customize the grammar check in order to use all possible rules so that you can see it at its potential best.

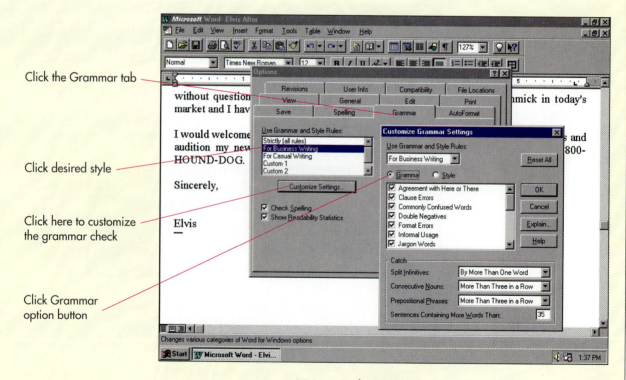

(e) Customize the Grammar Check (step 6)

FIGURE 3.6   Hands-on Exercise 1 (continued)

- Click the **Grammar option button,** then scroll through the list box in order to place a check next to every option as shown in Figure 3.6d.
- Click the **Style option button,** then scroll through its list box in order to place a check next to every option.

➤ Click **OK** to accept the settings for the Grammar Check. Click **OK** a second time to exit the Options dialog box and return to your document.

STEP 7: Check the Document

➤ Press **Ctrl+Home** to move to the beginning of the document. Pull down the **Tools menu** a second time. Click **Grammar** to begin checking the document. Suggestions for correction will be returned one at a time; you can accept or reject the suggestions as you see fit.

➤ Click the **Explain button** at any time to display an explanation of the rule as shown in Figure 3.6f. Click the **Close button** (or press Esc) to close the explanation window.
- We elected to keep the phrase *in the public eye* by clicking the **Ignore button,** but we accepted the next suggestion to change *concepts* to ideas.
- We deleted the phrase *as soon as possible,* by selecting the phrase in the Sentence box, pressing the **Del key,** then clicking the **Change button.**
- The grammar check is not perfect, but it does detect one very significant error: the incorrect use of *form* rather than *from* in the last sentence.

➤ Click **OK** after viewing the readability statistics to return to the document. Save the document.

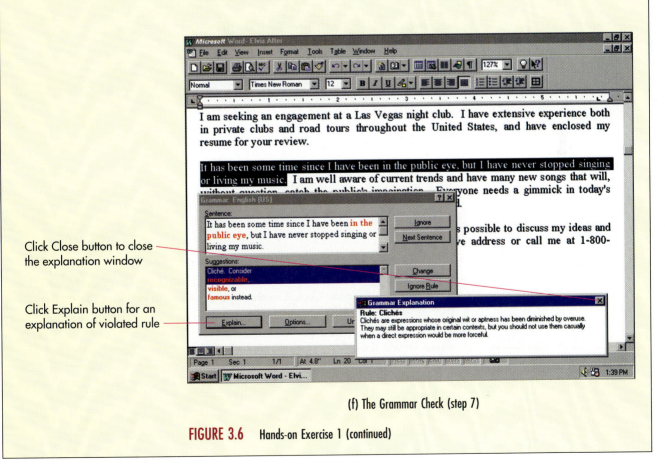

(f) The Grammar Check (step 7)

FIGURE 3.6 Hands-on Exercise 1 (continued)

STEP 8: Special Characters

➤ The proper spelling of résumé places accents over both e's. Click before the first e in resume (in the first paragraph of the letter).

➤ Pull down the **Insert menu,** click **Symbol,** and choose **normal text** from the Font list box.

➤ Click the **é** as shown in Figure 3.6g. Click the **Insert button** to insert the character into the document.

➤ Click in the document window and delete the unaccented e. Click before the second e. Click **Insert.** Click **Close.** Delete the second unaccented e.

➤ Save the document.

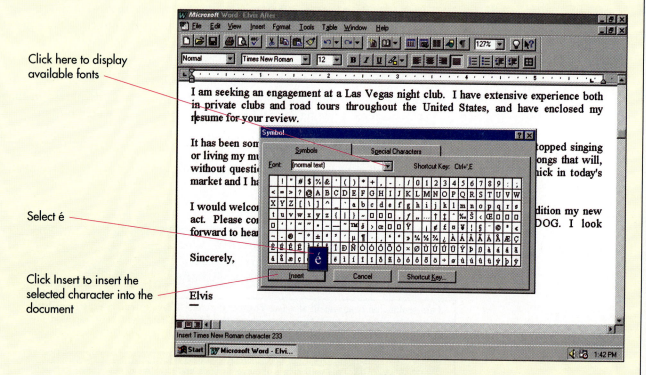

(g) Special Characters (step 8)

FIGURE 3.6 Hands-on Exercise 1 (continued)

STEP 9: Create an Envelope

➤ Click and drag to select the three lines in David Letterman's address. Pull down the **Tools menu.** Click **Envelopes and Labels** to produce the dialog box in Figure 3.6h.

➤ David Letterman's address should be in the Delivery address box because you selected the address prior to executing the Envelopes and Labels command. If this is not the case, you can enter (or edit) the address in the Envelopes and Labels dialog box. You can also enter (or edit) the return address.

➤ Click the **Add to document command button.** Click **Yes** or **No,** depending on whether you want to change the default return address.

➤ Save the document.

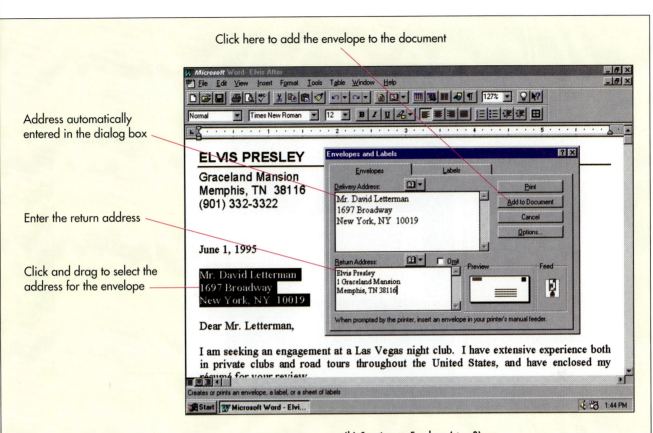

(h) Creating an Envelope (step 9)

FIGURE 3.6 Hands-on Exercise 1 (continued)

CUSTOMIZE THE TOOLBAR

The Create Envelope button is a perfect addition to the Standard toolbar if you print envelopes frequently. Pull down the Tools menu, click Customize, then click the Toolbars tab in the dialog box. If necessary, click the arrow in the Categories list box, select Tools, then drag the Create Envelope button to the Standard toolbar. Close the Customize dialog box. The Create Envelope button appears on the Standard toolbar and can be used the next time you need to create an envelope or label.

STEP 10: The Completed Document

▶ Click the **Page Layout icon** on the status bar. Click the **Zoom Control arrow** on the Standard toolbar and select **Two Pages.** You should see the completed letter and envelope as shown in Figure 3.6i.

▶ Do *not* print the envelope unless you can manually feed an envelope to the printer. Click the page containing the letter (page two in our document).

▶ Pull down the **File menu.** Click **Print.** Click the **Current Page option button.** Click **OK** to print only the letter. Exit Word if you do not want to continue with the next exercise at this time.

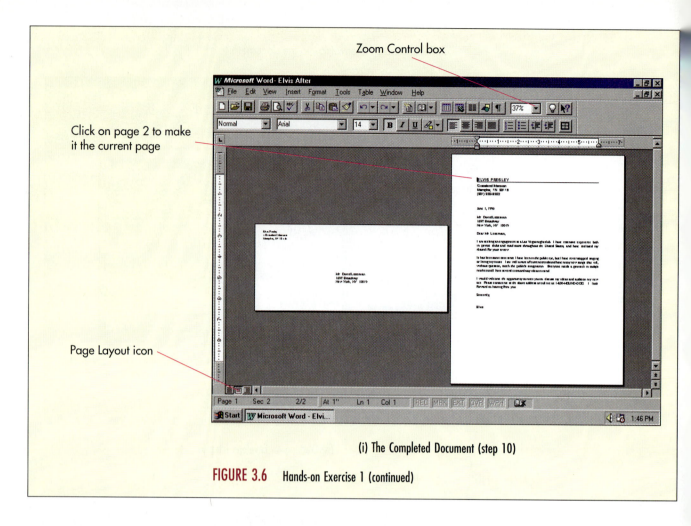

(i) The Completed Document (step 10)

FIGURE 3.6 Hands-on Exercise 1 (continued)

WIZARDS AND TEMPLATES

A *template* is a partially completed document that contains formatting, text, and/or graphics. It may be as simple as a memo or as complex as a résumé or newsletter. Word provides a variety of templates for common documents including a résumé, letter, memo, report, or fax cover sheet. You can design your own templates, or you can use the ones built into Word. A *wizard* attempts to make the process even easier by asking questions, then creating the template for you.

Figure 3.7 illustrates the use of wizards and templates in conjunction with a résumé. You can choose from one of three existing templates (contemporary, elegant, and professional) as shown in Figure 3.7a. Each of these templates is a partially completed résumé to which you add personal information to create your own résumé according to the formatting stored within the template.

We prefer, however, to use the **Résumé Wizard** to create a custom template. This is accomplished by selecting the wizard in Figure 3.7a, then answering the questions posed by the Wizard. We specify the type of résumé in Figure 3.7b, enter some personal information in Figure 3.7c, and choose the categories in Figure 3.7d. (The wizard continues to ask additional questions not shown in Figure 3.7.)

The end product of the Résumé Wizard is the template in Figure 3.7e. You save the finished product as a regular document, then you complete the résumé by entering the specifics of your employment. You can copy and paste information within the résumé, just as you would with a regular document. It takes a little practice, but the end result is a professional résumé.

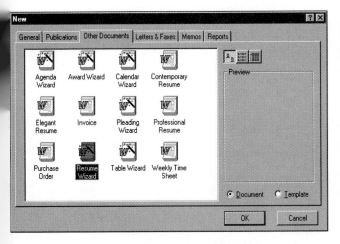
(a) Résumé Wizards and Templates

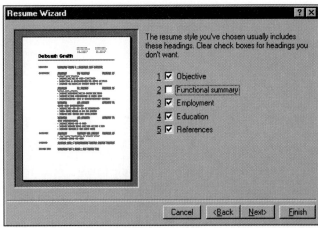
(d) Choose the Categories

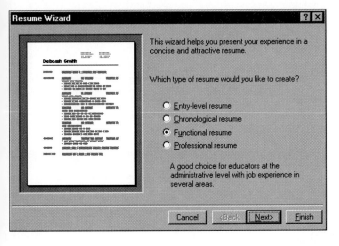
(b) Résumé Wizard

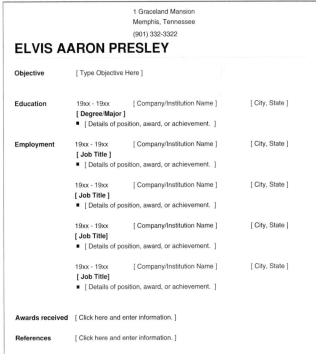
(e) The Template

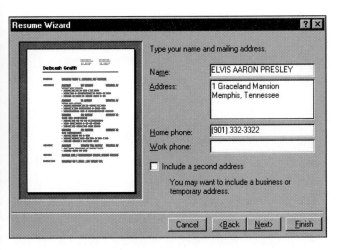
(c) Supply the Information

FIGURE 3.7 Creating a Résumé

ENHANCING A DOCUMENT

(a) Calendar

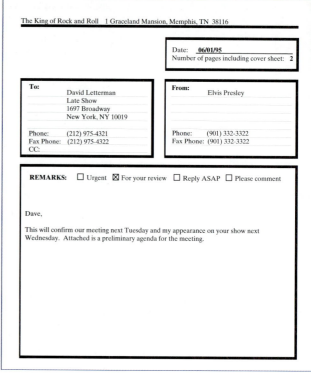
(b) Fax Cover Sheet

(c) Agenda

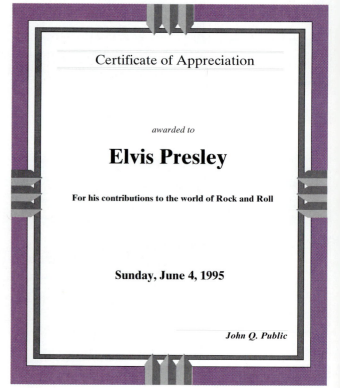
(d) Award

FIGURE 3.8 What You Can Do with Wizards

The Résumé Wizard is one of several different wizards available within Microsoft Word. Look carefully at the tabs within the dialog box of Figure 3.7a, and you can infer that Word supplies both templates and wizards for reports, memos, letters, and faxes. The Other Documents tab provides access to the Agenda, Award, and Calendar wizards as well as several other documents. Figure 3.8 shows four attractive documents that were created by using the respective wizards.

Wizards and templates help you to create professionally designed documents, but they are only a beginning. The content is still up to you. Some wizards are easier to use than others. The **Calendar Wizard,** for example, asks you for the month, year, and type of calendar, then completes the document for you. The **Fax Cover Sheet, Agenda,** and **Award Wizards** create a template, but require you to enter additional information.

Any document that is created with a wizard or template can be saved under its own name, then edited like any other document. Wizards and templates are illustrated in the following exercise.

HANDS-ON EXERCISE 2

Wizards and Templates

Objective: To use wizards and templates to create two documents based on existing templates. To view multiple documents at the same time. Use Figure 3.9 as a guide in the exercise.

STEP 1: The File New Command

- Start Word. Pull down the **File menu.** Click **New** to produce the New dialog box shown in Figure 3.9a.
- Click the **Letters & Faxes tab** to display the indicated wizards and templates. Check that the **Document option button** is selected.
- Double click the **Fax Wizard** to begin creating a fax cover sheet.

STEP 2: The Fax Wizard

- The Fax Wizard asks a series of questions in order to build a template:
  - Click **Portrait** as shown in Figure 3.9b. Click **Next.**
  - Choose a style for the cover sheet. (We chose **Jazzy.**) Click **Next.**
  - Click the text box(es) to enter (or change) your name, company name, and address. Click **Next.**
  - Click the text box(es) to enter (or change) your telephone number and your fax number. Click **Next.**
  - Click the text box(es) to enter the recipient's name, company name, and address. Click **Next.**
  - Click the text box(es) to enter the recipient's phone and fax number. Click **Next.**
- The final screen of the Fax Wizard indicates that the wizard has all the information it needs and asks whether you want help in completing the fax cover sheet. Click **No,** then click the **Finish command button.**
- Save the document as **Elvis Fax Cover Sheet.**

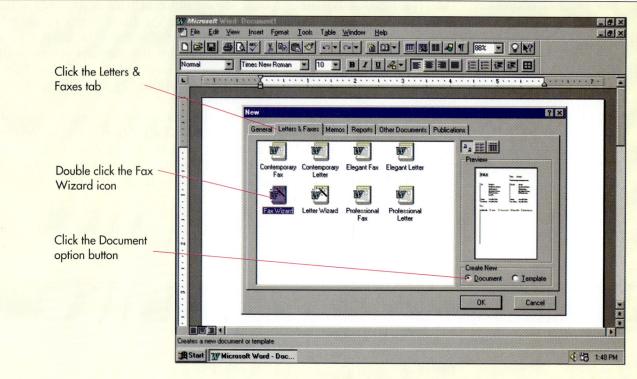

(a) The File New Command (step 1)

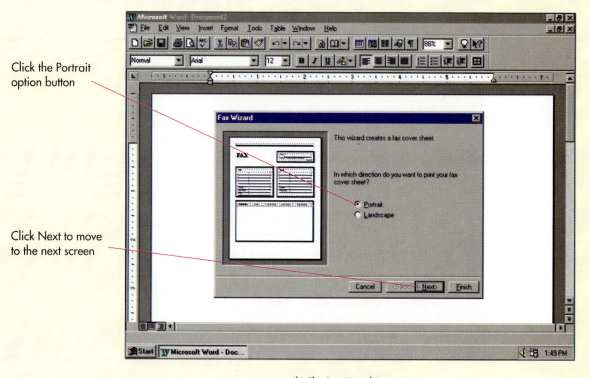

(b) The Fax Wizard (step 2)

FIGURE 3.9 Hands-on Exercise 2

124 EXPLORING MICROSOFT WORD 7.0

RETRACE YOUR STEPS

The *Fax Wizard* guides you every step of the way, but what if you make a mistake or change your mind? Click the Back command button at any time to return to a previous screen in order to enter different information, then continue working with the wizard.

STEP 3: Complete the Fax

➤ If necessary, zoom to **Page Width.** Figure 3.9c displays the Fax cover sheet created by the Fax Wizard based on the answers you entered through the Fax Wizard.

➤ Click in the **Remarks area.** Type the text of the fax as shown in Figure 3.9c.

➤ Click the **Spelling button** to begin the spell check. Correct any misspellings or other errors. Enter the number of pages in the upper right corner. Click the check box "For your review".

➤ Save the document. Click the **Print button** on the Standard toolbar to print the completed document.

➤ Pull down the **File menu.** Click **Close** to close the Fax document but remain in Word.

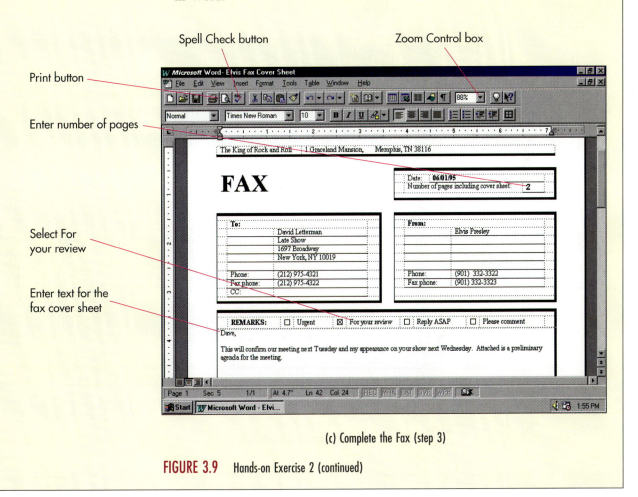

(c) Complete the Fax (step 3)

FIGURE 3.9 Hands-on Exercise 2 (continued)

ENHANCING A DOCUMENT 125

MICROSOFT FAX

The ***Microsoft Fax accessory*** enables you to send and receive fax messages provided you have a fax modem on your computer or local area network. The easiest way to fax an existing document is to right click the document from within My Computer or the Windows Explorer, click the Send To command, click Fax Recipient from the shortcut menu, then follow the on-screen instructions. If you are unable to load Microsoft Fax, it is most likely because it was not installed properly. Open My Computer, double click Control Panel, then double click the icon to Add/Remove programs. Click the Windows Setup tab, then check that Microsoft Exchange and Microsoft Fax are both installed.

STEP 4: The Other Documents Tab

➤ Pull down the **File menu.** Click **New** to produce the New dialog box. Click the **Other Documents tab** to display the documents shown in Figure 3.9d.

➤ Click the **Details button** to switch to the Details view to see the file name, type, size, and date of last modification.

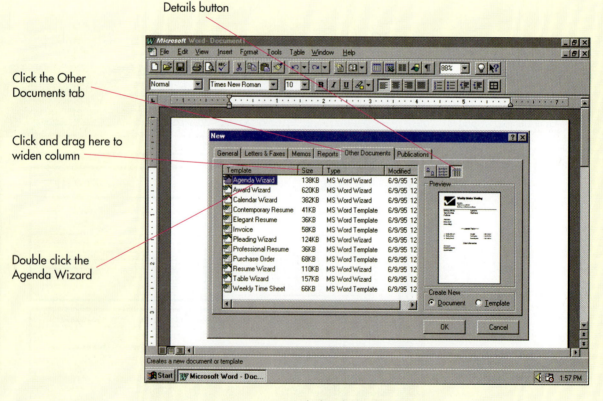

(d) The Other Documents (step 4)

FIGURE 3.9 Hands-on Exercise 2 (continued)

- Click and drag the vertical line between the Template and Size columns, to increase the size of the Template column, so that you can see the complete document name.
- Double click the **Agenda Wizard** to open the wizard and create an agenda.

STEP 5: The Agenda Wizard (continued)

- The Agenda Wizard asks a series of questions in order to build a template. Click the option button for the style you want—for example, **Boxes** in Figure 3.9e. Click **Next**.
- Enter the Date and Starting Time of the meeting. Click **Next**. Enter the main topic and location of the meeting. Click **Next**.
- Check (clear) the boxes corresponding to the items you want (don't want) placed on the agenda; for example, check the boxes for **Please read** and **Please bring.** Click **Next**.
- Check the boxes for the persons you want mentioned on the agenda; for example, check the boxes for note taker and the attendees. Click **Next**.

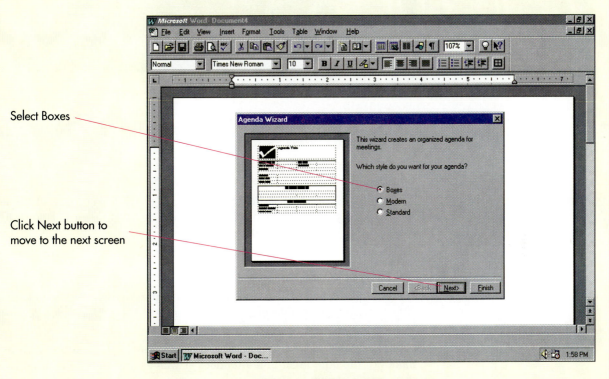

(e) The Agenda Wizard (step 5)

FIGURE 3.9 Hands-on Exercise 2 (continued)

STEP 6: The Agenda Wizard (continued)

- Enter the Agenda topics as shown in Figure 3.9f. Press the **Tab key** to move from one text box to the next. Click the **Next command button** when you have completed the topics.
- If necessary, reorder the topics by clicking the desired topic, then clicking the **Move Up** or **Move Down command button.** Click **Next** when you are satisfied with the agenda.

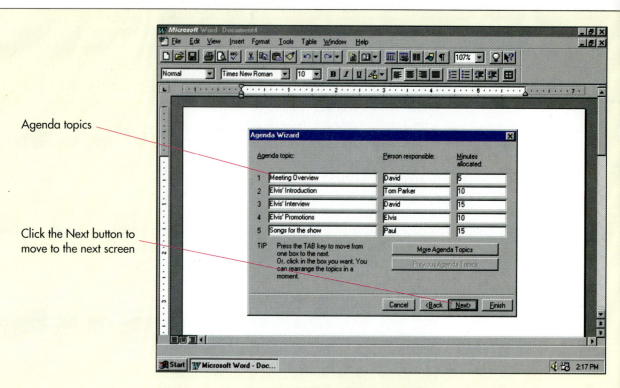

(f) The Agenda Wizard, continued (step 6)

FIGURE 3.9 Hands-on Exercise 2 (continued)

➤ Click the **Yes** or **No button,** depending on whether or not you want a form to record the minutes of the meeting. Click **Next.**

➤ You will see a message indicating that the Agenda Wizard has all the information it needs. Click **Yes** or **No,** depending on whether or not you want to seek help as you complete the agenda.

➤ Click the **Finish command button.** Save the document as **Elvis Agenda.**

STEP 7: Complete the Agenda

➤ If necessary, change to the **Normal view** and zoom to **Page Width.** Figure 3.9g displays the agenda created by Agenda Wizard based on the answers you supplied.

➤ Complete the Agenda by entering the additional information, such as the names of the note taker and attendees as well as the specifics of what to read or bring, as shown in the figure.

➤ Save the document. Click the **Print button** on the Standard toolbar to print the completed document.

➤ Pull down the **File menu** and click the **Close command** to close the document and remain in Word.

STEP 8: Award Yourself

➤ Use the **Award Wizard** to create a certificate for yourself, citing the outstanding work you have done so far. The Award Wizard lets you choose one of four styles (formal, modern, decorative, or jazzy) in either portrait or landscape orientation. It's fun, it's easy, and you deserve it.

➤ Exit Word if you do not want to continue with the next exercise at this time.

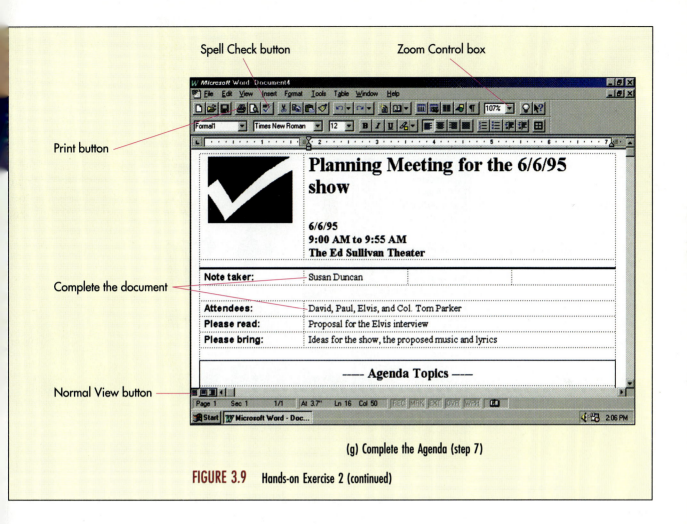

(g) Complete the Agenda (step 7)

FIGURE 3.9 Hands-on Exercise 2 (continued)

THE INSERT OBJECT COMMAND

One of the primary advantages of the Windows environment is the ability to create a *compound document* containing data from multiple applications. One way this can be accomplished is through the *Insert Object command* by which an *object* (any piece of data created by a Windows application) is embedded into a Word document.

The Microsoft Office includes not only Word, Excel, PowerPoint, and Access, but also several additional applications, including the ClipArt Gallery and Microsoft WordArt. The following discussion shows you how to insert objects created by these applications into a Word document, and in so doing, create some truly impressive documents.

Microsoft ClipArt Gallery

The right picture adds immeasurably to a document. *Clip art* (graphic images) is available from a variety of sources, including the Microsoft ClipArt Gallery, which is part of the Microsoft Office. The *ClipArt Gallery* contains more than 1,100 clip art images in 26 different categories as shown in Figure 3.10a. Select a category such as Cartoons, select an image such as the duck smashing the computer, then click the Insert command button to insert the clip art into a document.

After clip art has been inserted into a document, it should be placed into a frame to facilitate moving the image. A *frame* is a special type of (invisible) *container* that holds an object (e.g., a piece of clip art), and it provides the easiest

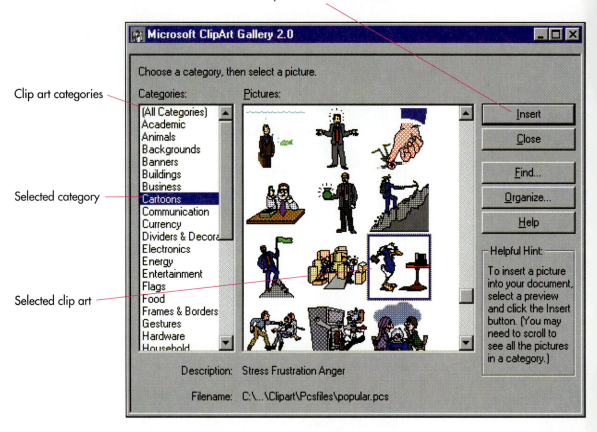

(a) The ClipArt Gallery

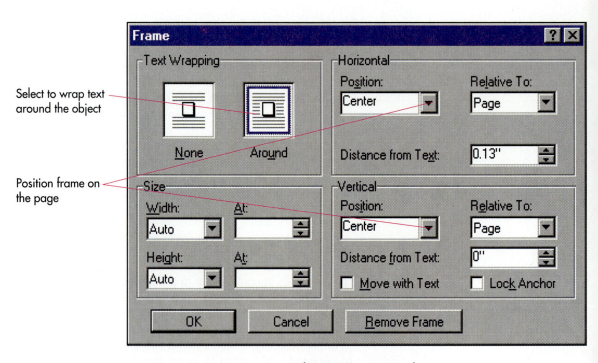

(b) Format Frame Command

FIGURE 3.10   Inserting Clip Art into a Document

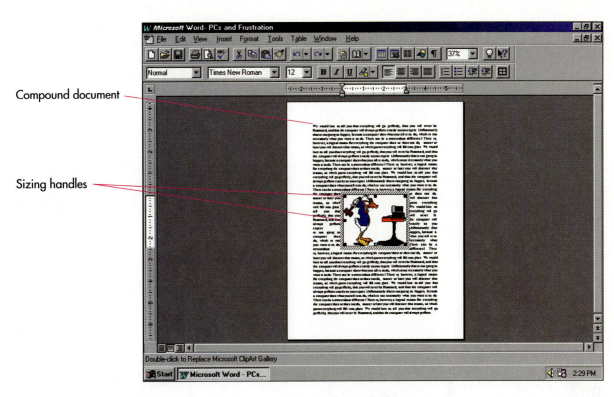

(c) The Completed Document

FIGURE 3.10 Inserting Clip Art into a Document (continued)

way to position the object within a document. Anything at all can be placed in a frame—a picture, a table, a dropped capital letter, or an object created by another application such as a spreadsheet created by Excel.

A frame (and its contents) can be dragged into position using the mouse or aligned more precisely using the *Format Frame command* shown in Figure 3.10b. Enclosing an object in a frame enables you to move the object freely on the page and/or wrap text around the object. Without a frame, the object is treated as an ordinary paragraph and movement is restricted to one of three positions (left, center, or right). Text cannot be wrapped around an unframed object.

Figure 3.10c displays the compound document containing text and the clip art cartoon. The text wraps around the graphic in accordance with the specifications in the Format Frame command of Figure 3.10b. The horizontal and vertical placement of the graphic is also consistent with the placement options within the command.

The graphic in Figure 3.10c is selected and surrounded by eight *sizing handles* that function identically in every Windows application. Click and drag any one of the four corner handles in the direction you want to go to change the length and width simultaneously and keep the graphic in proportion. Click and drag a border handle to change one dimension at a time.

Microsoft WordArt

Clip art is wonderful, but what if you cannot find an appropriate graphic? Microsoft Word anticipates this situation and includes a delightful application, *Microsoft WordArt,* that enables you to create special effects with text. It lets you rotate and/or flip text, display it vertically on the page, shade it, slant it, arch it, or even print it upside down.

WordArt is intuitively easy to use. In essence, you enter the text in the dialog box of Figure 3.11a, then choose a shape for the text from among the selections shown in Figure 3.11b. You can create special effects by choosing one of several different shadows as shown in Figure 3.11c. You can use any TrueType font on your system, and you can change the color of the WordArt object. Figure 3.11d shows the completed WordArt object. It's fun, it's easy, and you can create some truly dynamite documents.

(a) Enter Text

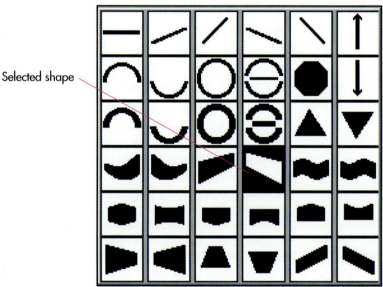

(b) Text Shapes

(c) Shadows

FIGURE 3.11 WordArt

(d) Completed Text

FIGURE 3.11 WordArt (continued)

OBJECT LINKING AND EMBEDDING

Object Linking and Embedding (OLE) enables you to create a compound document containing objects (data) from multiple Windows applications. In actuality, there are two distinct techniques, linking and embedding, and each can be implemented in different ways. OLE is one of the major benefits of working in the Windows environment, but it would be impossible to illustrate all of the techniques in a single exercise. Accordingly, we have created the icon at the left to help you identify the many examples of object linking and embedding that appear throughout the Exploring Windows series.

HANDS-ON EXERCISE 3

The ClipArt Gallery and WordArt

Objective: Enhance the appearance of a document through the Microsoft ClipArt Gallery and Microsoft WordArt. Insert an object into a frame, then move and size the frame within the document. Use Figure 3.12 as a guide in the exercise.

STEP 1: Insert Object Command

➤ Start Word. Open the **About the Internet** document in the Exploring Word folder. Save the document as **Modified Internet.** Check that the insertion point is at the beginning of the document.

➤ Pull down the **Insert menu.** Click **Object** to display the dialog box shown in Figure 3.12a. Click the **Create New tab** if necessary. (You may see a different set of object types from those in the figure, depending on the applications that are installed on your system.)

➤ Select the **Microsoft ClipArt Gallery.** Click **OK.**

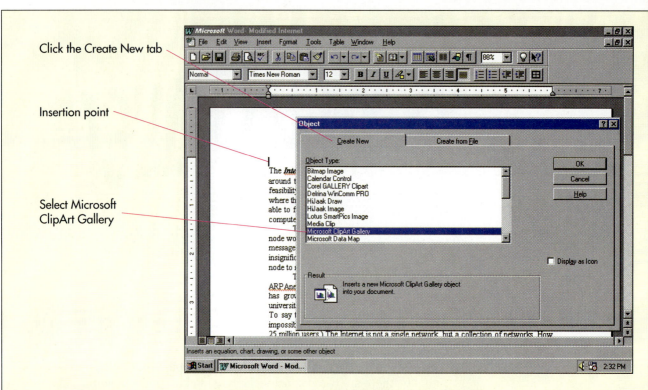

(a) Insert Object Command (step 1)

FIGURE 3.12 Hands-on Exercise 3

STEP 2: The ClipArt Gallery

➤ The dialog box for the Microsoft ClipArt Gallery should appear on your screen as shown in Figure 3.12b. Select (click) the **Maps - International** category as shown in the figure.

➤ Click the **World Map clip art image** to select the image. Click the **Insert command button** to place the clip art into your document.

➤ Click the **Save button** on the Standard toolbar to save the document.

MISSING CLIP ART

The ClipArt Gallery contains more than 1,100 clip art images in 26 different categories. If you do not see all of the clip art, it is because the clip art was not included in the original installation of Microsoft Office. Ask your instructor to reinstall the ClipArt Gallery (from the CD version of Microsoft Office) to obtain the full complement of clip art images. Be sure to include the clip art in the Value Pack folder.

STEP 3: Frame the Clip Art Object

➤ Click on the **clip art image** to select the image as indicated by the sizing handles shown in Figure 3.12c. (If you do not see the sizing handles, just point to the object and click the left mouse button.)

Click to select the clip art image

Click to select the clip art category

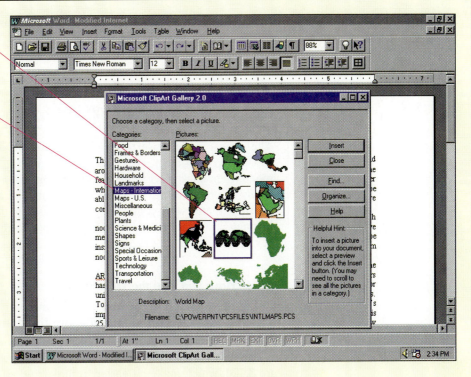

(b) The ClipArt Gallery (step 2)

Click Frame to frame the object

Sizing handles indicate that the image is selected

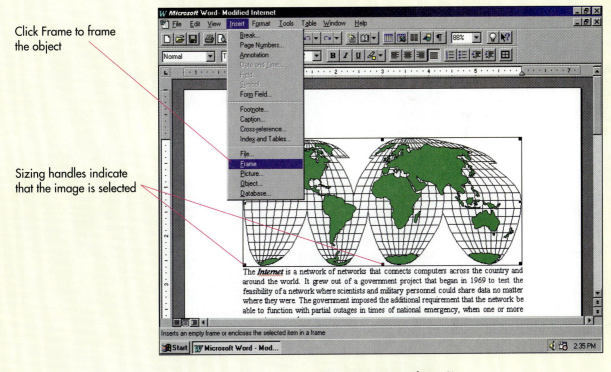

(c) Insert Frame Command (step 3)

FIGURE 3.12 Hands-on Exercise 3 (continued)

ENHANCING A DOCUMENT 135

➤ Pull down the **Insert menu.** Click **Frame** as shown in Figure 3.12c. The clip art will still be selected but will be surrounded by a shaded border to indicate that it is contained in a frame.

> ### USE THE RIGHT MOUSE BUTTON
>
> The easiest way to insert a frame is to use the right mouse button. Point to the clip art object, click the right mouse button to display a shortcut menu, then click the Frame Picture command. Point to the border of the newly inserted frame, click the right mouse button to display a different shortcut menu with commands appropriate to the frame, then click the Format Frame command to move and/or size the frame.

STEP 4: Move and Size the Object
➤ Pull down the **View menu** and check that you are in the Page Layout view (or click the **Page Layout button** above the status bar).
➤ Click the **drop-down arrow** in the **Zoom Control box** and change the magnification to **Whole Page.** You can see the entire document as shown in Figure 3.12d, which makes it easier to move and size the clip art.

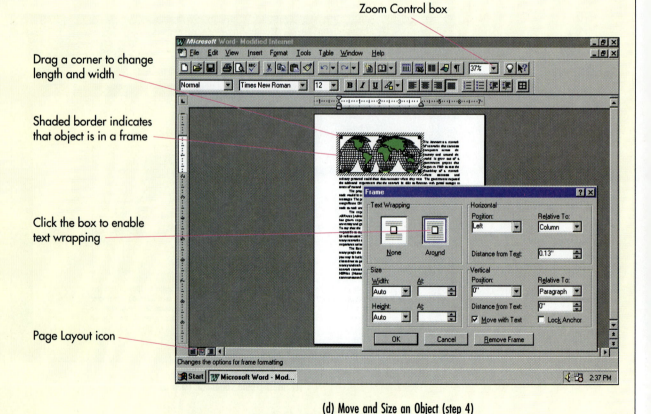

(d) Move and Size an Object (step 4)

FIGURE 3.12 Hands-on Exercise 3 (continued)

- Size the frame within the document:
  - Drag a corner handle (the mouse pointer changes to a double arrow) to change the length and width of the frame simultaneously and keep the graphic in proportion.
  - Drag a handle on the horizontal or vertical border to change one dimension only (which distorts the object in the frame).
- Point to a border of the clip art, click the **right mouse button** to display a shortcut menu, then click the **Format Frame** command from the resulting shortcut menu.
- Click the box to wrap text around the object as shown in Figure 3.12d. (You must allow at least one inch of text on each side of the object if you want to wrap text on both sides.) Click **OK.**
- Position the graphic along the right margin at the top of the second paragraph. (You can use the Format Frame command instead of the mouse for more precision.)
- Save the document.

TO CLICK OR DOUBLE CLICK

Clicking an object selects the object and produces the sizing handles to move and/or size the object. Double clicking an object loads the application that created the object and enables you to modify the object using that application.

STEP 5: Change the Clip Art
- Double click the **clip art image** to reload the ClipArt Gallery as shown in Figure 3.12e.
- Select (click) a different image such as the globe of the **Western hemisphere.** Click the **Insert command button** to insert the new image in place of the existing image.
- The frame in which the clip art image is contained retains its approximate position within the document. The size of the image has changed due to the different shape. Move and/or size the image as desired.
- Save the document.

FIND THE RIGHT CLIP ART

The Find command within the ClipArt Gallery enables you to search for clip art images containing specific text in their description. Some searches yield fruitful results such as a search on the word "computer," which returns multiple images in several categories. Other searches are less productive because there is less clip art. To initiate a search, click the Find button, click the down arrow on the description box, click and drag over the current contents in the Description box, then enter the desired text (e.g., "soccer"). Click the Find Now command button, then click the Insert button to insert the found image into a document.

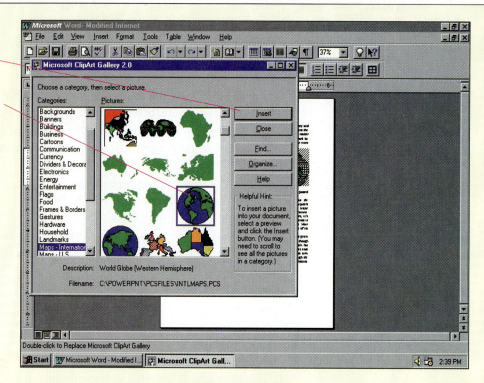

(e) Replace the Clip Art (step 5)

FIGURE 3.12   Hands-on Exercise 3 (continued)

STEP 6: WordArt

▸ Press **Ctrl+Home** to move to the beginning of the document. Pull down the **Insert menu** and click **Object** to produce the Insert Object dialog box.

▸ If necessary, click the **Create New tab,** then scroll until you can select **Microsoft WordArt 2.0** from the Object Type list box. Click **OK.**

▸ You should see a screen similar to Figure 3.12f. Type **About the Internet** as shown in the figure. Click **Update Display.**

▸ Click the **down arrow** on the **Shapes list box.** Click the **Deflate shape** as shown in Figure 3.12f. The shape of the text changes to match the shape you selected.

▸ Pull down the **Format menu** and click **Shadow** (or click the **Shadow button** on the WordArt toolbar) to display the available shadow effects. Choose (click) the effect that appeals to you. Click **OK.**

▸ Pull down the **Format menu** a second time. Click **Shading.** Choose a different foreground color (e.g., blue) and a different shading pattern. Click **OK.**

▸ Pull down the **Format menu** a third and final time and (if necessary) click the **Stretch to Frame** command. This ensures that the WordArt object will maintain its size and shape within its frame.

▸ Click outside the WordArt to deselect the object and return to Word.

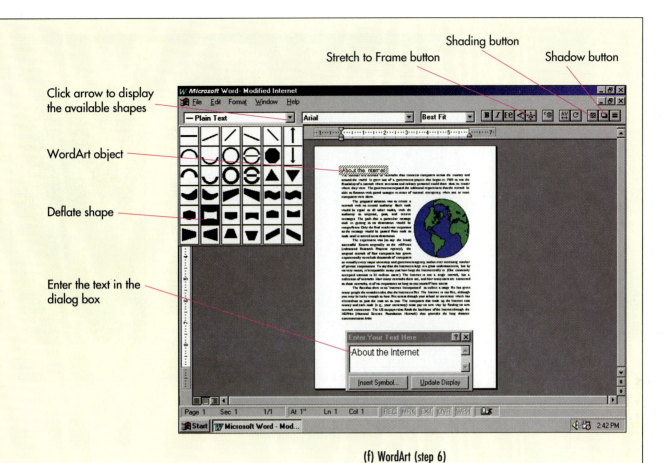

(f) WordArt (step 6)

FIGURE 3.12 Hands-on Exercise 3 (continued)

IN-PLACE EDITING

In-place editing enables you to double click a WordArt object within a Word document to edit the embedded object. You remain in Word (the client application), but the toolbar and pull-down menus are those of WordArt (the server application). The File menu is an exception and contains Word commands in order to save the compound document containing the embedded object.

STEP 7: Frame the WordArt Object

➤ The WordArt object should be selected with the sizing handles displayed. Pull down the **Insert menu** and click **Frame** (or right click the object to display the shortcut menu from where you can click the Frame Picture command).

➤ Move and/or size the WordArt frame to match the document in Figure 3.12g.

➤ Save the completed document. Print the completed document and submit it to your instructor as proof that you did the exercise. Exit Word.

ENHANCING A DOCUMENT **139**

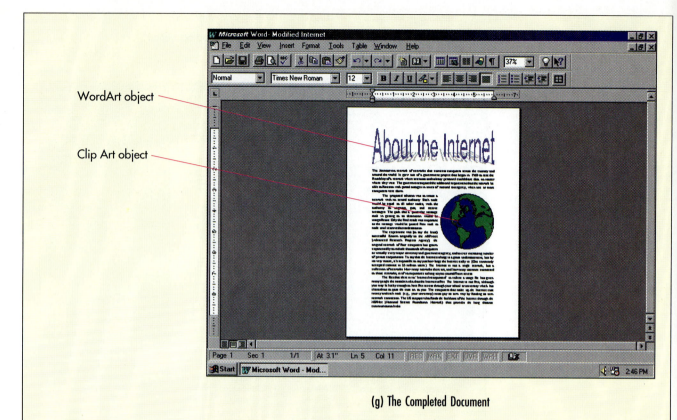

(g) The Completed Document

FIGURE 3.12 Hands-on Exercise 3 (continued)

DROP CAPS

Drop caps add interest to a document and are created through the Drop Cap command in the Format menu. Click at the beginning of a paragraph (where the drop cap is to appear), pull down the Format Menu, and click Drop Cap. Choose the type of drop cap you want, its font, and the lines to drop, then click OK. The drop cap will be inserted into a frame and will add interest to the document.

SUMMARY

The spell check compares the words in a document to those in a standard and/or custom dictionary. It will detect misspellings, duplicated phrases, and/or irregular capitalization, but will not flag properly spelled words that are used incorrectly.

The thesaurus suggests synonyms and/or antonyms. It can also recognize multiple forms of a word (noun, verb, and adjective) and offers suggestions for each. The grammar check searches for mistakes in punctuation, writing style, and word usage, by comparing strings of text within a document to a series of predefined rules.

An envelope is based on a different physical document from the letter it will contain. Microsoft Word saves you the trouble of having to change margins and orientation by providing the Envelopes and Labels command in the Tools menu.

The Insert Date and Time command places the date and/or time into a document either as a specific value or as a field. The latter is updated automatically whenever the document is opened in the Page Layout view or when it is printed.

The Insert Symbol command provides easy access to special characters, making it easy to place typographic characters into a document. Many special symbols are found in the Normal text, Wingdings, and Symbol fonts. All TrueType fonts are scaleable and may be displayed in any point size.

Wizards and templates help create professionally designed documents with a minimum of time and effort. A template is a partially completed document that contains formatting and other information. A wizard is an interactive program that creates a customized template based on the answers you supply.

One of the primary advantages of the Windows environment is the ability to create a compound document—that is, a document containing data from multiple applications. This can be accomplished through the Insert Object command where an object (any piece of data created by a Windows application) is inserted into a Word document.

The ClipArt Gallery contains more than 1,100 clip art images in 26 different categories. Microsoft WordArt enables you to add special effects to text. Each object (e.g., a clip art image or WordArt text) should be placed into a frame to facilitate moving it within a document. A frame (and its contents) can be dragged into position using the mouse or aligned more precisely using the dialog box within the Format Frame command. It can be sized by dragging the sizing handles.

KEY WORDS AND CONCEPTS

Agenda Wizard
Award Wizard
Calendar Wizard
Clip Art
ClipArt Gallery
Compound document
Container
Date field
Drop Cap
Envelopes and Labels command
Fax Wizard
Field
Field code
Field result
Format Frame command
Frame
Grammar check
In-place editing
Insert Date and Time command
Insert Frame command
Insert Object command
Insert Symbol command
Microsoft Fax accessory
Microsoft WordArt
Object
Résumé Wizard
Sizing handle
Spell check
Template
Thesaurus
Wizard
WordArt

MULTIPLE CHOICE

1. Which of the following will be detected by the spell check?
   (a) Duplicate words
   (b) Irregular capitalization
   (c) Both (a) and (b)
   (d) Neither (a) nor (b)

2. Which of the following is true about the thesaurus?
   (a) It recognizes different forms of a word such as a noun and a verb
   (b) It provides antonyms as well as synonyms
   (c) Both (a) and (b)
   (d) Neither (a) nor (b)

3. Which of the following is true about the Insert Symbol command?
   (a) It can insert a symbol in different type sizes
   (b) It can access any font installed on the system
   (c) Both (a) and (b)
   (d) Neither (a) nor (b)

4. Which of the following is true about the date field?
   (a) It is equivalent to typing the current date except that it is faster
   (b) It may be displayed during editing as either a field code or a field result
   (c) It may be displayed in only one format
   (d) All of the above are true

5. The grammar check:
   (a) Implements the identical rules for casual and business writing
   (b) Can be customized to include (omit) specific rules
   (c) Is run automatically in conjunction with a spell check
   (d) All of the above

6. The easiest way to create an envelope is to:
   (a) Use the Envelopes and Labels command in the Tools menu
   (b) Use the Envelopes command in the Insert menu
   (c) Change the margins and orientation using the Page Setup command in the File menu
   (d) All of the above are equally easy to implement

7. Which of the following is a true statement about wizards?
   (a) They are accessed through the New command in the File menu
   (b) They always produce a finished document
   (c) Both (a) and (b)
   (d) Neither (a) nor (b)

8. How do you access the wizards built into Microsoft Word?
   (a) Pull down the Wizards and Templates menu
   (b) Pull down the Insert menu and choose Wizards and Templates
   (c) Pull down the File menu and choose the New command
   (d) None of the above

9. Which of the following is true regarding wizards and templates?
   (a) A wizard may create a template
   (b) A template may create a wizard
   (c) Both (a) and (b)
   (d) Neither (a) nor (b)

10. Which of the following is controlled by the Format Frame command?
    (a) The horizontal and/or vertical placement of the frame
    (b) Wrapping (not wrapping) text around the framed object
    (c) Both (a) and (b)
    (d) Neither (a) nor (b)

11. What is the difference between clicking and double clicking an object?
    (a) Clicking selects the object; double clicking opens the application that created the object
    (b) Double clicking selects the object; clicking opens the application that created the object
    (c) Clicking changes to Normal view; double clicking changes to Page Layout view
    (d) Double clicking changes to Normal view; clicking changes to Page Layout view

12. The Microsoft ClipArt Gallery:
    (a) Is accessed through the Object command in the Insert menu
    (b) Is available to every application in the Microsoft Office
    (c) Enables you to search for a specific piece of ClipArt by specifying a key word in the description of the clip art
    (d) All of the above

13. Which view, and which magnification, offers the most convenient way to position a graphic within a document?
    (a) Page Width in the Page Layout view
    (b) Full Page in the Page Layout view
    (c) Page Width in the Normal view
    (d) Full Page in the Normal view

14. How do you frame a graphic object?
    (a) Click to select the object, pull down the Insert menu, and choose the Frame command
    (b) Right click the object, then select the Frame Picture command from the shortcut menu
    (c) Both (a) and (b)
    (d) Neither (a) nor (b)

15. How do you insert a date into a document so that the date is automatically updated when the document is retrieved?
    (a) Type the date manually
    (b) Use the Date and Time command in the Insert menu and clear the box to insert the date as a field
    (c) Use the Insert Date and Time command in the Insert menu and check the box to insert the date as a field
    (d) It cannot be done

ANSWERS

1. c	6. a	11. a
2. c	7. a	12. d
3. c	8. c	13. b
4. b	9. a	14. c
5. b	10. c	15. c

Exploring Microsoft Word

1. Use Figure 3.13 to match each action with its result; a given action may be used more than once or not at all.

Action

a. Click at 1
b. Click at 2
c. Click at 10, then click at 3
d. Click at 4
e. Click at 11, then click at 5
f. Click at 7, then click at 6
g. Click and drag at 8
h. Click and drag at 9
i. Double click at 9
j. Click at 12

Result

____ Insert the current date into the masthead
____ Spell check the document
____ Add a drop cap to the first paragraph
____ Save the document
____ Change the view to Whole Page
____ Move the clip art image
____ Size the clip art image
____ Change to a different clip art image
____ Find a synonym for "network"
____ Create a fax cover sheet

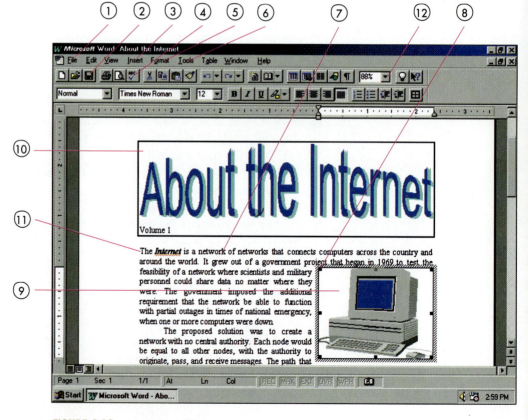

FIGURE 3.13 Screen for Problem 1

2. The need to check a document: The human eye is generally uncritical and sees what it wants or expects to see. For example, read the sentence in the box below, once, and only once, counting the number of times the letter "F" appears in the sentence.

> *Finished files are the result of years of scientific study combined with the experience of years*

The average person spots only three or four, and you can feel reasonably proud if you found all six. Our point in this seemingly trivial exercise is that our eyes are less discriminating than we would like to believe, allowing misspellings and simple typos to go unnoticed. Use the spell check in every document!

3. The grammar check: Answer the following with respect to the screen in Figure 3.14:
   a. Which command displayed the dialog box in the figure?
   b. Which options are currently in effect? How do you change these settings?
   c. What is a cliché? How was the explanation displayed in the figure?
   d. What is a homonym? Will the grammar check look for homonyms?
   e. What is the effect of clicking the drop down arrow in the Use Grammar and Styles Rules list box?
   f. What is the effect of clicking the Grammar option button?
   g. What happens if you click the OK command button? the Cancel command button?

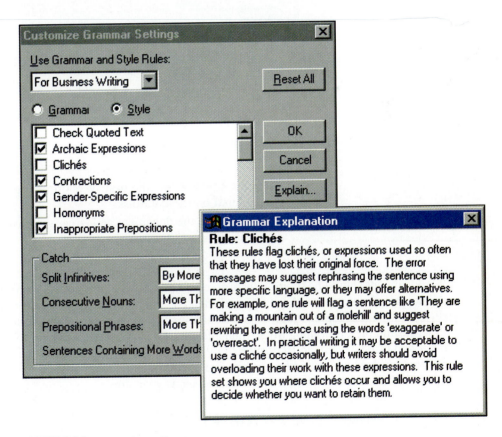

FIGURE 3.14   Screen for Problem 3

4. Answer the following with respect to the screen in Figure 3.15:
   a. Which command displayed the dialog box in the figure?
   b. Which font is selected? Which character is selected?
   c. How do you insert the selected character into the current document? What is the shortcut key to insert the character?
   d. How do you insert the copyright, registered, and trademark (©, ®, and ™) symbols into a document?
   e. What is a nonbreaking space? When would you want to insert this special character into a document?

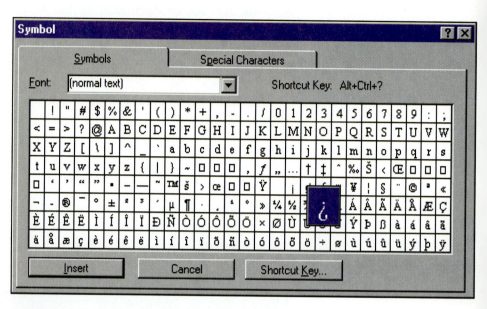

FIGURE 3.15 Screen for Problem 4

Practice with Microsoft Word

1. Figure 3.16 contains the draft version of the *Chapter 3 Practice 1* document contained on the data disk.
   a. Proofread the document and circle any mistakes in spelling, grammar, capitalization, or punctuation.

> All documents should be thoroughly proofed before they be printed and distributed. This means that documents, at a minimum should be spell cheked,, grammar cheked, and proof read by the author. A documents that has spelling errors and/or grammatical errors makes the Author look unprofessional and illiterate and their is nothing worse than allowing a first impression too be won that makes you appear slopy and disinterested, and a document full or of misteakes will do exactly that. Alot of people do not not realize how damaging a bad first impression could be, and documents full of misteakes has cost people oppurtunities that they trained and prepared many years for.

FIGURE 3.16 Document for Practice with Word Exercise 1

b. Open the document in Word and run the spell check. Did Word catch any mistakes you missed? Did you find any errors that were missed by the program?

c. Use the thesaurus to come up with alternate words for *document,* which appears entirely too often within the paragraph.

d. Run the grammar check on the revised document. Did the program catch any grammatical errors you missed? Did you find any mistakes that were missed by the program?

e. Add your name to the revised document, save it, print it, and submit the completed document to your instructor.

f. Submit a title page with this assignment using WordArt, the ClipArt Gallery, or the Insert Symbol command to create a unique design.

2. Inserting Objects: Figure 3.17 illustrates a flyer that we created for a hypothetical computer sale. We embedded clip art and WordArt and created what we believe is an attractive flyer. Try to duplicate our advertisement, or better yet, create your own. Include your name somewhere in the document as a sales associate. Be sure to spell check your ad, then print the completed flyer and submit it to your instructor.

3. Exploring TrueType: Installing Windows 95 also installs several TrueType fonts, which in turn are accessible from any application. Two of the fonts, Symbol and Wingdings, contain a variety of special characters that can be used to create some unusual documents. Use the Insert Symbol command, your imagination, and the fact that TrueType fonts are scaleable to any point size, to recreate the documents in Figure 3.18. Better yet, use your imagination to create your own documents.

4. It's easier than it looks: The document in Figure 3.19 was created to illustrate the automatic formatting and correction facilities that are built into Microsoft Word. We want you to create the document, include your name at the bottom, then submit the completed document to your instructor as proof that you did the exercise. All you have to do is follow the instructions within the document and let Word do the formatting and correcting for you.

The only potential difficulty is that the options on your system may be set to negate some of the features to which we refer. Accordingly, you need to pull down the Tools menu, click the Options command, click the AutoFormat tab, then click the AutoFormat As You Type option button in order to verify that the options referenced in the document are in effect. You also need to review the table of predefined substitutions in the AutoCorrect command (pull down the Tools menu and click the AutoCorrect command) to learn the typewritten characters that will trigger the smiley faces, copyright, and registered trademark substitutions.

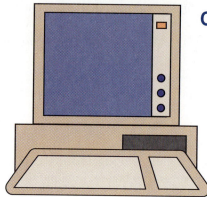

Computer World's Annual Pre-Inventory Sale

When: Saturday, October 21, 1995
            8:00AM - 10:00 PM

Where: 13640 South Dixie Highway

Computer World

- Computers
- Printers
- Fax/Modems
- CD-ROM drives
- Sound systems
- Software
- Etc.

Pre-Inventory Sale

Sales Associate: Bianca Costo

FIGURE 3.17   Document for Practice with Word Exercise 2

Valentine's Day
We'll serenade your sweetheart
Call 284-LOVE

STUDENT COMPUTER LAB
Fall Semester Hours

FIGURE 3.18 Documents for Practice with Word Exercise 3

It's Easier Than It Looks

This document was created to demonstrate the AutoCorrect and AutoFormat features that are built into Microsoft Word. In essence, you type as you always did and enter traditional characters, then let Word perform its "magic" by substituting symbols and other formatting for you. Among the many features included in these powerful commands are the:

1. Automatic creation of numbered lists by typing a number followed by a period, tab, or right parenthesis. Just remember to press the return key twice to turn off this feature.
2. Symbols for common fractions such as ½ or ¼.
3. Ordinal numbers with superscripts created automatically such as 1st, 2nd, or 3rd.
4. Copyright © and Registered trademark ® symbols.

AutoFormat will even add a border to a paragraph any time you type three or more hyphens, equal signs, or underscores on a line by itself.

===
_____

And finally, the AutoCorrect feature has built-in substitution for smiley faces that look best when set in a larger point size such as 72 points.

FIGURE 3.19   Document for Practice with Word Exercise 4

Case Studies

The Letterhead

A well-designed letterhead adds impact to your correspondence. Collect samples of professional stationery, then design your own letterhead, including your name, address, phone, and any other information you deem relevant. Include a fax number and/or e-mail address as appropriate. Use your imagination and design the letterhead for your planned career. Try different fonts and/or the Format Border command to add horizontal line(s) under the text. Consider a graphic logo, but keep it simple. You might also want to decrease the top margin so that the letterhead prints closer to the top of the page. Submit the completed letterhead for entry into a class contest.

An Ad for Travel

The ClipArt Gallery includes the maps and flags of many foreign countries. It also has maps of all 50 states as well as pictures of many landmarks. Design a one-page flyer for a place you want to visit, in the United States or abroad. Collect the assignments, then ask your instructor to hold a contest to decide the most appealing document. It's fun, it's easy, and it's educational. Bon voyage!

The Cover Page

Use WordArt and/or the ClipArt Gallery to create a truly original cover page that you can use with all of your assignments. The cover page should include the title of the assignment, your name, course information, and date. (Insert the date as a field so that it will be updated automatically every time you retrieve the document.) The formatting is up to you. Print the completed cover page and submit it to your instructor, then use the cover page for all future assignments.

A Junior Year Abroad

How lucky can you get? You are spending the second half of your junior year in Paris. The problem is you will have to submit your work in French, and the English version of Microsoft Word won't do. Is there a foreign language version available? What about the dictionary and thesaurus? How do you enter the accented characters that occur so frequently? You are leaving in two months, so you had better get busy. What are your options? Bon voyage.

APPENDIX A: OBJECT LINKING AND EMBEDDING

OVERVIEW

The ability to create a ***compound document*** is one of the primary advantages of the Windows environment. A compound document, such as the memo in Figure A.1, is a document that contains data (objects) from multiple applications. The memo was created in Microsoft Word, and it contains an object (a worksheet) that was created in Microsoft Excel. The ***container*** (the Word document) is created in the ***client application*** (Microsoft Word in this example). The object it contains (a worksheet) is created in the ***server application*** (Microsoft Excel in this example). ***Object Linking and Embedding*** (OLE—pronounced "OH-lay") is the means by which you develop compound documents.

The essential difference between linking and embedding is whether the object is stored within the compound document (embedding) or in its own file (linking). An ***embedded object*** is stored in the compound document, which in turn becomes the only user (client) of that object. A ***linked object*** is stored in its own file, and the compound document is one of many potential containers of that object. The compound document does not contain the linked object per se, but only a representation of the object as well as a pointer (link) to the file containing the object. The advantage of linking is that the object in the compound document is updated automatically if the object is changed in the source file in which it was created.

The choice between linking and embedding depends on how the object will be used. Linking is preferable if the object is likely to change, and the compound document requires the latest version. Linking should also be used when the same object is placed in many documents so that any change to the object has to be made in only one place. Embedding is preferable if you intend to edit the compound document on a computer other than the one on which it was created.

The exercise that follows shows you how to create the compound document in Figure A.1. The exercise uses the ***Insert Object command*** to embed a copy of the Excel worksheet into a Word document. (The

Lionel Douglas
402 Mahoney Hall • Coral Gables, Florida 33124

June 25, 1995

Dear Folks,

I heard from Mr. Black, the manager at University Commons, and the apartment is a definite for the Fall. Ken and I are very excited, and can't wait to get out of the dorm. The food is poison, not that either of us are cooks, but anything will be better than this! I have been checking into car prices (we are definitely too far away from campus to walk!), and have done some estimating on what it will cost. The figures below are for a Jeep Wrangler, the car of my dreams:

Price of car	$11,995			
Manufacturer's rebate	$1,000			
Down payment	$3,000		**My assumptions**	
Amount to be financed	$7,995		Interest rate	7.90%
Monthly payment	$195		Term (years)	4
Gas	$40			
Maintenance	$50			
Insurance	$100			
Total per month	$385			

My initial estimate was $471 based on a $2,000 down payment and a three year loan at 7.9%. I know this is too much so I plan on earning an additional $1,000 and extending the loan to four years. That will bring the total cost down to a more manageable level (see the above calculations). If that won't do it, I'll look at other cars.

Lionel

FIGURE A.1   A Compound Document

Insert Object command was introduced in Chapter 3 to embed objects from the Microsoft ClipArt Gallery and from Microsoft WordArt into a Word document.)

Once an object has been embedded into a document, it can be modified through *in-place editing.* In-place editing enables you to double click an embedded object (the worksheet) and change it, using the tools of the server application (Excel). In other words, you remain in the client application (Microsoft Word in this example), but you have access to the Excel toolbar and pull-down menus. In-place editing modifies the copy of the embedded object in the compound document. It does *not* change the original object because there is no connection (or link) between the object and the compound document.

HANDS-ON EXERCISE 1

Embedding

Objective: To embed an Excel worksheet into a Word document; to use in-place editing to modify the worksheet within Word. Use Figure A.2 as a guide in the exercise.

STEP 1: Open the Word Document

➤ Start Word. Open the **Car Request document** in the **Exploring Word folder**. Zoom to **Page Width** so that the display on your monitor matches ours.

➤ Save the document as **Modified Car Request** so that you can return to the original document if you edit the duplicated file beyond redemption.

➤ The date displayed on your monitor will be May 31, 1995, and needs to be updated. Point to the date field, click the **right mouse button** to display the shortcut menu in Figure A.2a, then click the **Update Field command.**

THE DATE FIELD

The Insert Date and Time command enables you to insert the date as a specific value (the date on which a document is created) or as a field. The latter will be updated automatically whenever the document is printed or when the document is opened in Page Layout view. Opening the document in the Normal view requires the date field to be updated manually.

Point to the date and click the right mouse button to produce the shortcut menu

Click Update Field to change the date to the current date

(a) The Word Document (step 1)

FIGURE A.2 Hands-on Exercise 1

APPENDIX A 155

STEP 2: Insert an Object

➤ Click the blank line above paragraph two as shown in Figure A.2b. This is the place in the document where the worksheet is to go.

➤ Pull down the **Insert menu,** and click the **Object command** to display the Object dialog box in Figure A.2b.

➤ Click the **Create from File tab,** then click the **Browse command button** in order to open the Browse dialog box and select the object.

➤ Click (select) the **Car Budget workbook** (note the Excel icon), which is in the Exploring Word folder.

➤ Click **OK** to select the workbook and close the Browse dialog box.

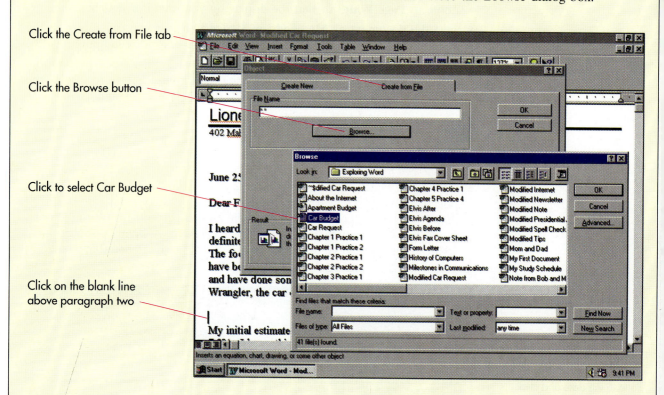

(b) Insert Object Command (step 2)

FIGURE A.2 Hands-on Exercise 1 (continued)

STEP 3: Insert an Object (continued)

➤ The file name of the object (Car Budget.xls) has been placed into the File Name text box, as shown in Figure A.2c.

➤ Verify that the Link to File and Display as Icon check boxes are clear, as shown in Figure A.2c. Note, too, the description at the bottom of the Object dialog box, which indicates that you will be able to edit the object using the application that created the file.

➤ Click **OK** to insert the Excel worksheet into the Word document. Save the document.

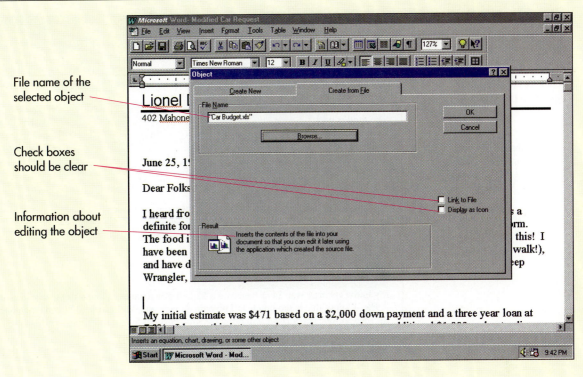

(c) Insert Object Command, continued (step 3)

FIGURE A.2 Hands-on Exercise 1 (continued)

STEP 4: Frame the Worksheet

➤ Point to the worksheet, then click the **right mouse button** to select the worksheet and display a shortcut menu. Click the **Frame Picture** command to frame the worksheet in order to position it more easily within the document.

➤ You will see the informational box in Figure A.2d, asking whether you want to switch to the Page Layout view. Click **Yes.** The worksheet is surrounded by a shaded (thatched) border to indicate a frame.

THE FORMAT FRAME COMMAND

All objects should be placed into a frame, a special type of (invisible) container in Microsoft Word that facilitates positioning an object within a Word document. An unframed object is treated as an ordinary paragraph, and movement is restricted to one of three alignments (left, center, or right). Additionally, text cannot be wrapped around an unframed object. A framed object, however, can be precisely positioned by right clicking the object, selecting the Format Frame command, then entering the information about the object's desired position.

Informational box

Click Yes to switch to the Page Layout view

Point to the object and click the right mouse button to produce a shortcut menu

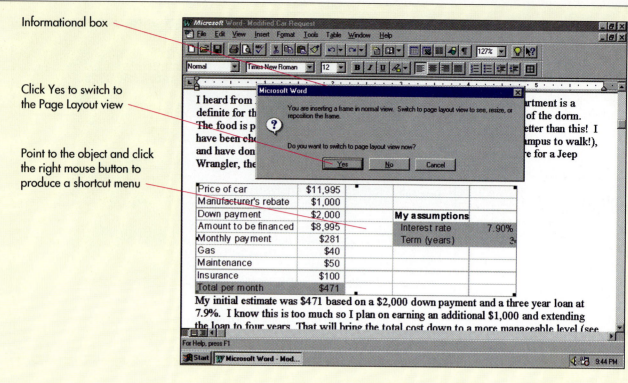

(d) Frame the Worksheet (step 4)

FIGURE A.2 Hands-on Exercise 1 (continued)

STEP 5: The Format Frame Command

➤ Pull down the **Format menu** and click **Frame** to display the Frame dialog box shown in Figure A.2e.

➤ Click the box for no text wrapping.

➤ Click the **drop-down arrow** on the list box for the Horizontal position and click **Center.** Click **OK** to accept the settings and close the Frame dialog box.

➤ The worksheet is centered within the memo, but you may want to insert a blank line(s) between the paragraphs to give the worksheet additional room.

➤ Save the document.

STEP 6: In-place Editing

➤ The worksheet should still be selected as indicated by the sizing handles. The monthly total of $471 needs to be changed to reflect Lionel's additional $1,000 for the down payment. Double click the worksheet object to edit the worksheet in place.

➤ Be patient as this step takes a while, even on a fast machine. The Excel grid, consisting of the row and column labels, will appear around the worksheet, as shown in Figure A.2f.

➤ You are still in Word, as indicated by the title bar (Microsoft Word - Modified Car Request), but the Excel toolbars are displayed.

➤ Click in cell **B3,** type the new down payment of **$3,000,** and press **enter.**

➤ Click in cell **E5,** type **4,** and press **enter.** The Monthly payment (cell B5) and Total per month (cell B9) drop to $195 and $385, respectively.

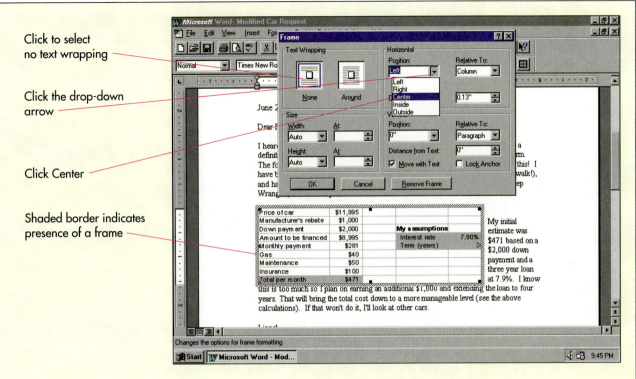

(e) Format Frame Command (step 5)

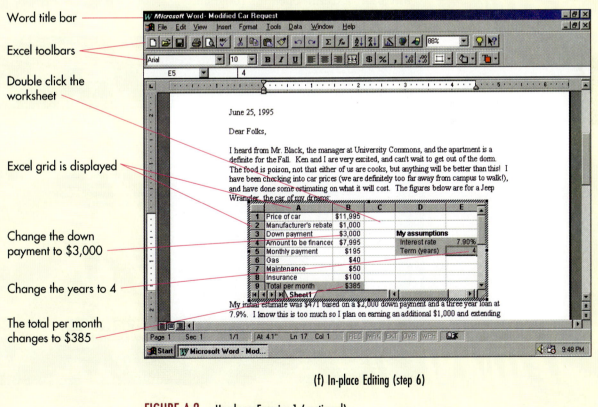

(f) In-place Editing (step 6)

FIGURE A.2 Hands-on Exercise 1 (continued)

APPENDIX A

IN-PLACE EDITING

In-place editing enables you to edit an embedded object using the toolbar and pull-down menus of the server application. Thus, when editing an Excel worksheet embedded into a Word document, the title bar is that of the client application (Microsoft Word), but the toolbars and pull-down menus reflect the server application (Excel). There are, however, two exceptions; the File and Window menus are those of the client application (Word) so that you can save the compound document and/or arrange multiple documents within the client application.

STEP 7: Save the Word Document

➤ Click anywhere outside the worksheet to deselect it and view the completed word document as shown in Figure A.2g.

➤ Pull down the **File menu** and click **Save** (or click the **Save button** on the Standard toolbar).

➤ Pull down the **File menu** a second time. Click **Exit** if you do not want to continue with the next hands-on exercise once this exercise is completed; otherwise click **Close** to remove the document from memory but leave Word open.

STEP 8: View the Original Object

➤ Click the **Start Button,** click (or point to) the **Programs menu,** then click **Microsoft Excel** to open the program.

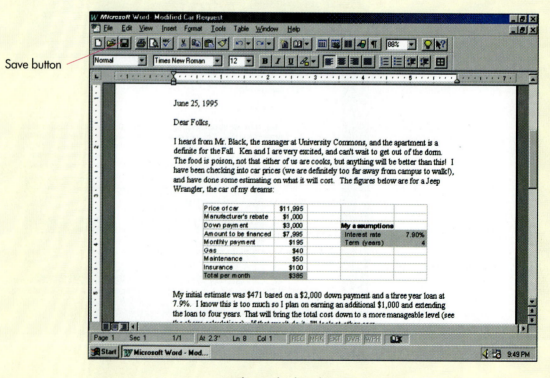

(g) The Completed Word Document (step 7)

FIGURE A.2 Hands-on Exercise 1 (continued)

➤ If necessary, click the **Maximize button** in the application window so that Excel takes the entire desktop, as shown in Figure A.2h.

➤ Pull down the **File menu** and click **Open** (or click the **Open button** on the Standard toolbar) to display the Open dialog box.

- Click the **drop-down arrow** on the Look In list box. Click the appropriate drive, drive C or drive A, depending on the location of your data.
- Double click the **Exploring Word folder** to make it the active folder.
- Click (select) **Car Budget** to select the workbook that we have used throughout the exercise.
- Click the **Open command button** to open the workbook, as shown in Figure A.2h.
- Click the **Maximize button** in the document window (if necessary) so that the document window is as large as possible.

➤ You should see the original (unmodified) worksheet, with a down payment of $2,000, a three-year loan, a monthly car payment of $281, and total expenses per month of $471. The changes that were made in step 6 were made to the compound document and are *not* reflected in the source file.

➤ Pull down the **File menu.** Click **Exit** to exit Microsoft Excel.

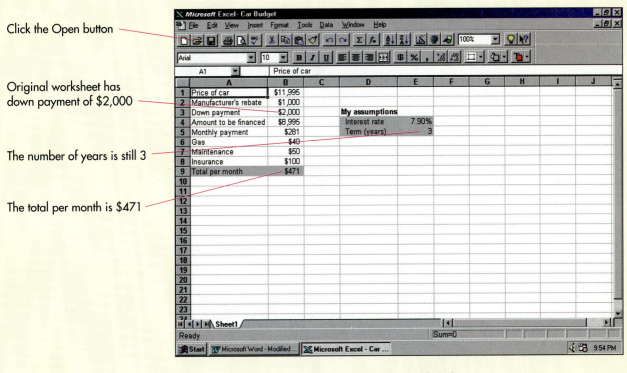

(h) The Original and Unmodified File (step 8)

FIGURE A.2   Hands-on Exercise 1 (continued)

LINKING

The exercise just completed used embedding rather than linking to place a copy of the Excel worksheet into the Word document. The last step in the exercise demonstrated that the original worksheet was unaffected by changes made to the embedded copy within the compound document.

Linking is very different from embedding as you shall see in the next exercise. Linking maintains a dynamic connection between the server and client. Embedding does not. With linking, the object created by the server application

Lionel Douglas
402 Mahoney Hall • Coral Gables, Florida 33124

Dear Mom and Dad,

Enclosed please find the budget for my apartment at University Commons. As I told you before, it's a great apartment and I can't wait to move.

	Total	Individual
Rent	$895	$298
Utilities	$125	$42
Cable	$45	$15
Phone	$60	$20
Food	$600	$200
Total		$575
Persons	3	

I really appreciate everything that you and Dad are doing for me. I'll be home next week after finals.

Lionel

(a) First Document (Mom and Dad)

Lionel Douglas
402 Mahoney Hall • Coral Gables, Florida 33124

Dear Ken,

I just got the final figures for our apartment next year and am sending you an estimate of our monthly costs. I included the rent, utilities, phone, cable, and food. I figure that food is the most likely place for the budget to fall apart, so learning to cook this summer is critical. I'll be taking lessons from the Galloping Gourmet, and suggest you do the same. Enjoy your summer and Bon Appetit.

	Total	Individual
Rent	$895	$298
Utilities	$125	$42
Cable	$45	$15
Phone	$60	$20
Food	$600	$200
Total		$575
Persons	3	

Guess what - the three bedroom apartment just became available which saves us more than $100 per month over the two bedroom we had planned to take. Jason Adler has decided to transfer and he can be our third roommate.

Lionel

(b) Second Document (Note to Ken)

	Total	Individual
Rent	$895	$298
Utilities	$125	$42
Cable	$45	$15
Phone	$60	$20
Food	$600	$200
Total		$575
Persons	3	

(c) Worksheet (Apartment Budget)

FIGURE A.3 Linking

(e.g., an Excel worksheet) is tied to the compound document (e.g., a Word document) in such a way that any changes in the Excel worksheet are automatically reflected in the Word document. The Word document does not contain the worksheet per se, but only a representation of the worksheet, as well as a pointer (or link) to the Excel workbook.

Linking requires that an object be saved in its own file because the object does not actually exist within the compound document. Embedding, on the other hand, lets you place the object directly in a compound document without having to save it as a separate file. (The embedded object simply becomes part of the compound document.)

Consider now Figure A.3, in which the same worksheet is linked to two different documents. Both documents contain a pointer to the worksheet, which may be edited by double clicking the object in either compound document. Alternatively, you may open the server application and edit the object directly. In either case, changes to the Excel workbook are reflected in every compound document that is linked to the workbook.

The next exercise links a single Excel worksheet to two different Word documents. During the course of the exercise both applications (client and server) will be explicitly open, and it will be necessary to switch back and forth between the two. Thus, the exercise also demonstrates the multitasking capability within Windows 95 and the use of the taskbar to switch between the open applications.

HANDS-ON EXERCISE 2

Linking

Objective: To demonstrate multitasking and the ability to switch between applications; to link an Excel worksheet to multiple Word documents. Use Figure A.4 as a guide in the exercise.

STEP 1: Open the Word Document

➤ Check the taskbar to see whether there is a button for Microsoft Word indicating that the application is already active in memory. Start Word if you do not see its button on the taskbar.

➤ Open the **Mom and Dad document** in the **Exploring Word folder** as shown in Figure A.4a. The document opens in the Normal view (the view in which it was last saved). If necessary, zoom to **Page Width** so that the display on your monitor matches ours.

➤ Save the document as **Modified Mom and Dad.**

STEP 2: Open the Excel Worksheet

➤ Click the **Start button,** click (or point to) the **Programs menu,** then click **Microsoft Excel** to open the program.

➤ If necessary, click the **Maximize button** in the application window so that Excel takes the entire desktop. Click the **Maximize button** in the document window (if necessary) so that the document window is as large as possible.

➤ The taskbar should now contain buttons for both Microsoft Word and Microsoft Excel. Click either button to move back and forth between the open applications. End by clicking the Microsoft Excel button, since you want to work in that application.

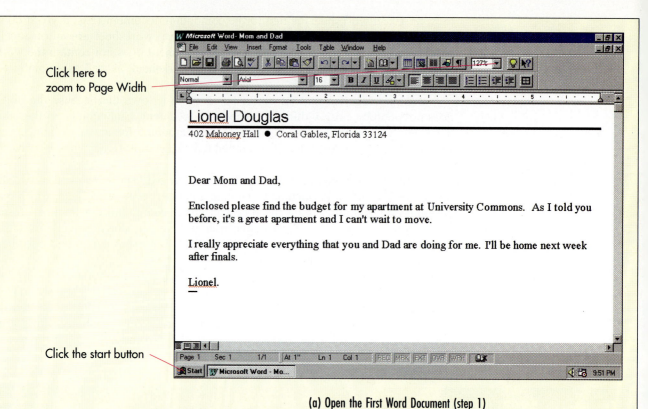

(a) Open the First Word Document (step 1)

FIGURE A.4   Hands-on Exercise 2

➤ Pull down the **File menu** and click **Open** (or click the **Open button** on the Standard toolbar) to display the Open dialog box in Figure A.4b.
➤ Click the **drop-down arrow** on the Look In list box. Click the appropriate drive, drive C or drive A, depending on the location of your data. Double click the **Exploring Word folder** to make it the active folder. Double click **Apartment Budget** to open the workbook.

THE COMMON USER INTERFACE

The *common user interface* provides a sense of familiarity from one Windows application to the next. Even if you have never used Excel, you will recognize many of the elements present in Word. Both applications share a common menu structure with consistent ways to execute commands from those menus. The Standard and Formatting toolbars are present in both applications. Many keyboard shortcuts are also common—for example Ctrl+Home and Ctrl+End to move to the beginning and end of a document.

STEP 3: Copy the Worksheet to the Clipboard
➤ Click in cell **A1**. Drag the mouse over cells **A1 through C9** so that the entire worksheet is selected as shown in Figure A.4c.

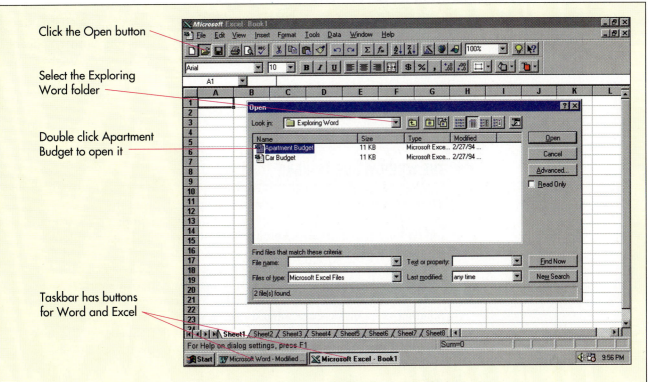

(b) Open the Excel Workbook (step 2)

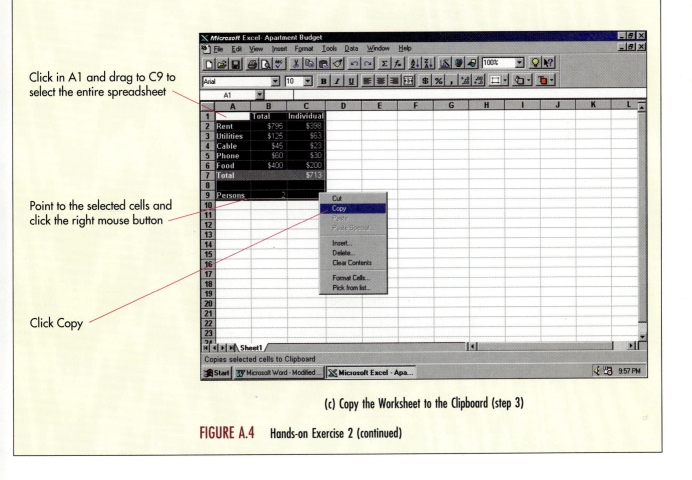

(c) Copy the Worksheet to the Clipboard (step 3)

FIGURE A.4   Hands-on Exercise 2 (continued)

- Point to the selected cells, then click the **right mouse button** to display the shortcut menu shown in the figure. Click **Copy.** A moving border appears around the selected area in the worksheet, indicating that it has been copied to the clipboard.
- Click the **Microsoft Word button** on the taskbar to return to the Word document.

THE WINDOWS 95 TASKBAR

Multitasking, the ability to run multiple applications at the same time, is one of the primary advantages of the Windows environment. Each button on the taskbar appears automatically when its application or folder is opened and disappears upon closing. (The buttons on are resized automatically according to the number of open windows.) You can customize the taskbar by right clicking an empty area to display a shortcut menu, then clicking the Properties command. You can resize the taskbar by pointing to its inside edge, then dragging when you see a double-headed arrow. You can also move the taskbar to the left or right edge of the desktop, or to the top of the desktop, by dragging a blank area of the taskbar to the desired position.

STEP 4: Create the Link
- Click in the document between the two paragraphs. Press **enter** to enter an additional blank line.
- Pull down the **Edit menu.** Click **Paste Special** to produce the dialog box in Figure A.4d.
- Click the **Paste Link option button.** Click **Microsoft Excel Worksheet Object.** Click **OK** to insert the worksheet into the document. You may want to insert a blank line before and/or after the worksheet to make it easier to read.
- Save the document containing the letter to Mom and Dad.

LINKING VERSUS EMBEDDING

The *Paste Special command* will link or embed an object, depending on whether the Paste Link or Paste Option button is checked. Linking stores a pointer to the file containing the object together with a reference to the server application, and changes to the object are automatically reflected in all compound documents that are linked to the object. Embedding stores a copy of the object with a reference to the server application, but any changes to the copy of the object within the compound document are not reflected in the original object. With both linking and embedding, however, you can double click the object in the compound document to edit the object by using the tools of the server application.

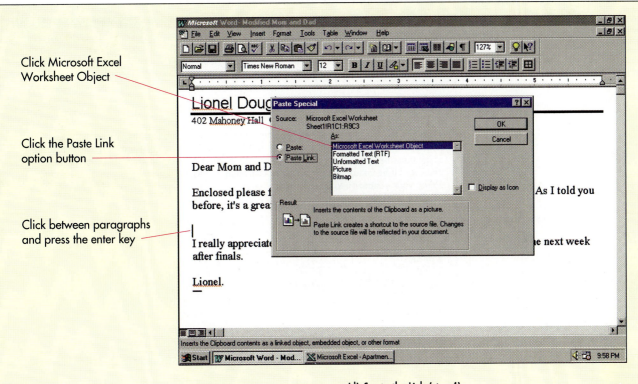

(d) Create the Link (step 4)

FIGURE A.4 Hands-on Exercise 2 (continued)

STEP 5: Open the Second Word Document

➤ Open the **Note to Ken document** in the **Exploring Word folder.** Save the document as **Modified Note to Ken** so that you can always return to the original document.

➤ The Apartment Budget worksheet is still in the clipboard since the contents of the clipboard have not been changed. Click at the end of the first paragraph (after the words Bon Appetit). Press the **enter key** to insert a blank line after the paragraph.

➤ Pull down the **Edit menu.** Click **Paste Special.** Click the **Paste Link option button.** Click **Microsoft Excel Worksheet Object.** Click **OK** to insert the worksheet into the document, as shown in Figure A.4e.

➤ If necessary, enter a blank line before or after the object to improve the appearance of the document. Save the document.

➤ Click anywhere on the worksheet to select the worksheet, as shown in Figure A.4e. The message on the status bar indicates you can double click the worksheet to edit the object.

STEP 6: Modify the Worksheet

➤ The existing spreadsheet indicates the cost of a two-bedroom apartment, but you want to show the cost of a three-bedroom apartment. Double click the worksheet in order to change it.

➤ The system pauses (the faster your computer, the better) as it switches back to Excel. Maximize the document window.

➤ Cells **A1 through C9** are still selected from step 3. Click outside the selected range to deselect the worksheet.

APPENDIX A 167

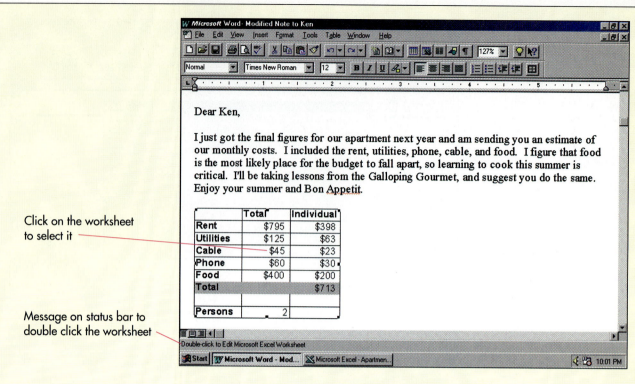

(e) Open the Second Document (step 5)

FIGURE A.4 Hands-on Exercise 2 (continued)

➤ Click in cell **B2.** Type **$895** (the rent for a three-bedroom apartment).

➤ Click in cell **B6.** Type **$600** (the increased amount for food).

➤ Click in cell **B9.** Type **3** to change the number of people sharing the apartment. Press **enter.** The total expenses (in cell C9) change to $575, as shown in Figure A.4f.

➤ Save the worksheet.

STEP 7: View the Modified Document

➤ Click the **Microsoft Word button** on the taskbar to return to Microsoft Word and the note to Ken, as shown in Figure A.4g.

➤ The note to Ken displays the modified worksheet because of the link established earlier.

➤ Click at the end of the worksheet and to add the additional text shown in Figure A.4g to let Ken know about the new apartment.

➤ Save the document.

STEP 8: View the Completed Note to Mom and Dad

➤ Pull down the **Window menu.** Click **Modified Note to Mom and Dad** to switch to this document.

➤ The note to your parents also contains the updated worksheet (with three roommates) because of the link established earlier.

➤ Save the completed document.

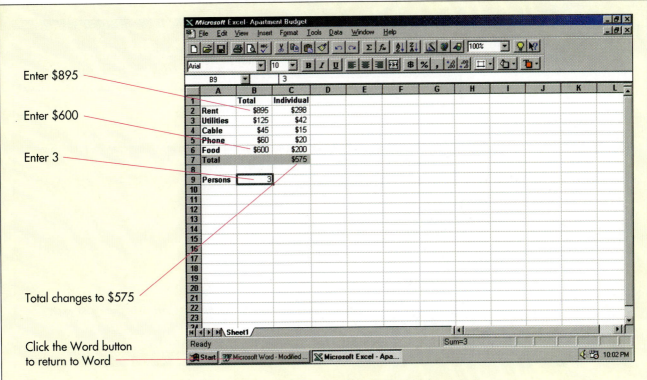

(f) Modify the Worksheet (step 6)

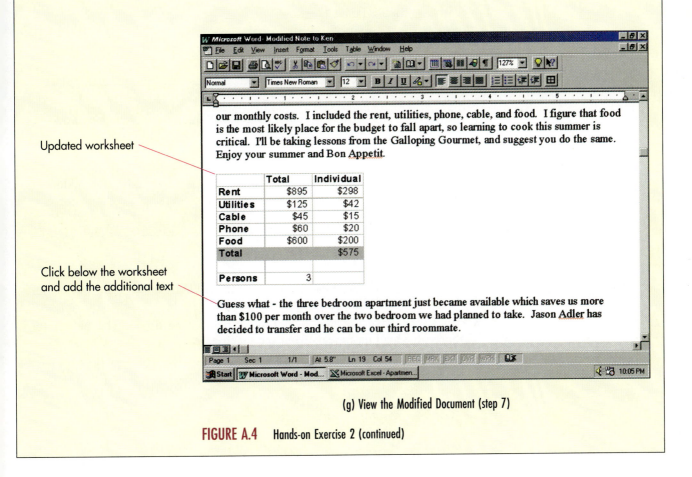

(g) View the Modified Document (step 7)

FIGURE A.4 Hands-on Exercise 2 (continued)

APPENDIX A 169

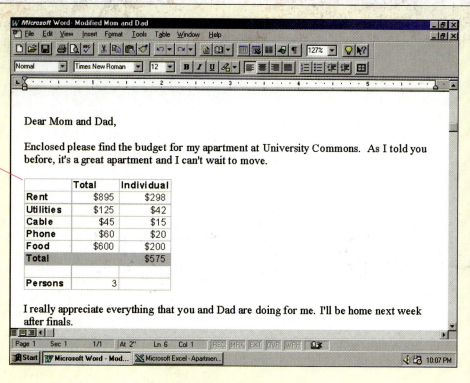

(h) View the Modified Document (step 8)

FIGURE A.4 Hands-on Exercise 2 (continued)

ALT+TAB STILL WORKS

Alt+Tab was a treasured shortcut in Windows 3.1 that enabled users to switch back and forth between open applications. The shortcut also works in Windows 95. Press and hold the Alt key while you press and release the Tab key repeatedly to cycle through the open applications. Note that each time you release the Tab key the icon of a different application is selected in the small rectangular window that is displayed in the middle of the screen. Release the Alt key when you have selected the icon for the application you want.

STEP 9: Exit

➤ Exit Word. Save the files if you are requested to do so. The button for Microsoft Word disappears from the taskbar.

➤ Exit Excel. Save the files if you are requested to do so. The button for Microsoft Excel disappears from the taskbar.

APPENDIX B: TOOLBARS

OVERVIEW

Microsoft Word has nine predefined toolbars, which provide access to commonly used commands. The toolbars are displayed in Figure B.1 and are listed here for convenience. They are: the Borders, Database, Drawing, Formatting, Forms, Microsoft, Standard, TipWizard, and Word 2.0 toolbars. The Standard and Formatting toolbars are displayed by default and appear immediately below the menu bar.

In addition to the predefined toolbars, which are displayed continually, seven other toolbars appear only when their corresponding feature is in use. These toolbars appear (and disappear) automatically and are shown in Figure B.2. They are: the Equation Editor, Header/Footer, Macro, Mail Merge, Master Document, Outlining, and Picture toolbars.

The buttons on the toolbars are intended to be indicative of their function. Clicking the Printer button (the fourth button from the left on the Standard toolbar), for example, executes the Print command. If you are unsure of the purpose of any toolbar button, point to it, and a ToolTip will appear that displays its name.

You can display multiple toolbars at one time, move them to new locations on the screen, customize their appearance, or suppress their display.

- To display or hide a toolbar, pull down the View menu and click the Toolbars command. Select (deselect) the toolbar(s) that you want to display (hide). The selected toolbar(s) will be displayed in the same position as when last displayed. You may also point to any toolbar and click with the right mouse button to bring up a shortcut menu, after which you can select the toolbar to be displayed (hidden).
- To change the size of the buttons, display them in monochrome rather than color, suppress the display of the ToolTips or display the associated shortcut key (if available), pull down the View

menu, click Toolbars, and then select (deselect) the appropriate check box. Alternatively, you can click on any toolbar with the right mouse button, select Toolbars, and then select (deselect) the appropriate check box.

- Toolbars may be either docked (along the edge of the window) or left floating (in their own window). A toolbar moved to the edge of the window will dock along that edge. A toolbar moved anywhere else in the window will float in its own window. Docked toolbars are one tool wide (high), whereas floating toolbars can be resized by clicking and dragging a border or corner as you would with any other window.
  - To move a docked toolbar, click anywhere in the gray background area and drag the toolbar to its new location.
  - To move a floating toolbar, drag its title bar to its new location.
- To customize a toolbar, display the toolbar on the screen, pull down the View menu, click Toolbars, click the Customize command button, and select the Toolbars tab. Alternatively, you can click on any toolbar with the right mouse button, select Customize from the shortcut menu, and then click the Toolbars tab.
  - To move a button, drag the button to its new location on that toolbar or any other displayed toolbar.
  - To copy a button, press the Ctrl key as you drag the button to its new location on that toolbar or any other displayed toolbar.
  - To delete a button, drag the button off the toolbar and release the mouse button.
  - To add a button, select the category containing the button from the Categories list box and then drag the button to the desired location on the toolbar. (To see a description of a tool's function prior to adding it to a toolbar, click the tool in the Customize dialog box and read the displayed description.)
  - To restore a predefined toolbar to its default appearance, pull down the View menu, click Toolbars, select (highlight) the desired toolbar, and click the Reset command button.
- Buttons can also be moved, copied, or deleted without displaying the Customize dialog box.
  - To move a button, press the Alt key as you drag the button to the new location.
  - To copy a button, press the Alt and Ctrl keys as you drag the button to the new location.
  - To delete a button, press the Alt key and drag the button off the toolbar.
- To create your own toolbar, pull down the View menu, click Toolbars, and click the New command button. Alternatively, you can click on any toolbar with the right mouse button, select Toolbars from the shortcut menu, and then click the New command button.
  - Enter a name for the toolbar in the dialog box that follows. The name can be any length and can contain spaces.
  - The new toolbar will appear at the top left of the screen. Initially it will be big enough to hold only one button. Add, move, and delete buttons following the same procedures as outlined above. The toolbar will automatically size itself as new buttons are added and deleted.
  - To delete a custom toolbar, pull down the View menu, click Toolbars, and make sure that the custom toolbar to be deleted is the only one selected (highlighted). Click the Delete command button. Click Yes to confirm the deletion. (Note that a predefined toolbar cannot be deleted.)

Borders Toolbar

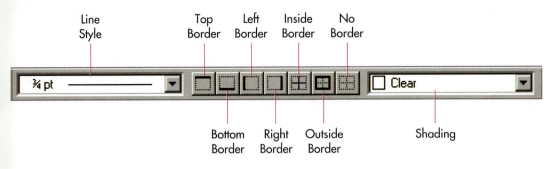

Database Toolbar

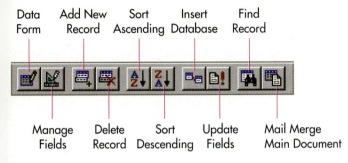

Drawing Toolbar

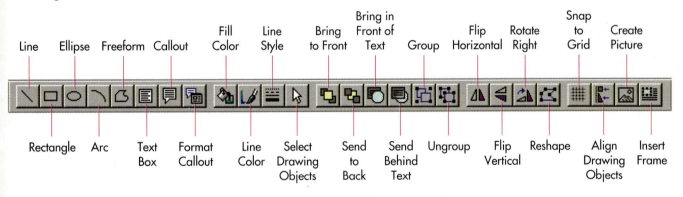

Formatting Toolbar

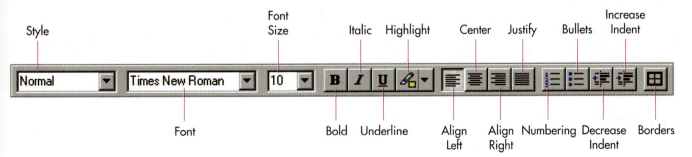

FIGURE B.1 Predefined Toolbars

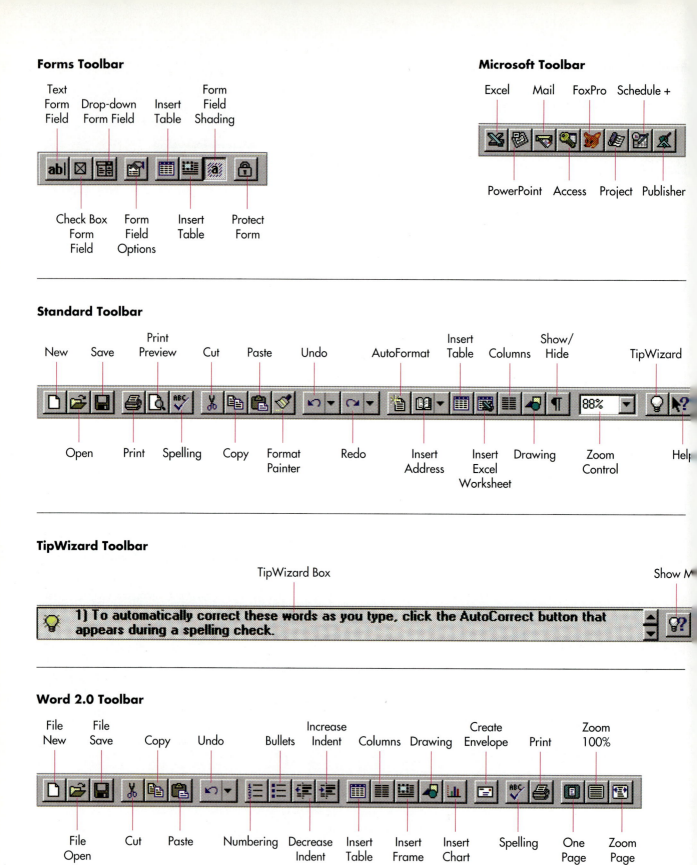

FIGURE B.1 Predefined Toolbars (continued)

Equation Editor Toolbar

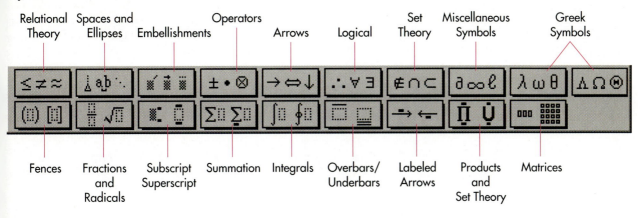

Header/Footer Toolbar

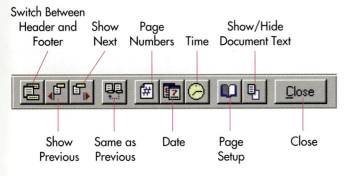

Macro Toolbar

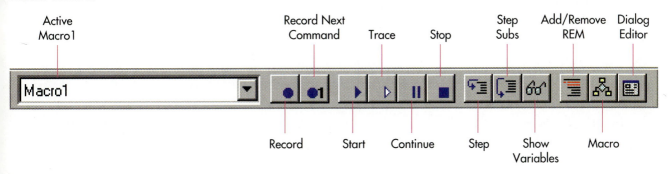

FIGURE B.2   Feature Toolbars

Mail Merge Toolbar

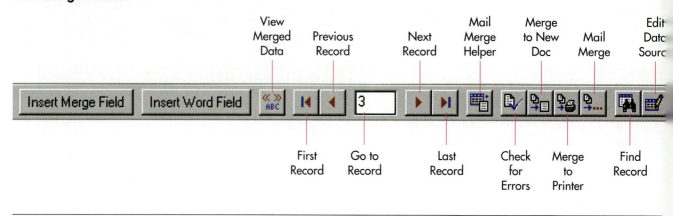

Master Document Toolbar

Picture Toolbar

Outlining Toolbar

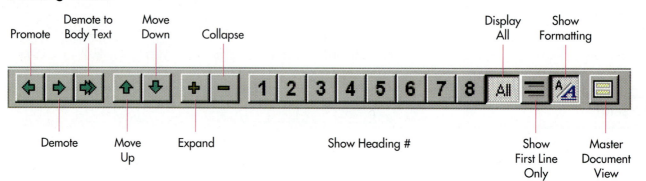

FIGURE B.2 Feature Toolbars (continued)

INTRODUCTION TO MICROSOFT EXCEL: WHAT IS A SPREADSHEET?

OBJECTIVES

After reading this chapter you will be able to:

1. Describe a spreadsheet and suggest several potential applications; explain how the rows and columns of a spreadsheet are identified, and how its cells are labeled.
2. Distinguish between a formula and a constant; explain the use of a predefined function within a formula.
3. Open an Excel workbook; add and delete rows and columns of a worksheet; save and print the modified worksheet.
4. Distinguish between a pull-down menu, a shortcut menu, and a toolbar.
5. Describe the three-dimensional nature of an Excel workbook; distinguish between a workbook and a worksheet.
6. Print a worksheet two ways: to show the computed values or the cell formulas.
7. Use the Page Setup command to print a worksheet with or without gridlines and/or row and column headings; preview a worksheet before printing.

OVERVIEW

This chapter provides a broad-based introduction to spreadsheets in general, and to Microsoft Excel in particular. The spreadsheet is the microcomputer application that is most widely used by managers and executives. Our intent is to show the wide diversity of business and other uses to which the spreadsheet model can be applied. For one example, we draw an analogy between the spreadsheet and the accountant's ledger. For a second example, we create an instructor's grade book.

The chapter covers the fundamentals of spreadsheets as implemented in Excel, which uses the term worksheet rather than spreadsheet. It discusses how the rows and columns of an Excel worksheet are labeled, the difference between a formula and a constant, and the ability of a worksheet to recalculate itself after a change is made. We also distinguish between a worksheet and a workbook.

The hands-on exercises in the chapter enable you to apply all of the material at the computer, and are indispensable to the learn-by-doing philosophy we follow throughout the text. As you do the exercises, you may recognize many commands from other Windows applications, all of which share a common user interface and consistent command structure. Excel will be even easier to learn if you already know another application in Microsoft Office.

INTRODUCTION TO SPREADSHEETS

A *spreadsheet* is the computerized equivalent of an accountant's ledger. As with the ledger, it consists of a grid of rows and columns that enables you to organize data in a readily understandable format. Figures 1.1a and 1.1b show the same information displayed in ledger and spreadsheet format, respectively.

"What is the big deal?" you might ask. The big deal is that after you change an entry (or entries), the spreadsheet will, automatically and almost instantly, recompute all of the formulas. Consider, for example, the profit projection spreadsheet shown in Figure 1.1b. As the spreadsheet is presently constructed, the unit price is $20 and the projected sales are 1,200 units, producing gross sales of $24,000 ($20/unit × 1,200 units). The projected expenses are $19,200, which yields a profit of $4,800 ($24,000 − $19,200). If the unit price is increased to $22 per unit, the spreadsheet recomputes every formula, adjusting the values of gross sales and net profit. The modified spreadsheet of Figure 1.1c appears automatically.

With a calculator and bottle of correction fluid or a good eraser, the same changes could also be made to the ledger. But imagine for a moment a ledger with hundreds of entries, many of which depend on the entry you wish to change. You can appreciate the time required to make all the necessary changes to the ledger by hand. The same spreadsheet, with hundreds of entries, will be recomputed automatically by the computer. And the computer will not make mistakes. Herein lies the advantage of a spreadsheet—the ability to make changes, and to have the com-

(a) The Accountant's Ledger

FIGURE 1.1   The Accountant's Ledger

Unit price is increased to $22

Formulas recompute automatically

	A	B
1	Profit Projection	
2		
3	Unit Price	$20
4	Unit Sales	1,200
5	Gross Sales	$24,000
6		
7	Expenses	
8	Production	$10,000
9	Distribution	$1,200
10	Marketing	$5,000
11	Overhead	$3,000
12	Total Expenses	$19,200
13		
14	Net Profit	$4,800

(b) Original Spreadsheet

	A	B
1	Profit Projection	
2		
3	Unit Price	$22
4	Unit Sales	1,200
5	Gross Sales	$26,400
6		
7	Expenses	
8	Production	$10,000
9	Distribution	$1,200
10	Marketing	$5,000
11	Overhead	$3,000
12	Total Expenses	$19,200
13		
14	Net Profit	$7,200

(c) Modified Spreadsheet

FIGURE 1.1 The Accountant's Ledger (continued)

puter carry out the recalculation faster and more accurately than could be accomplished manually.

The Professor's Grade Book

A second example of a spreadsheet, one with which you can easily identify, is that of a professor's grade book. The grades are recorded by hand in a notebook, which is nothing more than a different kind of accountant's ledger. Figure 1.2 contains both manual and spreadsheet versions of a grade book.

Figure 1.2a shows a handwritten grade book as it has been done since the days of the little red schoolhouse. For the sake of simplicity, only five students are shown, each with three grades. The professor has computed class averages for each exam, as well as a semester average for every student, in which the final counts *twice* as much as either test; for example, Adams's average is equal to $(100+90+81+81)/4 = 88$.

Figure 1.2b shows the grade book as it might appear in a spreadsheet, and is essentially unchanged from Figure 1.2a. Walker's grade on the final exam in Figure 1.2b is 90, giving him a semester average of 85 and producing a class average on the final of 75.2 as well. Now consider Figure 1.2c, in which the grade on Walker's final has been changed to 100, causing Walker's semester average to change from 85 to 90, and the class average on the final to go from 75.2 to 77.2. As with the profit projection, a change to any entry within the grade book automatically recalculates all other dependent formulas as well. Hence, when Walker's final exam was regraded, all dependent formulas (the class average for the final as well as Walker's semester average) were recomputed.

As simple as the idea of a spreadsheet may seem, it provided the first major reason for managers to have a personal computer on their desks. Essentially, anything that can be done with a pencil, a pad of paper, and a calculator can be done faster and far more accurately with a spreadsheet.

Final counts twice so average is computed as (100 + 90 + 81 + 81)/4

	TEST 1	TEST 2	FINAL	AVERAGE
ADAMS	100	90	81	88
BAKER	90	76	87	85
GLASSMAN	90	78	78	81
MOLDOF	60	60	40	50
WALKER	80	80	90	85
CLASS AVERAGE	84.0	76.8	75.2	
NOTE: FINAL COUNTS DOUBLE				

(a) The Professor's Grade Book

	A	B	C	D	E
1	Student	Test 1	Test 2	Final	Average
2					
3	Adams	100	90	81	88.0
4	Baker	90	76	87	85.0
5	Glassman	90	78	78	81.0
6	Moldof	60	60	40	50.0
7	Walker	80	80	90	85.0
8					
9	Class Average	84.0	76.8	75.2	

(b) Original Grades

Grade on Walker's final is changed to 100

	A	B	C	D	E
1	Student	Test 1	Test 2	Final	Average
2					
3	Adams	100	90	81	88.0
4	Baker	90	76	87	85.0
5	Glassman	90	78	78	81.0
6	Moldof	60	60	40	50.0
7	Walker	80	80	100	90.0
8					
9	Class Average	84.0	76.8	77.2	

Formulas recompute automatically

(c) Modified Spreadsheet

FIGURE 1.2 The Professor's Grade Book

Row and Column Headings

A spreadsheet is divided into rows and columns, with each row and column assigned a heading. Rows are given numeric headings ranging from 1 to 16,384 (the maximum number of rows allowed). Columns are assigned alphabetic headings from column A to Z, then continue from AA to AZ and then from BA to BZ and so on, until the last of 256 columns (column IV) is reached.

The intersection of a row and column forms a *cell,* with the number of cells in a spreadsheet equal to the number of rows times the number of columns. The professor's grade book in Figure 1.2, for example, has 5 columns labeled A through E, 9 rows numbered from 1 to 9, and a total of 45 cells. Each cell has a unique *cell reference;* for example, the cell at the intersection of column A and row 9 is known as cell A9. The column heading always precedes the row heading in the cell reference.

Formulas and Constants

Figure 1.3 shows an alternate view of the spreadsheet for the professor's grade book that displays the *cell contents* rather than the computed *values.* This figure displays the actual entries (formulas and constants) that were entered into the individual cells, which enable the spreadsheet to recalculate formulas whenever any entry changes.

A *constant* is an entry that does not change; that is, it may be a number, such as a student's grade on an exam, or it may be descriptive text (a label), such as a student's name. A *formula* is a combination of numeric constants, cell references, arithmetic operators, and/or functions (described below) that displays the result of a calculation. Every cell in a spreadsheet contains either a formula or a constant.

A formula always begins with an equal sign; a constant does not. Consider, for example, the formula in cell E3, =(B3+C3+2*D3)/4, which computes Adams's semester average. The formula is built in accordance with the professor's rules for computing a student's semester average, which counts the final twice as much as either exam. Excel uses symbols +, −, *, /, and ^ to indicate addition, subtraction, multiplication, division, and exponentiation, respectively, and follows the normal rules of arithmetic precedence. Any expression in parentheses is evaluated first, then within an expression exponentiation is performed first, followed by multiplication or division in left to right order, then finally addition or subtraction, also in left-to-right order.

The formula in cell E3 takes the grade on the first exam (in cell B3), plus the grade on the second exam (in cell C3), plus two times the grade on the final (in cell D3), and divides the result by four. Because we entered a formula for the semester average (rather than a constant), should any of the exam grades change, the semester average (a formula whose results depend on the individual exam grades) will also change. This, in essence, is the basic principle behind the spreadsheet and explains why, when one number changes, various other numbers throughout the spreadsheet change as well.

A formula may also include a *function,* or predefined computational task, such as the *AVERAGE function* in cells B9, C9, and D9. The function in cell B9, for example, =AVERAGE(B3:B7), is interpreted to mean the average of all cells starting at cell B3 and ending at cell B7 and is equivalent to the formula =(B3+B4+B5+B6+B7)/5. You can appreciate that functions are often easier to use than the corresponding formulas, especially with larger spreadsheets (and classes with many students).

Constant (entry that does not change)

Formula (displays the result of a calculation)

Function (predefined computational task)

	A	B	C	D	E
1	Student	Test 1	Test 2	Final	Average
2					
3	Adams	100	90	81	=(B3+C3+2*D3)/4
4	Baker	90	76	87	=(B4+C4+2*D4)/4
5	Glassman	90	78	78	=(B5+C5+2*D5)/4
6	Moldof	60	60	40	=(B6+C6+2*D6)/4
7	Walker	80	80	90	=(B7+C7+2*D7)/4
8					
9	Class Average	=AVERAGE(B3:B7)	=AVERAGE(C3:C7)	=AVERAGE(D3:D7)	

FIGURE 1.3 The Professor's Grade Book (cell formulas)

INTRODUCTION TO MICROSOFT EXCEL

Figure 1.4 displays the professor's grade book as it is implemented in Microsoft Excel. Microsoft Excel is a Windows application, and thus shares the common user interface with which you are already familiar. You should recognize, therefore, that the desktop in Figure 1.4 has two open windows—an application window for Microsoft Excel and a document window for the workbook, which is currently open.

Each window has its own Minimize, Maximize (or Restore), and Close buttons. Both windows have been maximized and thus the title bars have been merged into a single title bar that appears at the top of the application window. The title bar reflects the application (Microsoft Excel) as well as the name of the workbook (Grade Book) on which you are working. A menu bar appears immediately below the title bar. Two toolbars, which are discussed in depth on page 8, appear below the menu bar. The TipWizard appears immediately under the toolbars and offers suggestions to enable you to work more efficiently. Vertical and horizontal scroll bars appear at the right and bottom of the document window. The Windows 95 taskbar appears at the bottom of the screen and shows the open applications.

The terminology is important, and we distinguish here between spreadsheet, worksheet, and workbook. Excel refers to a spreadsheet as a **worksheet**. Spreadsheet is a generic term; *workbook* and *worksheet* are unique to Excel. An Excel **workbook** contains one or more worksheets. The professor's grades for this class are contained in the CIS120 worksheet within the Grade Book workbook. This workbook also contains additional worksheets (CIS223 and CIS316) as indicated by the worksheet tabs at the bottom of the window. These worksheets contain the professor's grades for other courses that he or she is teaching this semester. (See practice problem 1 at the end of the chapter.)

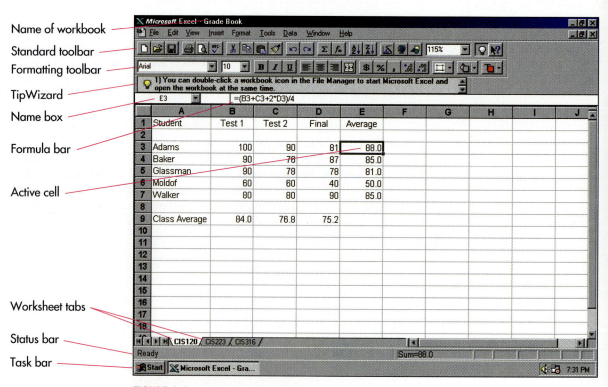

FIGURE 1.4   Professor's Grade Book

Figure 1.4 resembles the grade book shown earlier, but it includes several other elements that enable you to create and/or edit the worksheet. The heavy border around cell E3 indicates that it (cell E3) is the ***active cell.*** Any entry made at this time is made into the active cell, and any commands that are executed affect the contents of the active cell. The active cell can be changed by clicking a different cell, or by using the arrow keys to move to a different cell.

The displayed value in cell E3 is 88.0, but as indicated earlier, the cell contains a formula to compute the semester average rather than the number itself. The contents of the active cell, =(B3+C3+2*D3)/4, are displayed in the ***formula bar*** near the top of the worksheet. The cell reference for the active cell, cell E3 in Figure 1.4, appears in the ***Name box*** at the left of the formula bar.

The ***status bar*** at the bottom of the worksheet keeps you informed of what is happening as you work within Excel. It displays information about a selected command or an operation in progress. It also shows the status of the keyboard toggle switches, such as the Caps Lock key or the Ins key, neither of which has been toggled on in the figure.

> **THE EXCEL WORKBOOK**
>
> An Excel workbook is the electronic equivalent of the three-ring binder. A workbook contains one or more worksheets (or chart sheets), each of which is identified by a ***tab*** at the bottom of the workbook. The worksheets in a workbook are normally related to one another; for example, each worksheet may contain the sales for a specific division within a company. The advantage of a workbook is that all of its worksheets are stored in a single file, which is accessed as a unit.

Toolbars

Excel provides several different ways to accomplish the same task. Commands may be accessed from a pull-down menu, from a shortcut menu (which is displayed by pointing to an object and clicking the right mouse button), and/or through keyboard equivalents. Commands can also be executed from one of many ***toolbars*** that appear immediately below the menu bar. The Standard and Formatting toolbars are displayed by default. (All toolbars can be displayed or hidden by using the View menu as described on page 25 later in the chapter.)

The ***Standard toolbar*** contains buttons corresponding to the most basic commands in Excel—for example, opening and closing a workbook, printing a workbook, and so on. The icon on the button is intended to be indicative of its function (e.g., a printer to indicate the Print command). You can also point to the button to display a ***ToolTip*** showing the name of the button. The ***Formatting toolbar*** appears under the Standard toolbar, and provides access to common formatting operations such as boldface, italics, or underlining. The easiest way to master the toolbars is to view the buttons in groups according to their general function, as shown in Figure 1.5.

The toolbars may appear overwhelming at first, but there is absolutely no need to memorize what the individual buttons do. That will come with time. Indeed, if you use another office application such as Microsoft Word, you may already recognize many of the buttons on the Standard and Formatting toolbars. Most individuals start by using the pull-down menus, then look for shortcuts along the way.

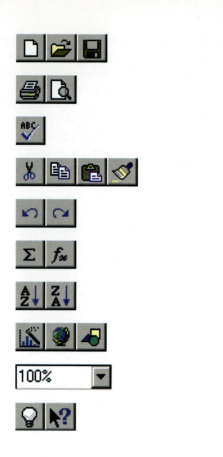

Opens a new workbook; opens an existing workbook; saves the workbook to disk

Prints the workbook; previews the workbook prior to printing

Checks spelling

Cuts or copies the selection to the clipboard; pastes the clipboard contents; copies the format of the selected cells

Undoes or redoes the previously executed command

Sums the suggested range; displays the Function Wizard dialog box

Performs an ascending or descending sort

Creates a chart; creates a map; toggles the Drawing toolbar on and off

Changes the zoom percentage

Displays the TipWizard; accesses online help

(a) The Standard Toolbar

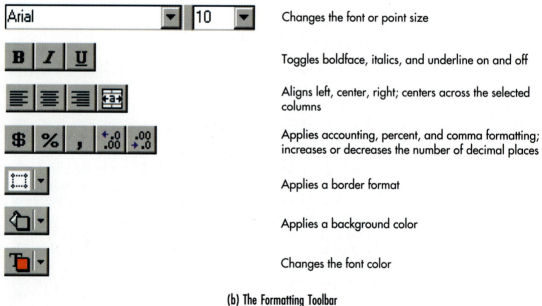

Changes the font or point size

Toggles boldface, italics, and underline on and off

Aligns left, center, right; centers across the selected columns

Applies accounting, percent, and comma formatting; increases or decreases the number of decimal places

Applies a border format

Applies a background color

Changes the font color

(b) The Formatting Toolbar

FIGURE 1.5   Toolbars

> **READ THE MANUAL**
>
> The answer to almost any question about Microsoft Excel is available through online help if only you take the trouble to look. The Help facility is intuitive and easy to use. The help displays are task specific and fit in a single screen to keep you from having to scroll through large amounts of information.

Entering Data

Data is entered into a worksheet by selecting a cell, then typing the constant or formula that is to go into that cell. The entry is displayed in the formula bar at the top of the window as it is being typed. The entry is completed by pressing the enter key, which moves the active cell to the cell immediately below the current cell, or by pressing any of the arrow keys to move to the next cell in the indicated direction. Pressing the right arrow key, for example, completes the entry and moves the active cell to the next cell in the same row. You can also complete the entry by clicking in a new cell, or by clicking the green check that appears to the left of the formula bar as data is entered.

To replace an existing entry, select the cell by clicking in the cell, or by using the keyboard to move to the cell. Type the corrected entry (as though you were entering it for the first time), then complete the entry as described above.

THE FILE MENU

The *File menu* is a critically important menu in virtually every Windows application. It contains the *Save command* to save a workbook to disk, and the *Open command* to subsequently retrieve (open) the workbook at a later time. The File Menu also contains the *Print command* to print a workbook, the *Close command* to close the current workbook but continue working in Excel, and the *Exit command* to quit Excel altogether.

The *Save command* copies the workbook that is currently being edited (the workbook in memory) to disk. The Save As dialog box appears the first time a workbook is saved so that you can specify the filename and other required information. All subsequent executions of the Save command save the workbook under the assigned name, replacing the previously saved version with the new version.

The Save As dialog box requires a filename (e.g., My First Spreadsheet in Figure 1.6a), which can be up to 255 characters in length. The filename may contain spaces and commas. The dialog box also requires the drive (and folder) in which the file is to be saved, as well as the file type that determines which application the file is associated with. (Long-time DOS users will remember the three-character extension at the end of a filename such as XLS to indicate an Excel workbook. The extension is generally hidden in Windows 95, according to options that are set through the View menu in My Computer. See page 30 in the Windows appendix.)

The Open command brings a copy of a previously saved workbook into memory, enabling you to edit the workbook. The Open command displays the Open dialog box in which you specify the file to retrieve. You indicate the drive (and optionally the folder) that contains the file, as well as the type of file you want to retrieve. Excel will then list all files of that type on the designated drive (and folder), enabling you to open the file you want.

INTRODUCTION TO MICROSOFT EXCEL

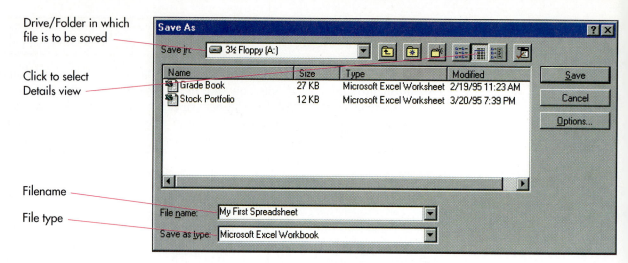

(a) Save As Dialog Box

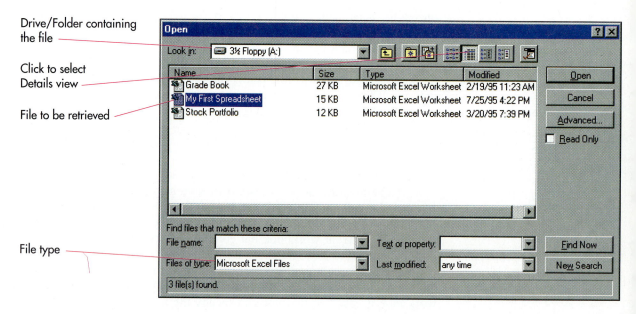

(b) File Open Dialog Box

FIGURE 1.6 The Save and Open Commands

The Save and Open commands work in conjunction with one another. The Save As dialog box in Figure 1.6a, for example, saves the file *My First Spreadsheet* onto the disk in drive A. The Open dialog box in Figure 1.6b brings that file back into memory so that you can work with the file, after which you can save the revised file for use at a later time.

The Save As and Open dialog boxes share a common toolbar that enables you to display the files on a specific drive (or folder) in different ways. The Details view is selected in both dialog boxes and displays the file size as well as the date and time a file was last modified. The drop-down arrow on the Look-in box enables you to display files on a different drive or folder.

> **THE SAVE AS COMMAND**
>
> The *Save As command* saves a workbook under a different name, and is useful when you want to retain a copy of the original workbook. The Save As command provides you with two copies of a workbook. The original workbook is kept on disk under its original name. A copy of the workbook is saved on disk under a new name and remains in memory. All subsequent editing is done on the new (renamed) workbook.

LEARNING BY DOING

We come now to the first of two hands-on exercises in this chapter that implement our learn-by-doing philosophy. The exercise shows you how to start Microsoft Excel and open the professor's grade book from the *data disk* that is referenced throughout the text. You can obtain a copy of the data disk from your instructor, or you can download the files on the data disk as described in the exercise. The data disk contains a series of Excel workbooks that are used in various exercises throughout the text. It can also be used to store the workbooks you create (or you can store the workbooks on a hard disk if you have access to your own computer).

HANDS-ON EXERCISE 1

Introduction to Microsoft Excel

Objectives: To start Microsoft Excel; to open, modify, and print an existing worksheet. Use Figure 1.7 as a guide in the exercise.

Step 1: Welcome to Windows 95

- Turn on the computer and all of its peripherals. The floppy drive should be empty prior to starting your machine. This ensures that the system starts by reading from the hard disk, which contains the Windows files, as opposed to a floppy disk, which does not.
- Your system will take a minute or so to get started, after which you should see the desktop in Figure 1.7a. Do not be concerned if the appearance of your desktop is different from ours.
- If you are new to Windows 95 and you want a quick introduction, click the **What's New** or **Windows Tour command buttons.** (Follow the instructions in the boxed tip to display the dialog box if it does not appear on your system.)
- Click the **Close button** to close the Welcome window and continue with the exercise.

Click if you are new to Windows 95 for a quick introduction

Click to close Welcome window and continue with the exercise

Click to display the Start menu

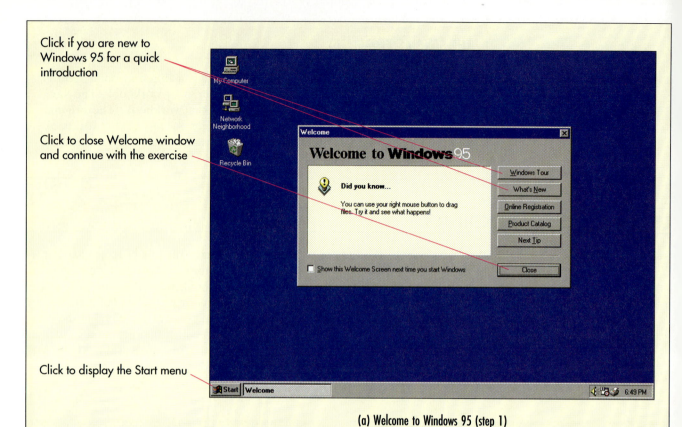

(a) Welcome to Windows 95 (step 1)

FIGURE 1.7 Hands-on Exercise 1

> ### TAKE THE WINDOWS 95 TOUR (REQUIRES CD-ROM INSTALLATION)
>
> Windows 95 greets you with a Welcome window that contains a command button to take you on a 10-minute tour of Windows 95. Click the command button and enjoy the show. You might also try the What's New command button for a quick overview of changes from Windows 3.1. If you do not see the Welcome window when you start Windows 95, click the Start button, click Run, type C:\WINDOWS\WELCOME in the Open *text box,* and press enter.

STEP 2: Install the Data Disk

➤ Do this step *only* if you have your own computer and you want to install (copy) the files from the data disk to the hard drive. Place the data disk in drive A.

➤ Click the **Start button** to display the Start menu. Click the **Run command** to display the Run dialog box.

➤ Type **A:\Install C** in the text box. (The drive letter, drive C in the example, is variable and indicates the drive on which to install the data disk.)

➤ Click **OK** or press the **enter key.** Follow the on-screen instructions to complete the installation.

DOWNLOAD THE DATA DISK

The data disk for all books in the Exploring Windows series can be downloaded from the Prentice Hall Web site (http://www.prenhall.com). Use any Web browser to log onto the site, select Business and Economics, then move to the Exploring Windows page. To download the files for a single application, go to the page for that book, then click the icon to download the data disk. To download the files for all Office applications simultaneously, go to the Exploring Microsoft Office page.

STEP 3: Start Microsoft Excel

➤ Click the **Start button** to display the Start menu. Click (or point to) the **Programs menu,** then click **Microsoft Excel** to start the program.

➤ If necessary, click the **Maximize button** in the application window so that Excel takes the entire desktop as shown in Figure 1.7b. Click the **Maximize button** in the document window (if necessary) so that the document window is as large as possible.

POINT AND SLIDE

Click the Start button, then slowly slide the mouse pointer over the various menu options. Notice that each time you point to a submenu, its items are displayed. Point to (don't click) the Programs menu, then click the Microsoft Excel item to start the program. In other words, you don't have to click a submenu—you can just point and slide!

STEP 4: Open the Workbook

➤ Pull down the **File menu** and click **Open** (or click the **Open button** on the Standard toolbar). You should see a dialog box similar to the one in Figure 1.7b.

➤ Click the **Details button** to change to the Details view. Click and drag the vertical border between two columns to increase (or decrease) the size of a column.

➤ Click the **drop-down arrow** on the Look In list box. Click the appropriate drive, drive C or drive A, depending on the location of your data. Double click the **Exploring Excel folder** to make it the active folder (the folder from which you will retrieve and into which you will save the workbook).

➤ Click the **down scroll arrow** if you need to scroll in order to click **Grade Book** to select the professor's grade book. Click the **Open command button** to open the workbook and begin the exercise.

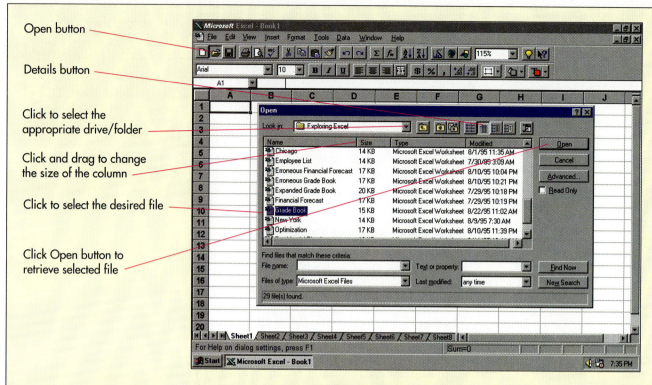

(b) Open the Grade Book (steps 3 & 4)

FIGURE 1.7 Hands-on Exercise 1 (continued)

A VERY USEFUL TOOLBAR

The Open and Save As dialog boxes share a common toolbar with several very useful buttons. Click the Details button to switch to the Details view and see the date and time the file was last modified as well as its size. Click the List button to display an icon for each file, enabling you to see many more files at the same time than in the Details view. The Preview button lets you see a workbook before you open it. The Properties button displays information about the workbook, including the number of revisions.

STEP 5: The Active Cell and Formula Bar

➤ You should see the workbook in Figure 1.7c. Click in **cell B3,** the cell containing Adams's grade on the first test. Cell B3 is now the active cell and is surrounded by a heavy border. The Name box indicates that cell B3 is the active cell, and its contents are displayed in the formula bar.

➤ Click in **cell B4** (or press the **down arrow key**) to make it the active cell. The Name box indicates cell B4 while the formula bar indicates a grade of 90.

➤ Click in **cell E3,** the cell containing the formula to compute Adams's semester average; the worksheet displays the computed average of 88.0, but the formula bar displays the formula, =(B3+C3+2*D3)/4, to compute that average based on the test grades.

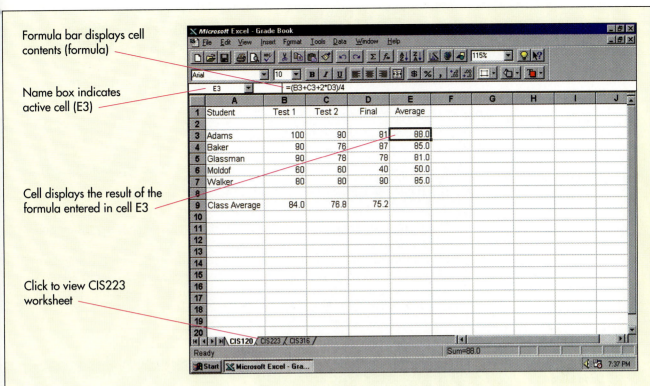

(c) The Active Cell and Formula Bar (step 5)

FIGURE 1.7 Hands-on Exercise 1 (continued)

➤ Continue to change the active cell (with the mouse or arrow keys) and notice how the display in the Name box and formula bar change to reflect the active cell.

THE ANSWER WIZARD

The Answer Wizard enables you to request help by posing a question in English. Pull down the Help menu and click the Answer Wizard command. Type your question in the text box, for example, "How do I get help?", then click the Search command button. The wizard will return a list of help topics that answer your question together with a list of related topics that may be of interest to you.

STEP 6: View the Other Worksheets

➤ Click the **CIS223 tab** to view a different worksheet within the same workbook. This worksheet contains the grades for a different class.

➤ Click the **CIS316 tab** to view this worksheet. Click the **CIS120 tab** to return to this worksheet and continue with the exercise.

STEP 7: Experiment (What If?)

➤ Click in **cell C4,** the cell containing Baker's grade on the second test. Enter a corrected value of **86** (instead of the previous entry of 76). Press **enter** (or click in another cell).

➤ The effects of this change ripple through the worksheet, automatically changing the computed value for Baker's average in cell E4 to 87.5. The class average on the second test in cell C9 changes to 78.8.

➤ Change Walker's grade on the final from 90 to **100.** Press **enter** (or click in another cell). Walker's average in cell E7 changes to 90.0, while the class average in cell D9 changes to 77.2.

➤ Your worksheet should match Figure 1.7d.

> ### THE UNDO COMMAND
>
> The *Undo command* reverses the effect of the most recent operation and is invaluable at any time, but especially when you are learning. Pull down the Edit menu and click Undo (or click the Undo button on the Standard toolbar) to cancel the effects of the preceding command. Use the Undo command whenever something happens to your worksheet that is different from what you intended.

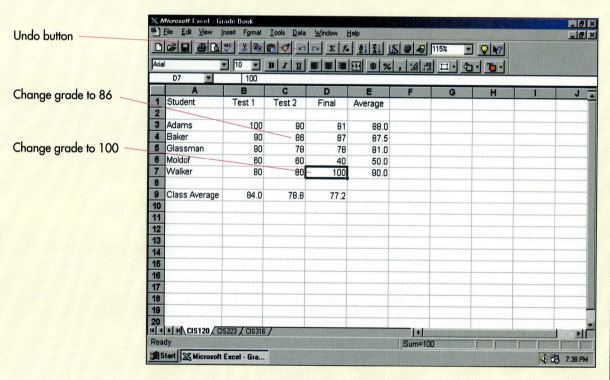

(d) What If (step 7)

FIGURE 1.7 Hands-on Exercise 1 (continued)

STEP 8: Print the Worksheet

➤ Pull down the **File menu** and click **Save** (or click the **Save button** on the Standard toolbar).

16 EXPLORING MICROSOFT EXCEL 7.0

▶ Pull down the **File menu.** Click **Print** to produce a dialog box requesting information about the Print command as shown in Figure 1.7e. Click **OK** to accept the default options (you need to print only the selected worksheet).

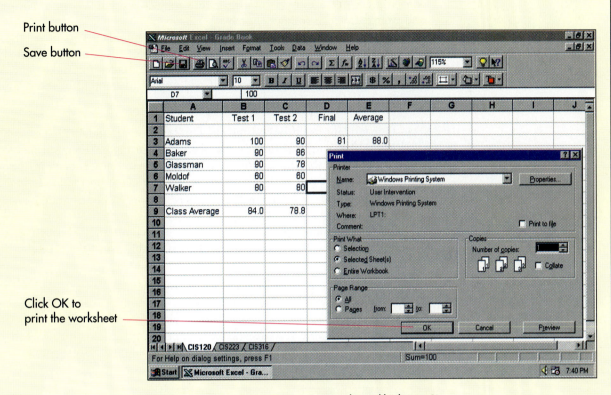

(e) Print the Workbook (step 8)

FIGURE 1.7 Hands-on Exercise 1 (continued)

ABOUT MICROSOFT EXCEL

Pull down the Help menu and click About Microsoft Excel to display the specific release number as well as other licensing information, including the product serial number. This help screen also contains two very useful command buttons, System Info and Technical Support. The first button displays information about the hardware installed on your system, including the amount of memory and available space on the hard drive. The Technical Support button provides the telephone numbers to call for technical assistance.

STEP 9: Close the Workbook

▶ Pull down the **File menu.** Click **Close** to close the workbook but leave Excel open.

▶ Pull down the **File menu** a second time. Click **Exit** if you do not want to continue with the next exercise at this time.

MODIFYING THE WORKSHEET

We trust that you completed the hands-on exercise without difficulty and that you are more confident in your ability than when you first began. The exercise was not complicated, but it did accomplish several objectives and set the stage for a second exercise, which follows shortly.

Consider now Figure 1.8, which contains a modified version of the professor's grade book. Figure 1.8a shows the grade book at the end of the first hands-on exercise and reflects the changes made to the grades for Baker and Walker. Figure 1.8b shows the worksheet as it will appear at the end of the second exercise. Several changes bear mention:

1. One student has dropped the class and two other students have been added. Moldof appeared in the original worksheet in Figure 1.8a, but has somehow managed to withdraw; Coulter and Courier did not appear in the original grade book but have been added to the worksheet in Figure 1.8b.
2. A new column containing the students' majors has been added.

The implementation of these changes is accomplished through a combination of the Insert and Delete commands that enable you to add or remove rows or columns as necessary.

Insert and Delete Commands

The *Insert command* adds row(s) or column(s) to an existing worksheet. The *Delete command* removes existing row(s) or column(s). Both commands auto-

	A	B	C	D	E
1	Student	Test 1	Test 2	Final	Average
2					
3	Adams	100	90	81	88.0
4	Baker	90	86	87	87.5
5	Glassman	90	78	78	81.0
6	Moldof	60	60	40	50.0
7	Walker	80	80	100	90.0
8					
9	Class Average	84.0	78.8	77.2	

(a) After Hands-on Exercise 1

A new column has been added (Major)

Two new students have been added

Moldof has been deleted

	A	B	C	D	E	F
1	Student	Major	Test 1	Test 2	Final	Average
2						
3	Adams	CIS	100	90	81	88.0
4	Baker	MKT	90	86	87	87.5
5	Coulter	ACC	85	95	100	95.0
6	Courier	FIN	75	75	85	80.0
7	Glassman	CIS	90	78	78	81.0
8	Walker	CIS	80	80	100	90.0
9						

(b) After Hands-on Exercise 2

FIGURE 1.8 The Modified Grade Book

matically adjust the cell references in existing formulas to account for the insertion or deletion of rows and columns within the worksheet.

Figure 1.9 displays the cell formulas in the professor's grade book and corresponds to the worksheets in Figure 1.8. The "before" and "after" worksheets reflect the insertion of a new column containing the students' majors, the addition of two new students, Coulter and Courier, and the deletion of an existing student, Moldof.

Let us consider the formula to compute Adams's semester average, which is contained in cell E3 of the original grade book, but in cell F3 in the modified grade book. The formula in Figure 1.9a referenced cells B3, C3, and D3 (the grades on test 1, test 2, and the final). The corresponding formula in Figure 1.9b reflects the fact that a new column has been inserted, and references cells C3, D3, and E3. The change in the formula is made automatically by Excel, without any action on the part of the user other than to insert the new column. The formulas for all other students have been adjusted in similar fashion.

Some students (all students below Baker) have had a further adjustment to reflect the addition of the new students through insertion of new rows in the worksheet. Glassman, for example, appeared in row 5 of the original worksheet, but appears in row 7 of the revised worksheet. Hence the formula to compute Glassman's semester average now references the grades in row 7, rather than in row 5 as in the original worksheet.

Finally, the formulas to compute the class averages have also been adjusted. These formulas appeared in row 9 of Figure 1.9a and averaged the grades in rows 3 through 7. The revised worksheet has a net increase of one student, which automatically moves these formulas to row 10, where the formulas are adjusted to average the grades in rows 3 through 8.

	A	B	C	D	E
1	Student	Test1	Test2	Final	Average
2					
3	Adams	100	90	81	=(B3+C3+2*D3)/4
4	Baker	90	86	87	=(B4+C4+2*D4)/4
5	Glassman	90	78	78	=(B5+C5+2*D5)/4
6	Moldof	60	60	40	=(B6+C6+2*D6)/4
7	Walker	80	80	100	=(B7+C7+2*D7)/4
8					
9	Class Average	=AVERAGE(B3:B7)	=AVERAGE(C3:C7)	=AVERAGE(D3:D7)	

Formula references grades in B3, C3, and D3

Function references grades in rows 3–7

(a) Before

	A	B	C	D	E	F
1	Student	Major	Test1	Test2	Final	Average
2						
3	Adams	CIS	100	90	81	=(C3+D3+2*E3)/4
4	Baker	MKT	90	86	87	=(C4+D4+2*E4)/4
5	Coulter	ACC	85	95	100	=(C5+D5+2*E5)/4
6	Courier	FIN	75	75	85	=(C6+D6+2*E6)/4
7	Glassman	CIS	90	78	78	=(C7+D7+2*E7)/4
8	Walker	CIS	80	80	100	=(C8+D8+2*E8)/4
9						
10	Class Average		=AVERAGE(C3:C8)	=AVERAGE(D3:D8)	=AVERAGE(E3:E8)	

Function changes to reference grades in rows 3–8 (due to addition of 2 new students and deletion of 1)

Formula changes to reference grades in C3, D3, and E3 due to addition of new column

(b) After

FIGURE 1.9 The Insert and Delete Commands

THE PAGE SETUP COMMAND

The Print command was used at the end of the first hands-on exercise to print the completed workbook. The *Page Setup command* gives you complete control of the printed worksheet as illustrated in Figure 1.10. Many of the options may not appear important now, but you will appreciate them as you develop larger and more complicated worksheets later in the text.

The Page tab in Figure 1.10a determines the orientation and scaling of the printed page. *Portrait orientation* (8½ × 11) prints vertically down the page. *Landscape orientation* (11 × 8½) prints horizontally across the page and is used

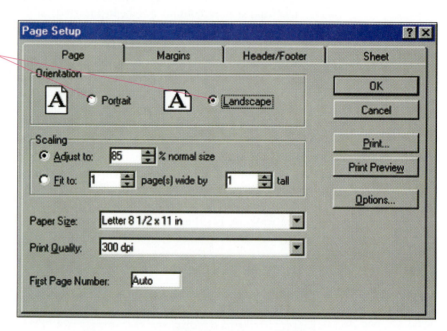

(a) The Page Tab

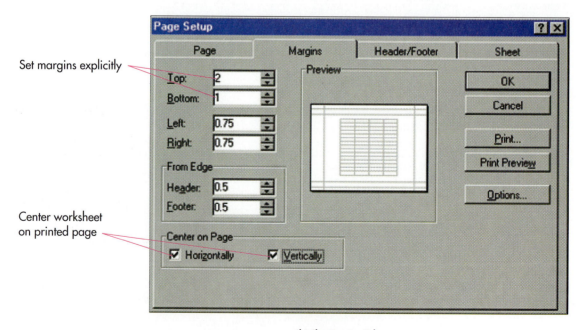

(b) The Margins Tab

FIGURE 1.10   The Page Setup Command

when the worksheet is too wide to fit on a portrait page. The option buttons indicate mutually exclusive items, one of which *must* be selected; that is, a worksheet must be printed in either portrait or landscape orientation. Option buttons are also used to choose the scaling factor. You can reduce (enlarge) the output by a designated scaling factor, or you can force the output to fit on a specified number of pages. The latter option is typically used to force a worksheet to fit on a single page.

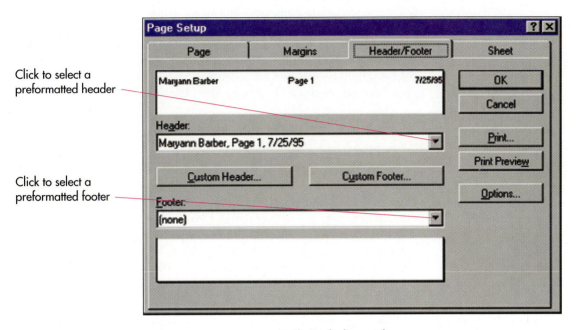

(c) The Header/Footer Tab

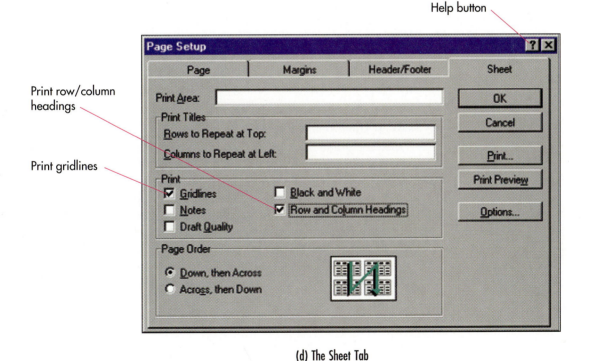

(d) The Sheet Tab

FIGURE 1.10   The Page Setup Command (continued)

The Margins tab in Figure 1.10b not only controls the margins, but will also center the worksheet horizontally and/or vertically. Check boxes are associated with the centering options and indicate that multiple options can be chosen; for example, horizontally and vertically are both selected. The Margins tab also determines the distance of the header and footer from the edge of the page.

The Header/Footer tab in Figure 1.10c lets you create a header (and/or footer) that appears at the top (and/or bottom) of every page. The pull-down list boxes let you choose from several preformatted entries, or alternatively, you can click the appropriate command button to customize either entry.

The Sheet tab in Figure 1.10d offers several additional options. The Gridlines option prints lines to separate the cells within the worksheet. The Row and Column Headings option displays the column letters and row numbers. Both options should be selected for most worksheets. Information about the additional entries can be obtained by clicking the Help button.

THE PRINT PREVIEW COMMAND

The *Print Preview command* displays the worksheet as it will appear when printed. The command is invaluable and will save you considerable time as you don't have to rely on trial and error to obtain the perfect printout. The Print Preview command can be executed from the File menu, via the Print Preview button on the Standard toolbar, or from the Print Preview command button within the Page Setup command.

HANDS-ON EXERCISE 2

Modifying a Worksheet

Objective: To open an existing workbook; to insert and delete rows and columns in a worksheet; to print cell formulas and displayed values; to use the Page Setup command to modify the appearance of a printed workbook. Use Figure 1.11 as a guide in doing the exercise.

STEP 1: Open the Workbook

▶ Open the grade book as you did in the previous exercise. Pull down the **File menu** and click **Open** (or click the **Open button** on the Standard toolbar) to display the Open dialog box.

▶ Click the **drop-down arrow** on the Look In list box. Click the appropriate drive, drive C or drive A, depending on the location of your data. Double click the **Exploring Excel folder** to make it the active folder (the folder in which you will save the workbook).

▶ Click the **down scroll arrow** until you can select (click) the **Grade Book** workbook. Click the **Open command button** to open the workbook and begin the exercise.

THE MOST RECENTLY OPENED FILE LIST

The easiest way to open a recently used workbook is to select the workbook directly from the File menu. Pull down the File menu, but instead of clicking the Open command, check to see if the workbook appears on the list of the most recently opened workbooks located at the bottom of the menu. If it does, you can click the workbook name rather than having to make the appropriate selections through the Open dialog box.

STEP 2: The Save As Command

➤ Pull down the **File menu.** Click **Save As** to display the dialog box shown in Figure 1.11a.

➤ Enter **Finished Grade Book** as the name of the new workbook. (A filename may contain up to 255 characters. Spaces and commas are allowed in the filename.)

➤ Click the **Save button.** Press the **Esc key** or click the **Close button** if you see a Properties dialog box.

➤ There are now two identical copies of the file on disk: "Grade Book," which is the completed workbook from the previous exercise, and "Finished Grade Book," which you just created. The title bar shows the latter name, which is the workbook currently in memory.

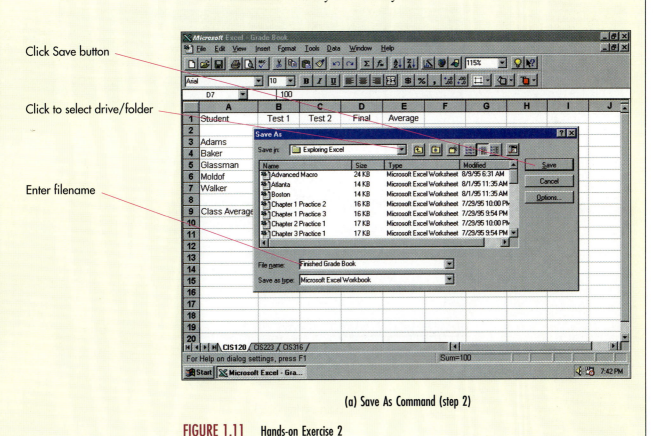

(a) Save As Command (step 2)

FIGURE 1.11   Hands-on Exercise 2

FILE PROPERTIES

Excel automatically stores summary information and other properties for each workbook you create, and prompts for that information when the workbook is saved initially. The information is interesting, but is typically not used by beginners, and hence we suggest you suppress the prompt for this information. Pull down the Tools menu, click Options, click the General tab, then clear the box to Prompt for File Properties. You can view (edit) the properties of any workbook by clicking the Properties command in the File menu.

STEP 3: Delete a Row

➤ Click any cell in **row 6** (the row you will delete). Pull down the **Edit menu.** Click **Delete** to display the dialog box in Figure 1.11b. Click **Entire Row.** Click **OK** to delete row 6.

➤ Moldof has disappeared from the grade book, and the class averages (now in row 8) have been updated automatically to reflect the fact that Moldof is gone.

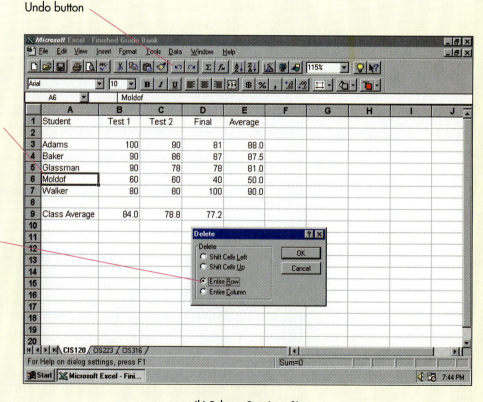

(b) Delete a Row (step 3)

FIGURE 1.11   Hands-on Exercise 2 (continued)

24   EXPLORING MICROSOFT EXCEL 7.0

ERASING VERSUS DELETING

The Edit Delete command deletes the selected cell, row, or column from the worksheet. It is very different from the Edit Clear command, which erases the contents (and/or formatting) of the selected cells, but does not delete the cells from the worksheet. The Edit Delete command causes Excel to adjust cell references throughout the worksheet. The Edit Clear command does not adjust cell references as no cells are moved.

STEP 4: The Undo Command

➤ Pull down the **Edit menu** and click **Undo Delete** (or click the **Undo button** on the Standard toolbar) to reverse the last command and put Moldof back in the worksheet.

➤ Click any cell in **row 6,** and this time delete the entire row for good.

MISSING TOOLBARS

The Standard and Formatting toolbars are displayed by default, but either or both can be hidden from view. To display (or hide) a toolbar, point to any toolbar, click the right mouse button to display the Toolbar shortcut menu, then click the individual toolbars on or off as appropriate. If you do not see any toolbars at all, pull down the View menu, click Toolbars to display a dialog box listing the available toolbars, check the toolbars you want displayed, and click OK.

STEP 5: Insert a Row

➤ Click any cell in **row 5** (the row containing Glassman's grades).

➤ Pull down the **Insert menu.** Click **Rows** to add a new row above the current row. Row 5 is now blank (it is the newly inserted row), and Glassman (who was in row 5) is now in row 6.

➤ Enter the data for the new student in row 5 as shown in Figure 1.11c:
- Click in **cell A5.** Type **Coulter.** Press the **right arrow key** or click in **cell B5.**
- Type **85.** Press the **right arrow key** or click in **cell C5.**
- Type **95.** Press the **right arrow key** or click in **cell D5.**
- Type **100.** Press the **right arrow key** or click in **cell E5.**
- Enter the formula to compute the semester average, **=(B5+C5+2*D5)/4.** Be sure to begin the formula with an equal sign. Press **enter.**
- Click the **Save button** on the Standard toolbar, or pull down the **File menu** and click **Save** to save the changes made to this point.

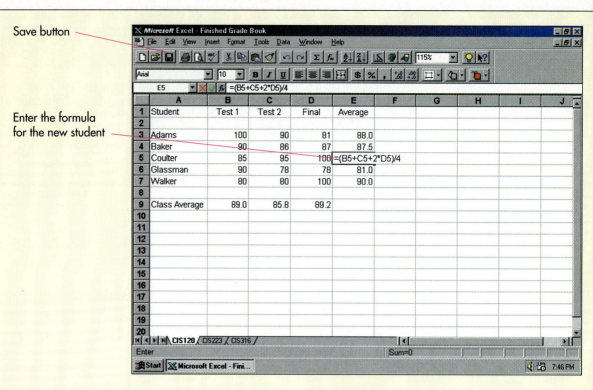

(c) Insert a Row (step 5)

FIGURE 1.11 Hands-on Exercise 2 (continued)

INSERTING (DELETING) ROWS AND COLUMNS

The fastest way to insert or delete a row is to point to the row number, then click the right mouse button to simultaneously select the row and display a shortcut menu. Click Insert to add a row above the selected row, or click Delete to delete the selected row. Use a similar technique to insert or delete a column, by pointing to the column heading, then clicking the right mouse button to display a shortcut menu from which you can select the appropriate command.

STEP 6: Insert a Second Row

➤ Point to the row heading for **row 6** (which now contains Glassman's grades), then click the **right mouse button** to select the row and display a shortcut menu. Click **Insert** to insert a new row 6, which moves Glassman to row 7.

➤ Click in **cell A6.** Type **C,** the first letter in "Courier," which also happens to be the first letter in "Coulter," a previous entry in column A. If the Auto-Complete feature is on (see boxed tip), Coulter's name will be automatically inserted in cell A6 with "oulter" selected. Type **ourier** (the remaining letters in "Courier," which replace "oulter."

➤ Enter Courier's grades in the appropriate cells (75, 75, and 85 in cells B6, C6, and D6, respectively).

➤ Click in **cell E6.** Enter the formula to compute the semester average, **=(B6+C6+2*D6)/4.** Press **enter.**

➤ Save the workbook.

> ### AUTOCOMPLETE
>
> The *AutoComplete* feature is Excel's way of trying to speed data entry. As soon as you begin typing a label into a cell, Excel searches for and (automatically) displays any other label in that column that matches the letters you typed. It's handy if you want to repeat a label, but it can be distracting if you want to enter a different label that just happens to begin with the same letter. To turn the feature on (off), pull down the Tools menu, click Options, then click the Edit tab. Check (clear) the box to enable the AutoComplete feature.

STEP 7: Insert a Column

➤ Point to the column heading for column B, then click the **right mouse button** to display a shortcut menu as shown in Figure 1.11d. Click **Insert** to insert a new column, which becomes the new column B. All existing columns have been moved to the right.

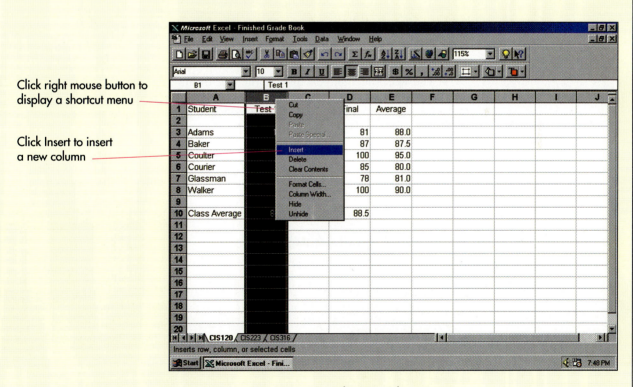

(d) Insert a Column (step 7)

FIGURE 1.11   Hands-on Exercise 2 (continued)

INTRODUCTION TO MICROSOFT EXCEL   **27**

- Click in **cell B1**. Type **Major**.
- Click in **cell B3**. Enter **CIS** as Adams's major. Press the **down arrow** to move automatically to the major for the next student.
- Type **MKT** in cell B4. Press the **down arrow**. Type **ACC** in cell B5. Press the **down arrow**. Type **FIN** in cell B6.
- Press the **down arrow** to move to cell B7. Type **C** (AutoComplete will automatically enter "IS" to complete the entry). Press the **down arrow** to move to cell B8. Type **C** (the AutoComplete feature again enters "IS"), then press **enter** to complete the entry.
- Save the workbook.

SHORTCUT MENUS

Shortcut menus provide an alternate way to execute commands. Point to any object in a worksheet—a cell, a row or column heading, a worksheet tab, or a toolbar—then click the right mouse button to display a shortcut menu with commands appropriate to the object. Click the left mouse button to select a command from the shortcut menu, or press the Esc key (or click outside the menu) to close the shortcut menu without executing a command.

STEP 8: Display the Cell Formulas
- Pull down the **Tools menu**. Click **Options** to display the Options dialog box. Click the **View tab**. Check the box for **Formulas**. Click **OK**.
- The worksheet should display the cell formulas as shown in Figure 1.11e. If necessary, click the **right scroll arrow** on the horizontal scroll bar until column F, the column containing the formulas to compute the semester averages, comes into view.
- If necessary (i.e., if the formulas are not completely visible), double click the border between the column headings for columns F and G. This increases the width of column F to accommodate the widest entry in that column.

DISPLAY CELL FORMULAS

A worksheet should always be printed twice, once to show the computed results, and once to show the cell formulas. The fastest way to toggle (switch) between cell formulas and displayed values is to use the Ctrl+` keyboard shortcut. (The ` is on the same key as the ~ at the upper left of the keyboard.) Press Ctrl+` and you switch from displayed values to cell formulas. Press Ctrl+` a second time and you are back to the displayed values.

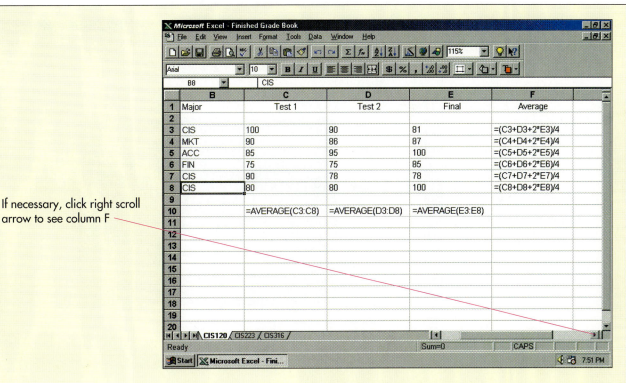

If necessary, click right scroll arrow to see column F

(e) Display the Cell Formulas (step 8)

FIGURE 1.11 Hands-on Exercise 2 (continued)

STEP 9: The Page Setup Command

➤ Pull down the **File menu.** Click the **Page Setup command** to display the Page Setup dialog box as shown in Figure 1.11f.
  - Click the **Page tab.** Click the **Landscape option button.** Click the option button to **Fit to 1 page.**
  - Click the **Margins tab.** Check the box to center the worksheet horizontally.
  - Click the **Header/Footer tab.** Click the **drop-down arrow** on the Header list box. Scroll to the top of the list and click **(none)** to remove the header. Click the **drop-down arrow** on the Footer list box. Scroll to the top of the list and click **(none)** to remove the footer.
  - Click the **Sheet tab.** Check the boxes to print Row and Column Headings and Gridlines.

➤ Click **OK** to exit the Page Setup dialog box. Save the workbook.

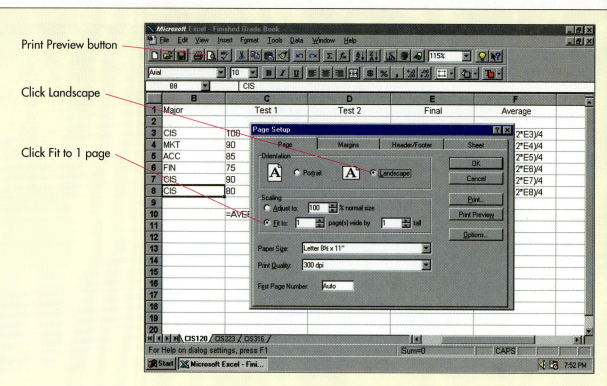

(f) The Page Setup Command (step 9)

FIGURE 1.11 Hands-on Exercise 2 (continued)

> **KEYBOARD SHORTCUTS—THE DIALOG BOX**
>
> Press Tab or Shift+Tab to move forward (backward) between fields in a dialog box, or press the Alt key plus the underlined letter to move directly to an option. Use the space bar to toggle check boxes on or off and the up (down) arrow keys to move between options in a list box. Press enter to activate the highlighted command button and Esc to exit the dialog box without accepting the changes.

STEP 10: The Print Preview Command

➤ Pull down the **File menu** and click **Print Preview** (or click the **Print Preview button** on the Standard toolbar). Your monitor should match the display in Figure 1.11g.

➤ Click the **Print command button** to display the Print dialog box, then click **OK** to print the worksheet.

➤ Press **Ctrl+`** to switch to displayed values rather than cell formulas. Click the **Print button** on the Standard toolbar to print the worksheet without displaying the Print dialog box.

➤ Save the workbook.

➤ Pull down the **File menu.** Click **Exit** to leave Excel.

30 EXPLORING MICROSOFT EXCEL 7.0

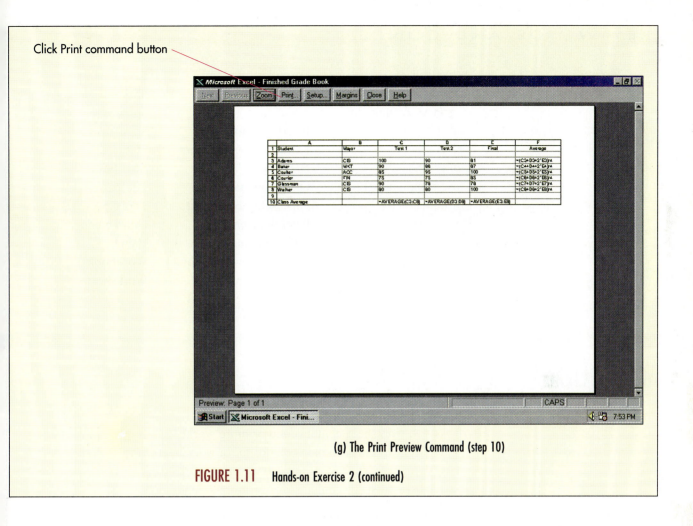

(g) The Print Preview Command (step 10)

FIGURE 1.11   Hands-on Exercise 2 (continued)

SUMMARY

A spreadsheet is the computerized equivalent of an accountant's ledger. It is divided into rows and columns, with each row and column assigned a heading. The intersection of a row and column forms a cell.

Spreadsheet is a generic term. Workbook and worksheet are Excel specific. An Excel workbook contains one or more worksheets.

Every cell in a worksheet (spreadsheet) contains either a formula or a constant. A formula begins with an equal sign, a constant does not. A constant is an entry that does not change and may be numeric or descriptive text. A formula is a combination of numeric constants, cell references, arithmetic operators, and/or functions that produces a new value from existing values.

The Insert and Delete commands add or remove rows or columns from a worksheet. The Open command brings a workbook from disk into memory. The Save command copies the workbook in memory to disk.

The Page Setup command provides complete control over the printed page, enabling you to print a worksheet with or without gridlines or row and column headings. The Page Setup command also controls margins, headers and footers, centering, and orientation. The Print Preview command shows the worksheet as it will print and should be used prior to printing.

A worksheet should always be printed twice, once with displayed values and once with cell formulas. The latter is an important tool in checking the accuracy of a worksheet, which is far more important than its appearance.

KEY WORDS AND CONCEPTS

Active cell	Formula	Save command
AutoComplete	Formula bar	Shortcut menu
AVERAGE function	Function	Spreadsheet
Cell	Insert command	Standard toolbar
Cell contents	Landscape orientation	Status bar
Cell reference	Name box	Text box
Close command	Open command	Toolbar
Constant	Page Setup command	ToolTips
Delete command	Portrait orientation	Undo command
Exit command	Print command	Value
File menu	Print Preview command	Workbook
Formatting toolbar	Save As command	Worksheet

MULTIPLE CHOICE

1. Which of the following is true?
   (a) A worksheet contains one or more workbooks
   (b) A workbook contains one or more worksheets
   (c) A spreadsheet contains one or more worksheets
   (d) A worksheet contains one or more spreadsheets

2. A worksheet is superior to manual calculation because:
   (a) The worksheet computes its entries faster
   (b) The worksheet computes its results more accurately
   (c) The worksheet recalculates its results whenever cell contents are changed
   (d) All of the above

3. The cell at the intersection of the second column and third row has the cell reference:
   (a) B3
   (b) 3B
   (c) C2
   (d) 2C

4. A right-handed person will normally:
   (a) Click the right and left mouse button to access a pull-down menu and shortcut menu, respectively
   (b) Click the left and right mouse button to access a pull-down menu and shortcut menu, respectively
   (c) Click the left mouse button to access both a pull-down menu and a shortcut menu
   (d) Click the right mouse button to access both a pull-down menu and a shortcut menu

5. What is the effect of typing F5+F6 into a cell without a beginning equal sign?
   (a) The entry is equivalent to the formula =F5+F6
   (b) The cell will display the contents of cell F5 plus cell F6
   (c) The entry will be treated as a text entry and display F5+F6 in the cell
   (d) The entry will be rejected by Excel, which will signal an error message

6. The Open command:
   (a) Brings a workbook from disk into memory
   (b) Brings a workbook from disk into memory, then erases the workbook on disk
   (c) Stores the workbook in memory on disk
   (d) Stores the workbook in memory on disk, then erases the workbook from memory

7. The Save command:
   (a) Brings a workbook from disk into memory
   (b) Brings a workbook from disk into memory, then erases the workbook on disk
   (c) Stores the workbook in memory on disk
   (d) Stores the workbook in memory on disk, then erases the workbook from memory

8. How do you open an Excel workbook?
   (a) Pull down the File menu and click the Open command
   (b) Click the Open button on the Standard toolbar
   (c) Either (a) or (b)
   (d) Neither (a) nor (b)

9. In the absence of parentheses, the order of operation is:
   (a) Exponentiation, addition or subtraction, multiplication or division
   (b) Addition or subtraction, multiplication or division, exponentiation
   (c) Multiplication or division, exponentiation, addition or subtraction
   (d) Exponentiation, multiplication or division, addition or subtraction

10. Given that cells A1, A2, and A3 contain the values 10, 20, and 40, respectively, what value will be displayed in a cell containing the cell formula =A1/A2*A3+1?
    (a) 1.125
    (b) 21
    (c) 20.125
    (d) Impossible to determine

11. The entry =AVERAGE(A4:A6):
    (a) Is invalid because the cells are not contiguous
    (b) Computes the average of cells A4 and A6
    (c) Computes the average of cells A4, A5, and A6
    (d) None of the above

12. Which of the following was suggested with respect to printing a workbook?
    (a) Print the displayed values only
    (b) Print the cell formulas only
    (c) Print both the displayed values and cell formulas
    (d) Print neither the displayed values nor the cell formulas

13. Which of the following is true regarding a printed worksheet?
    (a) It may be printed with or without the row and column headings
    (b) It may be printed with or without the gridlines
    (c) Both (a) and (b) above
    (d) Neither (a) nor (b)

14. Which options are mutually exclusive in the Page Setup menu?
    (a) Portrait and landscape orientation
    (b) Cell gridlines and row and column headings
    (c) Headers and footers
    (d) Left and right margins

15. Which of the following is controlled by the Page Setup command?
    (a) Headers and footers
    (b) Margins
    (c) Orientation
    (d) All of the above

ANSWERS

1. b
2. d
3. a
4. b
5. c
6. a
7. c
8. c
9. d
10. b
11. c
12. c
13. c
14. a
15. d

Exploring Excel 7.0

1. Use Figure 1.12 to identify the elements of a Microsoft Excel screen by matching each element with the appropriate number.

   ___ Formatting toolbar   ___ Standard toolbar
   ___ Active cell   ___ Contains the Open command
   ___ Contains the Delete command   ___ Name box
   ___ Help button   ___ Formula bar
   ___ Tip Wizard button   ___ Contains the Print command

2. Troubleshooting: The informational messages in Figure 1.13 appeared (or could have appeared) in response to various commands issued during the chapter.
   a. The message in Figure 1.13a is produced when the user exits Excel, but only under a specific circumstance. When will that message be produced? When would "No" be an appropriate response to this message?
   b. The message in Figure 1.13b appeared in response to a File Print command. What is the most likely corrective action?
   c. The message in Figure 1.13c appeared in response to a File Open command. What corrective action needs to be taken?

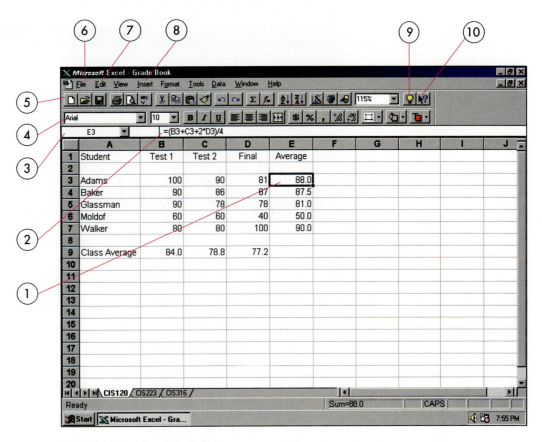

FIGURE 1.12 Screen for Problem 1

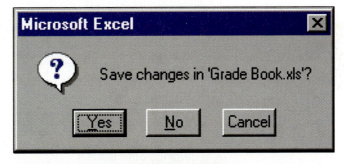

(a) Informational Message 1

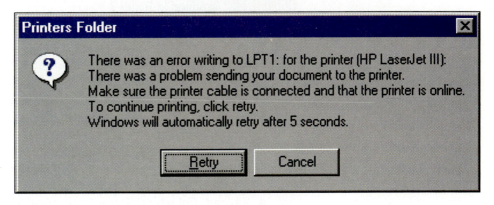

(b) Informational Message 2

FIGURE 1.13 Informational Messages for Problem 2

(c) Informational Message 3

FIGURE 1.13 Informational Messages for Problem 2 (continued)

3. Figure 1.14 contains a simple worksheet showing the earnings for Widgets of America, before and after taxes. The cell values in cells B6, B7, and B9 may be produced in several ways, two of which are shown below. For example:

	Method 1	**Method 2**
Cell B6	=10000−4000	=B3−B4
Cell B7	=.30*6000	=.30*B6
Cell B9	=6000−1800	=B6−B7

Which is the better method and why?

	A	B
1	Widgets of America	
2		
3	Revenue	10000
4	Expenses	4000
5		
6	Earnings before taxes	6000
7	Taxes	1800
8		
9	Earnings after taxes	4200

FIGURE 1.14 Spreadsheet for Problem 3

4. Answer the following with respect to Figure 1.15, which depicts the use of a worksheet in a simplified calculation for income tax. (Assume that all cells in column C contain a formula rather than a constant.)
   a. What is the active cell? What are the contents of the active cell?
   b. Assume that the income in cell B2 changes to $125,000. What other numbers will change automatically?
   c. Assume that an additional deduction for local income taxes of $3,000 is entered between rows 9 and 10. Which formula (if any) has to be explicitly changed to accommodate the new deduction?
   d. Which formula(s) will change automatically after the formula(s) in part c is (are) changed to accommodate the new deduction?

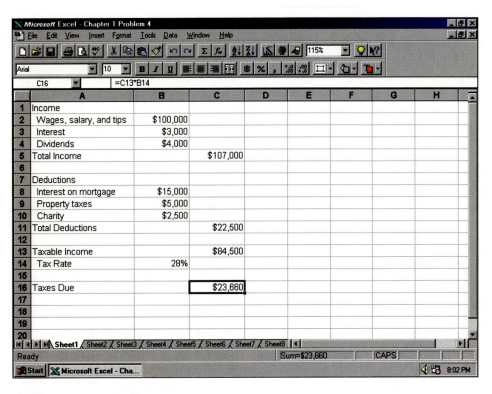

FIGURE 1.15 Screen for Problem 4

Practice with Excel 7.0

1. Your professor is very impressed with the way you did the hands-on exercises in the chapter and has hired you as his grading assistant to handle all of his classes this semester. He would like you to take the Finished Grade Book that you used in the chapter, and save it as *Chapter 1 Practice 1*. Make the following changes in the new workbook:

   a. Click the worksheet tab for CIS120 to move to this worksheet. Add Milgrom as a new student majoring in Finance with grades of 88, 80, and 84, respectively. Delete Baker. Be sure that the class averages adjust automatically for the insertion and deletion of these students.

   b. Click the worksheet tab for CIS223. Enter the formulas to compute the class averages on all tests as well as each student's semester average. All tests count equally.

   c. Click the worksheet tab for CIS316 to move to this worksheet. Insert a new column for the Final, then enter the following grades for the students in this class (Bippen, 90; Freeman, 75; Manni, 84; Peck, 93; Tanney, 87).

   d. Enter the formulas to compute the semester average for each student in the class. (Tests 1, 2, and 3 each count 20%. The final counts 40%.)

   e. Enter the formulas to compute the class average on each test and the final.

   f. Enter the label *Grading Assistant* followed by your name on each worksheet. Print the entire workbook and submit all three pages of the printout to your instructor as proof that you did this exercise.

INTRODUCTION TO MICROSOFT EXCEL

2. The worksheet in Figure 1.16 displays the last week's sales from the Exotic Gardens Nurseries. There are four different locations, each of which divides its sales into three general areas.
   a. Open the partially completed *Chapter 1 Practice 2* workbook on the data disk. Save the workbook as *Finished Chapter 1 Practice 2*.
   b. Enter the appropriate formulas in row 5 of the worksheet to compute the total sales for each location. Use the SUM function to compute the total for each location; for example, type =SUM(B2:B4) in cell B5 (as opposed to =B2+B3+B4) to compute the total sales for the Las Olas location.
   c. Insert a new row 4 for a new category of product. Type *Insecticides* in cell A4, and enter $1,000 for each store in this category. The total sales for each store should adjust automatically to include the additional business.
   d. Enter the appropriate formulas in column F of the worksheet to compute the total sales for each category.
   e. Delete column D, the column containing the sales for the Galleria location. Check to be sure that the totals for each product adjust automatically.
   f. Add your name somewhere in the worksheet as the bookkeeper.
   g. Print the completed worksheet two times, to show both displayed values and cell formulas. Submit both pages to your instructor.

	A	B	C	D	E	F
1		Las Olas	Coral Gables	Galleria	Miracle Mile	Total
2	Indoor Plants	1,500	3,000	4,500	800	
3	Accessories	350	725	1,200	128	
4	Landscaping	3,750	7,300	12,000	1,500	
5	Total					
6						
7						
8						

FIGURE 1.16 Spreadsheet for Practice Exercise 2

3. Formatting is not covered until Chapter 2, but we think you are ready to try your hand at basic formatting now. Most formatting operations are done in the context of select-then-do. You select the cell or cells you want to format, then you execute the appropriate formatting command, most easily by clicking the appropriate button on the Formatting toolbar. The function of each button should be apparent from its icon, but you can simply point to a button to display a ToolTip that is indicative of the button's function.

   Open the unformatted version of the *Chapter 1 Practice 3* workbook on the data disk, and save it as *Finished Chapter 1 Practice 3*. Add a new row 6 and enter data for Hume Hall as shown in Figure 1.17. Format the

Residential Colleges

	Freshmen	Sophomores	Juniors	Seniors	Graduates	Totals
Broward Hall	176	143	77	29	13	438
Graham Hall	375	112	37	23	7	554
Hume Hall	212	108	45	43	12	420
Jennings Hall	89	54	23	46	23	235
Rawlings Hall	75	167	93	145	43	523
Tolbert Hall	172	102	26	17	22	339
Totals	1099	686	301	303	120	2509

FIGURE 1.17 Spreadsheet for Practice Exercise 3

remainder of the worksheet so that it matches the completed worksheet in Figure 1.17. Add your name in bold italics somewhere in the worksheet as the Residence Hall Coordinator, then print the completed worksheet and submit it to your instructor.

4. Create a worksheet that shows your income and expenses for a typical semester according to the format in Figure 1.18. Enter your budget rather than ours by entering your name in cell A1.

   a. Enter at least five different expenses in consecutive rows, beginning in A6, and enter the corresponding amounts in column B.

   b. Enter the text *Total Expenses* in the row immediately below your last expense item and then enter the formula to compute the total in the corresponding cells in columns B through E.

   c. Skip one blank row and then enter the text *What's Left For Fun* in column A and the formula to compute how much money you have left at the end of the month in columns B through E.

   d. Insert a new row 8. Add an additional expense that you left out, entering the text in A8 and the amount in cells B8 through E8. Do the formulas for total expenses reflect the additional expense? If not, change the formulas so they adjust automatically.

   e. Save the workbook as *Chapter 1 Practice 4*. Center the worksheet horizontally, then print the worksheet two ways, to show cell formulas and displayed values. Submit both printed pages to your instructor.

	A	B	C	D	E
1	Maryann Barber's Budget				
2		Sept	Oct	Nov	Dec
3	Monthly Income	$ 1,000	$ 1,000	$ 1,000	$ 1,400
4					
5	Monthly Expenses				
6	Food	$ 250	$ 250	$ 250	$ 250
7	Rent	$ 350	$ 350	$ 350	$ 350
8	Utilities	$ 100	$ 100	$ 125	$ 140
9	Phone	$ 30	$ 30	$ 30	$ 20
10	Gas	$ 40	$ 40	$ 40	$ 75
11	Total Expenses	$ 770	$ 770	$ 795	$ 835
12					
13	What's left for fun	$ 230	$ 230	$ 205	$ 565

FIGURE 1.18 Spreadsheet for Practice Exercise 4

Case Studies

Buying a Computer

You have decided to buy a PC and have settled on a minimum configuration consisting of an entry-level Pentium, with 8MB of RAM, a quad-speed CD-ROM, and a 500MB hard disk. You would like a modem if it fits into the budget, and you need a printer. You also need Windows 95 and Microsoft Office 95. You can spend up to $2500 and hope, that at today's prices, you can find a system that goes beyond your minimum requirements; for example, a system with a faster processor and 16MB of RAM. We suggest you shop around and look for educational discounts on software to save money.

Create a spreadsheet based on real data that presents several alternatives. Show different configurations from the same vendor and/or comparable systems from different vendors. Include the vendor's telephone number with its estimate. Bring the spreadsheet to class together with the supporting documentation in the form of printed advertisements.

Portfolio Management

A spreadsheet is an ideal vehicle to track the progress of your investments. You need to maintain the name of the company, the number of shares purchased, the date of the purchase, and the purchase price. You can then enter the current price and see immediately the potential gain or loss on each investment as well as the current value of the portfolio. Retrieve the *Stock Portfolio* workbook from the data disk, enter the closing prices of the listed investments, and compute the current value of the portfolio.

Accuracy Counts

The *Underbid* workbook on the data disk was the last assignment completed by your predecessor prior to his unfortunate dismissal. The worksheet contains a significant error, which caused your company to underbid a contract and assume a subsequent loss of $100,000. As you look for the error, don't be distracted by the attractive formatting. The shading, lines, and other touches are nice, but accuracy is more important than anything else. Write a memo to your instructor describing the nature of the error. Include suggestions in the memo on how to avoid mistakes of this nature in the future.

Planning for Disaster

This case has nothing to do with spreadsheets per se, but it is perhaps the most important case of all, as it deals with the question of backup. Do you have a backup strategy? Do you even know what a backup strategy is? Now is a good time to learn, because sooner or later you will wish you had one. You will erase a file, be unable to read from a floppy disk, or worse yet, suffer a hardware failure in which you are unable to access the hard drive. The problem always seems to occur the night before an assignment is due. The ultimate disaster is the disappearance of your computer, by theft or natural disaster (e.g., Hurricane Andrew, the floods in the Midwest, or the Los Angeles earthquake). Describe in 250 words or less the backup strategy you plan to implement in conjunction with your work in this class.

GAINING PROFICIENCY: COPYING, FORMATTING, AND ISOLATING ASSUMPTIONS

2

OBJECTIVES

After reading this chapter you will be able to:

1. Explain the importance of isolating assumptions within a worksheet.
2. Define a cell range; select and deselect ranges within a worksheet.
3. Copy and/or move cells within a worksheet; differentiate between relative, absolute, and mixed addresses.
4. Format a worksheet to include boldface, italics, shading, and borders; change the font and/or alignment of a selected entry.
5. Change the width of a column; explain what happens if a column is too narrow to display the computed result.
6. Describe in general terms the steps to build a worksheet for a financial forecast.
7. Define the TipWizard and explain how it can make you more proficient in Excel; explain the need to reset the TipWizard.

OVERVIEW

This chapter continues the grade book example of Chapter 1. It is perhaps the most important chapter in the entire text as it describes the basic commands to create a worksheet. We begin with the definition of a cell range and the commands to build a worksheet without regard to its appearance. We focus on the Copy command and the difference between relative and absolute addresses. We stress the importance of isolating the assumptions within a worksheet so that alternative strategies may be easily evaluated.

The second half of the chapter presents formatting commands to improve the appearance of a worksheet after it has been created. You will be pleased with the dramatic impact you can achieve with a few simple commands, but we emphasize that accuracy in a worksheet is much more important than appearance.

The hands-on exercises are absolutely critical if you are to master the material. As you do the exercises, you will realize that there are many different ways to accomplish the same task. Our approach is to present the most basic way first and the shortcuts later. You will like the shortcuts better, but you may not remember them and hence you need to understand the underlying concepts. You can always find the necessary command from the appropriate menu, and if you don't know which menu, you can always look to online help.

A BETTER GRADE BOOK

Figure 2.1 contains a much improved version of the professor's grade book over the one from the previous chapter. The most obvious difference is in the appearance of the worksheet, as a variety of formatting commands have been used to make it more attractive. The exam scores and semester averages are centered under the appropriate headings. Boldface and italics are used for emphasis. Shading and borders are used to highlight different areas of the worksheet. The title has been centered over the worksheet and is set in a larger typeface.

The most *significant* differences, however, are that the weight of each exam is indicated within the worksheet, and that the formulas to compute the students' semester averages reference these cells in their calculations. The professor can change the contents of the cells containing the exam weights and see immediately the effect on the student averages.

The isolation of cells whose values are subject to change is one of the most important concepts in the development of a spreadsheet. This technique lets the professor explore alternative grading strategies. He may notice, for example, that the class did significantly better on the final than on either of the first two exams. He may then decide to give the class a break and increase the weight of the final relative to the other tests. But before he says anything to the class, he wants to know the effect of increasing the weight of the final to 60%. What if he decides that the final should count 70%? The effect of these changes can be seen immediately by entering the new exam weights in the appropriate cells at the bottom of the worksheet.

Title is centered and in a larger typeface

Boldface, italics, shading, and borders are used for emphasis

Exam scores are centered

Exam weights are used to calculate the students' semester averages

	A	B	C	D	E
1		CIS 120 - Spring 1996			
2					
3	**Student**	Test 1	Test 2	Final	Average
4	Costa, Frank	70	80	90	82.5
5	Ford, Judd	70	65	80	73.8
6	Grauer, Jessica	90	80	98	91.5
7	Howard, Lauren	80	78	98	88.5
8	Krein, Darren	85	70	95	86.3
9	Moldof, Adam	75	75	80	77.5
10					
11	**Class Averages**	78.3	74.7	90.2	
12					
13	**Exam Weights**	25%	25%	50%	

FIGURE 2.1 A Better Grade Book

CELL RANGES

Every command in Excel operates on a rectangular group of cells known as a *range*. A range may be as small as a single cell or as large as the entire worksheet. It may consist of a row or part of a row, a column or part of a column, or multiple rows and/or columns. The cells within a range are specified by indicating the diagonally opposite corners, typically the upper-left and lower-right corners of the rectangle. Many different ranges could be selected in conjunction with the worksheet of Figure 2.1. The exam weights, for example, are found in the range B13:D13. The semester averages are found in the range E4:E9. The student data is contained in the range A4:E9.

The easiest way to select a range is to click and drag—click at the beginning of the range, then press and hold the left mouse button as you drag the mouse to the end of the range where you release the mouse. Once selected, the range is highlighted and its cells will be affected by any subsequent command. The range remains selected until another range is defined or until you click another cell anywhere on the worksheet.

COPY COMMAND

The ***Copy command*** duplicates the contents of a cell, or range of cells, and saves you from having to enter the contents of every cell individually. It is much easier, for example, to enter the formula to compute the class average once (for test 1), then copy it to obtain the average for the remaining tests, rather than explicitly entering the formula for every test.

Figure 2.2 illustrates how the Copy command can be used to duplicate the formula to compute the class average. The cell(s) that you are copying from, cell B11, is called the ***source range.*** The cells that you are copying to, cells C11 and D11, are the ***destination*** (or target) ***range***. The formula is not copied exactly, but is adjusted as it is copied, to compute the average for the pertinent test.

The formula to compute the average on the first test was entered in cell B11 as =AVERAGE(B4:B9). The range in the formula references the cell seven rows above the cell containing the formula (i.e., cell B4 is seven rows above cell B11) as well as the cell two rows above the formula (i.e., cell B9). When the formula in cell B11 is copied to C11, it is adjusted so that the cells referenced in the new formula are in the same relative position as those in the original formula; that is,

	A	B	C	D	E
1			CIS 120 - Spring 1996		
2					
3	Student	Test 1	Test 2	Final	Average
4	Costa, Frank	70	80	90	=$B$13*B4+$C$13*C4+$D$13*D4
5	Ford, Judd	70	65	80	=$B$13*B5+$C$13*C5+$D$13*D5
6	Grauer, Jessica	90	80	98	=$B$13*B6+$C$13*C6+$D$13*D6
7	Howard, Lauren	80	78	98	=$B$13*B7+$C$13*C7+$D$13*D7
8	Krein, Darren	85	70	95	=$B$13*B8+$C$13*C8+$D$13*D8
9	Moldof, Adam	75	75	80	=$B$13*B9+$C$13*C9+$D$13*D9
10					
11	Class Averages	=AVERAGE(B4:B9)	=AVERAGE(C4:C9)	=AVERAGE(D4:D9)	
12					
13	Exam Weights	25%	25%	50%	

Absolute reference → column E formulas
Relative reference → column E formulas
Source range (B11)
Destination range (C11:D11)

FIGURE 2.2 The Copy Command

seven and two rows above the formula itself. Thus, the formula in cell C11 becomes =AVERAGE(C4:C9). In similar fashion, the formula in cell D11 becomes =AVERAGE(D4:D9).

Figure 2.2 also illustrates how the Copy command is used to copy the formula for a student's semester average, from cell E4 (the source range) to cells E5 through E9 (the destination range). This is slightly more complicated than the previous example because the formula is based on a student's grades, which vary from one student to the next, and on the exam weights, which do not. The cells referring to the student's grades should adjust as the formula is copied, but the addresses referencing the exam weights should not.

The distinction between cell references that remain constant versus cell addresses that change is made by means of a dollar sign. An *absolute reference* remains constant throughout the copy operation and is specified with a dollar sign in front of the column and row designation, for example, $B$13. A *relative reference*, on the other hand, adjusts during a copy operation and is specified without dollar signs; for example, B4. (A *mixed reference* uses a single dollar sign to make the column absolute and the row relative; for example, $A5. Alternatively, you can make the column relative and the row absolute as in A$5. Mixed references are not discussed further.)

Consider, for example, the formula to compute a student's semester average as it appears in cell E4 of Figure 2.2:

=$B$13*B4+$C$13*C4+$D$13*D4

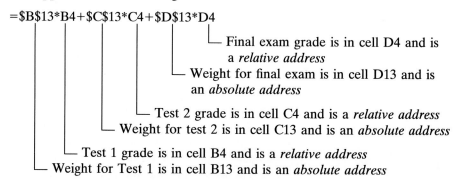

The formula in cell E4 uses a combination of relative and absolute addresses to compute the student's semester average. Relative addresses are used for the exam grades (found in cells B4, C4, and D4) and change automatically when the formula is copied to the other rows. Absolute addresses are used for the exam weights (found in cells B13, C13, and D13) and remain constant from student to student.

The copy operation is implemented by using the Windows *clipboard* and a combination of the *Copy* and *Paste commands* from the Edit menu. The contents of the source range are copied to the clipboard, from where they are pasted to the destination range. The contents of the clipboard are replaced with each subsequent Copy command but are unaffected by the Paste command. Thus, you can execute the Paste command several times in succession to paste the contents of the clipboard to multiple locations.

MOVE OPERATION

The *move operation* is not used in the grade book, but its presentation is essential for the sake of completeness. The move operation transfers the contents of a cell (or range of cells) from one location to another. After the move is completed, the cells where the move originated (that is, the source range) are empty. This is in contrast to the Copy command, where the entries remain in the source range and are duplicated in the destination range.

A simple move operation is depicted in Figure 2.3a, in which the contents of cell A3 are moved to cell C3, with the formula in cell C3 unchanged after the move. In other words, the move operation simply picks up the contents of cell A3 (a formula that adds the values in cells A1 and A2) and puts it down in cell C3. The source range, cell A3, is empty after the move operation has been executed.

Figure 2.3b depicts a situation where the formula itself remains in the same cell, but one of the values it references is moved to a new location; that is, the entry in A1 is moved to C1. The formula in cell A3 is adjusted to follow the moved entry to its new location; that is, the formula is now =C1+A2.

The situation is different in Figure 2.3c as the contents of all three cells—A1, A2, and A3—are moved. After the move has taken place, cells C1 and C2 contain the 5 and the 2, respectively, with the formula in cell C3 adjusted to reflect the movement of the contents of cells A1 and A2. Once again the source range (A1:A3) is empty after the move is completed.

Figure 2.3d contains an additional formula in cell B1, which is *dependent* on cell A3, which in turn is moved to cell C3. The formula in cell C3 is unchanged

Source range is empty after move

	A	B	C
1	5		
2	2		
3	=A1+A2		

	A	B	C
1	5		
2	2		
3			=A1+A2

(a) Example 1 (only cell A3 is moved)

Cell reference is adjusted to follow moved entry

	A	B	C
1	5		
2	2		
3	=A1+A2		

	A	B	C
1			5
2	2		
3	=C1+A2		

(b) Example 2 (only cell A1 is moved)

Both cell references adjust to follow moved entries

	A	B	C
1	5		
2	2		
3	=A1+A2		

	A	B	C
1			5
2			2
3			=C1+C2

(c) Example 3 (all three cells in column A are moved)

Cell reference adjusts to follow moved entry

Moved formula is unchanged

	A	B	C
1	5	=A3*4	
2	2		
3	=A1+A2		

	A	B	C
1	5	=C3*4	
2	2		
3			=A1+A2

(d) Example 4 (dependent cells)

Cell reference adjusts to follow moved entry

	A	B	C
1	5	=$A$3*4	
2	2		
3	=$A$1+$A$2		

	A	B	C
1		=$C$3*4	5
2			2
3			=$C$1+$C$2

Both cell references adjust to follow moved entries

(e) Example 5 (absolute cell addresses)

FIGURE 2.3   The Move Command

after the move because *only* the formula was moved, *not* the values it referenced. The formula in cell B1 changes (even though the contents of cell B1 were not moved) because cell B1 refers to an entry (cell A3) that was moved to a new location (cell C3).

Figure 2.3e shows that the specification of an absolute reference has no meaning in a move operation, because absolute references are adjusted as necessary to reflect a move. Moving a formula that contains an absolute reference does not adjust the formula. Moving a value that is specified as an absolute reference, however, adjusts the formula to follow the cell to its new location. Thus all of the absolute references in Figure 2.3e are changed to reflect the entries that were moved.

The move operation is a convenient way to improve the appearance of a worksheet after it has been developed. It is subtle in its operation, and we suggest you think twice before moving cell entries because of the complexities involved.

The move operation is implemented by using the Windows clipboard and a combination of the ***Cut*** and ***Paste commands*** from the Edit menu. The contents of the source range are transferred to the clipboard, from which they are pasted to the destination range. (Executing a Paste command after a Cut command empties the clipboard. This is different from pasting after a Copy command, which does not affect the contents of the clipboard.)

THE TIPWIZARD

The ***TipWizard*** greets you with a *tip of the day* every time you start Excel, but that is only one of its capabilities. The true purpose of the TipWizard is to introduce you to new features by suggesting more efficient ways to accomplish the tasks you are doing.

The TipWizard monitors your work and offers advice throughout a session. The TipWizard button on the Standard toolbar "lights up" whenever there is a suggestion. (Click the button to display the TipWizard; click the button a second time to close it.) You can read the suggestions as they occur and/or review them at the end of a session. You needn't always follow the advice of the TipWizard (at first you may not even understand all of its suggestions), but over time it will make you much more proficient.

The TipWizard will not repeat a tip from one session to the next unless it is specifically reset as described in step one of the following exercise. This is especially important in a laboratory situation when you are sharing the same computer with other students.

LEARNING BY DOING

As we have already indicated, there are many different ways to accomplish the same task. You can execute commands using a pull-down menu, a shortcut menu, a toolbar, or the keyboard. In the exercise that follows we emphasize pull-down menus (the most basic technique) but suggest various shortcuts as appropriate. We also direct you to reset the TipWizard so that Excel can monitor your actions and offer additional suggestions.

Realize, however, that while the shortcuts are interesting, it is far more important to focus on the underlying concepts in the exercise, rather than specific key strokes or mouse clicks. The professor's grade book was developed to emphasize the difference between relative and absolute cell references. The grade book also illustrates the importance of isolating assumptions so that alternative strategies (e.g., different exam weights) can be considered.

HANDS-ON EXERCISE 1

Creating a Worksheet

Objective: To create a formula containing relative and absolute references; to use the Copy command within a worksheet. Use Figure 2.4 as a guide.

STEP 1: Start Excel

➤ Start Microsoft Excel as described in the previous chapter. If necessary, click the **TipWizard button** on the Standard toolbar to display the tip of the day as shown in Figure 2.4a. Do not be concerned if your tip is different from ours.

➤ Pull down the **Tools menu,** click **Options,** then click the **General tab** to display the dialog box in Figure 2.4a.

➤ Click the check box to **Reset TipWizard.** Click **OK.** The contents of the TipWizard box change to indicate that you have reset the TipWizard and that the tips may repeat.

➤ Click the **TipWizard button** to close the TipWizard box.

(a) Reset the TipWizard (step 1)

FIGURE 2.4 Hands-on Exercise 1

STEP 2: Enter the Column Headings

➤ Click in **cell A1.** Enter the title of the worksheet, **CIS120 - Spring 1996** as in Figure 2.4b.

➤ Press the **down arrow key** twice to move to cell A3. Type **Student.**

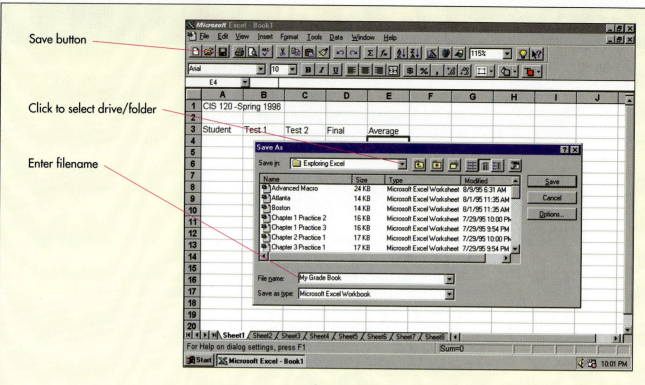

(b) Dialog Box for the Save Command (step 3)

FIGURE 2.4   Hands-on Exercise 1 (continued)

➤ Press the **right arrow key** to move to cell B3. Type **Test 1.**
➤ Press the **right arrow key** to move to cell C3. Type **Test 2.**
➤ Press the **right arrow key** to move to cell D3. Type **Final.**
➤ Press the **right arrow key** to move to cell E3. Type **Average.** Press **enter.**

STEP 3: Save the Workbook

➤ Pull down the **File menu** and click **Save** (or click the **Save button** on the Standard toolbar).
➤ Click the **drop-down arrow** on the Save In list box. Click the appropriate drive, drive C or drive A, depending on whether or not you installed the data disk.

LONG FILENAMES

Windows 95 allows filenames of up to 255 characters (spaces and commas are permitted). Anyone using Windows 95 for the first time will take descriptive names such as *My Grade Book* for granted, but veterans of MS-DOS and Windows 3.1 will appreciate the improvement over the earlier 8.3 naming convention (an eight-character name followed by a three-letter extension to indicate the file type).

- Double click the **Exploring Excel folder** to make it the active folder (the folder in which you will save the document).
- Click and drag **Book1** (the default entry) in the File name text box. Type **My Grade Book** as the name of the workbook. Click **Save** or press the **enter key.**
- The title bar changes to reflect the name of the workbook.

STEP 4: Enter Student Data and Literal Information

- Click in **cell A4** and type **Costa, Frank.** Move across row 4 and enter Frank's grades on the two tests and the final. Use Figure 2.4c as a guide.
  - Do *not* enter Frank's average in cell E4 as that will be entered as a formula in step 6.
  - Do *not* be concerned that you cannot see Frank's entire name because the default width of column A is not wide enough to display the entire name.
- Enter the names and grades for the other students in rows 5 through 9. Do *not* enter their averages.
- Complete the entries in column A by typing **Class Averages** and **Exam Weights** in cells **A11** and **A13,** respectively.
- Click the **Save button** on the Standard toolbar to save the workbook.

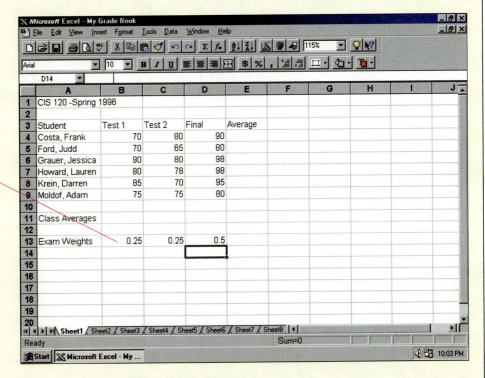

(c) Grade Book (steps 4 & 5)

FIGURE 2.4 Hands-on Exercise 1 (continued)

SAVE YOUR WORK

We cannot overemphasize the importance of periodically saving a workbook, so if something goes wrong, you won't lose everything. Nothing is more frustrating than to lose two hours of effort, due to an unexpected problem in Windows or to a temporary loss of power. Save your work frequently, at least once every 15 minutes. Click the Save button on the Standard toolbar or pull down the File menu and click Save. Do it!

STEP 5: Enter Exam Weights

➤ Click in **cell B13** and enter **.25,** the weight for the first exam.

➤ Press the **right arrow key** to move to cell C13 and enter **.25,** the weight for the second exam.

➤ Press the **right arrow key** to move to cell D13 and enter **.5,** the weight for the final. Press **enter.** Do *not* be concerned that the exam weights do not appear as percentages; they will be formatted in the second exercise later in the chapter.

➤ The worksheet should match Figure 2.4c except that column A is too narrow to display the entire name of each student.

STEP 6: Compute the Semester Average

➤ Click in **cell E4** and type the formula **=$B$13*B4+$C$13*C4+$D$13*D4** to compute the semester average for the first student. Press the **enter key** when you have completed the formula.

➤ Check that the displayed value in cell E4 is 82.5, which indicates you entered the formula correctly.

➤ Save the workbook.

CORRECTING MISTAKES

The fastest way to change the contents of an existing cell is to double click in the cell in order to make the changes directly in the cell rather than on the formula bar. Use the mouse or arrow keys to position the insertion point at the point of correction. Press the Ins key to toggle between insert and overtype and/or use the Backspace or Del key to erase a character. Press the Home and End keys to move to the first and last characters in the cell, respectively.

STEP 7: Copy the Semester Average

➤ Click in **cell E4.** Pull down the **Edit menu** as in Figure 2.4d. Click **Copy.** A moving border will surround cell E4, indicating that its contents have been copied to the clipboard.

➤ Click **cell E5.** Drag the mouse over cells **E5** through **E9** to select the destination range as in Figure 2.4e.

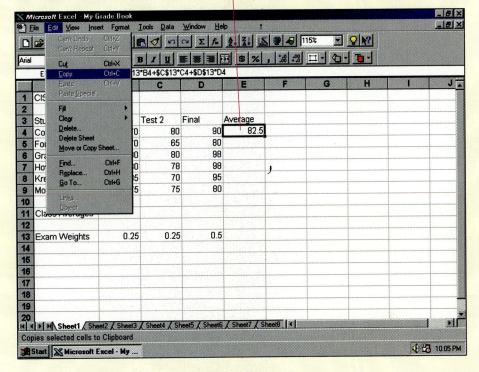

(d) The Copy Command (step 7)

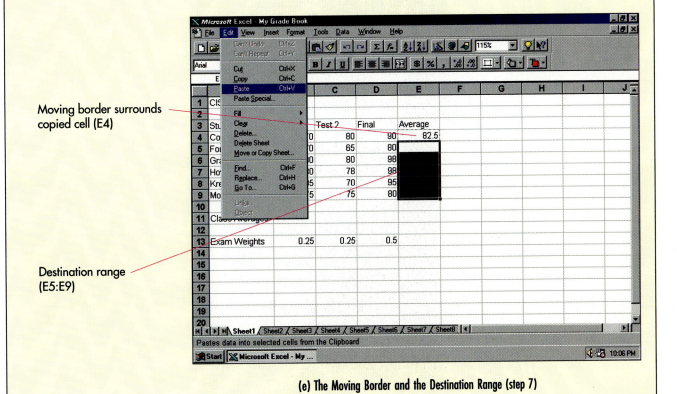

(e) The Moving Border and the Destination Range (step 7)

FIGURE 2.4 Hands-on Exercise 1 (continued)

- Pull down the **Edit menu** and click **Paste** to copy the contents of the clipboard to the destination range. You should see the semester averages for the other students in cells E5 through E9.
- Press **Esc** to remove the moving border around cell E4. Click anywhere in the worksheet to deselect cells E5 through E9.
- Click in **cell E5** and look at the formula. The cells that reference the grades have changed to B5, C5, and D5. The cells that reference the exam weights—$B$13, $C$13, and $D$13—are the same as in cell E4.
- Save the workbook.

CUT, COPY AND PASTE

Ctrl+X (the X is supposed to remind you of a pair of scissors), Ctrl+C, and Ctrl+V are keyboard equivalents to cut, copy, and paste, respectively, and apply to Excel, Word, PowerPoint and Access, as well as Windows applications in general. (The keystrokes are easier to remember when you realize that the operative letters, X, C, and V, are next to each other at the bottom-left side of the keyboard.) Alternatively, you can use the Cut, Copy, and Paste buttons on the Standard toolbar, which are also found on the Standard toolbar in the other Office applications.

STEP 8: Compute Class Averages
- Click in **cell B11** and type the formula **=AVERAGE(B4:B9)** to compute the class average on the first test. Press the **enter key** when you have completed the formula.
- Point to **cell B11,** then click the **right mouse button** to display the shortcut menu in Figure 2.4f. Click **Copy,** which produces the moving border around cell B11.
- Click **cell C11.** Drag the mouse over cells **C11** and **D11,** the destination range for the Copy command.
- Click the **Paste button** on the Standard toolbar (or press Ctrl+V) to paste the contents of the clipboard to the destination range.
- Press **Esc** to remove the moving border. Click anywhere in the worksheet to deselect cells C11 through D11.

DEFINING A RANGE WITH A KEYBOARD

To define a range with the keyboard, move to the first cell in the range, that is, the cell in the upper-left corner. Press and hold the Shift key as you use the arrow keys to extend the selection over the remaining cells in the range.

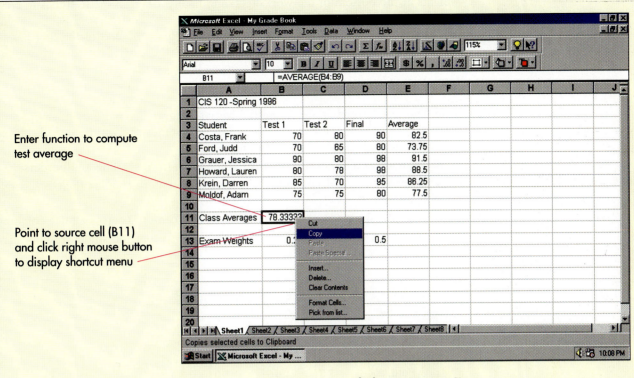

(f) Shortcut Menu (step 8)

FIGURE 2.4 Hands-on Exercise 1 (continued)

STEP 9: What If? Change Exam Weights

► Change the entries in cells B13 and C13 to **.20** and the entry in cell D13 to **.60**. The semester average for every student changes automatically; for example, Costa and Moldof change to 84 and 78, respectively.

► The professor decides this does not make a significant difference and goes back to the original weights; reenter .25, .25, and .50 in cells B13, C13, and D13, respectively.

► Click the **Save button** on the Standard toolbar to save the workbook.

STEP 10: Review the TipWizard

► Click the **TipWizard button** on the Standard toolbar to display the TipWizard dialog box.

► Read the displayed tip, then click the **up arrow** to read the previous tip. Continue in this fashion until you have read all of the suggested tips.

► Close the workbook. Exit Excel if you are not ready to begin the next exercise at this time.

FORMATTING

In this chapter the professor's grade book is developed in two stages, as shown in Figure 2.5. The exercise just completed created the grade book, but paid no attention to its appearance. It had you enter the data for every student, develop the formulas to compute the semester average for every student based on the exam weights at the bottom of the worksheet, and finally, develop the formulas to compute the class averages for each exam.

Figure 2.5a shows the grade book as it exists at the end of the first hands-on exercise. Figure 2.5b shows the grade book at the end of the second exercise after it has been formatted. The differences between the two are due entirely to formatting. Consider:

- The exam weights are formatted as percentages in Figure 2.5b, as opposed to decimals in Figure 2.5a. The class and semester averages are displayed with a single decimal point in Figure 2.5b.
- Boldface and italics are used for emphasis, as are shading and borders.
- Exam grades and computed averages are centered under their respective headings.
- The worksheet title is set in larger type and centered across all five columns.
- The width of column A has been increased so that the students' names are completely visible.

	A	B	C	D	E
1	CIS 120 - Spring 1996				
2					
3	Student	Test 1	Test 2	Final	Average
4	Costa, F	70	80	90	82.5
5	Ford, Jud	70	65	80	73.75
6	Grauer, J	90	80	98	91.5
7	Howard,	80	78	98	88.5
8	Krein, Da	85	70	95	86.25
9	Moldof, A	75	75	80	77.5
10					
11	Class Av	78.333	74.667	90.167	
12					
13	Exam We	0.25	0.25	0.5	

(a) At the End of Hands-on Exercise 1

Title is centered across the worksheet and set in larger typeface

Column A is wider

Boldface, italics, shading, and borders used for emphasis

Grades are centered in column

Results are displayed with 1 decimal place

Exam weights are formatted as %

	A	B	C	D	E
1	CIS 120 - Spring 1996				
2					
3	*Student*	*Test 1*	*Test 2*	*Final*	*Average*
4	Costa, Frank	70	80	90	82.5
5	Ford, Judd	70	65	80	73.8
6	Grauer, Jessica	90	80	98	91.5
7	Howard, Lauren	80	78	98	88.5
8	Krein, Darren	85	70	95	86.3
9	Moldof, Adam	75	75	80	77.5
10					
11	*Class Averages*	78.3	74.7	90.2	
12					
13	*Exam Weights*	25%	25%	50%	

(b) At the End of Hands-on Exercise 2

FIGURE 2.5 Developing the Grade Book

Column Widths

A column is often too narrow to display the contents of one or more cells in that column. When this happens, the display depends on whether the cell contains a text or numeric entry, and if it is a text entry, on whether or not the adjacent cell is empty.

The student names in Figure 2.5a, for example, are partially hidden because column A is too narrow to display the entire name. Cells A4 through A9 contain the complete names of each student, but because the adjacent cells in column B contain data, the displayed entries in column A are truncated (cut off) at the cell width. The situation is different for the worksheet title in cell A1. This time the adjacent cell (cell B1) is empty, so that the contents of cell A1 overflow into that cell and are completely visible.

Numbers are treated differently from text and do not depend on the contents of the adjacent cell. Excel displays a series of number signs (######) when a cell containing a numeric entry is too narrow to display the entry in its current format. You may be able to correct the problem by changing the format of the number (e.g., display the number with fewer decimal places). Alternatively, you can increase the *column width* by using the **Column command** in the Format menu.

Row Heights

The *row height* changes automatically as the font size is increased. Row 1 in Figure 2.5b, for example, has a greater height than the other rows to accommodate the larger font size in the title of the worksheet. The row height can also be changed manually through the **Row command** in the Format menu.

FORMAT CELLS COMMAND

The **Format Cells command** controls the formatting for numbers, alignment, fonts, borders, and patterns (color). Execution of the command produces a tabbed dialog box in which you choose the particular formatting category, then enter the desired options. (Almost every formatting option can also be specified from the Formatting toolbar.)

All formatting is done within the context of *select-then-do*. You select the cells to which the formatting is to apply, then you execute the Format Cells command or click the appropriate button on the Formatting toolbar.

FORMATS VERSUS VALUES

Changing the format of a number changes the way the number is displayed but does *not* change its value. If, for example, you entered 1.2345 into a cell but displayed the number as 1.23, the actual value (1.2345) would be used in all calculations involving that cell.

Numeric Formats

General format is the default format for numeric entries and displays a number according to the way it was originally entered. Numbers are shown as integers (e.g., 123), decimal fractions (e.g., 1.23), or in scientific notation (e.g., 1.23E+10) if the number is larger than the width of the cell or if it exceeds 11 digits. You can also display any number in one of several formats as shown in Figure 2.6a:

- ***Number format,*** which displays a number with or without the 1000 separator (e.g., a comma) and with any number of decimal places.
- ***Currency format,*** which displays a number with the 1000 separator, an optional dollar sign (which is placed immediately to the left of the number), and negative values preceded by a minus sign or shown in red.
- ***Accounting format,*** which displays a number with the 1000 separator, an optional dollar sign (at the left of the cell that vertically aligns the dollar signs within a column), negative values in parentheses, and zero values as hyphens.
- ***Date format,*** which displays the date in different ways, such as March 4, 1994, 3/4/94, or 4-Mar-94.
- ***Time format,*** which displays the time in different formats, such as 10:50 PM or the equivalent 22:50 (24-hour time).
- ***Percentage format,*** whereby the number is multiplied by 100 for display purposes only, a percent sign is included, and any number of decimal places can be specified.
- ***Fraction format,*** which displays a number as a fraction, and is appropriate when there is no exact decimal equivalent, for example, ⅓.
- ***Scientific format,*** which displays a number as a decimal fraction followed by a whole number exponent of 10; for example, the number 12345 would appear as 1.2345E+04. The exponent, +04 in the example, is the number of places the decimal point is moved to the left (or right if the exponent is negative). Very small numbers have negative exponents; for example, the entry .0000012 would be displayed as 1.2E−06. Scientific notation is used only with very large or very small numbers.
- ***Text format,*** which left aligns the entry and is useful for numerical values that are treated as text, such as zip codes.

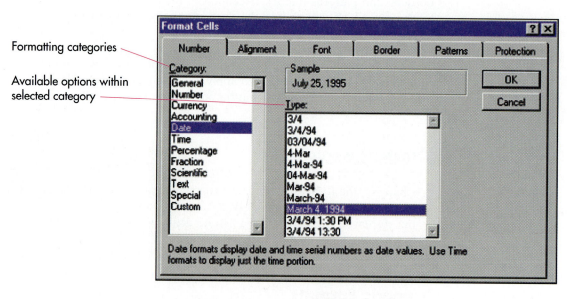

(a) The Number Tab

FIGURE 2.6 The Format Cells Command

- **Special format,** which displays a number with editing characters, such as hyphens in a social security number or parentheses around the area code of a telephone number.
- **Custom format,** which allows you to develop your own formats.

> **DATES VERSUS FRACTIONS**
>
> A fraction may be entered into a cell by preceding the fraction with an equal sign, for example, =1/3. The fraction is converted to its decimal equivalent and displayed in that format in the worksheet. Omission of the equal sign causes Excel to treat the entry as a date; that is, 1/3 will be stored as January 3 (of the current year).

Alignment

The contents of a cell (whether text or numeric) may be aligned horizontally and/or vertically as indicated by the dialog box of Figure 2.6b. The options for horizontal *alignment* include left (the default for text), center, right (the default for numbers), and justify. You can also center an entry across a range of selected cells, as in the grade book of Figure 2.5b, which centered the title that was entered in cell A1 across columns A through E. The Fill option duplicates the characters in the cell across the entire width of that cell.

Vertical alignment is important only if the row height is changed and the characters are smaller than the height of the row. Entries may be vertically aligned at the top, center, or bottom (the default) of a cell.

It is also possible to wrap the text within a cell to emulate the word wrap of a word processor. And finally, you can achieve some very interesting effects by choosing from one of the four orientations within the alignment window.

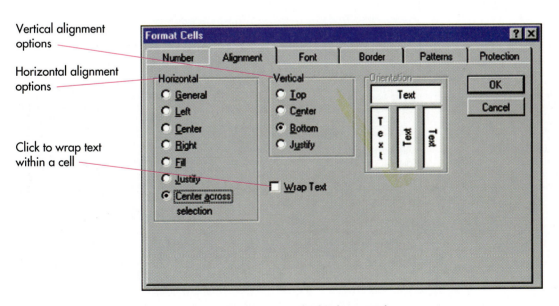

(b) The Alignment Tab

FIGURE 2.6   The Format Cells Command (continued)

Fonts

You can use the same fonts (typefaces) in Excel as you can in any other Windows application. Windows itself includes a limited number of fonts (Arial, Times New Roman, Courier New, Symbol, and Wingdings) to provide variety in creating documents. Additional fonts can be obtained from Microsoft and/or other vendors. All fonts are WYSIWYG (What You See Is What You Get), meaning that the worksheet you see on the monitor will match the worksheet produced by the printer.

Any entry in a worksheet may be displayed in any font, style, or point size as indicated by the dialog box of Figure 2.6c. The example shows Arial, Bold Italic, and 14 points, and corresponds to the selection for the worksheet title in the improved grade book. Special effects, such as subscripts or superscripts, are also possible. You can even select a different color, but you will need a color printer to see the effect on the printed page. The Preview box shows the text as it will appear in the worksheet.

USE RESTRAINT

More is not better, especially in the case of too many typefaces and styles, which produce cluttered worksheets that impress no one. Limit yourself to a maximum of two typefaces per worksheet, but choose multiple sizes and/or styles within those typefaces. Use boldface or italics for emphasis, but do so in moderation, because if you emphasize too many elements, the effect is lost.

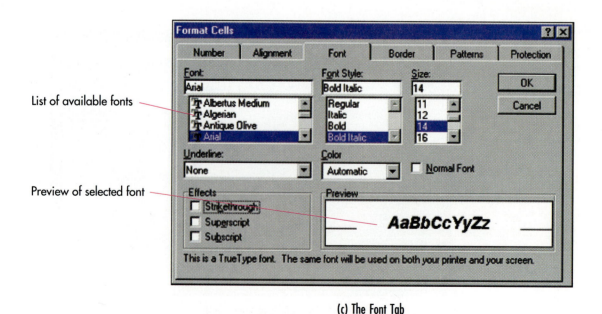

(c) The Font Tab

FIGURE 2.6 The Format Cells Command (continued)

Borders, Patterns, and Shading

The *Border tab* in Figure 2.6d enables you to create a border around a cell (or cells) for additional emphasis. You can outline the entire selection, or you can choose the specific side or sides; for example, thicker lines on the bottom and right sides produce a drop shadow, which is very effective. You can also specify a different color for the border, but you will need a color printer to see the effect on the printed output.

The *Patterns tab* in Figure 2.6e lets you choose a different color in which to shade the cell and further emphasize its contents. The Pattern drop-down list box lets you select an alternate pattern, such as dots or slanted lines.

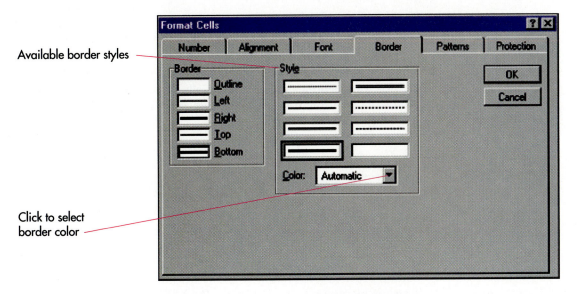

(d) The Border Tab

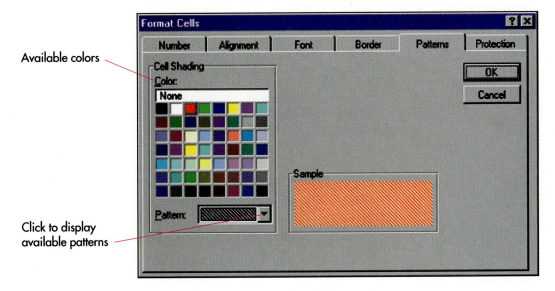

(e) The Patterns Tab

FIGURE 2.6   The Format Cells Command (continued)

HANDS-ON EXERCISE 2

Formatting a Worksheet

Objective: To format a worksheet using both pull-down menus and the Formatting toolbar; to use boldface, italics, shading, and borders; to change the font and/or alignment of a selected entry; to change the width of a column; to print the cell contents as well as the computed values. Use Figure 2.7 as a guide in the exercise.

STEP 1: Fonts

➤ Open **My Grade Book** from the previous exercise. Pull down the **Tools menu,** click **Options,** click the **General Tab,** then check the box to **Reset TipWizard.** Click **OK.**

➤ Click in **cell A1** to select the cell containing the title of the worksheet.

➤ Pull down the **Format menu.** Click **Cells.** If necessary, click the **Font tab.** Click **Arial** from the Font list box, **Bold Italic** from the Font Style box, and **14** from the Size box. Click **OK.**

CHANGE THE DEFAULT FILE LOCATION

The *default file location* is the folder Excel uses to open (save) a workbook unless it is otherwise instructed. To change the default location, pull down the Tools menu, click Options, and click the General tab. Type the name of the new folder (e.g., C:\Exploring Excel) in the Default File Location text box, then click OK. The next time you access the Open or Save commands from the File menu, the Look In text box will reflect the change.

STEP 2: Alignment

➤ Click and drag to select cells **A1** through **E1,** which represents the width of the entire worksheet.

➤ Pull down the **Format menu** a second time. Click **Cells.** Click the **Alignment tab.** Click the **Center Across Selection option button** as in Figure 2.7a. Click **OK** to center the entry in cell A1 over the selected range (cells A1 through E1).

➤ If necessary, click the **TipWizard button** to open the TipWizard toolbar. The TipWizard suggests that you click the **Center Across Selection button** on the Formatting toolbar as a more efficient way to center text.

➤ Click and drag over cells **B3** through **E13.** Click the **Centering button** on the Formatting toolbar.

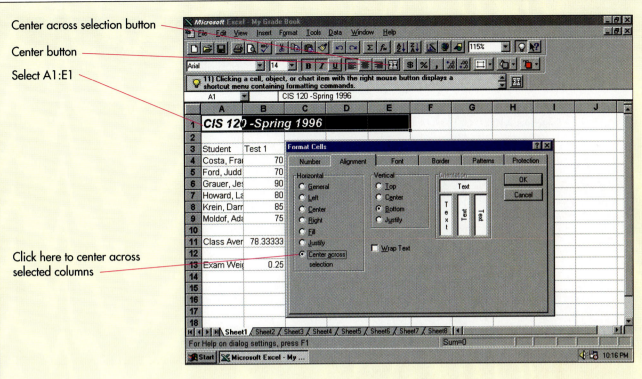

(a) Center across Columns (step 2)

FIGURE 2.7 Hands-on Exercise 2

> **QUIT WITHOUT SAVING**
>
> There will be times when you do not want to save the changes to a workbook—for example, when you have edited it beyond recognition and wish you had never started. The Undo command, useful as it is, reverses only the most recent operation and is of no use if you need to cancel all changes. Pull down the File menu and click the Close command, then click No in response to the message asking whether to save the changes. Pull down the File menu, click the file's name at the bottom of the menu to reopen the file, then begin all over.

STEP 3: Increase the Width of Column A

▶ Click in **cell A4.** Drag the mouse over cells **A4** through **A13.**

▶ Pull down the **Format menu,** click **Column,** then click **AutoFit Selection** as shown in Figure 2.7b. The width of the selected cells increases to accommodate the longest entry in the selected range.

▶ Save the workbook.

GAINING PROFICIENCY **61**

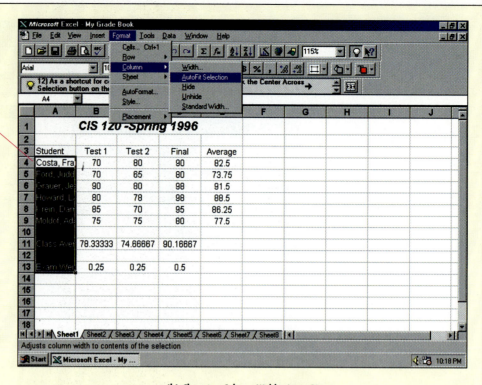

(b) Changing Column Widths (step 3)

FIGURE 2.7 Hands-on Exercise 2 (continued)

COLUMN WIDTHS AND ROW HEIGHTS

Drag the border between column headings to change the column width; for example, to increase (decrease) the width of column A, drag the border between column headings A and B to the right (left). Double click the right boundary of a column heading to change the column width to accommodate the widest entry in that column. Use the same techniques to change the row heights.

STEP 4: Format the Exam Weights

▶ Click and drag to select cells **B13** through **D13**. Point to the selected cells and click the **right mouse button** to display the shortcut menu in Figure 2.7c. Click **Format Cells** to produce the Format Cells dialog box.

▶ If necessary, click the **Number tab.** Click **Percentage** in the Category list box. Click the **down arrow** in the Decimal Places box to reduce the number of decimals to zero, then click **OK.** The exam weights are displayed with percent signs and no decimal places.

▶ Click the **Undo button** on the Standard toolbar to cancel the formatting command.

▶ Click the **% button** on the Formatting toolbar to reformat the exam weights as percentages.

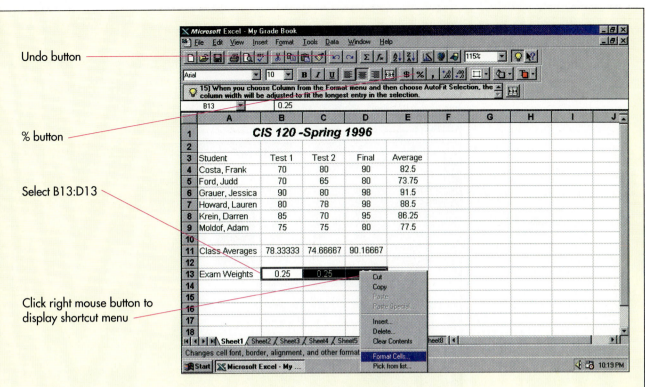

(c) Format Exam Weights (step 4)

FIGURE 2.7 Hands-on Exercise 2 (continued)

AUTOMATIC FORMATTING

Excel converts any number entered with a beginning dollar sign to currency format, and any number entered with an ending percent sign to percentage format. The automatic formatting enables you to save a step by typing $100,000 or 7.5% directly into a cell, rather than entering 100000 or .075 and having to format the number. The formatting is applied to the cell and affects any subsequent numbers in that cell.

STEP 5: Noncontiguous Ranges

➤ Select cells **B11** through **D11,** the cells that contain the class averages for the three exams.

➤ Press *and* hold the **Ctrl key** as you click and drag to select cells **E4** through **E9.** Release the **Ctrl key.**

➤ You will see two noncontiguous (nonadjacent) ranges highlighted, cells B11:D11 and cells E4:E9 as in Figure 2.7d. Format the selected cells using either the Formatting toolbar or the Format menu:

  • To use the Formatting toolbar, click the appropriate button to increase or decrease the number of decimal places to one.

GAINING PROFICIENCY 63

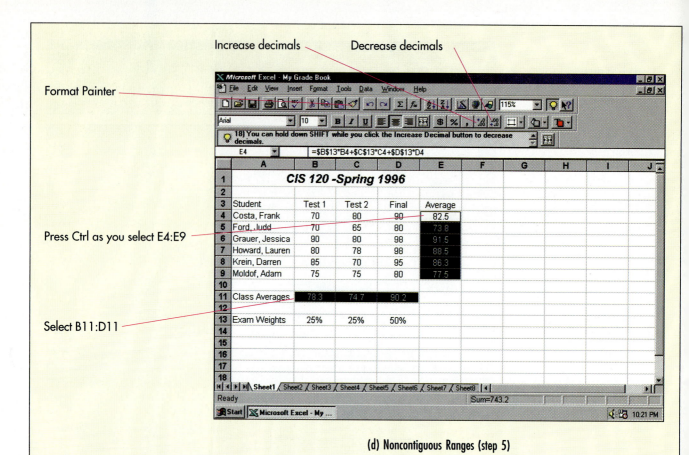

(d) Noncontiguous Ranges (step 5)

FIGURE 2.7 Hands-on Exercise 2 (continued)

- To use the Format menu, pull down the **Format menu,** click **Cells,** click the **Number tab,** then click **Number** in the Category list box. Click the **down arrow** in the Decimal Places text box to reduce the decimal places to one. Click **OK.**

> ### THE FORMAT PAINTER
>
> The *Format Painter* copies the formatting of the selected cell to other cells in the worksheet. Click the cell whose formatting you want to copy, then double click the Format Painter button on the Standard toolbar. The mouse pointer changes to a paintbrush to indicate that you can copy the current formatting; just click and drag the paintbrush over the additional cells that you want to assume the identical formatting as the original cell. Repeat the painting process as often as necessary, then click the Format Painter button a second time to return to normal editing.

STEP 6: Borders

➤ Click and drag to select cells **A3** through **E3.** Press *and* hold the **Ctrl key** as you click and drag to select the range **A11:E11.** Continue to press the **Ctrl key** as you click and drag to select cells **A13:E13.**

➤ Pull down the **Format menu** and click **Cells** (or click the **right mouse button** to produce a shortcut menu, then click **Format Cells**). Click the **Border tab** to access the dialog box in Figure 2.7e.

➤ Choose a line width from the Style section. Click the **Top** and **Bottom** boxes in the Border section. Click **OK** to exit the dialog box and return to the worksheet.

> ### SELECTING NONCONTIGUOUS RANGES
>
> Dragging the mouse to select a range always produces some type of rectangle; that is, a single cell, a row or column, or a group of rows and columns. You can, however, select *noncontiguous* (nonadjacent) *ranges* by selecting the first range in the normal fashion, then pressing and holding the Ctrl key as you select the additional range(s). This is especially useful when the same command is to be applied to multiple ranges within a worksheet.

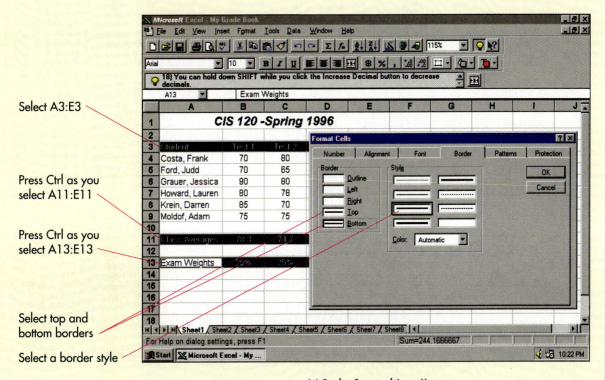

(e) Border Command (step 6)

FIGURE 2.7 Hands-on Exercise 2 (continued)

STEP 7: Color

➤ Check that all three ranges are still selected (A3:E3, A11:E11, *and* A13:E13).

➤ Click the **down arrow** on the **Color button** on the Formatting toolbar. Click light gray (or whatever color appeals to you) as shown in Figure 2.7f.

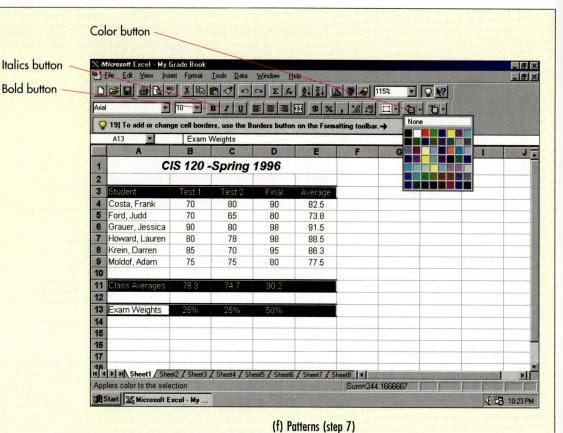

(f) Patterns (step 7)

FIGURE 2.7 Hands-on Exercise 2 (continued)

➤ Click the **boldface** and **italics buttons** on the Formatting toolbar. Click outside the selected cells to see the effects of the formatting change.

➤ Save the workbook.

> ### DESELECTING A RANGE
>
> The effects of a formatting change are often difficult to see when the selected cells are highlighted. Thus, you may need to deselect the range by clicking elsewhere in the worksheet to see the results of a formatting command.

STEP 8: Enter Your Name and Social Security Number

➤ Click in **cell A15.** Type **Grading Assistant.** Press the **down arrow key.** Type your name, press the **down arrow key,** and enter your social security number *without* the hyphens. Press **enter.**

➤ Point to **cell A17,** then click the **right mouse button** to display a shortcut menu. Click **Format Cells** to display the dialog box in Figure 2.7g.

➤ Click the **Number tab,** click **Special** in the Category list box, then click **Social Security Number** in the Type list box. Click **OK.** Hyphens have been inserted into your social security number.

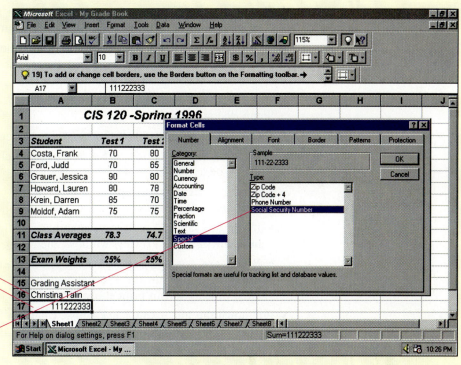

(g) Add Your Name and Social Security Number (step 8)

FIGURE 2.7 Hands-on Exercise 2 (continued)

STEP 9: The Page Setup Command

➤ Pull down the **File menu.** Click **Page Setup** to display the Page Setup dialog box.

- Click the **Margins tab.** Check the box to center the worksheet Horizontally.
- Click the **Sheet tab.** Check the boxes to print Row and Column Headings and Gridlines.
- Click the **Header/Footer tab.** Click the **drop-down arrow** on the Header list box. Scroll to the top of the list and click **(none)** to remove the header. Click the **drop-down arrow** on the Footer list box. Scroll to the top of the list and click **(none)** to remove the footer.
- Click **OK** to exit the Page Setup dialog box.

➤ Click the **Print Preview button** to preview the worksheet before printing:

- If you are satisfied with the appearance of the worksheet, click the **Print button** within the Preview window, then click **OK** to print the worksheet.
- If you are not satisfied with the appearance of the worksheet, click the **Setup button** within the Preview window to make the necessary changes, after which you can print the worksheet.

➤ Save the workbook.

STEP 10: Print the Cell Formulas

➤ Pull down the **Tools menu,** click **Options,** click the **View tab,** check the box for **Formulas,** then click **OK** (or use the keyboard shortcut **Ctrl+`**). The worksheet should display the cell formulas.

➤ If necessary, click the arrow to the right of the horizontal scroll box so that column E, the column containing the cell formulas, comes into view.

➤ Double click the border between the column headings for columns E and F to increase the width of column E to accommodate the widest entry in the column.

➤ Pull down the **File menu.** Click the **Page Setup** command to display the Page Setup dialog box.

- Click the **Page tab.** Click the **Landscape orientation button.**
- Click the option button to **Fit to 1 page.** Click **OK** to exit the Page Setup dialog box.

➤ Click the **Print Preview button** to preview the worksheet before printing. It should match the display in Figure 2.7h:

- If you are satisfied with the appearance of the worksheet, click the **Print button** within the Preview window, then click **OK** to print the worksheet.
- If you are not satisfied with the appearance of the worksheet, click the **Setup button** within the Preview window to make the necessary changes, after which you can print the worksheet.

➤ Pull down the **File menu.** Click **Close.** Click **No** if prompted to save changes.

➤ Exit Excel if you do not want to continue with the next exercise at this time.

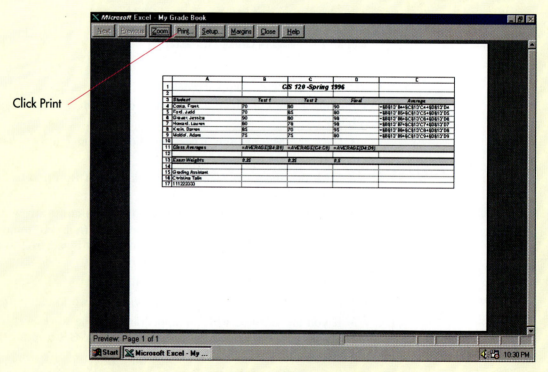

Click Print

(h) Print Preview Command (step 10)

FIGURE 2.7 Hands-on Exercise 2 (continued)

A FINANCIAL FORECAST

Financial forecasting is one of the most common business applications of spreadsheets. Figure 2.8 depicts one such illustration, in which the income and expenses of Get Rich Quick Enterprises are projected over a five-year period. The displayed values are shown in Figure 2.8a, and the cell formulas are shown in Figure 2.8b.

Income in any given year is equal to the number of units sold times the unit price. The projected income in 1996, for example, is $300,000 based on sales of 100,000 units at a price of $3.00 per unit. The variable costs for the same year are estimated at $150,000 (100,000 units times $1.50 per unit). The production facility costs an additional $50,000, and administrative expenses add another $25,000.

	A	B	C	D	E	F
1		Get Rich Quick Enterprises				
2		1996	1997	1998	1999	2000
3	Income					
4	Units Sold	100,000	110,000	121,000	133,100	146,410
5	Unit Price	$3.00	$3.15	$3.31	$3.47	$3.65
6	Gross Revenue	$300,000	$346,500	$400,208	$462,240	$533,887
7						
8	Fixed costs					
9	Production facility	$50,000	$54,000	$58,320	$62,986	$68,024
10	Administration	$25,000	$26,250	$27,563	$28,941	$30,388
11	Variable cost					
12	Unit mfg cost	$1.50	$1.65	$1.82	$2.00	$2.20
13	Variable mfg cost	$150,000	$181,500	$219,615	$265,734	$321,538
14						
15	Earnings before taxes	$75,000	$84,750	$94,710	$104,579	$113,936
16						
17	Initial conditions			Annual increase		
18	First year sales	100,000		10%		
19	Selling price	$3.00		5%		
20	Unit mfg cost	$1.50		10%		
21	Production facility	$50,000		8%		
22	Administration	$25,000		5%		
23	First year of forecast	1996				

100,000 units at $3.00 per unit → (points to $300,000 in row 6)

100,000 units at $1.50 per unit → (points to $150,000 in row 13)

Assumptions and initial conditions are isolated and are used in developing formulas

(a) Displayed Values

	A	B	C	D	E	F
1	Get Rich Quick Enterprises					
2		=B23	=B2+1	=C2+1	=D2+1	=E2+1
3	Income					
4	Units Sold	=B18	=B4+B4*$D$18	=C4+C4*$D$18	=D4+D4*$D$18	=E4+E4*$D$18
5	Unit Price	=B19	=B5+B5*$D$19	=C5+C5*$D$19	=D5+D5*$D$19	=E5+E5*$D$19
6	Gross Revenue	=B4*B5	=C4*C5	=D4*D5	=E4*E5	=F4*F5
7						
8	Fixed costs					
9	Production facility	=B21	=B9+B9*$D$21	=C9+C9*$D$21	=D9+D9*$D$21	=E9+E9*$D$21
10	Administration	=B22	=B10+B10*$D$22	=C10+C10*$D$22	=D10+D10*$D$22	=E10+E10*$D$22
11	Variable cost					
12	Unit mfg cost	=B20	=B12+B12*$D$20	=C12+C12*$D$20	=D12+D12*$D$20	=E12+E12*$D$20
13	Variable mfg cost	=B4*B12	=C4*C12	=D4*D12	=E4*E12	=F4*F12
14						
15	Earnings before taxes	=B6-(B9+B10+B13)	=C6-(C9+C10+C13)	=D6-(D9+D10+D13)	=E6-(E9+E10+E13)	=F6-(F9+F10+F13)
16						
17	Initial conditions			Annual increase		
18	First year sales	100,000		10%		
19	Selling price	$3.00		5%		
20	Unit mfg cost	$1.50		10%		
21	Production facility	$50,000		8%		
22	Administration	$25,000		5%		
23	First year of forecast	1996				

(b) Cell Formulas

FIGURE 2.8 The Financial Forecast

Subtracting the total expenses from the estimated income yields a net income before taxes of $75,000.

The estimated income and expenses for each succeeding year are based on an assumed percentage increase over the previous year. The projected rates of increase as well as the initial conditions are shown at the bottom of the worksheet. We cannot overemphasize the importance of isolating *assumptions* and *initial conditions* in this manner, and further, that all entries in the body of the spreadsheet be developed as formulas that reference these cells. The entry in cell B4, for example, is *not* the constant 100,000, but rather a reference to cell B18, which contains the value 100,000.

The distinction may seem trivial, but most assuredly it is not, as two important objectives are achieved. The user sees at a glance which factors affect the results of the spreadsheet (i.e., the cost and earnings projections), and further, the user can easily change any of those values to see their effect on the overall forecast. Assume, for example, that the first-year forecast changes to 80,000 units and that this number will increase at 8 percent a year (rather than 10). The only changes in the worksheet are to the entries in cells B18 and D18, because the projected sales are calculated using the values in these cells.

Once you appreciate the necessity of isolating the assumptions and initial conditions, you can design the actual spreadsheet. Ask yourself why you are building the spreadsheet in the first place and what you hope to accomplish. (The financial forecast in this example is intended to answer questions regarding projected rates of growth, and more important, how changes in the assumptions and initial conditions will affect the income, expenses, and earnings in later years.) By clarifying what you hope to accomplish, you facilitate the creation of the spreadsheet, which is done in five general stages:

1. Enter the row and column headings, and the values for the initial conditions and the assumed rates of change.
2. Develop the formulas for the first year of the forecast based on the initial conditions at the bottom of the spreadsheet.
3. Develop the formulas for the second year based on the values in year one and the assumed rates of change.
4. Copy the formulas for year two to the remaining years of the forecast.
5. Format the spreadsheet, then print the completed forecast.

Perhaps the most critical step is the development of the formulas for the second year (1997 in Figure 2.8), which are based on the results of 1996 and the assumptions about how these results will change for the next year. The units sold in 1997, for example, are equal to the sales in 1996 (cell B4) plus the estimated increase (B4*$D$18); that is,

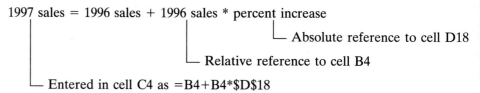

The formula to compute the sales for 1997 uses both absolute and relative references, so that it will be copied properly to the other columns for the remaining years in the forecast. An absolute reference ($D$18) is used for the cell containing the percent increase in sales, because this reference should remain the same when the formula is copied. A relative reference (B4) is used for the sales from the previous year, because this reference should change when the formula is copied. Many of the other formulas in column C are also based on percentage increases from column B, and are developed in similar fashion, as shown in Figure 2.8b.

The formulas for year two (1997) are parallel to those in the remaining years of the forecast (1998 through 2000), and so they can be copied directly to obtain the finished worksheet.

HANDS-ON EXERCISE 3

A Financial Forecast

Objective: Develop a spreadsheet for a financial forecast based on the principles of absolute and relative addresses, and the importance of isolating assumptions and initial conditions. Use Figure 2.9 as a guide in the exercise.

STEP 1: Enter the Formulas for Year One

- Start Excel and reset the TipWizard. Pull down the **Tools menu,** click **Options,** click the **General tab,** then click the check box to **Reset TipWizard.** Click **OK.**
- Open the **Financial Forecast** workbook in the **Exploring Excel folder** to display the workbook in Figure 2.9a. (Cells B4 through B15 will be empty on your worksheet.)
- Save the workbook as **Finished Financial Forecast.**

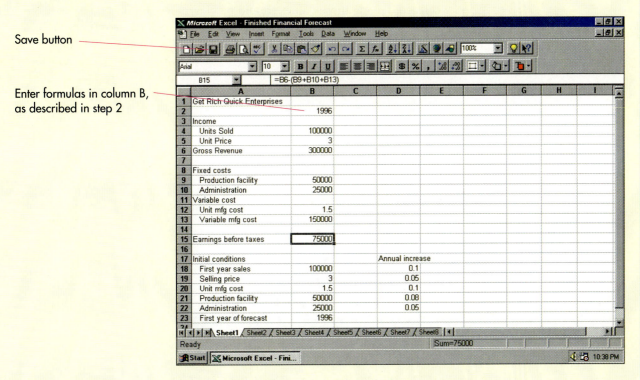

Save button

Enter formulas in column B, as described in step 2

(a) Enter Formulas for Year One (step 2)

FIGURE 2.9   Hands-on Exercise 3

STEP 2: Enter the Formulas for Year One

➤ Click in **cell B2.** Type **=B23** and press **enter.** This is very different from entering 1996 in cell B2 as described in the boxed tip on isolating assumptions.

➤ Enter the remaining formulas for year one:
- Click in **cell B4.** Type **=B18.**
- Click in **cell B5.** Type **=B19.**
- Click in **cell B6.** Type **=B4*B5.**
- Click in **cell B9.** Type **=B21.**
- Click in **cell B10.** Type **=B22.**
- Click in **cell B12.** Type **=B20.**
- Click in **cell B13.** Type **=B4*B12.**
- Click in **cell B15.** Type **=B6−(B9+B10+B13).**

➤ The cell contents for year one (1996) are complete. The displayed values in this column should match the numbers shown in Figure 2.9a.

➤ Save the workbook.

ISOLATE ASSUMPTIONS

The formulas in a worksheet should be based on cell references rather than specific values; for example, B17 or $B$17 rather than 100,000. The cells containing these values should be clearly labeled and set apart from the rest of the worksheet. You can then vary the inputs (assumptions) to the worksheet and immediately see the effect. The chance for error is also minimized because you are changing the contents of a single cell, rather than changing multiple formulas.

STEP 3: Enter the Formulas for Year Two

➤ Click in **cell C2.** Type **=B2+1,** which is the formula to determine the second year of the forecast.

➤ Click in **cell C4.** Type **=B4+B4*$D$18.** This formula computes the sales for year two as a function of the sales in year one and the assumed rate of increase.

➤ Enter the remaining formulas for year two:
- Click in **cell C5.** Type **=B5+B5*$D$19.**
- Click in **cell C6.** Type **=C4*C5.**
- Click in **cell C9.** Type **=B9+B9*$D$21.**
- Click in **cell C10.** Type **=B10+B10*$D$22.**
- Click in **cell C12.** Type **=B12+B12*$D$20**
- Click in **cell C13.** Type **=C4*C12.**
- Click in **cell C15.** Type **=C6−(C9+C10+C13).**

➤ The cell contents for the second year (1997) are complete. The displayed values in this column should match the numbers shown in Figure 2.9b.

➤ Save the workbook.

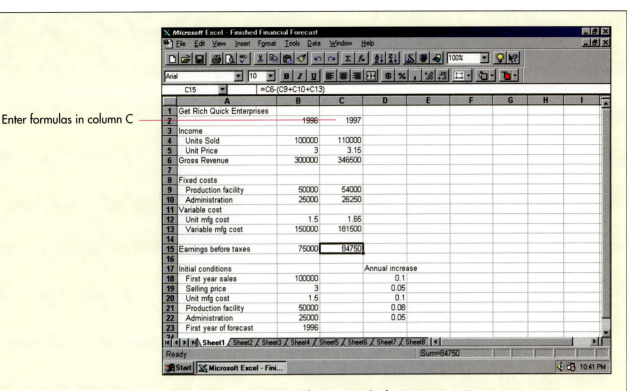

(b) Enter Formulas for Year Two (step 3)

FIGURE 2.9 Hands-on Exercise 3 (continued)

STEP 4: Copy the Formulas to the Remaining Years

➤ Click and drag to select cells **C2** through **C15** (the cells containing the formulas for year two). Click the **Copy button** on the Standard toolbar. A moving border will surround these cells to indicate that their contents have been copied to the clipboard.

➤ Click and drag to select cells **D2** through **F15** (the cells that will contain the formulas for years three to five). Point to the selection and click the **right mouse button** to display the shortcut menu in Figure 2.9c.

➤ Click **Paste** to paste the contents of the clipboard into the selected cells. The displayed values for the last three years of the forecast should be visible in the worksheet. (You should see earnings before taxes of 113936.384 for the year 2000.)

➤ Press **Esc** to remove the moving border. Save the workbook.

THE HELP BUTTON

Click the Help button on the Standard toolbar (the mouse pointer changes to include a large question mark), then click any other toolbar button to display a help screen with information about that button. Double click the Help button to open online help, which functions identically in every Office application. Click the Answer Wizard tab, for example, and you can ask a question in your own words.

GAINING PROFICIENCY

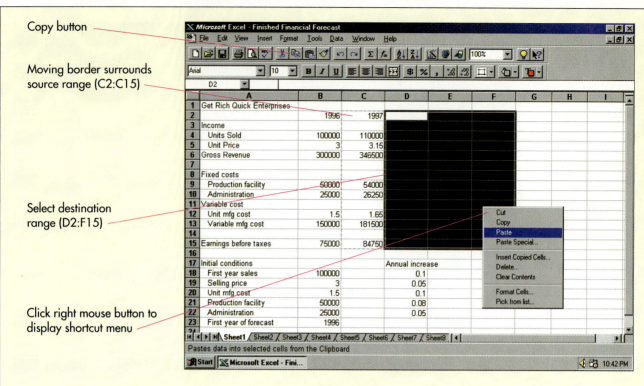

(c) Copy Formulas to Remaining Years (step 4)

FIGURE 2.9   Hands-on Exercise 3 (continued)

STEP 5: Format the Spreadsheet

➤ The hard part is done, and you are ready to format the worksheet. The specifics of the formatting operation are left to you, but Figure 2.9d is provided to guide you to the completed result.

➤ Formatting is done within the context of select-then-do; that is, you select the cell(s) to which you want the formatting to apply, then you execute the appropriate formatting command.

➤ Remember to press and hold the Ctrl key if you want to select noncontiguous cells prior to executing a formatting command as described in the tip on page 65.

THE FORMATTING TOOLBAR

The **Formatting toolbar** is the fastest way to implement most formatting operations. There are buttons for boldface, italics, and underlining, alignment (including centering across columns), currency, percent, and comma formats, as well as buttons to increase or decrease the number of decimal places. There are also several list boxes, which enable you to choose the font, point size, and font color, as well as the type of border and shading.

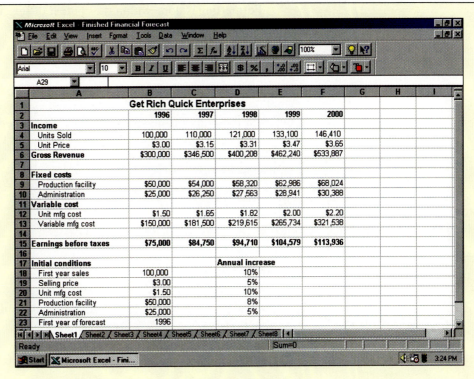

(d) The Completed Spreadsheet (step 5)

FIGURE 2.9 Hands-on Exercise 3 (continued)

STEP 6: Print the Completed Spreadsheet

➤ Add your name somewhere in the worksheet to prove to your instructor that you did the exercise.

➤ Print the completed spreadsheet twice, once to show the displayed values and once to show the cell formulas. Submit both printouts to your instructor.

➤ Review the suggestions of the TipWizard. Exit Excel.

➤ Congratulations on a job well done!

SUMMARY

All worksheet commands operate on a cell or group of cells known as a range. A range is selected by dragging the mouse to highlight the range. The range remains selected until another range is defined or you click another cell in the worksheet. Noncontiguous (nonadjacent) ranges may be selected in conjunction with the Ctrl key.

The formulas in a cell or range of cells may be copied or moved anywhere within a worksheet. An absolute reference remains constant throughout a copy operation, whereas a relative address is adjusted for the new location. Absolute and relative references have no meaning in a move operation. The copy and move operations are implemented through the Copy and Paste commands, and the Cut and Paste commands, respectively.

Formatting is done within the context of select-then-do; that is, select the cell or range of cells, then execute the appropriate command. The Format Cells command controls the formatting for Numbers, Alignment, Fonts, Borders, and Patterns (colors). The Formatting toolbar simplifies the formatting process.

A spreadsheet is first and foremost a tool for decision making, and as such, the subject of continual what-if speculation. It is critical, therefore, that the initial conditions and assumptions be isolated and clearly visible, and further that all formulas in the body of the spreadsheet be developed using these cells.

The TipWizard suggests more efficient ways to accomplish the tasks you are doing. The TipWizard will not repeat a tip from one session to the next unless it is specifically reset at the beginning of a session.

KEY WORDS AND CONCEPTS

Absolute reference	Date format	Percentage format
Accounting format	Destination range	Range
Alignment	Format cells command	Relative reference
Assumptions	Format menu	Row command
Automatic formatting	Format Painter	Row height
Border tab	Formatting toolbar	Scientific format
Cell formulas	Fraction format	Select-then-do
Clipboard	General format	Source range
Column command	Initial conditions	Special format
Column width	Move operation	Text format
Copy command	Noncontiguous range	Time format
Currency format	Number format	TipWizard
Custom format	Paste command	
Cut command	Patterns tab	

MULTIPLE CHOICE

1. Cell F6 contains the formula =AVERAGE(B6:D6). What will be the contents of cell F7 if the entry in cell F6 is *copied* to cell F7?
    (a) =AVERAGE(B6:D6)
    (b) =AVERAGE(B7:D7)
    (c) =AVERAGE($B$6:$D$6)
    (d) =AVERAGE($B$7:$D$7)

2. Cell F6 contains the formula =AVERAGE(B6:D6). What will be the contents of cell F7 if the entry in cell F6 is *moved* to cell F7?
    (a) =AVERAGE(B6:D6)
    (b) =AVERAGE(B7:D7)
    (c) =AVERAGE($B$6:$D$6)
    (d) =AVERAGE($B$7:$D$7)

3. A formula containing the entry =$A$4 is copied to a cell one column over and two rows down. How will the entry appear in its new location?
   (a) Both the row and column will change
   (b) Neither the row nor column will change
   (c) The row will change but the column will remain the same
   (d) The column will change but the row will remain the same

4. Which commands are necessary to implement a move?
   (a) Cut and Paste commands
   (b) Move command from the Edit menu
   (c) Either (a) or (b)
   (d) Neither (a) nor (b)

5. A cell range may consist of:
   (a) A single cell
   (b) A row or set of rows
   (c) A column or set of columns
   (d) All of the above

6. Which command will take a cell, or group of cells, and duplicate them elsewhere in the worksheet, without changing the original cell references?
   (a) Copy command, provided relative addresses were specified
   (b) Copy command, provided absolute addresses were specified
   (c) Move command, provided relative addresses were specified
   (d) Move command, provided absolute addresses were specified

7. The contents of cell B4 consist of the formula =B2*B3, yet the displayed value in cell B4 is a series of pound signs. What is the most likely explanation for this?
   (a) Cells B2 and B3 contain text entries rather than numeric entries and so the formula in cell B4 cannot be evaluated
   (b) Cell B4 is too narrow to display the computed result
   (c) Both (a) and (b)
   (d) Neither (a) nor (b)

8. The Formatting toolbar contains buttons to
   (a) Change to percent format
   (b) Increase or decrease the number of decimal places
   (c) Center an entry across columns
   (d) All of the above

9. Given that the percentage format is in effect, and that the number .056 has been entered into the active cell, how will the contents of the cell appear?
   (a) .056
   (b) 5.6%
   (c) .056%
   (d) 56%

10. Which of the following entries is equivalent to the decimal number .2?
    (a) ⅕
    (b) =1/5
    (c) Both (a) and (b)
    (d) Neither (a) nor (b)

11. What is the effect of two successive Undo commands, one right after the other?
   (a) The situation is not possible because the Undo command is not available in Microsoft Excel
   (b) The situation is not possible because the Undo command cannot be executed twice in a row
   (c) The Undo commands cancel each other out; that is, the worksheet is as it was prior to the first Undo command
   (d) The last two commands prior to the first Undo command are reversed

12. Which of the following fonts are included in Windows?
   (a) Arial and Times New Roman
   (b) Courier New
   (c) Wingdings and Symbol
   (d) All of the above

13. A numerical entry may be
   (a) Displayed in boldface and/or italics
   (b) Left, centered, or right aligned in a cell
   (c) Displayed in any TrueType font in any available point size
   (d) All of the above

14. Which of the following best describes the formula to compute the sales in the second year of the financial forecast?
   (a) It contains a relative reference to the assumed rate of increase and an absolute reference to the sales from the previous year
   (b) It contains an absolute reference to the assumed rate of increase and a relative reference to the sales from the previous year
   (c) It contains absolute references to both the assumed rate of increase and the sales from the previous year
   (d) It contains relative references to both the assumed rate of increase and the sales from the previous year

15. The estimated sales for the first year of a financial forecast are contained in cell B3. The sales for year two are assumed to be 10% higher than the first year, with the rate of increase (10%) stored in cell C23 at the bottom of the spreadsheet. Which of the following is the best way to enter the projected sales for year two, assuming that this formula is to be copied to the remaining years of the forecast?.
   (a) =B3+B3*.10
   (b) =B3+B3*C23
   (c) =B3+B3*$C$23
   (d) All of the above are equivalent entries

ANSWERS

1. b	6. b	11. c
2. a	7. b	12. d
3. b	8. d	13. d
4. a	9. b	14. b
5. d	10. b	15. c

Exploring Excel 7.0

1. Use Figure 2.10 to match each action with its result; a given action may be used more than once or not at all.

Action

a. Click at 8, then click at 15
b. Click at 6, then click at 15
c. Click at 7, drag to 3, click at 16
d. Click at 4, drag to 2, click at 16
e. Click at 5, drag to 1, click at 20
f. Click at 12, drag to 10, click at 19
g. Click at 12, then click at 13
h. Click at 11, drag to 9, click at 14

Result

_____ Format the exam weights as percentages

_____ Copy the formula to calculate the semester average for Frank Costa to the clipboard

_____ Change the font size of the worksheet title

_____ Paste the formula to calculate the semester average for the remaining students

_____ Create a bottom border that separates the column titles from the students' names and grades

_____ Copy the formula to calculate the average for Test 1 to the clipboard

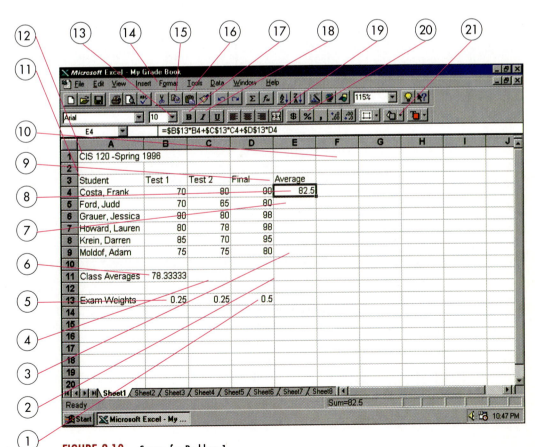

FIGURE 2.10   Screen for Problem 1

GAINING PROFICIENCY   79

Action	Result
i. Click at 8, drag to 3, click at 21	_____ Apply boldface and italic formatting to the worksheet title
j. Click at 12, click at 17, click at 18	_____ Paste the formula to calculate the test average for Test 2 and the final
	_____ Shade the student averages a light gray
	_____ Center the worksheet title over the width of the worksheet

2. Figure 2.11 contains a worksheet depicting simplified payroll calculations for gross pay, withholding tax, social security tax (FICA), and net pay.

   a. What formula should be entered in cell E3 to compute an individual's gross pay? (An individual receives time and a half for overtime.)

   b. What formula should be entered in cell F3 to compute the withholding tax?

   c. What formula should be entered in cell G3 to compute the social security tax?

   d. What formula should be entered in cell H3 to compute the net pay?

   e. What formula should be entered in cell E10 to compute the total gross pay for the company? What formulas should be entered in cells F10 through H10 to compute the remaining totals?

	A	B	C	D	E	F	G	H
1	Employee	Hourly	Regular	Overtime	Gross	Withholding	Social Security	Net
2	Name	Wage	Hours	Hours	Pay	Tax	Tax	Pay
3	Adams	$8.00	40	3	$356.00	$99.68	$23.14	$233.18
4	Hall	$6.25	40	0	$250.00	$70.00	$16.25	$163.75
5	Costo	$9.50	25	0	$237.50	$66.50	$15.44	$155.56
6	Lee	$4.50	40	5	$213.75	$59.85	$13.89	$140.01
7	Arnold	$6.25	35	0	$218.75	$61.25	$14.22	$143.28
8	Vedo	$5.50	40	2	$236.50	$66.22	$15.37	$154.91
9								
10			Totals		$1,512.50	$423.50	$98.31	$990.69
11								
12	Assumptions:							
13	Withholding Tax:		28.0%					
14	Social Security Tax:		6.5%					

FIGURE 2.11 Spreadsheet for Problem 2

3. Relative versus Absolute Addressing: Figure 2.12 contains two versions of a worksheet in which sales, costs, and profits are to be projected over a five-year horizon. The worksheets are only partially completed, and the intent in both is to copy the entries from year 2 (cells C2 through C4) to the remainder of the worksheet. As you can see, the first worksheet uses only relative references and the second uses only absolute references. Both worksheets are in error.

   a. Show the erroneous formulas that will result when column C is copied to columns D, E, and F for both worksheets.

   b. What are the correct formulas for column C so that the formulas will copy correctly?

	A	B	C	D	E	F
1		Year 1	Year 2	Year 3	Year 4	Year 5
2	Sales	1000	=B2+B2*C7			
3	Cost	800	=B3+B3*C8			
4	Profit	200	=C2-C3			
5						
6	Assumptions:					
7	Annual Sales Increase		10%			
8	Annual Cost Increase		8%			

(a) Error 1 (relative cell addresses)

	A	B	C	D	E	F
1		Year 1	Year 2	Year 3	Year 4	Year 5
2	Sales	1000	=$B$2+$B$2*$C$7			
3	Cost	800	=$B$3+$B$3*$C$8			
4	Profit	200	=$C$2-$C$3			
5						
6	Assumptions:					
7	Annual Sales Increase		10%			
8	Annual Cost Increase		8%			

(b) Error 2 (absolute cell addresses)

FIGURE 2.12 Spreadsheets for Problem 3

4. The spreadsheet is an invaluable tool in decision making, but what if the spreadsheet contains an error? Unfortunately, it is all too easy to get caught up in the appearance of an attractively formatted spreadsheet without paying attention to its underlying accuracy.

   Figure 2.13 contains a modified (and erroneous) version of the financial forecast in which the initial selling price has been revised downward to $2.25. The lower selling price is *not* to be considered an error as it reflects the results of a more recent marketing survey. Look carefully at the displayed values in Figure 2.13 and see if you can detect the underlying error(s) in the revised spreadsheet. Should you recommend the project based on the revised selling price?

	A	B	C	D	E	F
1		Get Rich Quick Enterprises				
2		1996	1997	1998	1999	2000
3	Income					
4	Units Sold	100,000	110,000	121,000	133,100	146,410
5	Unit Price	$2.25	$2.36	$2.48	$2.60	$2.73
6	Gross Revenue	$225,000	$259,875	$300,156	$346,680	$400,415
7						
8	Fixed costs					
9	Production facility	$50,000	$54,000	$54,000	$54,000	$54,000
10	Administration	$25,000	$26,250	$27,563	$28,941	$30,388
11	Variable cost					
12	Unit mfg cost	$1.50	$1.65	$1.82	$2.00	$2.20
13	Variable mfg cost	$150,000	$181,500	$219,615	$265,734	$321,538
14						
15	Earnings before taxes	$25,000	$24,375	$26,541	$26,946	$24,877
16						
17	Initial conditions			Annual increase		
18	First year sales	100,000		10%		
19	Selling price	$2.25		5%		
20	Unit mfg cost	$1.50		10%		
21	Production facility	$50,000		8%		
22	Administration	$25,000		5%		
23	First year of forecast	1996				

FIGURE 2.13 Spreadsheet for Problem 4

Practice with Excel 7.0

1. Figure 2.14 contains a worksheet that was used to calculate the difference between the Asking Price and Selling Price on various real estate listings that were sold during June, as well as the commission paid to the real estate agency as a result of selling those listings. Complete the worksheet, following the steps outlined below:

   a. Open the partially completed *Chapter 2 Practice 1* workbook on the data disk, then save the workbook as *Finished Chapter 2 Practice 1*.

   b. Click cell E5 and enter the formula to calculate the difference between the asking price and the selling price for the property belonging to Mr. Landry.

   c. Click cell F5 and enter the formula to calculate the commission paid to the agency as a result of selling the property. (Pay close attention to the difference between relative and absolute cell references.)

   d. Select cells E5:F5 and copy the formulas to E6:F11 to calculate the difference and commission for the rest of the properties.

   e. Click cell C13 and enter the formula to calculate the total asking price, which is the sum of the asking prices for the individual listings in cells C5:C11.

   f. Copy the formula in C13 to the range D13:F13 to calculate the other totals.

   g. Select the range C5:F13 and format the numbers so that they display with dollar signs and commas, and no decimal places (e.g., $450,000).

   h. Click cell B15 and format the number as a percentage.

   i. Click cell A1 and center the title across the width of the worksheet. With the cell still selected, select cells A3:F4 as well and change the font to 12 point Arial bold italic.

   j. Select cells A4:F4 and create a bottom border to separate the headings from the data.

   k. Select cells F5:F11 and shade the commissions.

   l. Print the worksheet.

	A	B	C	D	E	F
1	Coaches Realty - Sales for June					
2						
3			Asking Price	Selling Price		
4	Customer	Address	Price	Price	Difference	Commission
5	Landry	122 West 75 Terr.	450000	350000		
6	Spurrier	4567 S.W. 95 Street	750000	648500		
7	Shula	123 Alamo Road	350000	275000		
8	Lombardi	9000 Brickell Place	275000	250000		
9	Johnson	5596 Powerline Road	189000	189000		
10	Erickson	8900 N.W. 89 Street	456000	390000		
11	Bowden	75 Maynada Blvd.	300000	265000		
12						
13		Totals:				
14						
15	Commission %:		0.035			

FIGURE 2.14 Spreadsheet for Practice Exercise 1

2. **The Sales Invoice:** Use Figure 2.15 as the basis for a sales invoice that you will create and submit to your instructor. Your spreadsheet should follow the general format shown in the figure with respect to including a uniform discount for each item. Your spreadsheet should also include the sales tax. The discount percentage and sales tax percentage should be entered in a separate area so that they can be easily modified.

    Use your imagination and sell any product at any price. You must, however, include at least four items in your invoice. Formatting is important, but you need not follow our format exactly. See how creative you can be, then submit your completed invoice to your instructor for inclusion in a class contest for the best invoice. Be sure your name appears somewhere on the worksheet as a sales associate. If you are really ambitious, you might include an object from the ClipArt Gallery.

	A	B	C	D	E	F
1		**Bargain Basement Shopping**				
2						
3	*Item*	*Quantity*	*List Price*	*Discount*	*Your Price*	*Total*
4	Hayes 28.8 Fax/Modem	2	$169.00	$33.80	$135.20	$270.40
5	Sony 4X CD-ROM	6	$329.00	$65.80	$263.20	$1,579.20
6	Seagate 1Gb Hard Drive	4	$338.00	$67.60	$270.40	$1,081.60
7	Iomega Zip Drive	10	$199.00	$39.80	$159.20	$1,592.00
8						
9	Subtotal					$4,523.20
10	Tax					$294.01
11	Amount Due					$4,817.21
12						
13	Discount Percentage	20%				
14	Sales Tax Percentage	6.50%				
15	Sales Associate	Serena Cruz				

FIGURE 2.15 Spreadsheet for Practice Exercise 2

3. **The Probability Expert:** How much would you bet *against* two people in your class having the same birthday? Don't be too hasty, for the odds of two classmates sharing the same birthday (month and day) are much higher than you would expect. For example, there is a fifty percent chance (.5063) in a class of 23 students that two people will have been born on the same day, as shown in the spreadsheet in Figure 2.16. The probability jumps to seventy percent (.7053) in a class of 30, and to ninety percent (.9025) in a class of 41. Don't take our word for it, but try the experiment in your class.

    You need a basic knowledge of probability to create the spreadsheet. In essence you calculate the probability of individuals not having the same birthday, then subtract this number from one, to obtain the probability of the event coming true. In a group of two people, for example, the probability of not being born on the same day is 365/366; i.e., the second person can be born on any of 365 days and still have a different birthday. The probability of two people having the same birthday becomes 1 − 365/366.

    The probability for different birthdays in a group of three is (365/366)*(364/366); the probability of not having different birthdays—that is, of two people having the same birthday, is one minus this number. Each row in the spreadsheet is calculated from the previous row. It's not as hard as it looks, and the results are quite interesting!

	A	B	C
1		The Birthday Problem	
2	Number of People	Probability of Different Birthdays	Probability of the Same Birthday
3	2	99.73%	0.27%
4	3	99.18%	0.82%
5	4	98.37%	1.63%
6	5	97.29%	2.71%
7	6	95.96%	4.04%
8	7	94.39%	5.61%
9	8	92.59%	7.41%
10	9	90.56%	9.44%
11	10	88.34%	11.66%
⋮	⋮	⋮	⋮
24	23	49.37%	50.63%
⋮	⋮	⋮	⋮
42	41	9.75%	90.25%
⋮	⋮	⋮	⋮
51	50	2.99%	97.01%

FIGURE 2.16   Spreadsheet for Practice Exercise 3

4. Help for Your Sibling: Develop the multiplication table for a younger sibling shown in Figure 2.17. Creating the row and column headings is easy in that you can enter the numbers manually, or you can use online help to learn about the AutoFill feature. The hard part is creating the formulas in the body of the worksheet (we don't want you to enter the numbers manually). The trick is to use mixed references for the formula in cell B4, then copy that single cell to the remainder of the table.

Add your name to the worksheet and submit it to your instructor. Remember, this worksheet is for a younger sibling, and so formatting is important. Print the cell formulas as well so that you can see how the mixed reference changes throughout the worksheet. Submit the complete assignment (title page, displayed values, and cell formulas) to your instructor. Using mixed references correctly is challenging, but once you arrive at the correct solution, you will have learned a lot about mixed references.

	A	B	C	D	E	F	G	H	I	J	K	L	M
1					A Multiplication Table for My Younger Sister								
2													
3		1	2	3	4	5	6	7	8	9	10	11	12
4	1	1	2	3	4	5	6	7	8	9	10	11	12
5	2	2	4	6	8	10	12	14	16	18	20	22	24
6	3	3	6	9	12	15	18	21	24	27	30	33	36
7	4	4	8	12	16	20	24	28	32	36	40	44	48
8	5	5	10	15	20	25	30	35	40	45	50	55	60
9	6	6	12	18	24	30	36	42	48	54	60	66	72
10	7	7	14	21	28	35	42	49	56	63	70	77	84
11	8	8	16	24	32	40	48	56	64	72	80	88	96
12	9	9	18	27	36	45	54	63	72	81	90	99	108
13	10	10	20	30	40	50	60	70	80	90	100	110	120
14	11	11	22	33	44	55	66	77	88	99	110	121	132
15	12	12	24	36	48	60	72	84	96	108	120	132	144

FIGURE 2.17   Spreadsheet for Practice Exercise 4

Case Studies

Establishing a Budget

You want to join a sorority, and you really would like a car. Convince your parents that you can afford both by developing a detailed budget for your four years at school. Your worksheet should include all sources of income (scholarships, loans, summer jobs, work-study, etc.) as well as all expenses (tuition, books, room and board, and entertainment). Make the budget as realistic as possible by building in projected increases over the four-year period.

Be sure to isolate the assumptions and initial conditions so that your spreadsheet is amenable to change. Print the spreadsheet twice, once to show displayed values, and once to show the cell formulas. Submit both pages to your instructor together with a cover page for your assignment.

The Entrepreneur

You have developed the perfect product and are seeking venture capital to go into immediate production. Your investors are asking for a projected income statement for the first four years of operation. The sales of your product are estimated at $200,000 the first year and are projected to grow at 10 percent annually. The cost of goods sold is 60 percent of the sales amount, which is expected to remain constant. You also have to pay a 10 percent sales commission, which is also expected to remain constant.

Develop a financial forecast that will show the projected profits before and after taxes (assuming a tax rate of 36 percent). Your worksheet should be completely flexible and capable of accommodating a change in any of the initial conditions or projected rates of increase, *without* having to edit or recopy any of the formulas.

Break-even Analysis

Widgets of America has developed the perfect product and is ready to go into production, pending a review of a five-year break-even analysis. The manufacturing cost in the first year is $1.00 per unit and is estimated to increase at 5% annually. The projected selling price is $2.00 per unit and can increase at 10% annually. Overhead expenses are fixed at $100,000 per year over the life of the project. The advertising budget is $50,000 in the first year but will decrease 15% a year as the product gains acceptance. How many units have to be sold each year for the company to break even, given the current cost estimates and projected rates of increase?

As in the previous case, your worksheet should be completely flexible and capable of accommodating a change in any of the initial conditions or projected rates of increase or decrease. Be sure to isolate all of the assumptions (i.e., the initial conditions and rates of increase) in one area of the worksheet, and then reference these cells as absolute references when building the formulas.

The Corporate Balance Sheet

A balance sheet is a snapshot of a firm's condition at a given point in time. One part of the balance sheet shows the firm's assets and includes items such as cash on hand, accounts receivable, and inventory. It also includes the value of fixed assets, such as the land and/or buildings owned by the firm. The other part of the balance sheet shows the firm's liabilities and includes accounts payable, accrued wages, and debt. It also includes owner's equity and retained earnings.

The best place to see examples of a real balance sheet is in an annual report, which is easily obtained from any public corporation. Obtain a copy of the annual report, find the balance sheet, then recreate the balance sheet for your instructor. Formatting and accuracy are important so do the best job you can. Include your name somewhere on the balance sheet as the financial auditor.

SPREADSHEETS IN DECISION MAKING: WHAT IF?

OBJECTIVES

After reading this chapter you will be able to:

1. Describe the use of spreadsheets in decision making; explain how the Goal Seek command and Scenario Manager facilitate the decision making process.
2. List the arguments of the PMT function and describe its use in financial decisions.
3. Use the Function Wizard to select a function, identify the function arguments, then enter the function into a worksheet.
4. Use the fill handle to copy a cell range to a range of adjacent cells; use the AutoFill capability to enter a series into a worksheet.
5. Use pointing to create a formula; explain the advantage of pointing over explicitly typing cell references.
6. Use the AVERAGE, MAX, MIN, and COUNT functions in a worksheet.
7. Use the IF function to implement a decision; explain the VLOOKUP function and how it is used in a worksheet.
8. Describe the additional measures needed to print large worksheets; explain how freezing panes may help in the development of a large worksheet.

OVERVIEW

Excel is a truly fascinating program, but it is only a means to an end. A spreadsheet is first and foremost a tool for decision making, and the objective of this chapter is to show you just how valuable that tool can be. We begin by presenting two worksheets that we think will be truly useful to you. The first evaluates the purchase of a car and helps you determine just how much car you can afford. The second will be of interest when you are looking for a mortgage to buy a home.

The chapter continues to develop your knowledge of Excel with emphasis on the predefined functions that are built into the program. We consider financial functions such as the PMT function to determine the monthly payment on a loan. We introduce the MAX, MIN, COUNT, and COUNTA statistical functions. We also present the IF and VLOOKUP functions that provide decision making within a worksheet.

The chapter also discusses two important commands that facilitate the decision-making process. The Goal Seek command lets you enter the desired end result (such as the monthly payment on a car loan) and from that, determines the input (e.g., the price of the car) to produce that result. The Scenario Manager enables you to specify multiple sets of assumptions and input conditions (scenarios), then see at a glance the results of any given scenario.

The examples in this chapter review the important concepts of relative and absolute cell references, as well as the need to isolate the assumptions and initial conditions in a worksheet. The hands-on exercises introduce new techniques in the form of powerful shortcuts that will make you more proficient in Excel. We show you how to use the fill handle to copy cells within a worksheet and how to use the AutoFill capability to enter a data series. We also explain how to enter formulas by pointing to cells within a worksheet, as opposed to having to explicitly type the cell references.

ANALYSIS OF A CAR LOAN

Figure 3.1 shows how a worksheet might be applied to the purchase of a car. In essence, you need to know the monthly payment, which depends on the price of the car, the down payment, and the terms of the loan. In other words:

- Can you afford the monthly payment on the car of your choice?
- What if you settle for a less expensive car and receive a manufacturer's rebate?
- What if you work next summer to earn money for a down payment?
- What if you extend the life of the loan and receive a more favorable interest rate?

The answers to these and other questions determine whether you can afford a car, and if so, which car, and how you will pay for it. The decision is made easier by developing the worksheet in Figure 3.1, and then by changing the various parameters as indicated.

Figure 3.1a contains the ***template***, or "empty" worksheet, in which the text entries and formulas have already been entered, the formatting has already been applied, but no specific data has been input. The template requires that you enter the price of the car, the manufacturer's rebate, the down payment, the interest rate, and the length of the loan. The worksheet uses these parameters to compute the monthly payment. (Implicit in this discussion is the existence of a PMT function within the worksheet program, which is explained in the next section.)

The availability of the worksheet lets you consider several alternatives, and therein lies its true value. You quickly realize that the purchase of a $14,999 car as shown in Figure 3.1b is prohibitive because the monthly payment is almost $500. Settling for a less expensive car, coming up with a substantial down payment, and obtaining a manufacturer's rebate in Figure 3.1c helps considerably, but the $317 monthly payment is still too steep. Extending the loan to a fourth year at a lower interest rate in Figure 3.1d reduces the monthly payment to (a more affordable) $244.

(a) The Template

	A	B
1	Price of car	
2	Manufacturer's rebate	
3	Down payment	
4	Amount to finance	=B1-(B2+B3)
5	Interest rate	
6	Term (in years)	
7	Monthly payment	=PMT(B5/12,B6*12,-B4)

No specific data has been input → (points to rows 1, 2, 3, 5, 6)

(b) Initial Parameters

	A	B
1	Price of car	$14,999
2	Manufacturer's rebate	
3	Down payment	
4	Amount to finance	$14,999
5	Interest rate	9%
6	Term (in years)	3
7	Monthly payment	$476.96

Data entered

(c) Less Expensive Car with Down Payment and Rebate

	A	B
1	Price of car	$13,999
2	Manufacturer's rebate	$1,000
3	Down payment	$3,000
4	Amount to finance	$9,999
5	Interest rate	9%
6	Term (in years)	3
7	Monthly payment	$317.97

Less expensive car — *Rebate* — *Down payment made*

(d) Longer Term and Better Interest Rate

	A	B
1	Price of car	$13,999
2	Manufacturer's rebate	$1,000
3	Down payment	$3,000
4	Amount to finance	$9,999
5	Interest rate	8%
6	Term (in years)	4
7	Monthly payment	$244.10

Lower interest rate — *Longer term*

FIGURE 3.1 Spreadsheets in Decision Making

PMT Function

A ***function*** is a predefined formula that accepts one or more ***arguments*** as input, performs the indicated calculation, then returns another value as output. Excel has more than 100 different functions in various categories. Financial functions, such as the PMT function we are about to study, are especially important in business.

The ***PMT function*** requires three arguments (the interest rate per period, the number of periods, and the amount of the loan) from which it computes the associated payment on a loan. The arguments are placed in parentheses and are separated by commas. Consider, for example, the PMT function as it might apply to Figure 3.1b:

```
=PMT(.09/12,36,−14999)
           │     │      └─ Amount of loan (entered as a negative amount)
           │     └─ Number of periods (3 years × 12 months/year)
           └─ Interest rate per period (annual rate divided by 12)
```

Instead of using specific values, however, the arguments in the PMT function are supplied as cell references, so that the computed payment can be based on values supplied by the user elsewhere in the worksheet. Thus, the PMT function is entered as =PMT(B5/12,B6*12,−B4) to reflect the terms of a specific loan whose arguments are in cells B4, B5, and B6. (The principal is entered as a negative amount because the money is lent to you and represents an outflow of cash from the bank.)

The Goal Seek Command

The analysis in Figure 3.1 enabled us to reduce the projected monthly payment from $476 to a more affordable $244. What if, however, we can afford a payment of only $200, and we want to know how much money to borrow in order to keep the payment to the specified amount. The **Goal Seek command** is designed to solve this type of problem as it enables you to set an end result (e.g., the monthly payment) in order to determine the input (the price of the car) to produce that result. Only one parameter (e.g., the price of the car *or* the interest rate) can be varied at a time.

Figure 3.2 extends our earlier analysis to illustrate the Goal Seek command. You create the spreadsheet as usual, then you pull down the Tools menu, and select the Goal Seek command to display the dialog box in Figure 3.2a. Enter the address of the cell containing the dependent formula (the monthly payment in cell B7) and the desired value of this cell ($200). Indicate the cell whose contents will change (the price of the car in cell B1), then click OK to execute the command. The Goal Seek command then varies the price of the car until the monthly payment returns the desired value of $200. (Not every problem has a solution, however, in which case Excel will return a message indicating that a solution cannot be found.)

In this example the Goal Seek command is able to find a solution and returns a purchase price of $12,192 as shown in Figure 3.2b. You now have all the information you need. Find a car that sells for $12,192 (or less), hold the other parameters to the values shown in the figure, and your monthly payment will be (at most) $200.

The analyses in Figures 3.1 and 3.2 illustrate how a worksheet is used in the decision-making process. An individual defines a problem, then develops a worksheet that includes all of the associated parameters. He or she can then plug in specific numbers, changing one or more of the variables until a decision can be reached.

> **LIMITATIONS OF THE GOAL SEEK COMMAND**
>
> The Goal Seek command, powerful as it is, is limited to a single variable; that is, you set the desired result but are limited to changing the value of a single input variable. Excel does, however, provide a more powerful tool known as Solver, which can vary multiple input variables. This is a much more complex analysis and is beyond the scope of the present discussion.

Cell containing dependent formula

Desired value for cell containing dependent formula

Cell whose contents are to be changed

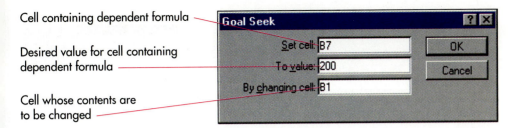

(a) Set the Maximum Payment

Required purchase price for a $200 monthly payment

	A	B
1	Price of car	$12,192
2	Manufacturer's rebate	$1,000
3	Down payment	$3,000
4	Amount to finance	$8,192
5	Interest rate	8%
6	Term (in years)	4
7	Monthly payment	$200.00

(b) Solution

FIGURE 3.2 The Goal Seek Command

HANDS-ON EXERCISE 1

Analysis of a Car Loan

Objective: To create a spreadsheet that will analyze a car loan; to illustrate the PMT function and the Goal Seek command. Use Figure 3.3 as a guide.

Step 1: Enter the Descriptive Labels

➤ Start Excel. If necessary, click the **New button** on the Standard toolbar to open a new workbook.

➤ Click in **cell A1,** type the label **Price of car,** then press the **enter key** or **down arrow** to complete the entry and move automatically to cell A2.

➤ Enter the remaining labels for column A as shown in Figure 3.3a.

> **THE SPELL CHECK**
>
> Anyone familiar with a word processor takes the spell check for granted, but did you know the same capability exists within Excel? Click the Spelling button on the Standard toolbar to initiate the spell check, then implement corrections just as you do in Microsoft Word. All of the applications in Microsoft Office share the same custom dictionary, so that any words you add to the custom dictionary in one application are automatically recognized in the other applications.

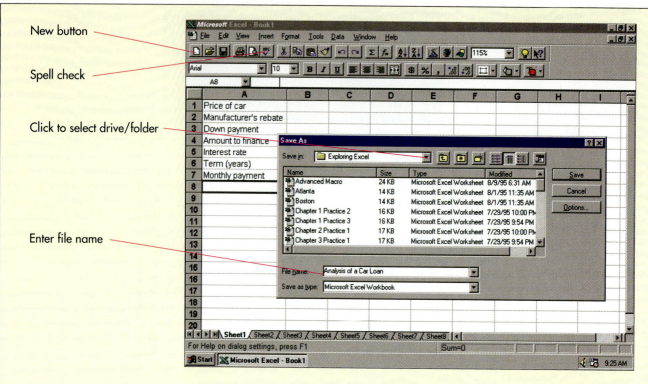

(a) Enter the Descriptive Labels (step 1)

FIGURE 3.3 Hands-on Exercise 1

- Click and drag the column border between columns A and B to increase the width of column A to accommodate its widest entry.
- Save the workbook as **Analysis of a Car Loan** in the **Exploring Excel folder** as shown in Figure 3.3a.

Step 2: Enter the PMT Function and Its Parameters

- Enter **14999** in cell B1 as shown in Figure 3.3b.
- Click in **cell B4.** Enter **=B1−(B2+B3),** which calculates the amount to finance (i.e., the principal of the loan).
- Enter **9%** and **3** in cells B5 and B6 as shown in Figure 3.3b.
- Click in **cell B7.** Enter **=PMT(B5/12,B6*12,−B4)** as the payment function. The arguments in the PMT function are the interest rate per period, the number of periods, and the principal, and correspond to the parameters of the loan.

THE FORMATTING IS IN THE CELL

Once a number format has been assigned to a cell, either by including the format as you entered a number or through execution of a formatting command, the formatting remains in the cell. Thus, to change the contents in a formatted cell, all you need to do is enter the new number without the formatting. Entering 5000, for example, in a cell that was previously formatted as currency will display the number as $5,000.

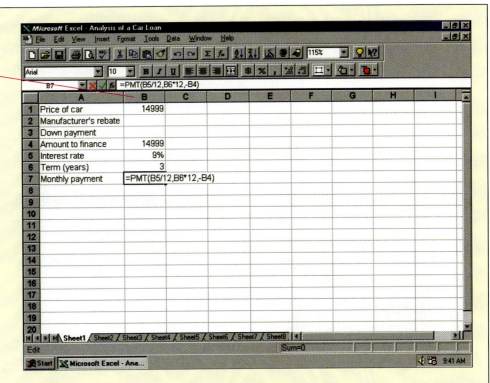

(b) Enter the PMT Function and Its Parameters (step 2)

FIGURE 3.3 Hands-on Exercise 1 (continued)

➤ Click and drag to select cells **B1** through **B4**. Format these cells in **currency format** with no decimals. You should see $476.96 as the displayed value in cell B7.

➤ Save the workbook.

Step 3: What If?

➤ Click in **cell B1** and change the price of the car to **$13,999.** The monthly payment drops to $445.16.

➤ Click in **cell B2** and enter a manufacturer's rebate of **$1,000.** Click in **cell B3** and enter a down payment of **$3,000.** The monthly payment drops to $317.97.

➤ Change the interest rate to **8%** and the term of the loan to **4** years. The payment drops to $244.10.

Step 4: The Goal Seek Command

➤ Click in **cell B7,** the cell containing the formula for the monthly payment. This is the cell whose value we want to set to a fixed amount.

➤ Pull down the **Tools menu.** Click **Goal Seek** to display the dialog box in Figure 3.3c.

➤ Click in the **To value** text box. Type **200** (the desired value of the monthly payment).

➤ Click in the **By changing cell** text box. Type **B1,** the cell containing the price of the car. This is the cell whose value will be determined.

➤ Click **OK.**

SPREADSHEETS IN DECISION MAKING   93

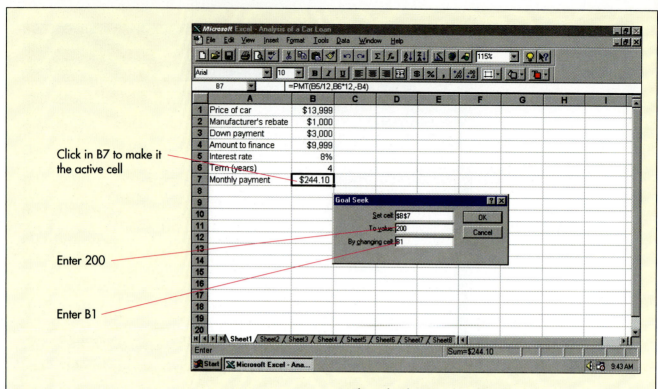

(c) The Goal Seek Command (step 4)

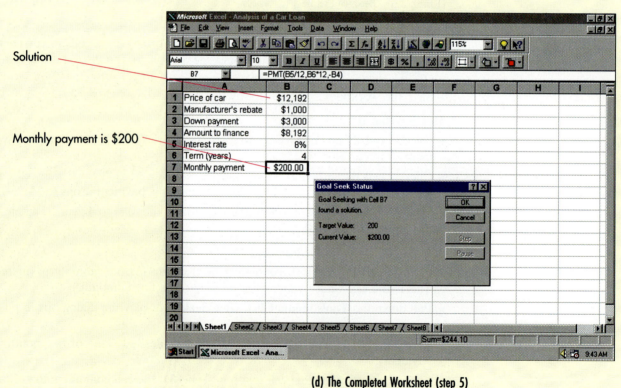

(d) The Completed Worksheet (step 5)

FIGURE 3.3   Hands-on Exercise 1 (continued)

> **Step 5: The Goal Seek Command (continued)**
>
> ➤ The Goal Seek command returns a successful solution as indicated by the dialog box in Figure 3.3d. The worksheet changes to display $12,192 and $200 in cells B1 and B7, respectively, corresponding to the parameters in the Goal Seek command:
>
> - Click **OK** to accept the solution and close the Goal Seek dialog box, *or*
> - Click **Cancel** if you don't like the solution and want to return to the original values.
>
> ➤ Save the workbook. Close the workbook. Exit Excel if you do not want to continue with the next exercise at this time.

HOME MORTGAGES

The PMT function is used in our next example in conjunction with the purchase of a home. The example also reviews the concept of relative and absolute addresses from Chapter 2. In addition, it introduces several other techniques to make you more proficient in Excel.

The spreadsheet in Figure 3.4 illustrates a variable rate mortgage, which will be developed over the next several pages. The user enters the amount he or she wishes to borrow and a starting interest rate, and the spreadsheet displays the associated monthly payment. The spreadsheet enables the user to see the monthly payment at varying interest rates, and to contrast the amount of the payment for a 15- and a 30-year mortgage.

Most first-time buyers opt for the longer term, but they would do well to consider a 15-year mortgage. Note, for example, that the difference in monthly payments for a $100,000 mortgage at 7.5% is only $227.80 (the difference between $927.01 for a 15-year mortgage versus $699.21 for the 30-year mortgage). This is a significant amount of money, but when viewed as a percentage of the total cost of a home (property taxes, maintenance, and so on), it becomes less significant, and it results in significant savings in reducing the amount of interest you will pay over the life of the mortgage.

Figure 3.5 expands the spreadsheet to show the total interest over the life of the loan for both the 15- and the 30-year mortgage. The total interest on a $100,000 loan at 7.5% is $151,717 for a 30-year mortgage, but only $66,862 for a 15-year mortgage. In other words, you will pay back the $100,000 in principal plus another $151,717 in interest if you select the longer term. This is more than twice the interest for the 15-year mortgage.

Difference between a 30-year and a 15-year mortgage at 7.5%

	A	B	C	D
1	Amount Borrowed		$100,000	
2	Starting Interest		7.50%	
3				
4		Monthly Payment		
5	Interest	30 Years	15 Years	Difference
6	7.50%	$699.21	$927.01	$227.80
7	8.50%	$768.91	$984.74	$215.83
8	9.50%	$840.85	$1,044.22	$203.37
9	10.50%	$914.74	$1,105.40	$190.66
10	11.50%	$990.29	$1,168.19	$177.90
11	12.50%	$1,067.26	$1,232.52	$165.26

FIGURE 3.4 Variable Rate Mortgages

Less interest is paid on a 15-year loan ($66,862 vs $151,717 on a 30-year loan)

	A	B	C	D	E
1	Amount Borrowed			$100,000	
2	Starting Interest			7.50%	
3					
4		30 Years		15 Years	
5	Interest	Monthly Payment	Total Interest	Monthly Payment	Total Interest
6	7.50%	$699.21	$151,717	$927.01	$66,862
7	8.50%	$768.91	$176,809	$984.74	$77,253
8	9.50%	$840.85	$202,708	$1,044.22	$87,960
9	10.50%	$914.74	$229,306	$1,105.40	$98,972
10	11.50%	$990.29	$256,505	$1,168.19	$110,274
11	12.50%	$1,067.26	$284,213	$1,232.52	$121,854

(a) Total Interest

	A	B	C	D
1		Amortization Schedule		
2				
3	Principal		$100,000	
4	Annual Interest		7.50%	
5	Term (in years)		30	
6	Monthly Payment		$699.21	
7				
8	Month	Toward Interest	Toward Principal	Balance
9				$100,000.00
10	1	$625.00	$74.21	$99,925.79
11	2	$624.54	$74.68	$99,851.11
12	3	$624.07	$75.15	$99,775.96
13	4	$623.60	$75.61	$99,700.35
14	5	$623.13	$76.09	$99,624.26
15	6	$622.65	$76.56	$99,547.70
...	.	.	.	.
65	56	$594.67	$104.55	$95,042.20
66	57	$594.01	$105.20	$94,937.00
67	58	$593.36	$105.86	$94,831.14
68	59	$592.69	$106.52	$94,724.62
69	60	$592.03	$107.19	$94,617.44

Less than $6,000 of the principal has been paid off

5 years (60 months)

(b) Amortization Schedule

FIGURE 3.5 15- vs 30-Year Mortgage

If, like most people, you move before you pay off the mortgage, you will discover that almost all of the early payments in the 30-year loan go to interest rather than principal. The amortization schedule in Figure 3.5b shows that if you were to move at the end of five years (60 months), less than $6,000 (of the $44,952 you paid during those five years) goes toward the principal. (A 15-year mortgage, however, would pay off almost $22,000 during the same five-year period. The latter number is not shown, but can be displayed by changing the term of the mortgage in cell C5.)

Our objective is not to convince you of the merits of one loan over another, but to show you how useful a worksheet can be in the decision-making process. If you do eventually buy a home, and you select a 15-year mortgage, think of us.

Relative versus Absolute Addresses

Figure 3.6 displays the cell formulas for the mortgage analysis. All of the formulas are based on the amount borrowed and the starting interest, in cells C1 and C2, respectively. You can vary either or both of these parameters, and the worksheet will automatically recalculate the monthly payments.

The similarity in the formulas from one row to the next implies that the copy operation will be essential to the development of the worksheet. You must, however, remember the distinction between a *relative* and an *absolute reference*—that is, a cell reference that changes during a copy operation (relative) versus one that does not (absolute). Consider the PMT function as it appears in cell B6:

=PMT(A6/12,30*12,−$C$1)

— The amount of the loan, −$C$1, is an absolute reference that remains constant

— Number of periods (30 years*12 months/year)

— The interest rate, A6/12, is a relative reference that changes

The entry A6/12 (which is the first argument in the formula in cell B6) is interpreted to mean "divide the contents of the cell one column to the left by 12." Thus, when the PMT function in cell B6 is copied to cell B7, it (the copied formula) is adjusted to maintain this relationship and will contain the entry A7/12. The Copy command does not duplicate a relative address exactly, but adjusts it from row to row (or column to column) to maintain the relative relationship. The cell reference for the amount of the loan should not change when the formula is copied, and hence it is specified as an absolute address.

> ### ISOLATE ASSUMPTIONS
>
> The formulas in a worksheet should be based on cell references rather than specific values—for example, C1 or $C$1 rather than $100,000. The cells containing these values should be clearly labeled and set apart from the rest of the worksheet. You can then vary the inputs (assumptions) to the worksheet and immediately see the effect. The chance for error is also minimized because you are changing the contents of a single cell, rather than changing multiple formulas.

Relative reference (adjusts during copy operation)

Absolute reference (doesn't adjust during copy operation)

	A	B	C	D
1	Amount Borrowed		$100,000	
2	Starting Interest		7.50%	
3				
4		Monthly Payment		
5	Interest	30 Years	15 Years	Difference
6	=C2	=PMT(A6/12,30*12,-$C$1)	=PMT(A6/12,15*12,-$C$1)	=C6-B6
7	=A6+0.01	=PMT(A7/12,30*12,-$C$1)	=PMT(A7/12,15*12,-$C$1)	=C7-B7
8	=A7+0.01	=PMT(A8/12,30*12,-$C$1)	=PMT(A8/12,15*12,-$C$1)	=C8-B8
9	=A8+0.01	=PMT(A9/12,30*12,-$C$1)	=PMT(A9/12,15*12,-$C$1)	=C9-B9
10	=A9+0.01	=PMT(A10/12,30*12,-$C$1)	=PMT(A10/12,15*12,-$C$1)	=C10-B10
11	=A10+0.01	=PMT(A11/12,30*12,-$C$1)	=PMT(A11/12,15*12,-$C$1)	=C11-B11

FIGURE 3.6 Cell Formulas

THE POWER OF EXCEL

You already know enough about Excel to develop the worksheet for the mortgage analysis. Excel is so powerful, however, and offers so many shortcuts, that we would be remiss not to show you alternative techniques. This section introduces the fill handle as a shortcut for copying cells, and pointing as a more accurate way to enter cell formulas. It also presents the Function Wizard, which helps you to enter the arguments in a function correctly.

The Fill Handle

The ***fill handle*** is a tiny black square that appears in the lower-right corner of the selected cells—it is the fastest way to copy a cell (or range of cells) to an *adjacent* cell (or range of cells). The process is quite easy, and you get to practice in the exercise (see Figure 3.8b) that follows shortly. In essence, you:

- Select the cell or cells to be copied.
- Point to the fill handle for the selected cell(s), which changes the mouse pointer to a thin crosshair.
- Click and drag the fill handle over the destination range. A border appears to outline the destination range.
- Release the mouse to complete the copy operation.

Pointing

A cell address is entered into a formula by typing the reference explicitly (as we have done throughout the text) or by pointing. If you type the address, it is all too easy to make a mistake, such as typing A40 when you really mean A41. ***Pointing*** is more accurate, since you use the mouse or arrow keys to select the cell directly as you build the formula. The process is much easier than it sounds, and you get to practice in the hands-on exercise (see Figure 3.8d). In essence, you:

- Select (click) the cell to contain the formula.
- Type an equal sign to begin entering the formula. The status bar indicates that you are in the **Enter mode,** which means that the formula bar is active and the formula can be entered.
- Click the cell you want to reference in the formula (or use the arrow keys to move to the cell). A moving border appears around the cell, and the cell reference is displayed in both the cell and formula bar. The status bar indicates the **Point mode.**
- Type any arithmetic operator to place the cell reference in the formula and return to the Enter mode.
- Continue pointing to additional cells and entering arithmetic operators until you complete the formula. Press the enter key to complete the formula.

As with everything else, the more you practice, the easier it is. The hands-on exercises will give you ample opportunity to practice everything that you have learned.

The Function Wizard

The ***Function Wizard*** helps you to select the appropriate function, then helps you enter the correct arguments for that function. The functions in Excel are grouped into categories, as shown in the open list box in Figure 3.7a. Select the function

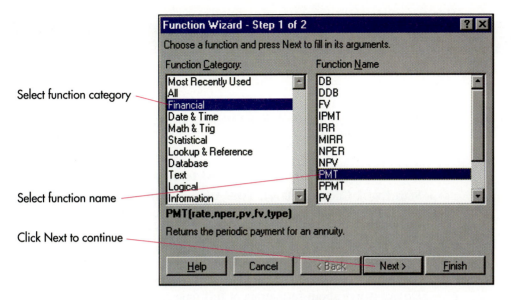

(a) Step 1

(b) Step 2

FIGURE 3.7 The Function Wizard

category you want, then choose the desired function from within that category. Click the Next command button to produce the dialog box in Figure 3.7b, in which you specify the arguments for the function.

The Function Wizard displays a text box for each argument, a description of each argument (as the text box is selected), and an indication of whether or not the argument is required. (Only the first three arguments are required in the PMT function.) Enter the value, cell reference, or formula for each argument by clicking in the text box and typing the entry, or by clicking the appropriate cell(s) in the worksheet.

Excel displays the calculated value for each argument immediately to the right of the argument. It also shows the computed value for the function as a whole at the top of the dialog box. All you need to do is click the Finish button to insert the function into the worksheet. The Function Wizard is illustrated in step 5 of the following exercise.

HANDS-ON EXERCISE 2

Mortgage Analysis

Objective: To develop the worksheet for the mortgage analysis; to use pointing to enter a formula and drag-and-drop to copy a formula. Use Figure 3.8 as a guide in the exercise.

Step 1: Enter the Descriptive Labels and Initial Conditions

➤ Start Excel. Click in **cell A1**. Type **Amount Borrowed.** Do not be concerned that the text is longer than the cell width, as cell B1 is empty and thus the text will be displayed in its entirety. Press the **enter key** or **down arrow** to complete the entry and move to cell A2.

➤ Type **Starting Interest** in cell A2. Click in **cell A4**. Type **Monthly Payment.** Enter the remaining labels in cells A5 through D5 as shown in Figure 3.8a. Do not worry about formatting at this time as all formatting will be done at the end of the exercise.

➤ Click in **cell C1**. Type **$100,000** (include the dollar sign and comma). Press the **enter key** or **down arrow** to complete the entry and move to cell C2. Type **7.5%** (include the percent sign). Press **enter**.

➤ Save the workbook as **Variable Rate Mortgage** in the **Exploring Excel folder**.

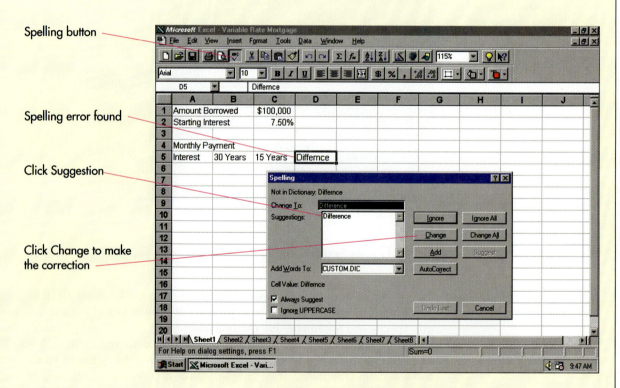

(a) Enter the Descriptive Labels and Spell Check (steps 1 & 2)

FIGURE 3.8 Hands-on Exercise 2

> **RESET THE TIPWIZARD**
>
> The TipWizard will not repeat a suggestion (from an earlier session) unless you reset it at the start of the new session. This is especially important in a laboratory situation where you are sharing a computer with many other students. Pull down the Tools menu, click Options, and click the General tab. Click the check box to Reset TipWizard, then click OK. Click the TipWizard button on the Standard toolbar to open (close) the TipWizard toolbar to view suggestions. You can view the suggestions as they occur, or you can wait until the end of the session to view all of the suggestions at one time.

Step 2: The Spell Check
- Click in **cell A1** to begin the spell check at the beginning of the worksheet.
- Click the **Spelling button** on the Standard toolbar to initiate the spell check as shown in Figure 3.8a. Make corrections, as necessary, just as you would in Microsoft Word.
- Save the workbook.

Step 3: Copy the Column of Interest Rates (the Fill Handle)
- Click in **cell A6.** Type **=C2** to reference the starting interest rate in cell C2.
- Click in **cell A7.** Type the formula **=A6+.01** to compute the interest rate in this cell, which is one percent more than the interest rate in row 6. Press **enter.**
- Click in **cell A7.** Point to the **fill handle** in the lower corner of cell A7. The mouse pointer changes to a thin crosshair.
- Drag the **fill handle** over cells **A8** through **A11.** A border appears, indicating the destination range as in Figure 3.8b. Release the mouse to complete the copy operation. The formula and associated percentage format in cell A7 have been copied to cells A8 through A11.
- Click in **cell C2.** Type **5%.** The entries in cells A6 through A11 change automatically. Click the **Undo button** on the Standard toolbar to return to the 7.5% interest rate.
- Save the workbook.

> **THE EDIT CLEAR COMMAND**
>
> The Edit Clear command erases the contents of a cell and/or its formatting. Select the cell or cells to erase, pull down the Edit menu, click the Clear command, then click All, Formats, Contents, or Notes from the cascaded menu. Pressing the Del key is equivalent to executing the Edit Clear Contents command; that is, it clears the contents of a cell but not the formatting.

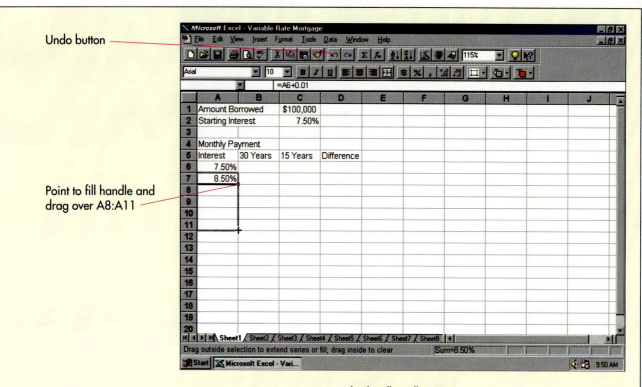

(b) The Fill Handle (step 3)

FIGURE 3.8 Hands-on Exercise 2 (continued)

Step 4: Determine the 30-Year Payments

➤ Click in **cell B6.** Type the formula **=PMT(A6/12,30*12,−$C$1).** Press the **enter key.** Cell B6 should display $699.21.

➤ Click in **cell B6.** Point to the **fill handle** in the bottom-right corner of cell B6. The mouse pointer changes to a thin crosshair. Drag the **fill handle** over cells **B7** through **B11.** A border appears to indicate the destination range. Release the mouse to complete the copy operation.

➤ The PMT function in cell B6 has been copied to cells B7 through B11. The payment amounts are visible in cells B7 through B10, but cell B11 displays a series of pound signs, meaning that the cell (column) is too narrow to display the computed results in the selected format.

> ### THE OPTIMAL (BEST FIT) COLUMN WIDTH
>
> The appearance of pound signs within a cell indicates that the cell width (column width) is insufficient to display the computed results in the selected format. Double click the right border of the column heading to change the column width to accommodate the widest entry in that column. For example, to increase the width of column B, double click the border between the column headings for columns B and C.

➤ Check that cell B11 is still selected. Pull down the **Format menu,** click **Column,** then click **AutoFit Selection** from the cascaded menu. Cell B11 should display $1,067.26.

➤ Save the workbook.

Step 5: The Function Wizard

➤ Click in **cell C6.** Pull down the **Insert menu** and click **Function** (or click the **Function Wizard button** on the Standard toolbar) to display step 1 of the Function Wizard.

➤ Click **Financial** in the Function Category list box. Click **PMT** in the Function Name list box. Click the **Next command button** to display the dialog box in Figure 3.8c.

➤ Click the text box for **rate.** Type **A6/12.** The Function Wizard displays the computed value of .00625.

➤ Click the text box for the number of periods **(nper).** Type **15*12,** corresponding to 15 years and 12 months per year.

➤ Click the text box for the present value **(pv).** Type **−$C$1.** Be sure to include the minus sign in front of the absolute reference.

➤ Check that the computed values on your monitor match those in Figure 3.8c. Make corrections as necessary. Click the **Finish command button** to insert the function into the worksheet. Cell C6 should display $927.01.

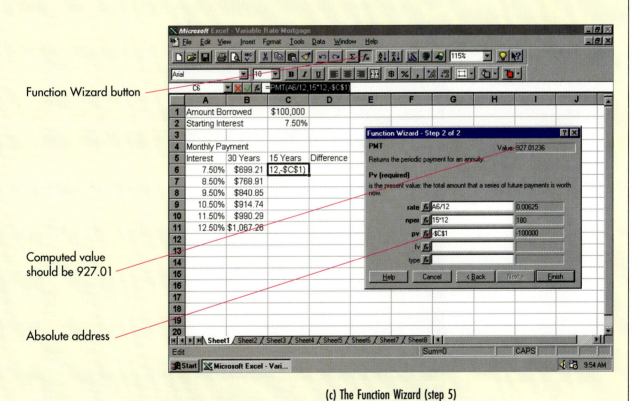

(c) The Function Wizard (step 5)

FIGURE 3.8 Hands-on Exercise 2 (continued)

Step 6: Copy the 15-Year Payments

➤ Check that cell C6 is still selected. Point to the **fill handle** in the lower-right corner of cell C6. The mouse pointer changes to a thin crosshair.

- Drag the **fill handle** to copy the PMT function to cells **C7** through **C11.** Adjust the width of these cells so that you can see the displayed values.
- Cell C11 should display $1,232.52 if you have done this step correctly. Save the workbook.

> ### MORE ABOUT THE FILL HANDLE
>
> Use the fill handle as a shortcut for the Edit Clear command. To clear the contents of a cell, drag the fill handle to the top of the cell (the cell will be shaded in gray) and release the mouse. To clear the contents *and* the format, press and hold the Ctrl key as you drag the fill handle to the top of the cell. You can apply the same technique to a cell range by selecting the range, then dragging the fill handle to the top (or left) of the range.

Step 7: Compute the Monthly Difference (Pointing)

- Click in **cell D6.** Type = to begin the formula. Press the **left arrow key** (or click in **cell C6**), which produces the moving border around the entry in cell C6. The status bar indicates the point mode as shown in Figure 3.8d.
- Press the **minus sign,** then press the **left arrow key** twice (or click in **cell B6**).
- Press **enter** to complete the formula. Cell D6 should display $227.80.

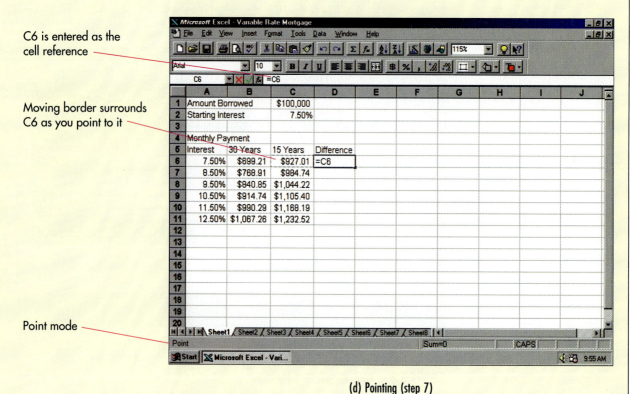

(d) Pointing (step 7)

FIGURE 3.8 Hands-on Exercise 2 (continued)

- Use the **fill handle** to copy the contents of cell D6 to cells **D7** through **D11**. If you have done the step correctly, cell D11 will display $165.26 as shown in Figure 3.8e.
- Save the workbook.

Step 8: The Finishing Touches

- Type **Financial consultant:** in cell A13. Enter **your name** in cell C13.
- Add formatting as necessary, using Figure 3.8e as a guide:
  - Click **cell A4.** Drag the mouse over cells **A4** through **D4.** Click the **Center Across Columns button** on the Formatting toolbar to center the entry in cell A4.
  - Center the column headings in row 5. Add boldface and/or italics to the text and/or numbers as you see fit.
- Save the workbook.

Step 9: Print the Worksheet

- Pull down the **File menu** and click **Print Preview** (or click the **Print Preview button** on the Standard toolbar).
- Click the **Setup command button** to display the Page Setup dialog box.
  - Click the **Margins tab.** Check the box to center the worksheet Horizontally.

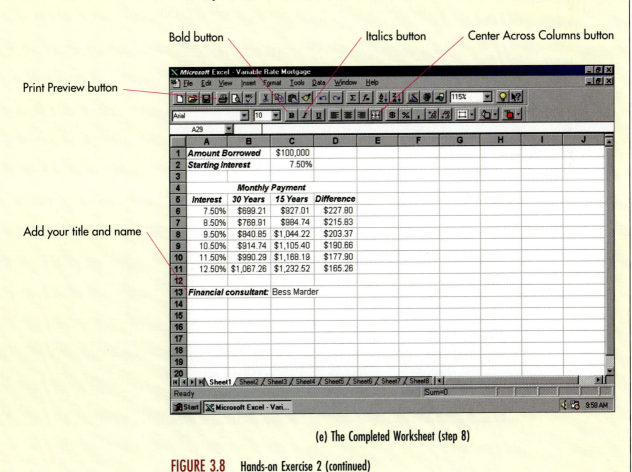

(e) The Completed Worksheet (step 8)

FIGURE 3.8   Hands-on Exercise 2 (continued)

> - Click the **Sheet tab.** Check the boxes to include Row and Column Headings and Gridlines.
> - Click **OK** to exit the Page Setup dialog box.
>
> ➤ Click the **Print command button** to display the Print dialog box, then click **OK** to print the worksheet.
>
> ➤ Press **Ctrl+`** to display the cell formulas. (The left quotation mark is on the same key as the ~.) Widen the cells as necessary to see the complete cell formulas.
>
> ➤ Click the **Print button** on the Standard toolbar to print the cell formulas.
>
> ➤ Close the workbook. Click **No** when asked whether you want to save the changes, or else you will save the workbook with the settings to print the cell formulas rather than the displayed values.
>
> ➤ Exit Excel if you do not want to continue with the next exercise at this time.

THE GRADE BOOK REVISITED

Financial functions are only one of several categories of functions that are included in Excel. Our next example presents an expanded version of the professor's grade book. It introduces several new functions and shows how those functions can aid in the professor's determination of a student's grade. The worksheet shown in Figure 3.9 illustrates several additional features. Consider:

Statistical functions: The AVERAGE, MAX, and MIN functions are used to compute the statistics on each test for the class as a whole. The range on each test is computed by subtracting the minimum value from the maximum value.

	A	B	C	D	E	F	G	H	I	J
1					Professor's Grade Book					
2										
3	Name	Student ID	Test 1	Test 2	Test 3	Test 4	Test Avg	Homework	Semester Avg	Grade
4	Adams, John	011-12-2333	80	71	70	84	77.8	Poor	77.8	C
5	Barber, Maryann	444-55-6666	96	98	97	90	94.2	OK	97.2	A
6	Boone, Dan	777-88-9999	78	81	70	78	77.0	OK	80.0	B
7	Borow, Jeff	123-45-6789	65	65	65	60	63.0	OK	66.0	D
8	Brown, James	999-99-9999	92	95	79	80	85.2	OK	88.2	B
9	Carson, Kit	888-88-8888	90	90	90	70	82.0	OK	85.0	B
10	Coulter, Sara	100-00-0000	60	50	40	79	61.6	OK	64.6	D
11	Fegin, Richard	222-22-2222	75	70	65	95	80.0	OK	83.0	B
12	Ford, Judd	200-00-0000	90	90	80	90	88.0	Poor	88.0	B
13	Glassman, Kris	444-44-4444	82	78	62	77	75.2	OK	78.2	C
14	Goodman, Neil	555-55-5555	92	88	65	78	80.2	OK	83.2	B
15	Milgrom, Marion	666-66-6666	94	92	86	84	88.0	OK	91.0	A
16	Moldof, Adam	300-00-0000	92	78	65	84	80.6	OK	83.6	B
17	Smith, Adam	777-77-7777	60	50	65	80	67.0	Poor	67.0	D
18										
19	Average		81.9	78.3	71.4	80.6	HW Bonus:	3	Grading Criteria	
20	Highest Grade		96	98	97	95			(No Curve)	
21	Lowest Grade		60	50	40	60				F
22	Range		36	48	57	35			60	D
23									70	C
24	Exam Weights		20%	20%	20%	40%			80	B
25									90	A

Statistical functions   IF function   Table Lookup function

FIGURE 3.9 The Expanded Grade Book

IF function: The IF function conditionally adds a homework bonus of three points to the semester average, prior to determining the letter grade. The bonus is awarded to those students whose homework is "OK." Students whose homework is not "OK" do not receive the bonus.

VLOOKUP function: The expanded grade book converts a student's semester average to a letter grade, in accordance with the table shown in the lower-right portion of the worksheet. A student with an average of 60 to 69 will receive a D, 70 to 79 a C, and so on. Any student with an average less than 60 receives an F.

Scenario Manager: The table for grading criteria indicates that grades (in this worksheet) are determined without a curve. The professor also has the capability to enter an alternative set of criteria (scenario) in which he or she assigns grades based on a curve.

Statistical Functions

The **MAX, MIN,** and **AVERAGE** functions return the highest, lowest, and average values, respectively, from an argument list. The list may include individual cell references, ranges, numeric values, functions, or mathematical expressions (formulas). The ***statistical functions*** are illustrated in the worksheet of Figure 3.10.

The first example, =AVERAGE(A1:A3), computes the average for cells A1 through A3 by adding the values in the indicated range (70, 80, and 90), then dividing the result by three, to obtain an average of 80. Additional arguments in the form of values and/or cell addresses can be specified within the parentheses; for example, the function =AVERAGE(A1:A3,200), computes the average of cells A1, A2, and A3, and the number 200.

Cells that are empty or cells that contain text values are *not* included in the computation. Thus, since cell A4 is empty, the function =AVERAGE(A1:A4)

Function	Value
=AVERAGE(A1:A3)	80
=AVERAGE(A1:A3,200)	110
=AVERAGE(A1:A4)	80
=AVERAGE(A1:A3,A5)	80
=MAX(A1:A3)	90
=MAX(A1:A3,200)	200
=MAX(A1:A4)	90
=MAX(A1:A3,A5)	90
=MIN(A1:A3)	70
=MIN(A1:A3,200)	70
=MIN(A1:A4)	70
=MIN(A1:A3,A5)	70
=COUNT(A1:A3)	3
=COUNT(A1:A3,200)	4
=COUNT(A1:A4)	3
=COUNT(A1:A3,A5)	3
=COUNTA(A1:A3)	3
=COUNTA(A1:A3,200)	4
=COUNTA(A1:A4)	3
=COUNTA(A1:A3,A5)	4

Empty and/or text values are not included in the computation

Empty and/or text values are not included in the computation (COUNT)

Empty cells are not included in the computation (COUNTA)

Text values are included in the computation (COUNTA)

	A
1	70
2	80
3	90
4	
5	Study hard

Empty cell — 4
Text value — 5

The spreadsheet

Illustrative functions

FIGURE 3.10   Statistical Functions with a Text Entry

also returns an average of 80 (240/3). In similar fashion, the function =AVERAGE(A1:A3,A5) includes only three values in its computation (cells A1, A2, and A3), because the text entry in cell A5 is excluded. The results of the MIN and MAX functions are obtained in a comparable way, as indicated in Figure 3.10. As with the AVERAGE function, empty cells and text entries are not included in the computation.

The COUNT and COUNTA functions each tally the number of entries in the argument list and are subtly different. The **COUNT function** returns the number of cells containing a numeric entry, including formulas that evaluate to numeric results. The **COUNTA function** includes cells with text as well as numeric values. In Figure 3.10, the functions =COUNT(A1:A3) and =COUNTA(A1:A3) both return a value of 3 as do the two functions =COUNT(A1:A4) and =COUNTA(A1:A4). (Cell A4 is empty and is excluded from the latter computations.) The function =COUNT(A1:A3,A5) also returns a value of 3 because it does not include the text entry in cell A5. However, the function =COUNTA(A1:A3,A5) returns a value of 4 because it includes the text entry in cell A5.

Arithmetic Expressions versus Functions

Many worksheet calculations, such as an average or a sum, can be performed in two ways. You can enter a formula such as =(A1+A2+A3)/3, or you can use the equivalent function =AVERAGE(A1:A3). *The use of functions is generally preferable* as shown in Figure 3.11.

The two worksheets in Figure 3.11a may appear equivalent, but the SUM function is superior to the arithmetic expression. This is true despite the fact that the entries in cell A5 of both worksheets return a value of 100.

Consider what happens if a new row is inserted between existing rows 2 and 3, with the entry in the new cell equal to 25. The **SUM function** adjusts automatically to include the new value (returning a sum of 125) because the SUM function was defined originally for the cell range *A1 through A4*. The new row is inserted within these cells, moving the entry in cell A4 to cell A5, and changing the range to include cell A5.

No such accommodation is made in the arithmetic expression, which was defined to include four *specific* cells rather than a range of cells. The addition of the new row modifies the cell references (since the values in cells A3 and A4 have been moved to cells A4 and A5), and does not include the new row in the adjusted expression.

Similar reasoning holds for deleting a row. Figure 3.11c deletes row two from the *original* worksheets, which moves the entry in cell A4 to cell A3. The SUM function adjusts automatically to =SUM(A1:A3) and returns the value 80. The formula, however, returns an error (to indicate an illegal cell reference) because it is still attempting to add the entries in four cells, one of which no longer exists. In summary, a function expands and contracts to adjust for insertions or deletions, and should be used wherever possible.

#REF!—ILLEGAL CELL REFERENCE

The #REF! error occurs when you refer to a cell that is not valid. The error is displayed whenever Excel is unable to evaluate a formula because of an illegal cell reference. The most common cause of the error is deleting the row, column, or cell that contained the original cell reference.

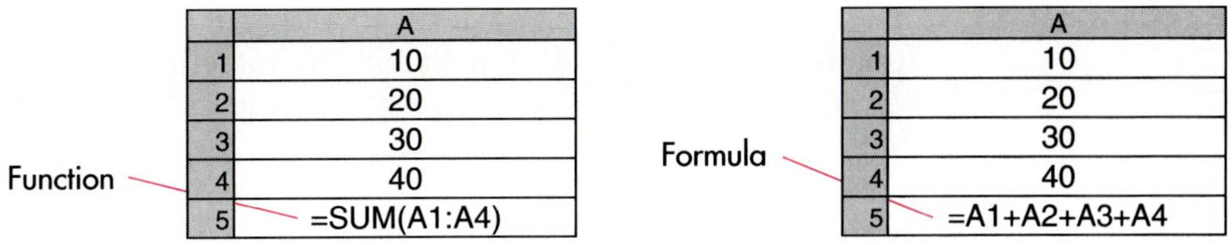

FIGURE 3.11 Arithmetic Expressions vs. Functions

(a) Spreadsheets as Initially Entered

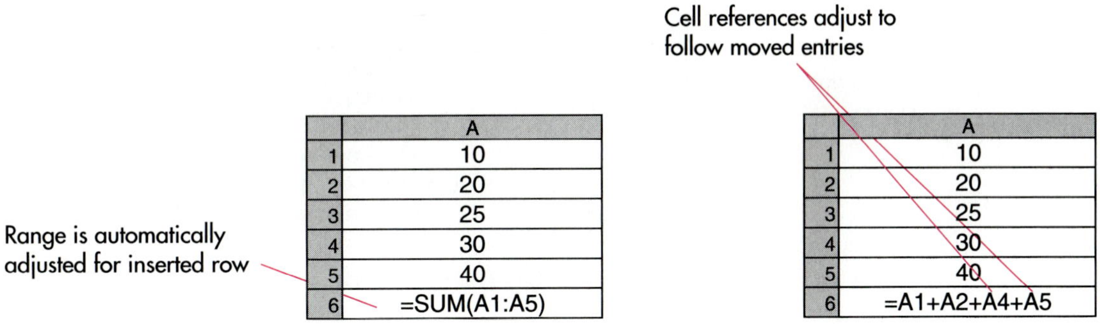

(b) Spreadsheets after the Addition of a New Row

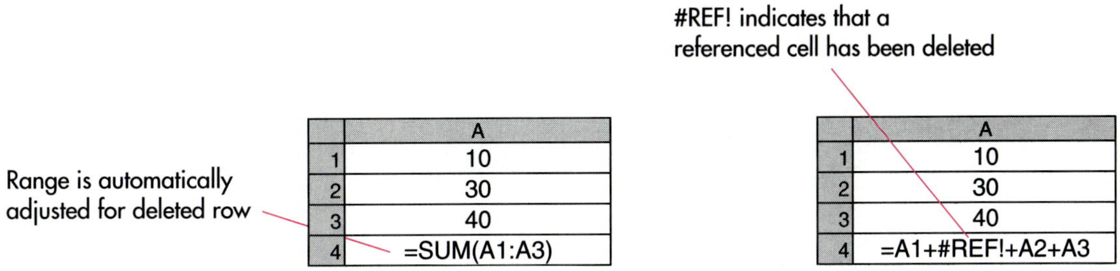

(c) Spreadsheets after the Deletion of a Row

IF Function

The *IF function* enables decision making to be implemented within a worksheet—for example, a conditional bonus for students whose homework is satisfactory. Students with inferior homework do not get this bonus.

The IF function has three arguments: a condition that is evaluated as true or false, the value to be returned if the condition is true, and the value to be returned if the condition is false. Consider:

=IF(condition,value-if-true,value-if-false)

— Value returned for a false condition
— Value returned for a true condition
— Condition is either true or false

The IF function returns either the second or third argument, depending on the result of the condition; that is, if the condition is true, the function returns the second argument, whereas if the condition is false, the function returns the third argument.

The condition uses one of the six ***relational operators*** in Figure 3.12a to perform ***logical tests.*** The IF function is illustrated in the worksheet in Figure 3.12b, which is used to create the examples in Figure 3.12c. In every instance the condition is evaluated, then the second or third argument is returned, depending on whether the condition is true or false. The arguments may be numeric (1000 or 2000), a cell reference to display the contents of the specific cell (B1 or B2), a formula (=B1+10 or =B1−10), a function (MAX(B1:B2) or MIN(B1:B2)), or a text entry enclosed in quotation marks ("Go" or "Hold").

Operator	Description
=	Equal to
<>	Not equal to
<	Less than
>	Greater than
<=	Less than or equal to
>=	Greater than or equal to

(a) Relational Operators

	A	B	C
1	10	15	April
2	10	30	May

(b) The Spreadsheet

IF Function	Evaluation	Result
=IF(A1=A2,1000,2000)	10 is equal to 10: TRUE	1000
=IF(A1<>A2,1000,2000)	10 is not equal to 10: FALSE	2000
=IF(A1<>A2,B1,B2)	10 is not equal to 10:FALSE	30
=IF(A1<B2,MAX(B1:B2),MIN(B1:B2))	10 is less than 30: TRUE	30
=IF(A1<A2,B1+10,B1-10)	10 is less than 10:FALSE	5
=IF(A1=A2,C1,C2)	10 is equal to 10: TRUE	April
=IF(SUM(A1:A2)>20,"Go","Hold")	10+10 is greater than 20:FALSE	Hold

(c) Examples

FIGURE 3.12 The IF Function

The IF function is used in the grade book of Figure 3.9 to award a bonus for homework. Students whose homework is "OK" receive the bonus, whereas other students do not. The IF function to implement this logic for the first student is entered in cell H4 as follows:

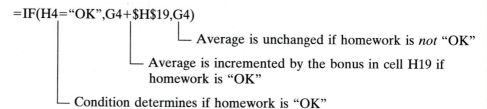

The IF function compares the value in cell H4 (the homework grade) to the literal "OK." If the condition is true (the homework is "OK"), the bonus in cell H19 is added to the student's test average in cell G4. If, however, the condition is false (the homework is not "OK"), the average is unchanged.

The bonus is specified as a cell address rather than a specific value so that the number of bonus points can be easily changed; that is, the professor can make a single change to the worksheet by increasing (decreasing) the bonus in cell H19 and see immediately the effect on every student without having to edit or retype any other formula. An absolute (rather than a relative) reference is used to reference the homework bonus so that when the IF function is copied to the other rows in the column, the address will remain constant. A relative reference, however, was used for the student's homework and semester averages, in cells H4 and G4, because these addresses change from one student to the next.

VLOOKUP Function

Consider, for a moment, how the professor assigns letter grades to students at the end of the semester. He or she computes a test average for each student and conditionally awards the bonus for homework. The professor then determines a letter grade according to a predetermined scale; for example, 90 or above is an A, 80 to 89 is a B, and so on.

The **VLOOKUP** (vertical lookup) *function* duplicates this process within a worksheet, by assigning an entry to a cell based on a numeric value contained in another cell. In other words, just as the professor knows where on the grading scale a student's numerical average will fall, the VLOOKUP function determines where within a specified table (the grading criteria) a numeric value (a student's average) is found, and retrieves the corresponding entry (the letter grade).

The VLOOKUP function requires three arguments: the numeric value to look up, the range of cells containing the table in which the value is to be looked up, and the column-number within the table that contains the result. These concepts are illustrated in Figure 3.13, which was taken from the expanded grade book in Figure 3.9. The table in Figure 3.13 extends over two columns (I and J), and five rows (21 through 25); that is, the table is located in the range I21:J25. The **breakpoints** or matching values (the lowest numeric value for each grade) are contained in column I (the first column in the table) and are in ascending order. The corresponding letter grades are found in column J.

= VLOOKUP(I4,$I$21:$J$25,2)

	A	B	G	H	I	J
1			Professor's Grade Book			
2						
3	Name		Test Avg	Homework	Semester Avg	Grade
4	Adams, John		77.8	Poor	77.8	C
...						
18						
19	Average		HW Bonus:	3	Grading Criteria	
20	Highest Grade				(No Curve)	
21	Lowest Grade					F
22	Range				60	D
23					70	C
24	Exam Weights				80	B
25					90	A

Breakpoints (in ascending order)

Grades are in column 2 of the table

FIGURE 3.13 Table Lookup Function

The VLOOKUP function in cell J4 determines the letter grade (for John Adams) based on the computed average in cell I4. Consider:

=VLOOKUP(I4,$I$21:$J$25,2)

- The column number containing the letter grade
- The range of the table
- Numeric value to look up the student's average

The first argument is the value to look up, which in this example is Adams's computed average, found in cell I4. A relative reference is used so that the address will adjust when the formula is copied to the other rows in the worksheet.

The second argument is the range of the table, found in cells I21 through J25, as explained earlier. Absolute references are specified so that the addresses will not change when the function is copied to determine the letter grades for the other students. The first column in the table (column I in this example) contains the breakpoints, which must be in ascending order.

The third argument indicates the column containing the value to be returned (the letter grades). To determine the letter grade for Adams (whose computed average is 77.8), the VLOOKUP function searches cells I21 through I25 for the largest value less than or equal to 77.8 (the computed average in cell I4). The lookup function finds the number 70 in cell I23. It then retrieves the corresponding letter grade from the second column in that row (cell J23). Adams, with an average of 77.8, is assigned a grade of C.

Scrolling

A large worksheet, such as the extended grade book, can seldom be seen on the monitor in its entirety; that is, only a portion of the worksheet is in view at any given time. The specific rows and columns that are displayed are determined by an operation called *scrolling,* which shows different parts of a worksheet at different times. Scrolling enables you to see any portion of the worksheet at the expense of not seeing another portion. The worksheet in Figure 3.14a, for example, displays column J containing the students' grades, but not columns A and B, which contain the students' names and social security numbers. In similar fashion, you can see rows 21 through 25 that display the grading criteria, but you cannot see the column headings, which identify the data in those columns.

Scrolling comes about automatically as the active cell changes and may take place in both horizontal and vertical directions. Clicking the right arrow on the horizontal scroll bar (or pressing the right arrow key when the active cell is already in the rightmost column of the screen) causes the entire screen to move one column to the right. In similar fashion, clicking the down arrow in the vertical scroll bar (or pressing the down arrow key when the active cell is in the bottom row of the screen) causes the entire screen to move down one row.

Freezing Panes

Scrolling brings distant portions of a large worksheet into view, but it also moves the descriptive headings for existing rows and/or columns off the screen. You can, however, retain these headings by freezing panes as shown in Figure 3.14b. The grades and grading criteria are visible as in the previous figure, but so too are the student names at the left of the worksheet and the column headings at the top.

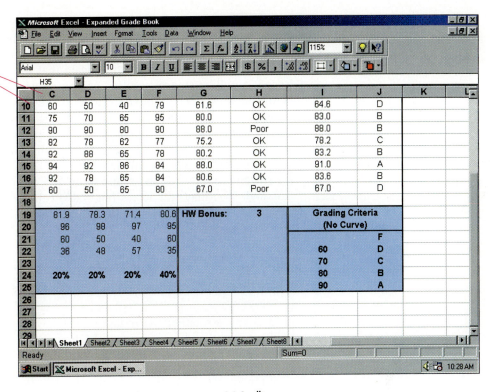

(a) Scrolling

(b) Freezing Panes

FIGURE 3.14 Large Spreadsheets

Look closely at Figure 3.12b and you will see that columns B through D (social security number, test 1, and test 2) are missing, as are rows 4 through 9 (the first six students). You will also notice a horizontal line under row 3, and a vertical line after column A, to indicate that these rows and columns have been frozen. Scrolling still takes place as you move beyond the rightmost column or below the bottom row, but you will always see column A and rows 1, 2, and 3 displayed on the monitor.

The ***Freeze Panes command,*** in the Window menu, displays the desired row or column headings regardless of the scrolling in effect. It is especially helpful when viewing or entering data in a large worksheet. The rows and/or columns that are frozen are the ones above and to the left of the active cell when the command is issued. You may still access (and edit) cells in the frozen area by clicking the desired cell. The ***Unfreeze command,*** also in the Window menu, returns to normal scrolling.

SCROLLING: THE MOUSE VERSUS THE KEYBOARD

You can use either the mouse or the keyboard to scroll within the worksheet, but there is one critical difference. Scrolling with the keyboard also changes the active cell. Scrolling with the mouse does not.

Scenario Manager

The ***Scenario Manager*** enables you to evaluate multiple sets of initial conditions and assumptions (scenarios). Each ***scenario*** represents a different set of what-if conditions that you want to consider in assessing the outcome of a spreadsheet model. You could, for example, look at optimistic, most likely, and pessimistic assumptions in a financial forecast. Our professor will use the Scenario Manager to evaluate his semester grades with and without a curve.

Figure 3.15 illustrates the use of the Scenario Manager in conjunction with the expanded grade book. Each scenario is stored under its own name, such as "Curve" and "No Curve" as shown in Figure 3.15a. Each scenario is comprised of a set of cells whose values vary from scenario to scenario, as well as the values for those cells. Figure 3.15b shows the scenario when no curve is in effect and contains the values for the homework bonus and the breakpoints for the grade distribution table. Figure 3.15c displays a different scenario in which the professor increases the homework bonus and introduces a curve in computing the grades for the class.

Once the individual scenarios have been defined, you can display the worksheet under any scenario by clicking the Show button in the Scenario Manager dialog box. The professor can consider the outcome (the grades assigned to individual students) under the different scenarios and arrive at the best possible decision (the grading criteria to use).

AutoFill

The ***AutoFill capability*** is a wonderful shortcut and the fastest way to enter certain series into adjacent cells. In essence, you enter the first value(s) of a series, then drag the fill handle to the adjacent cells that are to contain the remaining values in that series. Excel creates the series for you based on the initial value(s) you supply. If, for example, you wanted the months of the year to appear in 12 successive cells, you would enter January (or Jan) in the first cell, then drag the

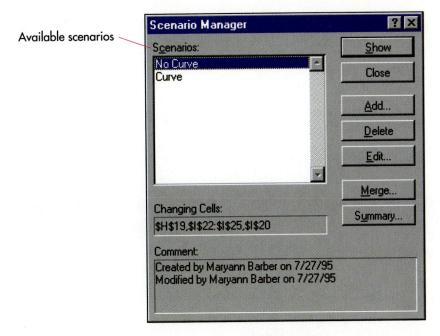

(a) Existing Scenarios

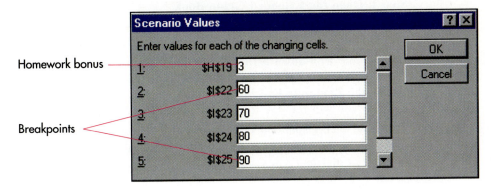

(b) Scenario Values (No Curve)

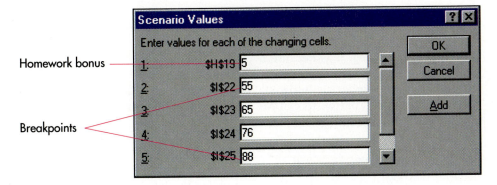

(c) Scenario Values (Curve)

FIGURE 3.15   Scenario Manager

fill handle over the next 11 cells in the direction you want to fill. Excel will enter the remaining months of the year in those cells.

Excel "guesses" at the type of series you want and fills the cells accordingly. You can type Monday (rather than January), and Excel will return the days of the week. You can enter a text and numeric combination, such as Quarter 1 or 1st Quarter, and Excel will extend the series appropriately. You can also create a numeric series by entering the first two numbers in that series; for example, to enter the years 1990 through 1999, type 1990 and 1991 in the first two cells, select both of these cells, and drag the fill handle in the appropriate direction over the destination range.

HANDS-ON EXERCISE 3

The Expanded Grade Book

Objective: To develop the expanded grade book; to use statistical (AVERAGE, MAX, and MIN) and logical (IF and VLOOKUP) functions; to demonstrate scrolling and the Freeze Panes command; to illustrate the AutoFill capability and the Scenario Manager. Use Figure 3.16 as a guide in the exercise.

Step 1: Open the Extended Grade Book

➤ Pull down the **File menu** and click **Open** (or click the **Open button** on the Standard toolbar) to display the Open dialog box.

➤ Click the **drop-down arrow** on the Look In list box. Click the appropriate drive, drive C or drive A, depending on the location of your data. Double click the **Exploring Excel folder** to make it the active folder (the folder from which you will retrieve the workbook).

➤ Double click **Expanded Grade Book** to open the workbook.

➤ Pull down the **File menu** and save the workbook as **Finished Expanded Grade Book** so that you can always return to the original workbook if necessary.

> ### MISSING SCROLL BARS
>
> The horizontal and vertical scroll bars are essential, especially with larger worksheets that cannot be seen in their entirety. If either scroll bar is missing, it is because a previous user elected to hide it. Pull down the Tools menu, click Options, and click the View tab. Click the check boxes to display the horizontal and vertical scroll bars, then click the OK command button to exit the dialog box and return to the worksheet.

Step 2: The AutoFill Capability

➤ Click in **cell C3,** the cell containing the label Test 1. Point to the **fill handle** in the lower-right corner, as shown in Figure 3.16a. The mouse pointer changes to a thin crosshair.

➤ Click and drag the **fill handle** over cells **D3, E3,** and **F3,** then release the mouse. Cells D3, E3, and F3 now contain the labels Test 2, Test 3, and Test 4, respectively.

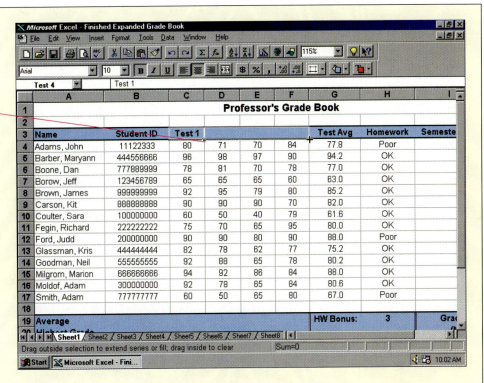

(a) The AutoFill Command (step 2)

FIGURE 3.16 Hands-on Exercise 3

CREATE A CUSTOM SERIES

A custom series is very helpful if you repeatedly enter the same lists of data. Pull down the Tools menu, click Options, then click the Custom Lists tab. Click New List in the Custom Lists box to position the insertion point in the List Entries box. Enter the items in the series (e.g., Tom, Dick, and Harry), using a comma or the enter key to separate one item from the next. Click the Add button. Click OK. The next time you type Tom, Dick, or Harry in a cell and drag the fill handle, you will see the series Tom, Dick, and Harry repeated through the entire range.

Step 3: Format the Social Security Numbers

➤ Click and drag to select cells **B4** through **B17**, the cells containing the unformatted social security numbers.

➤ Point to the selected cells and click the **right mouse button** to display a shortcut menu. Click the **Format Cells command,** click the **Number tab,** then click **Special** in the Category list box.

➤ Click **Social Security Number** in the Type box, then click **OK** to accept the formatting and close the Format Cells dialog box. The social security numbers are displayed with hyphens.

➤ Save the workbook.

Step 4: Scrolling and Freezing Panes

➤ Press **Ctrl+Home** to move to cell A1. Click the **right arrow** on the horizontal scroll bar until column A scrolls off the screen. Cell A1 is still the active cell, as can be seen in the Name box, because scrolling with the mouse does not change the active cell.

➤ Press **Ctrl+Home**. Press the **right arrow key** until column A scrolls off the screen. The active cell changes as you scroll with the keyboard.

➤ Press **Ctrl+Home** to return to cell A1. Click the **down arrow** on the vertical scroll bar (or press the **down arrow key** until row 1 scrolls off the screen). Note whether the active cell changes or not.

➤ Press **Ctrl+Home** again, then click in **cell B4**. Pull down the **Window menu**. Click **Freeze Panes** as shown in Figure 3.16b. You will see a line to the right

---

KEYBOARD SHORTCUTS: MOVING WITHIN A WORKSHEET

Press PgUp or PgDn to scroll an entire screen in the indicated direction. Press Ctrl+Home or Ctrl+End to move to the beginning and end of a worksheet—that is, to cell A1 and to the cell in the lower-right corner, respectively. If these keys do not work, it is because the transition navigation keys (i.e., Lotus 1-2-3 conventions) are in effect. Pull down the Tools menu, click Options, and click the Transition tab. Clear the check in the Transition Navigation Keys check box, then click OK.

Click in B4 to make it the active cell (rows 1–3 and column A will be frozen)

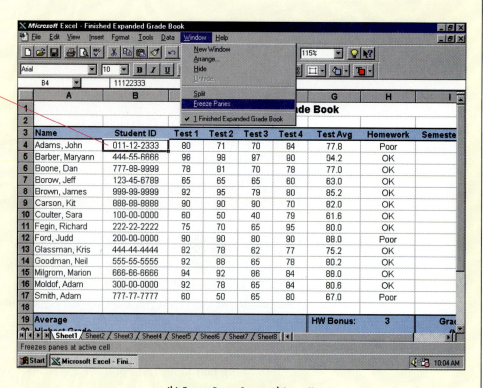

(b) Freeze Panes Command (step 4)

FIGURE 3.16   Hands-on Exercise 3 (continued)

of column A and below row 3; that is, column A and rows 1 through 3 will always be visible regardless of scrolling.

➤ Click the **right arrow** on the horizontal scroll bar (or press the **right arrow key**) repeatedly until column J is visible. Note that column A is visible (frozen), but that one or more columns are not shown.

➤ Click the **down arrow** on the vertical scroll bar (or press the **down arrow key**) repeatedly until row 25 is visible. Note that rows one through three are visible (frozen), but that one or more rows are not shown.

Step 5: The IF Function

➤ Scroll to the top of the worksheet, then scroll until Column I is visible on the screen. Click in **cell I4**.

➤ Click the **Function Wizard button** on the Standard toolbar. Click **Logical** in the Function Category list box. Click **IF** in the Function Name list box, then click the **Next command button** to move to step 2 of the Function Wizard and display the dialog box in Figure 3.16c.

➤ Enter the arguments for the IF function as shown in the figure. You can enter the arguments directly, or you can use pointing as follows:

- Click the **logical_test** text box. Click **cell H4** in the worksheet. (You may need to move the dialog box to access cell H4. Click and drag the title bar of the dialog box to move it out of the way.) Type =**"OK"** to complete the logical test.

- Click the **value_if_true** text box. Click **cell G4** in the worksheet, type a **plus sign,** click **cell H19** in the worksheet (scrolling if necessary), and finally press the **F4 key** (see boxed tip) to convert the reference to cell H19 to an absolute reference ($H$19).

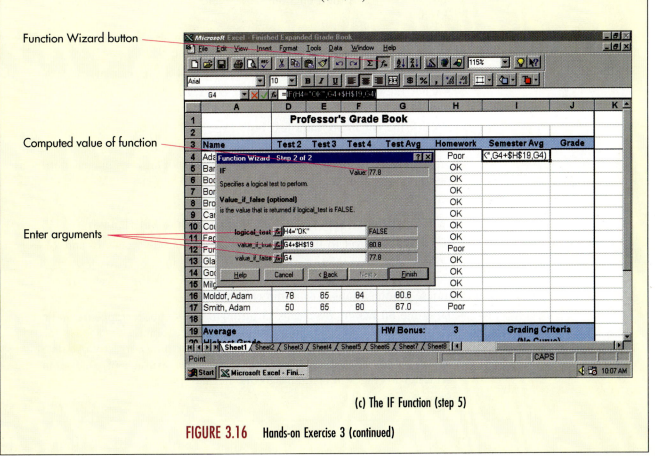

(c) The IF Function (step 5)

FIGURE 3.16   Hands-on Exercise 3 (continued)

- Click the **value_if_false** text box. Click **cell G4** in the worksheet, scrolling if necessary.
➤ Check that the dialog box on your worksheet matches the one in Figure 3.16c. Make corrections as necessary. Click the **Finish command button** to insert the function into your worksheet.
➤ Save the workbook.

> **THE F4 KEY**
>
> The F4 key cycles through relative, absolute, and mixed addresses. Click on any reference within the formula bar; for example, click on A1 in the formula =A1+A2. Press the F4 key once, and it changes to an absolute reference. Press the F4 key a second time, and it becomes a mixed reference, A$1; press it again, and it is a different mixed reference, $A1. Press the F4 key a fourth time, and it returns to the original relative address, A1.

Step 6: The VLOOKUP Function

➤ Click in **cell J4**.
➤ Click the **Function Wizard button** on the Standard toolbar. Click **Lookup & Reference** in the Function Category list box. Scroll in the Function name list box until you can select **VLOOKUP.** Click the **Next command button** to move to step 2 of the Function Wizard and display the dialog box in Figure 3.16d.
➤ Enter the arguments for the VLOOKUP function as shown in the figure. You can enter the arguments directly, or you can use pointing as follows:
- Click the **lookup_value** text box. Click **cell I4** in the worksheet.
- Click the **table_array** text box. Click **cell I21** and drag to cell **J25** (scrolling if necessary). Press the **F4 key** to convert to an absolute reference.
- Click the **col_index_num** text box. Type **2.**
➤ Check that the dialog box on your worksheet matches the one in Figure 3.16d. Make corrections as necessary. Click the **Finish command button** to insert the function into your worksheet.
➤ Save the workbook.

Step 7: Copy the IF and VLOOKUP Functions (the Fill Handle)

➤ If necessary, scroll to the top of the worksheet. Select cells **I4** and **J4** as in Figure 3.16e.
➤ Point to the **fill handle** in the lower-right corner of the selected range. The mouse pointer changes to a thin crosshair.
➤ Drag the **fill handle** over cells **I5** through **J17**. A border appears, indicating the destination range as shown in Figure 3.16e. Release the mouse to complete the copy operation. If you have done everything correctly, Adam Smith should have a grade of D based on a semester average of 67. Format the semester averages in column I to one decimal place.
➤ Save the workbook.

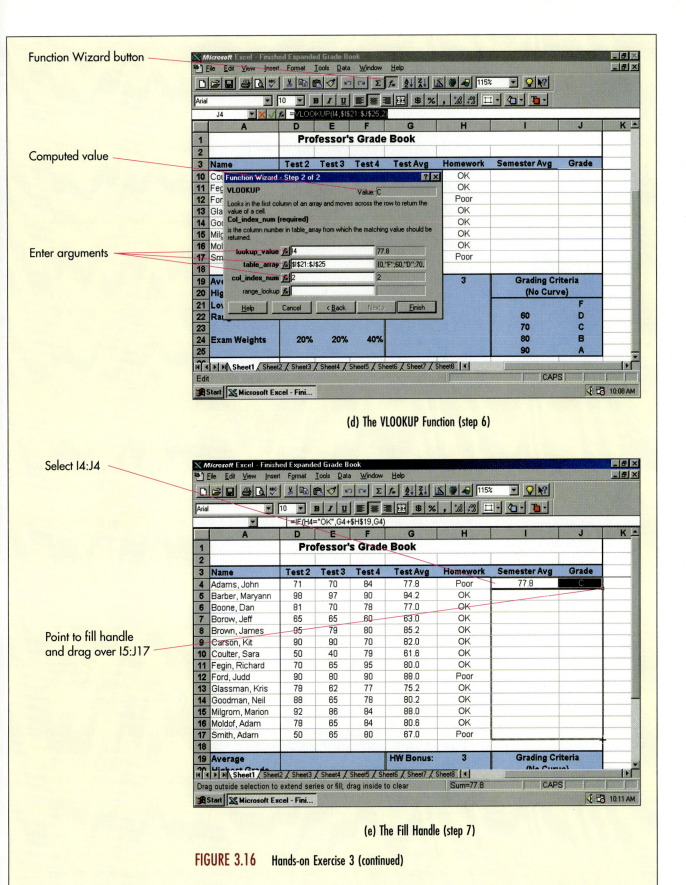

FIGURE 3.16 Hands-on Exercise 3 (continued)

Step 8: Statistical Functions

➤ Click in **cell C19**. Type **=AVERAGE(C4:C17)**. Press **enter**. Cell C19 should display 81.857. Format the average to one decimal place.

➤ Click in **cell C20**. Type **=MAX(C4:C17)**. Press **enter**. Cell C20 should display a value of 96.

➤ Click in **cell C21**. Type **=MIN(C4:C17)**. Press **enter**. Cell C21 should display a value of 60.

➤ Click in **cell C22**. Type **=C20-C21**. Press **enter**. Cell C22 should display 36.

#NAME? AND OTHER ERRORS

Excel displays an error value when it is unable to calculate the formula in a cell. Misspelling a function name (e.g., using AVG instead of AVERAGE) results in #NAME?, which is perplexing at first, but easily corrected once you know the meaning of the error. All error values begin with a pound sign (#). Pull down the Help menu, click Microsoft Excel Help topics, click the Index tab, then enter # for a list of the error values. Click the desired error value, then click the Display button for an explanation.

Step 9: Copy the Statistical Functions (Shortcut Menu)

➤ Select cells **C19** through **C22** as shown in Figure 3.16f. Click the **right mouse button** to display the shortcut menu shown in the figure. Click **Copy**. A moving border appears around the selected cells.

➤ Drag the mouse over cells **D19** through **F19**. Click the **Paste button** on the Standard toolbar to complete the copy operation, then press **Esc** to remove the moving border. If you have done everything correctly, cells F19, F20, F21, and F22 will display 80.6, 95, 60, and 35, respectively.

➤ Save the workbook.

SEE THE WHOLE WORKSHEET

Press Ctrl+Home to move to the beginning of the worksheet. Press the F8 key to enter the extended selection mode (EXT will appear on the status bar), then press Ctrl+End to move to the end of the worksheet and simultaneously select the entire worksheet. Pull down the View menu, click Zoom, then click the Fit Selection option button. Click OK to close the dialog box. The magnification shrinks to display the entire worksheet on the screen; how well you can read the display depends on the size of your monitor and the size of the worksheet.

Step 10: Create the No Curve Scenario

➤ Click in **cell H19**. Pull down the **Tools menu**. Click **Scenarios** to display the Scenario Manager dialog box. Click the **Add command button** to display the Add Scenario dialog box in Figure 3.16g.

Click the right mouse button to display the shortcut menu

Select C19:C22

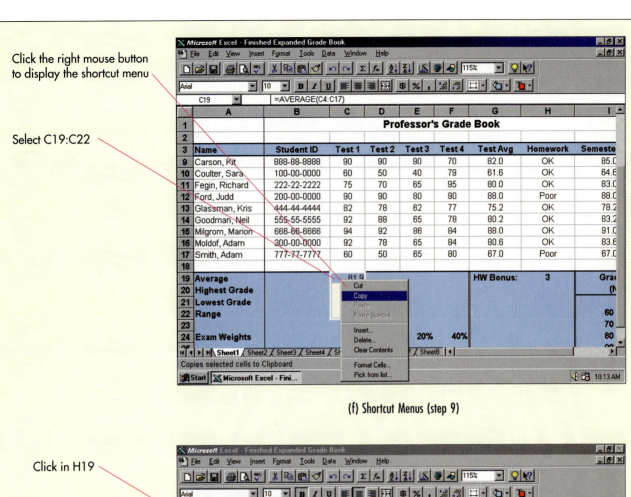

(f) Shortcut Menus (step 9)

Click in H19

Enter No Curve as the scenario name

Enter the changing cells

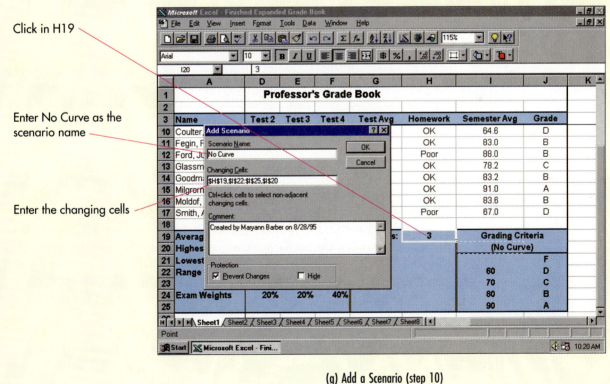

(g) Add a Scenario (step 10)

FIGURE 3.16 Hands-on Exercise 3 (continued)

SPREADSHEETS IN DECISION MAKING

- Type **No Curve** in the Scenario Name text box.
- Click in the **Changing Cells text box** to the right of $H$19. Cell H19 (the active cell) is already entered as the first cell in the scenario. Type a **comma,** then click and drag to select cells **I22** through **I25** (the cells containing the breakpoints for the grade distribution table). Scroll to these cells if necessary.
- Type another **comma,** then click in **cell I20.** The Add Scenarios dialog box should match the display in Figure 3.16g. Click **OK.**
- You should see the Scenario Values dialog box with the values of this scenario (No Curve) already entered. Only the first five cells are displayed, and you must scroll to see the others.
- Click **OK** to complete the No Curve scenario and close the Scenario Values dialog box.

Step 11: Add the Curve Scenario

- The Scenario Manager dialog box should still be open. Click the **Add button** to add a second scenario and display the Add Scenario dialog box.
- Type **Curve** in the Scenario Name text box. The changing cells are already entered and match the changing cells in the No Curve scenario. Click **OK.**
- Enter **5** as the new value for cell H19 (the bonus for homework). Press the **Tab key** to move to the text box for the next cell. Enter 55, 65, 76, and 88 as the values for cells I22 through I25, respectively.
- Enter **(Curve)** as the value for cell I20. Click **OK** to complete the scenario and close the Scenario Values dialog box.

INCLUDE THE SCENARIO NAME

A scenario is composed of one or more changing cells whose values you want to consider in evaluating the outcome of a spreadsheet model. We find it useful to include an additional cell within the scenario that contains the name of the scenario itself, so that the scenario name appears within the worksheet when the worksheet is printed.

Step 12: View the Scenarios

- The Scenario Manager dialog box should still be open as shown in Figure 3.16h. (If necessary, pull down the **Tools menu** and click the **Scenarios command** to reopen the Scenario Manager.) There should be two scenarios listed, No Curve and Curve, corresponding to the scenarios that were just created.
- Select the **Curve** scenario, then click the **Show button** to display the grade book under this scenario. Some, but not all, of the grades will change under the easier criteria. Ford, for example, goes from a B to an A.
- Select the **No Curve** scenario. Click the **Show button** to display the grades under the initial set of assumptions. Click the **Close button** and review the changes. Ford goes from an A back to a B.
- Show the grades under the **Curve** scenario a second time, then click the **Close button** to exit the Scenario Manager.
- Save the workbook.

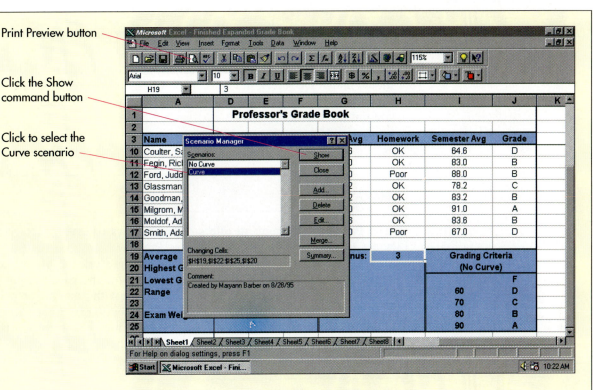

(h) View the Scenarios (step 12)

FIGURE 3.16 Hands-on Exercise 3 (continued)

THE SCENARIO MANAGER LIST BOX

The Scenario Manager List Box enables you to select a scenario directly from a toolbar. Point to any toolbar, click the right mouse button to display a shortcut menu, then click Customize to display the Customize dialog box. Select Utility in the Categories list box, then click and drag the Scenario list box to an empty space on the toolbar. Click Close to close the dialog box and return to the workbook. Click the down arrow on the Scenario list box, which now appears on the toolbar, to choose from the scenarios that have been defined within the current workbook.

Step 13: Print the Worksheet

- Add your name and title (**Grading Assistant**) in cells G26 and G27. Save the workbook.
- Pull down the **File menu.** Click **Page Setup** to display the Page Setup dialog box:
  - Click the **Page tab.** Click the **Landscape option button.** Click the option button to **Fit to 1 page.**
  - Click the **Margins tab.** Check the box to center the worksheet Horizontally on the page.
  - Click the **Header/Footer tab.** Click the **down arrow** on both the Header and Footer list boxes and select **none** for both of these items.

- Click the **Sheet tab.** Check the boxes for **Row and Column Headings** and for **Gridlines.**
➤ Click the **Print Preview button** to display the completed spreadsheet, which should match the screen in Figure 3.16i. Click the **Print command button** and click **OK** to print the workbook. Submit it to your instructor as proof that you did the exercise.
➤ Save the workbook. Exit Excel.

> **MAKE IT FIT**
>
> The Page Setup command offers different ways to make a large worksheet fit on one page. Click the Print Preview button on the Standard toolbar to view the worksheet prior to printing. Click the Margins command button to display (hide) sizing handles for the page margins and column widths, then drag any handle to adjust the margin or column width. You can also click the Setup command button from the Print Preview screen to display the Page Setup dialog box. Use the Page tab to change to landscape printing and/or to select the scaling option to Fit to 1 page.

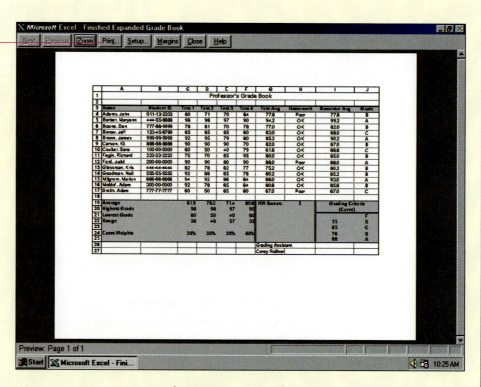

Click the Print command button

(i) The Print Preview Command (step 13)

FIGURE 3.16   Hands-on Exercise 3 (continued)

SUMMARY

Excel contains several different categories of built-in functions. The PMT function computes the periodic payment for a loan based on three arguments (the interest rate per period, the number of periods, and the amount of the loan). The PMT function was used in the analysis of a car loan and in the comparison of 15- and 30-year mortgages.

Statistical functions were also discussed. The AVERAGE, MAX, and MIN functions return the average, highest, and lowest values in the argument list. The COUNT function returns the number of cells with numeric entries. The COUNTA function displays the number of cells with numeric and/or text entries.

The IF and VLOOKUP functions implement decision making within a worksheet. The IF function has three arguments: a logical test, which is evaluated as true or false; a value if the test is true; and a value if the test is false. The VLOOKUP (table lookup) function also has three arguments: the numeric value to look up, the range of cells containing the table, and the column number within the table that contains the result.

The hands-on exercises introduced several techniques to make you more proficient. The fill handle is used to copy a cell or group of cells to a range of adjacent cells. Pointing is a more accurate way to enter a cell reference into a formula as it uses the mouse or arrow keys to select the cell as you build the formula. The Function Wizard helps you choose the appropriate function, then enter the arguments in the proper sequence. The AutoFill capability creates a series based on the initial value(s) you supply.

Scrolling enables you to view any portion of a large worksheet but moves the labels for existing rows and/or columns off the screen. The Freeze Panes command keeps the row and/or column headings on the screen while scrolling in a large worksheet.

A spreadsheet is first and foremost a tool for decision making, and thus Excel includes several commands to aid in that process. The Goal Seek command lets you enter the desired end result of a spreadsheet model (such as the monthly payment on a car loan) and determines the input (the price of the car) to produce that result. The Scenario Manager enables you to specify multiple sets of assumptions (scenarios), and see at a glance the results of any scenario.

KEY WORDS AND CONCEPTS

=AVERAGE	AutoFill capability	Pointing
=COUNT	AutoFit Selection	Relational operator
=COUNTA	Breakpoint	Relative reference
=IF	Custom series	Scenario
=MAX	Edit Clear command	Scenario Manager
=MIN	Enter mode	Scrolling
=PMT	Fill handle	Spell check
=SUM	Freeze Panes command	Statistical functions
=VLOOKUP	Function	Template
Absolute reference	Function Wizard	Unfreeze command
Arguments	Goal Seek command	
Assumptions	Logical test	

Multiple Choice

1. Which of the following options may be used to print a large worksheet?
   (a) Landscape orientation
   (b) Scaling
   (c) Reduced margins
   (d) All of the above

2. If the results of a formula contain more characters than can be displayed according to the present format and cell width,
   (a) The extra characters will be truncated under all circumstances
   (b) All of the characters will be displayed if the cell to the right is empty
   (c) A series of asterisks will be displayed
   (d) A series of pound signs will be displayed

3. Which cell—A1, A2, or A3—will contain the amount of the loan, given the function =PMT(A1,A2,A3)?
   (a) A1
   (b) A2
   (c) A3
   (d) Impossible to determine

4. Which of the following will compute the average of the values in cells D2, D3, and D4?
   (a) The function =AVERAGE(D2:D4)
   (b) The function =AVERAGE(D2,D4)
   (c) Both (a) and (b)
   (d) Neither (a) nor (b)

5. The function =IF(A1>A2,A1+A2,A1*A2) returns
   (a) The product of cells A1 and A2 if cell A1 is greater than A2
   (b) The sum of cells A1 and A2 if cell A1 is less than A2
   (c) Both (a) and (b)
   (d) Neither (a) nor (b)

6. Which of the following is the preferred way to sum the values contained in cells A1 to A4?
   (a) =SUM(A1:A4)
   (b) =A1+A2+A3+A4
   (c) Either (a) or (b) is equally good
   (d) Neither (a) nor (b) is correct

7. Which of the following will return the highest and lowest arguments from a list of arguments?
   (a) HIGH/LOW
   (b) LARGEST/SMALLEST
   (c) MAX/MIN
   (d) All of the above

8. Which of the following is a *required* technique to develop the worksheet for the mortgage analysis?
   (a) Pointing
   (b) Copying with the fill handle
   (c) Both (a) and (b)
   (d) Neither (a) nor (b)

9. Given that cells B6, C6, and D6 contain the numbers 10, 20, and 30, respectively, what value will be returned by the function =IF(B6>10,C6*2,D6*3)?
   (a) 10
   (b) 40
   (c) 60
   (d) 90

10. Which of the following is not an input to the Goal Seek command?
    (a) The cell containing the end result
    (b) The desired value of the end result
    (c) The cell whose value will change to reach the end result
    (d) The value of the input cell that is required to reach the end result

11. Each scenario in the Scenario Manager:
    (a) Is stored in a separate worksheet
    (b) Contains the value of a single assumption or input condition
    (c) Both (a) and (b)
    (d) Neither (a) nor (b)

12. Which function will return the number of nonempty cells in the range A2 through A6, including in the result cells that contain text as well as numeric entries?
    (a) =COUNT(A2:A6)
    (b) =COUNTA(A2:A6)
    (c) =COUNT(A2,A6)
    (d) =COUNTA(A2,A6)

13. What happens if you select a range, then press the right (alternate) mouse button?
    (a) The range will be deselected
    (b) Nothing; that is, the button has no effect
    (c) The Edit and Format menus will be displayed in their entirety
    (d) A shortcut menu with commands from both the Edit and Format menus will be displayed

14. The worksheet displayed in the monitor shows columns A and B, skips columns D, E, and F, then displays columns G, H, I, J, and K. What is the most likely explanation for the missing columns?
    (a) The columns were previously deleted
    (b) The columns are empty and thus are automatically hidden from view
    (c) Either (a) or (b) is a satisfactory explanation
    (d) Neither (a) nor (b) is a likely reason

15. Given the function =VLOOKUP(C6,D12:F18,3)
    (a) The entries in cells D12 through D18 are in ascending order
    (b) The entries in cells D12 through D18 are in descending order
    (c) The entries in cells F12 through F18 are in ascending order
    (d) The entries in cells F12 through F18 are in descending order

ANSWERS

1. d	6. a	11. d
2. d	7. c	12. b
3. c	8. d	13. d
4. a	9. d	14. d
5. d	10. d	15. a

EXPLORING EXCEL 7.0

1. Use Figure 3.17 to match each action with its result; a given action may be used more than once or not at all.

    Action
    a. Click at 10, type =AVERAGE(, then click at 6, drag to 8, and press enter
    b. Click at 7, then click at 16
    c. Click at 12
    d. Click at 13
    e. Click at 14
    f. Click in the lower-right corner of 9, then drag to 11
    g. Click at 10, drag to 4, then click at 18
    h. Click at 19, click at 17
    i. Click at 7, drag to 5, click at 15
    j. Click at 1, type =, click at 3, type −, click at 2, then press enter

    Result
    _____ Freeze column A and rows 1, 2, and 3 on the screen for scrolling
    _____ Use the AutoFill feature to enter the column titles for Test 2, Test 3, and Test 4
    _____ Increase the number of decimal places for the test averages
    _____ Use the Function Wizard to enter the IF function for the semester averages in column I
    _____ Preview the worksheet prior to printing
    _____ Save the workbook
    _____ Enter the formula to compute the range for the scores on Test 1
    _____ Format the social security number with hyphens
    _____ Enter the function to compute the test average for John Adams
    _____ Spell check the worksheet

2. Consider the two worksheets shown in Figure 3.18 and the entries, =AVERAGE(A1:A4) versus =(A1+A2+A3+A4)/4, both of which calculate the average of cells A1 through A4. Assume that a new row is inserted in the worksheet between existing rows 2 and 3, with the entry in the new cell equal to 100.
    a. What value will be returned by the AVERAGE function in worksheet 1 after the new row has been inserted?
    b. What value will be returned by the formula in worksheet 2 after the new row has been inserted?
    c. In which cell will the AVERAGE function itself be located after the new row has been inserted?

    Return to the original problem, but this time delete row 2.

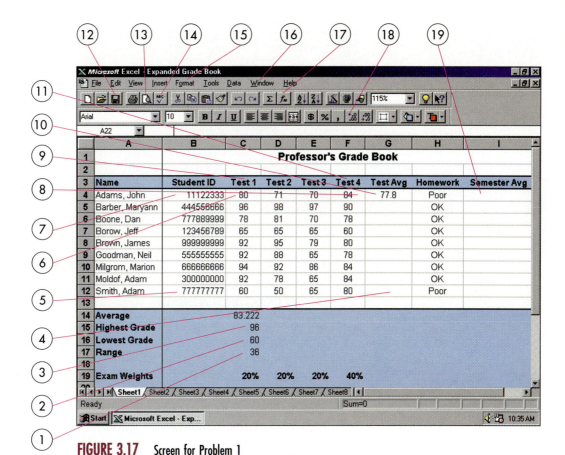

FIGURE 3.17 Screen for Problem 1

d. What value will be returned by the AVERAGE function in worksheet 1 after the row has been deleted?
e. What will be returned by the formula in worksheet 2 after the row has been deleted?

	A
1	10
2	20
3	30
4	40
5	=AVERAGE(A1:A4)

(a) Worksheet 1

	A
1	10
2	20
3	30
4	40
5	=(A1+A2+A3+A4)/4

(b) Worksheet 2

FIGURE 3.18 Spreadsheets for Problem 2

3. Answer the following with respect to Figure 3.19. (Cell B5 is empty.) What value will be returned by the worksheet functions?
   a. =IF(A1=0,A2,A3)
   b. =SUM(A1:A5)
   c. =MAX(A1:A5,B1:B5)
   d. =MIN(A1:A3,5,A5)
   e. =AVERAGE(B1:B4)
   f. =AVERAGE(B1:B5)

	A	B
1	10	60
2	20	70
3	30	80
4	40	90
5	50	

FIGURE 3.19 Spreadsheet for Problem 3

g. =MIN(10,MAX(A2:A4))
h. =MAX(10,MIN(A2:A4))
i. =COUNTA(A1:A5)
j. =COUNTA(B1:B5)
k. =COUNT(A1:A5)
l. =COUNT(B1:B5)
m. =VLOOKUP(15,A1:B5,2)
n. =VLOOKUP(20,A1:B5,2)

4. The spreadsheet in Figure 3.20 illustrates the use of the PMT function to compute the amortization schedule on a loan. The mortgagee is trying to pay off the note in less time than the indicated 15 years, and so he pays an additional amount every month toward the principal.

   a. What formula should be entered in cell C6 to compute the monthly payment?
   b. What formula should be entered in cell B10? (The amount of each payment that goes toward interest is the interest rate per period times the unpaid balance of the loan.)

	A	B	C	D	E
1			Amortization Schedule		
2					
3	Principal		$100,000		
4	Annual Interest		7.50%		
5	Term (in years)		15		
	Extra principal		$100		
6	Monthly Payment		$927.01		
7					
8	Month	Toward Interest	Toward Principal	Extra Payment	Balance
9					$100,000.00
10	1	$625.00	$302.01	$100.00	$99,597.99
11	2	$622.49	$304.52	$100.00	$99,193.46
12	3	$619.96	$307.05	$100.00	$98,786.41
13	4	$617.42	$309.60	$100.00	$98,376.81
14	5	$614.86	$312.16	$100.00	$97,964.65
15	6	$612.28	$314.73	$100.00	$97,549.92
	.	.	.	.	.
65	56	$460.69	$466.32	$100.00	$73,144.11
66	57	$457.15	$469.86	$100.00	$72,574.25
67	58	$453.59	$473.42	$100.00	$72,000.83
68	59	$450.01	$477.01	$100.00	$71,423.82
69	60	$446.40	$480.61	$100.00	$70,843.21

FIGURE 3.20 Spreadsheet for Problem 4

c. What formula should be entered in cell C10? (The amount of each payment that goes toward principal is the monthly payment minus the amount that goes toward interest.)

d. What formula should be entered in cell E10 to compute the new balance?

e. The mortgagee wants to pay off the loan even faster and has as his goal a balance of $50,000 at the end of five years. Explain how to use the Goal Seek command to determine the amount of extra principal needed each month (beginning in the first month) to reach the stated goal.

PRACTICE WITH EXCEL 7.0

1. **Startup Airlines:** The partially completed spreadsheet in Figure 3.21 is used by a new airline to calculate the fuel requirements and associated cost for its available flights. The airline has only two types of planes, B27s and DC-9s. The fuel needed for any given flight depends on the aircraft and number of flying hours; for example, a five-hour flight in a DC-9 can be expected to use 40,000 gallons. In addition, the plane must carry an additional 10% of the required fuel to maintain a holding pattern (4,000 gallons in this example) and an additional 20% as reserve (8,000 gallons in this example).

   Retrieve the partially completed *Chapter 3 Practice 1* from the data disk and save it as *Finished Chapter 3 Practice 1*. Compute the fuel necessary for the listed flights based on a fuel price of $1.00 per gallon. Your worksheet should be completely flexible and amenable to change; that is, the hourly fuel requirements, price per gallon, holding and reserve percentages are all subject to change at a moment's notice.

   After completing the cell formulas, format the spreadsheet as you see fit. Add your name somewhere in the worksheet, then print the completed worksheet and cell formulas, and submit the assignment to your instructor.

	A	B	C	D	E	F	G	H
1	Fuel Estimates							
2								
3	Plane	Flight	Flying Hours	Flying Fuel	Reserve Fuel	Holding Fuel	Total Fuel Needed	Estimated Fuel Cost
4	Boeing-727	MIA-JFK	2.75					
5	DC-9	MIA-ATL	1.25					
6	Boeing-727	MIA-IAH	2.25					
7	Boeing-727	MIA-LAX	5.5					
8	DC-9	MIA-MSY	1.5					
9		Totals						
10								
11	Fuel Facts:							
12	Gallons per hour: Boeing-727				10000			
13	Gallons per hour: DC-9				8000			
14	Fuel cost per gallon				1			
15								
16	% of Flying Fuel required for:							
17	Reserve Fuel				0.2			
18	Holding Fuel				0.1			

FIGURE 3.21 Spreadsheet for Practice Exercise 1

2. A partially completed version of the worksheet in Figure 3.22 can be found on the data disk as *Chapter 3 Practice 2*. Retrieve the workbook from the data disk and complete it so that it is identical to the worksheet in Figure 3.22. In completing the spreadsheet you need to understand the discount policy, which states that a discount is given if the total sale is equal to or greater than the discount threshold. (The amount of the discount is equal to the total sale multiplied by the discount percentage, which is contained in the assumption area at the bottom of the worksheet.) If the total sale is less than the discount threshold, no discount is given.

Complete the worksheet in Figure 3.22, then create two additional scenarios for different selling strategies. In one scenario lower the discount threshold and discount percentage to $3000 and 12%, respectively. Increase these values in a second scenario to $10,000 and 20%. Add your name somewhere in the worksheet, then print all three scenarios (the two you created plus the original set of numbers) and submit the completed assignment.

	A	B	C	D	E	F	G	H	I
1		Hot Spot Software Distributors							
2		Miami, Florida							
3									
4	Customer Name	Program	Current Price	Units Sold	Total Sale	Amount of Discount	Discounted Total	Sales Tax	Amount Due
5	AAA Software Sales	Windows 95	$62.99	23	$1,448.77	$0.00	$1,448.77	$94.17	$1,542.94
6	CompuSoft, Inc.	Microsoft Office 95	$335.99	45	$15,119.55	$2,267.93	$12,851.62	$835.36	$13,686.97
7	Kings Bay Software	Adobe Photoshop	$398.99	10	$3,989.90	$0.00	$3,989.90	$259.34	$4,249.24
8	MicroSales, Inc	Corel Draw	$300.99	30	$9,029.70	$1,354.46	$7,675.25	$498.89	$8,174.14
9	PC and Me Software	Microsoft Office 95	$335.99	17	$5,711.83	$0.00	$5,711.83	$371.27	$6,083.10
10	Personal Software Sales	Corel Draw	$300.99	25	$7,524.75	$1,128.71	$6,396.04	$415.74	$6,811.78
11	Service Software	Adobe Photoshop	$398.99	35	$13,964.65	$2,094.70	$11,869.95	$771.55	$12,641.50
12	Software and More	Windows 95	$62.99	25	$1,574.75	$0.00	$1,574.75	$102.36	$1,677.11
13	Software To Go	Windows 95	$62.99	35	$2,204.65	$0.00	$2,204.65	$143.30	$2,347.95
14	Unique Software Sales	Microsoft Office 95	$335.99	50	$16,799.50	$2,519.93	$14,279.58	$928.17	$15,207.75
15									
16	Discount Threshold	$6,000.00					Number of customers		10
17	Discount Percentage	15.0%					Highest current price		$398.99
18	Sales Tax	6.5%					Fewest units sold		10
19							Average Discount		$936.57
20							Total Amount Due		$72,422.48

FIGURE 3.22 Spreadsheet for Practice Exercise 2

3. Object Linking and Embedding: Figure 3.23 extends the analysis of a car loan to include monthly expenditures for gas, insurance, and maintenance. It also includes an IF function in cell B13 that compares the total monthly cost to $500 (the maximum you can afford), and prints "Yes" or "No" depending on the answer. And finally, it uses the Insert Object command to insert a picture of the car from the Microsoft ClipArt Gallery.

Enter parameters for the car of your dreams, together with realistic terms for a car loan in today's economy. Add your name somewhere in the worksheet, insert a clip art object, then print the completed worksheet and submit it to your instructor.

4. Scenario Summary: The report in Figure 3.24 illustrates the summary capability within Scenario Manager and is based on the completed financial forecast from Chapter 2. Return to the Finished Financial Forecast that you created in the third hands-on exercise, then add the Optimistic and Pessimistic scenarios as shown in Figure 3.24.

The changing cells in both scenarios are cells B18 and B19, which contain the first-year sales and selling price, and cells D18 and D19 containing the projected increase in these values. [Note, however, that the summary

	A	B
1	Price of car	$13,999
2	Manufacturer's rebate	$1,000
3	Down payment	$3,000
4	Amount to finance	$9,999
5	Interest rate	8%
6	Term (in years)	4
7	Monthly payment	$244.10
8	Insurance	$100.00
9	Gas	$75.00
10	Maintenance	$50.00
11	Total	$469.10
12		
13	Can I afford it?	Yes

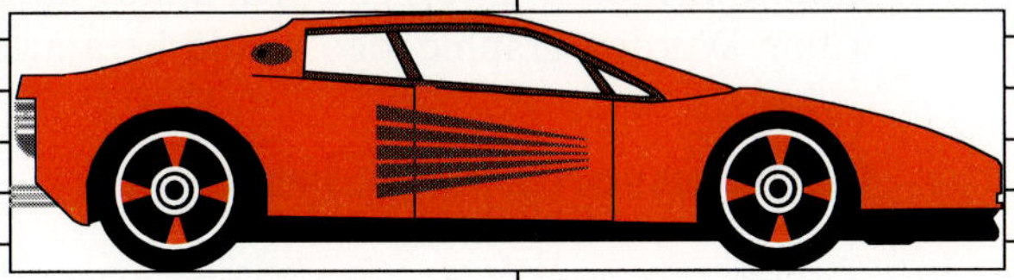

FIGURE 3.23 Spreadsheet for Practice Exercise 3

table uses descriptive names rather than cell references (e.g., FirstYearSales instead of cell B18) because the Insert Name command was used to assign a descriptive name to the associated cell reference. This should be done prior to using the Scenario Manager. (Use online help to learn how to name a formula or reference.)]

The Scenario Summary is created by clicking the Summary command button within Scenario Manager, then choosing the Scenario Summary option button from the available report types. To create the summary, you will need to specify the result cells (cells B15 through F15 in the financial forecast) whose values will be displayed in the summary table shown in the figure.

Create one additional scenario (with any values you like) that identifies you by name, then print the scenario summary and submit it to your instructor.

Scenario Summary			
	Current Values:	Optimistic	Pessimistic
Changing Cells:			
FirstYearSales	$100,000	$150,000	$75,000
SellingPrice	$3.00	$4.50	$2.50
SalesIncrease	10%	15%	8%
PriceIncrease	5%	8%	5%
Result Cells:			
EarningsYear1	$75,000	$375,000	$0
EarningsYear2	$84,750	$473,475	-$1,275
EarningsYear3	$94,710	$595,298	-$3,542
EarningsYear4	$104,579	$745,818	-$7,126
EarningsYear5	$113,936	$931,591	-$12,434

Notes: Current Values column represents values of changing cells at time Scenario Summary Report was created. Changing cells for each scenario are highlighted in gray.

FIGURE 3.24 Spreadsheet for Practice Exercise 4

Case Studies

The Financial Consultant

A friend of yours is in the process of buying a home and has asked you to compare the payments and total interest on a 15- and a 30-year loan. You want to do as professional a job as possible and have decided to analyze the loans in Excel, then incorporate the results into a memo written in Microsoft Word. As of now, the principal is $150,000, but it is very likely that your friend will change his mind several times, and so you want to use the OLE capability within Windows to dynamically link the worksheet to the word processing document. Your memo should include a letterhead that takes advantage of the formatting capabilities within Word; a graphic logo would be a nice touch.

Compensation Analysis

A corporation typically uses several different measures of compensation in an effort to pay its employees fairly. Most organizations closely monitor an employee's salary history, keeping both the present and previous salary in order to compute various statistics, including:

- The percent salary increase, which is computed by taking the difference between the present and previous salary, and dividing by the previous salary.
- The months between increase, which is the elapsed time between the date the present salary took effect and the date of the previous salary. (Assume 30 days per month for ease of calculation.)
- The annualized rate of increase, which is the percent salary increase divided by the months between increase; for example, a 5% raise after 6 months is equivalent to an annualized increase of 10%; a 5% raise after two years is equivalent to an annual increase of 2.5%.

Use the data in the *Compensation Analysis* workbook on the data disk to compute salary statistics for the employees who have had a salary increase; employees who have not received an increase should have a suitable indication in the cell. Compute the average, minimum, and maximum value for each measure of compensation for those employees who have received an increase.

The Automobile Dealership

The purchase of a car usually entails extensive bargaining between the dealer and the consumer. The dealer has an asking price but typically settles for less. The commission paid to a salesperson depends on how close the selling price is to the asking price. Exotic Motors has the following compensation policy for its sales staff:

- A 3% commission on the actual selling price for cars sold at 95% or more of the asking price.
- A 2% commission on the actual selling price for cars sold at 90% or more (but less than 95%) of the asking price
- A 1% commission on the actual selling price for cars sold at less than 90% of the asking price. The dealer will not go below 85% of his asking price.

The dealer's asking price is based on the dealer's cost plus a 20% markup; for example, the asking price on a car that cost the dealer $20,000 would be $24,000. Develop a worksheet to be used by the dealer that shows his profit (the selling price minus the cost of the car minus the salesperson's commission) on every sale. The worksheet should be completely flexible and allow the dealer to vary the markup or commission percentages without having to edit or recopy any of the formulas. Use the data in the *Exotic Motors* workbook to test your worksheet.

The Lottery

Many states raise money through lotteries that advertise prizes of several million dollars. In reality, however, the actual value of the prize is considerably less than the advertised value, although the winners almost certainly do not care. One state, for example, recently offered a twenty million dollar prize that was to be distributed in twenty annual payments of one million dollars each. How much was the prize actually worth, assuming a long-term interest rate of seven percent? What is the value of the prize if the interest rate decreases to six percent? If it increases to eight percent?

GRAPHS AND CHARTS: DELIVERING A MESSAGE

OBJECTIVES

After reading this chapter you will be able to:

1. Distinguish between the different types of charts, stating the advantages and disadvantages of each.
2. Distinguish between a chart embedded in a worksheet and one in a separate chart sheet; explain how many charts can be associated with the same worksheet.
3. Use the ChartWizard to create and/or modify a chart.
4. Enhance a chart by using arrows and text.
5. Differentiate between data series specified in rows and data series specified in columns.
6. Describe how a chart can be statistically accurate yet totally misleading.
7. Create a compound document consisting of a word processing memo, a worksheet, and a chart.

OVERVIEW

Business has always known that the graphic representation of data is an attractive, easy-to-understand way to convey information. Indeed, business graphics has become one of the most exciting Windows applications, whereby charts (graphs) are easily created from a worksheet, with just a few simple keystrokes or mouse clicks.

The chapter begins by emphasizing the importance of determining the message to be conveyed by a chart. It describes the different types of charts available within Excel and how to choose among them. It explains how to create a chart by using the ChartWizard, how to embed a chart within a worksheet, and how to create a chart in a separate chart sheet. It also describes how to enhance a chart with arrows and additional text.

The second half of the chapter explains how one chart can plot multiple sets of data, and how several charts can be based on the same worksheet. It also describes how to create a compound document, in which a chart and its associated worksheet are dynamically linked to a memo created by a word processor. All told, we think you will find this to be one of the most enjoyable chapters in the text.

CHART TYPES

A *chart* is a graphic representation of data in a worksheet. The chart is based on descriptive entries called *category labels,* and on numeric values called *data points*. The data points are grouped into one or more *data series* that appear in row(s) or column(s) on the worksheet. In every chart there is exactly one data point, in each data series, for each value of the category label.

The worksheet in Figure 4.1 will be used throughout the chapter as the basis for the charts we will create. Your manager believes that the sales data can be understood more easily from charts than from the strict numerical presentation of a worksheet. You have been given the assignment of analyzing the data in the worksheet and are developing a series of charts to convey that information.

	A	B	C	D	E	F
1		Superior Software Sales				
2						
3		*Miami*	*Denver*	*New York*	*Boston*	*Total*
4	**Word Processing**	$50,000	$67,500	$9,500	$141,000	$268,000
5	**Spreadsheets**	$44,000	$18,000	$11,500	$105,000	$178,500
6	**Database**	$12,000	$7,500	$6,000	$30,000	$55,500
7	**Total**	$106,000	$93,000	$27,000	$276,000	$502,000

FIGURE 4.1 Superior Software

The sales data in the worksheet can be presented several ways—for example, by city, by product, or by a combination of the two. Ask yourself which type of chart is best suited to answer the following questions:

- What percentage of total revenue comes from each city? from each product?
- What is the dollar revenue produced by each city? by each product?
- What is the rank of each city with respect to sales?
- How much revenue does each product contribute in each city?

In every instance realize that a chart exists only to deliver a message, and that you cannot create an effective chart unless you are sure of what that message is. The next several pages discuss the different types of business charts, each of which is best suited to a particular type of message.

KEEP IT SIMPLE

Keep it simple. This rule applies to both your message and the means of conveying that message. Excel makes it almost too easy to change fonts, styles, type sizes, and colors, but such changes will often detract from, rather than enhance, a chart. More is not necessarily better, and you do not have to use the features just because they are there. Remember that a chart must ultimately succeed on the basis of content, and content alone.

Pie Charts

A *pie chart* is the most effective way to display proportional relationships. It is the type of chart to select whenever words like *percentage* or *market share* appear in the message to be delivered. The pie, or complete circle, denotes the total amount. Each slice of the pie corresponds to its respective percentage of the total.

The pie chart in Figure 4.2a divides the pie representing total sales into four slices, one for each city. The size of each slice is proportional to the percentage of total sales in that city. The chart depicts a single data series, which appears in cells B7 through E7 on the associated worksheet. The data series has four data points corresponding to the total sales in each city.

To create the pie chart, Excel computes the total sales ($502,000 in our example), calculates the percentage contributed by each city, and draws each slice of the pie in proportion to its computed percentage. Boston's sales of $276,000 account for 55 percent of the total, and so this slice of the pie is allotted 55 percent of the area of the circle.

An *exploded pie chart,* as shown in Figure 4.2b, separates one or more slices of the pie for emphasis. Another way to achieve emphasis in a chart is to choose a title that reflects the message you are trying to deliver. The title in Figure 4.2a, for example, *Revenue by Geographic Area*, is neutral and leaves the reader to develop his or her own conclusion about the relative contribution of each area. By contrast, the title in Figure 4.2b, *New York Accounts for Only 5% of Revenue,* is more suggestive and emphasizes the problems in this office. Alternatively, the title could be changed to *Boston Exceeds 50% of Total Revenue* if the intent were to emphasize the contribution of Boston.

Three-dimensional pie charts may be created in exploded or nonexploded format as shown in Figures 4.2c and 4.2d, respectively. Excel also enables you to add arrows and text for emphasis.

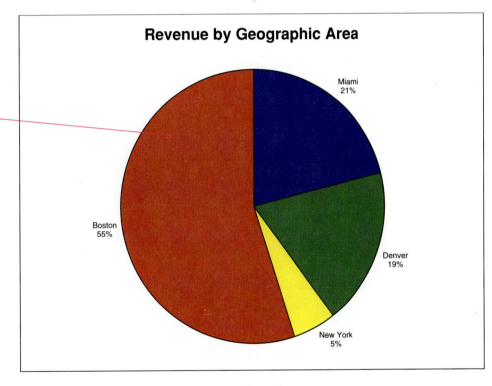

(a) Simple Pie Chart

FIGURE 4.2   Pie Charts

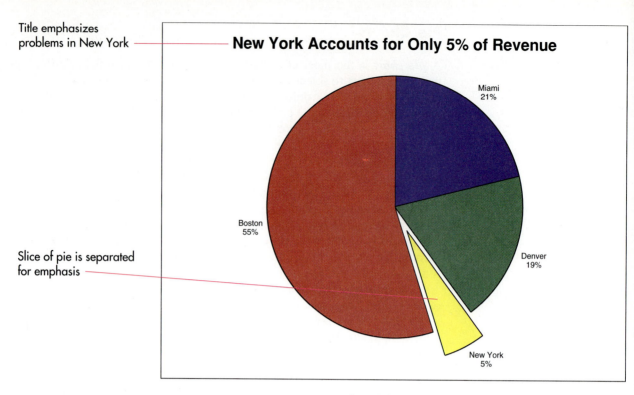

(b) Exploded Pie Chart

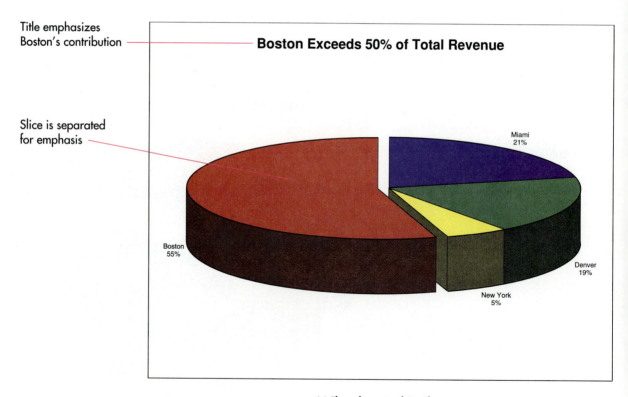

(c) Three-dimensional Pie Chart

FIGURE 4.2   Pie Charts (continued)

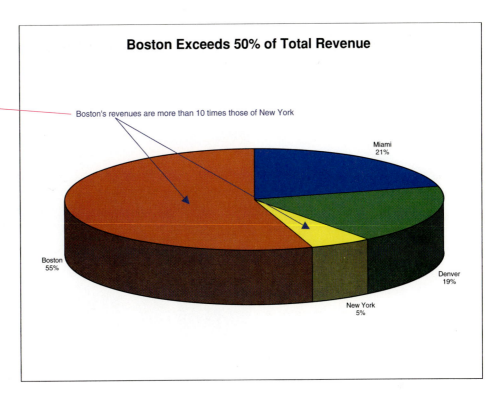

(d) Enhanced Pie Chart

FIGURE 4.2 Pie Charts (continued)

A pie chart is easiest to read when the number of slices is limited (not more than six or seven), and when small categories (percentages less than five) are grouped into a single category called "Other."

EXPLODED PIE CHARTS

Click and drag wedges out of a pie chart to convert an ordinary pie chart to an exploded pie chart. For best results pull the wedge out only slightly from the main body of the pie.

Column and Bar Charts

A *column chart* is used when there is a need to show actual numbers rather than percentages. The column chart in Figure 4.3a plots the same data series as the earlier pie chart, but displays it differently. The category labels (Miami, Denver, New York, and Boston) are shown along the *X* (horizontal) *axis.* The data points (monthly sales) are plotted along the *Y* (vertical) *axis,* with the height of each column reflecting the value of the data point.

A column chart can be given a horizontal orientation and converted to a *bar chart* as in Figure 4.3b. Some individuals prefer the bar chart over the corresponding column chart because the longer horizontal bars accentuate the difference between the cities. Bar charts are also preferable when the descriptive labels are long to eliminate the crowding that can occur along the horizontal axis of a

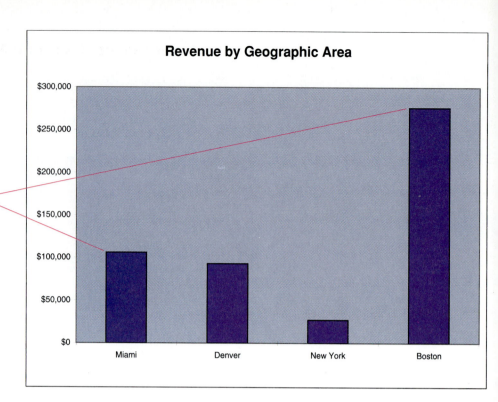

(a) Column Chart

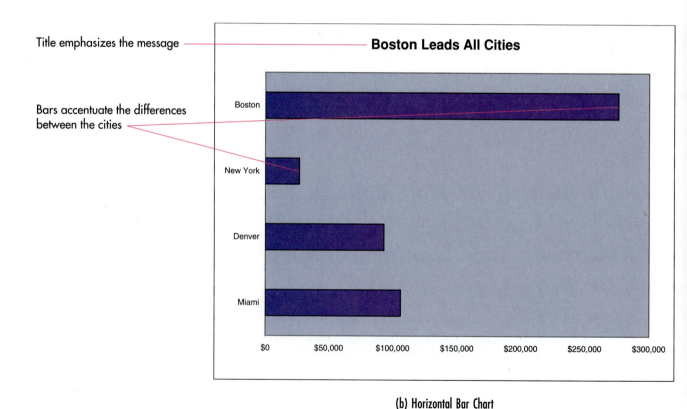

(b) Horizontal Bar Chart

FIGURE 4.3 Column/Bar Charts

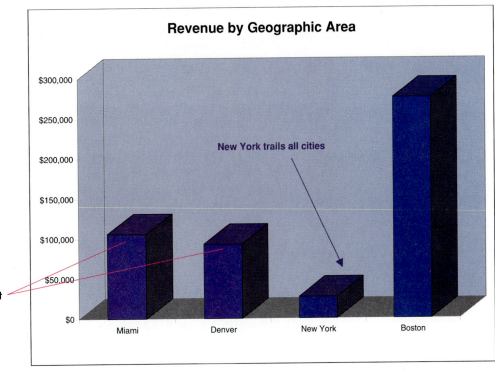

(c) Three-dimensional Column Chart

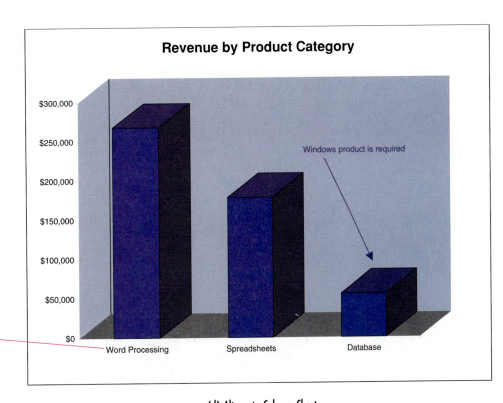

(d) Alternate Column Chart

FIGURE 4.3   Column/Bar Charts (continued)

column chart. As with the pie chart, a title can be developed to lead the reader and further emphasize the message, as with *Boston Leads All Cities* in Figure 4.3b.

A three-dimensional effect can produce added interest as shown in Figures 4.3c and 4.3d. Figure 4.3d plots a different set of numbers than we have seen so far (the sales for each application, rather than the sales for each city). The choice between the charts in Figures 4.3c and 4.3d depends on the message you want to convey—whether you want to emphasize the contribution of each city or each product. The title can be developed to emphasize the message. Arrows and text can be added to either chart to enhance the message.

As with a pie chart, column and bar charts are easiest to read when the number of categories is relatively small (seven or fewer). Otherwise the columns (bars) are plotted so close together that labeling becomes impossible.

CREATING A CHART

There are two ways to create a chart in Excel. You can embed the chart in a worksheet, or you can create the chart in a separate ***chart sheet.*** Figure 4.4a displays an embedded column chart. Figure 4.4b shows a pie chart in its own chart sheet. Both techniques are valid. The choice between the two depends on your personal preference.

Regardless of where it is kept (embedded in a worksheet or in its own chart sheet), a chart is linked to the worksheet on which it is based. The charts in Figure 4.4 plot the same data series (the total sales for each city). Change any of these data points on the worksheet, and both charts will be updated automatically to reflect the new data.

Both charts are part of the same workbook (Software Sales) as indicated in the title bar of each figure. The tabs within the workbook have been renamed to indicate the contents of the associated sheet. Additional charts may be created and embedded in the worksheet and/or placed on their own chart sheets. And, as previously stated, if you change the worksheet, the chart (or charts) based upon it will also change.

Study the column chart in Figure 4.4a to see how it corresponds to the worksheet on which it is based. The descriptive names on the X axis are known as ***category labels*** and match the entries in cells B3 through E3. The quantitative values (data points) are plotted on the Y axis and match the total sales in cells B7 through E7. Even the numeric format matches; that is, the currency format used in the worksheet appears automatically on the scale of the Y axis.

The ***sizing handles*** on the embedded chart indicate it is currently selected and can be sized, moved, or deleted the same way as any other Windows object:

- To size the selected chart, point to a sizing handle (the mouse pointer changes to a double arrow), then drag the handle in the desired direction.
- To move the selected chart, point to the chart (the mouse pointer is a single arrow), then drag the chart to its new location.
- To copy the selected chart, click the Copy button to copy the chart to the clipboard, click in the workbook where you want the copied chart to go, then click the Paste button to paste the chart at that location.
- To delete the selected chart, press the Del key.

The same operations apply to any of the objects within the chart (e.g., its title), as will be discussed in the section on enhancing a chart.

Workbook name

Sizing handles

Data points are plotted on the Y axis and reflect entries in B7:E7

Descriptive names (category labels) match entries in B3:E3

Tabs renamed to reflect content of sheet

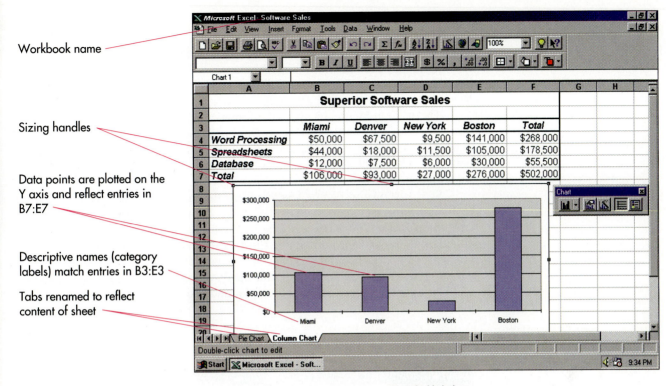

(a) Embedded Chart

Workbook name

Selected sheet

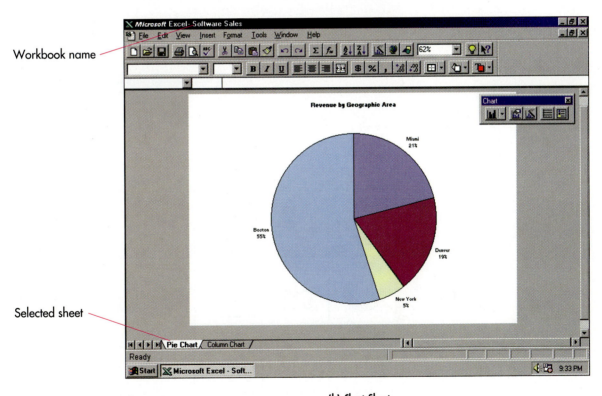

(b) Chart Sheet

FIGURE 4.4   Creating a Chart

GRAPHS AND CHARTS   147

The ChartWizard

The *ChartWizard* is the easiest way to create a chart. Just select the cells that contain the data, click the ChartWizard button on the Standard toolbar, and let the Wizard do the rest. The process is illustrated in Figure 4.5, which shows how the Wizard creates a column chart to plot total sales by geographic area.

The steps in Figure 4.5 appear automatically, one after the other, as you click the Next command button to move from one step to the next. You can retrace your steps at any time by pressing the Back command button, access the online help facility with the Help command button, or negate the process with the Cancel command button.

Step 1, shown in Figure 4.5a, confirms the range of selected cells, $B$3:$E$3 (containing the city names) and $B$7:$E$7 (containing the total sales for each city). Step 2 asks you to choose one of the available chart types, and step 3 has you choose the specific format for the type of chart you selected. Step 4 shows you a preview of the completed chart. (The distinction between data series in rows versus columns is explained after the hands-on exercise.) Step 5 enables you to add a title and a legend. It's that simple, and the entire process takes but a few minutes.

(a) Step 1—Define the Range

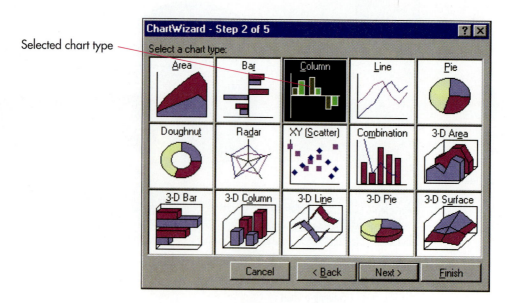

(b) Step 2—Select the Chart Type

FIGURE 4.5 The ChartWizard

Selected format

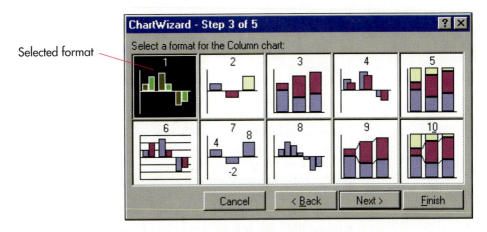

(c) Step 3—Select the Format for the Column Chart

Preview of chart

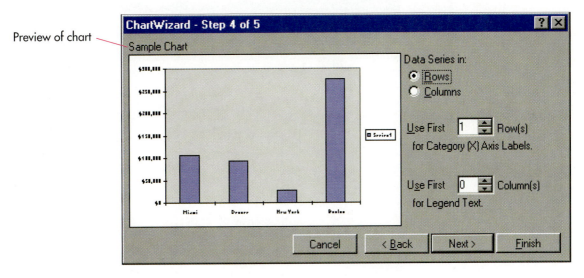

(d) Step 4—Preview the Chart

Specify whether a legend is to be displayed

Enter a title for the chart

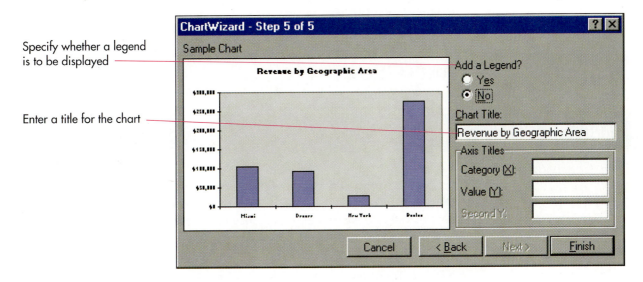

(e) Step 5—Add Legends and Titles

FIGURE 4.5   The ChartWizard (continued)

Enhancing a Chart

A chart can be enhanced in several ways. You can change the chart type, add (remove) a legend, and/or add (remove) gridlines. You can select any part of the chart (e.g., the title) and change its formatting. You can also add arrows and text.

Figure 4.6 displays an enhanced version of the column chart that was created by using the ChartWizard in Figure 4.5. The chart type has been changed to a *three-dimensional column chart,* and gridlines have been added. Both changes were accomplished by using buttons on the **Chart toolbar.**

A text box and an arrow have been added by using the corresponding tools on the **Drawing toolbar.** A *text box* is a block of text that is added to a chart (or worksheet) for emphasis. You can format all or part of the text by selecting it and choosing a different font or point size. You can also apply boldface or italics. Text wraps within the box as it is entered.

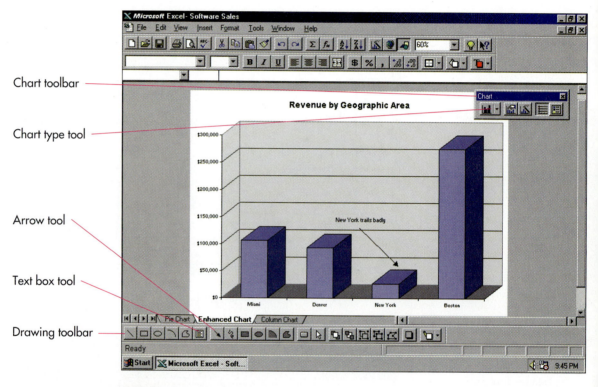

FIGURE 4.6 Enhancing a Chart

HANDS-ON EXERCISE 1

The ChartWizard

Objective: To create and modify a chart by using the ChartWizard; to embed a chart within a worksheet; to enhance a chart to include arrows and text. Use Figure 4.7 as a guide in the exercise.

STEP 1: Open the Software Sales Workbook

➤ Start Excel. Open the **Software Sales** workbook in the **Exploring Excel folder.** Save the workbook as **Finished Software Sales.**

➤ Pull down the **Tools menu,** click **Options,** click the **General tab,** check the box to **Reset TipWizard,** and click **OK.**

STEP 2: Start the ChartWizard

➤ Drag the mouse over **cells B3** through **E3** to select the category labels (the names of the cities) as shown in Figure 4.7a.

➤ Press and hold the **Ctrl key** as you drag the mouse over **cells B7** through **E7** to select the data series (the cells containing the total sales for the individual cities).

➤ Check that both ranges **B3:E3** and **B7:E7** are selected.

➤ Click the button for the **ChartWizard.** A moving border will appear around the selected ranges, and the mouse pointer changes to a tiny crosshair with a tiny bar chart.

➤ Click below **cell A7,** then drag the mouse to define the area to hold the chart as shown in Figure 4.7a. Release the mouse.

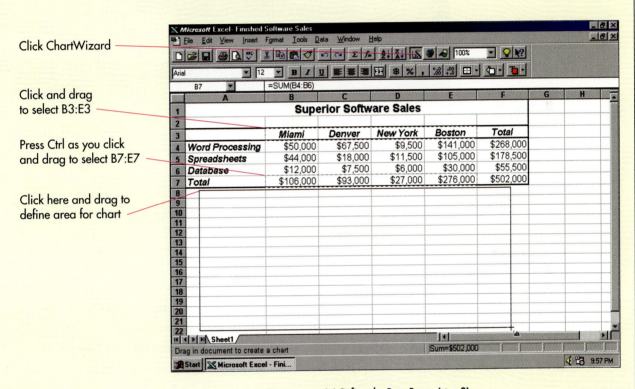

(a) Define the Data Range (step 2)

FIGURE 4.7   Hands-on Exercise 1

STEP 3: The ChartWizard (continued)

➤ You should see the dialog box for step 1 of the ChartWizard as shown in Figure 4.7b. If the range is correct (i.e., the ChartWizard displays $B$3:$E$3 and $B$7:$E$7), click the **Next command button.** If the range is incorrect, click **Cancel** and begin again, or click in the text box and enter the correct range.

➤ If necessary, click the icon for a **column chart** (the default). Click the **Next command button.**

➤ If necessary, click the column chart format in **box number 6** (the default). Click the **Next command button.**

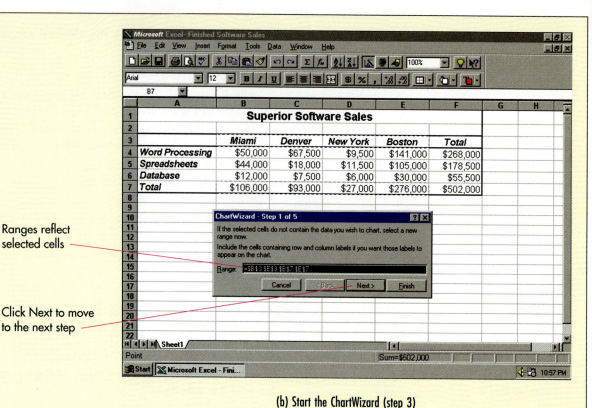

(b) Start the ChartWizard (step 3)

FIGURE 4.7 Hands-on Exercise 1 (continued)

- View the sample chart shown in step 4 of the ChartWizard:
  - If you are satisfied with your chart (do not be concerned about the legend at this time), click the **Next command button.**
  - If you are not satisfied, click the **Back command button** to return to the previous step, where you can change the chart type.

STEP 4: The ChartWizard (continued)

- Complete the chart in step 5 of the ChartWizard as shown in Figure 4.7c:
  - Click the **No option button** to suppress the legend.
  - Click in the text box to add the title. Type **Revenue by Geographic Area.**
  - Click the **Finish command button** to exit the ChartWizard and place the chart on the worksheet.
- Save the workbook.

STEP 5: The Column Chart

- You should see the chart in Figure 4.7d.
  - The sizing handles indicate that the chart is selected and will be affected by subsequent commands.
  - The Chart toolbar is automatically displayed when the chart is selected.
- Press the **Del key.** The chart (and Chart toolbar) disappears from the worksheet. Click the **Undo button** on the Standard toolbar to cancel the last command. The chart is back in the worksheet, and the Chart toolbar is redisplayed.
- Click anywhere outside the chart to deselect it.

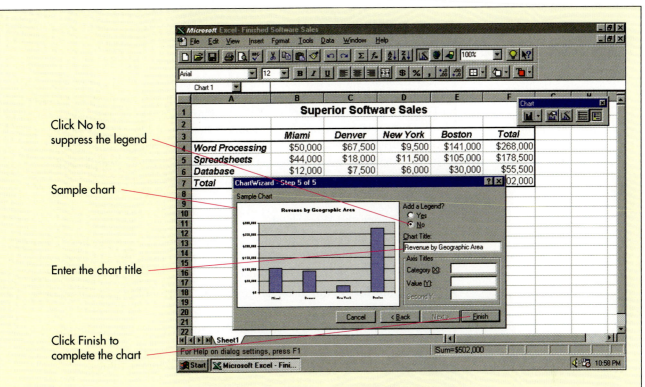

(c) The ChartWizard (step 4)

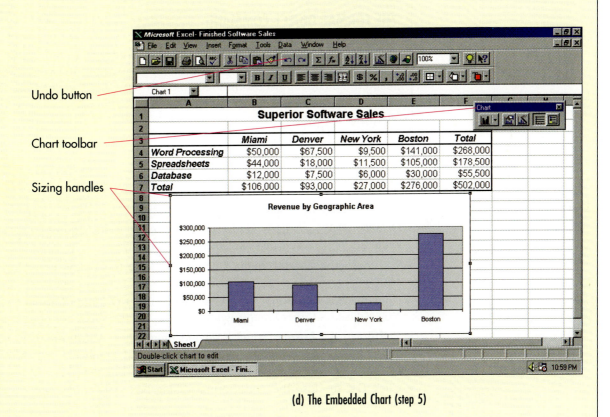

(d) The Embedded Chart (step 5)

FIGURE 4.7   Hands-on Exercise 1 (continued)

> ### FLOATING TOOLBARS
>
> Any toolbar can be docked along the edge of the application window, or it can be displayed as a floating toolbar within the application window. To move a docked toolbar, drag the toolbar background. To move a floating toolbar, drag its title bar. To size a floating toolbar, drag any border in the direction you want to go. Double click the background of any toolbar to toggle between a floating toolbar and a docked (fixed) toolbar.

STEP 6: Change the Worksheet

- Click in **cell B4.** Change the entry to **$300,000.** Press the **enter key.** The totals in cells F4, B7, and F7 change automatically to reflect the increased sales for word processing in the Miami office.
- The column for Miami also changes in the chart and is now larger than the column for Boston.
- Click the **Undo button** on the Standard toolbar to return to the initial value of $50,000.
- The worksheet and chart are restored to their original values.

> ### THE FORMAT OBJECT COMMAND
>
> Dress up an embedded chart by changing its border to include color or a different line thickness or style. Select the chart, pull down the Format menu, then click Object to produce the Format Object dialog box. Click the Patterns tab, which displays check boxes, to choose a shadow effect and rounded corners. You can also specify a different border style, thickness (weight), or color as well as a background color and/or pattern for the entire chart. Click OK to exit the dialog box.

STEP 7: Modify the Chart

- Double click anywhere in the chart to select it for editing. The chart is enclosed in a hashed line as shown in Figure 4.7e.
- Pull down the **Format menu.** Click **Chart Type** to display the dialog box in Figure 4.7e.
- Click the box containing a **Pie chart.** Click the **3-D option button.** Click **OK.** You will see a three-dimensional pie chart, but the slices are not yet labeled.
- Pull down the **Format menu** a second time. Click **AutoFormat** to display a dialog box with various pie charts. Click format **number 7,** which will label the slices of the pie with percentages and the city names.
- Click **OK** to close the AutoFormat dialog box. The completed pie chart is shown in Figure 4.7f.

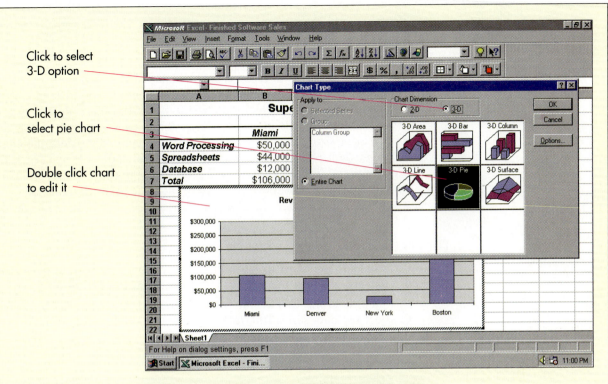

(e) Change the Chart Type (step 7)

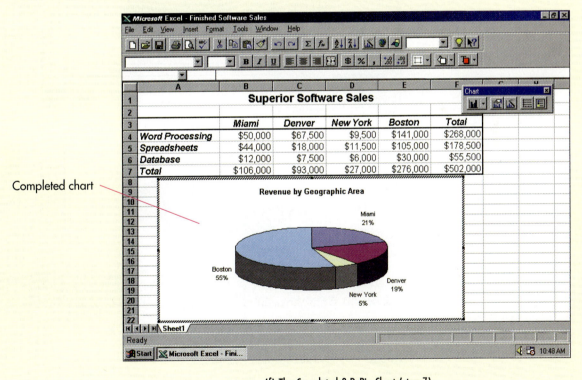

(f) The Completed 3-D Pie Chart (step 7)

FIGURE 4.7 Hands-on Exercise 1 (continued)

EMBEDDED CHARTS

An embedded chart is treated as an object that can be moved, sized, copied, or deleted just as any other Windows object. To move an embedded chart, click anywhere in the chart to select the chart, then drag it to a new location in the worksheet. To size the chart, select it, then drag any of the eight sizing handles in the desired direction. To delete the chart, select it, then press the Del key. To copy the chart, select it, click the Copy button on the Standard toolbar to copy the chart to the clipboard, click where you want the copied chart, then click the Paste button.

STEP 8: Create a Second Chart

➤ Click outside the chart to deselect the chart. Drag the mouse over **cells A4** through **A6** to select the category labels as shown in Figure 4.7g.

➤ Press and hold the **Ctrl key** as you drag the mouse over **cells F4** through **F6** to select the data series (the total sales for the product categories).

➤ Pull down the **Insert menu.** Click **Chart.** Click **As New Sheet.**

Click and drag to select A4:A6 (category labels)

Press Ctrl key as you click and drag to select F4:F6 (data series)

(g) Insert Chart Command (step 8)

FIGURE 4.7   Hands-on Exercise 1 (continued)

STEP 9: The ChartWizard

➤ You should see step 1 of the ChartWizard with the ranges A4:A6 and F4:F6 displayed in the text box.

  • Click the **Next command button** if the range is correct, or

- Click the **Cancel command button** if the range is incorrect, or click in the text box to enter the correct range.
▶ Click the icon for a **3-D Column chart.** Click the **Next command button.**
▶ Click the column chart format in **box number 1.** Click the **Next command button.**
▶ View the sample chart shown in step 4 of the ChartWizard:
- If you are satisfied, click the **Next command button** to move to step 5 of the ChartWizard.
- If you are not satisfied, click the **Back command button** to return to the previous step, where you can change the chart format.
▶ Complete the chart in step 5 of the ChartWizard:
- Click the **No option button** to suppress the legend.
- Click in the text box to add the title. Type **Revenue by Product Category.**
- Click the **Finish command button.**
▶ You should see the chart in Figure 4.7h, but without the text box and arrow. Save the workbook.

STEP 10: Workbook Tabs
▶ The 3-D column chart has been created in the chart sheet labeled Chart1. Click the **Sheet1 tab** to return to the worksheet and embedded chart from the first part of the exercise.
▶ Click the **Chart1 tab** to return to the chart sheet containing the 3-D column chart.

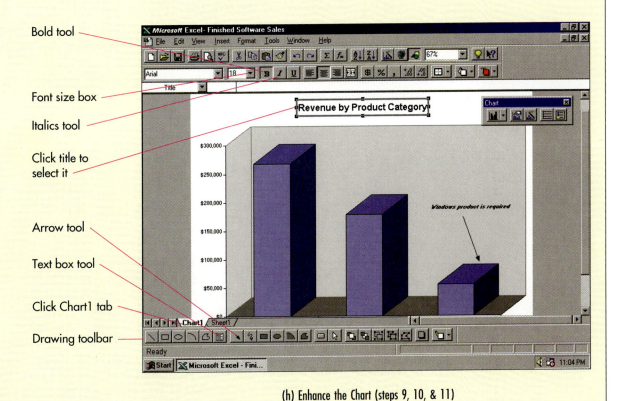

(h) Enhance the Chart (steps 9, 10, & 11)

FIGURE 4.7   Hands-on Exercise 1 (continued)

> **THE EXCEL WORKBOOK**
>
> The Excel workbook is the electronic equivalent of the three-ring binder. A workbook contains one or more worksheets and/or chart sheets, each of which is identified by a tab at the bottom of the workbook. The various sheets in a workbook are typically related to one another. One worksheet, for example, may contain data for several charts, each of which appears on a separate chart sheet in the workbook. The advantage of a workbook is that all of its sheets are stored in a single file, which is accessed as a unit.

STEP 11: Enhance the Chart

- Point to any visible toolbar. Click the **right mouse button** to display the Toolbar shortcut menu. Click **Drawing** to display the Drawing toolbar, which will be used to enhance the chart. (If necessary, click and drag the toolbar to dock it along an edge of the window.)
- Click the **black arrow button** on the Drawing toolbar. The mouse pointer changes to a thin crosshair. Click in the chart where you want the arrow to begin, drag the mouse to extend the arrow, then release the mouse to complete the arrow as shown in Figure 4.7h.
- Click the **text box button** on the Drawing toolbar. The mouse pointer changes to a thin crosshair. Click in the chart where you want the text box to begin, drag the mouse to extend the box, then release the mouse.
- Click the **Bold** and **Italic buttons** on the Formatting toolbar. Type **Windows product is required** as shown in Figure 4.7h. Click outside the text box to complete the entry.
- Click the title of the chart. You will see sizing handles around the title to indicate it has been selected.
- Click the **arrow** on the Font Size box on the Formatting toolbar. Click **18** to increase the size of the title.
- Use the text tool to add your name somewhere in the chart so that your instructor will know the assignment is from you. Save the workbook.

> **ENHANCEMENT TIPS**
>
> Arrows and text boxes are the basis of many chart enhancements. To draw an arrow that is perfectly horizontal, vertical, or at a forty-five degree angle, press and hold the Shift key as you drag the mouse to create the line. To change the appearance of the shaft or arrowhead, double click the arrow to display the Format Object dialog box, make your changes, then click OK. To resize a text box so that it fits the text exactly, select the text box, pull down the Format menu, and click Selected Object. Click the Alignment tab, check the Automatic Size box, and click OK. Move or size an arrow or text box just as you would any other Windows object.

STEP 12: Format the Data Series

➤ Click any of the columns to select the data series. (All three columns will be selected. However, clicking a column after the data series has been selected selects only that column and deselects the others.) Be sure that all three columns are selected as shown in Figure 4.7i.

➤ Point to any column and click the **right mouse button** to display the shortcut menu in Figure 4.7i. Click **Format Data Series** to display a dialog box, click the **Patterns tab,** select (click) a different color, then click **OK** to accept the change and close the dialog box.

➤ Point to the **X axis** (scrolling if necessary), click the **right mouse button** to display a shortcut menu, then click the **Format Axis command.** Experiment with different formatting options for the X axis, then close the dialog box.

➤ Save the workbook.

Click column to select the data series

Point to any column and click right mouse button to display shortcut menu

(i) Format the Data Series (step 12)

FIGURE 4.7   Hands-on Exercise 1 (continued)

STEP 13: Print the Workbook

➤ Pull down the **File menu** and click **Print** to display the dialog box in Figure 4.7j. Click the option button to print the **Entire Workbook.** Click **OK.**

➤ Click the **TipWizard button** to open the TipWizard box. Click the **up arrow** on the tip box to review the suggestions made by the TipWizard during the exercise. Close the TipWizard.

➤ Close the workbook. Exit Excel if you do not want to continue with the next exercise at this time.

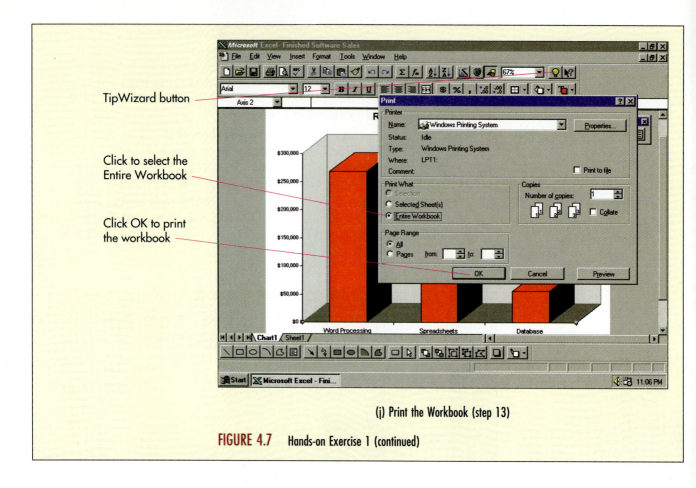

(j) Print the Workbook (step 13)

FIGURE 4.7 Hands-on Exercise 1 (continued)

MULTIPLE DATA SERIES

The charts presented so far displayed only a single data series—for example, the total sales by location or the total sales by product category. Although such charts are useful, it is often necessary to view *multiple data series* on the same chart.

Figure 4.8a displays the sales in each location according to product category. We see how the products compare within each city, and further, that word processing is the leading application in three of the four cities. Figure 4.8b plots the identical data but in *stacked columns* rather than side-by-side.

The choice between the two types of charts depends on your message. If, for example, you want your audience to see the individual sales in each product category, the side-by-side columns are more appropriate. If, on the other hand, you want to emphasize the total sales for each city, the stacked columns are preferable. Note, too, the different scale on the Y axis in the two charts. The side-by-side columns in Figure 4.8a show the sales of each product category and so the Y axis goes only to $160,000. The stacked columns in Figure 4.8b, however, reflect the total sales for each city and thus the scale goes to $300,000.

The biggest difference is that the stacked column explicitly totals the sales for each city while the side-by-side column does not. The advantage of the stacked column is that the city totals are clearly shown and can be easily compared, and further the relative contributions of each product category within each city are apparent. The disadvantage is that the segments within each column do not start at the same point, making it difficult to determine the actual sales for the individual product categories or to compare the product categories among cities.

Realize, too, that for a stacked column chart to make sense, its numbers must be additive. This is true in Figure 4.8b, where the stacked columns consist of three

160 EXPLORING MICROSOFT EXCEL 7.0

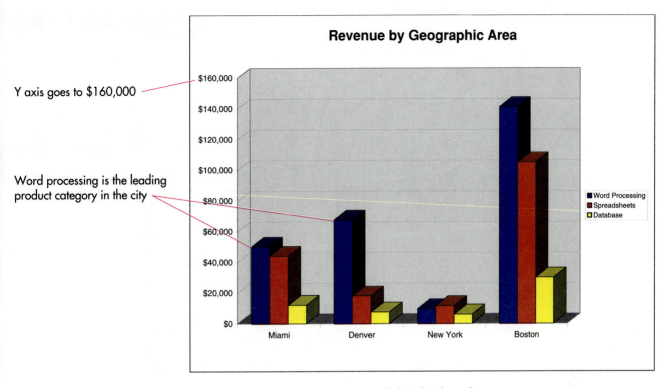

(a) Side-by-Side Column Chart

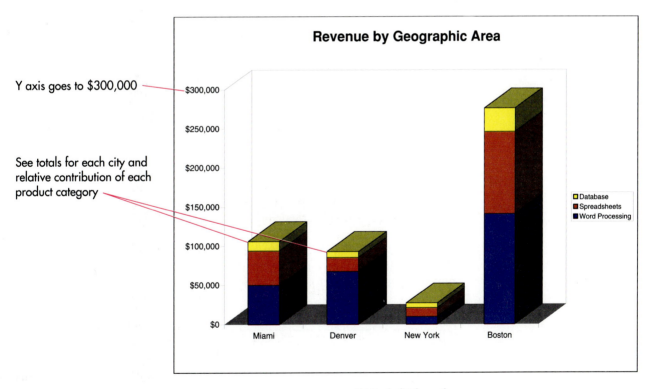

(b) Stacked Column Chart

FIGURE 4.8 Column Charts

components, each of which is measured in dollars, and which can be logically added together to produce a total. You shouldn't, however, automatically convert a side-by-side column chart to its stacked column equivalent. It would not make sense, for example, to convert a column chart that plots unit sales and dollar sales side-by-side, into a stacked column chart that adds the two, because units and dollars represent different physical concepts and are not additive.

Rows versus Columns

Figure 4.9 illustrates a critical concept associated with multiple data series—whether the data series are in rows or columns. Figure 4.9a displays the worksheet with multiple data series selected. (Column A and Row 3 are included in the selection to provide the category labels and legend.) Figure 4.9b contains the chart when the data series are in rows (B4:E4, B5:E5, and B6:E6). Figure 4.9c displays the chart based on data series in columns (B4:B6, C4:C6, D4:D6, and E4:E6).

Both charts plot a total of twelve data points (three product categories for each of four locations), but they group the data differently. Figure 4.9b displays the data by city; that is, the sales of three product categories are shown for each of four cities. Figure 4.9c is the reverse and groups the data by product category; this time the sales in the four cities are shown for each of the three product categories. The choice between the two depends on your message and whether you want to emphasize revenue by city or by product category. It sounds complicated, but it's not, and Excel will create either chart for you according to your specifications.

- If the data series are in rows (Figure 4.9b), the Wizard will:
  - Use the first row (cells B3 through E3) in the selected range for the category labels on the X axis
  - Use the first column (cells A4 through A6) for the legend text
- If the data series are in columns (Figure 4.9c), the Wizard will:
  - Use the first column (cells A4 through A6) in the selected range for the category labels on the X axis
  - Use the first row (cells B3 through E3) for the legend text

Stated another way, the data series in Figure 4.9b are in rows. Thus, there are three data series (B4:E4, B5:E5, and B6:E6), one for each product category. The first data series plots the word processing sales in Miami, Denver, New York, and Boston; the second series plots the spreadsheet sales for each city, and so on.

The data series in Figure 4.9c are in columns. This time there are four data series (B4:B6, C4:C6, D4:D6, and E4:E6), one for each city. The first series plots the Miami sales for word processing, spreadsheets, and database; the second series plots the Denver sales for each software category, and so on.

A3:E6 is selected

	A	B	C	D	E	F
1		Superior Software Sales				
2						
3		Miami	Denver	New York	Boston	Total
4	**Word Processing**	$50,000	$67,500	$9,500	$141,000	$268,000
5	**Spreadsheets**	$44,000	$18,000	$11,500	$105,000	$178,500
6	**Database**	$12,000	$7,500	$6,000	$30,000	$55,500
7	**Total**	$106,000	$93,000	$27,000	$276,000	$502,000

(a) The Worksheet

FIGURE 4.9 Multiple Data Series

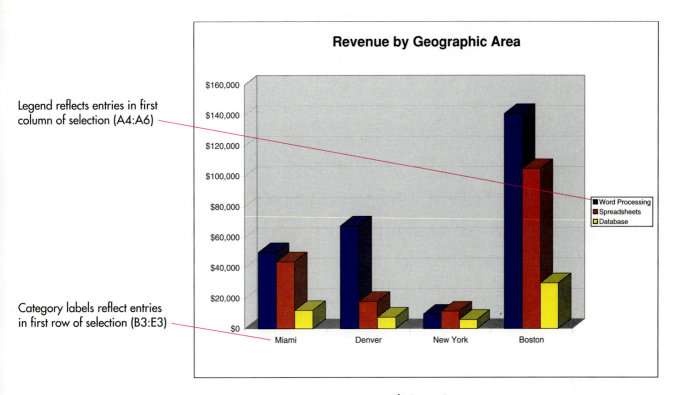

(b) Data in Rows

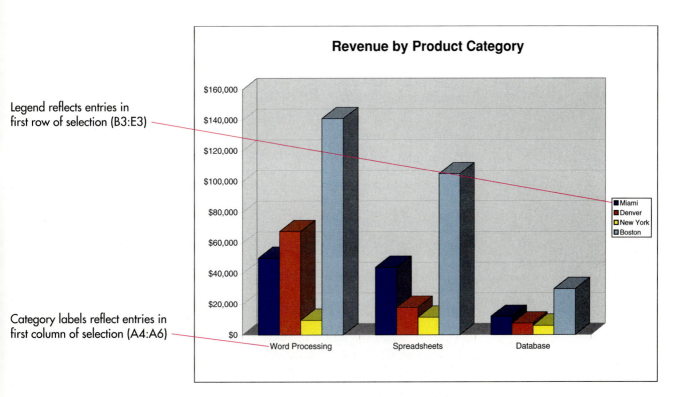

(c) Data in Columns

FIGURE 4.9   Multiple Data Series (continued)

GRAPHS AND CHARTS   163

Default Selections

Excel makes a default determination as to whether the data is in rows or columns by assuming that you want fewer data series than categories. Thus, if the selected cells contain fewer rows than columns (or if the number of rows and columns are equal), it assumes the data series are in rows. If, on the other hand, there are fewer columns than rows, it will assume the data series are in columns.

Be sure to include the text for both the category labels and legend in your selection so that Excel can create these elements for you. And remember, you can subsequently override any default selection by using the ChartWizard to edit the *default chart*.

HANDS-ON EXERCISE 2

Multiple Data Series

Objective: To plot multiple data series in the same chart; to differentiate between data series in rows and columns; to create and save multiple charts associated with the same worksheet. Use Figure 4.10 as a guide in doing the exercise.

STEP 1: Rename the Workbook Tabs

➤ Open the **Finished Software Sales workbook** from the previous exercise. Reset the TipWizard as you have been doing throughout the text so that you will see all of the tips the Wizard has to offer.

➤ Point to the workbook tab labeled **Sheet1** as shown in Figure 4.10a. Click the **right mouse button** to display a shortcut menu with commands pertaining to the worksheet tab.

➤ Click **Rename** to display the Rename Sheet dialog box in Figure 4.10a. Type **Sales Data.** Click **OK**.

➤ Point to the tab labeled **Chart1** (which contains the three-dimensional column chart created in the previous exercise). Click the **right mouse button** to display a shortcut menu.

➤ Click **Rename** to display the Rename Sheet dialog box in Figure 4.10a. Type **Revenue by Product Category.** Click **OK**.

➤ Save the workbook.

THE RIGHT MOUSE BUTTON

Point to a cell (or group of selected cells), a chart or worksheet tab, a toolbar, or chart (or a selected object on the chart), then click the right mouse button to display a shortcut menu. All shortcut menus are context sensitive and display commands appropriate for the selected object. Right clicking a toolbar, for example, enables you to display (hide) additional toolbars. Right clicking a sheet tab enables you to rename, move, copy, or delete the sheet. Right clicking a chart displays commands that enable you to edit the chart.

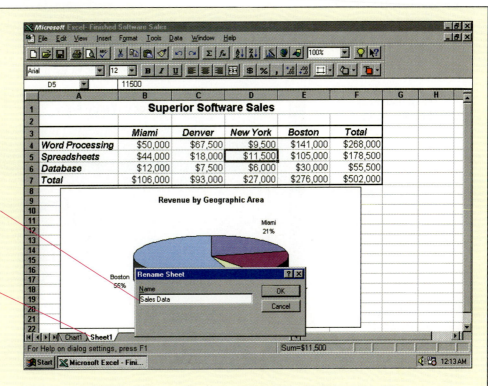

(a) Rename the Worksheet Tab (step 1)

FIGURE 4.10 Hands-on Exercise 2

STEP 2: Multiple Data Series

➤ Click the **Sales Data tab,** then click and drag to select **cells A3** through **E6** as shown in Figure 4.10b.

➤ Pull down the **Insert menu.** Click **Chart.** Click **As New Sheet** to bring up step 1 of the ChartWizard as shown in Figure 4.10b.

➤ Click the **Finish command button** to skip the remaining steps in the ChartWizard and create the default chart with no additional input from you.

➤ The new chart is in its own chart sheet labeled Chart1 (The tab may reflect a higher number, depending on how many charts you have created this session.)

➤ Save the workbook.

THE F11 KEY

The F11 key is the fastest way to create a chart in its own sheet. Select the data series, including the legends and category labels, then press the F11 key to create the chart according to the default format built into Excel. After the chart has been created, you can use the menu bar, Chart toolbar, or shortcut menus to choose a different chart type and/or customize the formatting.

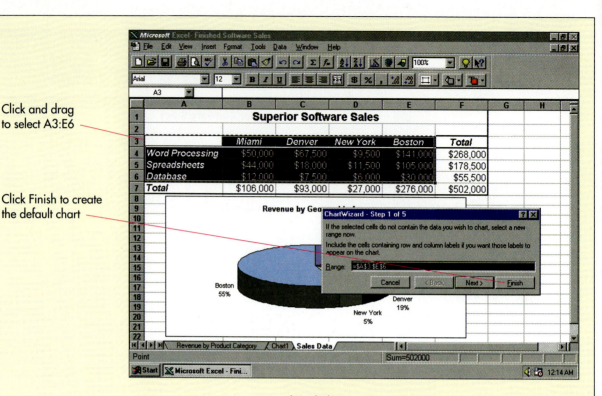

(b) Multiple Data Series (step 2)

FIGURE 4.10   Hands-on Exercise 2 (continued)

STEP 3: Insert the Title

➤ Click the tab for the newly created chart sheet. Pull down the **Insert menu.** Click **Titles** to bring up the Titles dialog box. Click the **check box** next to Chart Title. Click **OK.**

➤ Type the title of the chart, **Revenue by Geographic Area.** Press the **enter key.** The title should still be selected, enabling you to change its font and/or the point size.

➤ Click the **arrow** on the Font Size box on the Formatting toolbar as shown in Figure 4.10c. Click **18** to increase the size of the title. Click outside the title to deselect it.

➤ Save the workbook.

STEP 4: Change the Chart Type

➤ Pull down the **Format menu** and click **AutoFormat.** (You can also point to the chart and click the **right mouse button,** then select AutoFormat from the shortcut menu.)

➤ Click the **down arrow** on the Galleries list box to scroll through the available chart types. Click **3-D Column** to produce the dialog box in Figure 4.10d.

➤ Click **Format 1.** Click **OK.** The chart changes to a three-dimensional column chart.

➤ Point to the tab containing this chart, click the **right mouse button** to display a shortcut menu, then click the **Rename command.** Enter **Revenue by Area** as the new name. Click **OK.**

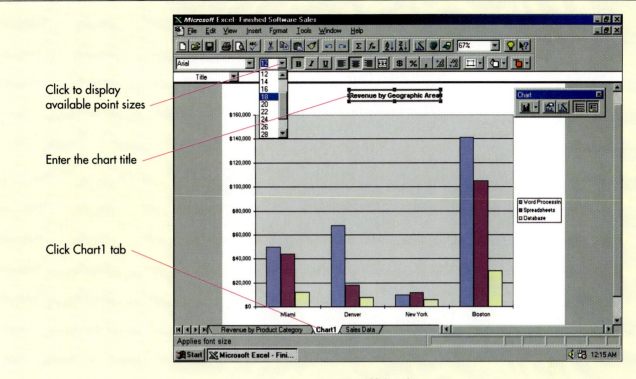

(c) Add the Title (step 3)

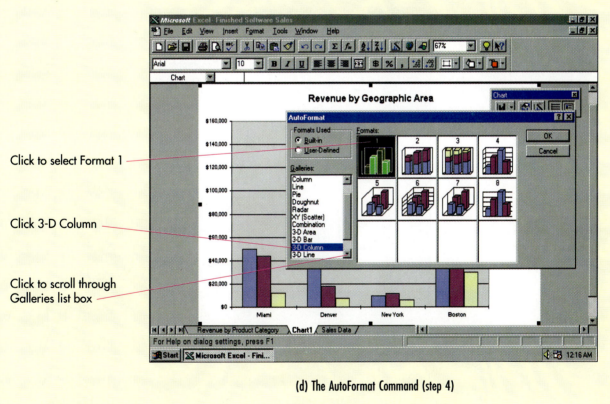

(d) The AutoFormat Command (step 4)

FIGURE 4.10 Hands-on Exercise 2 (continued)

STEP 5: Copying Sheets

➤ Point to the tab named **Revenue by Area.** Click the **right mouse button.** Click **Move** or **Copy** to display the dialog box in Figure 4.10e.

➤ Click **Sales Data** in the Before Sheet list box. Click the check box to **Create a Copy.** Click **OK** to create a duplicate worksheet called Revenue by Area (2) and insert it before (to the left of) the Sales Data worksheet.

➤ Rename the copied sheet **Revenue by Product.** Save the workbook.

MOVING AND COPYING A CHART SHEET

The fastest way to move or copy a chart sheet is to drag its tab. To move a sheet, point to its tab, then click and drag the tab to its new position. To copy a sheet, press and hold the Ctrl key as you drag the tab to the desired position for the second sheet. Rename the copied sheet (or any other sheet) by pointing to its tab and clicking the right mouse button to produce a shortcut menu. Click Rename, then enter the new name in the resulting dialog box.

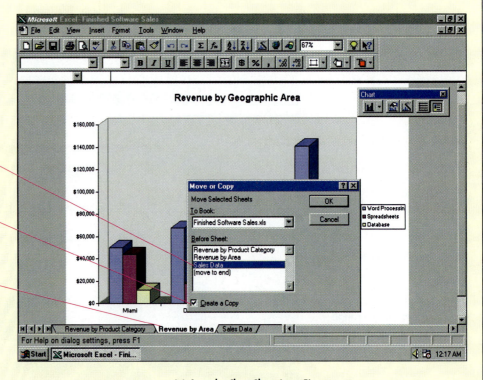

Click Sales Data to insert duplicated sheet to the left of it (i.e., before it)

Click to select option to create a copy

Rename tab, then point to tab and click right mouse button to display a shortcut menu

(e) Copy the Chart Sheet (step 5)

FIGURE 4.10 Hands-on Exercise 2 (continued)

STEP 6: Change the Data Series

➤ Click the **Revenue by Product tab** to make it the active sheet. Click anywhere in the chart to select it.

➤ Click the **ChartWizard button** on the Chart toolbar. The Sales Data sheet is displayed on the screen, and you will see a dialog box indicating step 1 of 2 in ChartWizard.

➤ Click the **Next command button** to redisplay the Revenue by Product chart and produce the dialog box in Figure 4.10f.

➤ Click the **Columns option button** to change the data series to columns; this will display the data by product category rather than location. Click **OK**.

➤ The orientation of the chart changes so that the applications appear as the category labels on the X axis. The legend contains the names of the cities. This was done automatically by the ChartWizard in conjunction with the options shown in Figure 4.10f.

➤ Click anywhere in the title of the chart to select the title. Drag the mouse over **Geographic Area** to select this text. Type **Product Category.** Click outside the title to deselect it.

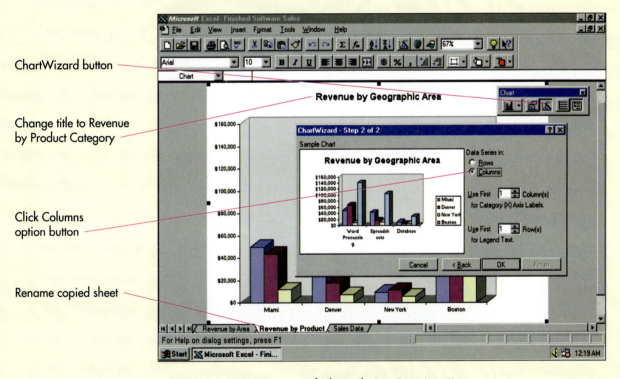

(f) Change the Data Series (step 6)

FIGURE 4.10 Hands-on Exercise 2 (continued)

STEP 7: The Stacked Column Chart

➤ Pull down the **Format menu** and click **AutoFormat.** (You can also point to the chart and click the **right mouse button,** then select AutoFormat from the shortcut menu.)

➤ Click **Format 2** in the Formats area. Click **OK.** The chart changes to a stacked bar chart as shown in Figure 4.10g.

➤ Save the workbook a final time.

> ### THE HORIZONTAL SCROLL BAR
>
> The horizontal scroll bar contains four scrolling buttons to scroll through the worksheet tabs in a workbook. Click ◄ or ► to scroll one tab to the left or right. Click |◄ or ►| to scroll to the first or last tab in the workbook. Once the desired tab is visible, click the tab to select it. Five tabs are visible simultaneously (the default workbook has 16 worksheets); you can, however, drag the tab split box to change the number of tabs that can be seen at one time.

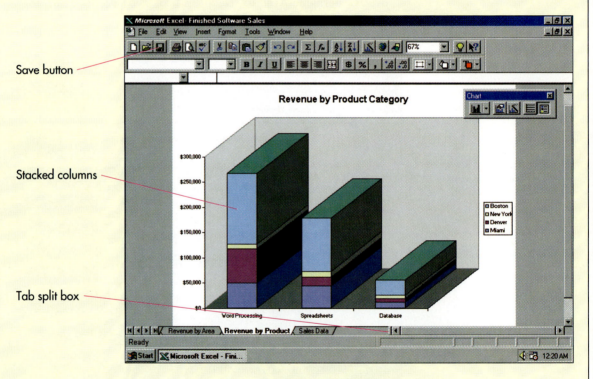

(g) Stacked Column Chart (step 7)

FIGURE 4.10 Hands-on Exercise 2 (continued)

STEP 8: Print the Completed Workbook

➤ Pull down the **File menu,** click the **Print command,** then click the option button to print the **Entire Workbook.** (Clicking the Print button on the Standard toolbar prints only the selected sheet, as opposed to the entire workbook.)

➤ Click **OK** to print the workbook, and submit it to your instructor as proof that you completed the exercise.

➤ Close the workbook. Exit Excel if you do not want to continue with the next exercise at this time.

OBJECT LINKING AND EMBEDDING

One of the primary advantages of the Windows environment is the ability to create a **compound document** that contains data **(objects)** from multiple applications. The memo in Figure 4.11 is an example of a compound document. The memo was created in Microsoft Word (the **client application**), and it contains objects (a worksheet and a chart) that were developed in Microsoft Excel (the **server application**). **Object Linking and Embedding** (**OLE,** pronounced "oh-lay") is the means by which you create the compound document.

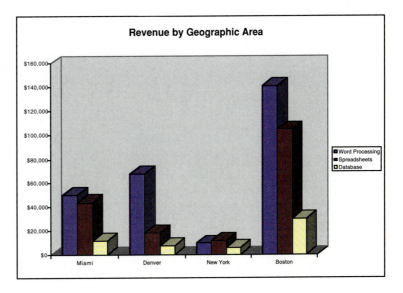

Superior Software

Miami, Florida

To: Mr. White
Chairman, Superior Software

From: Heather Bond
Vice President, Marketing

Subject: May Sales Data

The May sales data clearly indicate that Boston is outperforming our other geographic areas. It is my feeling that Ms. Brown, the office supervisor, is directly responsible for its success and that she should be rewarded accordingly. In addition, we may want to think about transferring her to New York, as they are in desperate need of new ideas and direction. I will be awaiting your response after you have time to digest the information presented.

Superior Software Sales					
	Miami	*Denver*	*New York*	*Boston*	*Total*
Word Processing	$50,000	$67,500	$9,500	$141,000	$268,000
Spreadsheets	$44,000	$18,000	$11,500	$105,000	$178,500
Database	$12,000	$7,500	$6,000	$30,000	$55,500
Total	$106,000	$93,000	$27,000	$276,000	$502,000

FIGURE 4.11   A Compound Document

The essential difference between linking and embedding is whether the object is stored within the compound document *(embedding)* or in its own file *(linking).* An *embedded object* is stored in the compound document, which in turn becomes the only client for that object. A *linked object* is stored in its own file, and the compound document is one of many potential clients for that object. The compound document does not contain the linked object per se, but only a representation of the object as well as a pointer (link) to the file containing the object. The advantage of linking is that any document that is linked to the object is updated automatically if the object is changed.

The choice between linking and embedding depends on how the object will be used. Linking is preferable if the object is likely to change and the compound document requires the latest version. Linking should also be used when the same object is placed in many documents, so that any change to the object has to be made in only one place. Embedding should be used if you need to take the object with you—for example, if you intend to edit the compound document on a different computer.

The following exercise uses linking to create a Word document containing an Excel worksheet and chart. As you do the exercise, both applications (Word and Excel) will be open, and it will be necessary to switch back and forth between the two. This in turn demonstrates the *multitasking* capability within Windows 95 and the use of the Windows 95 taskbar to switch between the open applications.

OBJECT LINKING AND EMBEDDING

Object Linking and Embedding (OLE) enables you to create a compound document containing objects (data) from multiple Windows applications. In actuality, there are two distinct techniques, linking and embedding, and each can be implemented in different ways. OLE is one of the major benefits of working in the Windows environment, but it would be impossible to illustrate all of the techniques in a single exercise. Accordingly, we have created the icon at the left to help you identify the many examples of object linking and embedding that appear throughout the Exploring Windows series.

HANDS-ON EXERCISE 3

Object Linking and Embedding

Objective: To create a compound document consisting of a memo, worksheet, and chart. Use Figure 4.12 as a guide in the exercise.

STEP 1: Open the Software Memo
- Click the **Start button** on the taskbar to display the Start menu.
- Click (or point to) the **Programs menu,** then click **Microsoft Word** to start the program.
- Word is now active, and the taskbar contains a button for Microsoft Word. It may (or may not) contain a button for Microsoft Excel, depending on whether or not you closed Excel at the end of the previous exercise.
- If necessary, click the **Maximize button** in the application window so that Word takes the entire desktop as shown in Figure 4.12a. (The Open dialog

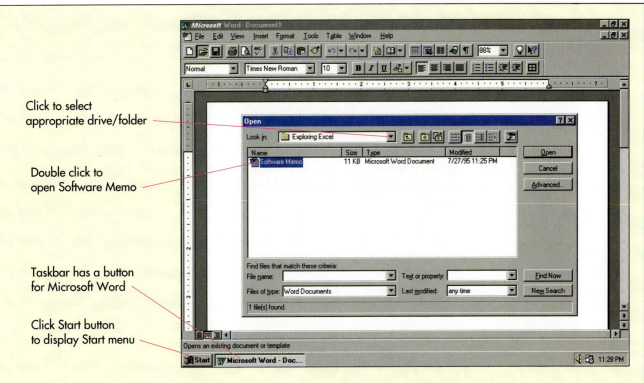

(a) Open the Software Sales Document (step 1)

FIGURE 4.12   Hands-on Exercise 3

box is not yet visible.) Click the **Maximize button** in the document window (if necessary) so that the document window is as large as possible.

➤ Pull down the **File menu** and click **Open** (or click the **Open button** on the Standard toolbar).

- Click the **drop-down arrow** on the Look In list box. Click the appropriate drive, drive C or drive A, depending on the location of your data.
- Double click the **Exploring Excel folder** (we placed the Word memo in the Excel folder) to open the folder. Double click the **Software Memo** to open the document.
- Save the document as **Finished Software Memo**.

➤ Pull down the **View menu.** Click **Page Layout** to change to the Page Layout view. Pull down the **View menu.** Click **Zoom.** Click **Page Width.**

THE MICROSOFT TOOLBAR

The Microsoft toolbar contains a button for each application in Microsoft Office and provides a quick and easy way to launch any of these applications. To display the toolbar, point to any visible toolbar, then click the right mouse button to produce a shortcut menu containing the available toolbars. Click (check) Microsoft to display the toolbar and close the menu. Click and drag the newly displayed toolbar to position it as desired.

STEP 2: Copy the Worksheet

➤ Open (or return to) the **Finished Software Sales workbook** from the previous exercise.
- If you did not close Microsoft Excel at the end of the previous exercise, you will see its button on the taskbar. Click the **Microsoft Excel button** to return to the Finished Software Sales workbook.
- If you closed Microsoft Excel, click the **Start button** to start Excel, then open the Finished Software Sales workbook.

➤ The taskbar should now contain a button for both Microsoft Word and Microsoft Excel. Click either button to move back and forth between the open applications. End by clicking the Microsoft Excel button so that you see the Finished Software Sales workbook.

➤ Click the tab for **Sales Data.** Click and drag to select **A1** through **F7** to select the entire worksheet as shown in Figure 4.12b.

➤ Point to the selected area and click the **right mouse button** to display the shortcut menu. Click **Copy.** A moving border appears around the entire worksheet, indicating that it has been copied to the clipboard.

THE WINDOWS 95 TASKBAR

Multitasking, the ability to run multiple applications at the same time, is one of the primary advantages of the Windows environment. Each button on the taskbar appears automatically when its application or folder is opened, and disappears upon closing. (The buttons are resized automatically according to the number of open windows.) You can customize the taskbar by right clicking an empty area to display a shortcut menu, then clicking the Properties command. You can resize the taskbar by pointing to the inside edge and then dragging when you see the double-headed arrow. You can also move the taskbar to the left or right edge of the desktop, or to the top of the desktop, by dragging a blank area of the taskbar to the desired position.

STEP 3: Create the Link

➤ Click the **Microsoft Word button** on the taskbar to return to the memo as shown in Figure 4.12c. Press **Ctrl+End** to move to the end of the memo, which is where you will insert the Excel worksheet.

➤ Pull down the **Edit menu.** Click **Paste Special** to display the dialog box in Figure 4.12c.

➤ Click **Microsoft Excel 5.0 Worksheet Object** in the As list. Click the **Paste Link option button.** Click **OK** to insert the worksheet into the document.

➤ Press the **enter key** twice (to create a blank line between the worksheet and the chart that will be added in step 5).

➤ Pull down the **File menu** and click **Save** (or click the **Save button** on the Standard toolbar) to save the memo.

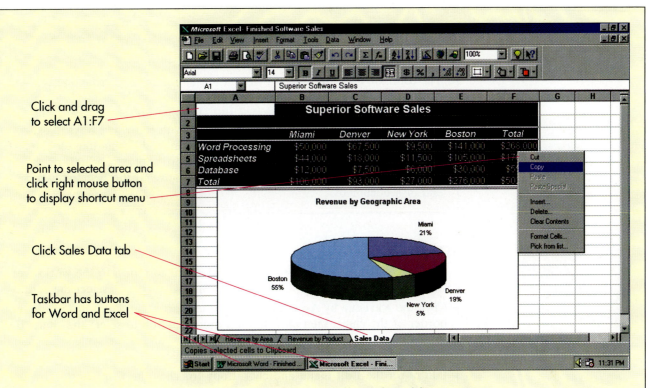

(b) Copy the Worksheet (step 2)

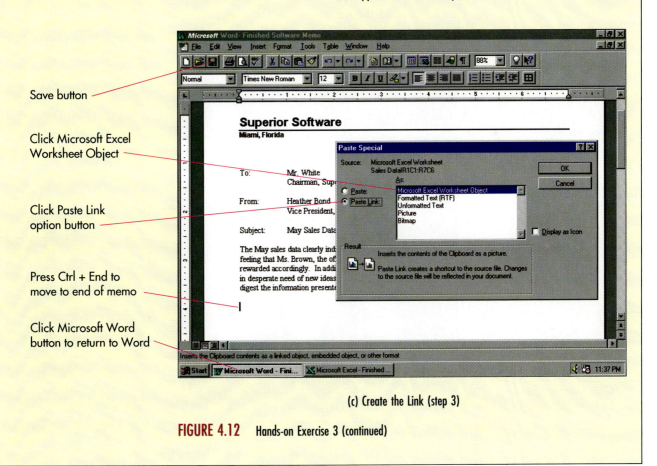

(c) Create the Link (step 3)

FIGURE 4.12 Hands-on Exercise 3 (continued)

GRAPHS AND CHARTS

THE COMMON USER INTERFACE

The common user interface provides a sense of familiarity from one Windows application to the next. Even if you have never used Microsoft Word, you will recognize many of the elements present in Excel. The applications share a common menu structure with consistent ways to execute commands from those menus. The Standard and Formatting toolbars are present in both applications. Many keyboard shortcuts are also common, such as Ctrl+Home and Ctrl+End to move to the beginning and end of a document.

STEP 4: Copy the Chart

➤ Click the **Microsoft Excel button** on the taskbar to return to the worksheet. Click outside the selected area (cells A1 through F7) to deselect the cells.

➤ Click the **Revenue by Area tab** to select the chart sheet. Point just inside the border of the chart, then click the left mouse button to select the chart. Be sure you have selected the entire chart and that you see the same sizing handles as in Figure 4.12d.

➤ Pull down the **Edit menu** and click **Copy** (or click the **Copy button** on the Standard toolbar).

STEP 5: Add the Chart

➤ Click the **Microsoft Word button** on the taskbar to return to the memo. If necessary, press **Ctrl+End** to move to the end of the Word document.

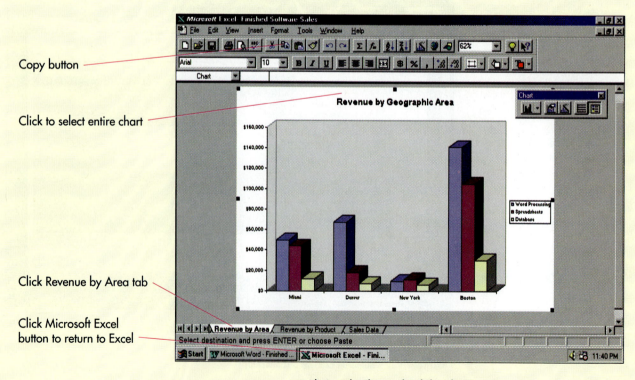

(d) Copy the Chart to the Clipboard (step 4)

FIGURE 4.12 Hands-on Exercise 3 (continued)

- Pull down the **Edit menu.** Click **Paste Special.** Click the **Paste Link** option button. If necessary, click **Microsoft Excel 5.0 Chart Object.** Click **OK** to insert the chart into the document.
- Click on the chart to select it and display the sizing handles. Click and drag a corner sizing handle inward to make the chart smaller.
- Click the **up** or **down arrow** on the vertical scroll bar so that you will be able to see the worksheet and the chart as shown in Figure 4.12e. (Do not be concerned if you do not see all of the chart.)

> **LINKING VERSUS EMBEDDING**
>
> The *Paste Special command* will link or embed an object, depending on whether the *Paste Link command* or *Paste command* option button is checked. Linking stores a pointer to the file containing the object together with a reference to the server application, and changes to the object are automatically reflected in all compound documents that are linked to the object. Embedding stores a copy of the object with a reference to the server application, but changes to the copy of the object within the compound document are not reflected in the original object. With both linking and embedding, however, you can double click the object in the compound document to edit the object, using the tools of the server application.

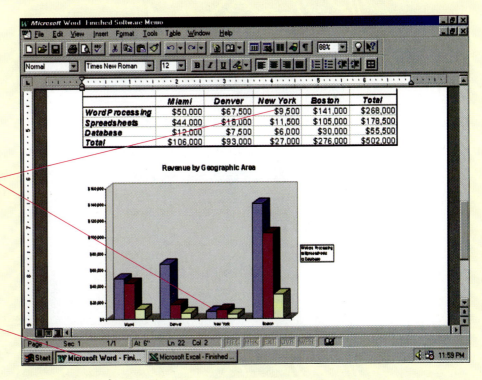

Sales for word processing in New York are $9,500

Click the Microsoft Word button to return to Word

(e) Add the Chart (step 5)

FIGURE 4.12   Hands-on Exercise 3 (continued)

- Look carefully at the worksheet and chart in the document. The sales for word processing in New York are currently $9,500, and the chart reflects this amount. Save the memo.
- Point to the **Microsoft Excel button** on the taskbar and click the **right mouse button** to display a shortcut menu. Click **Close** to close Excel. Click **Yes** if prompted whether to save the changes to the Finished Software Sales workbook.
- The Microsoft Excel button disappears from the taskbar, indicating that Excel has been closed. Word is now the only open application.

STEP 6: Modify the Worksheet
- Click anywhere in the worksheet to select the worksheet and display the sizing handles as shown in Figure 4.12f. (We suggest you do not move or size the object until step 8 in the exercise.)
- The status bar indicates that you can double click to edit the worksheet. Double click anywhere within the worksheet to reopen Excel in order to change the data.
- The system pauses as it loads Excel and reopens the Finished Software Sales workbook. If necessary, click the **Maximize button** to maximize the Excel window.
- Click the **Sales Data tab** within the workbook. Click in **cell D4**. Type **$200,000**. Press **enter**. You may need to widen the column in order to display the larger number.
- Click the **Revenue by Area tab** to select the chart sheet. The chart has been modified automatically and reflects the increased sales for New York.

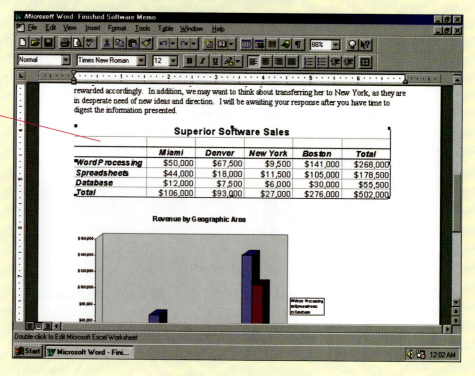

Click worksheet to select it; double click to edit it

(f) Modify the Worksheet (step 6)

FIGURE 4.12 Hands-on Exercise 3 (continued)

ALT+TAB STILL WORKS

Alt+Tab was a treasured shortcut in Windows 3.1 that enabled users to switch back and forth between open applications. The shortcut also works in Windows 95. Press and hold the Alt key while you press and release the Tab key repeatedly to cycle through the open applications, whose icons are displayed in a small rectangular window in the middle of the screen. Release the Alt key when you have selected the icon for the application you want.

STEP 7: Update the Links

➤ Use the taskbar to return to Microsoft Word and the Software Memo. The links for the worksheet and chart may (or may not) be updated automatically, according to the options that are set in Microsoft Word.

- Point to the worksheet, click the **right mouse button** to display the shortcut menu, then click the **Update Link command.** The New York word processing sales should be $200,000.

- Point to the chart, click the **right mouse button** to display the shortcut menu in Figure 4.12g, then click the **Update Link command.**

➤ Save the Word document.

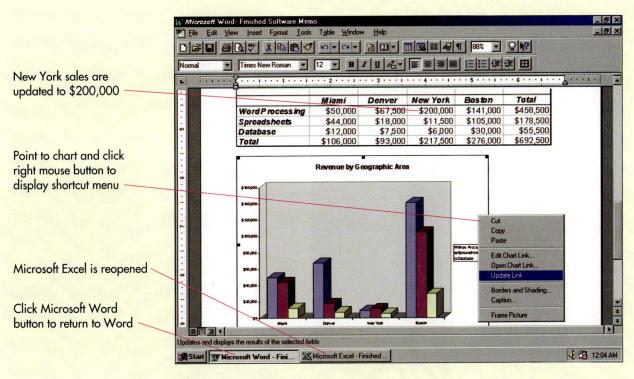

(g) Update the Link (step 7)

FIGURE 4.12 Hands-on Exercise 3 (continued)

STEP 8: The Completed Memo

➤ Pull down the **View menu.** Click **Zoom.** Click **Whole Page.** Click **OK.** You should see the completed memo as shown in Figure 4.12h.

➤ Point to the chart, then click the **right mouse button** to display the shortcut menu. Click **Frame Picture** to place the chart in a frame, which facilitates moving the chart within a document. Frame the worksheet in similar fashion.

➤ Click and drag the worksheet and chart until you are satisfied with the appearance of the completed memo. Save the memo a final time.

➤ Print the memo. Exit Word. Exit Excel. (Save the changes to Finished Software Sales.) Congratulations on a job well done.

THE FORMAT FRAME COMMAND

All objects should be placed into a frame, a special type of (invisible) container in Microsoft Word that facilitates positioning an object within a Word document. An unframed object is treated as an ordinary paragraph, and movement is restricted to one of three positions (left, center, or right). A second limitation is that text cannot be wrapped around an unframed object. A framed object, however, can be precisely positioned by right clicking the object, selecting the Format Frame command, then entering the information about the object's desired position.

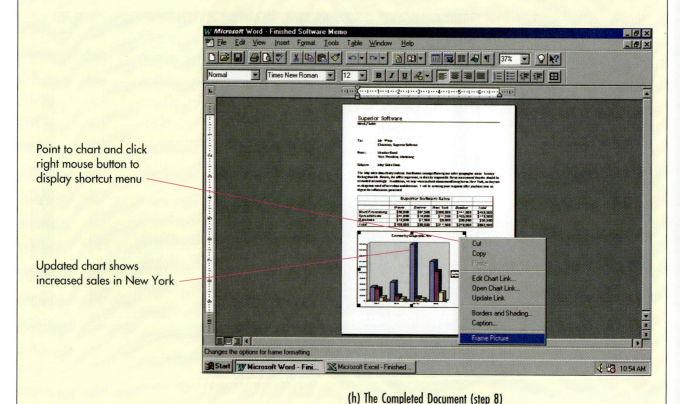

(h) The Completed Document (step 8)

FIGURE 4.12   Hands-on Exercise 3 (continued)

ADDITIONAL CHART TYPES

Excel offers a total of 15 **chart types,** each with several formats. The chart types are displayed in the ChartWizard (see Figure 4.5b) and are listed here for convenience. The chart types are Area, Bar, Column, Line, Pie, Doughnut, Radar, XY (scatter), Combination, 3-D Area, 3-D Bar, 3-D Column, 3-D Line, 3-D Pie, and 3-D Surface.

It is not possible to cover every type of chart, and so we concentrate on the most common. We have already presented the bar, column, and pie charts and continue with the line and combination charts. We use a different example, the worksheet in Figure 4.13a, which plots financial data for the National Widgets Corporation in Figures 4.13b and 4.13c. Both charts were created through the ChartWizard, then modified as necessary using the techniques from the previous exercises.

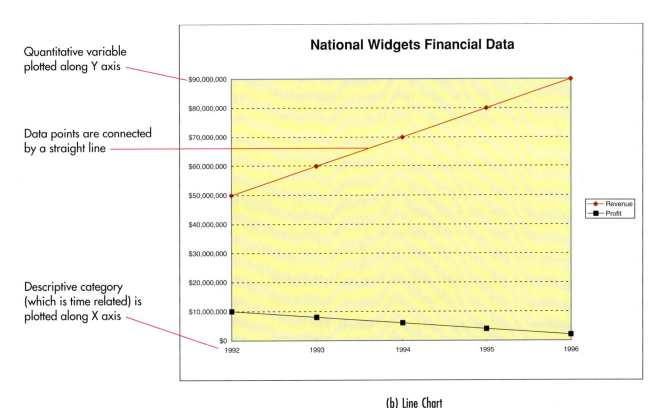

FIGURE 4.13   National Widgets Financial Data

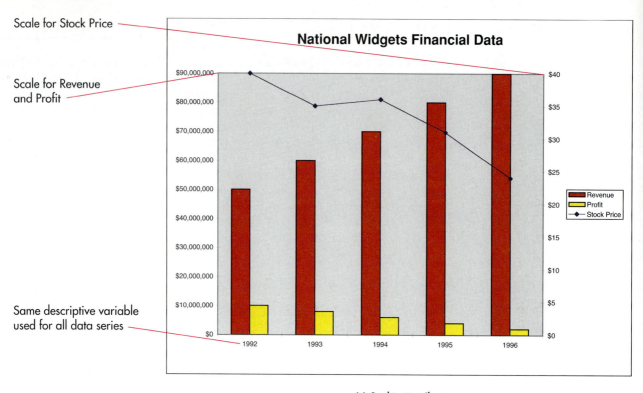

(c) Combination Chart

FIGURE 4.13 National Widgets Financial Data (continued)

Line Chart

A *line chart* is best to display time-related information, such as the five-year trend of revenue and profit in Figure 4.13b. A line chart plots one or more data series (e.g., revenue and profit) against a descriptive category (e.g., year). As with a column chart, the quantitative values are plotted along the vertical scale (Y axis) and the descriptive category along the horizontal scale (X axis).

Combination Chart

A *combination chart* is used when different scales are required for multiple data series that are plotted against the same descriptive variable. The chart in Figure 4.13c plots revenue, profit, and stock price over the five-year period. The same scale can be used for revenue and profit (both are in millions of dollars), but an entirely different scale is needed for the stock price. Investors in National Widgets can see at a glance the true status of their company.

USE AND ABUSE OF CHARTS

The hands-on exercises in the chapter demonstrate how easily numbers in a worksheet can be converted to their graphic equivalent. *The numbers can, however, just as easily be converted into erroneous or misleading charts, a fact that is often overlooked.* Indeed, some individuals are so delighted just to obtain the charts, that they accept the data without question. Accordingly, we present two examples of statistically accurate yet entirely misleading graphical data, drawn from charts submitted by our students in response to homework assignments.

> Lying graphics cheapen the graphical art everywhere... When a chart on television lies, it lies millions of times over; when a *New York Times* chart lies, it lies 900,000 times over to a great many important and influential readers. The lies are told about the major issues of public policy—the government budget, medical care, prices, and fuel economy standards, for example. The lies are systematic and quite predictable, nearly always exaggerating the rate of recent change.
>
> **Edward Tufte**

Improper (Omitted) Labels

The difference between *unit sales* and *dollar sales* is a concept of great importance, yet one which is often missed. Consider, for example, the two pie charts in Figures 4.14a and 4.14b, both of which are intended to identify the leading salesperson, based on the underlying worksheet in Figure 4.14c. The charts yield two different answers, Jones and Smith, respectively, depending on which chart you use.

As you can see, the two charts reflect different percentages and would appear therefore to contradict each other. Both charts, however, are technically correct, as the percentages depend on whether they express unit sales or dollar sales. *Jones is the leader in terms of units, whereas Smith is the leader in terms of dollars.* The

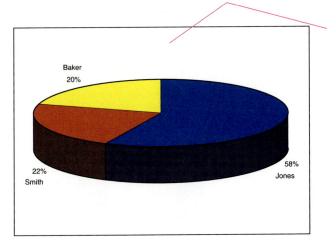
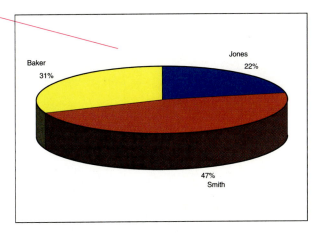

(a) Units   (b) Dollars

		Jones		Smith		Baker	
	Price	Units	Dollars	Units	Dollars	Units	Dollars
Product 1	$1	200	$200	20	$20	30	$30
Product 2	$5	50	$250	30	$150	30	$150
Product 3	$20	5	$100	50	$1,000	30	$600
	Totals	255	$550	100	$1,170	90	$780

Sales Data - First Quarter

(c) Underlying Spreadsheet

FIGURE 4.14 Omitted Labels

latter is generally more significant, and hence the measure that is probably most important to the reader. Neither chart, however, was properly labeled (there is no indication of whether units or dollars are plotted), which in turn may lead to erroneous conclusions on the part of the reader.

Good practice demands that every chart have a title and that as much information be included on the chart as possible to help the reader interpret the data. Use titles for the X axis and Y axis if necessary. Add text boxes for additional explanation.

Adding Dissimilar Quantities

The conversion of a side-by-side column chart to a stacked column chart is a simple matter, requiring only a few mouse clicks. Because the procedure is so easy, however, it can be done without thought, and in situations where the stacked column chart is inappropriate.

Figures 4.15a and 4.15b display a side-by-side and a stacked column chart, respectively. One chart is appropriate and one chart is not. The side-by-side columns in Figure 4.15a indicate increasing sales in conjunction with decreasing profits. This is a realistic portrayal of the company, which is becoming less efficient because profits are decreasing as sales are increasing.

The stacked column chart in Figure 4.15b plots the identical numbers. It is deceptive, however, as it implies an optimistic trend whose stacked columns reflect a nonsensical addition. The problem is that although sales and profits are both measured in dollars, they should not be added together because the sum does not represent a meaningful concept.

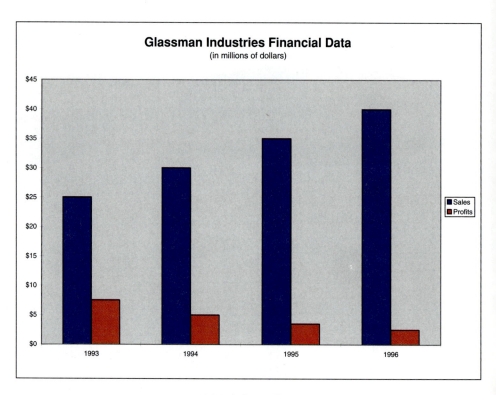

(a) Multiple Bar Chart

FIGURE 4.15 Adding Dissimilar Quantities

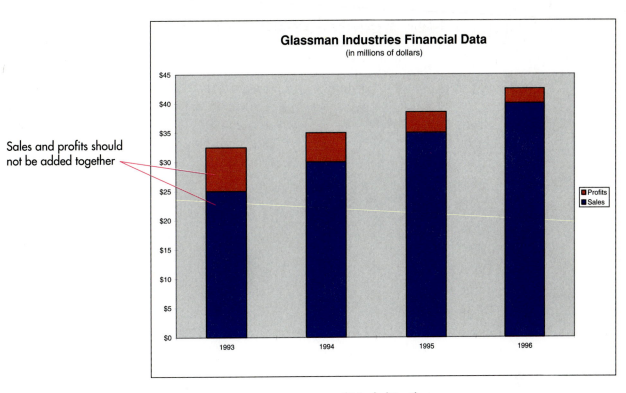

(b) Stacked Bar Chart

FIGURE 4.15 Adding Dissimilar Quantities (continued)

SUMMARY

A chart is a graphic representation of data in a worksheet. The type of chart chosen depends on the message to be conveyed. A pie chart is best for proportional relationships. A column or bar chart is used to show actual numbers rather than percentages. A line chart is preferable for time-related data.

The ChartWizard is the easiest way to create a chart. Once created, a chart can be enhanced with arrows and text boxes found on the Drawing toolbar.

A chart may be embedded in a worksheet or created in a separate chart sheet. An embedded chart may be moved within a worksheet by selecting it and dragging it to its new location. An embedded chart may be sized by selecting it and dragging any of the sizing handles in the desired direction.

Multiple data series may be specified in either rows or columns. If the data is in rows, the first row is assumed to contain the category labels, and the first column is assumed to contain the legend. Conversely, if the data is in columns, the first column is assumed to contain the category labels, and the first row the legend. The ChartWizard makes it easy to switch from rows to columns and vice versa.

Object Linking and Embedding enables the creation of a compound document containing data (objects) from multiple applications. The essential difference between linking and embedding is whether the object is stored within the compound document (embedding) or in its own file (linking). An embedded object is stored in the compound document, which in turn becomes the only user (client) of that object. A linked object is stored in its own file, and the compound document is one of many potential clients of that object.

KEY WORDS AND CONCEPTS

Bar chart	Drawing toolbar	Paste Link command
Category label	Embedded chart	Paste Special command
Chart	Embedded object	Pie chart
Chart sheet	Embedding	Server application
Chart toolbar	Exploded pie chart	Sheet tab
Chart type	Floating toolbar	Sizing handles
ChartWizard	Legend	Stacked columns
Client application	Line chart	Taskbar
Column chart	Linked object	Text box
Combination chart	Linking	Three-dimensional column chart
Common user interface	Multiple data series	
Compound document	Multitasking	Three-dimensional pie chart
Data point	Object	
Data series	Object Linking and Embedding (OLE)	X axis
Default chart		Y axis
Docked toolbar	Paste command	

Multiple Choice

1. Which type of chart is best to portray proportion or market share?
   (a) Pie chart
   (b) Line
   (c) Column chart
   (d) Combination chart

2. Which type of chart is typically used to display time-related data?
   (a) Pie chart
   (b) Line chart
   (c) Column chart
   (d) Combination chart

3. Which of the following chart types is *not* suitable to display multiple data series?
   (a) Pie chart
   (b) Horizontal bar chart
   (c) Column chart
   (d) All of the above are equally suitable

4. Which of the following is best to display additive information from multiple data series?
   (a) A column chart with the data series stacked one on top of another
   (b) A column chart with the data series side by side
   (c) Both (a) and (b) are equally appropriate
   (d) Neither (a) nor (b) is appropriate

5. A workbook must contain:
   (a) A separate chart sheet for every worksheet
   (b) A separate worksheet for every chart sheet
   (c) Both (a) and (b)
   (d) Neither (a) nor (b)

6. Which of the following is true regarding an embedded chart?
   (a) It can be moved elsewhere within the worksheet
   (b) It can be made larger or smaller
   (c) Both (a) and (b)
   (d) Neither (a) nor (b)

7. Which of the following will produce a shortcut menu?
   (a) Pointing to a workbook tab and clicking the right mouse button
   (b) Pointing to an embedded chart and clicking the right mouse button
   (c) Pointing to a selected cell range and clicking the right mouse button
   (d) All of the above

8. Which of the following is done *prior* to invoking the ChartWizard?
   (a) The data series are selected
   (b) The location of the embedded chart within the worksheet is specified
   (c) Both (a) and (b)
   (d) Neither (a) nor (b)

9. Which of the following will display sizing handles when selected?
   (a) An embedded chart
   (b) The title of a chart
   (c) A text box or arrow
   (d) All of the above

10. How do you switch between open applications?
    (a) Click the appropriate button on the taskbar
    (b) Use Alt+Tab to cycle through the applications
    (c) Both (a) and (b)
    (d) Neither (a) nor (b)

11. Which of the following is true regarding the compound document (the memo containing the worksheet and chart) that was created in the chapter?
    (a) The compound document contains more than one object
    (b) Excel is the server application and Word for Windows is the client application
    (c) Both (a) and (b)
    (d) Neither (a) nor (b)

12. In order to represent multiple data series on the same chart:
    (a) The data series must be in rows and the rows must be adjacent to one another on the worksheet
    (b) The data series must be in columns and the columns must be adjacent to one another on the worksheet
    (c) The data series may be in rows or columns so long as they are adjacent to one another
    (d) The data series may be in rows or columns with no requirement to be next to one another

13. If multiple data series are selected and rows are specified:
    (a) The first row will be used for the category (X axis) labels
    (b) The first column will be used for the legend
    (c) Both (a) and (b)
    (d) Neither (a) nor (b)

14. If multiple data series are selected and columns are specified:
    (a) The first column will be used for the category (X axis) labels
    (b) The first row will be used for the legend
    (c) Both (a) and (b)
    (d) Neither (a) nor (b)

15. Which of the following is true about the scale on the Y axis in a column chart that plots multiple data series side-by-side versus one that stacks the values one on top of another?
    (a) The scale for the stacked columns will contain larger values than if the columns are plotted side-by-side
    (b) The scale for the side-by-side columns will contain larger values than if the columns are stacked
    (c) The values on the scale will be the same regardless of whether the columns are stacked or side-by-side
    (d) The values on the scale will be different but it is not possible to tell which chart will contain the higher values

ANSWERS

1. a   6. c   11. c
2. b   7. d   12. d
3. a   8. a   13. c
4. a   9. d   14. c
5. d   10. c   15. a

EXPLORING EXCEL 7.0

1. Use Figure 4.16 to match each action with its result; a given action may be used more than once or not at all.

Action	Result
a. Click at 1	_____ Switch to the Sales Data sheet
b. Click at 2	_____ Create gridlines on the chart
c. Click right mouse button at 3	_____ Change the font used for the chart title
d. Click at 4	_____ Rename the current sheet
e. Click at 5	_____ Place an arrow on the chart
f. Click at 6	_____ Change the chart type
g. Click at 7	_____ Create a new chart on its own sheet

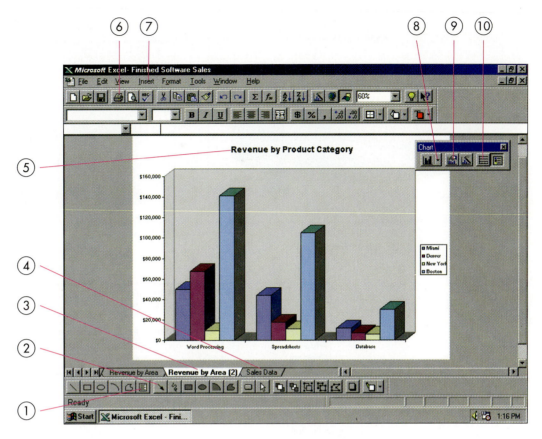

FIGURE 4.16 Screen for Problem 1

    h. Click at 8   _____ Print the chart
    i. Click at 9   _____ Place a text box on the chart
    j. Click at 10   _____ Change the data series from columns to rows

2. The value of a chart is aptly demonstrated by writing a verbal equivalent to a graphic analysis. Accordingly, write the corresponding written description of the information contained in Figure 4.8a. Can you better appreciate the effectiveness of the graphic presentation?

3. The worksheet of Figure 4.17c is the basis for the two charts of Figures 4.17a and 4.17b. Although the charts may at first glance appear to be satisfactory, each reflects a fundamental error. Discuss the problems associated with each chart.

4. Answer the following with respect to the worksheet and embedded chart of Figure 4.18:
    a. Are the data series in rows or columns? How many data series are there?
    b. Which cells contain the category labels? Which cells contain the legends?
    c. Which toolbars in the figure are docked? Which are floating?
    d. How do you change the size of an embedded chart? How do you move an embedded chart? How do you delete it?
    e. What is the difference between clicking and double clicking the embedded chart? Was the chart in Figure 4.18 clicked or double clicked?
    f. What is the easiest way to reverse the way the data is plotted (i.e., switch rows to columns or vice versa)? (Hint: look at the floating toolbar and ToolTip.)

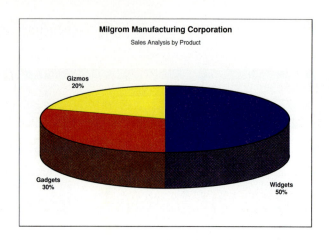

(a) Error 1

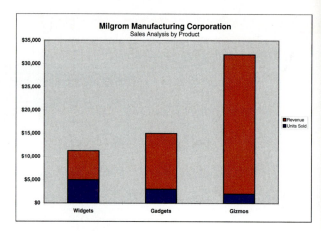

(b) Error 2

	Milgrom Manufacturing Corporation Sales Analysis by Product		
	Unit Price	Units Sold	Revenue
Widgets	$1.25	5000	$6,250
Gadgets	$4.00	3000	$12,000
Gizmos	$14.99	2000	$29,980

(c) The Worksheet

FIGURE 4.17 Spreadsheet and Graphs for Problem 3

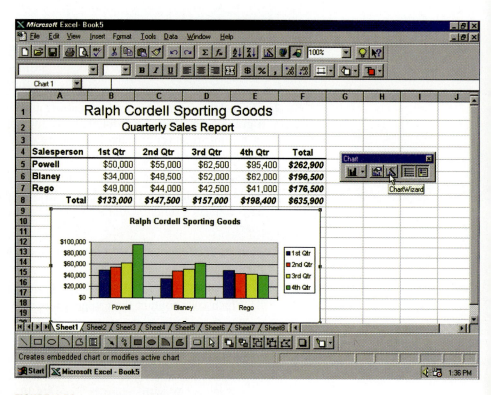

FIGURE 4.18 Screen for Problem 4

190 EXPLORING MICROSOFT EXCEL 7.0

PRACTICE WITH EXCEL 7.0

1. The worksheet in Figure 4.19 is to be used as the basis of several charts that analyze the sales data for the chain of four Michael Moldof clothing boutiques. The worksheet is found on the data disk in the *Chapter 4 Practice 1 workbook*. Use the worksheet to develop the following charts:

   a. A pie chart showing the percentage of total sales attributed to each store.
   b. A column chart showing the total sales for each store.
   c. A stacked column chart showing total sales for each store, broken down by clothing category.
   d. A stacked column chart showing total dollars for each clothing category, broken down by store.
   e. Create each chart in its own chart sheet. Rename the various chart sheets to reflect the charts they contain.
   f. Title each chart appropriately and enhance each chart as you see fit.
   g. Print the entire workbook (the worksheet and all four chart sheets).
   h. Add a title page with your name and date, then submit the completed assignment to your instructor.

	A	B	C	D	E	F
1		Michael Moldof Men's Boutique				
2		January Sales				
3						
4		Store 1	Store 2	Store 3	Store 4	Total
5	Slacks	$25,000	$28,750	$21,500	$9,400	$84,650
6	Shirts	$43,000	$49,450	$36,900	$46,000	$175,350
7	Underwear	$18,000	$20,700	$15,500	$21,000	$75,200
8	Accessories	$7,000	$8,050	$8,000	$4,000	$27,050
9						
10	Total	$93,000	$106,950	$81,900	$80,400	$362,250

FIGURE 4.19 Spreadsheet for Practice Exercise 1

2. The worksheet in Figure 4.20 is to be used by the corporate marketing manager in a presentation in which she describes sales over the past four years. The manager has placed the worksheet on the data disk (in the *Chapter 4 Practice 2 workbook*) and would like you, her student intern, to do all of the following:

   a. Format the worksheet attractively so that it can be used as part of the presentation. Include your name somewhere in the worksheet.
   b. Create any chart(s) you think appropriate to emphasize the successful performance enjoyed by the London office.
   c. Use the same data and chart type(s) as in part (a) but modify the title (and/or callouts) to emphasize the disappointing performance of the Paris office.
   d. Print the worksheet together with all charts and submit them to your instructor. Be sure to title all charts appropriately and to use the text and arrow tools to add the required emphasis.

	A	B	C	D	E	F
1	Unique Boutiques					
2	Sales for 1992-1995					
3						
4	Store	1992	1993	1994	1995	Totals
5	Miami	1500000	2750000	3000000	3250000	10500000
6	London	4300000	5500000	6700000	13000000	29500000
7	Paris	2200000	1800000	1400000	1000000	6400000
8	Rome	2000000	3000000	4000000	5000000	14000000
9	Totals	10000000	13050000	15100000	22250000	60400000

FIGURE 4.20 Spreadsheet for Practice Exercise 2

3. The worksheet in Figure 4.21 is to be used as the basis for several charts depicting information on hotel capacities. Each of the charts is to be created in its own chart sheet within the *Chapter 4 Practice 3 workbook* on the data disk. We describe the message we want to convey, but it is up to you to determine the appropriate chart and associated data range(s). Accordingly, you are to create a chart that:

   a. Compares the total capacity of the individual hotels to one another.
   b. Shows the percent of total capacity for each hotel.
   c. Compares the number of standard and deluxe rooms for all hotels, with the number of standard and deluxe rooms side-by-side for each hotel.
   d. Compares the standard and deluxe room rates for all hotels, with the two different rates side-by-side for each hotel.
   e. Add your name to the worksheet as the Hotel Manager, then print the complete workbook, which will consist of the original worksheet plus the four chart sheets you created.

	A	B	C	D	E	F
1		**Hotel Capacities and Room Rates**				
2						
3	Hotel	No. of Standard Rooms	Standard Rate	No. of Deluxe Rooms	Deluxe Rate	Total Number of Rooms
4	Holiday Inn	300	100	100	150	400
5	Hyatt	225	120	50	175	275
6	Ramada Inn	150	115	35	190	185
7	Sheraton	175	95	25	150	200
8	Marriott	325	100	100	175	425
9	Hilton	250	80	45	120	295
10	Best Western	150	75	25	125	175
11	Days Inn	100	50	15	100	115

FIGURE 4.21 Spreadsheet for Practice Exercise 3

4. Object Linking and Embedding: The compound document in Figure 4.22 contains a memo and combination chart. (The worksheet is contained in the *Chapter 4 Practice 4 workbook*. The text of the memo is in the *Chapter 4 Practice 4 Memo,* which exists as a Word document in the Exploring Excel folder on the data disk.) You are to complete the compound document and submit it to your instructor by completing the following steps:

   a. Create a letterhead for the memo containing your name, address, phone number, and any other information you deem appropriate.
   b. Create the combination chart that appears in the memo.
   c. Link the chart to the memo.
   d. Print the compound document and submit it to your instructor.

Steven Stocks

Financial Investments • 100 Century Tower • New York, NY 10020

To: Carlos Rosell

From: Steven Stocks

Subject: Status Report on National Widgets

I have uncovered some information that I feel is important to the overall health of your investment portfolio. The graph below clearly shows that while revenues for National Widgets have steadily increased since 1992, profits have steadily decreased. In addition, the stock price is continuing to decline. Although at one time I felt that a turnaround was imminent, I am no longer so optimistic and am advising you to cut your losses and sell your National Widgets stock as soon as possible.

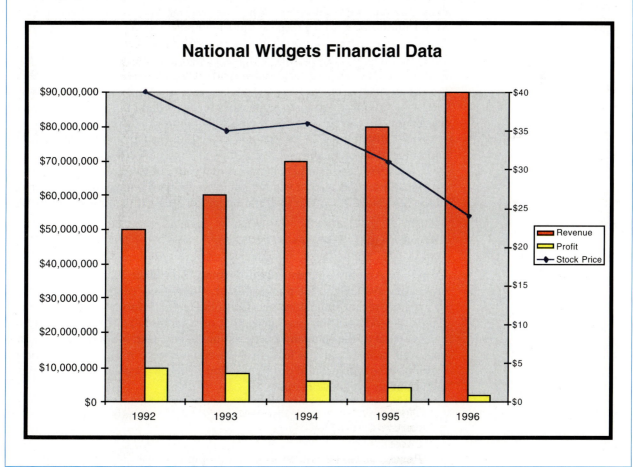

FIGURE 4.22   Compound Document for Practice Exercise 4

Case Studies

University Enrollments

Your assistantship next semester has placed you in the Provost's office, where you are to help create a presentation for the Board of Trustees. The Provost is expected to make recommendations to the Board regarding the expansion of some programs and the reduction of others. You are expected to help the Provost by developing a series of charts to illustrate enrollment trends. The Provost has created the *Student Enrollments workbook* on the data disk, which contains summary data over the last several years.

The Federal Budget

The National debt is staggering—nearly $5 trillion, or almost $20,000 for every man, woman, and child in the United States. The annual budget is approximately $1.5 trillion, with the deficit in the neighborhood of $200 billion. Medicare, defense, and interest on the debt itself are the largest expenditures and consume approximately 35%, 24%, and 14%, respectively. Personal income taxes and Social Security (including Medicare) taxes account for approximately 36% and 31% of the government's income.

Use the information on your most recent federal tax return to obtain exact figures for the current year, then create the appropriate charts to reflect the government's distribution of income and expenditures. Do some additional research and obtain data on the budget, the deficit, and the national debt for the years 1945, 1967, and 1980. The numbers may surprise you. For example, how does the interest expense for the current year compare to the total budget in 1967 (at the height of the Viet Nam War)? To the total budget in 1945 (at the end of World War II)?

The Annual Report

Corporate America spends a small fortune to produce its annual reports, which are readily available to the public at large. Choose any company and obtain a copy of its most recent annual report. Consolidate the information in the company's report to produce a two-page document of your own. Your report should include a description of the company's progress in the last year, a worksheet with any data you deem relevant, and at least two charts in support of the worksheet or written material. Use Microsoft Word in addition to the worksheet to present the information in an attractive manner.

Computer Mapping

Your boss has asked you to look into computer mapping in an effort to better analyze sales data for your organization. She suggested you use the online help facility to explore the Data Map feature within Excel, which enables you to create color-coded maps from columns of numerical data. You mentioned this assignment to a colleague who suggested that you open the *Mapstats workbook* that is installed with Excel to see the sample maps and demographic data included with Excel. You have two days to learn the potential for computer mapping. Your boss expects at least a three-page written report with real examples.

APPENDIX A: THE SPREADSHEET AUDIT

OVERVIEW

In one of the most celebrated spreadsheet errors of all time, the comptroller of James A. Cummings, Inc, a Florida construction company, used a spreadsheet to develop a bid on a multi-million dollar office complex. At the last minute, he realized that he had forgotten to include $254,000 for overhead, and so he inserted this number at the top of a column of numbers. Unfortunately for both the comptroller and the company, the $254,000 was not included in the final total, and the contract was underbid by that amount. The company was awarded the contract and forced to make good on its unrealistically low estimate.

Seeking to recover its losses, the construction company brought suit against the spreadsheet vendor, claiming that a latent defect within the spreadsheet failed to add the entry in question. The vendor contended that the mistake was in fact a *user error* and the court agreed, citing the vendor's licensing agreement:

> *"... Because software is inherently complex and may not be completely free of errors, you are advised to verify your work. In no event will the vendor be liable for direct, indirect, special, incidental, or consequential damages arising out of the use of or inability to use the software or documentation, even if advised of the possibility of such damages. In particular, said vendor is not responsible for any costs including, but not limited to, those incurred as a result of lost profits or revenue."*

The purpose of this appendix is to remind you that the spreadsheet is only a tool, and like all other tools it must be used properly, or there can be serious consequences. Think, for a moment, how business has become totally dependent on the spreadsheet, and how little validity checking is actually done. Ask yourself if any of your spreadsheets contained an error, and if so, what the consequences would have been if those spreadsheets represented real applications rather than academic exercises.

USE FUNCTIONS RATHER THAN FORMULAS

The entries =A1+A2+A3+A4 and =SUM(A1:A4) may appear equivalent, but the function is inherently superior and should be used whenever possible. A function adjusts automatically for the insertion (deletion) of rows within the designated range, whereas a formula does not. Including a blank row at the beginning and end of the function's range ensures that any value added to the top or bottom of a column of numbers will automatically be included in the sum. Had this technique been followed by the James A. Cummings company, the error would not have occurred.

A WORD OF CAUTION

The formatting capabilities within Excel make it all too easy to get caught up in the appearance of a worksheet without paying attention to its accuracy. Consider, for example, the grade book in Figure A.1, which is used by a hypothetical professor to assign final grades in a class. The grade book is nicely formatted, *but its calculations are wrong*, and no amount of fancy formatting can compensate for the erroneous results. Consider:

- Baker should have received an A rather than a B. He has an 87 average on his quizzes, he received an 87 on the final exam, and with two bonus points for each of his two homeworks, he should have had an overall final average of 91.

- Charles should have received a B rather than a C. True, he did not do any homework and he did do poorly on the final, but, with the semester quizzes and final exam counting equally, his semester average should have been 80.

	Name	HW 1	HW 2	HW 3	Quiz 1	Quiz 2	Quiz 3	Quiz Average	Final Exam	HW Bonus	Semester Average	Grade
1	Name	HW 1	HW 2	HW 3	Quiz 1	Quiz 2	Quiz 3	Quiz Average	Final Exam	HW Bonus	Semester Average	Grade
2	Baker		OK	OK	77	89	95	87	87	2	89	B
3	Charles				84	76	86	82	78	0	79	C
4	Goodman	OK	OK			95	94	63	95	4	89	B
5	Johnson	OK	OK		90	86	70	82	90	4	92	A
6	Jones		OK	OK	75	85	71	77	86	2	85	B
7	Irving	OK		OK	65	85	75	75	78	2	79	C
8	Lang				84	88	83	85	94	0	91	A
9	London		OK		72	69	75	72	82	2	81	B
10	Milgrom	OK	OK		100	65	90	85	100	4	100	A
11	Mills	OK	OK		75	85	80	80	65	4	74	C
12	Nelson	OK	OK		65	60	61	62	60	4	65	D
13												
14		Grading Criteria								Grading Scale		
15		Bonus for each homework					2			Average	Grade	
16		Weight of semester quizzes					50%			0	F	
17		Weight of final exam					50%			60	D	
18										70	C	
19										80	B	
20										90	A	

Baker should have received an A

Charles should have received a B

Goodman should have received an A

FIGURE A.1   The Professor's Grade Book

- Goodman should have received an A rather than a B. She aced both quizzes (she was excused from the first quiz) as well as the final, and in addition, she received a four-point bonus for homework.

The errors in our example are contrived, but they could occur. Consider:

- At the class's urging, the professor decided at the last minute to assign a third homework but neglected to modify the formulas to include the additional column containing the extra homework.
- The professor changed the grading scheme at the last minute and decided to count the semester quizzes and final exam evenly. (The original weights were 30% and 70%, respectively.) Unfortunately, however, the formulas to compute each student's semester average specify constants (.30 and .70) rather than absolute references to the cells containing the exam weights. Hence the new grading scheme is not reflected in the student averages.
- The professor forgot that he had excused Goodman from the first quiz and hence did not adjust the formula to compute Goodman's average on the basis of two quizzes rather than three.

Our professor is only human, but he would have done well to print the cell formulas in order to audit the mechanics of the worksheet and double check its calculations. Suffice it to say that the accuracy of a worksheet is far more important than its appearance, and you are well advised to remember this thought as you create and/or use a spreadsheet.

THE SPREADSHEET AUDIT

The *Auditing toolbar* helps you understand the relationships between the various cells in a worksheet. It enables you to trace the *precedents* for a formula and identify the cells in the worksheet that are referenced by that formula. It also enables you to trace the *dependents* of a cell and identify the formulas in the worksheet that reference that cell.

The identification of precedent and/or dependent cells is done graphically by displaying tracers on the worksheet. You simply click in the cell for which you want the information, then you click the appropriate button on the Auditing toolbar. The blue arrows (tracers) appear on the worksheet, and will remain on the worksheet until you click the appropriate removal button. The tracers always point forward, from the precedent cells to the dependent formula.

To see how valuable the tracers can be, consider Figure A.2, which contrasts the professor's original worksheet (Figure A.2a) with the corrected worksheet (Figure A.2b). Consider first the precedents for cell J2, which contains the formula to compute Baker's homework bonus. The tracers (the blue lines) in the invalid worksheet identify homeworks 1 and 2 (note the box around cells B2 and C2) as precedents. The corrected worksheet, however, shows that all three homeworks (cells B2, C2, and D2) are used in the determination of the bonus. (Both worksheets show that cell G15, which contains the homework bonus, is also a precedent for cell J2.)

The analysis of dependent cells is equally telling. There are no dependent cells for cell G16 in the invalid spreadsheet because the formulas to compute the students' semester averages do not reference this cell. The valid worksheet, however, corrects the error, and hence each cell in column K is dependent on cell G16.

The Auditing toolbar is displayed through the View menu and is shown in both Figures A.2a and A.2b. You can point to any button on the Auditing toolbar to display a ToolTip to indicate the purpose of that button.

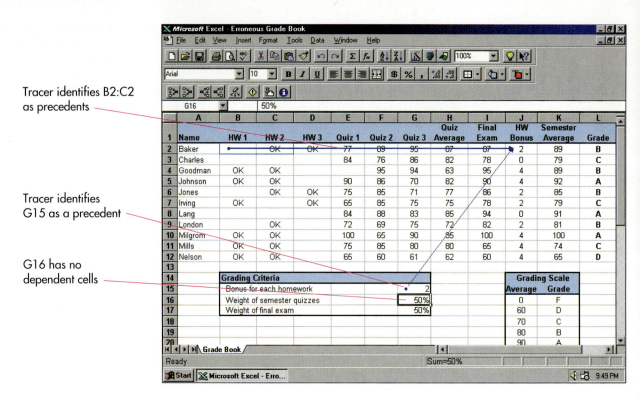

(a) The Invalid Worksheet

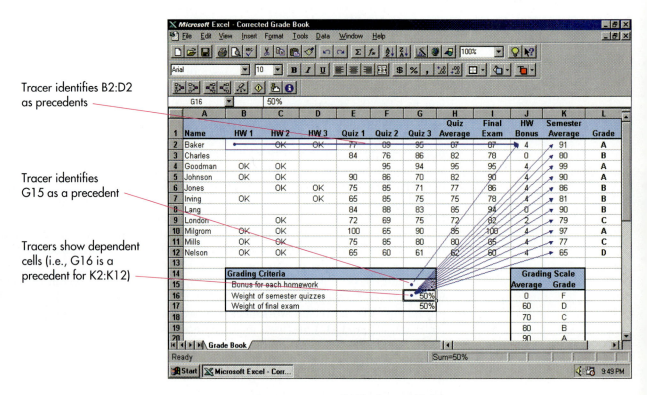

(b) The Corrected Worksheet

FIGURE A.2   The Spreadsheet Audit

> ### ANNOTATE YOUR SPREADSHEETS
>
> The Attach Note button on the Auditing Toolbar enables you to create the equivalent of your own ToolTip for any cell in a spreadsheet. It is an excellent way to annotate a spreadsheet and attach an explanation to any cell containing a complex formula. See step 5 in the hands-on exercise for details on attaching a note.

A SECOND EXAMPLE

Financial planning and budgeting is one of the most common business applications of spreadsheets. Figure A.3 contains a revised (and invalid) version of the financial forecast that was developed in Chapter 2 (see pages 69–75). As in the professor's grade book, the spreadsheet is nicely formatted, but its calculations are wrong, as will be explained shortly. Any decisions based on the spreadsheet will also be in error.

How do you know when a spreadsheet displays invalid results? One way is to "eyeball" the spreadsheet and try to approximate its results. Look for any calculations that are obviously incorrect. Look at the financial forecast, for example, and see whether all the values are growing at the projected rates of change. The number of units sold and the unit price increase every year as expected, but the cost of the production facility remains constant after 1997. This is an obvious error because the production facility is supposed to increase at eight percent annually, according to the assumptions at the bottom of the spreadsheet. The consequence of this error is that the production costs (after 1997) are too low and hence the projected earnings are too high. The error was easy to find, even without the use of a calculator.

	A	B	C	D	E	F
1		Get Rich Quick - Financial Forecast				
2		1996	1997	1998	1999	2000
3	Income					
4	Units sold	100,000	110,000	121,000	133,100	146,410
5	Unit price	$2.25	$2.36	$2.48	$2.60	$2.73
6	Gross revenue	$225,000	$259,875	$300,156	$346,680	$400,415
7						
8	Fixed costs					
9	Production facility	$50,000	$54,000	$54,000	$54,000	$54,000
10	Administration	$25,000	$26,250	$27,563	$28,941	$30,388
11	Variable cost					
12	Unit mfg cost	$1.50	$1.65	$1.82	$2.00	$2.20
13	Variable mft cost	$150,000	$181,500	$219,615	$265,734	$321,538
14						
15	Earnings before taxes	$25,000	$24,375	$26,541	$26,946	$24,877
16						
17	Initial conditions			Annual increase		
18	First year sales	100,000		10%		
19	Selling price	$2.25		5%		
20	Unit mfg cost	$1.50		10%		
21	Production facility	$50,000		8%		
22	Administration	$25,000		5%		
23	First year of forecast	1996				

Cost of the production facility is not increasing as expected after 1977

Earnings should be 0 ($225,000 – $225,000)

FIGURE A.3 The Erroneous Financial Forecast

A more subtle error occurs in the computation of the earnings before taxes. Look at the numbers for 1996. The gross revenue is $225,000. The total cost is also $225,000 ($50,000 for the production facility, $25,000 for administration, and $150,000 for the manufacturing cost). The projected earnings should be zero, but are shown incorrectly as $25,000, because the administration cost was not subtracted from the gross revenue in determining the profit.

The errors in the financial forecast are easy to discover if only you take the time to look. Unfortunately, however, too many people are prone to accept the results of a spreadsheet, simply because it is nicely formatted on a laser printer. We urge you, therefore, to "eyeball" every spreadsheet for obvious errors, and if a mistake is found, a spreadsheet audit is called for.

TEST WITH SIMPLE AND PREDICTABLE DATA

Test a spreadsheet initially with simple and predictable data that you create yourself so that you can manually verify the spreadsheet is performing as expected. Once you are confident the spreadsheet works with data you can control, test it again with real data to further check its validity. Adequate testing is time consuming, but it can save you from embarrassing, not to mention costly, mistakes.

HANDS-ON EXERCISE 1

The Auditing Toolbar

Objective: To illustrate the tools on the Auditing toolbar; to trace errors in spreadsheet formulas; to identify precedent and dependent cells; to attach a note to a cell. Use Figure A.4 as a guide in the exercise.

STEP 1: Display the Auditing Toolbar

➤ Load Excel. Open the **Erroneous Financial Forecast** workbook in the **Exploring Excel folder** as shown in Figure A.4a. Save the workbook as **Finished Erroneous Financial Forecast.**

➤ Point to any toolbar, click the **right mouse button** to display the shortcut menu in Figure A.4a, then click **Auditing** to display the Auditing toolbar.

➤ If necessary, click and drag the title bar of the Auditing toolbar to dock the toolbar under the Formatting toolbar.

FIXED VERSUS FLOATING TOOLBARS

Any toolbar can be docked along the edge of the application window, or it can be displayed as a floating toolbar within the application window. To move a docked toolbar, drag the toolbar background. To move a floating toolbar, drag its title bar. To size a floating toolbar, drag any border in the direction you want to go. Double click the background of any toolbar to toggle between a floating toolbar and a docked (fixed) toolbar.

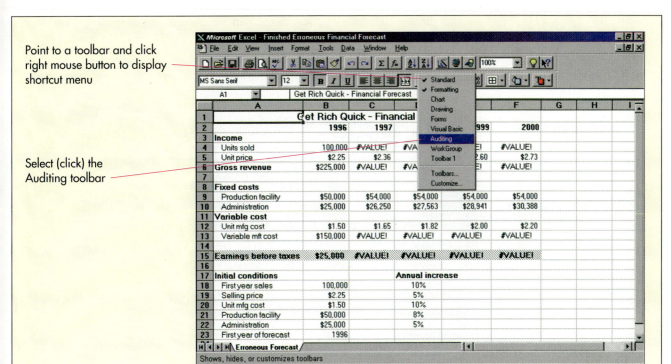

(a) Display the Auditing Toolbar (step 1)

FIGURE A.4 Hands-on Exercise 1

STEP 2: The Trace Error Command

➤ Click in **cell C4,** the first cell that displays the #VALUE error. Click the **Trace Error button** on the Auditing toolbar to display the tracers shown in Figure A.4b.

➤ The tracers identify the error in graphic fashion and show that cell C4 is dependent on cells A4 and D18 (i.e., cells A4 and D18 are precedents of cell C4). Cell A4 contains a text entry and is obviously incorrect.

➤ Click in the formula bar to edit the formula for cell C4 so that it references cell B4 rather than cell A4. (The correct formula is =B4+B4*$D$18). Press **enter** when you have corrected the formula.

➤ The tracer arrows disappear (they disappear automatically whenever you edit a formula to which they refer). The #VALUE errors are also gone because the formula has been corrected and all dependent formulas have been automatically recalculated.

THE #VALUE ERROR

The #VALUE error occurs when the wrong type of entry is used in a formula or as an argument in a function. It typically occurs when a formula references a text rather than a numeric entry. The easiest way to resolve the error is to display the Auditing toolbar, select the cell in question, then click the Trace Error button.

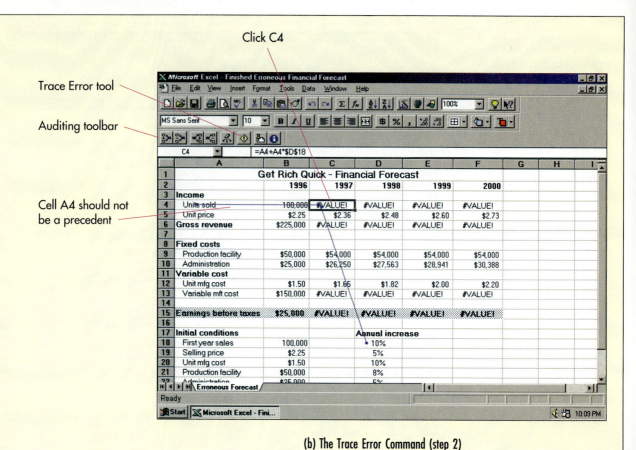

(b) The Trace Error Command (step 2)

FIGURE A.4 Hands-on Exercise 1 (continued)

STEP 3: Trace Dependents

➤ The worksheet is in error because the production costs do not increase after 1997. Click in **cell D21** (the cell containing the projected increase in the cost of the production facility).

➤ Click the **Trace Dependents button** to display the dependent cells as shown in Figure A.4c. Only one dependent cell (cell C9) is shown. This is clearly an error because cells D9 through F9 should also depend on cell D1.

➤ Click in **cell C9** to examine its formula (=B9+B9*D21). The production costs for the second year are based on the first-year costs (cell B9) and the rate of increase (cell D21). The latter, however, was entered as a relative rather than an absolute address.

➤ Change the formula in cell C9 to include an absolute reference to cell D21 (i.e., the correct formula is =B9+B9*$D$21). The tracer arrow disappears due to the correction.

➤ Drag the fill handle in **cell C9** to copy the corrected formula to **cells D9, E9,** and **F9**. (The displayed value for cell F9 should be $68,024.)

➤ Click in **cell D21**. Click the **Trace Dependents button,** and this time it points to the production costs for years 2 through 5 in the forecast. Click the **Remove Dependents button** to remove the arrows.

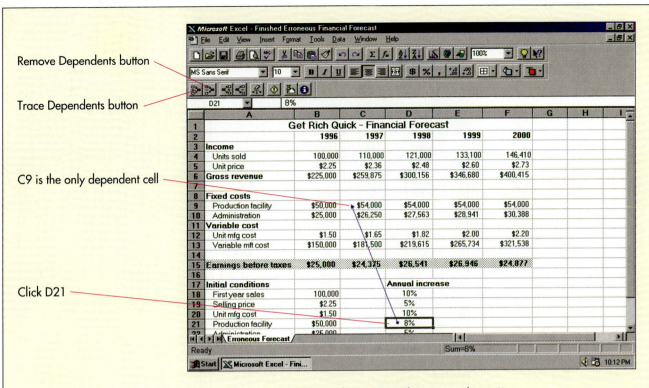

(c) The Trace Dependents Command (step 3)

FIGURE A.4 Hands-on Exercise 1 (continued)

ISOLATE ASSUMPTIONS AND INITIAL CONDITIONS

A spreadsheet is first and foremost a tool for decision making, and as such, the subject of continual what-if speculation. It is critical, therefore, that the input and assumptions be isolated and clearly visible, and further that all formulas in the spreadsheet accurately reflect the cells containing these values.

STEP 4: Trace Precedents

➤ The earnings before taxes in cell B15 should be zero. (The gross revenue is $225,000, as are the total expenses, which consist of production, administration, and manufacturing costs of $50,000, $25,000, and $150,000, respectively.) Click in **cell B15**.

➤ Click the **Trace Precedents button** to display the precedent cells as shown in Figure A.4d. The projected earnings depend on the revenue (cell B6) and various expenses (cells B9 and B13). The problem is that the administration expense (cell B10) is omitted, and hence the earnings are too high.

➤ Change the formula in cell B15 to **=B6−(B9+B10+B13)** so that the administration expense is included in the expenses that are deducted from the gross revenue. The tracer arrow disappears.

➤ Drag the fill handle in **cell B15** to copy the corrected formula to **cells C15 through F15**. (The displayed value in cell F15 is a *negative* $19,535.)

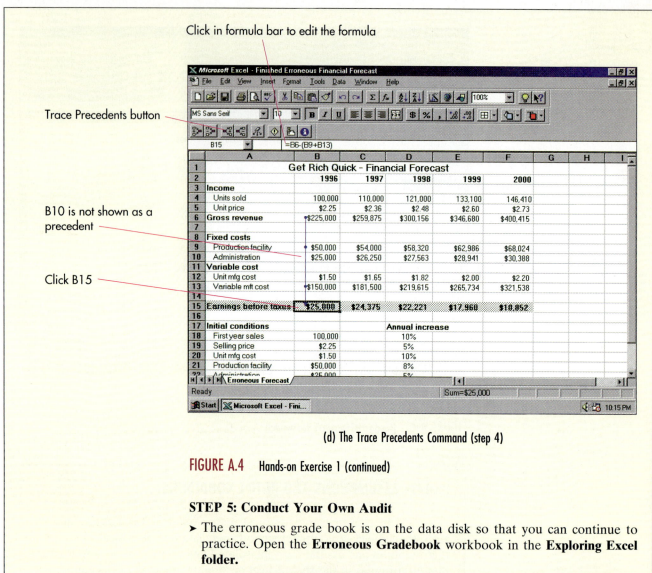

(d) The Trace Precedents Command (step 4)

FIGURE A.4 Hands-on Exercise 1 (continued)

STEP 5: Conduct Your Own Audit

➤ The erroneous grade book is on the data disk so that you can continue to practice. Open the **Erroneous Gradebook** workbook in the **Exploring Excel folder.**

➤ You should see the professor's grade book that was described at the beginning of the appendix. Conduct your own audit of the grade book, using the techniques in the exercise.

➤ Exit Excel when you have completed the exercise.

SUMMARY

A spreadsheet is only a tool, and like all other tools, it must be used properly, or else there can be serious consequences. The essential point in the grade book and financial forecast examples is that the potential for spreadsheet error does exist, and that you cannot blindly accept the results of a spreadsheet. Every spreadsheet should be checked for obvious errors, and if any are found, a spreadsheet audit is called for.

The Auditing toolbar helps you understand the relationships between the various cells in a worksheet. It enables you to trace the precedents for a formula and identify the cells in the worksheet that are referenced by that formula. It also enables you to trace the dependents of a cell and identify the formulas in the worksheet that reference that cell.

APPENDIX B: TOOLBARS

OVERVIEW

Microsoft Excel has thirteen predefined toolbars to provide access to commonly used commands. The toolbars are displayed in Figure B.1 and are listed here for convenience. They are: the Auditing, Chart, Drawing, Formatting, Forms, Full Screen, Microsoft, Query and Pivot, Standard, Stop Recording, TipWizard, Visual Basic, and WorkGroup toolbars. The Standard and Formatting toolbars are displayed by default and appear immediately below the menu bar. The other toolbars can be displayed as needed or, in some cases, may appear automatically when you access their corresponding feature (e.g., the Chart toolbar and the Query and Pivot toolbar).

The buttons on the toolbars are intended to be indicative of their function. Clicking the Printer button (the fourth button from the left on the Standard toolbar), for example, executes the Print command. If you are unsure of the purpose of any toolbar button, point to it, and a ToolTip will appear that displays its name.

You can display multiple toolbars at one time, move them to new locations on the screen, customize their appearance, or suppress their display.

- To display or hide a toolbar, pull down the View menu and click the Toolbars command. Select (deselect) the toolbar(s) that you want to display (hide). The selected toolbar(s) will be displayed in the same position as when last displayed. You may also point to any toolbar and click with the right mouse button to bring up a shortcut menu, after which you can select the toolbar to be displayed (hidden).
- To change the size of the buttons, display them in monochrome rather than color, or suppress the display of the ToolTips, pull down the View menu, click Toolbars, and then select (deselect) the appropriate check box. Alternatively, you can click on any

toolbar with the right mouse button, select Toolbars, and then select (deselect) the appropriate check box.

- Toolbars may be either docked (along the edge of the window) or left floating (in their own window). A toolbar moved to the edge of the window will dock along that edge. A toolbar moved anywhere else in the window will float in its own window. Docked toolbars are one tool wide (high), whereas floating toolbars can be resized by clicking and dragging a border or corner as you would with any window.
  - To move a docked toolbar, click anywhere in the gray background area and drag the toolbar to its new location.
  - To move a floating toolbar, drag its title bar to its new location.
- To customize one or more toolbars, display the toolbar(s) on the screen, pull down the View menu, click Toolbars, and then click the Customize command button. Alternatively, you can click on any toolbar with the right mouse button and select Customize from the shortcut menu.
  - To move a button, drag the button to its new location on that toolbar or any other displayed toolbar.
  - To copy a button, press the Ctrl key as you drag the button to its new location on that toolbar or any other displayed toolbar.
  - To delete a button, drag the button off the toolbar and release the mouse button.
  - To add a button, select the category from the Categories list box and then drag the button to the desired location on the toolbar. (To see a description of a tool's function prior to adding it to a toolbar, click the tool in the Customize dialog box and read the displayed description.)
  - To restore a predefined toolbar to its default appearance, pull down the View menu, click Toolbars, select (highlight) the desired toolbar, and click the Reset command button.
- The Borders, Color, and Font Color buttons on the Formatting toolbar, the Chart Type button on the Chart toolbar, and the Pattern button on the Drawing toolbar also function as movable tear-off palettes. Display the desired palette by clicking the associated down arrow, then drag the palette onto the worksheet in order to make it more accessible as you work. Click the Close button to close the palette.
- To create your own toolbar, pull down the View menu and click Toolbars. Alternatively, you can click on any toolbar with the right mouse button and select Toolbars from the shortcut menu.
  - Enter a name for the toolbar in the Toolbar Name text box. The name can be any length and can contain spaces.
  - Click the New command button.
  - The new toolbar will appear at the top left of the screen. Initially, it will be big enough to hold only one button. Add, move, and delete buttons following the same procedures as outlined above. The toolbar will automatically size itself as new buttons are added and deleted.
- To delete a custom toolbar, pull down the View menu, click Toolbars, and make sure that the custom toolbar to be deleted is the only one selected (highlighted). Click the Delete command button. Click OK to confirm the deletion. (Note that a predefined toolbar cannot be deleted.)

MICROSOFT EXCEL 7.0 TOOLBARS

Auditing Toolbar

Chart Toolbar

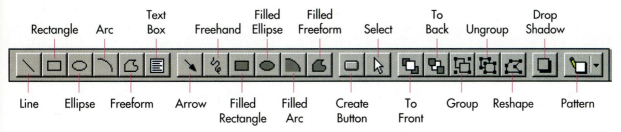

Drawing Toolbar

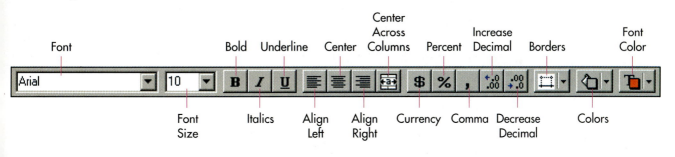

Formatting Toolbar

Forms Toolbar

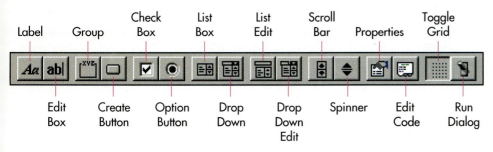

FIGURE B.1 Toolbars

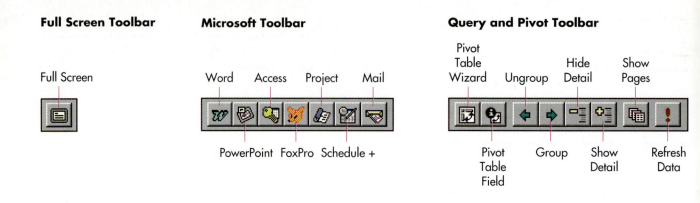

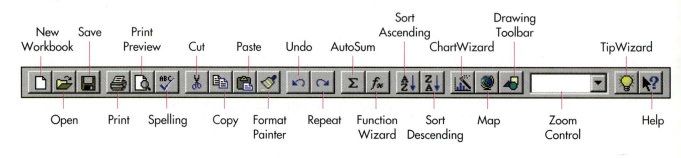

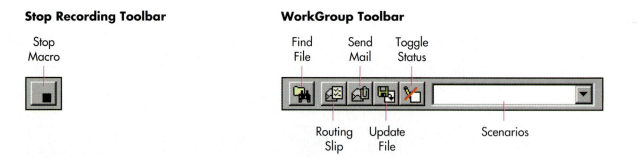

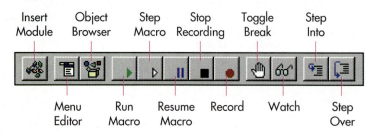

FIGURE B.1   Toolbars (continued)

INTRODUCTION TO MICROSOFT ACCESS: WHAT IS A DATABASE?

OBJECTIVES

After reading this chapter you will be able to:

1. Define the terms field, record, table, and database.
2. Start Microsoft Access; describe the Database window and the objects in an Access database.
3. Add, edit, and delete records within a table; use the Find command to locate a specific record.
4. Describe the record selector; explain when changes are saved to a database.
5. Explain the importance of data validation in table maintenance.
6. Describe a relational database; distinguish between a one-to-many and a many-to-many relationship.

OVERVIEW

All businesses and organizations maintain data of one kind or another. Companies store data about their employees. Schools and universities store data about their students and faculties. Magazines and newspapers store data about their subscribers. The list goes on and on, and while each of these examples refers to different types of data, they all operate under the same basic principles of database management.

This chapter provides a broad-based introduction to database management through the example of a college bookstore. We begin by showing how the mechanics of manual record keeping can be extended to a computerized system. We discuss the basic operations in maintaining data and stress the importance of data validation.

The chapter also introduces you to Microsoft Access, the fourth major application in the Microsoft Office Professional suite. We describe the objects within an Access database and show you how to add, edit, and delete records in an Access table. We also explain how the real power of Access is derived from a database with multiple tables that are related to one another.

The hands-on exercises in the chapter enable you to apply all of the material at the computer, and are indispensable to the learn-by-doing philosophy we follow throughout the text. As you do the exercises, you may recognize many commands from other Windows applications, all of which share a common user interface and consistent command structure.

CASE STUDY: THE COLLEGE BOOKSTORE

Imagine, if you will, that you are the manager of a college bookstore and that you maintain data for every book in the store. Accordingly, you have recorded the specifics of each book (the title, author, publisher, price, and so on) in a manila folder, and have stored the folders in one drawer of a file cabinet.

One of your major responsibilities is to order books at the beginning of each semester, which in turn requires you to contact the various publishers. You have found it convenient, therefore, to create a second set of folders with data about each publisher such as the publisher's phone number, address, discount policy, and so on. You also found it necessary to create a third set of folders with data about each order such as when the order was placed, the status of the order, which books were ordered, how many copies, and so on.

Normal business operations will require you to make repeated trips to the filing cabinet to maintain the accuracy of the data and keep it up to date. You will have to create a new folder whenever a new book is received, whenever you contract with a new publisher, or whenever you place a new order. Each of these folders must be placed in the proper drawer in the filing cabinet. In similar fashion, you will have to modify the data in an existing folder to reflect changes that occur, such as an increase in the price of a book, a change in a publisher's address, or an update in the status of an order. And, lastly, you will need to remove the folder of any book that is no longer carried by the bookstore, or of any publisher with whom you no longer have contact, or of any order that was canceled.

The preceding discussion describes the bookstore of 40 years ago—before the advent of computers and computerized databases. The bookstore manager of today needs the same information as his or her predecessor. Today's manager, however, has the information readily available, at the touch of a key or the click of a mouse, through the miracle of modern technology. The concepts are identical in both the manual and computerized systems.

You can think of the file cabinet, which contains the various sets of folders, as a ***database.*** Each set of folders in the file cabinet corresponds to a ***table*** within the database. In our example the bookstore database consists of three separate tables—for books, publishers, and orders. Each table, in turn, consists of multiple ***records,*** corresponding to the folders in the file cabinet. The Books table, for example, contains a record for every book title in the store. The Publishers table has a record for each publisher, just as the Orders table has a record for each order.

Each fact (or data element) that is stored within a record is called a ***field.*** In our example each book record consists of six fields—ISBN (a unique identifying number for the book), title, author, year of publication, price, and publisher. The table is constructed in such a way that every record has the same fields in the same order. In similar fashion, every record in the Publishers table will have the same fields for each publisher just as every record in the Orders table has the same fields for each order. This terminology (field, table, file, and database) is extremely important and will be used throughout the text.

INTRODUCTION TO MICROSOFT ACCESS

Microsoft Access is the fourth major application in the Microsoft Office and is used to create and manage a database such as the one for the college bookstore. Consider now Figure 1.1, which shows how Microsoft Access appears on the desktop. Our discussion assumes a basic familiarity with Windows 95 and the user interface that is common to all Windows applications. You should recognize, therefore, that the desktop in Figure 1.1 has two open windows—an application window for Microsoft Access and a document (database) window for the database that is currently open.

Each window has its own title bar and Minimize, Maximize (or Restore), and Close buttons. The title bar in the application window contains the name of the application (Microsoft Access). The title bar in the document (database) window contains the name of the database that is currently open (Bookstore). The application window for Access has been maximized to take up the entire desktop, and hence the Restore button is visible. The database window has not been maximized.

A menu bar appears immediately below the application title bar. A toolbar (similar to those in other Office applications) appears below the menu bar and offers alternative ways to execute common commands. The Windows 95 taskbar appears at the bottom of the screen and shows the open applications.

The Database Window

The *Database window* displays the various objects in an Access database. There are six different types of objects—tables, queries, forms, reports, macros, and modules. Every database must contain at least one table, and it may contain any

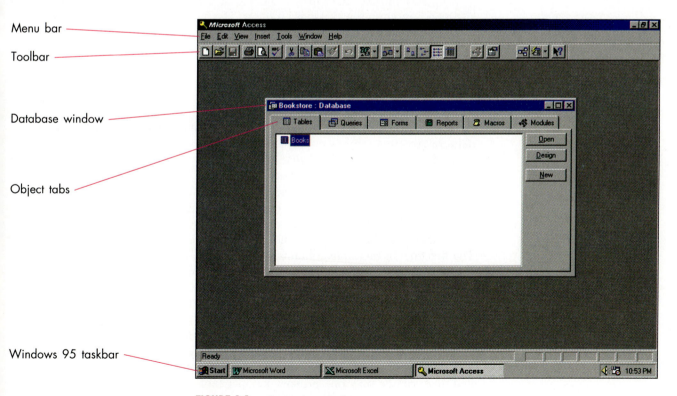

FIGURE 1.1   The Database Window

or all (or none) of the other objects. Each object type is accessed through the appropriate tab within the Database window. In this chapter we concentrate on tables, but we briefly describe the other types of objects as a preview of what you will learn as you read our book.

- A *table* stores data about an entity (a person, place, or thing) and is the basic element in any database. A table is made up of records, which in turn are made up of fields. It is columnar in appearance, with each record in a separate row of the table and each field in a separate column.
- A *form* provides a more convenient and attractive way to enter, display, and/or print the data in a table. Forms are discussed in Chapter 2.
- A *query* answers a question about the database. The most common type of query specifies a set of criteria, then searches the database to retrieve the records that satisfy the criteria. Queries are introduced in Chapter 3.
- A *report* presents the data in a table or query in attractive fashion on the printed page. Reports are described in Chapter 3.
- A *macro* is analogous to a computer program and consists of commands that are executed automatically one after the other. Macros are used to automate the performance of any repetitive task.
- A *module* provides a greater degree of automation through programming in Access Basic. Modules are beyond the scope of this text.

ONE FILE HOLDS ALL

All of the objects in an Access database (tables, forms, queries, reports, macros, and modules) are stored in a single file on disk. The database itself is opened through the Open command in the File menu or by clicking the Open button on the Database toolbar. The individual objects within a database are opened through the database window.

Tables

A table (or set of tables) is the heart of any database, as it contains the actual data. In Access a table is displayed in one of two views—the Table Design view or the Datasheet view. The **Table Design view** is used to define the table initially and to specify the fields it will contain. It is also used to modify the table definition if changes are subsequently necessary. The Table Design view is discussed in Chapter 2. The **Datasheet view** is the view you use to add, edit, or delete records. It is the view on which we focus in this chapter.

Figure 1.2 shows the Datasheet view for the Books table in our bookstore. The first row in the table contains the *field names.* Each additional row contains a record (the data for a specific book). Each column represents a field (one fact about a book). Every record in the table contains the same fields in the same order: ISBN Number, Title, Author, Year, List Price, and Publisher.

The ISBN number is the *primary key,* the field (or combination of fields) that must be unique for each record. The existence of the primary key ensures that every record in a table is different from every other record, and hence it prevents the occurrence of duplicate records. Every table must have a primary key, and there can be only one primary key per table.

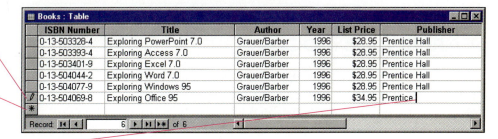

FIGURE 1.2 Tables

The status bar at the bottom of Figure 1.2a indicates that there are five records in the table and that you are positioned on the first record. This is the record you are working on and is known as the *current record.* (You can work on only one record at a time.) There is a *record selector symbol* (either a triangle or a pencil) next to the current record to indicate its status.

A *triangle* indicates that the record has been saved to disk. A *pencil* indicates that you are working on the record and that the changes have not yet been saved. As soon as you move to the next record, however, the pencil changes to a triangle to indicate that the record on which you were working has been saved. (Access, unlike other Office applications, automatically saves its changes without your having to execute the Save command.) An *asterisk* appears next to the blank record at the end of every table.

Figure 1.2a shows the table as it would appear immediately after you opened it. The first field in the first record is selected (highlighted), and anything you type at this point will replace the selected data. (This is the same convention as in any other Windows application.) The triangle next to the current record (record 1) indicates changes have not yet been made. An asterisk appears as the record selector symbol next to the blank record at the end of the table. The blank record is used to add a record to the table and is not counted in determining the number of records in the table.

Figure 1.2b shows the table as you are in the process of entering data for a new record at the end of the table. The current record is now record 6. The *insertion point* (a flashing vertical bar) appears at the point where text is being entered. The record selector for the current record is a pencil, indicating that the record has not yet been saved. The asterisk has moved to the blank record at the end of the table, which now contains one more record than the table in Figure 1.2a.

> **THE INTERNATIONAL STANDARD BOOK NUMBER**
>
> The International Standard Book Number (ISBN) is an internationally recognized number that uniquely identifies a book. The first part of the ISBN indicates the publisher; for example, every book published by Prentice Hall begins with 0-13. The founder of Prentice Hall was very superstitious and the selection of the number 13 was not an accident. Prentice Hall was founded in 1913, its first office was on 13th Street in New York City, and its first phone number ended in 1300. The original name of the company included a hyphen. "Prentice-Hall" (including the hyphen) is thirteen characters.

LEARNING BY DOING

We come now to the first of two hands-on exercises that implement our learn-by-doing philosophy. The exercise shows you how to start Microsoft Access and open the Bookstore database from the *data disk* that is used in conjunction with this text. The exercise tells you how to install the data disk on your computer if you are fortunate enough to have your own machine. Otherwise it tells you how to work from a floppy disk.

Access, like all other Office applications, provides different ways to accomplish the same task. Commands may be executed from a pull-down menu, from a shortcut menu (which is displayed by pointing to an object and clicking the right mouse button), through keyboard equivalents, and/or from a toolbar. The various techniques may at first appear overwhelming, but you will be surprised at how quickly you learn them. There is no need to memorize anything, nor is there a requirement to use every technique. Just be flexible and willing to experiment.

> **ABOUT THE DATA DISK**
>
> The data disk is almost full and should not be used to add or modify the data files referenced in the hands-on exercises. It is intended only to provide the necessary files, but should not be used in any other capacity. This is true even in a lab setting, where you should work from drive C (because it is faster) rather than from drive A. Use the Windows Explorer prior to the exercise to copy the necessary database from the network drive to drive C. Work from drive C throughout the exercise, then copy the modified database from drive C to a floppy disk (for your copy) as you leave the lab.

HANDS-ON EXERCISE 1

Introduction to Microsoft Access

Objective: To open an existing database; to add a record to a table within the database. The exercise introduces you to the data disk that accompanies the text. Use Figure 1.3 as a guide in the exercise.

STEP 1: Welcome to Windows 95

➤ Turn on the computer and all of its peripherals. The floppy drive should be empty prior to starting your machine. This ensures that the system starts by reading from the hard disk, which contains the Windows files, as opposed to a floppy disk, which does not.

➤ Your system will take a minute or so to get started, after which you should see the desktop in Figure 1.3a. Do not be concerned if the appearance of your desktop is different from ours.

➤ If you are new to Windows 95 and you want a quick introduction, click the **What's New** or **Windows Tour command buttons.** (Follow the instructions in the boxed tip to display the Welcome window if it does not appear on your system.)

➤ Click the **Close button** to close the Welcome window and continue with the exercise.

TAKE THE WINDOWS 95 TOUR (REQUIRES CD-ROM INSTALLATION)

Windows 95 greets you with a Welcome window that contains a command button to take you on a 10-minute tour of Windows 95. Click the command button and enjoy the show. You might also try the What's New command button for a quick overview of changes from Windows 3.1. If you do not see the Welcome window when you start Windows 95, click the Start button, click Run, type C:\WINDOWS\WELCOME in the Open text box, and press enter.

Click Windows Tour or What's New buttons if you are new to Windows 95

Click Close button to close Welcome window

(a) Welcome to Windows 95 (step 1)

FIGURE 1.3 Hands-on Exercise 1

STEP 2: Install the Data Disk

- Do this step *only* if you have your own computer and you want to install (copy) the files from the data disk to the hard drive. Place the data disk in drive A.
- Click the **Start button** to display the Start menu. Click the **Run command** to display the Run dialog box.
- Type **A:\Install C** in the text box. (The drive letter, drive C in the example, is variable and indicates the drive on which to install the data disk.)
- Click **OK** or press the **enter key.** Follow the on-screen instructions to complete the installation.

DOWNLOAD THE DATA DISK

The data disk for all books in the Exploring Windows series can be downloaded from the Prentice Hall Web site (http://www.prenhall.com). Use any Web browser to log onto the site, select Business and Economics, then move to the Exploring Windows page. To download the files for a single application, go to the page for that book, then click the icon to download the data disk. To download the files for all Office applications simultaneously, go to the Exploring Microsoft Office page.

STEP 3: Start Microsoft Access

- Click the **Start button** to display the Start menu. Click (or point to) the **Programs menu,** then click **Microsoft Access** to start the program.
- You should see the Microsoft Access dialog box with the option button to **Open an Existing Database** already selected. Click **More Files,** then click **OK** to display the Open dialog box in Figure 1.3b.
- Click the **Details button** to change to the Details view. Click and drag the vertical border between columns to increase (or decrease) the size of a column.
- Click the **drop-down arrow** on the Look In list box. Click the appropriate drive (drive C is recommended rather than drive A), depending on the location of your data. Double click the **Exploring Access folder** to make it the active folder (the folder from which you will retrieve and into which you will save the database).

WORK ON DRIVE C

Even in a lab setting it is preferable to work on the local hard drive, as opposed to a floppy disk. The hard drive is much faster, which becomes especially important when working with the large file sizes associated with Access. Use the Windows Explorer to copy the database from the network drive to the local hard drive prior to the exercise, then work on drive C throughout the exercise. Once you have completed the exercise, use the Explorer a second time to copy the modified database to a floppy disk that you can take with you.

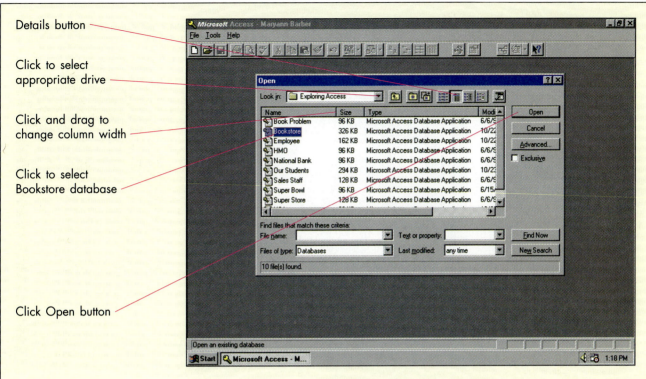

(b) Open an Existing Database (step 3)

FIGURE 1.3 Hands-on Exercise 1 (continued)

➤ Click the **down scroll arrow** (if needed) to click the **Bookstore database.** Click the **Open command button** to open the database.

STEP 4: Open the Books Table
➤ You should see the database window for the Bookstore database with the **Tables tab** already selected. Double click the icon next to **Books** to open the table as shown in Figure 1.3c.
➤ Click the **Maximize button** so that the Books table fills the Access window and reduces the clutter on the screen. If necessary, click the **Maximize button** in the application window so that Access takes the entire desktop.

A SIMPLER DATABASE

The real power of Access is derived from a database with multiple tables that are related to one another. For the time being, however, we focus on a database with only one table so that you can learn the basics of Access. After you are comfortable working with a single table, we will show you how to work with multiple tables and how to relate them to one another.

STEP 5: Moving within a Table
➤ Click in any field in the first record, and the status bar indicates record 1 of 18. The triangle symbol in the record selector indicates that the record has been saved.

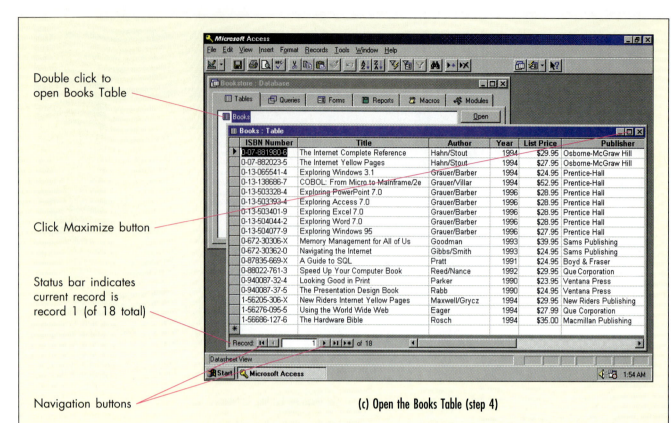

Double click to open Books Table

Click Maximize button

Status bar indicates current record is record 1 (of 18 total)

Navigation buttons

(c) Open the Books Table (step 4)

FIGURE 1.3 Hands-on Exercise 1 (continued)

➤ You can move from record to record (or field to field) using either the mouse or the arrow keys:
  • Click in any field in the second record. The status bar indicates record 2 of 18.
  • Press the **down arrow key** to move to the third record. The status bar indicates record 3 of 18.
  • Press the **left and right arrow keys** to move from field to field within the third record.

➤ You can also use the navigation buttons above the status bar to move from one record to the next:
  • Click |◄ to move to the first record in the table.
  • Click ► to move forward in the table to the next record.
  • Click ◄ to move back in the table to the previous record.

MOVING FROM FIELD TO FIELD

Press the Tab key, the right arrow key, or the enter key to move to the next field in the current record (or the first field in the next record if you are already in the last field of the current record). Press Shift+Tab or the left arrow key to return to the previous field in the current record (or the last field in the previous record if you are already in the first field of the current record).

- Click ▶| to move to the last record in the table.
- Click ▶* to move beyond the last record in order to insert a new record.

➤ Click |◀ to return to the first record in the table.

STEP 6: Add a Record

➤ Pull down the **Insert menu** and click **Record** (or click the **New Record button** on the toolbar). The record selector moves to the last record (record 19). The insertion point is positioned in the first field (ISBN Number).

➤ Enter data for the new record as shown in Figure 1.3d. The record selector changes to a pencil as soon as you enter the first character in the new record.

➤ Press the **enter key** when you have entered the last field for the record. The new record is saved, and the record selector changes to a triangle and moves automatically to the next record.

WHEN IS DATA SAVED?

There is one critical difference between Access and other Office applications such as Word for Windows or Microsoft Excel. *Access automatically saves any changes in the current record as soon as you move to the next record or when you close the table.* In other words, you do *not* have to execute the Save command explicitly to save the data in the table.

New Record button

The record selector is a pencil, indicating data has not yet been saved

(d) Add a New Record (step 6)

FIGURE 1.3 Hands-on Exercise 1 (continued)

INTRODUCTION TO MICROSOFT ACCESS

STEP 7: Add a Second Record

➤ The record selector is at the end of the table where you can add another record. Enter **0-13-504051-5** as the ISBN number for this record. Press the **Tab, enter,** or **right arrow key** to move to the Title field.

➤ Enter the title of this book as **Exploring teh Internet** (deliberately misspelling the word "the"). Try to look at the monitor as you type to see the Auto-Correct feature (common to all Office applications) in action. Access will correct the misspelling and change *teh* to *the*.

➤ If you did not see the correction being made, press the **backspace key** several times to erase the last several characters in the title, then re-enter the title.

➤ Complete the entry for this book. Enter **Marks** for the author. Enter **1996** for the year of publication. Enter **28.95** for the list price. Enter **Prentice Hall** for the publisher, then press **enter.**

CREATE YOUR OWN SHORTHAND

Use the AutoCorrect feature that is common to all Office applications to expand abbreviations such as "PH" for Prentice Hall. Pull down the Tools menu, click AutoCorrect, type the abbreviation in the Replace text box and the expanded entry in the With text box. Click the Add command button, then click OK to exit the dialog box and return to the document. The next time you type PH (in upper- or lowercase) as you enter a record, it will automatically be expanded to Prentice Hall.

STEP 8: Print the Table

➤ Pull down the **File menu.** Click **Page Setup** to display the Page Setup dialog box in Figure 1.3e.

➤ Click the **Page tab.** Click the **Landscape option button.** Click **OK** to accept the settings and close the dialog box.

➤ Click the **Print button** on the toolbar to print the table. Alternatively, you can pull down the **File menu,** click **Print** to display the Print dialog box, click the **All options button,** then click **OK.**

ABOUT MICROSOFT ACCESS

Pull down the Help menu and click About Microsoft Access to display the specific release number as well as other licensing information, including the product serial number. This help screen also contains two very useful command buttons, System Info and Tech Support. The first button displays information about the hardware installed on your system, including the amount of memory and available space on the hard drive. The Tech Support button provides telephone numbers for technical assistance.

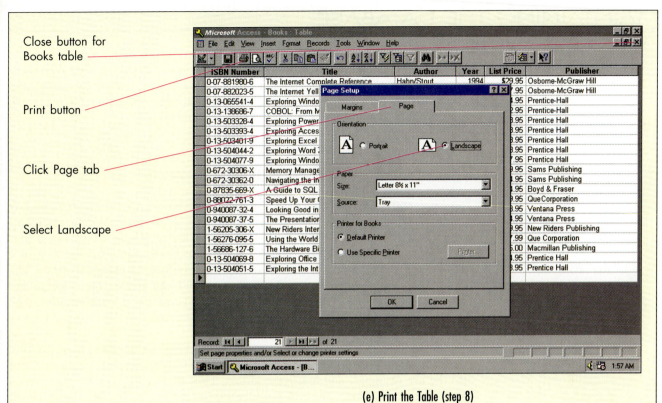

(e) Print the Table (step 8)

FIGURE 1.3 Hands-on Exercise 1 (continued)

STEP 9: Exit Access

➤ You need to close both the Books table and the Bookstore database:

- Pull down the **File menu** and click **Close** (or click the **Close button**) to close the Books table. Answer **Yes** if asked to save changes to the layout of the table.
- Pull down the **File menu** and click **Close** (or click the **Close button**) to close the Bookstore database.

➤ Pull down the **File menu** and click **Exit** to close Access if you do not want to continue with the next exercise at this time.

BACK UP THE DATABASE

You have invested time and effort into completing the first hands-on exercise. Now, when you are getting started, is the time to develop proper backup procedures. Use the Windows Explorer to copy the Bookstore database from drive C to a floppy disk that you will keep as backup.

INTRODUCTION TO MICROSOFT ACCESS   13

MAINTAINING THE DATABASE

The exercise just completed showed you how to open an existing table and **add records** to that table. You will also need to **edit** and/or **delete** existing **records** in order to maintain the data as changes occur. These operations require you to find the specific record and then make the change. You can search the table manually, or more easily through the Find and Replace commands.

Find and Replace Commands

The Find and Replace commands are similar in function to the corresponding commands in all other Office applications. The **Find command** in Microsoft Access enables you to locate a specific record(s) by searching a table for a particular value. You could, for example, search the Books table for the title of a book as in Figure 1.4a, then move to the appropriate field to change its price. The **Replace command** incorporates the Find command and allows you to locate and optionally replace (one or more occurrences of) one value with another. The Replace command in Figure 1.4b, for example, searches for *PH* in order to substitute *Prentice Hall*.

Searches can be made more efficient by making use of the various options. A case-sensitive search, for example, matches not only the specific characters, but also the use of upper- and lowercase letters. Thus, *PH* is different from *ph*, and a case-sensitive search on one will not identify the other. A case-insensitive search

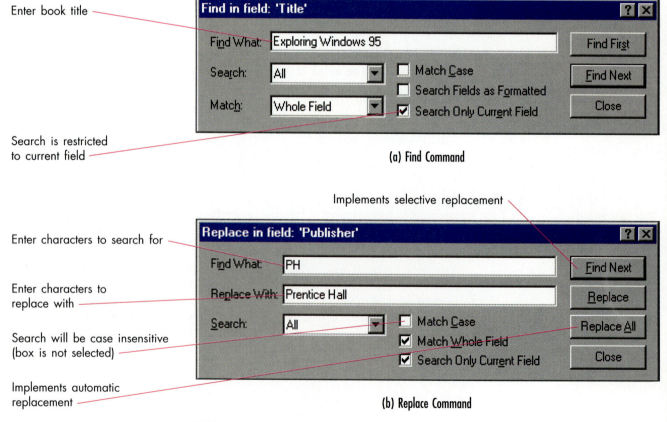

FIGURE 1.4   Find and Replace Commands

(where Match Case is *not* selected) will find both *PH* and *ph.* Any search may specify a match on whole fields to identify *Davis,* but not *Davison.* And finally, a search can also be made more efficient by restricting it to the current field (e.g., Publisher), as opposed to searching every field.

The replacement can be either selective or automatic. Selective replacement lets you examine each successful match in context and decide whether to replace it. Automatic replacement makes the substitution without asking for confirmation (and is generally not recommended). Selective replacement is implemented by clicking the Find Next command button, then clicking (or not clicking) the Replace button to make (or not make) the substitution. Automatic replacement (through the entire table) is implemented by clicking the Replace All button.

Data Validation

It is unwise to simply add (edit or delete) a record without adequate checks on the validity of the data. Ask yourself, for example, whether a search for all books by Prentice Hall (without a hyphen) will also return all books by *Prentice-Hall* (with a hyphen). The answer is *no* because the publisher's name is spelled differently and a search for one will not locate the other. *You* know the publisher is the same in both instances, but the computer does not.

Data validation is a crucial part of any system. Good systems will anticipate errors you might make and reject those errors prior to accepting data. Access automatically implements certain types of data validation. It will not, for example, let you enter letters where a numeric value is expected (such as the Year and Price fields in our example.) More sophisticated types of validation are implemented by the user when the table is created. You may decide, for example, to reject any record that omits the title or author. Data validation is described more completely in Chapter 2.

> ### GARBAGE IN, GARBAGE OUT (GIGO)
>
> A computer does exactly what you tell it to do, which is not necessarily what you want it to do. It is absolutely critical, therefore, that you validate the data that goes into a system, or else the associated information may not be correct. No system, no matter how sophisticated, can produce valid output from invalid input. In other words, *garbage in—garbage out.*

FORMS, QUERIES, AND REPORTS

As previously indicated, an Access database can contain as many as six different types of objects. Thus far we have concentrated on tables, but now we extend the discussion to include forms, queries, and reports as illustrated in Figure 1.5.

Figure 1.5a contains the Books table as it exists after the first hands-on exercise. There are 20 records in the table and six fields for each record. The status bar indicates that you are currently positioned in the first record. You can enter new records in the table as was done in the previous exercise. You can also edit or delete an existing record, as will be illustrated in the next exercise.

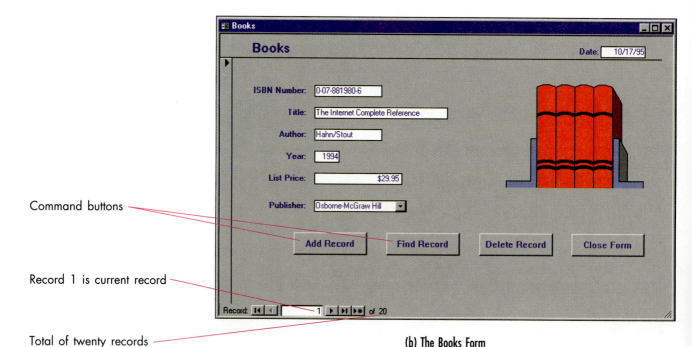

FIGURE 1.5 The Objects in a Database

Figure 1.5b displays a form that is based on the table of Figure 1.5a. A form provides a friendlier interface than does a table and is easier to understand and use. Note, for example, the command buttons in the form to add a new record, or to find and/or delete an existing record. The status bar at the bottom of the form indicates that you are on the first of 20 records, and is identical to the status bar for the table in Figure 1.5a.

Figure 1.5c displays a query to list the books for a particular publisher (Prentice Hall in this example). A query consists of a question (e.g., enter the publisher name) and an answer (the records that satisfy the query). The results of the query

Books are in sequence by author, and within the same author, by title

Publisher	Author	Title	ISBN Number	Year	List Price
Prentice Hall	Grauer/Barber	Exploring Access 7.0	0-13-503393-4	1996	$28.95
Prentice Hall	Grauer/Barber	Exploring Excel 7.0	0-13-503401-9	1996	$28.95
Prentice Hall	Grauer/Barber	Exploring Office 95	0-13-504069-8	1996	$34.95
Prentice Hall	Grauer/Barber	Exploring PowerPoint 7.0	0-13-503328-4	1996	$28.95
Prentice Hall	Grauer/Barber	Exploring Windows 3.1	0-13-065541-4	1994	$24.95
Prentice Hall	Grauer/Barber	Exploring Windows 95	0-13-504077-9	1996	$28.95
Prentice Hall	Grauer/Barber	Exploring Word 7.0	0-13-504044-2	1996	$28.95
Prentice Hall	Grauer/Villar	COBOL: From Micro to Mainframe/2e	0-13-138686-7	1994	$52.95
Prentice Hall	Marks	Exploring the Internet	0-13-504051-5	1996	$28.95

(c) The Publisher Query

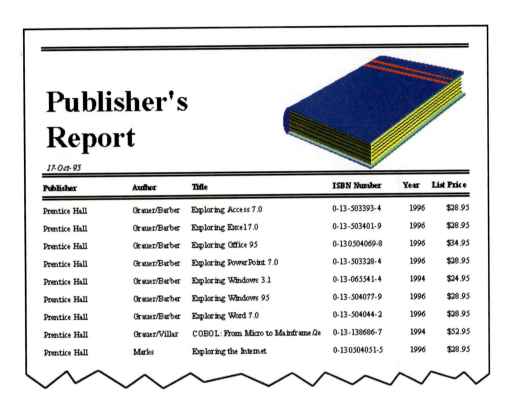

(d) The Publisher Report

FIGURE 1.5 The Objects in a Database (continued)

are similar in appearance to the underlying table, except that the query contains selected records and/or selected fields for those records. The query may also list the records in a different sequence from that of the table.

Figure 1.5d illustrates a report that includes only the books from Prentice Hall. A report provides presentation-quality output and is preferable to printing the results of a table or query. Note, too, that a report may be based on either a table or a query. You could, for example, base the report in Figure 1.5d on the Books table, in which case it would list every book in the table. Alternatively, the report could be based on a query, as in Figure 1.5d, and list only the books that satisfy the criteria within the query.

Later chapters discuss forms, queries, and reports in depth. The exercise that follows is intended only as a brief introduction to what can be accomplished in Access.

HANDS-ON EXERCISE 2

Maintaining the Database

Objective: To add records to, edit records in, and delete records from a table within a database; to use the Find and Replace commands; to demonstrate data validation; to introduce forms, queries, and reports. Use Figure 1.6 as a guide in doing the exercise.

STEP 1: Open the Bookstore Database

➤ Start Access as you did in the previous exercise. The Bookstore database should appear within the list of recently opened databases as shown in Figure 1.6a.

> ### THE DOCUMENTS SUBMENU
>
> One of the fastest ways to get to a recently used document, regardless of the application, is through the Windows 95 Start menu, which includes a Documents submenu containing the last 15 documents that were opened. Click the Start button, click (or point to) the Documents submenu, then click the document you wish to open (e.g., Bookstore), assuming that it appears on the submenu. Windows will start the application, then open the indicated document.

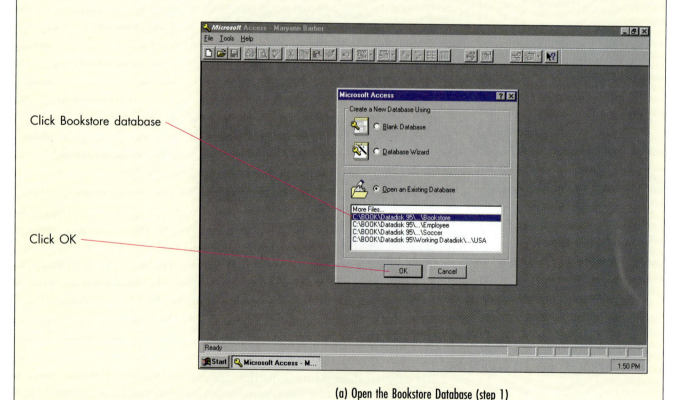

(a) Open the Bookstore Database (step 1)

FIGURE 1.6 Hands-on Exercise 2

18 EXPLORING MICROSOFT ACCESS 7.0

➤ Select the **Bookstore database** (its drive and folder may be different from that in Figure 1.6a). Click **OK** to open the database.

➤ Click the **Tables tab** in the Database window. Double click the icon for the **Books table** to open the table from the previous exercise.

STEP 2: The Find Command

➤ You should see the Books table in Figure 1.6b. (The Find dialog box is not yet displayed). If necessary, click the **Maximize button** to maximize the Books table within the Access window.

➤ Exploring Office 95 and Exploring the Internet, the books you added in the previous exercise, appear in sequence according to the ISBN number because this field is the primary key for the Books table.

➤ Click in the **Title field** for the first record. Pull down the **Edit menu** and click **Find** (or click the **Find button** on the toolbar) to display the dialog box in Figure 1.6b. (You are still positioned in the first record.)

➤ Enter **Exploring Windows 95** in the Find What text box. Check that the other parameters for the Find command match the dialog box in Figure 1.6b. Be sure that **Search Only Current Field** is selected.

➤ Click the **Find First command button.** Access moves to record 11, the record containing the designated character string, and selects the Title field for that record. Click **Close** to close the Find dialog box.

➤ Press the **tab key** three times to move from the Title field to the List Price field. The current price ($27.95) is already selected. Type **28.95,** then press the **enter key** to change the price to $28.95.

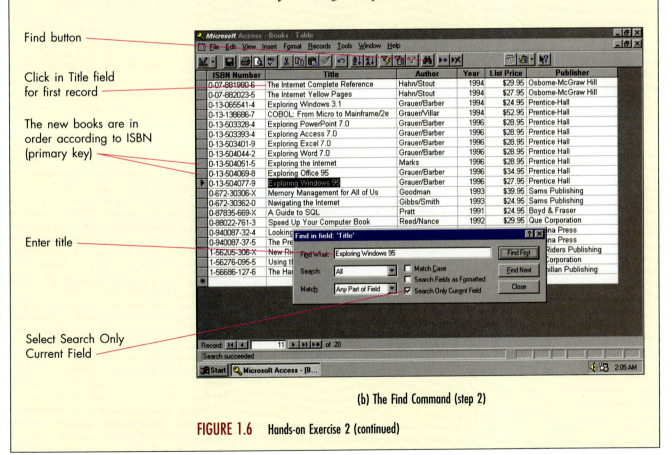

(b) The Find Command (step 2)

FIGURE 1.6 Hands-on Exercise 2 (continued)

INTRODUCTION TO MICROSOFT ACCESS | **19**

EDITING A RECORD

The fastest way to replace the value in an existing field is to select the field, then type the new value. Access automatically selects the field for you when you use the keyboard (Tab, enter, or arrow keys) to move from one field to the next. Click the mouse within the field (to deselect the field) if you are replacing only one or two characters rather than the entire field.

STEP 3: The Undo Command

➤ Pull down the **Edit menu** and click **Undo Current Field/Record** (or click the **Undo button** on the toolbar). The price for Exploring Windows 95 returns to its previous value.

➤ Pull down the **Edit menu** a second time. The Undo command is dim (as is the Undo button on the toolbar), indicating that you can no longer undo any changes. Press **Esc.**

➤ Correct the List Price field a second time and move to the next record to save your change.

THE UNDO COMMAND

The Undo command is common to all Office applications, but is implemented differently from one application to the next. Microsoft Word, for example, enables you to undo the last 100 operations. Access, however, because it saves changes automatically as soon as you move to the next record, enables you to undo only the most recent command.

STEP 4: The Delete Command

➤ Click any field in the record for **A Guide to SQL.** (You can also use the **Find command** to search for the title and move directly to its record.)

➤ Pull down the **Edit menu.** Click **Select Record** to highlight the entire record.

➤ Press the **Del key** to delete the record. You will see a dialog box as shown in Figure 1.6c, indicating that you are about to delete a record and asking you to confirm the deletion. Click **Yes.**

➤ Pull down the **Edit menu.** The Undo command is dim, indicating that you cannot undelete a record. Press **Esc** to continue working.

THE RECORD SELECTOR

Click the record selector (the box immediately to the left of the first field in a record) to select the record without having to use a pull-down menu. Click and drag the mouse over the record selector for multiple rows to select several sequential records at the same time.

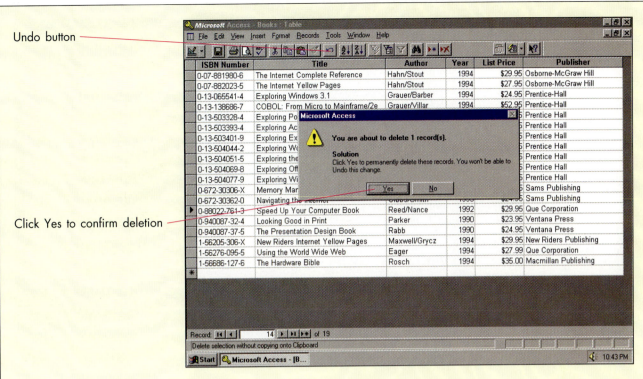

(c) The Delete Command (step 4)

FIGURE 1.6   Hands-on Exercise 2 (continued)

STEP 5: Data Validation

▶ Click the **New Record button** on the toolbar. The record selector moves to the last record (record 20).

▶ Add data as shown in Figure 1.6d, being sure to enter an invalid price by typing **XXX** in the List Price field. Press the **Tab key** to move to the Publisher field.

▶ Access displays the dialog box in Figure 1.6d, indicating that the value you entered (XXX) is inappropriate for the List Price field; in other words, you cannot enter letters when Access is expecting a numeric entry.

▶ Click the **OK command button** to close the dialog box and return to the table. Drag the mouse to select XXX, then enter the correct price of **$39.95**.

▶ Press the **Tab key** to move to the Publisher field. Type **IDG Books Worldwide.** Press the **Tab key, right arrow key,** or **enter key** to complete the record and move to the blank record at the end of the table.

▶ Click the **Close button** to close the Books table and return to the database window.

STEP 6: Open the Books Form

▶ Click the **Forms tab** in the Database window. Double click the **Books form** to open the form as shown in Figure 1.6e, then (if necessary) maximize the form so that it takes the entire window.

▶ Click the **Add Record command button** to move to a new record. The status bar shows record 21 of 21.

▶ Click in the text box for **ISBN number,** then use the **Tab key** to move from field to field as you enter data for the book as shown in Figure 1.6e. Click

INTRODUCTION TO MICROSOFT ACCESS   21

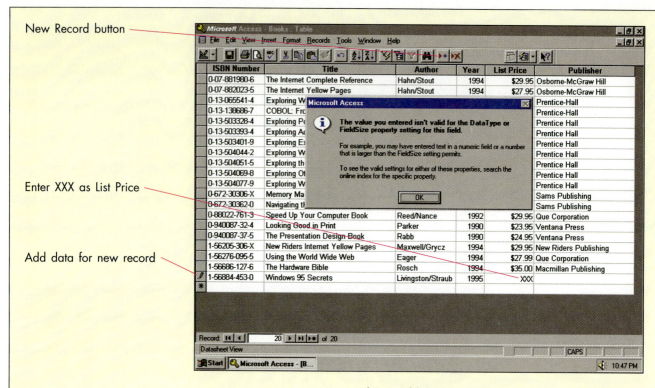

(d) Data Validation (step 5)

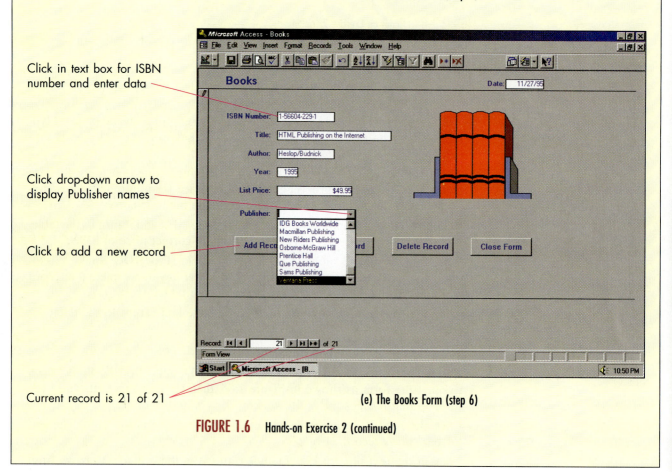

(e) The Books Form (step 6)

FIGURE 1.6 Hands-on Exercise 2 (continued)

the **drop-down arrow** on the Publisher's list box to display the available publishers and to select the appropriate one. The use of a list box ensures that you cannot misspell a publisher's name.

STEP 7: The Replace Command

➤ Pull down the **View menu.** Click **Datasheet** to switch from the Form view to the Datasheet view to display the table on which the form is based.

➤ Press **Ctrl+Home** to move to the first record in the Books table, then click in the **Publisher field** for that record. Pull down the **Edit menu.** Click **Replace** to display the dialog box in Figure 1.6f.

➤ Enter the parameters as they appear in Figure 1.6f, then click the **Find Next button** to move to the first occurrence of Prentice-Hall. Click **Replace** to make the substitution in this record and move to the next occurrence. Click **Replace** to make the second (and last) substitution, then close the dialog box when Access no longer finds the search string.

➤ Click the **Close button** to close the table.

THE COMMON USER INTERFACE

Ctrl+Home and Ctrl+End are keyboard shortcuts that apply universally to virtually every Windows application and move to the beginning and end of a document, respectively. Microsoft Access is no exception. Press Ctrl+Home to move to the first field in the first record of a table. Press Ctrl+End to move to the last field in the last record. Press Home and End to move to the first and last fields in the current record, respectively.

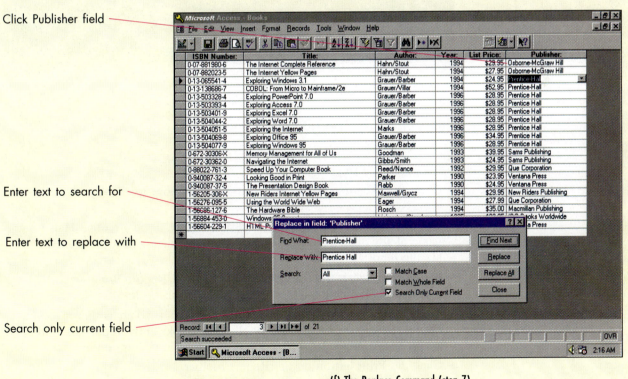

(f) The Replace Command (step 7)

FIGURE 1.6 Hands-on Exercise 2 (continued)

STEP 8: Run a Query

➤ Click the **Queries tab** in the Database window. Double click the **Publisher query** to run the query.

➤ You will see the Enter Parameter Value dialog box in Figure 1.6g. Type **Prentice Hall,** then press **enter** to see the results of the query, which should contain 9 books by Prentice Hall. (If you do not see all of the books, it is probably because you failed to replace Prentice-Hall with Prentice Hall in step 7.)

➤ Click the **Close button** to close the query, which returns you to the Database window.

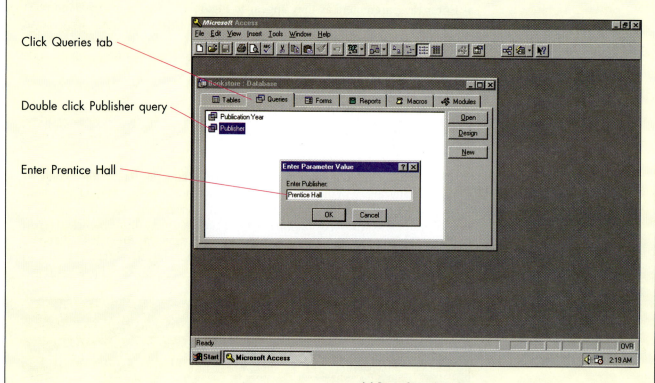

(g) Run a Query (step 8)

FIGURE 1.6 Hands-on Exercise 2 (continued)

STEP 9: Print a Report

➤ Click the **Reports tab** in the Database window to display the available reports.

➤ Double click the icon for the **Publisher report.** Type **Prentice Hall** (or the name of any other publisher) in the Parameter dialog box. Press **enter** to create the report.

➤ If necessary, click the **Maximize button** in the Report Window so that the report takes the entire screen as shown in Figure 1.6h.

➤ Click the **arrow** on the Zoom box on the Report toolbar, then click **Fit** to display the whole page. Note that all of the books in the report are published by Prentice Hall, which is consistent with the parameter you entered earlier.

➤ Click the **Print button** on the Report toolbar.

➤ Click the **Close Window button** to close the Report window.

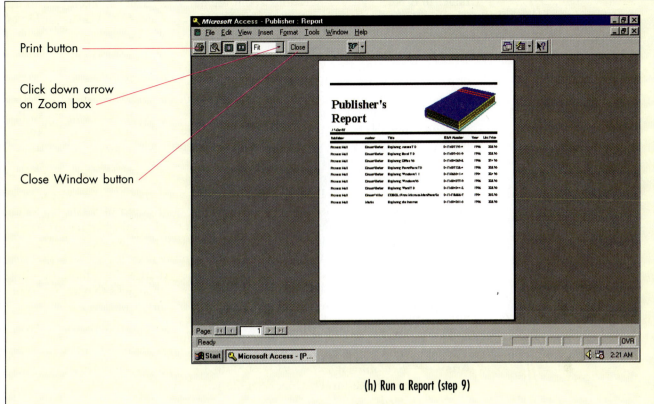

(h) Run a Report (step 9)

FIGURE 1.6   Hands-on Exercise 2 (continued)

> **TOOLBAR HELP**
>
> Point to any button on any toolbar and Access displays the name of the toolbar button, which is indicative of its function. If pointing to a button has no effect, pull down the View menu, click Toolbars, and check the box to Show ToolTips.

STEP 10: Exit Access
▶ Pull down the **File menu.** Click **Exit** to quit Access. Remember to use the Windows Explorer to copy the Bookstore database from drive C to a floppy disk that you will keep as backup.

LOOKING AHEAD: A RELATIONAL DATABASE

The database we have been using is a simple database in that it contains only one table. The real power of Access, however, is derived from multiple tables and the relationships between those tables. This type of database is known as a ***relational database.***

This section extends the Bookstore example by including the additional tables for Publishers and Orders. We will ask you to look at the data in those

INTRODUCTION TO MICROSOFT ACCESS   **25**

tables in order to answer questions about the database. You will need to consider several tables at the same time, but that is precisely what Access does. Once you see how the tables are related to one another, you will be well on your way to designing your own applications.

Pretend again that you are the manager of the bookstore and think about how you would actually use the database. You want information about the individual books, but you also need information about the publishers of those books. At the very least you need the publishers' addresses and phone numbers so that you can order the books. And once you order the books, you need to be able to track the orders, to know when each order was placed, which books were ordered, and how many of each. These requirements give rise to a database with several additional tables as shown in Figure 1.7.

The Books table in Figure 1.7a is the table as it exists at the end of the second exercise, with one modification. This is the substitution of a (shorter) PublisherID field instead of the publisher's name. The Books table contains only fields that pertain to a specific book, such as the book's ISBN, Title, Author, Year (of publication), List Price, and PublisherID. The Publishers table has fields that pertain to the publisher: PublisherID, Publisher Name, Address, City, State, Zipcode, and Phone. The PublisherID appears in both tables, enabling us to obtain the publisher's address and phone number for a particular book. Consider:

Query: What are the address and telephone number for the publisher of the book *Exploring Windows 95?*
Answer: *Exploring Windows 95* is published by Prentice Hall, which is located at 1 Lake Street, Upper Saddle River, NJ 07458. The telephone number is (800) 526-0485.

To determine the answer, Access would search the Books table for *Exploring Windows 95* to obtain the PublisherID (P4 in this example). It would then search the Publishers table for the publisher with this PublisherID and obtain the address and phone number from that record. The relationship between the publishers and books is an example of a *one-to-many relationship.* One publisher can have many books, but a book can have only one publisher.

Query: Which books are published by Ventana Press?
Answer: Three books—*Looking Good in Print, The Presentation Design Book,* and *HTML Publishing on the Internet*—are published by Ventana Press.

To answer this query, Access would begin in the Publishers table and search for Ventana Press to determine the PublisherID. It would then select all records in the Books table with a PublisherID of P6. It's easy once you recognize the relationship between the tables.

The Bookstore database in Figure 1.7 has a second one-to-many relationship between publishers and orders. One publisher can receive many orders, but a given order goes to only one publisher. Use this relationship to answer the following queries:

Query: What is the publisher and address associated with Order number O4?
Answer: Osborne-McGraw Hill at 2600 Tenth Street, Berkeley, CA 94710.

To determine the publisher's address, Access first has to identify the publisher. Thus it would search the Orders table (Figure 1.7c) for the specific order (order number O4 in this example) to obtain the corresponding PublisherID (P3). It would then search the Publishers table for the matching PublisherID and return the publisher's name and address.

(a) Books Table

ISBN	Title	Author	Year	List Price	PublisherID
0-07-881980-6	The Internet Complete Reference	Hahn/Stout	1994	$29.95	P3
0-07-882023-5	The Internet Yellow Pages	Hahn/Stout	1994	$27.95	P3
0-13-065541-4	Exploring Windows 3.1	Grauer/Barber	1994	$24.95	P4
0-13-138686-7	COBOL: From Micro to Mainframe/2e	Grauer/Villar	1994	$52.95	P4
0-13-503328-4	Exploring PowerPoint 7.0	Grauer/Barber	1996	$28.85	P4
0-13-503393-4	Exploring Access 7.0	Grauer/Barber	1996	$28.85	P4
0-13-503401-9	Exploring Excel 7.0	Grauer/Barber	1996	$28.85	P4
0-13-504044-2	Exploring Word 7.0	Grauer/Barber	1996	$28.85	P4
0-13-504051-5	Exploring the Internet	Marks	1996	$28.85	P4
0-13-504069-8	Exploring Office 95	Grauer/Barber	1996	$34.95	P4
0-13-504077-9	Exploring Windows 95	Grauer/Barber	1996	$28.95	P4
0-672-30306-X	Memory Management for All of Us	Goodman	1993	$39.95	P8
0-672-30362-0	Navigating the Internet	Gibbs/Smith	1993	$24.95	P8
0-88022-761-3	Speed Up Your Computer Book	Reed/Nance	1992	$29.95	P5
0-940087-32-4	Looking Good in Print	Parker	1990	$23.95	P6
0-940087-37-5	The Presentation Design Book	Rabb	1990	$24.95	P6
1-56205-306-X	New Riders Internet Yellow Pages	Maxwell/Grycx	1994	$29.95	P7
1-56276-095-5	Using the World Wide Web	Eager	1994	$27.99	P5
1-56604-229-1	HTML Publishing on the Internet	Heslop/Budnick	1995	$49.95	P6
1-56686-127-6	The Hardware Bible	Rosch	1994	$35.00	P2
1-56884-453-0	Windows 95 Secrets	Livingston/Straub	1995	$39.95	P1

(b) Publishers Table

PublisherID	Publisher Name	Address	City	State	Zipcode	Phone
P1	IDG Books Worldwide	919 E. Hillsdale Blvd.	Foster City	CA	94404	(800)762-2974
P2	Macmillan Publishing	201 West 103 Street	Indianapolis	IN	46290	(317)871-6724
P3	Osborne-McGraw Hill	2600 Tenth Street	Berkeley	CA	94710	(800)338-3987
P4	Prentice Hall	1 Lake Street	Upper Saddle River	NJ	07458	(800)526-0485
P5	Que Corporation	201 West 103 Street	Indianapolis	IN	46290	(317)581-3500
P6	Ventana Press	P.O. Box 2468	Chapel Hill	NC	27515	(800)743-5369
P7	New Riders Publishing	201 West 103 Street	Indianapolis	IN	46290	(317)581-3500
P8	Sams Publishing	11711 N. College Ave.	Carmel	IN	46032	(800)526-0465

(c) Orders Table

OrderID	Date	PublisherID
O1	1/12/96	P4
O2	3/15/96	P5
O3	11/15/95	P4
O4	2/3/96	P3
O5	1/15/96	P2
O6	12/16/95	P1
O7	3/30/96	P4
O8	11/11/95	P6
O9	12/15/95	P8
O10	2/2/96	P6

(d) Order Details Table

OrderID	ISBN	Quantity
O1	0-13-504077-9	200
O1	0-13-503393-4	200
O2	1-56276-095-5	35
O3	0-13-503393-4	450
O3	0-13-503401-9	450
O3	0-13-504044-2	450
O4	0-07-881980-6	50
O4	0-07-882023-5	75
O5	1-56686-127-6	25
O6	1-56884-453-0	30
O7	0-13-503328-4	60
O7	0-13-503401-9	60
O7	0-13-504044-2	60
O7	0-13-504069-8	350
O8	0-940087-32-4	75
O8	1-56604-229-1	125
O9	0-672-30362-0	150
O10	1-56604-229-1	50

FIGURE 1.7 The Bookstore Database

You probably have no trouble recognizing the need for the Books, Publishers, and Orders tables in Figure 1.7. You may be confused, however, by the presence of the Order Details table, which is made necessary by the ***many-to-many relationship*** between orders and books. One order can specify several books; and at the same time, one book can appear in many orders. Consider:

Query: Which books were included in Order number O7?
Answer: *Exploring PowerPoint 7.0, Exploring Excel 7.0, Exploring Word 7.0,* and *Exploring Office 95.*

To answer the query, Access would search the Order Details table for all records with an Order ID of O7. Access would then take the ISBN number found in each of these records and search the Books table for the records with matching ISBN numbers. Can you answer the next query, which is also based on the many-to-many relationship between books and orders?

Query: How many copies of *Exploring Access 7.0* were ordered?
Answer: A total of 650 copies.

This time, Access searches the Books table to obtain the ISBN number for *Exploring Access 7.0,* then searches the Order Details table for all records with this ISBN number (0-13-503393-4). It finds two such records (associated with orders 1 and 3), then it adds these quantities (200 and 450) to obtain the total number of copies that were ordered.

We trust that you were able to answer our queries by intuitively relating the tables to one another. Eventually, you will learn how to do this automatically in Access, but you must first gain a solid understanding of how to work with one table at a time. This is the focus of Chapters 2 and 3.

SUMMARY

A database consists of multiple tables that are related to each other. Each table in the database is composed of records, and each record is in turn composed of fields. Every record in a given table has the same fields in the same order.

An Access database has six different types of objects—tables, forms, queries, reports, macros, and modules. The database window displays these objects and enables you to open an existing object or create a new object.

A table is displayed in one of two views—the Table Design view or the Datasheet view. The Table Design view is used to define the table initially and to specify the fields it will contain. The Datasheet view is the view you use to add, edit, or delete records.

A record selector symbol is displayed next to the current record and signifies the status of that record. A triangle indicates that the record has been saved. A pencil indicates that the record has not been saved and that you are in the process of entering (or changing) the data. An asterisk appears next to the blank record present at the end of every table, where you add a new record to the table.

Access automatically saves any changes in the current record as soon as you move to the next record or when you close the table. The Undo Current Record command cancels (undoes) the changes to the previously saved record.

No system, no matter how sophisticated, can produce valid output from invalid input. Data validation is thus a critical part of any system. Access automatically imposes certain types of data validation during data entry. Additional checks can be implemented by the user.

A relational database contains multiple tables and enables you to extract information from multiple tables at the same time. The tables in the database are connected to one another through a one-to-many or many-to-many relationship.

KEY WORDS AND CONCEPTS

Add record
Asterisk (record selector) symbol
AutoCorrect
Current record
Data validation
Database
Database window
Datasheet view
Delete record
Edit record
Field
Field name
Find command
Form
GIGO (garbage in, garbage out)
Insertion point
Macro
Many-to-many relationship
Microsoft Access
Module
One-to-many relationship
Pencil (record selector) symbol
Primary key
Query
Record
Record selector symbol
Relational database
Replace command
Report
Table
Table Design view
Triangle (record selector) symbol
Undo command

MULTIPLE CHOICE

1. Which sequence represents the hierarchy of terms, from smallest to largest?
   (a) Database, table, record, field
   (b) Field, record, table, database
   (c) Record, field, table, database
   (d) Field, record, database, table

2. Which of the following is true regarding movement within a record (assuming you are not in the first or last field of that record)?
   (a) Press Tab or the right arrow key to move to the next field
   (b) Press Shift+Tab or the left arrow key to return to the previous field
   (c) Both (a) and (b)
   (d) Neither (a) nor (b)

3. You're performing routine maintenance on a table within an Access database. When should you execute the Save command?
   (a) Immediately after you add, edit, or delete a record
   (b) Periodically during a session—for example, after every fifth change
   (c) Once at the end of a session
   (d) None of the above since Access automatically saves the changes as they are made

4. Which of the following objects are contained within an Access database?
   (a) Tables and forms
   (b) Queries and reports
   (c) Macros and modules
   (d) All of the above

5. Which of the following is true about the objects in an Access database?
   (a) Every database must contain at least one object of every type
   (b) A database may contain at most one object of each type
   (c) Both (a) and (b)
   (d) Neither (a) nor (b)

6. Which of the following is true of an Access database?
   (a) Every record in a table has the same fields as every other record in that table
   (b) Every table contains the same number of records as every other table
   (c) Both (a) and (b)
   (d) Neither (a) nor (b)

7. Which of the following is a *false* statement about the Open Database command?
   (a) It can be executed from the File menu
   (b) It can be executed by clicking the Open button on the Database toolbar
   (c) It loads a database from disk into memory
   (d) It opens the selected table from the Database window

8. Which of the following is true regarding the record selector symbol?
   (a) A pencil indicates that the current record has already been saved
   (b) A triangle indicates that the current record has not changed
   (c) An asterisk indicates the first record in the table
   (d) All of the above

9. Which view is used to add, edit, and delete records in a table?
   (a) The Table Design view
   (b) The Datasheet view
   (c) Either (a) or (b)
   (d) Neither (a) nor (b)

10. Which of the following is true with respect to a table within an Access database?
    (a) Ctrl+End moves to the last field in the last record of a table
    (b) Ctrl+Home moves to the first field in the first record of a table
    (c) Both (a) and (b)
    (d) Neither (a) nor (b)

11. What does GIGO stand for?
    (a) Gee, I Goofed, OK
    (b) Grand Illusions, Go On
    (c) Global Indexing, Global Order
    (d) Garbage In, Garbage Out

12. The find and replace values in a Replace command must be:
    (a) The same length
    (b) The same case
    (c) Both (a) and (b)
    (d) Neither (a) nor (b)

13. An Access table containing 10 records, and 10 fields per record, requires two pages for printing. What, if anything, can be done to print the table on one page?
    (a) Print in Landscape rather than Portrait mode
    (b) Decrease the left and right margins
    (c) Both (a) and (b)
    (d) Neither (a) nor (b)

14. Which of the following best describes the relationship between publishers and books as implemented in the Bookstore database within the chapter?
    (a) One to one
    (b) One to many
    (c) Many to many
    (d) Impossible to determine

15. Which of the following best describes the relationship between books and orders as implemented in the Bookstore database within the chapter?
    (a) One to one
    (b) One to many
    (c) Many to many
    (d) Impossible to determine

ANSWERS

1. b	6. a	11. d
2. c	7. d	12. d
3. d	8. b	13. c
4. d	9. b	14. b
5. d	10. c	15. c

EXPLORING MICROSOFT ACCESS 7.0

1. Use Figure 1.8 to match each action with its result. A given action may be used more than once or not at all.

   Action
   a. Click and drag at 1
   b. Click at 2
   c. Click at 3
   d. Click at 4 and press the Del key
   e. Click at 5
   f. Click at 6
   g. Click and drag at 7
   h. Click at 8
   i. Click at 9
   j. Click at 10

   Result
   ____ Go to the first record in the table
   ____ Search for help on adding records
   ____ Size the window
   ____ Exit Access
   ____ Add a new record to the table
   ____ Move the window
   ____ Go to the next record in the table
   ____ Print the table
   ____ Delete *The Presentation Design Book* from the table
   ____ Find the book written by Parker

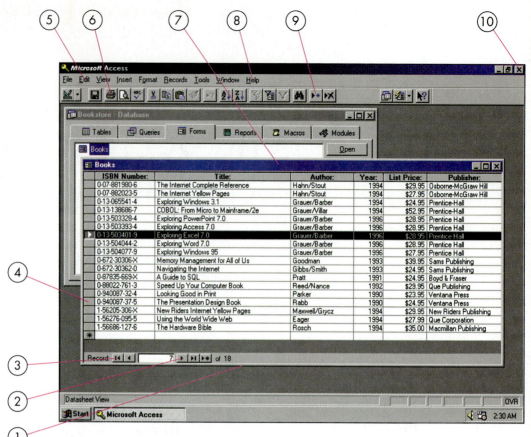

FIGURE 1.8 Screen for Problem 1

2. The error messages in Figure 1.9 appeared or could have appeared in conjunction with the hands-on exercises in the chapter. Indicate a potential cause of each error and a suggested course of action to correct the problem.

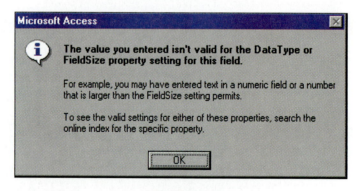

(a) Message 1

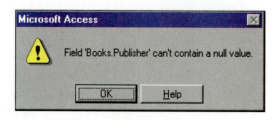

(b) Message 2

FIGURE 1.9 Screens for Problem 2

(c) Message 3

(d) Message 4

FIGURE 1.9   Screens for Problem 2 (continued)

3. Use what you know about the Help facility in other Office applications to answer the following:

   a. How do you display the dialog box in Figure 1.10?

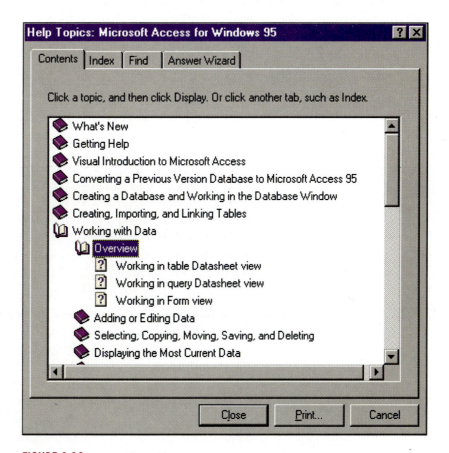

FIGURE 1.10   Screen for Problem 3

b. What is the difference between the Contents and Index tabs? Which tab is currently selected? How do you select a different tab?

c. Which books are open in the figure? Which books are closed? How do you open a closed book? How do you close an open book?

d. What is the Answer Wizard?

e. How is the dialog box in Figure 1.10 similar to the corresponding dialog boxes in other Office applications?

4. Answer the following with respect to the Bookstore database in Figure 1.7 on page 27:

a. Which publisher received Order number O8?

b. How many orders have been placed by the bookstore?

c. How many orders were sent to Prentice Hall?

d. What is the price of *The Hardware Bible?* Who is the author? Who is the publisher? How many copies of this book have been ordered?

Which table (or tables) have to be modified to accommodate the following changes in the Bookstore database?

e. The phone number for Sams Publishing is changed to (800) 526-1000.

f. The price of *Exploring Windows 3.1* is increased to $25.95.

g. Order number O3 was modified to include 500 copies of *Exploring Word 7.0* rather than the original 450.

h. Order number O11 was placed on January 6, 1996. The order is for 1,000 copies of *Exploring Windows 95, Exploring Word 7.0, Exploring Excel 7.0,* and *Exploring Access 7.0.*

i. The book *Looking Good in Print* is no longer carried by the bookstore.

j. Order number O4 is canceled. Which record(s) have to be deleted from which table(s)?

k. What problems, if any, would be caused by deleting the record for Ventana Press from the Publishers table?

PRACTICE WITH MICROSOFT ACCESS 7.0

1. Do the two hands-on exercises in the chapter, then modify the Bookstore database to accommodate the following:

a. Add the book *Welcome to CompuServe* (ISBN: 1-55828-353-6), written by Banks, published in 1994 by MIS Press, and selling for $24.95.

b. Change the price of *Memory Management for All of Us* to $29.95.

c. Delete *The Presentation Design Book.*

d. Print the *All Books Report* after these changes have been made.

2. The table in Figure 1.11 exists within the Employee database on the data disk. Open the table and do the following:

a. Add a new record for yourself. You have been hired as a trainee earning $20,000 in Boston.

b. Delete the record for Kelly Marder.

c. Change Pamela Milgrom's salary to $59,500.

d. Use the Replace command to change all occurrences of "Manager" to "Supervisor".

FIGURE 1.11 Screen for Practice Exercise 2

   e. Print the table after making the changes in parts a through d.
   f. Print the Employee Census Report after making the changes in parts a through d.
   g. Print the Location Report after making the changes in parts a through d.
   h. Create a cover page (in Microsoft Word), then submit the output from parts e, f, and g to your instructor.

3. Figure 1.12 displays a table from the United States (USA) database that is contained on the data disk. The database contains statistical data about all 50 states and enables you to produce various reports such as the 10 largest states in terms of population.

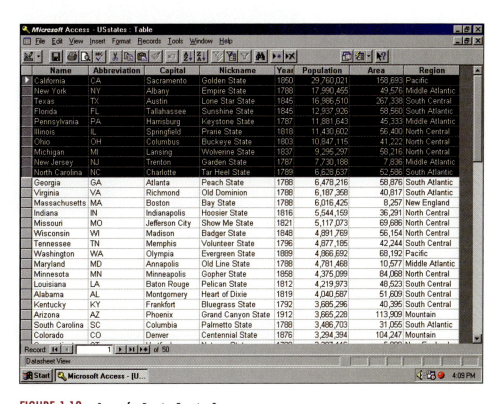

FIGURE 1.12 Screen for Practice Exercise 3

INTRODUCTION TO MICROSOFT ACCESS 35

a. Open the USA database, then open the USstates table. Click anywhere in the Population field, then click the Sort Descending button to list the states in descending order. Click and drag to select the first ten records so that you have selected the ten most populous states. Pull down the File menu, click the Print command, then click the option button to print the selected records. Be sure to print in Landscape mode so that all of the data fits on one page. (Use the Page Setup command in the File menu prior to printing.)

b. Repeat the procedure in step a, but this time print the ten states with the largest area.

c. Repeat the procedure once again to print the first thirteen states admitted to the Union.

d. Submit all three pages together with a title page (created in Microsoft Word) to your instructor.

4. This problem is different from our exercises in that it does not require you to complete a specific exercise. Instead we describe how to display a new type of Help screen that provides a visual introduction to Microsoft Access, then ask you to use that screen to review the chapter.

a. Pull down the Help menu, click Microsoft Access Help Topics, click the Contents tab, then double click to open the book entitled Visual Introduction to Microsoft Access. Select the topic, "Tables: What they are and how they work", then click the Display button to display the screen in Figure 1.13.

b. Click the various buttons on the screen of Figure 1.13 to review (and extend) the information about a relational database that was presented at the end of the chapter.

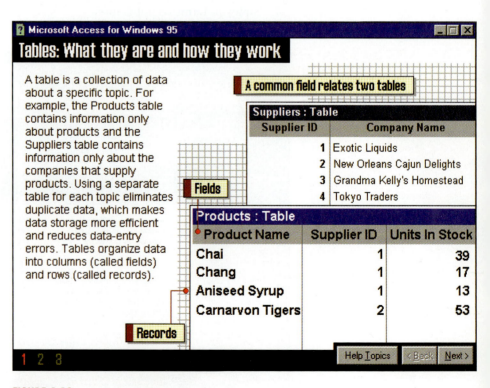

FIGURE 1.13   Screen for Practice Exercise 4

c. Click the Next button when you have viewed all of the topics to display the second of three screens (note the numbers 1, 2, and 3 at the bottom of Figure 1.13). Click the Help topics button when you have completed all three screens, then select the topic, "What is a database?" Go through the six available screens on this topic.
d. Was this a useful review? Did you learn anything new that was not covered directly in the chapter? Bring your comments to the next class to discuss your impression with your instructor and classmates.

Case Studies

Planning for Disaster

This case has nothing to do with databases per se, but it is perhaps the most important case of all, as it deals with the question of backup. Do you have a backup strategy? Do you even know what a backup strategy is? Now is a good time to learn because sooner or later you will wish you had one. There will come a time when you will accidentally erase a file, be unable to read from a floppy disk, or worse yet, suffer a hardware failure in which you are unable to access the hard drive. The problem always seems to occur the night before an assignment is due. The ultimate disaster is the disappearance of your computer, by theft or natural disaster (e.g., Hurricane Andrew, the floods in the Midwest, or the Los Angeles earthquake). Describe in 250 or fewer words the backup strategy you plan to implement in conjunction with your work in this class.

The Common User Interface

One of the most significant benefits of the Windows environment is the common user interface, which provides a sense of familiarity when you go from one application to another—for example, when you go from Excel to Access. How many similarities can you find between these two applications? Which menus are common to both? Which keyboard shortcuts? Which formatting conventions? Which toolbar icons? Which shortcut menus?

Garbage In, Garbage Out

Your excellent work in this class has earned you an internship in the registrar's office. Your predecessor has created a student database that appears to work well, but in reality has several problems in that many of its reports do not produce the expected information. One problem came to light in conjunction with a report listing business majors: the report contained far fewer majors than were expected. Open the GIGO database on the data disk and see if you can find and correct the problem.

The Database Consultant

The university's bookstore manager has gone to your instructor and asked for help in improving the existing database. The manager needs to know which books are used in which courses. One course may require several books, and the same book is often used in many courses. A book may be required in one course and merely recommended in a different course. The manager also needs to be able to contact the faculty coordinator in charge of each course. Which additional table(s) should be added to the database in Figure 1.7 on page 27 to provide this information? Which fields should be present in those tables?

TABLES AND FORMS: DESIGN, PROPERTIES, VIEWS, AND WIZARDS

OBJECTIVES

After reading this chapter you will be able to:

1. Describe in general terms how to design a table; discuss three guidelines you can use in the design process.
2. Describe the data types and properties available within Access and the purpose of each; set the primary key for a table.
3. Use the Table Wizard to create a table; add and delete fields in an existing table.
4. Discuss the importance of data validation and how it is implemented in Access.
5. Use the Form Wizard to create one of several predefined forms.
6. Distinguish between a bound control, an unbound control, and a calculated control; explain how each type of control is entered on a form.
7. Modify an existing form to include a combo box, command buttons, and color.
8. Switch between the Form view, Design view, and Datasheet view; use a form to add, edit, and delete records in a table.

OVERVIEW

This chapter introduces a new case study, that of a student database, which we use to present the basic principles of table and form design. Tables and forms are used to input data into a system from which information can be produced. The value of that information depends entirely on the quality of the underlying data, which must be both complete and accurate. We begin, therefore, with a conceptual discussion emphasizing the importance of proper design and develop essential guidelines that are used throughout the book.

After the design has been developed, we turn our attention to implementing that design in Access. We show you how to create a table using the Table Wizard, then show you how to refine its design by changing the properties of various fields within the table. We also stress the importance of data validation during data entry.

The second half of the chapter introduces forms as a more convenient way to enter and display data. We introduce the Form Wizard to create a basic form, then show you how to modify that form to include command buttons, a list box, a check box, and an option group.

As always, the hands-on exercises in the chapter enable you to apply the conceptual material at the computer. This chapter contains three exercises, after which you will be well on your way toward creating a useful database in Access.

CASE STUDY: A STUDENT DATABASE

As a student you are well aware that your school maintains all types of data about you. They have your social security number. They have your name and address and phone number. They know whether or not you are receiving financial aid. They know your major and the number of credits you have completed.

Think for a moment about the information your school requires, then write down all of the data to produce that information. This is the key to the design process as you must visualize the output the end user will require to determine the input to produce that output. Think of the specific fields you will need. Try to characterize each field according to the type of data it contains (such as text, numbers, or dates) as well as its size (length).

Our solution is shown in Figure 2.1, which may or may not correspond to what you have written down. The order of the fields within the table is not significant. Neither are the specific field names. What is important is that the table contain all necessary fields so that the system can perform as intended.

Field Name	Type
SSN	Text
FirstName	Text
LastName	Text
Address	Text
City	Text
State	Text
PostalCode	Text
PhoneNumber	Text
Major	Text
BirthDate	Date/Time
FinancialAid	Yes/No
Gender	Text
Credits	Number
QualityPoints	Number

FIGURE 2.1   The Students Table

Figure 2.1 may seem obvious upon presentation, but it does reflect the results of a careful design process based on three essential guidelines:

1. Include all of the necessary data
2. Store data in its smallest parts
3. Do not use calculated fields

Each guideline is discussed in turn. As you proceed through the text, you will be exposed to many different applications that help you develop the experience necessary to design your own systems.

Include the Necessary Data

How do you determine the necessary data? The best way is to create a rough draft of the reports you will need, then design the table so that it contains the fields necessary to create those reports. In other words, ask yourself what information will be expected from the system, then determine the data required to produce that information. Put another way, determine the input needed to produce the required output.

Consider, for example, the type of information that can and cannot be produced from the table in Figure 2.1:

- You can contact a student by mail or by telephone. You cannot, however, contact the student's parents if the student lives on campus or has an address different from his or her parents.
- You can calculate a student's grade point average (GPA) by dividing the quality points by the number of credits. You cannot produce a transcript listing the courses a student has taken.
- You can calculate a student's age from his or her date of birth. You cannot determine how long the student has been at the university because the date of admission is not in the table.

Whether or not these omissions are important depends on the objectives of the system. Suffice it to say that you must design a table carefully, so that you are not disappointed when it is implemented. *You must be absolutely certain that the data entered into a system is sufficient to provide all necessary information*, otherwise the system is almost guaranteed to fail.

DESIGN FOR THE NEXT 100 YEARS

Your system will not last 100 years, but it is prudent to design as though it will. It is a fundamental law of Information Technology that systems evolve continually and that information requirements will change. Try to anticipate what the future needs of the system will be, then build in the flexibility to satisfy those demands. Include the necessary data at the outset and be sure that the field sizes are large enough to accommodate future expansion.

Store Data in Its Smallest Parts

Figure 2.1 divides a student's name into two fields (first name and last name) to reference each field individually. You might think it easier to use a single field consisting of both the first and last name, but that approach is inadequate. Consider, for example, the following list in which the student's name is stored as a single field:

Allison Foster
Brit Reback
Carrie Graber
Danielle Ferrarro

The first problem in this approach is one of flexibility, in that you cannot separate a student's first name from her last name. You could not, for example, create a salutation of the form "Dear Allison" or "Dear Ms. Foster" because the first and last name are not accessible individually.

A second difficulty is that the list of students cannot be put into alphabetical order because the last name begins in the middle of the field. Indeed, whether you realize it or not, the names in the list are already in alphabetical order (according to the design criteria of a single field) because sorting always begins with the leftmost position in a field. Thus the "A" in Allison comes before the "B" in Brit, and so on. The proper way to sort a file is on the last name, which can be done only if the last name is stored as a separate field.

CITY, STATE, AND ZIP CODE: ONE FIELD OR THREE?

The city, state, and zip code should always be stored as separate fields. Any type of mass mailing requires you to sort on zip code to take advantage of bulk mail. Other applications may require you to select records from a particular state or zip code, which can be done only if the data is stored as separate fields. The guideline is simple—store data in its smallest parts.

Avoid Calculated Fields

A *calculated field* is a field whose value is derived from a formula or function that references an existing field or combination of fields. Calculated fields should not be stored in a table because they are subject to change, waste space, and are otherwise redundant.

The Grade Point Average (GPA) is an example of a calculated field as it is computed by dividing the number of quality points by the number of credits. It is both unnecessary and undesirable to store GPA in the Students table, because the table contains the fields on which the GPA is based. In other words, Access is able to calculate the GPA from these fields whenever it is needed, which is much more efficient than doing it manually. Imagine, for example, having to manually recalculate the GPA for 10,000 students each semester.

BIRTHDATE VERSUS AGE

A person's age and date of birth provide equivalent information, as one is calculated from the other. It might seem easier, therefore, to store the age rather than the birth date, and thus avoid the calculation. That would be a mistake because age changes continually (and would need to be updated continually), whereas the date of birth remains constant. Similar reasoning applies to an employee's length of service versus date of hire.

CREATING A TABLE

There are two ways to create a table. The easier way is to use the **Table Wizard,** an interactive coach that lets you choose from several predefined tables. The Table Wizard asks you questions about the fields you want to include in your table, then creates the table for you. Alternatively, you can create a table yourself by defining every field in the table. Regardless of how a table is created, you can modify it to include a new field or to delete an existing field.

Every field has a ***field name*** to identify the data that is entered into the field. The field name should be descriptive of the data and can be up to 64 characters in length, including letters, numbers, and spaces. We do not, however, use spaces in our field names, but use uppercase letters to distinguish the first letter of a new word. This is consistent with the default names provided by Access in its predefined tables. LastName, BirthDate, and Credits are examples of field names in Figure 2.1.

Every field also has a ***data type*** that determines the type of data that can be entered and the operations that can be performed on that data. Access recognizes eight different data types: Number, Text, Memo, Date/Time, Currency, Counter, Yes/No, and OLE Object. Text, Date/Time, Yes/No, and Number are the data types used in Figure 2.1.

- A ***Number field*** contains a value that can be used in a calculation such as the number of quality points or credits a student has earned. The contents of a number field are restricted to numbers, a decimal point, and a plus or minus sign.
- A ***Currency field*** can also be used in a calculation and is used for fields that contain monetary values.
- A ***Text field*** stores alphanumeric data such as a student's name or address. It can contain alphabetic characters, numbers, and/or special characters (e.g., an apostrophe in O'Malley). Fields that contain only numbers but which are not used in a calculation (e.g., social security number, telephone number, or zip code) should be designated as text fields for efficiency purposes. A text field can hold up to 255 characters.
- A ***Memo field*** can be up to 64,000 characters long. Memo fields are used to hold descriptive data (several sentences or paragraphs).
- A ***Date/Time field*** holds formatted dates or times (e.g., mm/dd/yy) and allows the values to be used in date or time arithmetic.
- A ***Yes/No field*** (also known as a Boolean or Logical field) assumes one of two values such as Yes or No, or True or False.
- An ***OLE field*** contains an object created by another application. OLE objects include pictures, sounds, or graphics.
- A ***Counter (or AutoNumber) field*** is a special data type that causes Access to assign the next consecutive number each time you add a record. By definition, the value of a Counter field is unique for each record in the file, and thus Counter fields are frequently used as the primary key.

Primary Key

The ***primary key*** is a field (or combination of fields) that uniquely identifies a record. There can be only one primary key per table and, by definition, every record in the table must have a different value for the primary key.

A person's name is not used as the primary key because names are not unique. A social security number, on the other hand, is unique and is a frequent choice for the primary key. Social security number is the primary key in the Students table. The primary key emerges naturally in many applications such as a part number in an inventory system, or the ISBN in the Books table of Chapter 1.

Views

A table has two views—the Datasheet view and the Design view. The Datasheet view is the view you used in Chapter 1 to add, edit, and delete records. The Design view is the view you will use in this chapter to create a table.

Figure 2.2a shows the Datasheet view corresponding to the table in Figure 2.1. (Not all of the fields are visible.) The **Datasheet view** displays the record selector symbol for the current record (a pencil or a triangle). It also displays an asterisk in the record selector next to the blank record at the end of the table.

Figure 2.2b shows the Design view of the same table. The **Design view** displays the field names in the table, the data type of each field, and the properties of the selected field. The Design view also displays a key indicator next to the field (or combination of fields) designated as the primary key.

(a) Datasheet View

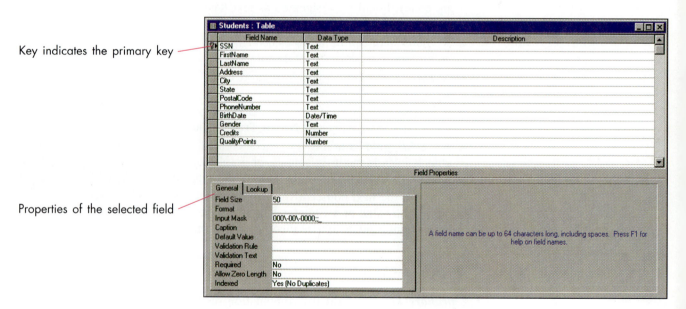

(b) Design View

FIGURE 2.2 The Views of a Table

Properties

A ***property*** is a characteristic or attribute of an object that determines how the object looks and behaves. Every Access object (tables, forms, queries, and reports) has a set of properties that determine the behavior of that object. The properties for an object are displayed and/or changed in a ***property sheet,*** which is described in more detail later in the chapter.

Each field has its own set of properties that determine how the data in the field are stored and displayed. The properties are set to default values according to the data type, but can be modified as necessary. The properties are displayed in the Design view and described briefly below:

- The ***Field Size property*** adjusts the size of a text field or limits the allowable value in a number field. Microsoft Access uses only the amount of space it needs even if the field size allows a greater number.
- The ***Format property*** changes the appearance of number and date fields but does not affect the stored value.
- The ***Input Mask property*** displays formatting characters, such as hyphens in a social security number, so that the formatting characters do not have to be entered. It also imposes data validation by ensuring that the data fits within the mask.
- The ***Caption property*** specifies a label other than the field name for forms and reports.
- The ***Default Value property*** automatically assigns a designated (default) value for the field in each record that is added to the table.
- The ***Validation Rule property*** rejects any record where the data does not conform to the specified validation rule.
- The ***Validation Text property*** specifies the error message that is displayed when the validation rule is violated.
- The ***Required property*** rejects any record that does not have a value entered for this field.
- The ***Allow Zero Length property*** allows text or memo strings of zero length.
- The ***Indexed property*** increases the efficiency of a search on the designated field. (The primary key in a table is always indexed.)

The following exercise has you create a table using the Table Wizard, then has you modify the table by including additional fields. It also has you change the properties for various fields within the table.

HANDS-ON EXERCISE 1

Creating a Table

Objective: Use the Table Wizard to create a table; add and delete fields in an existing table; change the primary key of an existing table; establish an input mask and validation rule for fields within a table; switch between the Design and Datasheet views of a table. Use Figure 2.3 as a guide.

STEP 1: Create a New Database

➤ Click the **Start button** to display the Start menu. Click (or point to) the **Programs menu,** then click **Microsoft Access** to start the program.

➤ You should see the Microsoft Access dialog box. Click the option button to create a new database using a **Blank Database.** Click **OK.** You should see the File New Database dialog box shown in Figure 2.3a.

➤ Click the **Details button** to change to the Details view. Click and drag the vertical border between columns to change the size of a column.

➤ Click the **drop-down arrow** on the Look In list box. Click the appropriate drive (e.g., drive C), depending on the location of your data. Double click the **Exploring Access folder** to make it the active folder.

➤ Click in the **File Name text box** and drag to select **db1.** Type **My First Database** as the name of the database you will create. Click the **Create button.**

CHANGE THE DEFAULT FOLDER

The default folder is the folder Access uses to retrieve (and save) a database unless it is otherwise instructed. To change the default folder, pull down the Tools menu, click Options, then click the General tab in the Options dialog box. Enter the name of the default database folder (e.g., C:\Exploring Access), then click OK to accept the settings and close the Options dialog box. The next time you access the File menu the default folder will reflect the change.

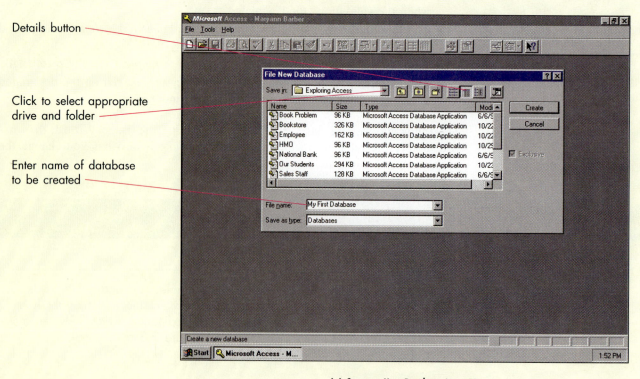

(a) Create a New Database (step 1)

FIGURE 2.3 Hands-on Exercise 1

STEP 2: Create the Table

► The Database window for My First Database should appear on your monitor. The **Tables tab** is selected by default.

► Click and drag an edge or border of the Database window to change its size to match that in Figure 2.3b. Click and drag the title bar of the Database window to change its position on the desktop.

► Click the **New command button** to display the New Table dialog box shown in Figure 2.3b. Click (select) **Table Wizard** in the New Table dialog box, then click **OK** to start the Table Wizard.

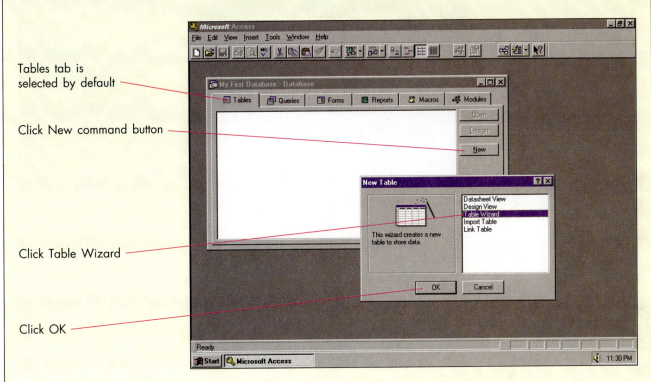

(b) The Table Wizard (step 2)

FIGURE 2.3 Hands-on Exercise 1 (continued)

STEP 3: The Table Wizard

► If necessary, click the **Business option button.** Click the **down arrow** on the **Sample Tables list box** to scroll through the available business tables. Click (select) **Students** within the list of sample tables. The tables are *not* in alphabetical order, and the Students table is found near the very bottom of the list.

► The **StudentID field** is already selected in the Sample Fields list box. Click the **>** **button** to enter this field in the list of fields for the new table as shown in Figure 2.3c.

► Enter the additional fields for the new table by selecting the field and clicking the **>** **button** (or by double clicking the field). The fields to enter are: **FirstName, LastName, Address, City,** and **StateOrProvince** as shown in the figure.

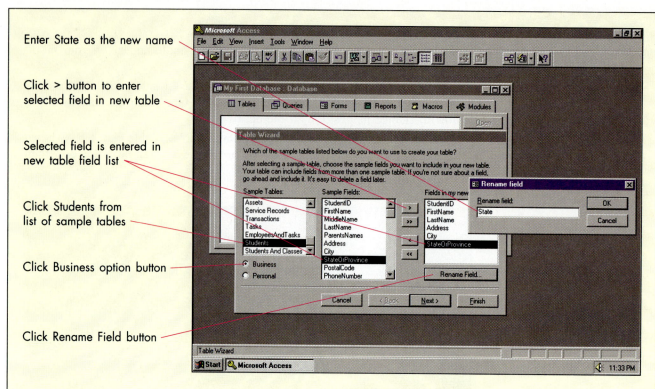

(c) The Table Wizard (step 3)

FIGURE 2.3   Hands-on Exercise 1 (continued)

➤ Click the **Rename Field command button** after adding the StateOrProvince field to display the Rename Field dialog box. Enter **State** to shorten the name of this field. Click **OK**.

➤ Add **PostalCode** and **PhoneNumber** as the last two fields in the table. Click the **Next command button** when you have entered all the fields.

WIZARDS AND BUTTONS

Many Wizards present you with two open list boxes and expect you to copy some or all fields from the list box on the left to the list box on the right. The > and >> buttons work from left to right. The < and << buttons work in the opposite direction. The > button copies the selected field from the list box on the left to the box on the right. The >> button copies all of the fields. The < button removes the selected field from the list box on the right. The << removes all of the fields.

STEP 4: The Table Wizard (continued)

➤ The next screen in the Table Wizard asks you to name the table and determine the primary key.
- Accept the Wizard's suggestion of **Students** as the name of the table.
- Make sure that the option button **Yes, set a primary key for me** is selected.
- Click the **Next command button** to accept both of these options.

➤ The final screen in the Table Wizard asks what you want to do next.
  - Click the option button to **Modify the table design.**
  - Click the **Finish command button.** The Students table should appear on your monitor.

➤ Pull down the **File menu** and click **Save** (or click the **Save button** on the Table Design toolbar) to save the table.

STEP 5: Add the Additional Fields

➤ Click the **Maximize button** to give yourself more room to work. Click the cell immediately below the last field in the table (PhoneNumber). Type **Birth-Date** as shown in Figure 2.3d.

➤ Press the **Tab key** to move to the Data Type column. Click the **down arrow** on the drop-down list box. Click **Date/Time** as the data type for the Birth-Date field.

➤ Add the remaining fields with the indicated data types to the Students table:
  - Add **Gender** as a Text field.
  - Add **Credits** as a Number field.
  - Add **QualityPoints** as a Number field. (There is no space in the field name.)

➤ Save the table.

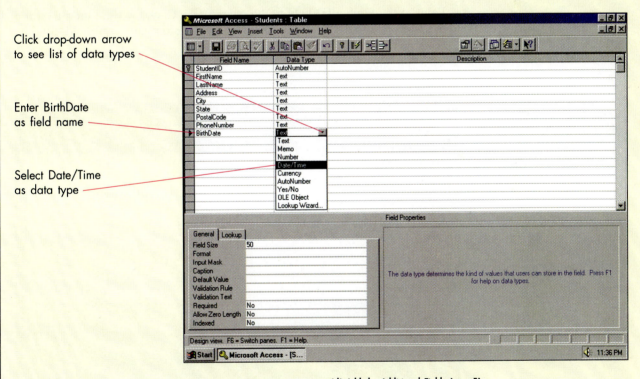

(d) Add the Additional Fields (step 5)

FIGURE 2.3 Hands-on Exercise 1 (continued)

CHOOSING A DATA TYPE

The fastest way to specify the data type is to type the first letter—T for Text, D for Date, N for Number, and Y for Yes/No. Text is the default data type and is entered automatically.

STEP 6: Change the Primary Key

➤ Point to the first row of the table and click the **right mouse button** to display the shortcut menu in Figure 2.3e. Click **Insert Field**.

➤ Click the **Field Name column** in the newly inserted row. Type **SSN** (for Social Security Number) as the name of the new field. Press **enter.** The data type will be set to Text by default.

➤ Click the **Required box** in the Properties area. Click the drop-down arrow and select **Yes.**

➤ Click in the Field Name column for **SSN,** then click the **Primary Key button** on the Table Design toolbar to change the primary key to social security number. The primary key symbol has moved from the StudentID field to SSN.

➤ Point to the **StudentID field** in the second row. Click the **right mouse button** to display the shortcut menu. Click **Delete Field** to remove this field from the table definition.

➤ Save the table.

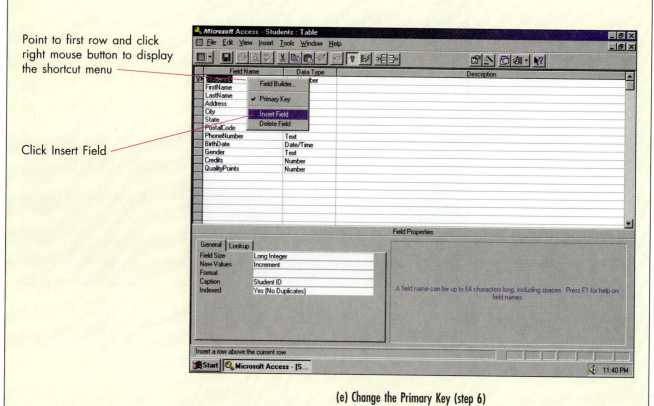

Point to first row and click right mouse button to display the shortcut menu

Click Insert Field

(e) Change the Primary Key (step 6)

FIGURE 2.3 Hands-on Exercise 1 (continued)

INSERTING OR DELETING FIELDS

To insert or delete a field, point to an existing field, then click the right mouse button to display a shortcut menu. Click Insert Row or Delete Row to add or remove a field as appropriate. To insert (or delete) multiple fields, point to the field selector to the left of the field name, click and drag the mouse over multiple rows to extend the selection, then click the right mouse button to display a shortcut menu.

STEP 7: Add an Input Mask

➤ Click the field selector column for **SSN.** Click the **Input Mask box** in the Properties area. (The box is currently empty.)

➤ Click the **Build button** to display the Input Mask Wizard. Click **Social Security Number** in the Input Mask Wizard dialog box as shown in Figure 2.3f.

➤ Click the **Try It** text box and enter a social security number to see how the mask works. If necessary, press the **left arrow key** until you are at the beginning of the text box, then enter a social security number (digits only). Click the **Finish command button** to accept the input mask.

➤ Click the field selector column for **BirthDate,** then follow the steps detailed above to add an input mask. (Choose the **Short Date** format.) Click **Yes** if asked whether to save the table.

➤ Save the table.

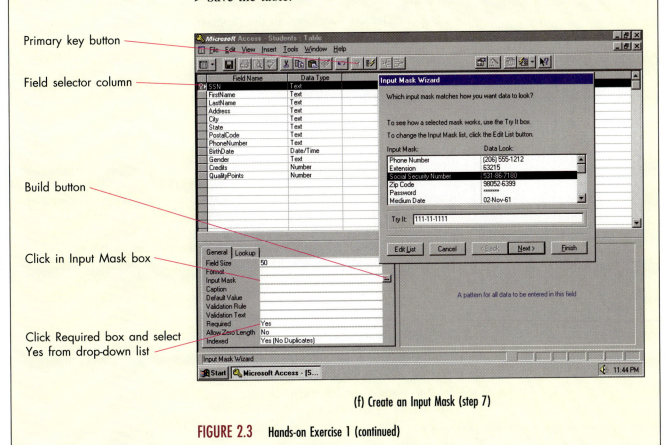

(f) Create an Input Mask (step 7)

FIGURE 2.3 Hands-on Exercise 1 (continued)

STEP 8: Change the Field Properties

➤ Click the field selector column for the **FirstName** field:
- Click the **Field Size box** in the Properties area and change the field size to **25.**
- Click the **Required box** in the Properties Area. Click the **drop-down arrow** and select **Yes.**

➤ Click the field selector column for the **LastName** field:
- Click the **Field Size box** in the Properties area and change the field size to **25.**
- Click the **Required box** in the Properties area. Click the **drop-down arrow** and select **Yes.**

➤ Click the field selector column for the **State** field.
- Click the **Field Size box** in the Properties area and change the field size to **2,** corresponding to the accepted abbreviation for a state.
- Click the **Format box** in the Properties area. Type a **>** **sign** to convert the data to uppercase.

➤ Click the field selector column for the **Credits** field:
- Click the **Field Size box** in the Properties area, click the **drop-down arrow** to display the available field sizes, then click **Integer.**
- Click the **Default Value box** in the Properties area. Delete the **0.**

➤ Click the field selector column for the **QualityPoints** field:
- Click the **Field Size box** in the Properties area, click the **drop-down arrow** to display the available field sizes, then click **Integer.**
- Click the **Default Value box** in the Properties area. Delete the **0.**

➤ Save the table.

THE FIELD SIZE PROPERTY

The field size property for a Text or Number field determines the maximum number of characters that can be stored in that field. The property should be set to the smallest possible setting because smaller data sizes are processed more efficiently. A text field can hold from 0 to 255 characters (50 is the default). Number fields (which do not contain a decimal value) can be set to Byte, Integer, or Long Integer field sizes, which hold values up to 255, or 32,767, or 2,147,483,647, respectively. The Single or Double sizes are required if the field is to contain a decimal value, as they specify the precision with which a value will be stored. (See online Help for details.)

STEP 9: Add a Validation Rule

➤ Click the field selector column for the **Gender** field. Click the **Field Size box** and change the field size to **1** as shown in Figure 2.3g.

➤ Click the **Format box** in the Properties area. Type a **>** **sign** to convert the data entered to uppercase.

➤ Click the **Validation Rule box.** Type **="M" or "F"** to accept only these values on data entry.
➤ Click the **Validation Text box.** Type **You must specify M or F.**
➤ Save the table.

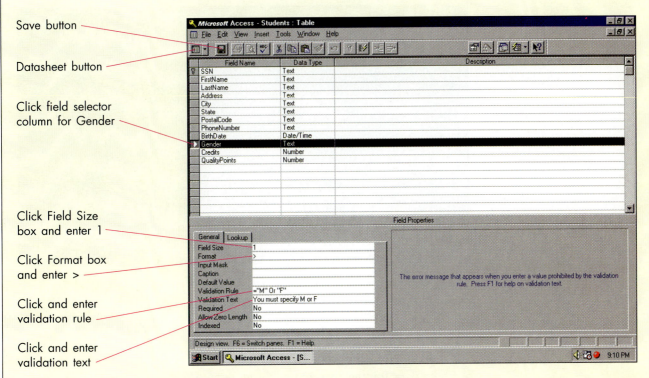

(g) Add a Validation Rule (step 9)

FIGURE 2.3 Hands-on Exercise 1 (continued)

STEP 10: The Datasheet View

➤ Pull down the **View menu** and click **Datasheet** (or click the **Datasheet button** on the toolbar) to change to the Datasheet view as shown in Figure 2.3h.
➤ The insertion point (a flashing vertical line indicating the position where data will be entered) is automatically set to the first field of the first record.
➤ Type **111111111** to enter the social security number for the first record. (The mask will appear as soon as you enter the first digit.)
➤ Press the **Tab key,** the **right arrow key,** or the **enter key** to move to the First-Name field. Enter the data for Ronnie Adili as shown in Figure 2.3h. Make up data for the fields you cannot see.
➤ Scrolling takes place automatically as you move within the record.

CHANGE THE FIELD WIDTH

Drag the border between field names to change the displayed width of a field. Double click the right boundary of a field name to change the width to accommodate the widest entry in that field.

TABLES AND FORMS 53

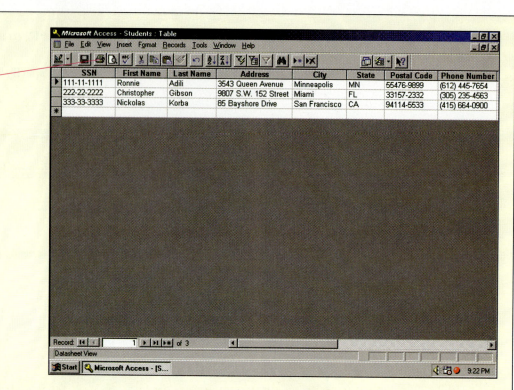

(h) Datasheet View (steps 10 & 11)

FIGURE 2.3 Hands-on Exercise 1 (continued)

STEP 11: Enter Additional Data

➤ Enter data for the two additional students shown in the figure, but enter deliberately invalid data to experiment with the validation capabilities built into Access. Some of the errors you may encounter:

- The message, *The value you entered isn't valid for the Data Type or Field Size property setting for this field,* implies that the data type is wrong—for example, alphabetic characters in a numeric field such as Credits.
- The message, *You must specify M or F,* means you entered a letter other than an "M" or an "F" in the Gender field (or you didn't enter a field at all).
- The message, *Duplicate value in index, primary key, or relationship,* indicates that the value of the primary key is not unique.
- The message, *Field 'Students.LastName' can't contain a null value,* implies that you left a required field blank.
- If you encounter a data validation error, press **Esc** (or click **OK**), then reenter the data.

STEP 12: Print the Students Table

➤ Pull down the **File menu** and click **Print** (or click the **Print button**).

➤ Click the **All option button** to print the entire table. Click the **OK command button** to begin printing. Do not be concerned if the table prints on multiple pages.

➤ Pull down the **File menu** and click **Close** to close the Students table. Click **Yes** if asked to save the changes to the table.

➤ Pull down the **File menu** and click **Close** to close the database and remain in Access. Pull down the **File menu** a second time and click **Exit** if you do not want to continue with the next exercise at this time.

> ### THE PAGE SETUP COMMAND
>
> The Page Setup command controls the margins and orientation of the printed page and may enable you to keep all fields for a single record on the same page. Pull down the File menu, click Page Setup, click the Margins tab, then decrease the left and right margins (to .5 inch each) to increase the amount of data that is printed on one line. Be sure to check the box to Print Headings so that the field names appear with the table. Click the Page tab, then click the Landscape option button to change the orientation, which further increases the amount of data printed on one line. Click OK to exit the Page Setup dialog box.

FORMS

A *form* provides an easy way to enter and display the data stored in a table. You type data into a form, such as the one in Figure 2.4, and Access stores the data in the corresponding (underlying) table in the database. One advantage of using a form (as opposed to entering records in the Datasheet view) is that you can see all of the fields in a single record without scrolling. A second advantage is that a form can be designed to resemble a paper form, and thus provide a sense of familiarity for the individuals who actually enter the data.

A form has different views, as does a table. The ***Form view*** in Figure 2.4a displays the completed form and is used to enter or modify the data in the underlying table. The ***Form Design view*** in Figure 2.4b is used to create or modify the form.

Controls

All forms consist of ***controls*** (objects) that accept and display data, perform a specific action, or add descriptive information. There are three types of controls—bound, unbound, and calculated. A ***bound control*** (such as the text boxes in Figure 2.4a) has a data source (a field in the underlying table) and is used to enter or modify the data in that table. An ***unbound control*** has no data source. Unbound controls are used to display titles, labels, lines, or rectangles. Note, too, that every bound control (***text box***) in Figure 2.4a is associated with an unbound control (***label***). The bound control for social security number, for example, is preceded by a label (immediately to the left of the control) that indicates to the user the value that is to be entered.

A ***calculated control*** has as its data source an expression rather than a field. An ***expression*** is a combination of operators (e.g., +, −, *, and /), field names, constants, and/or functions. A student's Grade Point Average (GPA in Figure 2.4a) is an example of a calculated control, since it is computed by dividing the number of quality points by the number of credits.

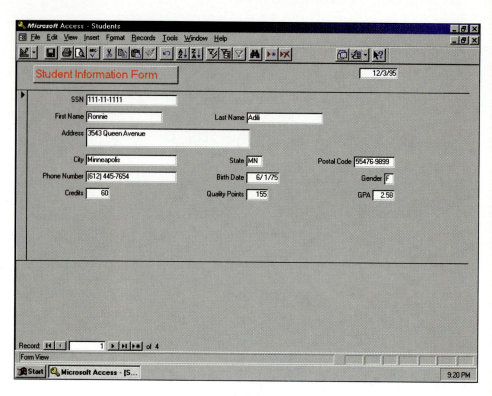

(a) Form View

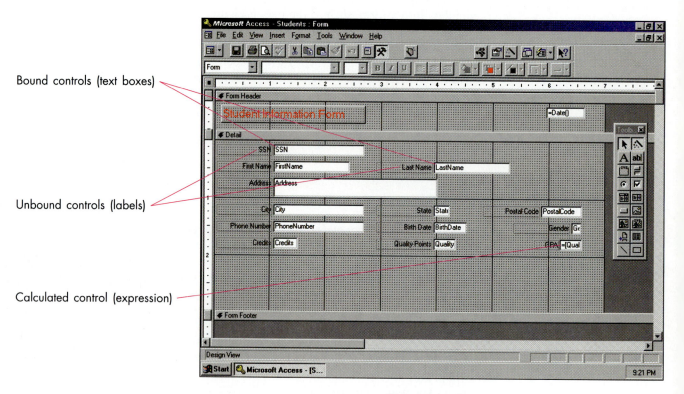

(b) Form Design View

FIGURE 2.4 Forms

ANATOMY OF A FORM

A form is divided into one or more sections. Virtually every form has a detail section to display or enter the records in the underlying table. You can, however, increase the effectiveness or visual appeal of a form by adding a header and/or footer. Either section may contain descriptive information about the form such as a title, instructions for using the form, or a graphic or logo.

Properties

As previously stated, a *property* is a characteristic or attribute of an object that determines how the object looks and behaves. Each control in a form has its own set of properties, just as every field in a table has its own set of properties. The properties for a control are displayed in a *property sheet,* such as Figure 2.5.

Figure 2.5a displays the property sheet for the Form Header Label. There are almost fifty different properties (note the vertical scroll bar) that control every aspect of the label's appearance. The properties are determined automatically as the object is created; that is, as you move and size the label on the form, the properties related to its size and position (Left, Top, Width, and Height in Figure 2.5a) are established for you.

Other actions, such as various formatting commands, set the properties that determine the font name and size (MS Sans Serif and 14 point in Figure 2.5a). You can change the appearance of an object in two ways—by executing a command to change the object on the form, which in turn changes the property sheet, *or* by changing the property within the property sheet, which in turn changes the object's appearance on the form.

Figure 2.5b displays the property sheet for the bound SSN control. The name of the control is SSN, which is the same as the name of the data source (the SSN field in the Students table). Other properties of the SSN control, such as the input mask, are inherited from the underlying table. Note, too, that the list of properties in Figure 2.5b, which reflects a bound control, is different from the list of properties in Figure 2.5a for an unbound control. Some properties, however (such as left, top, width, and height, which determine the size and position of an object), are present for every control and determine its location on the form.

The Form Wizard

The easiest way to create a form is with the **Form Wizard.** The Form Wizard asks a series of questions, then builds a form according to your answers. You can accept the form as it is created, or you can customize it to better suit your needs.

Figure 2.6a displays the New Form dialog box from which you call the Form Wizard. The Form Wizard, in turn, requires that you specify the table or query on which the form will be based. (Queries are discussed in Chapter 3.) The form in this example will be based on the Students table created in the previous exercise. Once you specify the underlying table, you select one or more fields from that table as shown in Figure 2.6b. Each field that is selected is entered automatically on the form as a bound control. The Form Wizard asks you to select a layout (e.g., Columnar in Figure 2.6c) and a style (e.g., Colorful 1 in Figure 2.6d). The Form Wizard then has all of the information it needs, and creates the form for you. You can enter data immediately, or you can modify the form in the Form Design view.

Scroll bar indicates that more properties exist than can currently be seen

Properties are set as object is moved and sized

Properties are determined as object is formatted

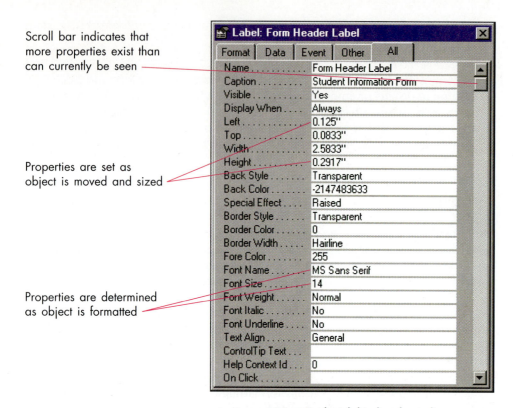

(a) Form Header Label (unbound control)

Name of data source within underlying table

Properties are inherited from underlying table

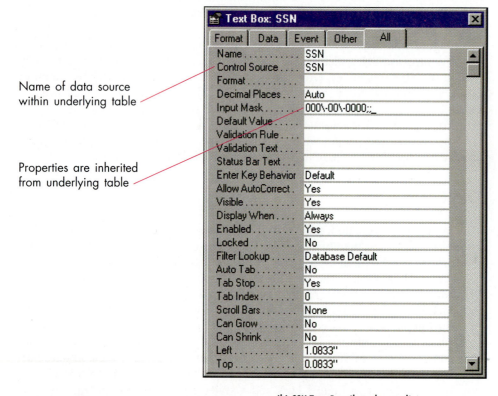

(b) SSN Text Box (bound control)

FIGURE 2.5 Property Sheets

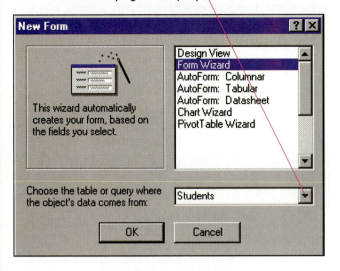
(a) Specify the Underlying Table

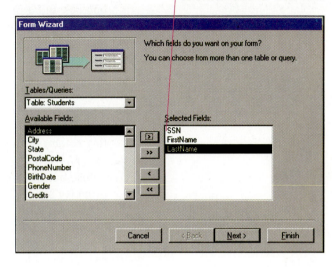
(b) Select the Fields

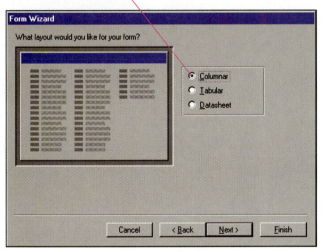
(c) Choose the Layout

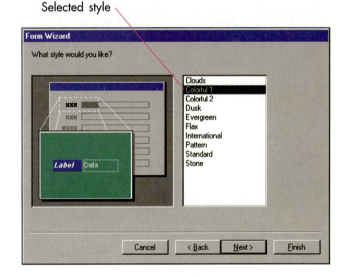
(d) Choose the Style

FIGURE 2.6 The Form Wizard

Modifying a Form

The Form Wizard provides an excellent starting point, but you typically need to customize the form by adding other controls (e.g., the calculated control for GPA) and/or by modifying the controls that were created by the Wizard. Each control is treated as an object, and moved or sized like any other Windows object. In essence, you select the control, then click and drag to resize the control or position it elsewhere on the form. You can also change the properties of the control through buttons on the various toolbars or by displaying the property sheet for the control and changing the appropriate property. Consider:

- *To select a bound control and its associated label (an unbound control),* click either the control or the label. If you click the control, the control has sizing handles and a move handle, but the label has only a move handle. If you click the label, the opposite occurs; that is, the label will have both sizing handles and a move handle, but the control will have only a move handle.

- *To size a control,* click the control to select the control and display the sizing handles, then drag the sizing handles in the appropriate direction. Drag the handles on the top or bottom to size the box vertically. Drag the handles on the left or right side to size the box horizontally. Drag the handles in the corner to size both horizontally and vertically.
- *To move a control and its label,* click and drag the border of either object. To move either the control or its label, click and drag the move handle (a tiny square in the upper left corner) of the appropriate object.
- *To change the properties of a control,* point to the control, click the right mouse button to display a shortcut menu, then click Properties to display the property sheet. Click the text box for the desired property, make the necessary change, then close the property sheet.
- *To select multiple controls,* press and hold the Shift key as you click each successive control. The advantage of selecting multiple controls is that you can modify the selected controls at the same time rather than working with them individually.

HANDS-ON EXERCISE 2

Creating a Form

Objective: Use the Form Wizard to create a form; move and size controls within a form; use the completed form to enter data into the associated table. Use Figure 2.7 as a guide in the exercise.

STEP 1: Open the Existing Database

➤ Start Access as you did in the previous exercise. Select (click) **My First Database** from the list of recently opened databases, then click **OK**. (Click the **Open Database button** on the Database toolbar if you do not see My First Database.)

➤ Click the **Forms tab** in the Database window. Click the **New command button** to display the New Form dialog box as shown in Figure 2.7a.

➤ Click **Form Wizard** in the list box. Click the **drop-down arrow** to display the available tables and queries in the database on which the form can be based.

➤ Click **Students** to select the Students table from the previous exercise. Click **OK** to start the Form Wizard.

> ### THE MOST RECENTLY OPENED FILE LIST
>
> The easiest way to open a recently used database is to select it from the Microsoft Access dialog box that appears when Access is first started. Check to see if your database appears on the list of the four most recently opened databases, and if so, simply double click the database to open it. The list of the most recently opened databases can also be found at the bottom of the File menu.

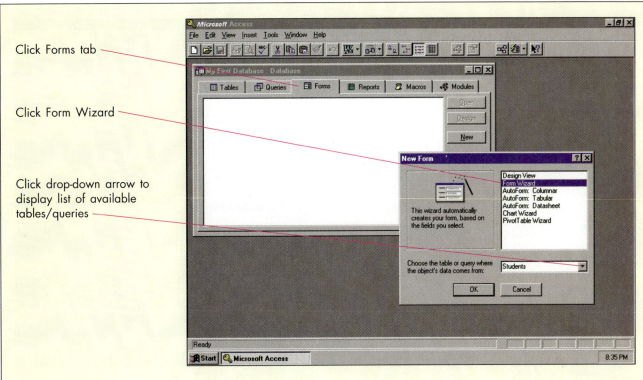

(a) Create a Form (step 1)

FIGURE 2.7 Hands-on Exercise 2

STEP 2: The Form Wizard

➤ You should see the dialog box in Figure 2.7b, which displays all of the fields in the Students table. Click the **>> button** to enter all of the fields in the table on the form. Click the **Next command button.**

➤ The **Columnar layout** is already selected. Click the **Next command button.**

➤ Click **Standard** as the style for your form. Click the **Next command button.**

➤ The Form Wizard asks you for the title of the form and what you want to do next.
  • The Form Wizard suggests **Students** as the title of the form. Keep this entry.
  • Click the option button to **Modify the form's design.**

➤ Click the **Finish command button** to display the form in Design view.

FLOATING TOOLBARS

A toolbar is typically docked (fixed) along the edge of the application window, but it can be displayed as a floating toolbar within the application window. To move a docked toolbar, drag the toolbar background. To move a floating toolbar, drag its title bar. To size a floating toolbar, drag any border in the direction you want to go. Double click the background of any toolbar to toggle between a floating toolbar and a docked (fixed) toolbar.

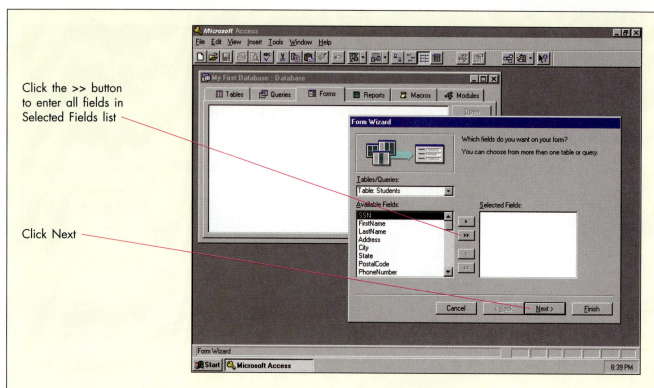

(b) The Form Wizard (step 2)

FIGURE 2.7 Hands-on Exercise 2 (continued)

STEP 3: Move the Controls

➤ If necessary, click the **Maximize button** so that the form takes the entire screen as shown in Figure 2.7c. The Form Wizard has arranged the controls in columnar format, but you need to rearrange the controls.

➤ Click the **LastName control** to select the control and display the sizing handles. (Be sure to select the text box and *not* the attached label.) Click and drag the **border** of the control (the pointer changes to a hand) so that the LastName control is on the same line as the FirstName control. Use the grid to space and align the controls.

➤ Click and drag the **Address control** under the FirstName control (to take the space previously occupied by the last name.)

➤ Click and drag the **border** of the form to **7 inches** so that the City, State, and PostalCode controls will fit on the same line. (Click and drag the title bar of the Toolbox toolbar to move the toolbar out of the way.)

➤ Click and drag the **State control** so that it is next to the City control, then click and drag the **PostalCode control** so that it is on the same line as the other two. Press and hold the **Shift key** as you click the **City, State,** and **PostalCode controls** to select all three, then click and drag the selected controls under the Address control.

➤ Place the controls for **PhoneNumber, BirthDate,** and **Gender** on the same line.

➤ Place the controls for **Credits** and **QualityPoints** on the same line.

➤ Pull down the **File menu** and click **Save** (or click the **Save button**) to save the form.

Click and drag title bar to move toolbar

Ruler

Click and drag border of control (pointer is a hand)

Sizing handles

Click and drag border of form to 7" (as indicated on ruler)

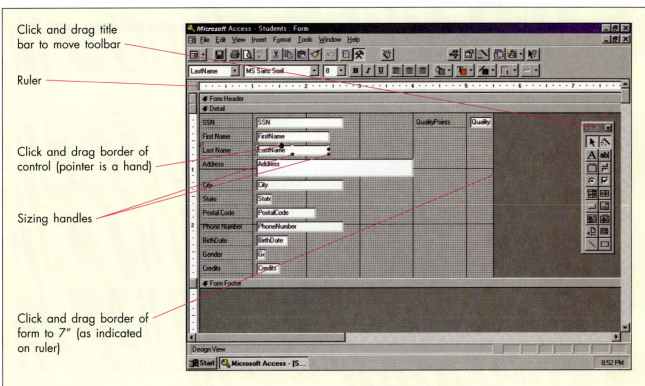

(c) Move the Controls (step 3)

FIGURE 2.7 Hands-on Exercise 2 (continued)

THE UNDO COMMAND

The Undo command is invaluable at any time, and is especially useful when moving and sizing controls. Pull down the Edit menu and click Undo (or click the Undo button on the toolbar) immediately to reverse the effects of the last command.

STEP 4: Add a Calculated Control (GPA)

➤ Click the **Textbox tool** in the toolbox as shown in Figure 2.7d. The mouse pointer changes to a tiny crosshair with a text box attached.

➤ Click and drag in the form where you want the text box (the GPA control) to go. Release the mouse. You will see an Unbound control and an attached label containing a field number (e.g., Text24) as shown in Figure 2.7d.

➤ Click in the **text box** of the control. The word Unbound will disappear, and you can enter a bound control:

- Enter **=[QualityPoints]/[Credits]** to calculate a student's GPA. Do not be concerned if you cannot see the entire entry as scrolling will take place as necessary.

- You must enter the field names *exactly* as they were defined in the table; that is, do *not* include a space between Quality and Points.

➤ Select the attached label (Text24), then click and drag to select the text in the attached label. Type **GPA** as the label for this control. Size the text box

TABLES AND FORMS 63

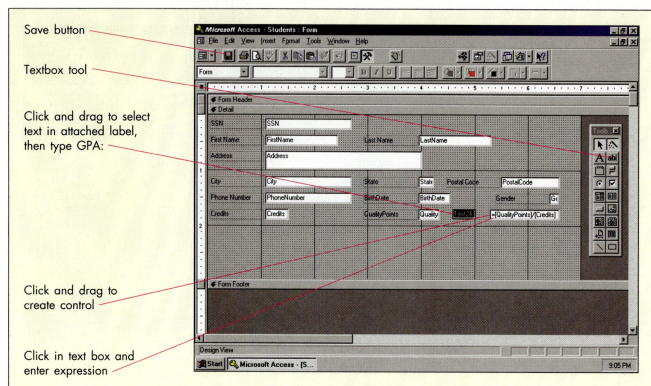

(d) Add a Calculated Control (step 4)

FIGURE 2.7 Hands-on Exercise 2 (continued)

appropriately for GPA. Click the **move handle** on the label so that you can move the label closer to the text box.

➤ Click the **Save button.**

SIZING OR MOVING A CONTROL AND ITS LABEL

A bound control is created with an attached label. Select (click) the control, and the control has sizing handles and a move handle, but the label has only a move handle. Select the label (instead of the control), and the opposite occurs; the control has only a move handle, but the label will have both sizing handles and a move handle. To move a control and its label, click and drag the border of either object. To move either the control or its label, click and drag the move handle (a tiny square in the upper left corner) of the appropriate object.

STEP 5: Modify the Property Sheet

➤ Point to the GPA control and click the **right mouse button** to display a shortcut menu. Click **Properties** to display the Properties dialog box.

➤ If necessary, click the **All tab** as shown in Figure 2.7e. The Control Source text box contains the entry =[QualityPoints]/[Credits] from the preceding step.

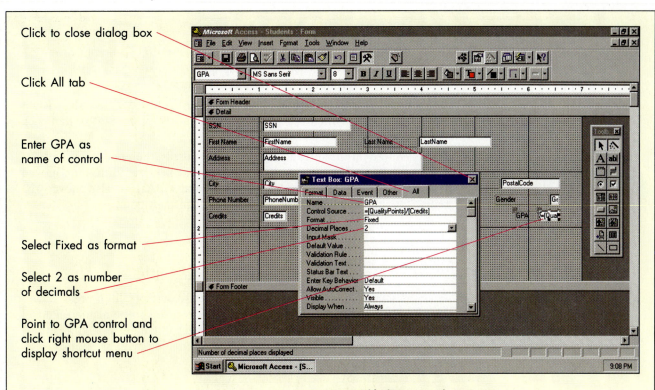

(e) Modify the Property Sheet (step 5)

FIGURE 2.7 Hands-on Exercise 2 (continued)

- Click the **Name text box.** Replace the original name (e.g., Text24) with **GPA**.
- Click the **Format box.** Click the **drop-down arrow,** then scroll until you can select **Fixed**.
- Click the box for the **Decimal places.** Click the **drop-down arrow** and select **2** as the number of decimal places.
- Close the Properties dialog box to accept these settings and return to the form.

USE THE PROPERTY SHEET

You can change the appearance or behavior of a control in two ways—by changing the actual control on the form itself or by changing the underlying property sheet. Anything you do to the control automatically changes the associated property, and conversely, any change to the property sheet is reflected in the appearance or behavior of the control. In general, you can obtain greater precision through the property sheet, but we find ourselves continually switching back and forth between the two techniques.

STEP 6: Align the Controls

➤ Press and hold the **Shift key** as you click the label for each control on the form. This enables you to select multiple controls at the same time in order to apply uniform formatting to the selected controls.

➤ All labels should be selected as shown in Figure 2.7f. Click the **Align Right button** on the Formatting toolbar to move the labels to the right so that each label is closer to its associated control.

➤ Click anywhere on the form to deselect the controls, then fine-tune the form as necessary to make it more attractive. We widened the form, then moved PostalCode so that it aligned with Gender and GPA. We also moved the Credits, QualityPoints, and GPA labels closer to their controls.

> **ALIGN THE CONTROLS**
>
> To align controls in a straight line (horizontally or vertically), press and hold the Shift key and click the labels of the controls to be aligned. Pull down the Format menu, click Align, then select the edge to align (Left, Right, Top, and Bottom). Click the Undo command if you are not satisfied with the result.

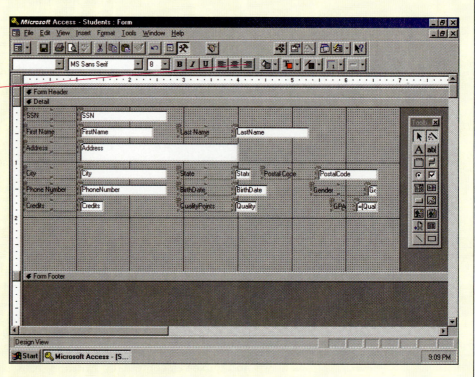

Right-align button

(f) Align the Controls (step 6)

FIGURE 2.7 Hands-on Exercise 2 (continued)

STEP 7: Create the Form Header

➤ Click and drag the line separating the border of the Form Header and Detail to provide space for a header as shown in Figure 2.7g.

➤ Click the **Label tool** on the Toolbox toolbar (the mouse pointer changes to a cross hair combined with the letter A). Click and drag the mouse pointer to create a label within the header. The insertion point (a flashing vertical line) is automatically positioned within the label.

➤ Type **Student Information Form.** Do not be concerned about the size or alignment of the text at this time. Click outside the label when you have completed the entry, then click the control to select it.

THE FORMATTING TOOLBAR

The Formatting toolbar contains many of the same buttons that are found on the Formatting toolbars of the other Office applications. These include buttons for boldface, italics, and underlining, as well as left, center, and right alignment. You will also find drop-down list boxes to change the font or point size. The Formatting toolbar also contains drop-down palettes to change the foreground or background color, the border width, and the special effect.

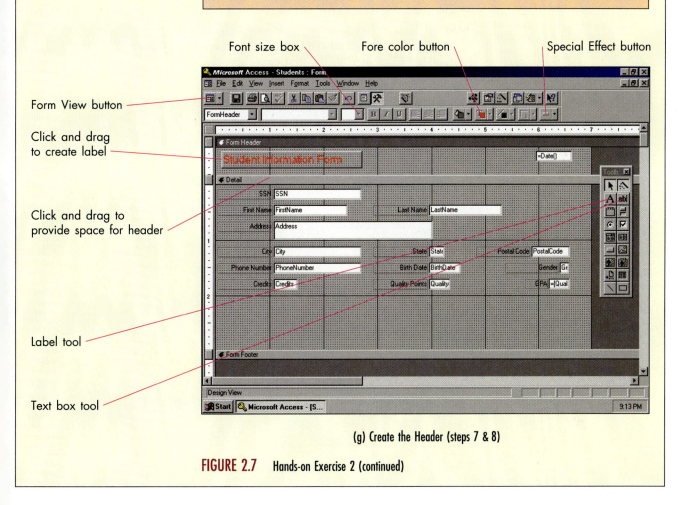

(g) Create the Header (steps 7 & 8)

FIGURE 2.7 Hands-on Exercise 2 (continued)

➤ Click the **drop-down arrow** on the **Font Size list box** on the Formatting toolbar. Click **14.** The size of the text changes to the larger point size.

➤ Click the **drop-down arrow** next to the **Special Effect button** on the Formatting toolbar to display the available effects. Click the **Raised button** to highlight the label.

➤ Click the **drop-down arrow** next to the **Fore Color button** on the Formatting toolbar. Click **Red.**

➤ Click outside the label to deselect it. Click the **Save button** to save the form.

STEP 8: Add the Date

➤ Click the **Textbox tool** on the Toolbox toolbar. The mouse pointer changes to a tiny crosshair with a text box attached. Click and drag in the form where you want the text box for the date, then release the mouse.

➤ You will see an Unbound control and an attached label containing a number (e.g., Text28). Click in the text box, and the word Unbound will disappear. Type =**Date().** Click the attached label. Press the **Del key** to delete the label.

STEP 9: The Form View

➤ Click the **Form view button** to switch to the Form view. You will see the first record in the table that was created in the previous exercise.

➤ Click the **New Record button** to move to the end of the table to enter a new record as shown in Figure 2.7h. Enter data for yourself:

- The record selector symbol changes to a pencil as you begin to enter data.
- Press the **Tab key** to move from one field to the next within the form. All properties (masks and data validation) have been inherited from the Students table created in the first exercise.

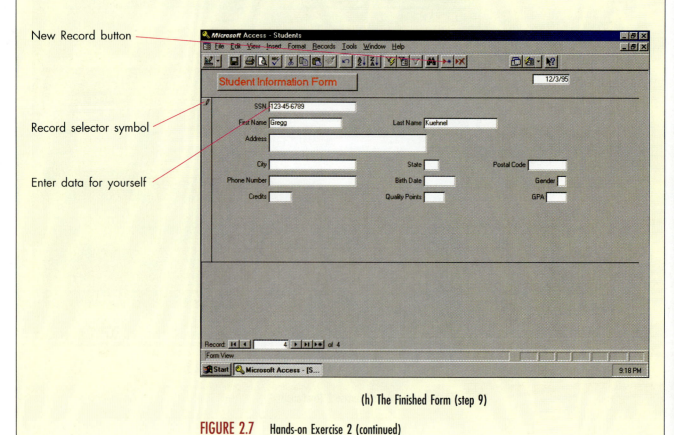

(h) The Finished Form (step 9)

FIGURE 2.7 Hands-on Exercise 2 (continued)

➤ Pull down the **File menu** and click **Close** to close the form. Click **Yes** if asked to save the changes to the form.

➤ Pull down the **File menu** and click **Close** to close the database and remain in Access. Pull down the **File menu** a second time and click **Exit** if you do not want to continue with the next exercise at this time.

> ### USE RESTRAINT
>
> More is not better, especially in the case of too many colors that detract from a form rather than enhance it. Access makes it almost too easy to switch foreground, background, and border colors and/or to change fonts and styles. Use restraint. A simple form is far more effective than one that uses too many fonts and colors simply because they are there.

A MORE SOPHISTICATED FORM

The Form Wizard provides an excellent starting point but stops short of creating the form you really want. The exercise just completed showed you how to add controls to a form that were not in the underlying table, such as the calculated control for the GPA. The exercise also showed how to move and size existing controls to create a more attractive and functional form.

Consider now Figure 2.8, which further improves on the form from the previous exercise. Three additional controls have been added for major, financial aid,

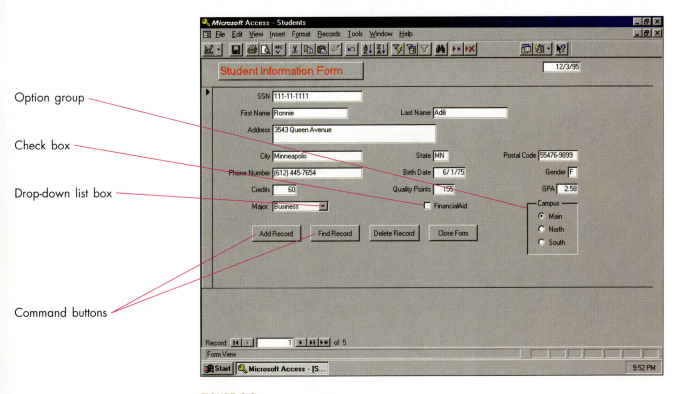

FIGURE 2.8   An Improved Form

and campus to illustrate other ways to enter data than through a text box. The student's major is selected from a *drop-down list box.* The indication of financial aid (a Yes/No field) is entered through a *check box.* The student's campus is selected from an *option group,* in which you choose one of three mutually exclusive options.

Command buttons have also been added to the bottom of the form to facilitate the way in which the user carries out certain procedures. To add a record, for example, the user simply clicks the Add Record command button, as opposed to having to click the New Record button on the Database toolbar or having to pull down the Insert menu. The next exercise has you retrieve the form you created in Hands-on Exercise 2 in order to add these enhancements.

HANDS-ON EXERCISE 3

A More Sophisticated Form

Objective: Add fields to an existing table; use the Lookup Wizard to create a combo box; add controls to an existing form to demonstrate inheritance; add command buttons to a form. Use Figure 2.9 as a guide in the exercise.

STEP 1: Modify the Table

➤ Open **My First Database** that we have been using throughout the chapter. If necessary, click the **Tables tab** in the Database window. The **Students table** is already selected since that is the only table in the database.

➤ Click the **Design command button** to open the table in Design view as shown in Figure 2.9a. (The FinancialAid, Campus, and Major fields have not yet been added.) Maximize the window.

➤ Click the **Field Name box** under QualityPoints. Enter **FinancialAid** as the name of the new field. Press the **enter (Tab, or right arrow) key** to move to the Data Type column. Type **Y** (the first letter in a Yes/No field) to specify the data type.

➤ Click the **Field Name box** on the next row. Type **Campus.** (There is no need to specify the Data Type since Text is the default.)

➤ Press the **down arrow key** to move to the Field Name box on the next row. Enter **Major.** Press the **enter (Tab, or right arrow) key** to move to the Data Type column. Click the **drop-down arrow** to display the list of data types as shown in Figure 2.9a. Click **Lookup Wizard.**

STEP 2: The Lookup Wizard

➤ The first screen in the Lookup Wizard asks how you want to look up the data. Click the option button that indicates **I will type in the values that I want.** Click **Next.**

➤ You should see the dialog box in Figure 2.9b. The number of columns is already entered as one. Click the **text box** to enter the first major. Type **Business.** Press **Tab** or the **down arrow key** (do *not* press the enter key) to enter the next major.

➤ Complete the entries shown in Figure 2.9b. Click **Next.** The Wizard asks for a label to identify the column. (Major is already entered.) Click **Finish** to exit the Wizard and return to the Design View.

➤ Click the **Save button** to save the table. Close the table.

70 EXPLORING MICROSOFT ACCESS 7.0

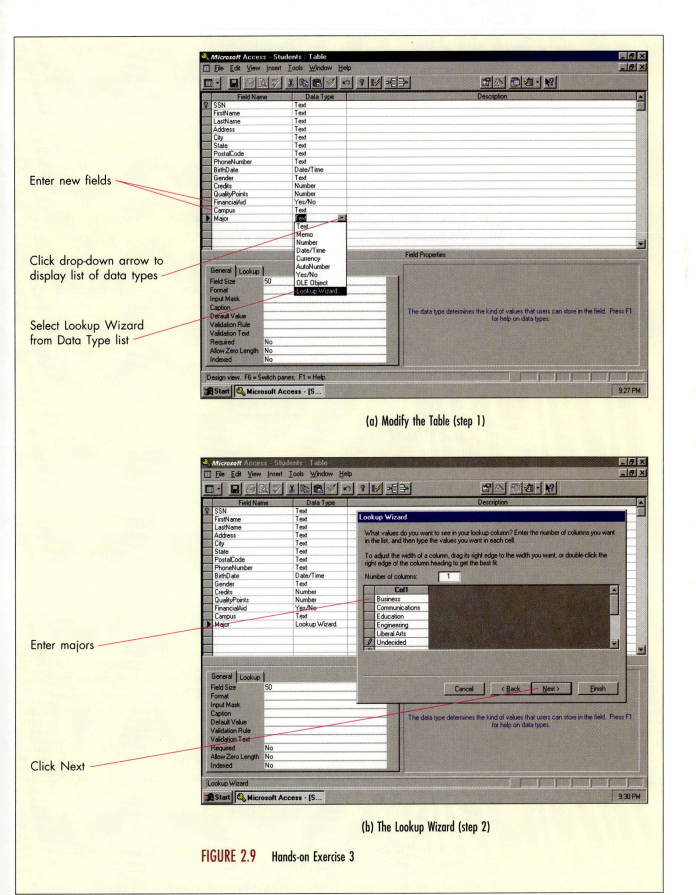

(a) Modify the Table (step 1)

(b) The Lookup Wizard (step 2)

FIGURE 2.9 Hands-on Exercise 3

STEP 3: Add the New Controls

- Click the **Forms tab** in the Database window. The Students form is already highlighted since there is only one form in the database.
- Click the **Design command button** to open the form from the previous exercise. If necessary, click the **Maximize button** so that the form takes the entire window.
- Pull down the **View menu.** Click **Field List** to display the field list for the table on which the form is based. You can move and size the field list just like any other Windows object.
  - Click and drag the **title bar** of the field list to the position in Figure 2.9c.
  - Click and drag a **corner** or **border** of the field list so that you can see all of the fields at the same time.
- Fields can be added to the form from the field list in any order. Click and drag the **Major field** from the field list to the form. The Major control is created as a list box because of the list in the underlying table.
- Click and drag the **FinancialAid field** from the list to the form. The FinancialAid control is created as a check box because FinancialAid is a Yes/No field in the underlying table.
- Save the form.

INHERITANCE

A bound control inherits the same properties as the associated field in the underlying table. A check box, for example, appears automatically next to any bound control that was defined as a Yes/No field. In similar fashion, a drop-down list will appear next to any bound control that was defined through the Lookup Wizard. Changing the property setting of a field *after* the form has been created will *not* change the property of the associated control. And finally, changing the property setting of a control does *not* change the property setting of the field because the control inherits the properties of the field rather than the other way around.

STEP 4: Create an Option Group

- Click the **Option Group button** on the Toolbox toolbar. The mouse pointer changes to a tiny crosshair attached to an option button when you point anywhere in the form. Click and drag in the form where you want the option group to go, then release the mouse.
- You should see the Option Group Wizard as shown in Figure 2.9d. Enter **Main** as the label for the first option, then press the **Tab key** to move to the next line. Type **North** and press **Tab** to move to the next line. Enter **South** as the third and last option. Click **Next**.
- The option button to select Main (the first label that was entered) as the default is selected. Click **Next**.
- Main, North, and South will be assigned the values 1, 2, and 3, respectively. (Numeric values are required for an option group). Click **Next**.
- Click the **drop-down arrow** to select the field in which to store the value of the option group, then scroll until you can select **Campus**. Click **Next**.

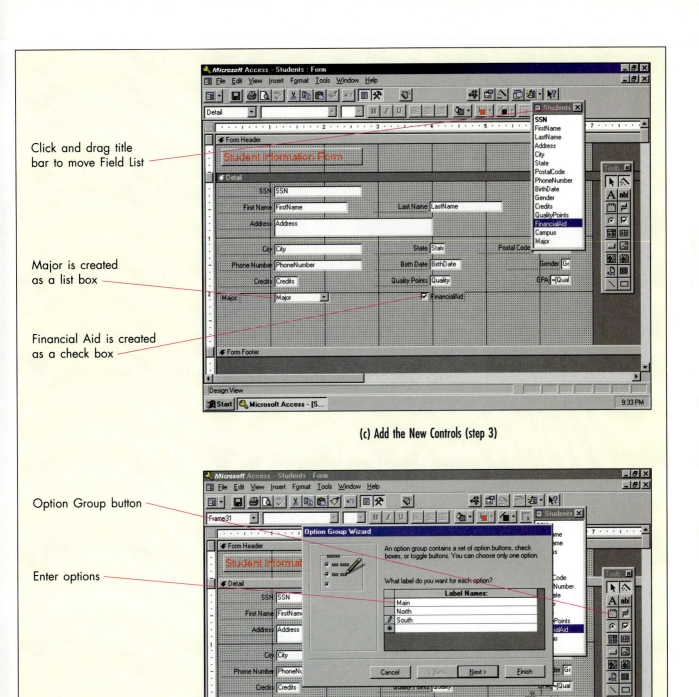

FIGURE 2.9 Hands-on Exercise 3 (continued)

- Click the option button for the **Sunken style** to match the other controls on the form. Click **Next**.
- Enter **Campus** as the label for the group. Click the **Finish command button** to create the option group on the form. Click and drag the option group to position it on the form next to the FinancialAid control.
- Point to the option group on the form, click the **right mouse button** to display a shortcut menu, and click **Properties**. Click the **All tab**. Change the caption to **Campus**. Close the dialog box.
- Save the form.

> **MISSING TOOLBARS**
>
> The Form Design, Formatting, and Toolbox toolbars appear by default in the Form Design view, but any (or all) of these toolbars may be hidden at the discretion of the user. Point to any visible toolbar, click the right mouse button to display a shortcut menu, then check the name of any toolbar you want to display. You can also click the Toolbox button on the Form Design toolbar to display (hide) the Toolbox toolbar.

STEP 5: Add a Command Button

- Click the **Command Button tool**. The mouse pointer changes to a tiny crosshair attached to a command button when you point anywhere in the form.
- Click and drag in the form where you want the button to go, then release the mouse. This draws a button and simultaneously opens the Command Button Wizard as shown in Figure 2.9e. (The number in your button may be different from ours.)
- Click **Record Operations** in the Categories list box. Choose **Add New Record** as the operation. Click **Next**.
- Click the **Text option button** in the next screen. Click **Next**.
- Type **Add Record** as the name of the button, then click the **Finish command button**. The completed command button should appear on your form. Save the form.

STEP 6: Create the Additional Command Buttons

- Click the **Command Button tool**. Click and drag on the form where you want the second button to go.
- Click **Record Navigation** in the Categories list box. Choose **Find Record** as the operation. Click the **Next command button**.
- Click the **Text option button**. Click the **Next command button**.
- Type **Find Record** as the name of the button, then click the **Finish command button**. The completed command button should appear on the form.
- Repeat these steps to add the command buttons to delete a record (Record Operations) and close the form (Form Operations).
- Save the form.

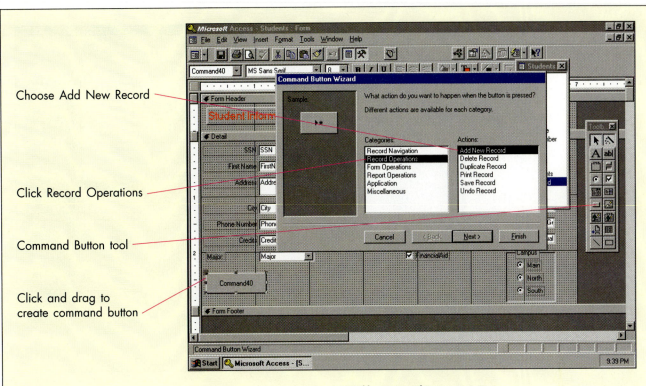

(e) Add a Command Button (step 5)

FIGURE 2.9   Hands-on Exercise 3 (continued)

STEP 7: Align the Command Buttons

▶ Select the four command buttons by pressing and holding the **Shift key** as you click each button. Release the Shift key when all buttons are selected.

▶ Pull down the **Format menu.** Click **Size** to display the cascade menu shown in Figure 2.9f. Click **to Widest** to set a uniform width.

▶ Pull down the **Format menu** a second time, click **Size,** then click **to Tallest** to set a uniform height.

▶ Pull down the **Format menu** again, click **Horizontal Spacing,** then click **Make Equal** so that each button is equidistant from the other buttons.

▶ Pull down the **Format menu** a final time, click **Align,** then click **Bottom** to complete the alignment. Drag the buttons to the center of the form.

MULTIPLE CONTROLS AND PROPERTIES

Press and hold the Shift key as you click one control after another to select multiple controls. To view or change the properties for the selected controls, click the right mouse button to display a shortcut menu, then click Properties to display a property sheet. If the value of a property is the same for all selected controls, that value will appear in the property sheet; otherwise the box for that property will be blank. Changing a property when multiple controls are selected changes the property for all selected controls.

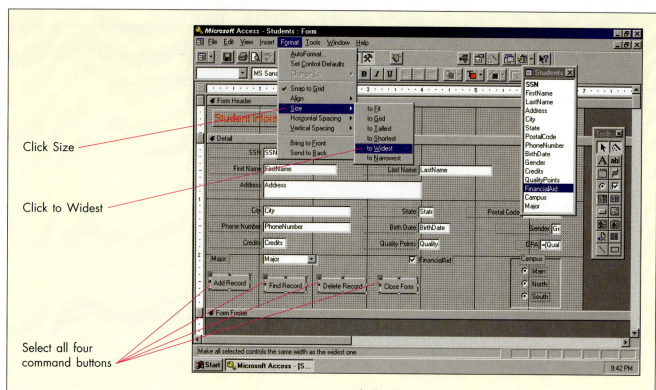

(f) Align the Buttons (step 7)

FIGURE 2.9   Hands-on Exercise 3 (continued)

STEP 8: Reset the Tab Order

➤ Click anywhere in the Detail section. Pull down the **View menu.** Click **Tab Order** to display the Tab Order dialog box in Figure 2.9g.

➤ Click the **AutoOrder command button** so that the tab key will move to fields in left-to-right, top-to-bottom order as you enter data in the form. Click **OK** to close the Tab Order dialog box.

➤ Check the form one more time in order to make any last-minute changes— for example, to move the label for Major closer to its control in Figure 2.9g.

➤ Save the form.

CHANGE THE TAB ORDER

The Tab key provides a shortcut in the finished form to move from one field to the next; that is, you press Tab to move forward to the next field and Shift+Tab to return to the previous field. The order in which fields are selected corresponds to the sequence in which the controls were entered onto the form, and need not correspond to the physical appearance of the actual form. To restore a left-to-right, top-to-bottom sequence, pull down the View menu, click Tab Order, then select Auto-Order. Alternatively, you can specify a custom sequence by clicking the selector for the various controls within the Tab Order dialog box, then moving the row up or down within the list.

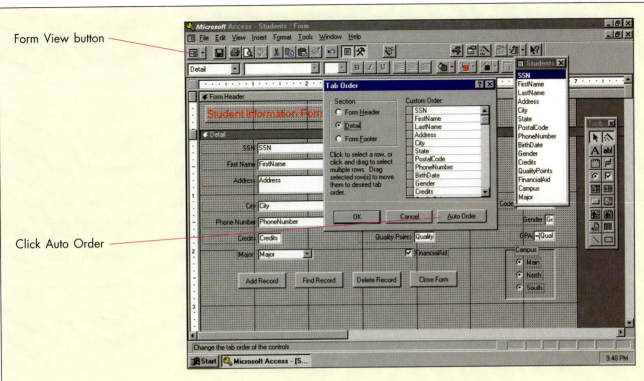

(g) Modify the Tab Order (step 8)

FIGURE 2.9 Hands-on Exercise 3 (continued)

STEP 9: The Page Setup Command

➤ Point to any blank area in the Detail section of the form. Click the **right mouse button** to display a shortcut menu, then click **Properties** to display the Properties dialog box for the Detail section. Click the **All tab.**

➤ Click the text box for **Height.** Enter **3.5** to change the height of the Detail section to three inches. Close the Properties dialog box.

➤ If necessary, click and drag the **right border** of the form so that all controls are fully visible. Do *not* exceed a width of 7 inches for the entire form.

➤ Pull down the **File menu.** Click **Page Setup** to display the Page Setup dialog box. If necessary, click the **Margins tab.**

➤ Change the left and right margins to **.75** inch. Click **OK** to accept the settings and close the Page Setup dialog box.

CHECK YOUR NUMBERS

The width of the form, plus the left and right margins, cannot exceed the width of the page. Thus increasing the width of a form may require a corresponding decrease in the left and right margins or a change to landscape (rather than portrait) orientation. Pull down the File menu and choose the Page Setup command to modify the dimensions of the form prior to printing.

STEP 10: The Completed Form

➤ Click the **Form View button** to switch to the Form view and display the first record in the table.

➤ Complete the record by adding appropriate data (choose any values you like) for the Major, FinancialAid, and Campus fields that were added to the form in this exercise.

➤ Click the **Add Record command button** to create a new record. Click the text box for **Social Security Number.** Add the record shown in Figure 2.9h. The record selector changes to a pencil as soon as you begin to enter data to indicate the record has not been saved.

➤ Press the **Tab key** or the **enter key** to move from field to field within the record. Click the **arrow** on the drop-down list box to display the list of majors, then click the desired major. Complete all of the information in the form.

➤ Click the **selection area** (the thin vertical column to the left of the form) to select only the last record. The record selector changes from a pencil to an arrow. The selection area is shaded to indicate that the record has been selected.

➤ Pull down the **File menu.** Click **Print** to display the Print dialog box. Click the option button to **print Selected Records**—that is, to print only the one record. Click **OK**.

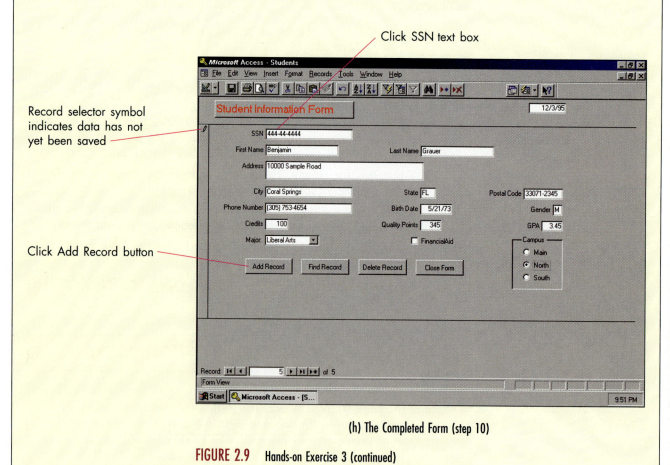

(h) The Completed Form (step 10)

FIGURE 2.9 Hands-on Exercise 3 (continued)

- Examine your printed output to be sure that the form fits on a single page. It if doesn't, you need to adjust the margins of the form itself and/or change the margins using the Page Setup command in the File menu, then print the form a second time.

> **KEYBOARD SHORTCUTS**
>
> Press Tab to move from one field to the next in a finished form. Press Shift+Tab to return to the previous field. Type the first letter of an item's name to select the first item in a drop-down list beginning with that letter; for example, type "B" to select the first item in Major beginning with that letter. Type the first two letters quickly—for example, Bu, and you will go directly to Business. Press the space bar to toggle a check box on and off. Press the down arrow key to move from one option to the next within an option group.

STEP 11: Exit Access

- Click the **Close Form command button** when you have completed the record. Click **Yes** if you see a message asking to save changes to the form.
- Pull down the **File menu.** Click **Exit** to leave Access. Congratulations on a job well done.

SUMMARY

The information produced by a system depends entirely on the underlying data. The design of the database is of critical importance and must be done correctly. Three guidelines were suggested. These are to include the necessary data, to store data in its smallest parts, and to avoid the use of calculated fields in a table.

The Table Wizard is the easiest way to create a table. It lets you choose from a series of business or personal tables, asks you questions about the fields you want, then creates the table for you.

A table has two views—the Design view and the Datasheet view. The Design view is used to create the table and display the fields within the table, as well as the data type and properties of each field. The Datasheet view is used after the table has been created to add, edit, and delete records.

A form provides a user-friendly way to enter and display data, in that it can be made to resemble a paper form. The Form Wizard is the easiest way to create a form. The Form Design view enables you to modify an existing form.

A form consists of objects called controls. A bound control has a data source such as a field in the underlying table. An unbound control has no data source. A calculated control contains an expression. Controls are selected, moved, and sized the same way as any other Windows object.

A property is a characteristic or attribute of an object that determines how the object looks and behaves. Every Access object (e.g., tables, fields, forms, and controls) has a set of properties that determine the behavior of that object. The properties for an object are displayed in a property sheet.

KEY WORDS AND CONCEPTS

Allow zero length property	Expression	Option group
AutoNumber field	Field name	Primary key
Bound control	Field Size property	Property
Calculated control	Form	Property sheet
Caption property	Form Design view	Required property
Check box	Form view	Table Wizard
Control	Form Wizard	Text box
Counter field	Format property	Text field
Currency field	Indexed property	Toolbox toolbar
Data type	Inherit	Unbound control
Datasheet view	Input Mask property	Validation Rule property
Date/Time field	Label	Validation Text property
Default Value property	Memo field	Yes/No field
Design view	Number field	
	OLE field	

MULTIPLE CHOICE

1. Which of the following is true?
   (a) The Table Wizard must be used to create a table
   (b) The Form Wizard must be used to create a form
   (c) Both (a) and (b)
   (d) Neither (a) nor (b)

2. Which of the following is implemented automatically by Access?
   (a) Rejection of a record with a duplicate value of the primary key
   (b) Rejection of numbers in a text field
   (c) Both (a) and (b)
   (d) Neither (a) nor (b)

3. Social security number, phone number, and zip code should be designated as:
   (a) Number fields
   (b) Text fields
   (c) Yes/No fields
   (d) Any of the above depending on the application

4. Which of the following is true of the primary key?
   (a) Its values must be unique
   (b) It must be defined as a text field
   (c) It must be the first field in a table
   (d) It can never be changed

5. Social security number rather than name is used as a primary key because:
   (a) The social security number is numeric, whereas the name is not
   (b) The social security number is unique, whereas the name is not

(c) The social security number is a shorter field
(d) All of the above

6. Which of the following is true regarding buttons within the Form Wizard?
   (a) The > button copies a selected field from a table onto a form
   (b) The < button removes a selected field from a form
   (c) Both (a) and (b)
   (d) Neither (a) nor (b)

7. Which of the following was *not* a suggested guideline for designing a table?
   (a) Include all necessary data
   (b) Store data in its smallest parts
   (c) Avoid calculated fields
   (d) Designate at least two primary keys

8. Which of the following are valid parameters for use with a form?
   (a) Portrait orientation, a width of 6 inches, left and right margins of 1¼ inch
   (b) Landscape orientation, a width of 9 inches, left and right margins of 1 inch
   (c) Both (a) and (b)
   (d) Neither (a) nor (b)

9. Which view is used to add, edit, or delete records in a table?
   (a) The Datasheet view
   (b) The Form view
   (c) Both (a) and (b)
   (d) Neither (a) nor (b)

10. Which of the following is true?
    (a) Any field added to a table after a form has been created is automatically added to the form as a bound control
    (b) Any calculated control that appears in a form is automatically inserted into the underlying table
    (c) Every bound and unbound control in a form has an underlying property sheet
    (d) All of the above

11. In which view will you see the record selector symbols of a pencil and a triangle?
    (a) Only the Datasheet view
    (b) Only the Form view
    (c) The Datasheet view and the Form view
    (d) The Form view, Form Design view, and the Datasheet view

12. To move a control (in the Form Design view), you select the control, then:
    (a) Point to a border (the pointer changes to an arrow) and click and drag the border to the new position
    (b) Point to a border (the pointer changes to a hand) and click and drag the border to the new position
    (c) Point to a sizing handle (the pointer changes to an arrow) and click and drag the sizing handle to the new position
    (d) Point to a sizing handle (the pointer changes to a hand) and click and drag the sizing handle to the new position

13. Which fields are commonly defined with an input mask?
    (a) Social security number and phone number
    (b) First name, middle name, and last name
    (c) City, state, and zip code
    (d) All of the above

14. Which data type appears as a check box in a form?
    (a) Text field
    (b) Number field
    (c) Yes/No field
    (d) All of the above

15. Which properties would you use to limit a user's response to two characters, and automatically convert the response to uppercase?
    (a) Field Size and Format
    (b) Input Mask, Validation Rule, and Default Value
    (c) Input Mask and Required
    (d) Field Size, Validation Rule, Validation Text, and Required

ANSWERS

1. d	**6.** c	**11.** c
2. a	**7.** d	**12.** b
3. b	**8.** c	**13.** a
4. a	**9.** c	**14.** c
5. b	**10.** c	**15.** a

EXPLORING MICROSOFT ACCESS 7.0

1. Use Figure 2.10 to match each action with its result. A given action may be used more than once or not at all.

   Action
   a. Click and drag at 1
   b. Click and drag at 2
   c. Click at 3
   d. Click at 4 and drag the detail section of the form
   e. Click at 5
   f. Click at 6
   g. Click at 7
   h. Click at 8
   i. Click at 9, click in the Form Header section
   j. Click at 10, click in the Form Header section

   Result
   ____ Create a command button
   ____ Move the selected control
   ____ Save the form design
   ____ Create a label in the Form Header
   ____ Suppress the display of the toolbox
   ____ Size the selected control
   ____ Change to the Form view
   ____ Change the tab order
   ____ Create an unbound control for the data in the Form Header
   ____ Add the Major field to the form

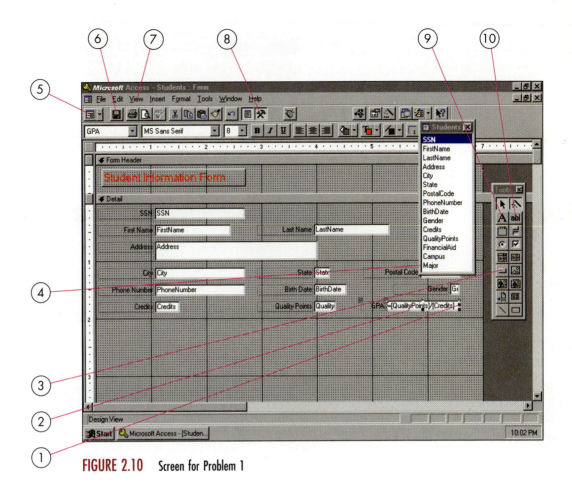

FIGURE 2.10 Screen for Problem 1

2. Careful attention must be given to designing a table, or else the resulting system will not perform as desired. Consider the following:
   a. An individual's age may be calculated from his or her birth date, which in turn can be stored as a field within a record. An alternate technique would be to store age directly in the record and thereby avoid the calculation. Which field, age or birth date, would you use? Why?
   b. Social security number is typically chosen as the primary key instead of a person's name. What attribute does the social security number possess that makes it the superior choice?
   c. Zip code is normally stored as a separate field to save money at the post office in connection with a mass mailing. Why?
   d. An individual's name is normally divided into two (or three) fields corresponding to the last name and first name (and middle initial). Why is this done; that is, what would be wrong with using a single field consisting of the first name, middle initial, and last name, in that order?
   e. An employee database has as one of its requirements the determination of an individual's percent salary increase. Which of the fields—present salary, previous salary, and percent salary increase—should be included in the underlying table in order to produce the desired information?

3. The error messages in Figure 2.11 appeared or could have appeared in conjunction with the hands-on exercises in the chapter. Indicate a potential cause of each error and a suggested course of action to correct the problem.

(a) Message 1

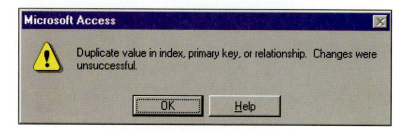

(b) Message 2

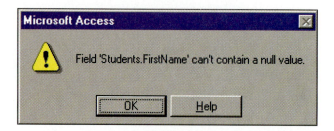

(c) Message 3

(d) Message 4

FIGURE 2.11   Screens for Problem 3

4. Answer the following with respect to the Help screen in Figure 2.12. (The screen was produced by pulling down the Help menu, clicking the Index tab, then entering FieldSize in the associated text box.)

   a. What is the significance of the underlined items? What happens if you click on Data Type or property sheet?

   b. What is the default setting of the Field Size property for a text field? What is the maximum field size for a text field?

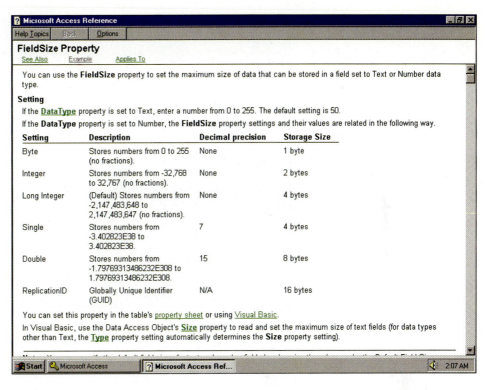

FIGURE 2.12 Screen for Problem 4

    c. What is the default setting of the Field Size property for a number field? Is this appropriate for fields such as Quality Points or Credits in the Students table that was developed in the chapter?

    d. What is the difference between the Byte, Integer, and Long Integer field sizes?

    e. What is to be gained (or lost) by changing the Field Size property in an existing table from Double to Integer?

    f. What is to be gained (or lost) by changing the Field Size property in an existing table from Integer to Long Integer?

PRACTICE WITH MICROSOFT ACCESS 7.0

1. Modify the Student form created in the hands-on exercises to match the form in Figure 2.13. (The form contains three additional controls that must be added to the Students table.)

    a. Add the DateAdmitted and EmailAddress as a date and a text field, respectively, in the Students table. Add a Yes/No field to indicate whether or not the student is an International student.

    b. Add controls for the additional fields as shown in Figure 2.13. Be sure to change the tab order after you have added the controls so that the user moves easily from one field to the next when entering data.

    c. Modify the State field in the underlying Students table to use the Lookup Wizard, and set CA, FL, NJ, and NY as the values for the list box. (These

TABLES AND FORMS

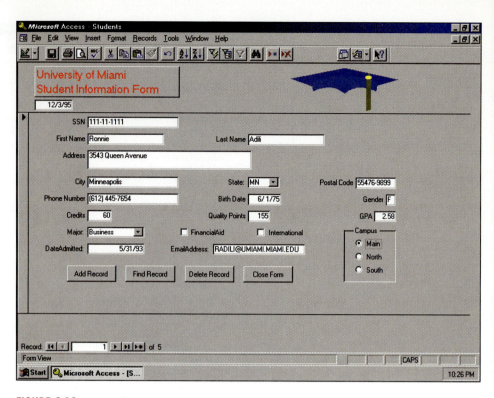

FIGURE 2.13   Screen for Practice Exercises 1 and 2

are the most common states in the Student population.) The control in the form will not, however, inherit the list box because it was added to the table after the form was created. Hence you have to delete the existing control in the form, display the field list, then click and drag the State field from the field list to the form.

d. Resize the control in the Form Header so that *University of Miami Student Information Form* takes two lines. Press Ctrl+Enter to force a line break within the control. Resize the Form Header.

e. Change the tab order to reflect the new fields in the form.

f. Add a graphic as described in problem 2.

2. This exercise is a continuation of problem 1 and describes how to insert a graphic created by another application onto an Access form. (The faster your machine, the more you will enjoy the exercise.)

a. Open the Students form in My First Database in the Design view. Move the date in the header under the label.

b. Click the Unbound Object Frame tool on the toolbox. (If you are unsure as to which tool to click, just point to the tool to display the name of the tool.)

c. Click and drag in the Form Header to size the frame, then release the mouse to display an Insert Object dialog box.

d. Click the Create New option button. Select the Microsoft ClipArt Gallery as the object type. Click OK.

e. Choose the category and picture you want from within the ClipArt Gallery. Click the Insert button to insert the picture into the Access form and simultaneously close the ClipArt Gallery dialog box. Do *not* be concerned if only a portion of the picture appears on the form.

f. Right click the newly inserted object to display a shortcut menu, then click Properties to display the Properties dialog box. Select (click) the Size Mode property and select Stretch from the associated list. Change the Back Style property to Transparent, the Special Effect property to Flat, and the Border Style property to Transparent. Close the Properties dialog box.

g. You should see the entire clip art image, although it may be distorted because the size and shape of the frame you inserted in steps (b) and (c) do not match the image you selected. Click and drag the sizing handles on the frame to size the object so that its proportions are correct. Click anywhere in the middle of the frame (the mouse pointer changes to a hand) to move the frame elsewhere in the form.

h. If you want to display a different object, double click the clip art image to return to the ClipArt Gallery in order to select another object.

3. Open the Employee database in the Exploring Access folder on the data disk to create a form similar to the one in Figure 2.14. (This is the same database that was referenced in problem 2 in Chapter 1.)

    a. The form was created using the Form Wizard and Colorful1 style. The various controls were then moved and sized to match the arrangement in the figure.

    b. The label in the Form Header, date of execution, and command buttons were added after the form was created, using the techniques in the third hands-on exercise.

    c. To add lines to the form, click the Line tool in the toolbox, then click and drag on the form to draw the line. To draw a straight line, press and hold the Shift key as you draw the line.

    d. You need not match our form exactly, and we encourage you to experiment with a different design.

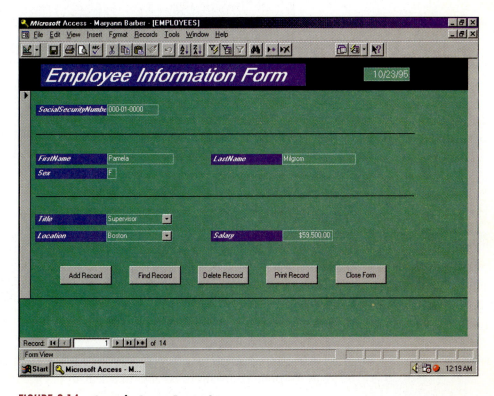

FIGURE 2.14   Screen for Practice Exercise 3

4. Open the USA database found in the Exploring Access folder on the data disk to create a form similar to the one in Figure 2.15. (This is the same database that was referenced in problem 3 in Chapter 1.)
   a. The form was created using the Form Wizard and Standard style. The various controls were then moved and sized to match the arrangement in the figure.
   b. Population density is a calculated control and is computed by dividing the population by the area.
   c. You need not match our form exactly, and we encourage you to experiment with different designs.
   d. The Find command can be used after the form has been created to search through the table and answer questions about the United States. The dialog box in Figure 2.15, for example, will identify the Empire State.
   e. Add the graphic by following the steps in the second exercise.

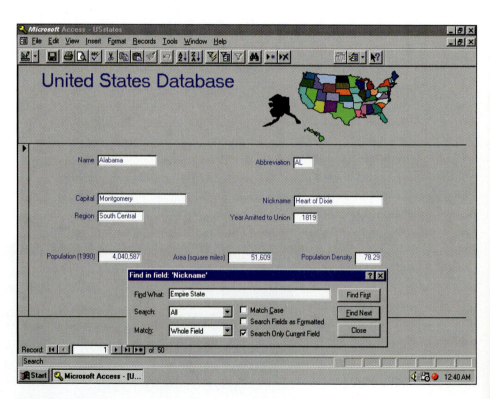

FIGURE 2.15   Screen for Practice Exercise 4

CASE STUDIES

Personnel Management

You have been hired as the Personnel Director for a medium-sized firm (500 employees) and are expected to implement a system to track employee compensation. You want to be able to calculate the age of every employee as well as the length of service. You want to know each employee's most recent performance evaluation. You want to be able to calculate the amount of the most recent salary increase, both in dollars and as a percentage of the previous salary. You also want to know how long the employee had to wait for that increase—that is, how much time elapsed between the present and previous salary. Design a table capable of providing this information.

The Stockbroker

A good friend has come to you for help. He is a new stockbroker whose firm provides computer support for existing clients, but does nothing in the way of data management for prospective clients. Your friend is determined to succeed and wants to use a PC to track the clients he is pursuing by telephone and through the mail. He wants to keep track of when he last contacted a person, how the contact was made (by phone or through the mail), and how interested the person was. He also wants to store the investment goals of each prospect, such as growth or income, and whether a person is interested in stocks, bonds, and/or a retirement account. And finally, he wants to record the amount of money the person has to invest. Design a table suitable for the information requirements of your friend.

Metro Zoo

Your job as Director of Special Programs at the Metro Zoo has put you in charge of this year's fund-raising effort. You have decided to run an "Adopt an Animal" campaign and are looking for contributions on three levels: $25 for a reptile, $50 for a bird, and $100 for a mammal. Adopting "parents" will receive a personalized adoption certificate, a picture of their animal, and educational information about the zoo. You already have a great mailing list—the guest book that is maintained at the zoo entrance. Your main job is to computerize that information and to store additional information about contributions that are received. Design a table that will be suitable for this project.

Form Design

Collect several examples of such real forms as a magazine subscription, auto registration, or employment application. Choose the form you like best and implement the design in Access. Start by creating the underlying table (with some degree of validation), then use the Form Wizard to create the form. How closely does the form you create resemble the paper form with which you began?

INFORMATION FROM THE DATABASE: REPORTS AND QUERIES

OBJECTIVES

After reading this chapter you will be able to:

1. Describe the different types of reports available through the Report Wizard.
2. Describe the different views in the Report Window and the purpose of each.
3. Describe the similarities between forms and reports with respect to bound, unbound, and calculated controls.
4. List the sections that may be present in a report and explain the purpose of each.
5. Differentiate between a query and a table; explain how the objects in an Access database (tables, forms, queries, and reports) interact with one another.
6. Use the Query By Example (QBE) grid to create and modify a select query.
7. Explain the use of multiple criteria rows within the QBE grid to implement AND and OR conditions in a query.
8. Describe the different views in the Query window and the purpose of each.

OVERVIEW

Data and information are not synonymous. Data refers to a fact or facts about a specific record, such as a student's name, major, quality points, or number of completed credits. Information can be defined as data that has been rearranged into a more useful format. The individual fields within a student record are considered data. A list of students on the Dean's List, however, is information that has been produced from the data about the individual students.

Chapters 1 and 2 described how to enter and maintain data through the use of tables and forms. This chapter shows how to convert the data to information through queries and reports. Queries enable you to ask questions about the database. Reports provide presentation quality output and display detail as well as summary information about the records in a database.

As you read the chapter, you will see that the objects in an Access database (tables, forms, reports and queries) have many similar characteristics. We use these similarities to build on what you have learned in previous chapters. You already know, for example, that the controls in a form inherit their properties from the corresponding fields in a table. The same concept applies to the controls in a report. And since you know how to move and size controls within a form, you also know how to move and size the controls in a report. As you read the chapter, look for these and other similarities to extend your existing knowledge to the new material.

REPORTS

A *report* is a printed document that displays information from a database. Figure 3.1 shows several sample reports, each of which will be created in this chapter. The reports were created with the Report Wizard and are based on the Students table that was presented in Chapter 2. (The table has been expanded to 24 records.) As you view each report, ask yourself how the data in the table was rearranged to produce the information in the report.

The *columnar (vertical) report* in Figure 3.1a is the simplest type of report. It lists every field for every record in a single column and typically runs for many pages. The records in this report are displayed in the same sequence (by social security number) as the records in the table on which the report is based.

The *tabular report* in Figure 3.1b displays fields in a row rather than in a column. Each record in the underlying table is printed in its own row. Unlike the previous report, only selected fields are displayed, so the tabular report is more concise than the columnar report of Figure 3.1a. Note, too, that the records in the report are listed in alphabetical order rather than by social security number.

The report in Figure 3.1c is also a tabular report, but it is very different from the report in Figure 3.1b. The report in Figure 3.1c lists only a selected set of students (those students with a GPA of 3.50 or higher), as opposed to the earlier reports, which listed every student. The students are listed in decreasing order according to their GPA.

The report in Figure 3.1d displays the students in groups, according to their major, then computes the average GPA for each group. The report also contains summary information (not visible in Figure 3.1d) for the report as a whole, which computes the average GPA for all students.

> ### DATA VERSUS INFORMATION
>
> Data and information are not synonymous although the terms are often interchanged. Data is the raw material and consists of the table (or tables) that compose a database. Information is the finished product. Data is converted to information by selecting records, performing calculations on those records, and/or changing the sequence in which the records are displayed. Decisions in an organization are made on the basis of information rather than raw data.

Student Roster

SSN	111-11-1111
First Name	Jared
Last Name	Berlin
Address	900 Main Highway
City	Charleston
State	SC
Postal Code	29410-0560
Phone Number	(803) 223-7868
BirthDate	1/15/72
Gender	M
Credits	100
QualityPoints	250
FinancialAid	Yes
Campus	1
Major	Engineering

Monday, December 04, 1995   Page 1 of 24

(a) Columnar Report

Student Master List

Last Name	First Name	Phone Number	Major
Adili	Ronnie	(612) 445-7654	Business
Berlin	Jared	(803) 223-7868	Engineering
Camejo	Oscar	(716) 433-3321	Liberal Arts
Coe	Bradley	(415) 235-6543	Undecided
Cornell	Ryan	(404) 755-4490	Undecided
DiGiacomo	Kevin	(305) 531-7652	Business
Faulkner	Eileen	(305) 489-8876	Communications
Frazier	Steven	(410) 995-8755	Undecided
Gibson	Christopher	(305) 235-4563	Business
Heltzer	Peter	(305) 753-4533	Engineering
Huerta	Carlos	(212) 344-5654	Undecided
Joseph	Cedric	(404) 667-8955	Communications
Korba	Nickolas	(415) 664-0900	Education
Ortiz	Frances	(303) 575-3211	Communications
Parulis	Christa	(410) 877-6565	Liberal Arts
Price	Lori	(310) 961-2323	Communications
Ramsay	Robert	(212) 223-9889	Business
Slater	Erica	(312) 545-6978	Communications
Solomon	Wendy	(305) 666-4532	Engineering
Watson	Ana	(305) 595-7877	Liberal Arts
Watson	Ana	(305) 561-2334	Business
Weissman	Kimberly	(904) 388-8605	Liberal Arts
Zacco	Michelle	(617) 884-3434	Undecided
Zimmerman	Kimberly	(713) 225-3434	Education

Monday, December 04, 1995   Page 1 of 1

(b) Tabular Report

Dean's List

First Name	Last Name	Major	Credits	Quality Points	GPA
Peter	Heltzer	Engineering	25	100	4.00
Cedric	Joseph	Communications	45	170	3.78
Erica	Slater	Communications	105	390	3.71
Kevin	DiGiacomo	Business	105	375	3.57
Wendy	Solomon	Engineering	50	175	3.50

Monday, December 04, 1995   Page 1 of 1

(c) Dean's List

GPA by Major

Major	Last Name	First Name	GPA
Business			
	Adili	Ronnie	2.58
	DiGiacomo	Kevin	3.57
	Gibson	Christopher	1.71
	Ramsay	Robert	3.24
	Watson	Ana	2.50
	Average GPA for Major:		**2.72**
Communications			
	Faulkner	Eileen	2.67
	Joseph	Cedric	3.78
	Ortiz	Frances	2.14
	Price	Lori	1.75
	Slater	Erica	3.71
	Average GPA for Major:		**2.81**
Education			
	Korba	Nickolas	1.66
	Zimmerman	Kimberly	3.29
	Average GPA for Major:		**2.48**
Engineering			
	Berlin	Jared	2.50
	Heltzer	Peter	4.00
	Solomon	Wendy	3.50
	Average GPA for Major:		**3.33**

Monday, December 04, 1995   Page 1 of 2

(d) Summary Report

FIGURE 3.1   Report Types

Anatomy of a Report

All reports are based on an underlying table or query within the database. (Queries are discussed later in the chapter, beginning on page 105.) A report, however, displays the data or information in a more attractive fashion because it contains various headings and/or other decorative items that are not present in either a table or a query.

The easiest way to learn about reports is to compare a printed report with its underlying design. Consider, for example, Figure 3.2a, which displays the tabular report, and Figure 3.2b, which shows the underlying design. The latter shows how a report is divided into sections, which appear at designated places when the report is printed. There are seven different types of sections, but a report need not contain all seven.

The *report header* appears once, at the beginning of a report. It typically contains information describing the report, such as its title and the date the report was printed. (The report header appears above the page header on the first page of the report.) The *report footer* appears above the page footer on the last page of the report and displays summary information for the report as a whole.

The *page header* appears at the top of every page in a report and can be used to display page numbers, column headings, and other descriptive information. The *page footer* appears at the bottom of every page and may contain page numbers (when they are not in the page header) or other descriptive information.

A *group header* appears at the beginning of a group of records to identify the group. A *group footer* appears after the last record in a group and contains summary information about the group. Headers and footers are used only when the records in a report are sorted (grouped) according to the value in a specific field. These sections do not appear in the report of Figure 3.2, but were shown earlier in the report of Figure 3.1d.

The *detail section* appears in the main body of a report and is printed once for every record in the underlying table (or query). It displays one or more fields for each record in columnar or tabular fashion, according to the design of the report.

The Report Wizard

The *Report Wizard* is the easiest way to create a report, just as the Form Wizard is the easiest way to create a form. The Report Wizard asks you questions about the report you want, then builds the report for you. You can accept the report as is, or you can customize it to better suit your needs.

Figure 3.3a displays the New Report dialog box, from which you can select the Report Wizard. The Report Wizard, in turn, requires you to specify the table or query on which the report will be based. The report in this example will be based on an expanded version of the Students table that was created in Chapter 2.

After you specify the underlying table, you select one or more fields from that table, as shown in Figure 3.3b. The Report Wizard then asks you to select a layout (e.g., Tabular in Figure 3.3c.) and a style (e.g., Soft Gray in Figure 3.3d). This is all the information the Report Wizard requires, and it proceeds to create the report for you. The controls on the report correspond to the fields you selected and are displayed in accordance with the specified layout.

Apply What You Know

The Report Wizard provides an excellent starting point, but typically does not create the report exactly as you would like it to be. Accordingly, you can modify a

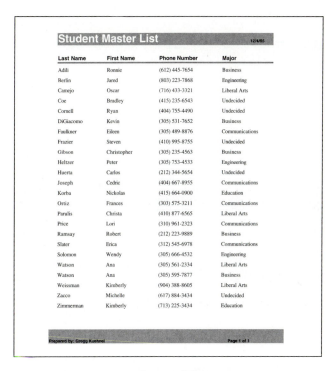

(a) The Printed Report

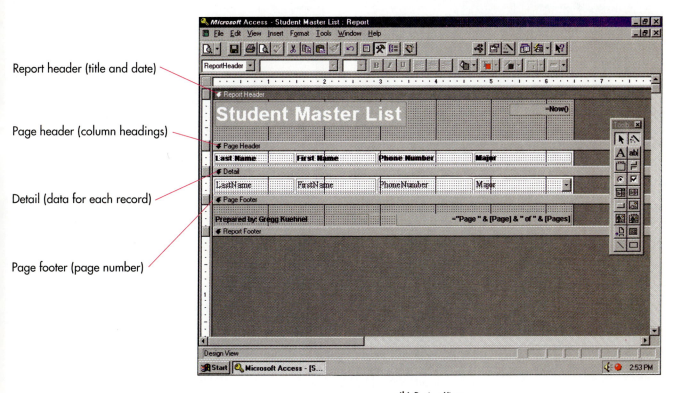

- Report header (title and date)
- Page header (column headings)
- Detail (data for each record)
- Page footer (page number)

(b) Design View

FIGURE 3.2 Anatomy of a Report

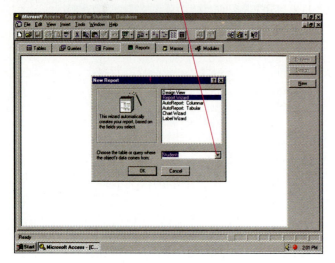
(a) Select the Underlying Table

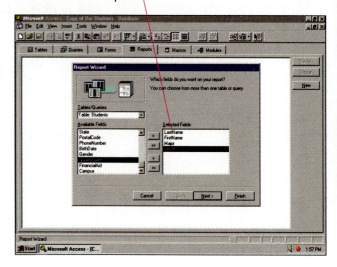
(b) Select the Fields

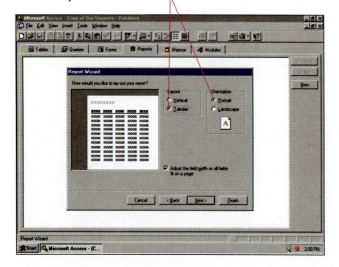
(c) Choose the Layout

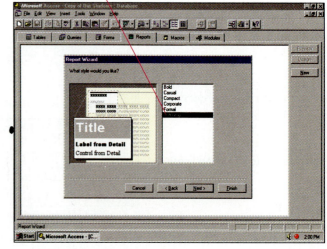
(d) Choose the Style

FIGURE 3.3 The Report Wizard

report created by the Report Wizard, just as you can modify a form created by the Form Wizard. The techniques are the same, and you should look for similarities between forms and reports so that you can apply what you already know. Knowledge of one is helpful in understanding the other.

Controls appear in a report just as they do in a form, and the same definitions apply. A ***bound control*** has as its data source a field in the underlying table. An ***unbound control*** has no data source and is used to display titles, labels, lines, or rectangles. A ***calculated control*** has as its data source an expression rather than a field. A student's Grade Point Average is an example of a calculated control since it is computed by dividing the number of quality points by the number of credits. The means for selecting, sizing, moving, aligning, and deleting controls are the same, regardless of whether you are working on a form or a report. Thus:

- To select a control, click anywhere on the control. To select multiple controls, press and hold the Shift key as you click each successive control.
- To size a control, click the control to select it, then drag the sizing handles. Drag the handles on the top or bottom to size the box vertically. Drag the handles on the left or right side to size the box horizontally. Drag the handles in the corner to size both horizontally and vertically.
- To move a control, point to any border, but not to a sizing handle (the mouse pointer changes to a hand), then click the mouse and drag the control to its new position.
- To change the properties of a control, point to the control, click the right mouse button to display a shortcut menu, then click Properties to display the property sheet. Click the text box for the desired property, make the necessary change, then close the property sheet.

INHERITANCE

A bound control inherits the same property settings as the associated field in the underlying table. Changing the property setting for a field after the report has been created does *not,* however, change the property of the corresponding control in the report. In similar fashion, changing the property setting of a control in a report does *not* change the property setting of the field in the underlying table.

HANDS-ON EXERCISE 1

The Report Wizard

Objective: To use the Report Wizard to create a new report; to modify an existing report by adding, deleting, and/or modifying its controls. Use Figure 3.4 as a guide in the exercise.

STEP 1: Open the Our Students Database
➤ Start Access. You should see the Microsoft Access dialog box with the option button to **Open an Existing Database** already selected.
➤ Double click the **More Files** selection to display the Open dialog box. Click the **drop-down arrow** on the Look In list box, click the drive containing the **Exploring Access folder,** then open that folder.

THE OUR STUDENTS DATABASE

The Our Students database has the identical design as the database you created in Chapter 2. We have, however, expanded the Students table so that it contains 24 records. The larger table enables you to create more meaningful reports and to obtain the same results as we do in the hands-on exercise.

➤ Click the **down scroll arrow** if necessary, and select the **Our Students** database. Click the **Open command button** to open the database.

➤ Click the **Reports tab** in the database window, then click the **New command button** to display the New Report dialog box in Figure 3.4a. Select the **Report Wizard** as the means of creating the report.

➤ Click the **drop-down arrow** to display the tables and queries in the database in order to select the one on which the report will be based. Click **Students** (the only table in the database). Click **OK** to start the Report Wizard.

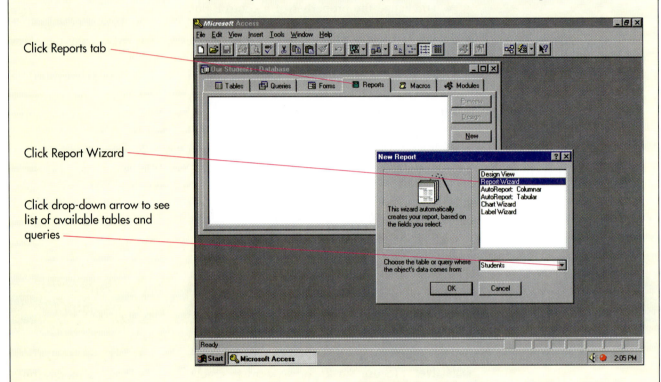

(a) Create a Report (step 1)

FIGURE 3.4 Hands-on Exercise 1

STEP 2: The Report Wizard

➤ You should see the dialog box in Figure 3.4b, which displays all of the fields in the Students table. Click the **LastName field** in the Available Fields list box, then click the **> button** to enter this field in the Selected Fields list as shown in Figure 3.4b.

➤ Enter the remaining fields (FirstName, PhoneNumber, and Major) one at a time, by selecting the field name, then clicking the **> button.** Click the **Next command button** when you have entered all fields.

WHAT THE REPORT WIZARD DOESN'T TELL YOU

The fastest way to select a field is by double clicking; that is, double click a field in the Available Fields list box, and it is automatically moved to the Selected Fields list for inclusion in the report. The process also works in reverse; that is, you can double click a field in the Selected Fields list to remove it from the report.

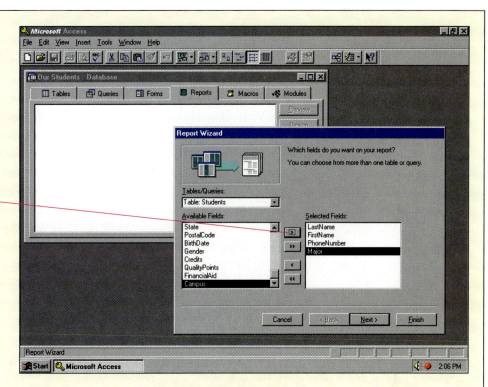

Click the > button to move selected field from Available Fields list to Selected Fields list

(b) The Report Wizard

FIGURE 3.4   Hands-on Exercise 1 (continued)

STEP 3: The Report Wizard (continued)

➤ The Report Wizard displays several additional screens asking about the report you want to create. The first screen asks whether you want to choose any grouping levels. Click **Next** without specifying a grouping level.

➤ The next screen asks whether you want to sort the records. Click the **drop-down arrow** to display the available fields, then select **LastName.** Click **Next.**

➤ The **Tabular layout** is selected, as is **Portrait orientation.** Be sure the box is checked to **Adjust field width so all fields fit on a page.** Click **Next.**

➤ Choose **Soft Gray** as the style. Click **Next.**

➤ Enter **Student Master List** as the title for your report. The option button to **Preview the Report** is already selected. Click the **Finish command button** to exit the Report Wizard and view the report.

AUTOMATIC SAVING

The Report Wizard automatically saves a report under the name you supply for the title of the report. To verify that a report has been saved, change to the Database window by pulling down the Window menu or by clicking the Database Window button that appears on every toolbar. Once you are in the Database window, click the Reports tab to see the list of existing reports. Note, however, that any subsequent changes must be saved explicitly by clicking the Save button in the Report Design view, or by clicking Yes in response to the warning prompt should you attempt to close the report without saving the changes.

INFORMATION FROM THE DATABASE

STEP 4: Preview the Report

➤ Click the **Maximize button** so the report takes the entire window as shown in Figure 3.4c. Note the report header at the beginning of the report, the page header (column headings) at the top of the page, and the page footer at the bottom of the page.

➤ Click the **drop-down arrow** on the Zoom Control box so that you can view the report at **75%**. Click the **scroll arrows** on the vertical scroll bar to view the names of additional students.

➤ Click the **Close button** to close the Print Preview window and change to the Report Design view.

> ### THE PRINT PREVIEW WINDOW
>
> The Print Preview window enables you to preview a report in various ways. Click the One Page or Two Page buttons to view one or two pages, respectively. Use the Zoom button to toggle between the full page and zoom (magnified) views, or use the Zoom Control box to choose a specific magnification. The Navigation buttons at the bottom of the Print Preview window enable you to preview a specific page, while the vertical scroll bar at the right side of the window lets you scroll within a page.

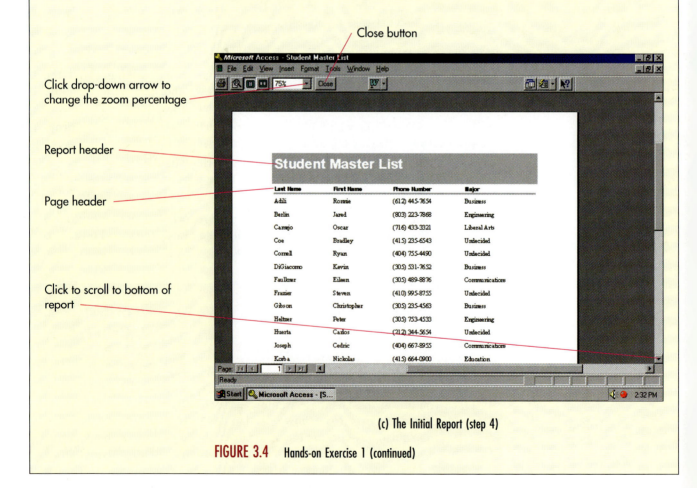

(c) The Initial Report (step 4)

FIGURE 3.4 Hands-on Exercise 1 (continued)

STEP 5: Modify an Existing Control

➤ Click and drag the control containing the **Now function** from the report footer to the report header as shown in Figure 3.4d. Size the control as necessary, then check that the control is still selected and click the **Align Right button** on the Formatting toolbar.

➤ Point to the control, then click the **right mouse button** to display a shortcut menu and click **Properties** to display the Properties sheet.

➤ Click the **Format tab** in the Properties sheet, click the **Format property,** then click the **drop-down arrow** to display the available formats. Click **Short Date,** then close the Properties sheet.

➤ Pull down the **File menu** and click **Save** (or click the **Save button**) to save the modified design

---

ACCESS FUNCTIONS

Access contains many built-in functions, each of which returns a specific value or the result of a calculation. The Now function, for example, returns the current date and time. The Page and Pages functions return the specific page number and total number of pages, respectively. The Report Wizard automatically adds these functions at appropriate places in a report. You can also add these (or other) functions explicitly, by creating a text box, then replacing the default unbound control by an equal sign, followed by the function name (and associated arguments if any)— for example, =Now to insert the current date and time.

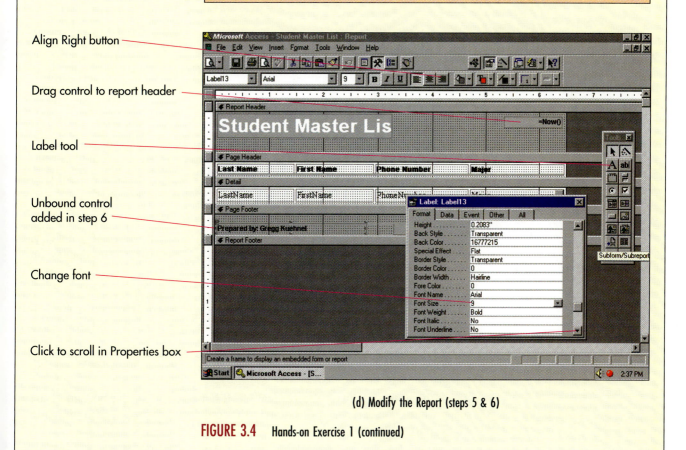

(d) Modify the Report (steps 5 & 6)

FIGURE 3.4 Hands-on Exercise 1 (continued)

STEP 6: Add an Unbound Control

- Click the **Label tool** on the Toolbox toolbar, then click and drag in the report footer where you want the label to go and release the mouse. You should see a flashing insertion point inside the label control. (If you see the word *Unbound* instead of the insertion point, it means you selected the Text box tool rather than the Label tool; delete the text box and begin again.)
- Type **Prepared by** followed by your name as shown. Press **enter** to complete the entry and also select the control. Point to the control, click the **right mouse button** to display the shortcut menu, then click **Properties** to display the Properties dialog box.
- Click the **down arrow** on the scroll bar, then scroll until you see the Font Size property. Click in the **Font Size text box,** click the **drop-down arrow,** then scroll until you can change the font size to **9.**
- Close the Property sheet. Save the report.

MISSING TOOLBARS

The Report Design, Formatting, and Toolbox toolbars appear by default in the Report Design view, but any (or all) of these toolbars may be hidden at the discretion of the user. If any of these toolbars do not appear, point to any visible toolbar, click the right mouse button to display a shortcut menu, then click the name of the toolbar you want to display. You can also click the Toolbox button on the Report Design toolbar to display (hide) the Toolbox toolbar.

STEP 7: Change the Sort Order

- Pull down the **View menu.** Click **Sorting and Grouping** to display the Sorting and Grouping dialog box. The students are currently sorted by last name.
- Click the **drop-down arrow** in the Field Expression box. Click **Major.** (The ascending sequence is selected automatically.)
- Click on the next line in the Field Expression box, click the **drop-down arrow** to display the available fields, then click **LastName** to sort the students alphabetically within major as shown in Figure 3.4e.
- Close the Sorting and Grouping dialog box. Save the report.

STEP 8: View the Modified Report

- Click the **Print Preview button** to preview the finished report. If necessary, click the **Zoom button** on the Print Preview toolbar so that the display on your monitor matches Figure 3.4f.
- The report has changed so that:
  - The date appears in the report header (as opposed to the report footer). The format of the date has changed to a numbered month, and the day of the week has been eliminated.
  - The students are listed by major and, within each major, alphabetically according to last name.
- Click the **down arrow** on the vertical scroll bar to move to the bottom of the page where you can see your name in the footer as the person who prepared the report.

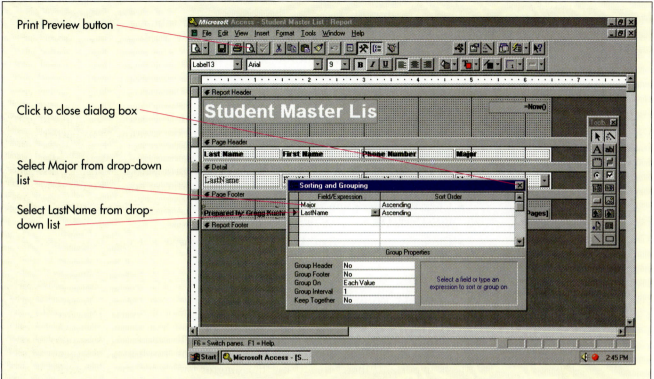

(e) Change the Sort Order (step 7)

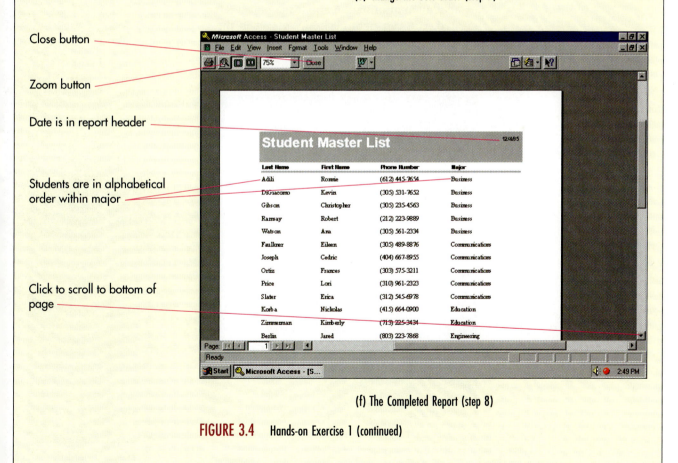

(f) The Completed Report (step 8)

FIGURE 3.4 Hands-on Exercise 1 (continued)

INFORMATION FROM THE DATABASE 103

➤ Click the **Print button** to print the report and submit it to your instructor. Click the **Close button** to exit the Print Preview window.

➤ Click the **Close button** in the Report Design window. Click **Yes** if asked whether to save changes to the Student Master List report.

STEP 9: Report Properties

➤ The Database window for the Our Students database should be displayed on the screen. Click the **Restore button** to restore the window to its earlier size.

➤ The **Reports tab** is already selected. Point to the **Student Master List** (the only report in the database), click the **right mouse button** to display a shortcut menu, then click **Properties** to display the dialog box in Figure 3.4g.

➤ Click the **Description text box,** then enter the description shown in the figure. Click **OK** to close the Properties dialog box.

➤ Close the database. Exit Access if you do not wish to continue with the next exercise at this time.

DESCRIBE YOUR OBJECTS

A working database will contain many different objects of the same type, making it all too easy to forget the purpose of the individual objects. It is important, therefore, to use meaningful names for the objects themselves, and further to take advantage of the Description property to enter additional information about the object. Once a description has been created, you can right click any object in the Database window, then click the Properties command from the shortcut menu to display the Properties dialog box with the description of the object.

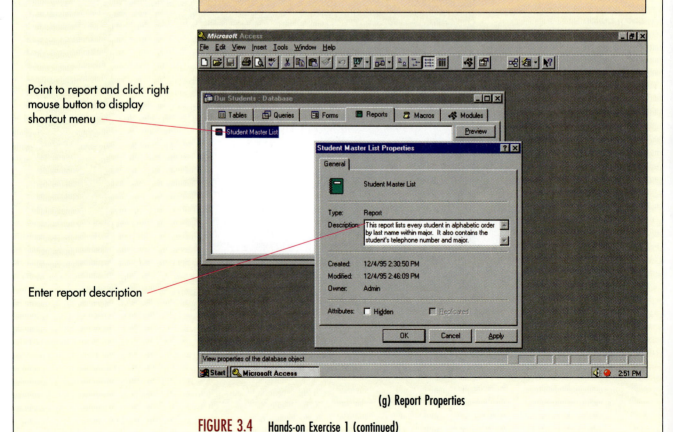

(g) Report Properties

FIGURE 3.4   Hands-on Exercise 1 (continued)

INTRODUCTION TO QUERIES

The report you just created displayed every student in the underlying table. What if, however, we wanted to see just the students who are majoring in Business? Or the students who are receiving financial aid? Or the students who are majoring in Business *and* receiving financial aid? The ability to ask questions such as these, and to see the answers to those questions, is provided through a query. Queries represent the real power of a database.

A *query* lets you see the data you want in the sequence that you want it. It lets you select specific records from a table (or from several tables) and show some or all of the fields for the selected records. It also lets you perform calculations to display data that is not explicitly stored in the underlying table(s), such as a student's GPA.

A query represents a question and an answer. The question is developed by using a graphical tool known as the ***Query By Example (QBE) grid.*** The answer is displayed in a ***dynaset,*** which contains the records that satisfy the criteria specified in the query.

A dynaset looks and acts like a table, but it isn't a table; it is a *dyna*mic *subset* of a table that selects and sorts records as specified in the query. A dynaset is similar to a table in appearance and, like a table, it enables you to enter a new record or modify or delete an existing record. Any changes made in the dynaset are automatically reflected in the underlying table.

Figure 3.5a displays the Students table we have been using throughout the chapter. (We omit some of the fields for ease of illustration.) Figure 3.5b contains the QBE grid used to select students whose major is "Undecided" and further, to list those students in alphabetical order. (The QBE grid is explained in the next section.) Figure 3.5c displays the answer to the query in the form of a dynaset.

The table in Figure 3.5a contains 24 records. The dynaset in Figure 3.5c has only five records, corresponding to the students who are undecided about their major. The table in Figure 3.5a has 15 fields for each record (some of the fields are hidden). The dynaset in Figure 3.5c has only four fields. The records in the table are in social security number order, whereas the records in the dynaset are in alphabetical order by last name.

The query in Figure 3.5 is an example of a ***select query,*** which is the most common type of query. A select query searches the underlying table (Figure 3.5a in the example) to retrieve the data that satisfies the query. The data is displayed in a dynaset (Figure 3.5c), which you can modify to update the data in the underlying table(s). The specifications for selecting records and determining which fields will be displayed for the selected records, as well as the sequence of the selected records, are established within the QBE grid of Figure 3.5b.

REPORTS, QUERIES, AND TABLES

Every report is based on either a table or a query. The design of the report may be the same with respect to the fields that are included, but the actual reports will be very different. A report based on a table contains every record in the table. A report based on a query contains only the records that satisfy the criteria in the query.

Query Window

The ***Query window*** has four different views. The ***Design view*** is displayed by default and is used to create (or modify) a select query. The ***Datasheet view***

Records in table are in order by SSN

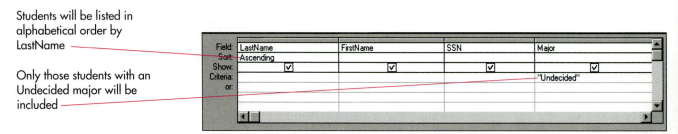

(a) Students Table

Students will be listed in alphabetical order by LastName

Only those students with an Undecided major will be included

(b) Query By Example (QBE) Grid

Records in dynaset are in alphabetical order by LastName

Only Undecided majors will be included

(c) Dynaset

FIGURE 3.5 Queries

displays the resulting dynaset. The **Print Preview** view shows how the dynaset will appear on the printed page. The **SQL view** enables you to use SQL (Structured Query Language) statements to modify the query and is beyond the scope of the present discussion. The Query Design toolbar contains the buttons to display all four views.

A select query is created in the Design view as shown in Figure 3.6a. The upper portion of the Design view window contains the field list for the table(s) on

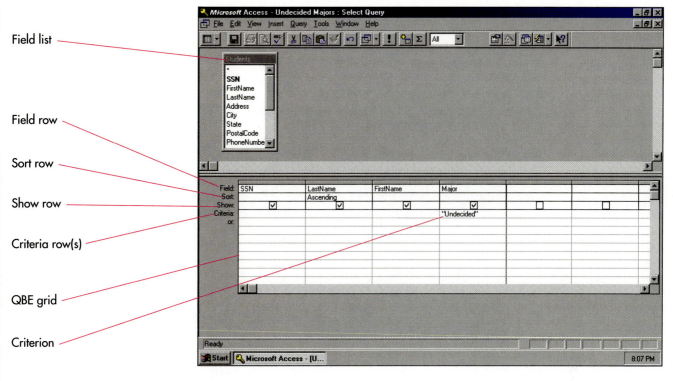

FIGURE 3.6   Query Design View

which the query is based (the Students table in this example). The lower portion of the window displays the QBE grid, which is where the specifications for the select query are entered.

The QBE grid consists of columns and rows. Each field in the query has its own column and is added by dragging it from the field list to the QBE grid. There are several rows for each field. The *Field row* displays the field name. The *Sort row* enables you to sort in *ascending* or *descending sequence.* The *Show row* controls whether or not the field will be displayed in the dynaset. The *Criteria row(s)* determine the records that will be selected, such as students with an undecided major as in Figure 3.6.

The data type of a field determines the way in which the criteria are specified for that field. The criterion for a text field is enclosed in quotation marks. The criteria for number, currency, and counter fields are shown as digits with or without a decimal point. (Commas and dollar signs are not allowed.) Dates are enclosed in pound signs and are entered in the mm/dd/yy format. The criterion for a Yes/No field is entered as Yes (or True) or No (or False).

CONVERSION TO STANDARD FORMAT

Access accepts values for text and date fields in the QBE grid in multiple formats. The value for a text field can be entered with or without quotation marks (Undecided or "Undecided"). A date can be entered with or without pound signs (1/1/94 or #1/1/94#). Access converts your entries to standard format as soon as you move to the next cell in the QBE grid. Thus, text entries are always shown in quotation marks, and dates are enclosed in pound signs.

Selection Criteria

To specify selection criteria in the QBE grid, enter a value or expression in the Criteria row of the appropriate column. Figure 3.7 contains several examples of simple criteria and provides a basic introduction to select queries.

The criterion in Figure 3.7a selects the students majoring in Business. The criteria for text fields are case insensitive. Thus, *"Business"* is the same as *"business"* or *"BUSINESS"*.

Values entered in multiple columns of the same Criteria row implement an **AND condition** in which the selected records must meet *all* of the specified criteria. The criteria in Figure 3.7b select students who are majoring in Business *and* who are from the state of Florida. The criteria in Figure 3.7c select Communications majors who are receiving financial aid.

Values entered in different Criteria rows are connected by an **OR condition** in which the selected records may satisfy *any* of the indicated criteria. The criteria in Figure 3.7d select students who are majoring in Business *or* who are from Florida or both.

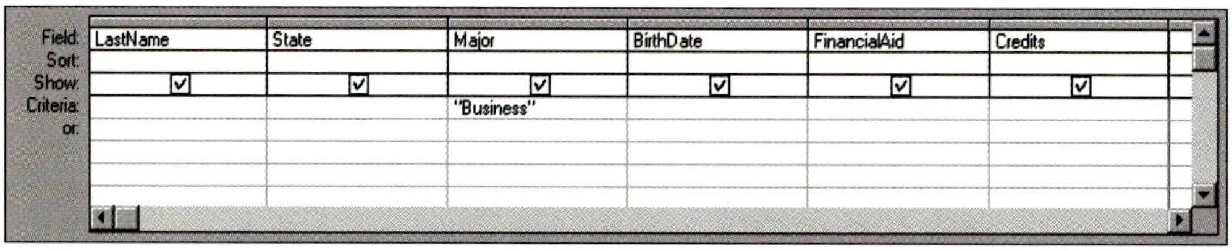

(a) Business Majors

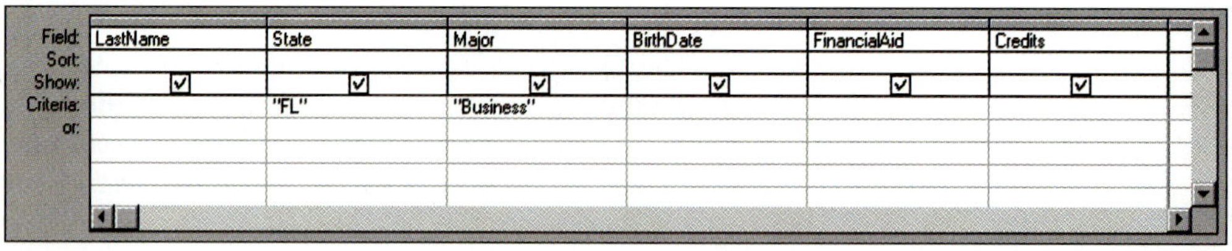

(b) Business Majors from Florida

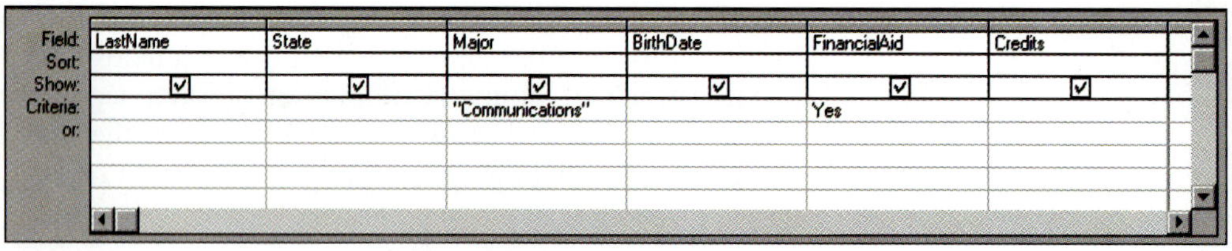

(c) Communications Majors Receiving Financial Aid

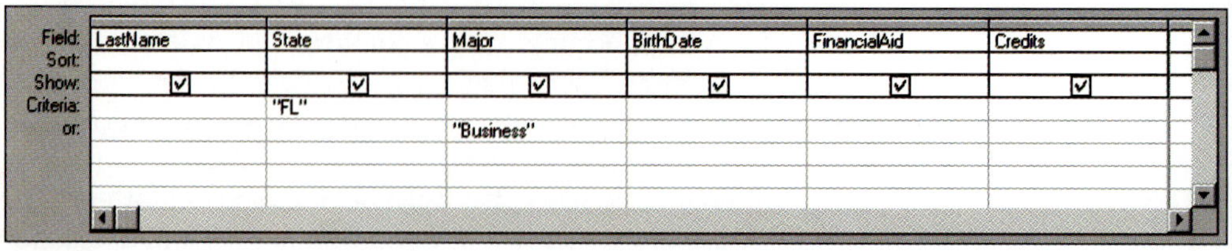

(d) Business Majors or Students from Florida

FIGURE 3.7 Criteria

Relational operators (>, <, >=, <=, =, and <>) are used with date or number fields to return records within a designated range. The criteria in Figure 3.7e select Engineering majors with fewer than 60 credits. The criteria in Figure 3.7f select Communications majors who were born on or after April 1, 1974.

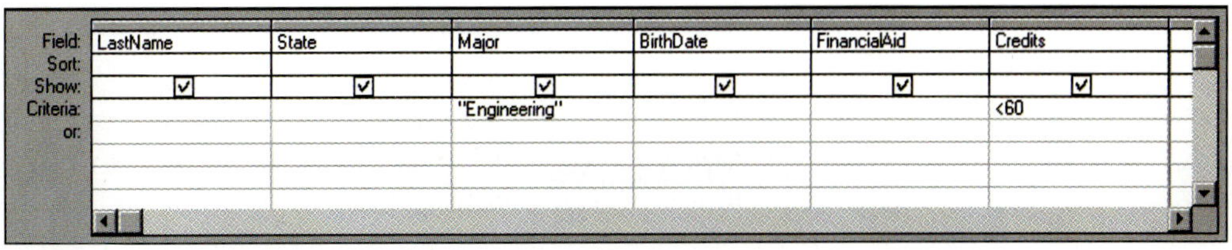

(e) Engineering Majors with Fewer than 60 Credits

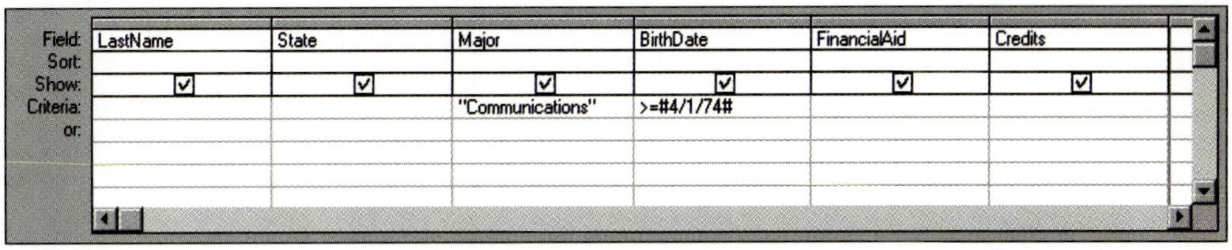

(f) Communications Majors Born on or after April 1, 1974

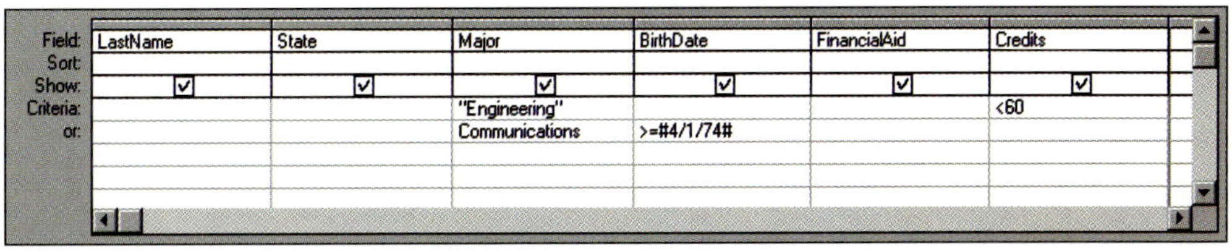

(g) Engineering Majors with Fewer than 60 Credits or Communications Majors Born on or after April 1, 1974

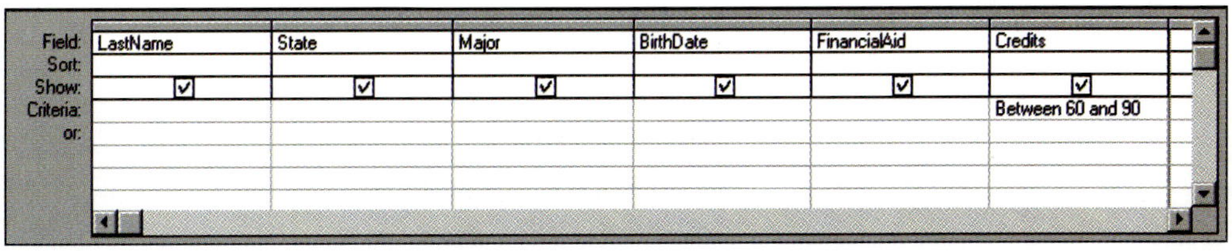

(h) Students with between 60 and 90 Credits

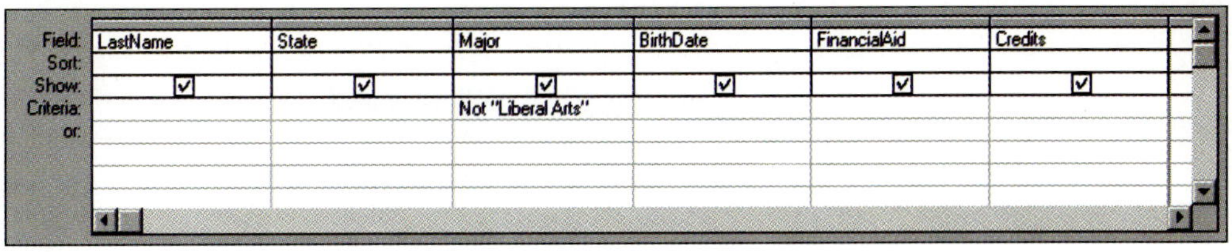

(i) Students with Majors Other Than Liberal Arts

FIGURE 3.7 Criteria (continued)

Criteria can grow more complex by combining multiple AND and OR conditions. The criteria in Figure 3.7g select Engineering majors with fewer than 60 credits *or* Communications majors who were born on or after April 1, 1974.

Other functions enable you to impose still other criteria. The ***Between function*** selects records that fall within a range of values. The criterion in Figure 3.7h selects students who have between 60 and 90 credits. The ***NOT function*** selects records that do not contain the designated value. The criterion in Figure 3.7i selects students with majors other than Liberal Arts.

> ### WILD CARDS
>
> Select queries recognize the question mark and asterisk wild cards that enable you to search for a pattern within a text field. A question mark stands for a single character in the same position as the question mark; thus H?ll will return Hall, Hill, and Hull. An asterisk stands for any number of characters in the same position as the asterisk; for example, S*nd will return Sand, Stand, and Strand.

HANDS-ON EXERCISE 2

Creating a Select Query

Objective: To create a select query using the Query By Example (QBE) grid; to show how changing values in a dynaset changes the values in the underlying table; to create a report based on a query. Use Figure 3.8 as a guide in the exercise.

STEP 1: Open the Existing Database

➤ Start Access as you did in the previous exercise. Our Students (the database you used in the previous exercise) should appear within the list of recently opened databases.

➤ Select (click) **Our Students,** then click **OK** (or simply double click the name of the database) to open the database and display the database window.

➤ Click the **Queries tab** in the database window. Click the **New command button** to display the New Query dialog box as shown in Figure 3.8a.

➤ **Design View** is already selected as the means of creating a query. Click **OK** to begin creating the query.

> ### THE SIMPLE QUERY WIZARD
>
> The Simple Query Wizard is exactly what its name implies—simple. It lets you select fields from an underlying table, but it does not let you enter values or a sort sequence. We prefer, therefore, to bypass the Wizard and to create the query entirely from the Query Design window.

Click Queries tab

Click New button

Click Design View

Click OK

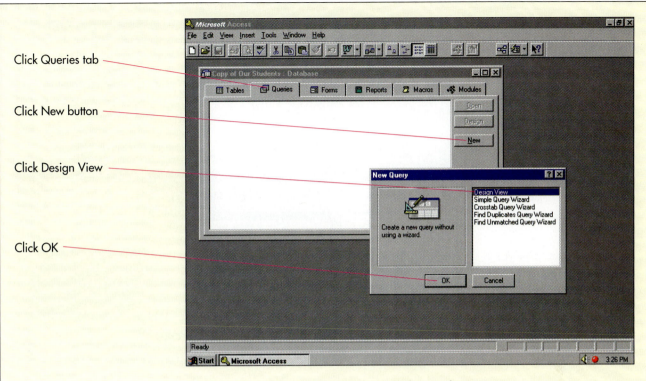

(a) Open the Our Students Database (step 1)

FIGURE 3.8 Hands-on Exercise 2

STEP 2: Add the Students Table

➤ The Show Table dialog box appears as shown in Figure 3.8b, with the **Tables tab** already selected.

➤ Click the **Add button** to add the Students table to the query (the field list should appear within the Query window). Click **Close** to close the Show Table dialog box.

➤ Click the **Maximize button** so that the Query Design window takes up the entire screen.

CUSTOMIZE THE QUERY WINDOW

The Query window displays the field list and QBE grid in its upper and lower halves, respectively. To increase (decrease) the size of either portion of the window, drag the line dividing the upper and lower sections. Drag the title bar to move a field list. You can also size a field list by dragging a border just as you would size any other window. Press the F6 key to toggle between the upper and lower halves of the Design window.

INFORMATION FROM THE DATABASE

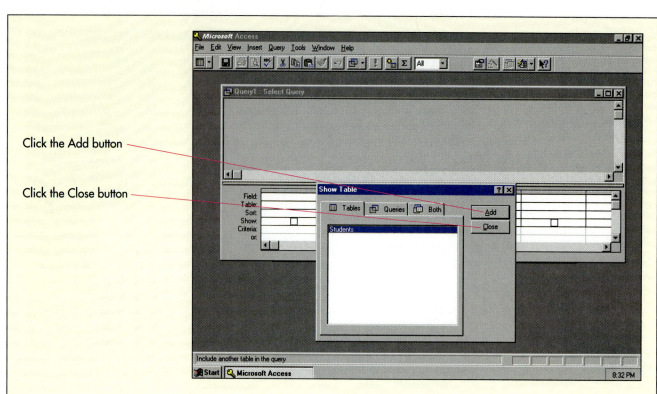

(b) Add the Students Table (step 2)

FIGURE 3.8   Hands-on Exercise 2 (continued)

STEP 3: Create the Query

➤ Click and drag the **LastName field** from the Students field list to the Field row in the first column of the QBE grid as shown in Figure 3.8c.

➤ Click and drag the **FirstName, PhoneNumber, Major,** and **Credits fields** (in that order) in similar fashion, dragging each field to the next available column in the Field row.

➤ A check appears in the Show row under each field name to indicate that the field will be displayed in the dynaset. (The check box functions as a toggle switch; thus, you can click the box to clear the check and hide the field in the dynaset. Click the box a second time to display the check and show the field.)

ADDING AND DELETING FIELDS

The fastest way to add a field to the QBE grid is to double click the field name in the field list. To add more than one field at a time, press and hold the Ctrl key as you click the fields within the field list, then drag the group to a cell in the Field row. To delete a field, click the column selector above the field name to select the column, then press the Del key.

STEP 4: Specify the Criteria

➤ Click the **Criteria row** for Major. Type **Undecided**.

➤ Click the **Sort row** under the LastName field, then select **Ascending** as the sort sequence.

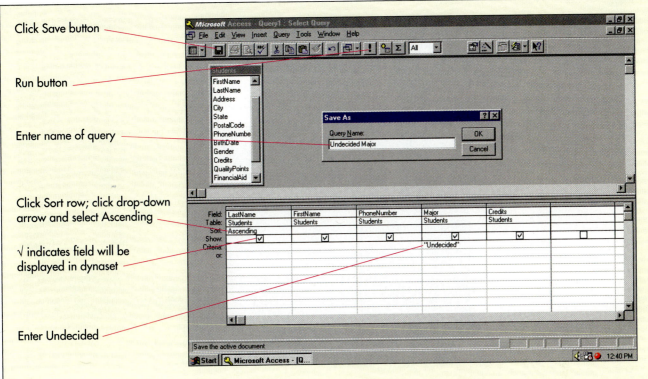

(c) Create the Query (steps 3 & 4)

FIGURE 3.8 Hands-on Exercise 2 (continued)

➤ Pull down the **File menu** and click **Save** (or click the **Save button**) to display the dialog box in Figure 3.8c.

➤ Type **Undecided Major** as the query name. Click **OK**.

FLEXIBLE CRITERIA

Access offers a great deal of flexibility in the way you enter the criteria for a text field. Quotation marks and/or an equal sign are optional. Thus "Undecided", Undecided, =Undecided, or ="Undecided" are all valid, and you may choose any of these formats. Access will convert your entry to standard format ("Undecided" in this example) after you have moved to the next cell.

STEP 5: Run the Query

➤ Pull down the **Query menu** and click **Run** (or click the **Run button**) to run the query and change to the Datasheet view.

➤ You should see the five records in the dynaset of Figure 3.8d. Change Ryan Cornell's major to Business by clicking in the **Major field,** clicking the **drop-down arrow,** then choosing **Business** from the drop-down list.

➤ Click the **Design view button** to change the query.

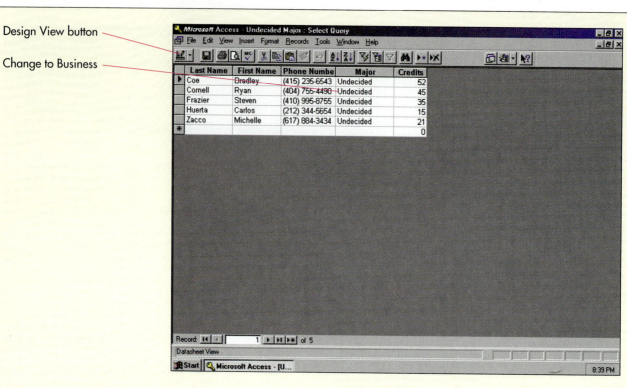

(d) Run the Query (step 5)

FIGURE 3.8   Hands-on Exercise 2 (continued)

STEP 6: Modify the Query

➤ Click the **Show check box** in the Major field to remove the check as shown in Figure 3.8e.

➤ Click the **Criteria row** under credits. Type **>30** to select only the Undecided majors with more than 30 credits.

➤ Click the **Save button** to save the revised query. Click the **Run button** to run the revised query. This time there are only two records (Bradley Coe and Steven Frazier) in the dynaset, and the major is no longer displayed.

• Ryan Cornell does not appear because he has changed his major.

• Carlos Huerta and Michelle Zacco do not appear because they do not have more than 30 credits.

STEP 7: Create a Report

➤ Pull down the **Window menu** and click **1 Our Students: Database** (or click the **Database window button** on the toolbar). You will see the Database window in Figure 3.8f.

➤ Click the **Reports tab,** then click the **New button** to create a report based on the query you just created. Select **Report Wizard** as the means of creating the report.

➤ Select **Undecided Major** from the drop-down list as shown in Figure 3.8f. Click **OK** to begin the Report Wizard.

➤ You should see the Report Wizard dialog box, which displays all of the visible fields (Major has been hidden) in the Undecided Major query. Click the **>> button** to select all of the fields from the query for the report. Click **Next**.

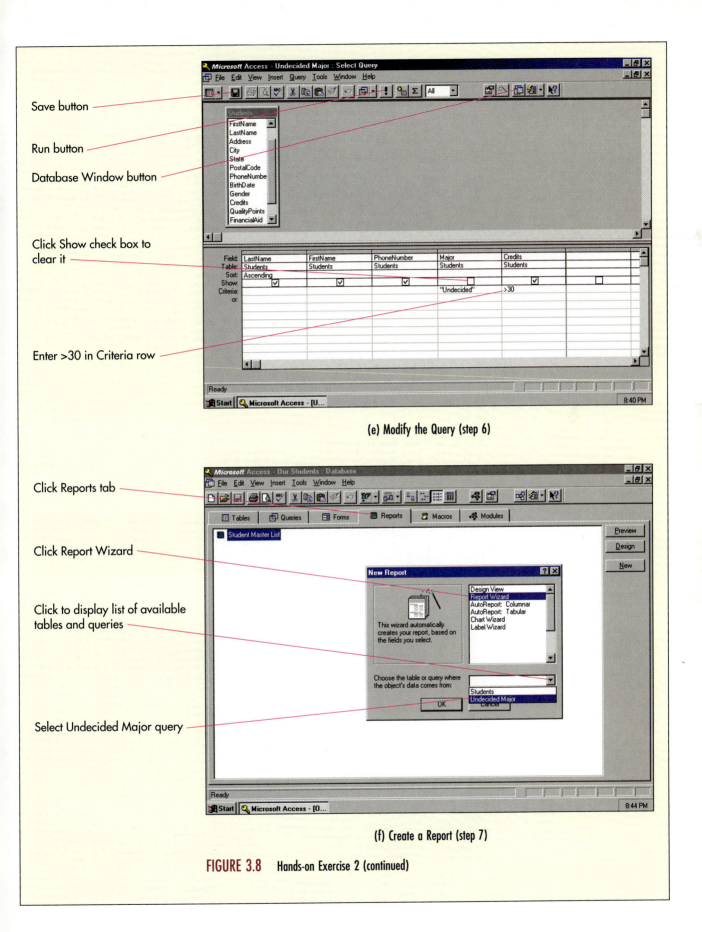

FIGURE 3.8 Hands-on Exercise 2 (continued)

➤ You do not want to choose additional grouping levels. Click **Next** to move to the next screen.

➤ There is no need to specify a sort sequence. Click **Next**.

➤ The **Tabular layout** is selected, as is **Portrait orientation**. Be sure the box is checked to **Adjust field width so all fields fit on a page**. Click **Next**.

➤ Choose **Soft Gray** as the style. Click **Next**.

➤ If necessary, enter **Undecided Major** as the title for your report. The option button to **Preview the Report** is already selected. Click the **Finish command button** to exit the Report Wizard and view the report.

THE BACK BUTTON

The Back button is present on every screen within the Report Wizard and enables you to recover from mistakes or simply to change your mind about how you want the report to look. Click the Back button at any time to return to the previous screen, then click it again if you want to return to the screen before that, and continue, if necessary, all the way back to the beginning.

STEP 8: View the Report

➤ If necessary, click the **Maximize button** to see the completed report as shown in Figure 3.8g. Click the **Zoom button** to see the full page.

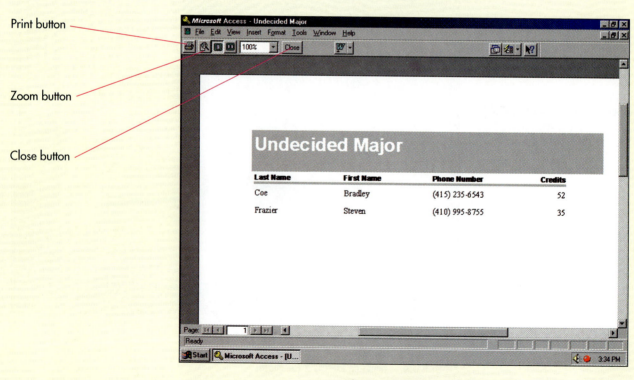

(g) The Completed Report (step 8)

FIGURE 3.8   Hands-on Exercise 2 (continued)

➤ Click the **Print button** to print the report and submit it to your instructor. Click the **Close button** to exit the Print Preview window.
➤ Click the **Close button** in the Report Design window.
➤ If necessary, click the **Database Window button** on the toolbar to return to the Database window. Click the **Maximize button**:
  - Click the **Queries tab** to display the names of the queries in the Our Students database. You should see the *Undecided Major* query created in this exercise.
  - Click the **Reports tab.** You should see two reports: *Student Master List* (created in the previous exercise) and *Undecided Major* (created in this exercise).
  - Click the **Forms tab.** You should see the *Students* form corresponding to the form you created in Chapter 2.
  - Click the **Tables tab.** You should see the *Students* table, which is the basis of all other objects in the database.
➤ Close the **Our Students database** and exit Access if you do not wish to continue with the next exercise. Click **Yes** if asked to save changes to any of the objects in the database.

DATABASE PROPERTIES

The tabs within the Database window display the objects within a database, but show only one type of object at a time. You can, for example, see all of the reports or all of the queries, but you cannot see the reports and queries at the same time. There is another way. Pull down the File menu, click Database Properties, then click the Contents tab to display the contents (objects) in the database. You cannot, however, use the Database Properties dialog box to open those objects.

GROUPING RECORDS

The records in a report are often grouped according to the value of a specific field. The report in Figure 3.9a, for example, groups students according to their major, sorts them alphabetically according to last name within each major, then calculates the average GPA for all students in each major. A group header appears before each group of students to identify the group and display the major. A group footer appears at the end of each group and displays the average GPA for students in that major.

Figure 3.9b displays the Design view of the report in Figure 3.9a, which determines the appearance of the printed report. Look carefully at the design to relate each section to the corresponding portion of the printed report:

- The report header contains the title of the report and appears at the beginning of the printed report.
- The page header contains the column headings that appear at the top of each page. The column headings are labels (or unbound controls) and are formatted in bold.

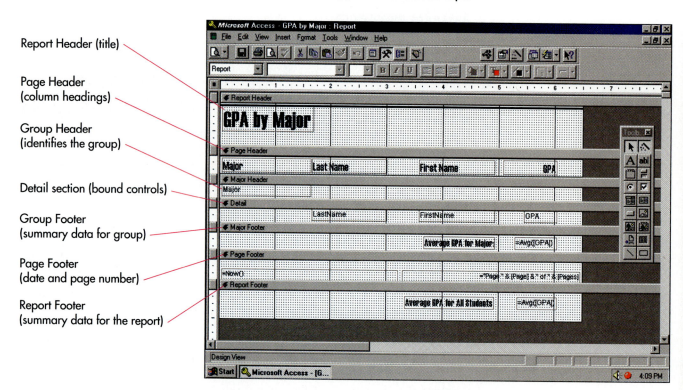

FIGURE 3.9 Summary Reports

- The group header consists of a single bound control that displays the value of the major field prior to each group of detail records.
- The detail section consists of bound controls that appear directly under the corresponding heading in the page header. The detail section is printed once for each record in each group.

- The group footer appears after each group of detail records. It consists of an unbound control (Average GPA for Major:) followed by a calculated control that computes the average GPA for each group of students.
- The page footer appears at the bottom of each page and contains the date, page number, and total number of pages in the report.
- The report footer appears at the end of the report. It consists of an unbound control (Average GPA for All Students:) followed by a calculated control that computes the average GPA for all students.

Grouping records within a report enables you to perform calculations on each group of records as was done in the group footer of Figure 3.9. The calculations in our example made use of the Avg function, but other types of calculations are possible:

- The ***Sum function*** computes the total of a specific field for all records in the group.
- The ***Min function*** computes the minimum value for all records in the group.
- The ***Max function*** computes the maximum value for all records in the group.
- The ***Count function*** counts the number of records in the group.

The following exercise has you create the report in Figure 3.9. The report is based on a query containing a calculated control, GPA, which is computed by dividing the QualityPoints field by the Credits field. The Report Wizard is used to design the basic report, but additional modifications are necessary to create the group header and group footer.

HANDS-ON EXERCISE 3

Grouping Records

Objective: Create a query containing a calculated control, then create a report based on that query; use the Sorting and Grouping command to add a group header and group footer to a report. Use Figure 3.10 as a guide in the exercise.

STEP 1: Create the Query
- Start Access and open the **Our Students database** from the previous exercise.
- Click the **Queries tab** in the database window, then click the **New command button** to display the New Query dialog box. **Design View** is already selected as the means of creating a query. Click **OK** to begin creating the query.
- The Show Table dialog box appears; the **Tables tab** is already selected, as is the **Students table.**
- Click the **Add button** to add the table to the query (the field list should appear within the Query window). Click **Close** to close the Show Table dialog box.
- Click the **Maximize button** so that the window takes up the entire screen as shown in Figure 3.10a.
- Scroll (if necessary) within the field list, then click and drag the **Major field** from the field list to the query. Click and drag the **LastName, FirstName, QualityPoints,** and **Credits fields** (in that order) in similar fashion.

INFORMATION FROM THE DATABASE 119

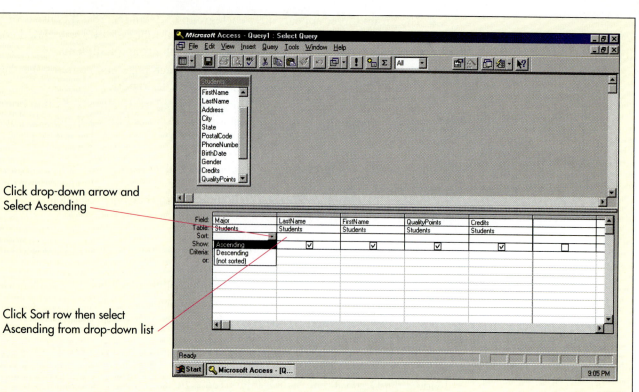

Click drop-down arrow and Select Ascending

Click Sort row then select Ascending from drop-down list

(a) Create the Query (step 1)

FIGURE 3.10 Hands-on Exercise 3

➤ Click the **Sort row** for the Major field. Click the **down arrow** to open the drop-down list box. Click **Ascending.**

➤ Click the **Sort row** for the LastName field. Click the **down arrow** to open the drop-down list box. Click **Ascending.**

> ### SORTING ON MULTIPLE FIELDS
>
> You can sort a query on more than one field, but you must be certain that the fields are in the proper order within the QBE grid. Access sorts from left to right (the leftmost field is the primary sort key), so the fields must be arranged in the desired sort sequence. To move a field within the QBE grid, click the column selector above the field name to select the column, then drag the column to its new position.

STEP 2: Add a Calculated Control

➤ Click in the first blank column in the Field row. Enter the expression **=[QualityPoints]/[Credits].** Do not be concerned if you cannot see the entire expression, but be sure you put **square brackets** around both field names.

➤ Press **enter.** Access has substituted Expr1: for the equal sign you typed initially. Drag the **column selector boundary** so that the entire expression is visible as in Figure 3.10b. (You may have to make some of the columns narrower to see all of the fields in the QBE grid.)

➤ Pull down the **File menu** and click **Save** (or click the **Save button**) to display the dialog box in Figure 3.10b. Enter **GPA By Major** for the Query Name. Click **OK**.

USE DESCRIPTIVE NAMES

An Access database contains multiple objects—tables, forms, queries, and reports. It is important, therefore, that the name assigned to each object be descriptive of its function so that you can select the proper object from the Database window. The name of an object can contain up to 64 characters and can include any combination of letters, numbers, and spaces. (Names may not, however, include leading spaces, a period, an exclamation mark, or brackets ([ ]).

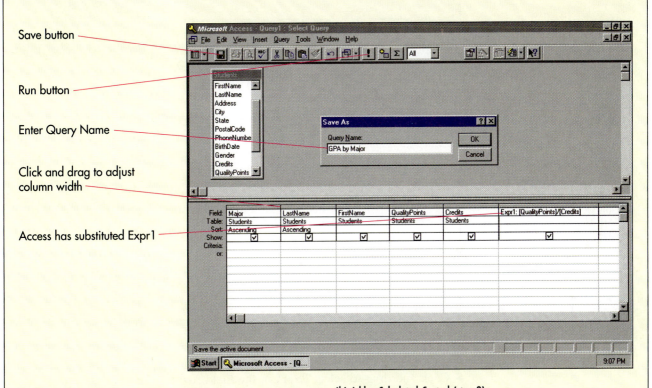

(b) Add a Calculated Control (step 2)

FIGURE 3.10 Hands-on Exercise 3 (continued)

STEP 3: Run the Query

➤ Pull down the **Query menu** and click **Run** (or click the **Run button** on the Query Design toolbar). You will see the dynaset in Figure 3.10c:
- Students are listed by major and alphabetically by last name within major.
- The GPA is calculated to several places (you may not even see the number to the left of the decimal) and appears in the Expr1 field.

➤ Click the **Design View button** in order to modify the query.

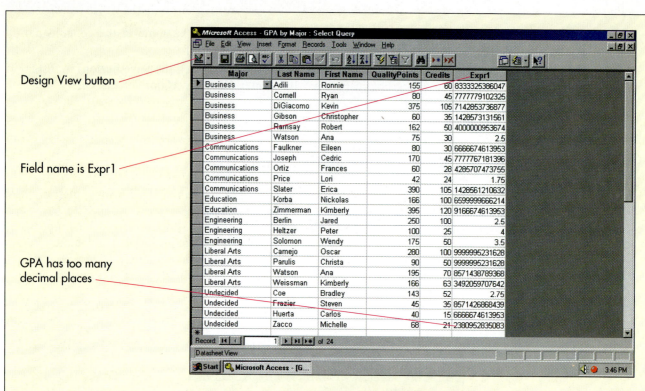

(c) Run the Query (step 3)

FIGURE 3.10 Hands-on Exercise 3 (continued)

ADJUST THE COLUMN WIDTH

Point to the right edge of the column you want to resize, then drag the mouse in the direction you want to go; drag to the right to make the column wider or to the left to make the column narrower. Alternatively, you can double click the column selector line (right edge) to fit the longest entry in that column. Adjusting the column width in the Design view does not affect the column width in the Datasheet view, but you can use the same technique in both views.

STEP 4: Modify the Query

▸ Click and drag to select **Expr1** in the Field row for the calculated field. (Do not select the colon). Type **GPA** to substitute a more meaningful field name.

▸ Point to the column and click the **right mouse button** to display a shortcut menu. Click **Properties** to display the Field Properties dialog box in Figure 3.10d. Click the **General tab** if necessary:

- Click the **Description text box.** Enter **GPA** as shown in Figure 3.10d.
- Click the **Format text box.** Click the **drop-down arrow** to display the available formats. Click **Fixed.**
- Close the Field Properties dialog box.

▸ Click the **Save button** to save the modified query.

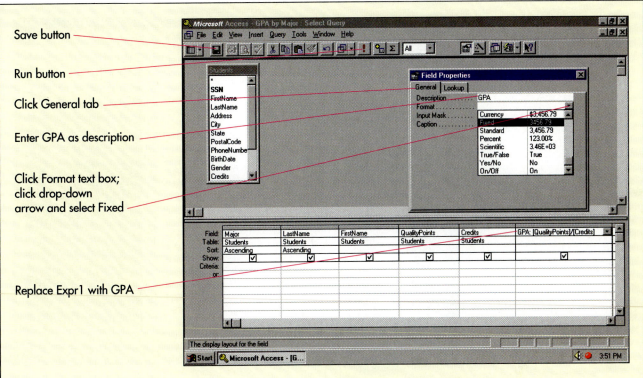

(d) Modify the Query (step 4)

FIGURE 3.10 Hands-on Exercise 3 (continued)

THE TOP VALUES PROPERTY

Can you create a query that lists only the five students with the highest or lowest GPA? It's easy, if you know about the Top Values property. First, sort the query according to the desired sequence—for example, students in descending order by GPA to see the students with the highest GPA. (Remove all other sort keys within the query.) Point anywhere in the gray area in the upper portion of the Query window, click the right mouse button to display a shortcut menu, then click Properties to display the Query Properties sheet. Click the Top Values box and enter the desired number of students (e.g., 5 for five students, or 5% for the top five percent). When you run the query you will see only the top five students. (You can see the bottom five instead if you specify ascending rather than descending as the sort sequence.)

STEP 5: Rerun the Query

▶ Click the **Run button** to run the modified query. You will see a new dynaset corresponding to the modified query as shown in Figure 3.10e. Resize the column widths (as necessary) within the dynaset.

- Students are still listed by major and alphabetically within major.
- The GPA is calculated to two decimal places and appears under the GPA field.

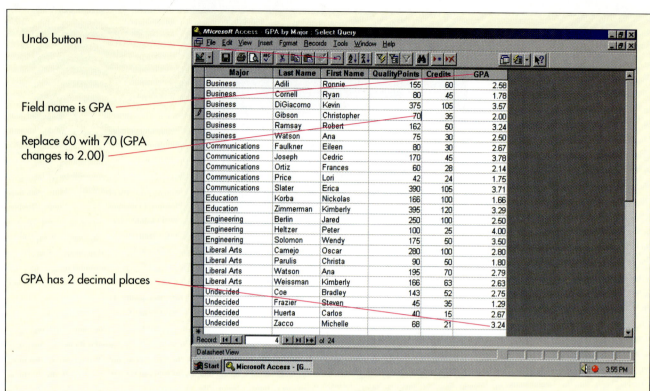

(e) Rerun the Query (step 5)

FIGURE 3.10 Hands-on Exercise 3 (continued)

➤ Click the **QualityPoints field** for Christopher Gibson. Replace 60 with **70**. Press **enter**. The GPA changes automatically to 2.

➤ Pull down the **Edit menu** and click **Undo Current Field/Record** (or click the **Undo button** on the Query toolbar). The GPA returns to its previous value.

➤ Tab to the **GPA field** for Christopher Gibson. Type **2**. Access will beep and prevent you from changing the GPA because it is a calculated field as indicated on the status bar.

➤ Click the **Close button** to close the query and return to the Database window. Click **Yes** if asked whether to save the changes.

THE DYNASET

A query represents a question and an answer. The question is developed by using the QBE (Query By Example) grid in the Query Design view. The answer is displayed in a dynaset that contains the records that satisfy the criteria specified in the query. A dynaset looks and acts like a table but it isn't a table; it is a dynamic subset of a table that selects and sorts records as specified in the query. A dynaset is like a table in that you can enter a new record or modify or delete an existing record. It is dynamic because the changes made to the dynaset are automatically reflected in the underlying table.

STEP 6: The Report Wizard

➤ You should see the Database window. Click the **Reports tab,** then click the **New button** to create a report based on the query you just created. Select **Report Wizard** as the means of creating the report.

➤ Select **GPA By Major** from the drop-down list at the bottom of the dialog box. Click **OK** to begin the Report Wizard. You should see the Report Wizard dialog box, which displays all of the fields in the GPA by Major query.

- Click (select) the **Major field** in the Available fields list box, then click the **> button.**
- Add the **LastName, FirstName,** and **GPA fields** one at a time.
- Do not include the QualityPoints or Credits fields. Click **Next.**

➤ You should see the screen asking whether you want to group the fields. Click (select) the **Major field,** then click the **> button** to display the screen in Figure 3.10f. The Major field appears above the other fields to indicate that the records will be grouped according to the value of the Major field. Click **Next.**

➤ The next screen asks you to specify the order for the detail records. Click the **drop-down arrow** on the list box for the first field. Click **LastName** to sort the records alphabetically by last name within each major. Click **Next.**

➤ The **Stepped Option button** is already selected for the report layout, as is **Portrait orientation.** Be sure the box is checked to **Adjust field width so all fields fit on a page.** Click **Next.**

➤ Choose **Compact** as the style. Click **Next.**

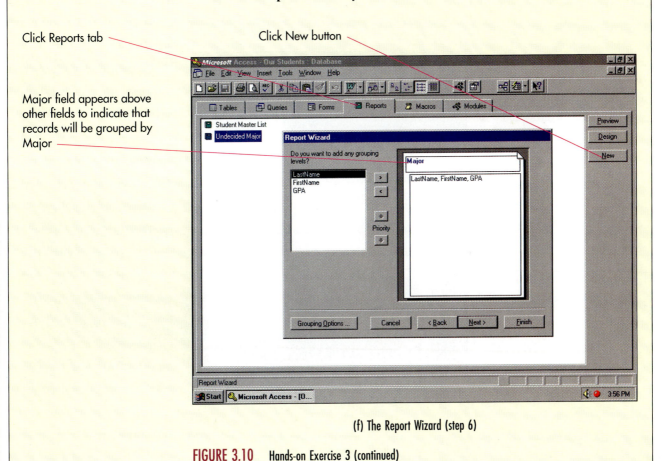

(f) The Report Wizard (step 6)

FIGURE 3.10 Hands-on Exercise 3 (continued)

➤ **GPA By Major** (which corresponds to the name of the underlying query) is already entered as the name of the report. Click the Option button to **Modify the report's design.** Click **Finish** to exit the Report Wizard.

STEP 7: Sorting and Grouping

➤ You should see the Report Design view as shown in Figure 3.10g. (The Sorting and Grouping dialog box is not yet visible.) Maximize the Report window (if necessary) so that you have more room in which to work.

➤ Move, size, and align the column headings and bound controls as shown in Figure 3.10g.

SELECTING MULTIPLE CONTROLS

Select (click) a column heading in the page header, then press and hold the Shift key as you select the corresponding bound control in the Detail section. This selects both the column heading and the bound control and enables you to move and size the objects in conjunction with one another. Continue to work with both objects selected as you apply formatting through various buttons on the Formatting toolbar, or change properties through the property sheet. Click anywhere on the report to deselect the objects when you are finished.

(g) Sorting and Grouping (step 7)

FIGURE 3.10 Hands-on Exercise 3 (continued)

➤ Pull down the **View menu.** Click **Sorting and Grouping** to display the Sorting and Grouping dialog box.

➤ The **Major field** should already be selected. Click the **Group Footer** property, click the **drop-down arrow,** then click **Yes** to create a group footer for the Major field.

➤ Close the dialog box. The Major footer has been added to the report. Click the Save button to save the modified report.

STEP 8: Create the Group Footer

➤ Click the **Text Box button** on the Toolbox toolbar. The mouse pointer changes to a tiny crosshair with a text box attached.

➤ Click and drag in the group footer where you want the text box (which will contain the average GPA) to go. Release the mouse. You will see an Unbound control and an attached label containing a field number (e.g., Text 15).

➤ Click in the **text box** of the control (Unbound will disappear). Enter **=Avg(GPA)** to calculate the average of the GPA for all students in this group as shown in Figure 3.10h.

➤ Click and drag to select the text in the attached label (Text15), then type **Average GPA for Major** as the label for this control. Size, move, and align the label as shown in the figure. (See the boxed tip on sizing or moving a control and its label.)

➤ Size the GPA control. Point to the **Average GPA control,** click the **right mouse button** to display a shortcut menu, then click **Properties** to display the

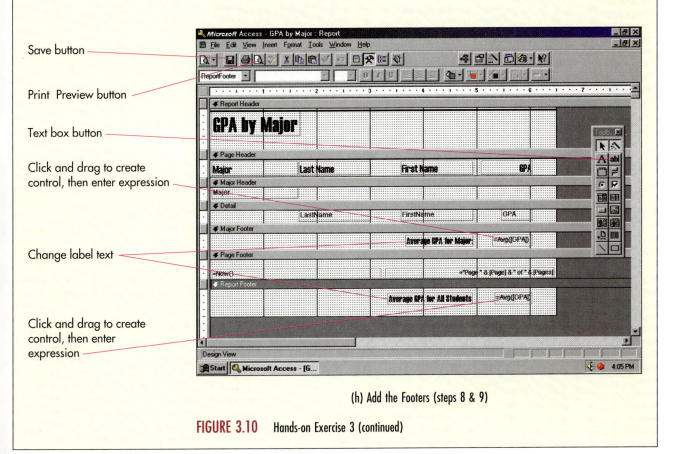

(h) Add the Footers (steps 8 & 9)

FIGURE 3.10 Hands-on Exercise 3 (continued)

INFORMATION FROM THE DATABASE

Properties dialog box. If necessary, click the **All tab,** then scroll to the top of the list to view and/or modify the existing properties:

- The Control Source text box contains the entry =Avg([GPA]) from the preceding step.
- Click the **Name text box.** Replace the original name (e.g., Text15) with **Average GPA for Major.**
- Click the **Format box.** Click the **drop-down arrow** and select **Fixed.**
- Click the box for the **Decimal places.** Click the **drop-down arrow** and select (click) **2.**
- Close the Properties dialog box to accept these settings and return to the report.

➤ Click the **Save button** on the toolbar.

SIZING OR MOVING A CONTROL AND ITS LABEL

A bound control is created with an attached label. Select (click) the control, and the control has sizing handles and a move handle, but the label has only a move handle. Select the label (instead of the control), and the opposite occurs: the control has only a move handle, but the label will have both sizing handles and a move handle. To move a control and its label, click and drag the border of either object. To move either the control or its label (but not both), click and drag the move handle (a tiny square in the upper left corner) of the appropriate object.

STEP 9: Create the Report Footer

➤ The report footer is created in similar fashion to the group footer. Click and drag the bottom of the report footer to extend the size of the footer as shown in Figure 3.10h.

➤ Click the **Text Box button** on the Toolbox toolbar, then click and drag in the report footer where you want the text box to go. Release the mouse. You will see an Unbound control and an attached label containing a field number (e.g., Text17).

➤ Click in the **text box** of the control (Unbound will disappear). Enter **=Avg(GPA)** to calculate the average of the grade point averages for all students in the report.

➤ Click and drag to select the text in the attached label (Text17), then type **Average GPA for All Students** as the label for this control. Move, size, and align the label appropriately. Size the GPA text box, then format the GPA control:

- Point to the control, click the **right mouse button** to display a shortcut menu, then click **Properties** to display the Properties dialog box. Change the properties to **Fixed Format** with **2 decimal places.** Change the name to **Average GPA for All Students.**
- Close the Properties dialog box to accept these settings and return to the report.

➤ Click the **Save button** on the toolbar.

> **SECTION PROPERTIES**
>
> Each section in a report has properties that control its appearance and behavior. Point to the section header, click the right mouse button to display a shortcut menu, then click Properties to display the property sheet and set the properties. You can hide the section by changing the Visible property to No. You can also change the Special Effect property to Raised or Sunken.

STEP 10: View the Report

➤ Click the **Print Preview button** to view the completed report as shown in Figure 3.10i. The status bar shows you are on page 1 of the report.

➤ Click the **Zoom button** to see the entire page. Click the **Zoom button** a second time to return to the higher magnification, which lets you read the report.

➤ Click the **Navigation button** to move to the next page (page 2). Click the **Navigation button** to return to page 1.

➤ Be sure that you are satisfied with the appearance of the report and that all controls align properly with their associated labels. If necessary, return to the Design view to modify the report.

➤ Pull down the **File menu** and click **Print** (or click the **Print button**) to display the Print dialog box. The **All option button** is already selected under Print Range. Click **OK** to print the report.

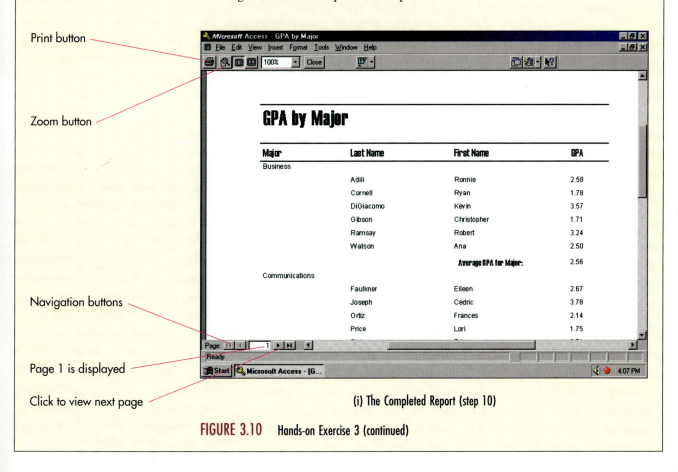

(i) The Completed Report (step 10)

FIGURE 3.10 Hands-on Exercise 3 (continued)

THE BORDER PROPERTY

The Border property enables you to display a border around any type of control. Point to the control (in the Design view), click the right mouse button to display a shortcut menu, then click Properties to display the Properties dialog box. Select the Format tab, click the Border Style property, then choose the type of border you want (e.g., solid to display a border or transparent to suppress a border). Use the Border Color and Border Width properties to change the appearance of the border.

STEP 11: Exit Access
- Pull down the **File menu** and click **Close** to close the GPA by Major report. Click **Yes** if asked to save design changes to the report.
- Close the **Our Students database** and exit Access.

COMPACTING A DATABASE

The size of an Access database is quite large even if the database contains only a limited number of records. It is not surprising to see simple databases, such as the Our Students database in this chapter, grow to 500KB or more. You can, however, reduce the storage requirements by compacting the database, a practice we highly recommend. Pull down the Help menu and ask the Answer Wizard about compacting a database. See problem 4 on page 136 for additional information.

SUMMARY

Data and information are not synonymous. Data refers to a fact or facts about a specific record. Information is data that has been rearranged into a more useful format. Data may be viewed as the raw material, whereas information is the finished product.

A report is a printed document that displays information from the database. Reports are created through the Report Wizard, then modified as necessary in the Design view. A report is made up of sections. Every section contains controls that are bound, unbound, or calculated, according to their data source.

Every report is based on either a table or a query. A report based on a table contains every record in that table. A report based on a query will contain only the records satisfying the criteria in the query.

A query enables you to select records from a table (or from several tables), display the selected records in any order, and perform calculations on fields within the query. A select query is the most common type of query and is created using the Query By Example grid. A select query displays its output in a dynaset that can be used to update the data in the underlying table(s).

The records in a report are often grouped according to the value of a specific field within the record. A group header appears before each group to identify the group. A group footer appears at the end of each group and can be used to display the summary information about the group.

All objects (tables, forms, queries, and reports) in an Access database are named according to the same rules. The name can contain up to 64 characters (letters or numbers) and can include spaces. A form and/or a report can have the same name as the table or query on which it is based to emphasize the relationship between the two.

KEY WORDS AND CONCEPTS

AND condition	Group footer	Report
Ascending sequence	Group header	Report footer
Between function	Inheritance	Report header
Bound control	Label tool	Report Wizard
Calculated control	Max function	Select query
Columnar report	Min function	Show row
Count function	NOT function	Sort row
Criteria row	OR condition	Sum function
Data type	Page footer	Tabular report
Datasheet view	Page header	Text box tool
Descending sequence	Print preview	Top Values property
Design view	QBE grid	Unbound control
Detail section	Query	Wild card
Dynaset	Query window	
Field row	Relational operators	

MULTIPLE CHOICE

1. Which of the following is a reason for basing a report on a query rather than a table?
   (a) To limit the report to selected records
   (b) To include a calculated field in the report
   (c) Both (a) and (b)
   (d) Neither (a) nor (b)

2. An Access database may contain:
   (a) One or more tables
   (b) One or more queries
   (c) One or more reports
   (d) All of the above

3. Which of the following is true regarding the names of objects within an Access database?
   (a) A form or report may have the same name as the underlying table
   (b) A form or report may have the same name as the underlying query

(c) Both (a) and (b)
(d) Neither (a) nor (b)

4. The dynaset created by a query may contain:
   (a) A subset of records from the associated table but must contain all of the fields for the selected records
   (b) A subset of fields from the associated table but must contain all of the records
   (c) Both (a) and (b)
   (d) Neither (a) nor (b)

5. Which toolbar contains a button to display the properties of a selected object?
   (a) The Query Design toolbar
   (b) The Report Design toolbar
   (c) Both (a) and (b)
   (d) Neither (a) nor (b)

6. Which of the following does *not* have both a Design view and a Datasheet view?
   (a) Tables
   (b) Forms
   (c) Queries
   (d) Reports

7. Which of the following is true regarding the wild card character within Access?
   (a) A question mark stands for a single character in the same position as the question mark
   (b) An asterisk stands for any number of characters in the same position as the asterisk
   (c) Both (a) and (b)
   (d) Neither (a) nor (b)

8. Which of the following will print at the top of every page?
   (a) Report header
   (b) Group header
   (c) Both (a) and (b)
   (d) Neither (a) nor (b)

9. A query, based on the Our Students database within the chapter, contains two fields from the Student table (QualityPoints and Credits) as well as a calculated field (GPA). Which of the following is true?
   (a) Changing the value of Credits or QualityPoints in the query's dynaset automatically changes these values in the underlying table
   (b) Changing the value of GPA automatically changes its value in the underlying table
   (c) Both (a) and (b)
   (d) Neither (a) nor (b)

10. Which of the following must be present in every report?
    (a) A report header and a report footer
    (b) A page header and a page footer

(c) Both (a) and (b)
(d) Neither (a) nor (b)

11. Which of the following may be included in a report as well as in a form?
    (a) Bound control
    (b) Unbound control
    (c) Calculated control
    (d) All of the above

12. The navigation buttons ▶ and ◀ will:
    (a) Move to the next or previous record in a table
    (b) Move to the next or previous page in a report
    (c) Both (a) and (b)
    (d) Neither (a) nor (b)

13. Assume that you created a query based on an Employee table, and that the query contains fields for Location and Title. Assume further that there is a single criteria row and that New York and Manager have been entered under the Location and Title fields, respectively. The dynaset will contain:
    (a) All employees in New York
    (b) All managers
    (c) Only the managers in New York
    (d) All employees in New York and all managers

14. You have decided to modify the query from the previous question to include a second criteria row. The Location and Title fields are still in the query, but this time New York and Manager appear in *different* criteria rows. The dynaset will contain:
    (a) All employees in New York
    (b) All managers
    (c) Only the managers in New York
    (d) All employees in New York and all managers

15. Which of the following is true about a query that lists employees by city and alphabetically within city?
    (a) The QBE grid should specify a descending sort on both city and employee name
    (b) The City field should appear to the left of the employee name in the QBE grid
    (c) Both (a) and (b)
    (d) Neither (a) nor (b)

ANSWERS

1. c
2. d
3. c
4. d
5. d
6. d
7. c
8. d
9. a
10. d
11. d
12. c
13. c
14. d
15. b

Exploring Microsoft Access 7.0

1. Use Figure 3.11 to match each action with its result. A given action may be used more than once or not at all.

   Action
   a. Click at 3 and enter >30, then click at 1 and enter >3.0
   b. Click at 3 and enter >30, then click at 2 and enter >3.0
   c. Click at 3 and enter >30
   d. Click at 4
   e. Click at 5
   f. Double click at 6
   g. Click at 7
   h. Click at 8

   Result
   ____ Sort the query by LastName
   ____ Limit the dynaset to students with more than 30 credits *and* a GPA higher than 3.0
   ____ Display the Database window
   ____ Rename the calculated field
   ____ Suppress the display of the Social Security Number
   ____ Add Major to the QBE grid
   ____ Limit the dynaset to students with more than 30 credits
   ____ Run the query

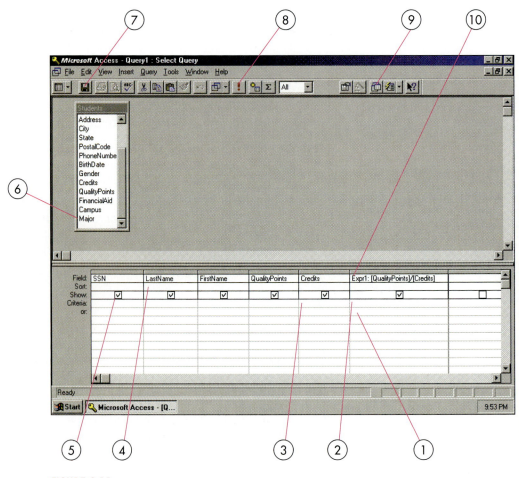

FIGURE 3.11   Screen for Problem 1

i. Click at 9
j. Click at 10, enter GPA, then press the Del key four times

___ Limit the dynaset to students with more than 30 credits *or* students with a GPA higher than 3.0
___ Save the query

2. Answer the following with respect to the window and dialog box shown in Figure 3.12:
   a. Which command displayed the Database window in Figure 3.12a? Which command displayed the dialog box in Figure 3.12b?
   b. What is the name of the database in Figure 3.12? How many objects does it contain? Which screen, Figure 3.12a or Figure 3.12b, gives you that information?
   c. Which objects in the database have a Design view? Which screen, Figure 3.12a or Figure 3.12b, do you use to open an object in the Design view?
   d. Which objects in the database are based on a table or query?
   e. Which objects in the database inherit properties from a table?
   f. Which objects in the database are associated with controls?

(a) Database Window

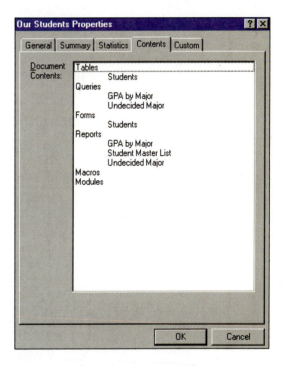

(b) Database Properties Window

FIGURE 3.12 Screen for Problem 2

3. Answer the following with respect to the query in Figure 3.13.
   a. What are the selection criteria?
   b. In which sequence will the selected records be displayed?
   c. Which fields (if any) are calculated fields?
   d. What is the difference between checking (or not checking) the Show box for Credits?

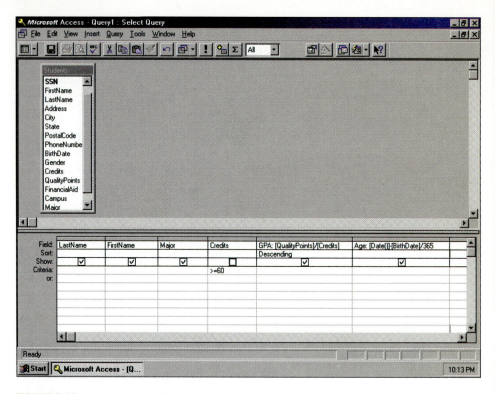

FIGURE 3.13 Screen for Problem 3

How would you modify the query to:
e. List all students in alphabetical order?
f. List all students by major and alphabetically within major?
g. List in alphabetical order students who are women *and* who are Business majors?
h. List in alphabetical order students who are women *or* who are Business majors?
i. List in alphabetical order all women who are Business majors, with at least 60 credits, a GPA higher than 3.00, and who are not receiving financial aid?

4. The size of an Access database containing multiple objects is likely to be quite large, even if the database contains only a limited number of records. Ask the Answer Wizard about compacting a database, then answer the following:
    a. What is meant by compacting a database? Why is this necessary?
    b. Describe how you would compact the Our Students database used in the chapter.
    c. What are the advantage(s) and disadvantage(s) of using the same name for the compacted database as for the original database?
    d. What is the file size of the Our Students database as it exists on the original data disk? What is the file size at the end of the third exercise?
    e. Follow the instructions in the Help screen to compact the Our Students database. What is the size of the database after it has been compacted?
    f. A friend of yours is working with a different database that, even after compacting, requires 2.1MB. What technique would you suggest to enable your friend to back up his (her) database onto a floppy disk?

Practice with Microsoft Access 7.0

1. Use the Our Students database as the basis for the following queries and reports:
   a. Create a select query for students on the Dean's List (GPA >= 3.50). Include the student's name, major, quality points, credits, and GPA. List the students alphabetically.
   b. Use the Report Wizard to prepare a tabular report based on the query in part a. Include your name in the report header as the academic advisor.
   c. Create a select query for students on academic probation (GPA < 2.00). Include the same fields as the query in part a. List the students in alphabetical order.
   d. Use the Report Wizard to prepare a tabular report similar to the report in part b.
   e. Print both reports and submit them to your instructor as proof that you did this exercise.

2. Use the Employee database in the Exploring Access folder to create the reports listed below. (This is the same database that was used earlier in Chapters 1 and 2.)
   a. A report containing all employees in sequence by location and alphabetically within location. Show the employee's last name, first name, location, title, and salary. Include summary statistics to display the total salaries in each location as well as for the company as a whole.
   b. A report containing all employees in sequence by title and alphabetically within title. Show the employee's last name, first name, location, title, and salary. Include summary statistics to show the average salary for each title as well as the average salary in the company.
   c. Add your name to the report header in the report so that your instructor will know the reports came from you. Print both reports and submit them to your instructor.

3. Use the United States database in the Exploring Access folder to create the report shown in Figure 3.14. (This is the same database that was used in problem 3 in both Chapters 1 and 2.) The report lists states by geographic region, and alphabetically within region. It includes a calculated field, Population Density, which is computed by dividing a state's population by its area. Summary statistics are also required as shown in the report.

   Note that the report header contains a map of the United States that was taken from the Microsoft ClipArt Gallery. The instructions for inserting an object can be found on page 86 in conjunction with an earlier problem. Be sure to include your name in the report footer so that your instructor will know that the report comes from you.

4. Use the Bookstore database in the Exploring Access folder to create the report shown in Figure 3.15. (This is the same database that was used in the hands-on exercises in Chapter 1.)

   The report header in Figure 3.15 contains a graphic object that was taken from the Microsoft ClipArt Gallery. You are not required to use this specific image, but you are required to insert a graphic. The instructions for inserting an object can be found on page 86 in conjunction with an earlier problem. Be sure to include your name in the report header so that your instructor will know that the report comes from you.

United States
by Region

Region	Name	Capital	Population	Area	Population Density
Middle Atlantic					
	Delaware	Dover	666,168	2,057	323.85
	Maryland	Annapolis	4,781,468	10,577	452.06
	New Jersey	Trenton	7,730,188	7,836	986.50
	New York	Albany	17,990,455	49,576	362.89
	Pennsylvania	Harrisburg	11,881,643	45,333	262.10
		Total for Region:	43,049,922	115,379	
		Average for Region:	8,609,984.40	23,075.80	477.48
Mountain					
	Arizona	Phoenix	3,665,228	113,909	32.18
	Colorado	Denver	3,294,394	104,247	31.60
	Idaho	Boise	1,006,749	83,557	12.05
	Montana	Helena	799,065	147,138	5.43
	Nevada	Carson City	1,201,833	110,540	10.87
	New Mexico	Sante Fe	1,515,069	121,666	12.45
	Utah	Salt Lake City	1,722,850	84,916	20.29
	Wyoming	Cheyenne	453,588	97,914	4.63
		Total for Region:	13,658,776	863,887	
		Average for Region:	1,707,347.00	107,985.88	16.19

Page 1 Of 4

FIGURE 3.14 Screen for Practice Exercise 3

University of Miami Book Store

Publisher	Author	ISBN Number	Title	List Price
IDG Books Worldwide				
	Livingston/Straub	1-56884-453-0	Windows 95 Secrets	$39.95
			Number of books:	1
			Average List Price:	$39.95
Macmillan Publishing				
	Rosch	1-56686-127-6	The Hardware Bible	$35.00
			Number of books:	1
			Average List Price:	$35.00
New Riders Publishing				
	Maxwell/Grycz	1-56205-306-X	New Riders Internet Yellow Pages	$29.95
			Number of books:	1
			Average List Price:	$29.95
Osborne-McGraw Hill				
	Hahn/Stout	0-07-882023-5	The Internet Yellow Pages	$27.95
	Hahn/Stout	0-07-881980-6	The Internet Complete Reference	$29.95
			Number of books:	2
			Average List Price:	$28.95
Prentice Hall				
	Grauer/Barber	0-13-503328-4	Exploring PowerPoint 7.0	$28.95
	Grauer/Barber	0-13-503393-4	Exploring Access 7.0	$28.95
	Grauer/Barber	0-13-065541-4	Exploring Windows 3.1	$24.95
	Grauer/Barber	0-13-504044-2	Exploring Word 7.0	$28.95

Page 1 Of 3

FIGURE 3.15   Screen for Practice Exercise 4

Case Studies

The Fortune 500

Research the Fortune 500 (or a similar list) to obtain the gross revenue and net income for the present and previous year for the 20 largest corporations. Create an Access database to hold a table for this data and an associated form to enter the data. Validate your data carefully, then produce at least three reports based on the data.

The United States of America

What is the total population of the United States? What is its area? Can you name the 13 original states or the last five states admitted to the Union? Do you know the 10 states with the highest population or the five largest states in terms of area? Which states have the highest population density (people per square mile)?

The answers to these and other questions can be obtained from the United States database that is available on the data disk. The key to the assignment is to use the Top Values property within a query that limits the number of records returned in the dynaset. Use the database to create several reports that you think will be of interest to the class.

The Super Bowl

How many times has the NFC won the Super Bowl? When was the last time the AFC won? What was the largest margin of victory? What was the closest game? What is the most points scored by two teams in one game? How many times have the Miami Dolphins appeared? How many times did they win? Use the data in the Super Bowl database to create a trivia sheet on the Super Bowl, then incorporate your analysis into a letter addressed to NBC Sports. Convince them you are a super fan and that you merit two tickets to next year's game.

Mail Merge

A mail merge takes the tedium out of sending form letters, as it creates the same letter many times, changing the name, address, and other information as appropriate from letter to letter. The form letter is created in a word processor (e.g., Microsoft Word), but the data file may be taken from an Access table or query. Use the Our Students database as the basis for two different form letters sent to two different groups of students. The first letter is to congratulate students on the Dean's list (GPA of 3.50 or higher). The second letter is a warning to students on academic probation (GPA of less than 2.00).

APPENDIX A: TOOLBARS

OVERVIEW

Microsoft Access has nineteen predefined toolbars, which provide access to commonly used commands. Twelve of the toolbars are tied to a specific view and are displayed automatically when you work in that view. Eleven of these toolbars are shown in Figure A.1 and are listed here for convenience: the Database, Relationships, Table Design, Table Datasheet, Query Design, Query Datasheet, Form Design, Form View, Report Design, Print Preview, and Macro toolbars. The twelfth, the Visual Basic toolbar, is not shown as it is beyond the scope of this book.

Four of the remaining seven toolbars are shown in Figure A.2. The Toolbox and Formatting (Form/Report Design) toolbars are displayed by default in both the Form Design and Report Design views. The Formatting (Datasheet) toolbar is displayed by default in both the Table Datasheet and Query Datasheet views. The Microsoft toolbar can be displayed as needed, and is used to quickly access the other Microsoft applications. The Utility1 and Utility2 toolbars are not displayed in the figure as they are used to create custom toolbars that can be used with any database, and are initially blank. The Filter/Sort toolbar is also not displayed as it is beyond the scope of this book.

The buttons on the toolbars are indicative of their function. Clicking the Print button, for example (the fourth button from the left on the Database toolbar), executes the Print command. If you are unsure of the purpose of any toolbar button, point to it, and a ToolTip will appear.

You can display multiple toolbars, move them to new locations on the screen, customize their appearance, or suppress their display.

> **SOME TOOLS ARE DIM**
>
> We don't know why, but Microsoft chose to include several buttons on various Toolbars that are rarely accessible. These buttons are dimmed initially. We reproduced the toolbars in this fashion so that our figures will match what you see on your monitor. We did, however, omit the captions from the dimmed buttons since they are rarely (if ever) used.

Database Toolbar

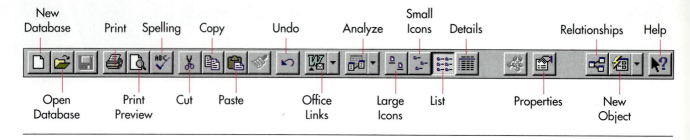

Relationships Toolbar

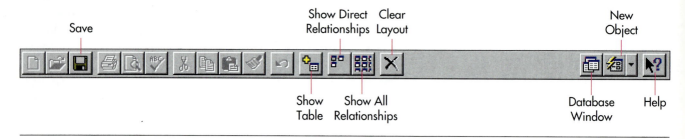

Table Design Toolbar

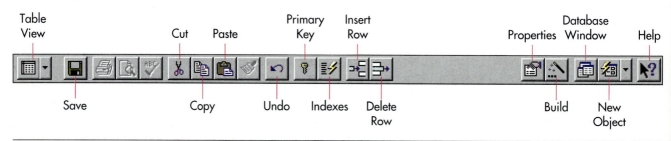

Table Datasheet Toolbar

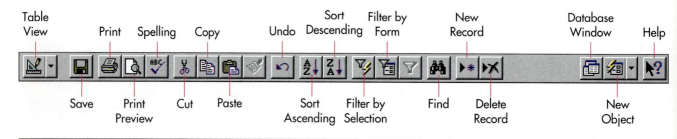

Query Design Toolbar

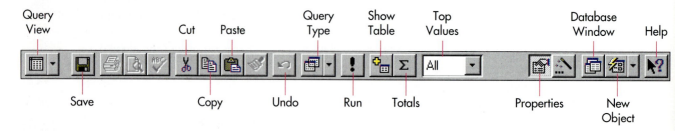

FIGURE A.1 Access Toolbars Tied to Specific Views

Query Datasheet Toolbar

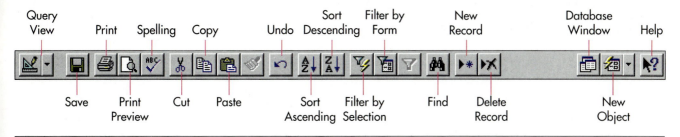

Form Design Toolbar

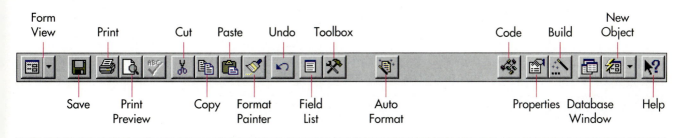

Form View Toolbar

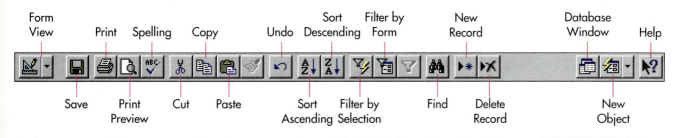

Report Design Toolbar

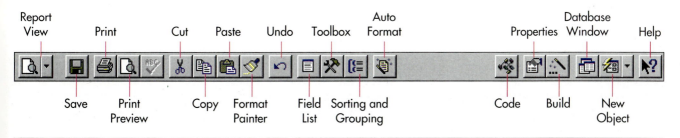

Print Preview Toolbar

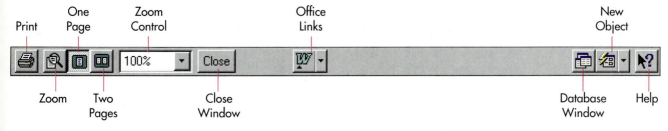

FIGURE A.1 Access Toolbars Tied to Specific Views (continued)

Macro Toolbar

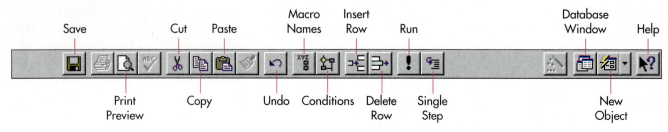

FIGURE A.1 Access Toolbars Tied to Specific Views (continued)

Toolbox Toolbar

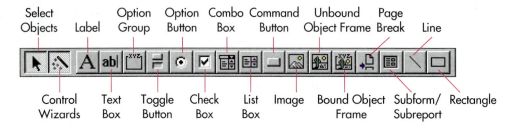

Formatting (Form/Report Design) Toolbar

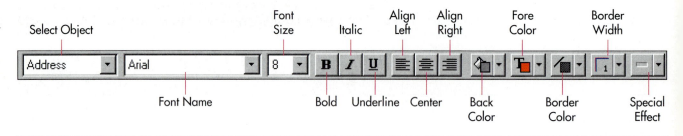

Formatting (Datasheet) Toolbar

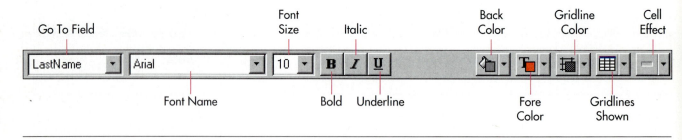

Microsoft Toolbar

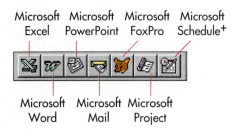

FIGURE A.2 Other Access Toolbars

INTRODUCTION TO POWERPOINT: PRESENTATIONS MADE EASY

OBJECTIVES

After reading this chapter you will be able to:

1. Describe the common user interface; give several examples of how PowerPoint follows the same conventions as other Microsoft applications.
2. Start PowerPoint; open, modify, and view an existing presentation.
3. Describe the different ways to print a presentation.
4. List the different views in PowerPoint; describe the unique features of each view.
5. Use the Outline view to add slides to, and/or delete slides from, an existing presentation and/or to modify the text on an existing slide.
6. Add clip art to an existing slide.
7. Use the Rehearse Timings feature to time a presentation.
8. Describe the Meeting Minder, Slide Navigator, and Pen; explain how these tools are used to enhance a presentation.

OVERVIEW

This chapter introduces you to PowerPoint, one of the four major applications in the Professional version of Microsoft Office (Microsoft Word, Microsoft Excel, and Microsoft Access are the other three). In essence, PowerPoint helps you to create a professional presentation without relying on others. It enables you to deliver a presentation on the computer (or via 35-mm slides or overhead transparencies) and to print that presentation in a variety of formats.

PowerPoint is easy to learn because it is a Windows application and follows all of the conventions associated with the common user interface. Thus, if you already use one Windows application, it is that much easier to learn PowerPoint because you can apply much of what you know. It's even easier if you use Microsoft Word, Excel, or Access, since there are over 100 commands that are common to the Microsoft Office.

The chapter begins by showing you an actual PowerPoint presentation so that you can better appreciate what you will be able to do. We describe the five different PowerPoint views and the unique capabilities of each view. We show you how to add slides to, and delete slides from, an existing presentation, how to modify the text of a presentation; and how to add clip art. (We will show you how to create your own presentation in Chapter 2.) We also provide three hands-on exercises, in which you apply the conceptual material at the computer. The exercises are essential to the learn-by-doing philosophy we follow throughout the text, and it is through the exercises that you will truly master the material.

One final point, before we begin, is that while PowerPoint can help you create attractive presentations, the content and delivery are still up to you. It is important that you express yourself clearly and that you deliver the presentation effectively. The chapter ends with several suggestions to help you in this regard.

A POWERPOINT PRESENTATION

A PowerPoint presentation consists of a series of slides such as those in Figure 1.1. Each slide contains different elements, including text, clip art, and/or a chart. Nevertheless, the presentation has a consistent look from slide to slide with respect to its overall design and color scheme.

You might think that creating a presentation such as Figure 1.1 is difficult, but it isn't. It is remarkably easy, and that is the beauty of PowerPoint. In essence, PowerPoint allows you to concentrate on the *content* of a presentation without worrying about its *appearance*. You supply the text and supporting elements and leave the formatting to PowerPoint.

In addition to helping you create the presentation, PowerPoint provides a variety of ways to deliver it. You can show the presentation on a computer using animated transition effects as you move from one slide to the next. You can include sound in the presentation, provided your system has a sound card and speakers. You can also automate the presentation and distribute it on a disk for display at a convention booth or kiosk. If you cannot show the presentation on a computer, you can convert it to 35-mm slides or overhead transparencies.

PowerPoint gives you the ability to print the presentation in various ways to distribute to your audience. You can print one slide per page, or you can print miniature versions of each slide and can choose between two, three, or six slides per page. You can prepare speaker notes for yourself, consisting of a picture of each slide together with notes for its delivery. You can also print the entire presentation in outline form. Giving the audience a copy of the presentation (in any format) enables them to follow it more closely, and to take it home when the session is over.

INTRODUCTION TO POWERPOINT

The desktop in Figure 1.2 should look somewhat familiar, even if you have never used PowerPoint, because PowerPoint shares the common user interface that is present in every Windows application. You should recognize, therefore, the two open windows in Figure 1.2—the application window for PowerPoint and the document window for the current presentation.

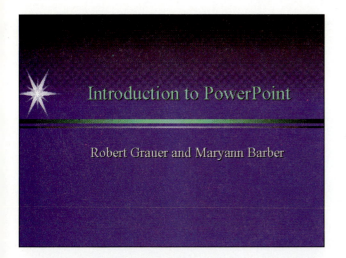
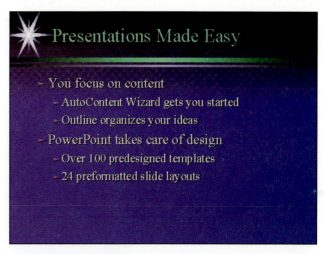

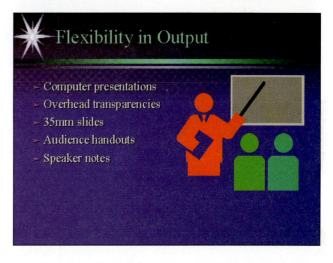
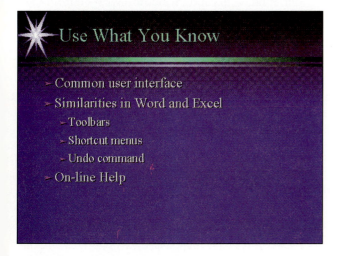
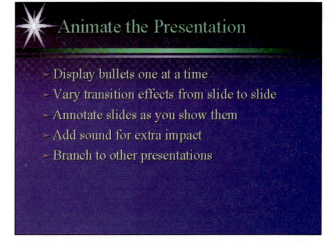

FIGURE 1.1   A PowerPoint Presentation

Each window has its own Minimize, Maximize (or Restore), and Close buttons. Both windows have been maximized, and thus the title bars have been merged into a single title bar that appears at the top of the application window. The title bar indicates the application (Microsoft PowerPoint) as well as the name

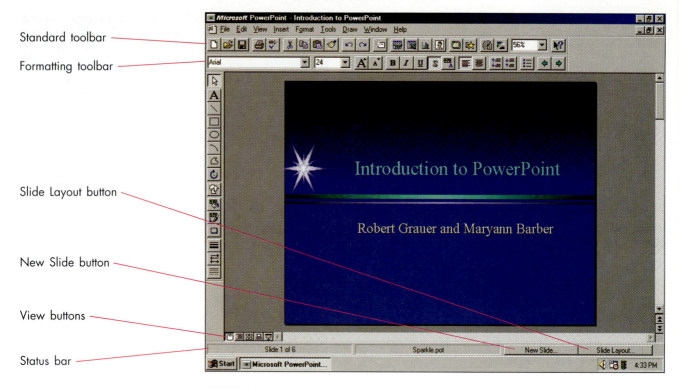

FIGURE 1.2 The PowerPoint Window

of the presentation (Introduction to PowerPoint) on which you are working. A *menu bar* appears immediately below the title bar. Two toolbars (which are discussed in the next section) appear below the menu bar. A *scroll bar* appears at the right (bottom) of the document window. The Windows 95 taskbar appears at the bottom of the screen and shows the open applications.

The *status bar* at the bottom of the application window displays information about what you are seeing and doing as you work on a presentation. It indicates the slide you are working on (e.g., Slide 1 in Figure 1.2), or it provides information about a command you have selected. The shortcut buttons on the right side of the status bar provide immediate access to two additional commands. The *New Slide button* is used to add a slide to the presentation. The *Slide Layout button* changes the layout of the current slide.

The *view buttons* are located to the left of the horizontal scroll bar immediately above the status bar and are used to switch between the five different views

THE COMMON USER INTERFACE

One of the most significant benefits of the Windows environment is the *common user interface,* which provides a sense of familiarity when you begin to learn a new application. In other words, once you know one Windows application, it will be that much easier for you to learn PowerPoint, because all applications work basically the same way. The benefits are magnified if you use other applications in Microsoft Office; indeed, if you use either Word or Excel, you already know more than 100 commands in PowerPoint.

of a presentation. (The Slide view is displayed in Figure 1.2.) Each view offers a different way of looking at a presentation and has unique capabilities. PowerPoint views are discussed later in the chapter.

Toolbars

The Standard and Formatting toolbars are similar to those in Word and Excel, and you may recognize several buttons from those applications. The **Standard toolbar** appears immediately below the menu bar and contains buttons for the most basic commands in PowerPoint—for example, opening, saving, and printing a presentation. The **Formatting toolbar,** under the Standard toolbar, provides access to formatting operations such as boldface, italics, and underlining.

As with all other Microsoft applications, you can point to any button on any toolbar and PowerPoint will display the name of the button, which indicates its function. You can also gain an overall appreciation for the toolbars by considering the buttons in groups, as shown in Figure 1.3.

Remember, too, that while PowerPoint is designed for a mouse, it provides keyboard equivalents for almost every command. The shortcut buttons on the status bar offer still other ways to accomplish two of the most frequent operations. You may at first wonder why there are so many different ways to do the same thing, but you will come to recognize the many options as part of PowerPoint's charm. The most appropriate technique depends on personal preference, as well as the specific situation.

If, for example, your hands are already on the keyboard, it is faster to use the keyboard equivalent. Other times, your hand will be on the mouse and that will be the fastest way. It is not necessary to memorize anything, nor should you even try; just be flexible and willing to experiment. The more you do, the easier it will be!

The File Menu

The **File menu** is a critically important menu in virtually every Windows application. It contains the **Save command** to save a presentation to disk and the **Open command** to retrieve (open) the presentation at a later time. The File menu also contains the **Print command** to print a presentation, the **Close command** to close the current presentation but continue working in PowerPoint, and the **Exit command** to quit PowerPoint altogether.

The Save command copies the presentation that is currently being edited (i.e., the presentation in memory) to disk. The File Save dialog box appears the first time a presentation is saved so that you can specify the file name and other required information. All subsequent executions of the Save command save the presentation under the assigned name, replacing the previously saved version with the new version.

The File Save dialog box requires a file name (e.g., *My First Presentation* in Figure 1.4a), which can be up to 255 characters in length and may contain both spaces and commas. The dialog box also requires the drive (and folder) in which the file is to be saved, as well as the file type, which determines the application the file is associated with. (Long-time DOS users will remember the three-character extension at the end of a file name, such as PPT to indicate a PowerPoint presentation. The extension is generally hidden in Windows 95, according to options set through the View menu in My Computer. See page 30 in the Windows appendix.)

The Open command brings a copy of a previously saved presentation into memory, enabling you to show, edit, and/or print the presentation. The Open command displays the Open dialog box in which you specify the file to retrieve. You

Starts a new document, opens an existing document, or saves the document to disk

Prints the document or checks the spelling in the document

Cuts or copies the selection to the clipboard; pastes the clipboard contents; copies the format of the selected text

Undoes or redoes a previously executed command

Inserts a new slide

Inserts a Microsoft Word table, a Microsoft Excel worksheet, a graph, or a ClipArt image

Applies a design template or an animation effect

Exports a PowerPoint outline to Microsoft Word; changes the display to black and white

Changes the zoom percentage

Accesses online help

(a) Standard Toolbar

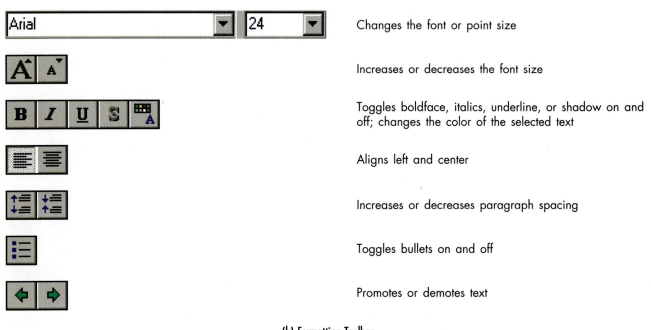

Changes the font or point size

Increases or decreases the font size

Toggles boldface, italics, underline, or shadow on and off; changes the color of the selected text

Aligns left and center

Increases or decreases paragraph spacing

Toggles bullets on and off

Promotes or demotes text

(b) Formatting Toolbar

FIGURE 1.3   Toolbars

indicate the drive (and the folder) that contains the file, as well as the type of file you want to retrieve. PowerPoint will then list all files of that type on the designated drive (and folder), enabling you to open the file you want.

The Save and Open commands work in conjunction with one another. The File Save dialog box in Figure 1.4a, for example, saves the file *My First Presentation* onto the disk in drive A. The Open dialog box in Figure 1.4b brings that file back into memory so that you can work with the file, after which you can save the revised file for use at a later time.

(a) File Save Dialog Box

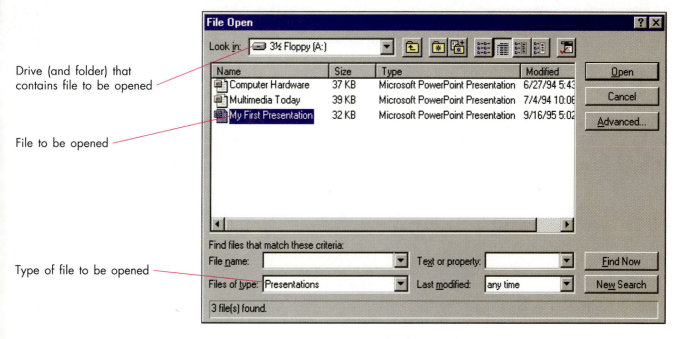

(b) File Open Dialog Box

FIGURE 1.4 The Save and Open Commands

> ### THE SAVE AS COMMAND
>
> The Save As command saves a presentation under a different name, and is useful when you want to retain a copy of the original presentation prior to making any changes. The original (unmodified) presentation is kept on disk under its original name. A second copy of the presentation is saved under a new name and remains in memory. All subsequent editing is done on the new presentation.

LEARNING BY DOING

We believe strongly in learning by doing, and thus there comes a point where you must sit down at the computer if the discussion is to have real meaning. The exercise introduces you to the data disk that is available from your instructor. The data disk contains the presentations referenced in the hands-on exercises throughout the text and can also be used to store the presentations you create. (Alternatively, you can store the presentations on a hard disk if you have access to your own computer.)

The following exercise has you retrieve the presentation of Figure 1.1 from the data disk. The exercise has you change the title slide to include your name, then directs you to view the presentation on the computer and to print the corresponding audience handouts.

HANDS-ON EXERCISE 1

Introduction to PowerPoint

Objective: To load PowerPoint, open an existing presentation, and modify the text on an existing slide. To show an existing presentation and print handouts of its slides. Use Figure 1.5 as a guide in the exercise.

STEP 1: Welcome to Windows 95

➤ Turn on the computer and all of its peripherals. The floppy drive should be empty prior to starting your machine. This ensures that the system starts by reading from the hard disk, which contains the Windows files, as opposed to a floppy disk, which does not.

➤ Your system will take a minute or so to get started, after which you should see the desktop in Figure 1.5a. Do not be concerned if the appearance of your desktop is different from ours.

➤ If you are new to Windows 95 and you want a quick introduction, click the **What's New** or **Windows Tour command button.** (Follow the instructions in the boxed tip to display the Welcome dialog box if it does not appear on your system.)

➤ Click the **Close button** to close the Welcome window and continue with the exercise.

Click buttons for a quick introduction to Windows 95

Click Close button to close Welcome window

(a) Welcome to Windows 95 (step 1)

FIGURE 1.5 Hands-on Exercise 1

TAKE THE WINDOWS 95 TOUR

Windows 95 greets you with a Welcome window that contains a command button to take you on a 10-minute tour of Windows 95. Click the command button and enjoy the show. You might also try the What's New command button for a quick overview of changes from Windows 3.1. If you do not see the Welcome window when you start Windows 95, click the Start button, click Run, type C:\WINDOWS\WELCOME in the Open text box, and press enter.

STEP 2: Install the Data Disk

➤ Do this step *only* if you have your own computer and you want to install (copy) the files from the data disk to the hard drive. Place the data disk in drive A.

➤ Click the **Start button** to display the Start menu. Click the **Run command** to display the Run dialog box.

➤ Type **A:\Install C** in the text box. (The drive letter, drive C in the example, is variable and indicates the drive on which to install the data disk.)

➤ Click **OK** or press the **enter key.** Follow the on-screen instructions to complete the installation.

INTRODUCTION TO POWERPOINT **9**

DOWNLOAD THE DATA DISK

The data disk for all books in the Exploring Windows series can be downloaded from the Prentice Hall Web site (http://www.prenhall.com). Use any Web browser to log onto the site, select Business and Economics, then move to the Exploring Windows page. To download the files for a single application, go to the page for that book, then click the icon to download the data disk. To download the files for all Office applications simultaneously, go to the Exploring Microsoft Office page.

STEP 3: Start PowerPoint

➤ Click the **Start button** to display the Start menu. Click (or point to) the **Programs menu,** then click **Microsoft PowerPoint** to start the program.

➤ Click **OK** to close the Tip of the Day dialog box (if it appears) in order to display the PowerPoint dialog box in Figure 1.5b. (If you do not see a tip of the day, and you want to, pull down the **Help menu** and click **Tip of the Day,** then check the box to **Show Tips at Startup.**)

➤ Click the **option button** to **Open an Existing Presentation,** then click **OK.** (If you do not see the PowerPoint dialog box, pull down the **File menu** and click **Open,** or click the **Open button** on the Standard toolbar.)

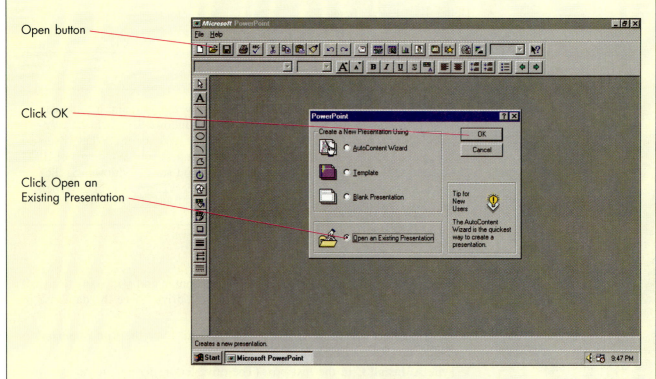

(b) Start PowerPoint (step 3)

FIGURE 1.5 Hands-on Exercise 1 (continued)

POINT AND SLIDE

Click the Start button, then slowly slide the mouse pointer over the various menu options. Notice that each time you point to a submenu, its items are displayed. Point to (don't click) the Programs menu, then click the Microsoft PowerPoint item to open the program. In other words, you don't have to click a submenu—you can just point and slide!

STEP 4: Open a Presentation

➤ You should see a File Open dialog box similar to the one in Figure 1.5c. Click the **Details button** to change to the Details view. If necessary, click and drag the vertical border between columns to increase (or decrease) the size of a column.

➤ Click the **drop-down arrow** on the Look In list box. Click the appropriate drive, drive C or drive A, depending on the location of your data. Double click the **Exploring PowerPoint folder** to make it the active folder (the folder from which you will retrieve and into which you will save the presentation).

➤ Click **Introduction to PowerPoint** to select the presentation. Click the **Open button** to open the presentation and begin the exercise.

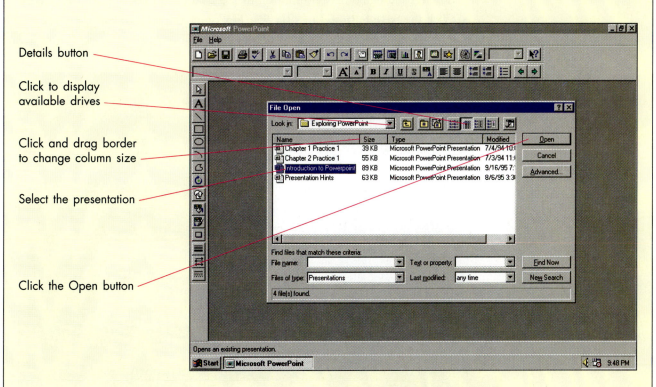

(c) Open an Existing Presentation (step 4)

FIGURE 1.5   Hands-on Exercise 1 (continued)

INTRODUCTION TO POWERPOINT **11**

A VERY USEFUL TOOLBAR

The File Open and File Save dialog boxes display similar toolbars with several common buttons. Click the Details button to switch to the Details view and see the date and time the file was last modified, as well as its size. Click the List button to display an icon for each file, enabling you to see many more files at the same time than in the Details view. The Preview button (available only in the File Open dialog box) lets you see a presentation before you open it. The Properties button displays information about the presentation, including the author's name and number of revisions.

STEP 5: The Save As Command

➤ If necessary, click the **Maximize button** in the application window so that PowerPoint takes the entire desktop. Click the **Maximize button** in the document window (if necessary) so that the document window is as large as possible.

➤ Pull down the **File menu.** Click **Save As** to display the dialog box shown in Figure 1.5d. Enter **Finished Introduction** as the name of the new presentation. (A file name may contain up to 255 characters; blanks are permitted.)

➤ Click the **Save button.** Press the **Esc key** or click the **Close button** if you see a Properties dialog box.

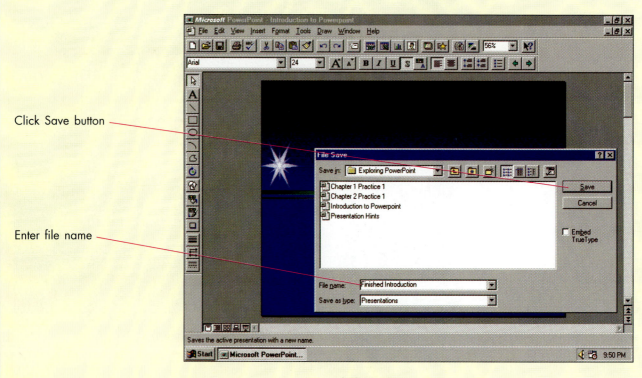

(d) The Save As Command (step 5)

FIGURE 1.5 Hands-on Exercise 1 (continued)

➤ There are now two identical copies of the file on disk: "Introduction to PowerPoint," which is the original presentation that we supplied, and "Finished Introduction," which you just created. The title bar shows the latter name, as it is the presentation currently in memory.

> **FILE PROPERTIES**
>
> PowerPoint automatically stores summary information and other properties for each presentation you create, and prompts for that information when the presentation is saved initially. The information is interesting, but is typically not used by beginners, and hence we suggest you suppress the prompt for this information. Pull down the Tools menu, click Options, click the General tab, then clear the box to Prompt for File Properties. You can view (edit) the properties of any presentation by clicking the Properties command in the File menu.

STEP 6: Modify a Slide

➤ Press and hold the left mouse button as you drag the mouse over the presenters' names (Robert Grauer and Maryann Barber). Release the mouse.

➤ The names should be highlighted (selected) as shown in Figure 1.5e. The selected text is the text that will be affected by the next command.

➤ Type your name, which automatically replaces the selected text. Click outside the placeholder to deselect it.

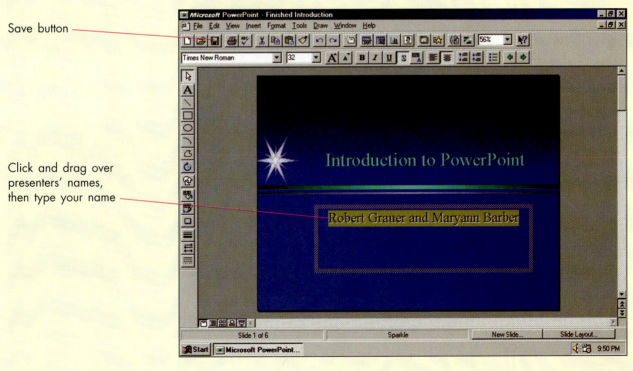

(e) Modify a Slide (step 6)

FIGURE 1.5 Hands-on Exercise 1 (continued)

➤ Pull down the **File menu** and click **Save** (or click the **Save button** on the Standard toolbar).

> ### THE HELP BUTTON
>
> Click the Help button on the Standard toolbar (the mouse pointer changes to include a large question mark), then click any other toolbar button to display a help screen with information about that button. Click anywhere to close the help screen and continue working.

STEP 7: Show the Presentation
➤ Pull down the **View menu** and click **Slide Show** to produce the Slide Show dialog box:
  • The **All option button** should be selected under Slides.
  • The **Manual Advance option button** should be selected under Advance.
  • Click the **Show command button** to begin the presentation.
➤ The presentation will begin with the first slide as shown in Figure 1.5f. You should see your name on the slide because of the modification you made in the previous step.
➤ Click the mouse to move to the second slide, which comes into the presentation from the left side of your monitor. (This is one of several transition

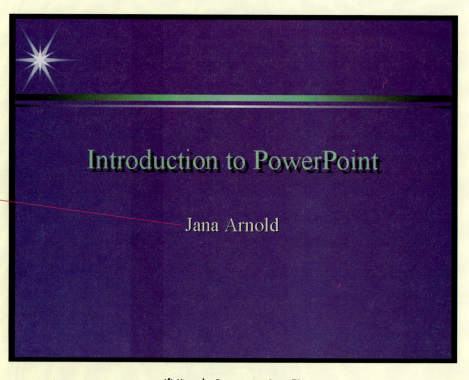

Your name should be displayed on the slide

(f) View the Presentation (step 7)

FIGURE 1.5 Hands-on Exercise 1 (continued)

effects available to add interest to a presentation.) Click the mouse again to move to the next (third) slide, which also comes in from the left.

➤ Continue to view the show until you come to the end of the presentation:
  • You can press the **Esc key** at any time to cancel the show and return to the PowerPoint window.
  • The last slide (Animate the Presentation) utilizes a build effect, which requires you to click the mouse to display each bullet on the slide.

➤ Click the left mouse button a final time to return to the regular PowerPoint window.

STEP 8: Print the Presentation

➤ Pull down the **File menu**. Click **Print** to produce the Print dialog box in Figure 1.5g.
  • Click the **down arrow** in the **Print What** drop-down list box.
  • Scroll to, then click, **Handouts (6 slides per page)** as shown in Figure 1.5g.
  • Check the box to **Frame Slides**.
  • Check that the **All option button** is selected under Print range.

➤ Click the **OK command button** to print the handouts for the presentation.

STEP 9: Exit PowerPoint

➤ Pull down the **File menu**. Click **Close** to close the presentation but remain in PowerPoint. Click **Yes** when asked whether to save the changes.

➤ Pull down the **File menu**. Click **Exit** to exit PowerPoint if you do not want to continue with the next exercise at this time.

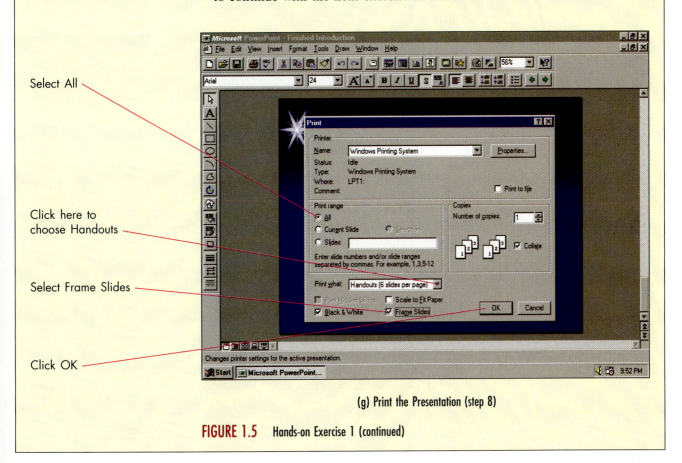

(g) Print the Presentation (step 8)

FIGURE 1.5 Hands-on Exercise 1 (continued)

INTRODUCTION TO POWERPOINT 15

FIVE DIFFERENT VIEWS

PowerPoint offers five different views in which to create, modify, and show a presentation. Figure 1.6 shows the five views for the introductory presentation from the first exercise. Each view represents a different way of looking at the presentation, and each view has unique capabilities. Some views display only a single slide, whereas others show multiple slides, making it easy to organize the presentation. You can switch back and forth between the views by clicking the appropriate view button at the bottom of the presentation window.

The ***Slide view*** in Figure 1.6a displays one slide at a time and enables all operations for that slide. You can enter, delete, or format text. You can draw or add objects such as a graph, clip art, or an organization chart. The ***Drawing Toolbar*** is displayed by default in this view.

The ***Slide Sorter view*** in Figure 1.6b displays multiple slides on the screen (each slide is in miniature) and lets you see the overall flow of the presentation. You can change the order of a presentation by clicking and dragging a slide from one position to another. You can delete a slide by clicking the slide and pressing the Del key. You can also set transition (animation) effects on each slide to add interest to the presentation. The Slide Sorter view has its own toolbar, which is discussed in Chapter 2 in conjunction with creating transition effects.

The ***Outline view*** in Figure 1.6c shows the presentation in outline form. You can see all of the text on every slide, but you cannot see the graphic elements that may be present on the individual slides. (A different icon appears next to the slides containing a graphic element.) The Outline view is the fastest way to enter or edit text, in that you type directly into the outline. You can copy and/or move text from one slide to another. You can also rearrange the order of the slides within the presentation. The Outline view has its own toolbar and is discussed more fully in Chapter 2.

The ***Notes Pages view*** in Figure 1.6d lets you create speaker's notes for some or all of the slides in a presentation. These notes do not appear when you show the presentation, but can be printed for use during the presentation to help you remember what you want to say about each slide.

The ***Slide Show view*** displays the slides one at a time as an electronic presentation on the computer. The show may be presented manually, where you click the mouse to move from one slide to the next. The presentation can also be shown automatically, where each slide stays on the screen for a predetermined amount of time, after which the next slide appears automatically. Either way, the slide show may contain transition effects from one slide to the next as was demonstrated in the first hands-on exercise.

The easiest way to switch from one view to another is by clicking the appropriate view button. The buttons are displayed in the lower-left part of the screen (above the status bar) in all views except the Slide Show view.

POWERPOINT VIEWS

PowerPoint has five different views of a presentation, each with unique capabilities. Anything you do in one view is automatically reflected in the other views. If, for example, you rearrange the slides in the Slide Sorter view, the new arrangement is reflected in the Outline view. In similar fashion, if you add or format text in the Outline view, the changes are also made in the Slide view.

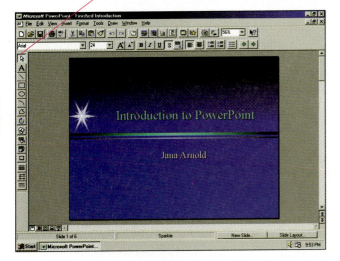
(a) Slide View

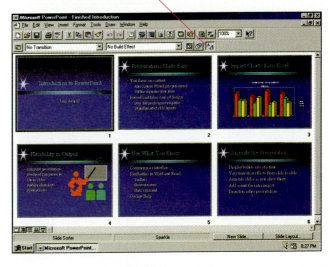
(b) Slide Sorter View

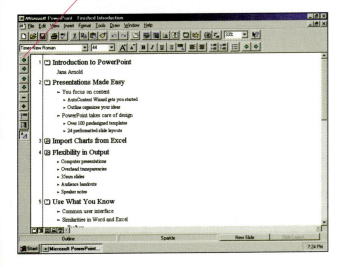
(c) Outline View

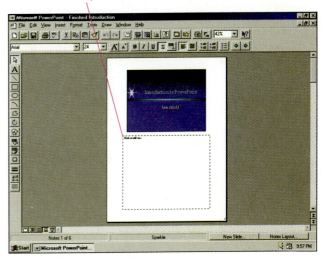
(d) Notes Pages View

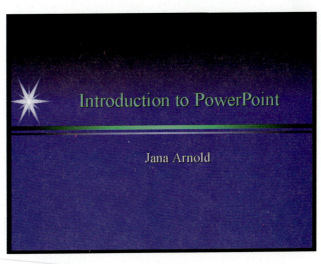
(e) Slide Show View

FIGURE 1.6 PowerPoint Views

INTRODUCTION TO POWERPOINT **17**

ADDING AND DELETING SLIDES

Slides are added to a presentation by using one of 24 predefined slide formats known as *AutoLayouts.* Click the New Slide button on the status bar to produce the dialog box in Figure 1.7a, then choose the type of slide you want. (The slide will be added to the presentation immediately after the current slide.)

Figure 1.7a depicts the addition of a bulleted slide with clip art. The user chooses the desired layout, then clicks the OK command button to switch to the slide view in Figure 1.7b. The AutoLayout contains *placeholders* for the various

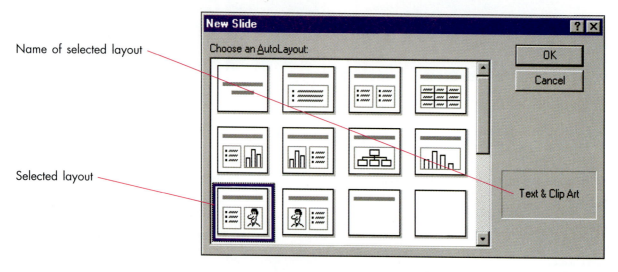

(a) AutoLayout

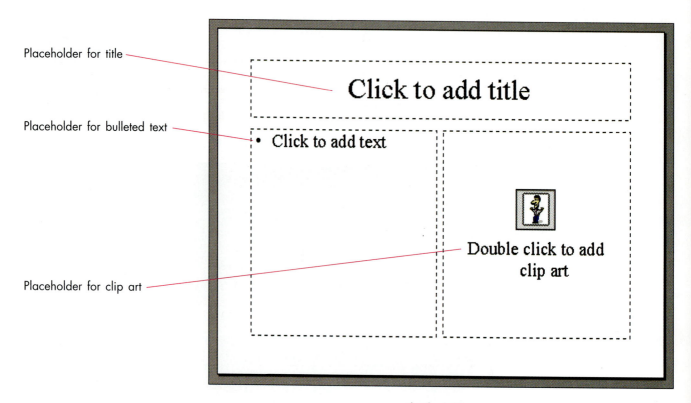

(b) Placeholders

FIGURE 1.7 Adding a Slide

objects on the slide that position the object on the slide. There are three placeholders in Figure 1.7b—one for the title, one for the bulleted text, and one for the clip art. Just follow the directions on the slide by clicking the appropriate place to add the title or text, or double clicking to add the clip art. It's that easy, as you will see in the exercise that follows shortly.

You can delete a slide from any view except the Slide Show view. To delete a slide from the Slide or Notes Pages view, select the slide by making it the current slide, pull down the Edit menu, and choose the Delete Slide command. To delete a slide from the Slide Sorter or Outline view, select the slide, then press the Del key.

HANDS-ON EXERCISE 2

PowerPoint Views

Objective: To switch between the different views while modifying a presentation; to use the ClipArt Gallery and add clip art to a slide; to add a slide to an existing presentation. Use Figure 1.8 as a guide in the exercise.

STEP 1: Add a New Slide

▶ Start PowerPoint. Follow the instructions from step 4 in the previous exercise to open the **Finished Introduction** presentation.

▶ Pull down the **Insert menu** and click **New slide** (or click the **New Slide command button** on the status bar). You will see the New Slide dialog box in Figure 1.8a.

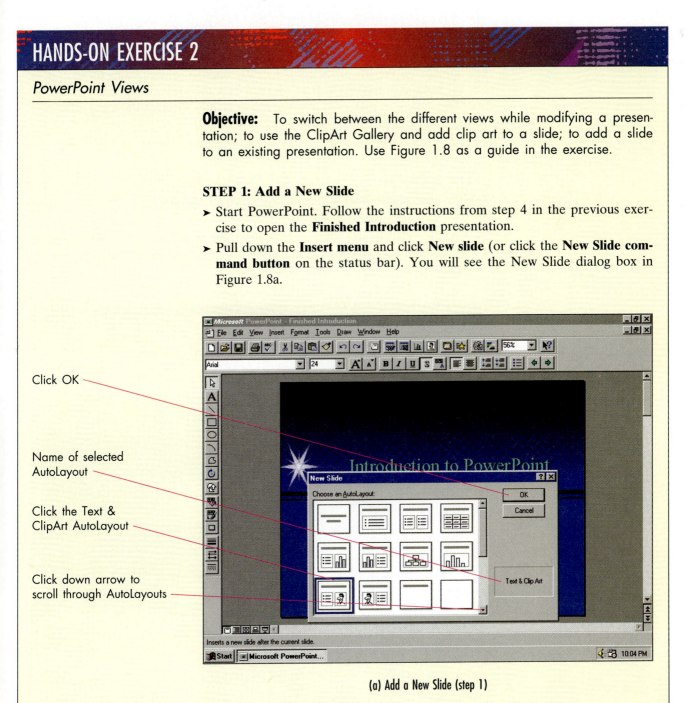

(a) Add a New Slide (step 1)

FIGURE 1.8 Hands-on Exercise 2

INTRODUCTION TO POWERPOINT 19

➤ Click the **down arrow** on the vertical scroll bar to scroll through AutoLayouts within PowerPoint.

➤ Select (click) the **Text & Clip Art layout** as shown in the figure. (The name of the selected layout appears in the lower-right corner of the dialog box.) Click the **OK command button.**

THE MOST RECENTLY OPENED FILE LIST

The easiest way to open a recently used presentation is to select the presentation directly from the File menu. Pull down the File menu, but instead of clicking the Open command, check to see if the presentation appears on the list of the most recently opened presentations located at the bottom of the menu. If so, you can click the presentation name rather than having to make the appropriate selections through the Open dialog box.

STEP 2: Click Here

➤ Click the **placeholder** where it says **Click to add title** in Figure 1.8b. Type **The ClipArt Gallery** as the title of the slide.

➤ Click the **placeholder** where it indicates **Click to add text.** Type **Choose from many different categories** as the first bullet. Press **enter** to move to the next bullet.

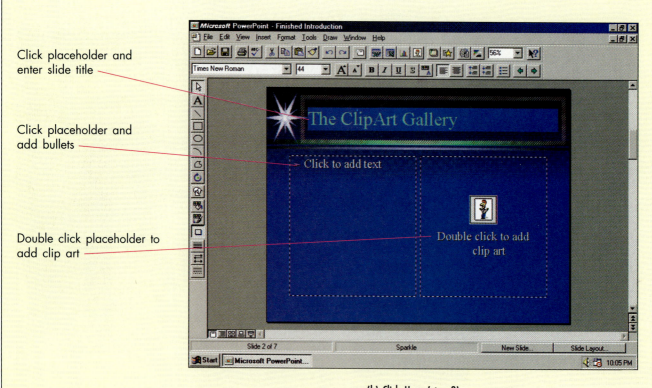

(b) Click Here (step 2)

FIGURE 1.8   Hands-on Exercise 2 (continued)

- Press **Tab** to indent the next bullet one level. Type **Cartoons.** Press **enter** to move to the next bullet.
- You do *not* have to press the Tab key because PowerPoint automatically aligns each succeeding bullet under the previous bullet. Type **Maps.** Press **enter** to move to the next bullet.
- Type **People.** Press **enter** to move to the next bullet.

➤ Press **Shift+Tab** to move the new bullet one level to the left. Enter **Valuepack on CD contains more than 1,000 images** as the final bullet. Do *not* press the enter key or else you will create another bullet.

BULLETS AND THE TAB (SHIFT+TAB) KEY

Bullets are entered one after another simply by typing the text of a bullet and pressing the enter key. A new bullet appears automatically under the previous bullet. Press the Tab key to indent the new bullet or press Shift+Tab to move the bullet back one level to the left.

STEP 3: Add Clip Art

➤ Double click the **placeholder** for the **clip art.** You will see the ClipArt Gallery dialog box shown in Figure 1.8c (although you may not see all of the categories listed in the figure).

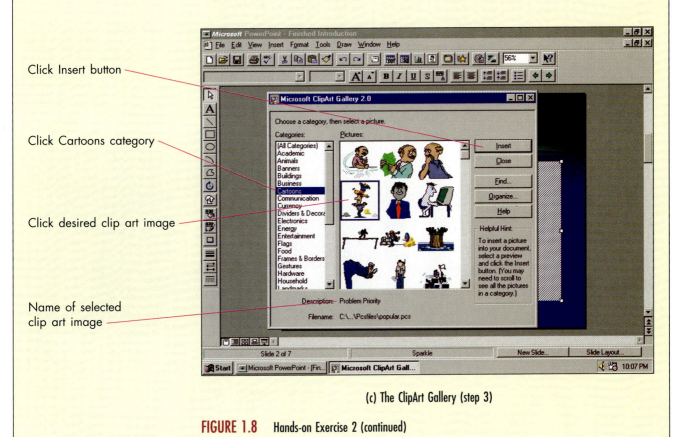

(c) The ClipArt Gallery (step 3)

FIGURE 1.8   Hands-on Exercise 2 (continued)

➤ Click the **Cartoons** category. If necessary, click the **down arrow** on the scroll bar to scroll through the available cartoons until you see the image you want.

➤ Select (click) the **Problem Priority** cartoon as shown in Figure 1.8c. Click the **Insert button** to insert the clip art onto the slide.

> ### MISSING CLIP ART—MS OFFICE VALUEPACK
>
> The default installation of PowerPoint includes only a limited number of clip art images and hence you may not see all of the images we display. Additional clip art is available from several sources, including the CD-ROM version of Microsoft Office, which has a Valuepack containing more than 1,000 images (see case study on page 46). To add clip art, click the Insert Clip Art button on the Standard toolbar, click Organize, then click Add Pictures. Select the folder containing the clip art (e.g., the Clip Art folder in the Valuepack), then click Open to add the clip art.

STEP 4: Select-Then-Do

➤ You should see the completed slide in Figure 1.8d. Click and drag to select the number 1,000.

• Click the **Bold button** on the Formatting toolbar to boldface the selected text.

(d) Select-Then-Do (step 4)

FIGURE 1.8 Hands-on Exercise 2 (continued)

- Click the **Italic button** on the Formatting toolbar to italicize the selected text.
- Click the **Text color button** on the Formatting toolbar to display the available text colors. Click **purple** (or any other color).

➤ Click outside the text area to deselect the text to see the results. Save the presentation.

> ### SELECT-THEN-DO
>
> All editing and formatting operations take place within the context of select-then-do; that is, you select a block of text, then you execute the command to operate on that text. Selected text is affected by any subsequent operation; for example, clicking the Boldface or Italic button changes the selected text to boldface or italics, respectively. In similar fashion, pressing the Del key deletes the selected text. And finally, the fastest way to replace existing text is to select the text, then type a new entry while the text is still selected. Selected text remains highlighted until you click elsewhere on the slide.

STEP 5: The Slide Sorter View

➤ Pull down the **View menu** and click **Slide Sorter** (or click the **Slide Sorter View button** on the status bar). This changes to the Slide Sorter view in Figure 1.8e.

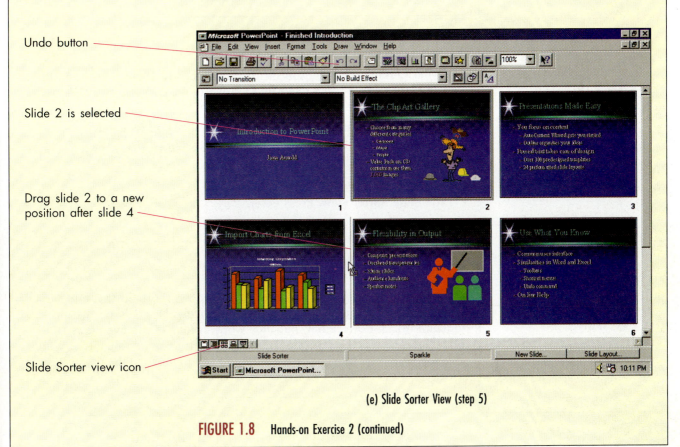

(e) Slide Sorter View (step 5)

FIGURE 1.8 Hands-on Exercise 2 (continued)

➤ Slide 2 (the slide you just created) is already selected as indicated by the heavy border around the slide.

➤ Click and drag slide 2 and move it after slide 4. (A vertical line appears in the presentation as you drag the slide to indicate where it will be placed.)

➤ Release the mouse. The existing slides are automatically renumbered to reflect the new sequence.

➤ Pull down the **Edit menu** and click **Undo Move** (or click the **Undo button** on the Standard toolbar). The slide containing the clip art goes back to its original position.

➤ Click and drag slide 2 and move it after slide 4.

➤ Save the presentation.

MULTIPLE LEVEL UNDO

The Undo command reverses (undoes) the most recent command. The command is executed from the Edit menu or more easily by clicking the Undo button on the Standard toolbar. Each click of the Undo button reverses one command; that is, click the Undo button and you reverse the last command. Click the Undo button a second time and you reverse the previous command. The Redo command works in reverse and undoes the most recent Undo command (i.e., it redoes the command you just undid). The maximum number of Undo commands (the default is 20) is set through the Tools menu. Pull down the Tools menu, click Options, click the Advanced tab, then enter the desired number.

STEP 6: The Outline View

➤ Click the **Outline View button** on the status bar to change to the Outline view in Figure 1.8f. Press **Ctrl+End** to move to the end of the outline where you will enter the next slide:

- Type **Five Different Views** (the title of the slide). Press **enter.**
- Press the **Tab key** to indent one level. Type **Slide view** as shown in Figure 1.8f. Press **enter** to move to the next bullet.
- Type **Outline view.** Press **enter.**
- Type **Slide Sorter view.** Press **enter.**

MOVING WITHIN THE PRESENTATION

Ctrl+Home and Ctrl+End are universal Windows shortcuts that move to the beginning or end of a document, respectively. Not only do the techniques work in PowerPoint, but they work in four of the five views (the Slide Show view is the exception). The shortcuts are quite valuable as you develop a presentation because you often need to move to the first or last slide.

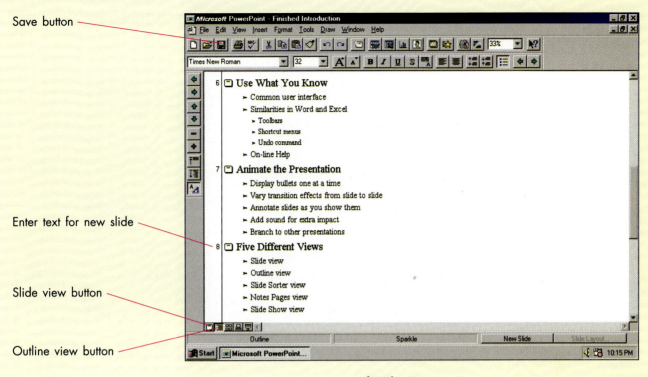

(f) Outline View (step 6)

FIGURE 1.8   Hands-on Exercise 2 (continued)

- Type **Notes Pages view.** Press **enter.**
- Type **Slide Show view.**
> The slide is complete. Click the **Save button** on the Standard toolbar to save the presentation.

STEP 7: The Slide View

> Click the **Slide View button** to change to the Slide view as shown in Figure 1.8g. You should see the Slide view of the slide created in the previous step.

> Click the **Previous Slide button** on the vertical scroll bar (or press the **PgUp key**) to move to the previous slide (slide 7) in the presentation.

> Click the **Next Slide button** on the vertical scroll bar (or press the **PgDn key**) to move to the next slide (slide 8).

THE SLIDE ELEVATOR

PowerPoint uses the scroll box (common to all Windows applications) in the vertical scroll bar as an elevator to move up and down within the presentation. Click and drag the elevator to go to a specific slide; as you drag, you will see a ToolTip indicating the slide you are about to display. Release the mouse when you see the number (title) of the slide you want.

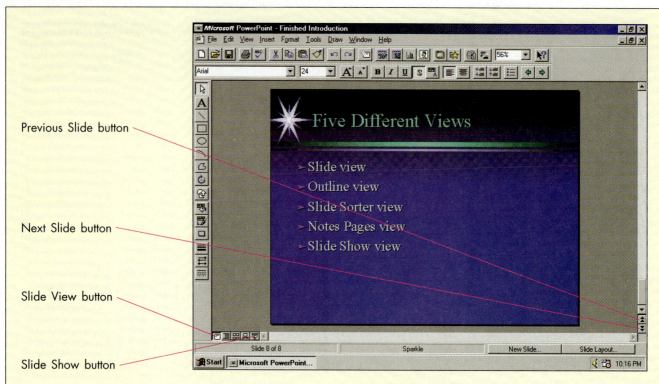

(g) Slide View (step 7)

FIGURE 1.8   Hands-on Exercise 2 (continued)

STEP 8: The Slide Show View

➤ Press **Ctrl+Home** to move to the beginning of the presentation. Click the **Slide Show button** to view the presentation as follows:

- Click the **left mouse button** (or press the **PgDn key**) to move forward in the presentation. Continue to click the left mouse button to move from one slide to the next.
- Click the **right mouse button** and click **Previous** from the shortcut menu (or press the **PgUp key**) to move backward in the presentation.
- Press the **Esc key** at any time to quit the presentation and return to the Slide view.

TRANSITIONS AND BUILDS

Transitions add interest and variety to a presentation by changing the way in which you progress from one slide to the next. Slides may move onto the screen from the left or right, be uncovered by horizontal or vertical blinds, fade, dissolve, etc. Transitions may also be applied to individual bullets to display the bullets one at a time. Transitions and builds are further described in Chapter 2.

STEP 9: The Notes Pages View

➤ Press **Ctrl+Home** to move to the beginning of the presentation. Click the **Notes Pages View button** to change to this view, as shown in Figure 1.8h. (If necessary, click the **down arrow** on the Zoom Control box to change to **100%** magnification so that you will be able to see what you are typing.)

➤ Click in the **notes placeholder,** then enter the text in Figure 1.8h. (The information is for the presenter rather than the audience.) Click outside the placeholder to deselect it. Save the presentation.

➤ Pull down the **File menu.** Click **Print** to produce the Print dialog box.

➤ Click the **down arrow** in the **Print What** drop-down list box. Scroll so that you can click **Notes Pages.** Click the **Current Slide option button** to print just this slide. Click **OK**.

➤ Pull down the **File menu.** Click **Close** to close the presentation but remain in PowerPoint. Click **Yes** if asked whether to save the changes.

➤ Pull down the **File menu** a second time (or click the **Close button**) to exit PowerPoint if you do not want to continue with the next exercise at this time.

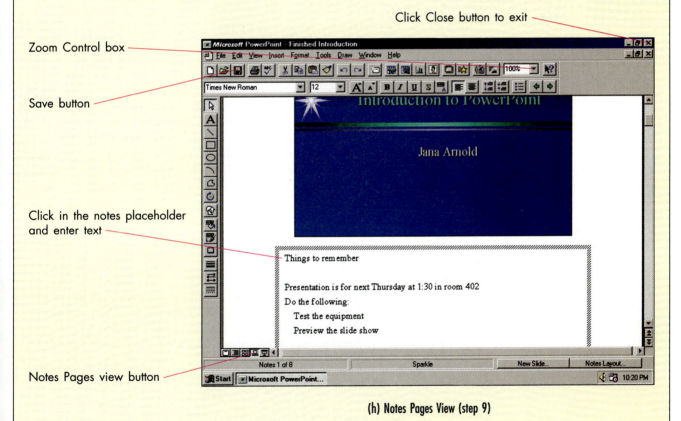

(h) Notes Pages View (step 9)

FIGURE 1.8 Hands-on Exercise 2 (continued)

SLIDE SHOW TOOLS

PowerPoint can help you create an attractive presentation, but it is up to you to deliver the presentation effectively. Accordingly, PowerPoint provides a series of Slide Show tools to help you accomplish this goal. The tools can be accessed from any slide during the slide show by clicking the right mouse button to display a shortcut menu. The tools are discussed briefly in conjunction with the presentation in Figure 1.9, then illustrated in detail in a hands-on exercise.

> **POLISH YOUR DELIVERY**
>
> The speaker is still the most important part of any presentation, and a poor delivery will kill even the best presentation. Look at the audience as you speak to open communication and gain credibility. Don't read from a prepared script. Speak clearly and try to vary your delivery. Pause to emphasize key points and be sure the person in the last row can hear you.

Rehearse Timings

The Slide Show view in Figure 1.9a displays a presentation consisting of five slides. It is similar to the Slide Show view shown earlier in the chapter, but with one significant difference. Look carefully under the slides and you will see a number preceded by a colon (e.g., :30 under slide 1) corresponding to the amount of time the presenter intends to devote to the slide. The timings were entered through the **Rehearse Timings** feature that enables you to time your presentation. This feature is extremely valuable because it provides a sense of timing as you practice your presentation. (The Rehearse Timings feature can also be used to automate a presentation so that each slide will be shown for the set time, after which the next slide will appear automatically.)

> **PRACTICE MAKES PERFECT**
>
> You have worked hard to gain the opportunity to present your ideas. Be prepared! You cannot bluff your way through a presentation. Practice aloud several times, preferably under the same conditions as the actual presentation. Everyone is nervous, but the more you practice, the more confident you will be.

Action Items

Questions arise during any presentation, suggestions are given, and action items are developed. The **Meeting Minder** enables you to keep track of these items as they occur and to summarize them at the end of the presentation. The slide in Figure 1.9b, for example, is not part of the original presentation (it does not appear in the Slide Sorter view) but will be created *during* the presentation, as explained in the hands-on exercise.

Note, too, the annotation that has been added to the Action Items slide. The mouse pointer has changed from an arrow to a pencil, changing the effect of the

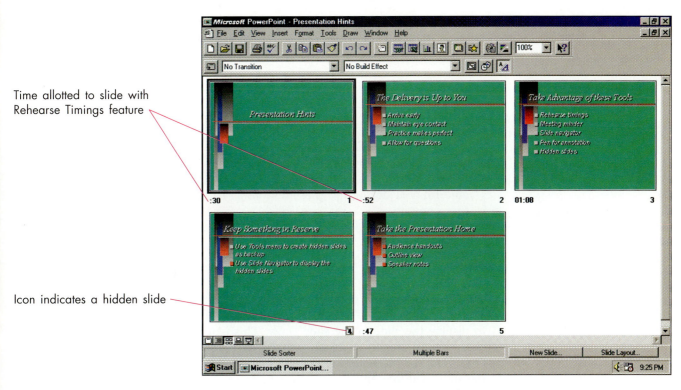

(a) Timings and Hidden Slides

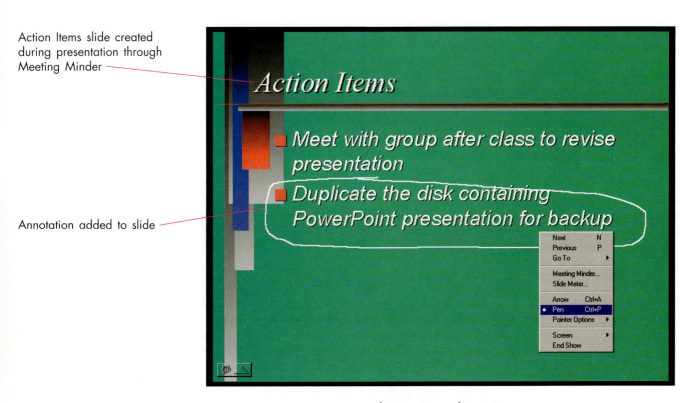

(b) Action Items and Annotation

FIGURE 1.9 Slide Show

mouse to an annotation tool. This enables you to click anywhere on the slide in order to **annotate the slide** as shown in Figure 1.9b. The **Pen** is a wonderful addition to any presentation.

> ### ARRIVE EARLY
>
> You will need plenty of time to gather your thoughts and set up the presentation. Start PowerPoint and open the presentation prior to beginning. Be sure your notes are with you or on the podium. Check that water is available for you during the presentation. Try to relax. Greet the audience as they come in.

Hidden Slides

The icon under slide number 4 in Figure 1.9a indicates that it is a **hidden slide**. The slide is contained within the presentation, but the presenter has elected not to display the slide in the slide show. This is a common practice among experienced speakers who anticipate probing questions that may arise during the presentation. The presenter prefers not to address the topic initially and elects to hide the slide. The presenter can, however, access the slide during the show (through the **Slide Navigator**) should it become necessary.

> ### BE FLEXIBLE
>
> Every presentation begins with its slides in a specific order. Each audience is different, however, and you may find it necessary to change the order, to jump to a later slide, or to return to an earlier slide. You may also find it necessary to display a hidden slide, a slide that you kept in reserve for a specific question, if that question arises. Be flexible and use the Slide Navigator to respond appropriately to questions from the audience.

HANDS-ON EXERCISE 3

Slide Show Tools

Objective: To use the Rehearse Timings feature to time a presentation; to hide a slide, then use the Slide Navigator to display that slide on demand; to use the Meeting Minder to create a list of action items during a presentation; and to annotate a slide for emphasis. Use Figure 1.10 as a guide in the exercise.

STEP 1: Open the Existing Presentation

➤ Start PowerPoint. Open **Presentation Hints** in the **Exploring PowerPoint folder** as shown in Figure 1.10a. Click where indicated to add your name to the title slide.

➤ Pull down the **File menu,** click the **Save As command** to display the File Save dialog box, then save the presentation as **Finished Presentation Hints.** (Press

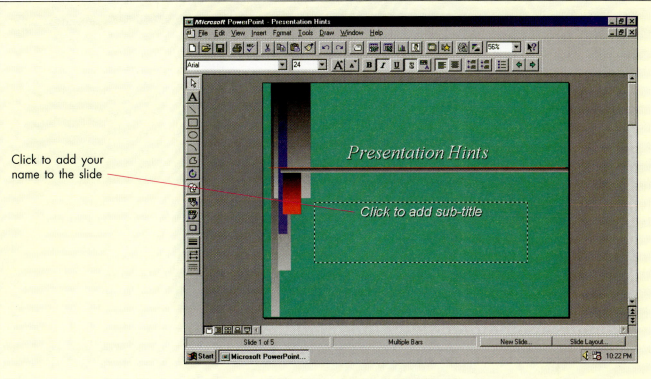

Click to add your name to the slide

(a) Open the Presentation (step 1)

FIGURE 1.10 Hands-on Exercise 3

the **Esc key** or click the **Close button** if you see a Properties dialog box after saving the file.)

CHANGE THE DEFAULT FOLDER

The default folder is the folder where PowerPoint retrieves (saves) presentations unless it is otherwise instructed. To change the default folder, pull down the Tools menu, click Options, click the Advanced tab, then enter the name of the default folder (for example, C:\Exploring PowerPoint) in the Default File Location text box. Click OK. The next time you execute the Open command, PowerPoint will automatically look in this folder.

STEP 2: Hide a Slide

➤ Click the **Slide Sorter View button** to change to this view as shown in Figure 1.10b. If necessary, click the **down arrow** on the Zoom Control box to zoom to 100%. The slides are larger and easier to read.

➤ Point to slide 4 (Keep Something in Reserve), then click the **right mouse button** to select the slide and simultaneously display a shortcut menu.

➤ Click **Hide Slide** as shown in Figure 1.10b. The menu closes and a hidden slide icon is displayed under slide 4. The slide remains in the presentation,

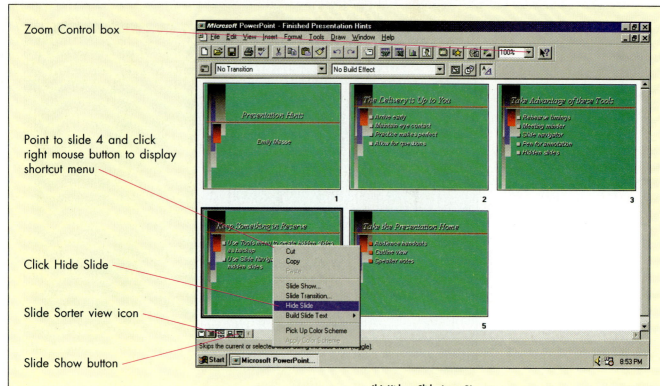

(b) Hide a Slide (step 2)

FIGURE 1.10 Hands-on Exercise 3 (continued)

but it will *not* be displayed during the slide show. (The Hide Slide command functions as a toggle switch. Click it once and the slide is hidden. Click the command a second time and the slide is no longer hidden.)

➤ Save the presentation. Click the **Slide Show button** to move quickly through the presentation. You will not see the slide titled Keep Something in Reserve because it has been hidden. (You can still access this slide through the Slide Navigator as described in step 5.)

STEP 3: Rehearse the Presentation

➤ Press **Ctrl+Home** to return to the first slide. Pull down the **View menu** and click **Slide Show** to display the Slide Show dialog box. Click the **option button** to **Rehearse New Timings,** then click the **Show button.**

➤ The first slide appears in the Slide Show view, and the Rehearsal dialog box is displayed in the lower-right corner of the screen. Speak as though you were presenting the slide, then click the mouse to register the elapsed time for that slide and move to the next slide.

➤ The second slide in the presentation should appear as shown in Figure 1.10c. Speak as though you were presenting the slide and note the times that appear in the dialog box. The cumulative time appears on the left (1 minute and 6 seconds). The time for this specific slide (39 seconds) is shown at the right.

• Click the **Repeat button** to redo the timing for the slide.

• Click the **Pause button** to (temporarily) stop the clock. Click the **Pause button** a second time to resume the clock.

• Click the **Next Slide button** to record the timing and move to the next slide.

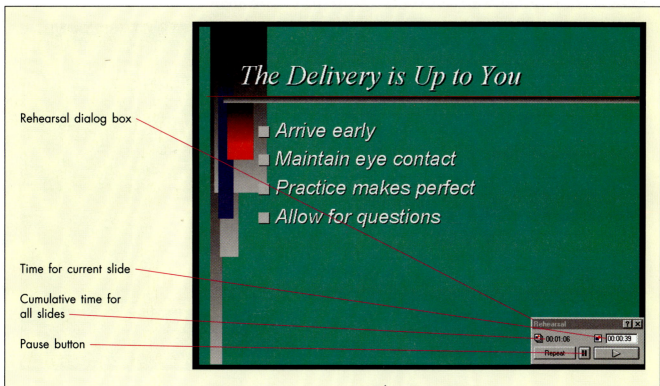

(c) Rehearse Timings (step 3)

FIGURE 1.10 Hands-on Exercise 3 (continued)

➤ Continue rehearsing the show until you reach the end of the presentation. (You will not see the hidden slide from the previous step.)

➤ You should see a dialog box at the end of the presentation that indicates the total time of the slide show. Click **Yes** when asked whether you want to record the new timings.

➤ PowerPoint returns to the Slide Sorter view and records the timings under each slide (except for the hidden slide). Note, too, the hidden icon under the fourth slide.

STEP 4: The Meeting Minder

➤ Click the **first slide** (or press **Ctrl+Home**) to move to the beginning of the presentation. Click the **Slide Show button** to show the presentation.

➤ You should see the title slide with your name as shown in Figure 1.10d. Point anywhere on the slide and click the **right mouse button** to display a shortcut menu containing the various slide show tools.

➤ Click **Meeting Minder** to display the Meeting Minder dialog box, then click the **Action Items tab** as shown in Figure 1.10d.

➤ Click in the work area of the dialog box and enter the first action item in Figure 1.10d. Press **enter,** then enter the second item. Click **OK** to close the dialog box and continue viewing the presentation.

➤ Click the **mouse button** to move from one slide to the next (you can enter an action item from any slide) until you reach the end of the presentation (the slide titled Action Items). A new slide has been created containing the action items you just supplied. Leave this slide on the screen (i.e., do not end the show at this time).

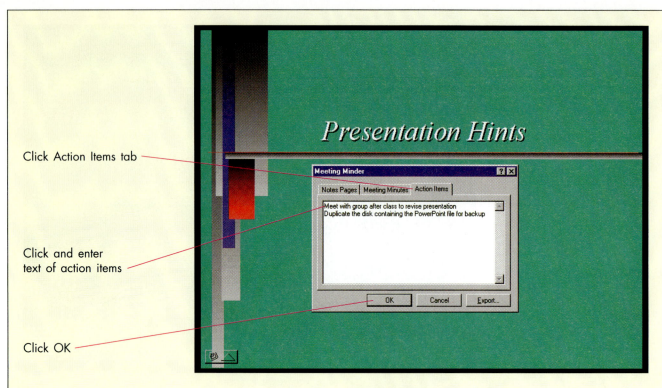

(d) Meeting Minder (step 4)

FIGURE 1.10 Hands-on Exercise 3 (continued)

> **BACK UP IMPORTANT FILES**
>
> We cannot overemphasize the importance of adequate backup. Hard disks die, files are accidentally deleted or lost, and viruses may infect a system. It takes only a few minutes to copy your data files to a floppy disk, so do it now. (See the Windows appendix for information on My Computer and the Windows Explorer to learn how to back up your files.) You will thank us when (not if) you lose an important file and wish you had another copy.

STEP 5: The Slide Navigator

➤ You should be positioned on the last slide (Action Items). Click the **right mouse button** to display a shortcut menu, click **Go to,** then click **Slide Navigator** to display the Slide Navigator dialog box as shown in Figure 1.10e.

➤ The titles of all slides (including the hidden slide) are displayed in the Slide Navigator dialog box. The number of the hidden slide, however, is enclosed in parentheses to indicate it is a hidden slide.

➤ Select (click) the **hidden slide,** then click the **Go To button** to display this slide.

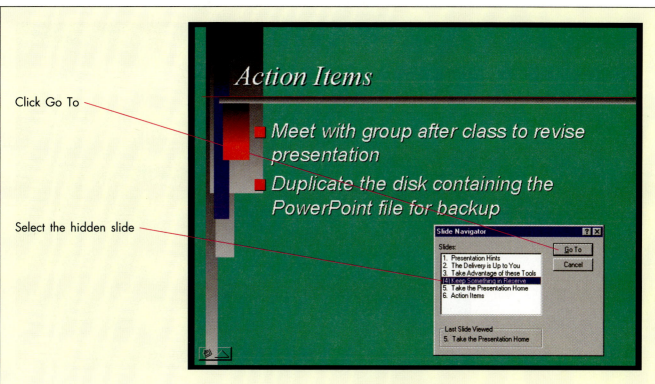

(e) Slide Navigator (step 5)

FIGURE 1.10   Hands-on Exercise 3 (continued)

QUESTIONS AND ANSWERS (Q & A))

Indicate at the beginning of your talk whether you will take questions during the presentation or collectively at the end. Announce the length of time that will be allocated to questions. Rephrase all questions so the audience can hear, then use the Slide Navigator to return to the appropriate slide in order to answer the question. Rephrase hostile questions in a neutral way and try to disarm the challenger by paying a compliment. If you don't know the answer, say so.

STEP 6: Annotate a Slide

➤ You should see the slide in Figure 1.10f. Click the **right mouse button** to display the shortcut menu containing the Slide Show tools. Click **Pen.** The mouse pointer changes from an arrow to a pencil.

➤ Click and drag on the slide to annotate the slide as shown in Figure 1.10f. The annotation is temporary and will be visible only as long as you display the slide.

➤ Press **N** (or the **PgDn key**) to move to the next slide, then press **P** (or the **PgUp key**) to return to the previous (i.e., this) slide. The annotation is gone.

➤ Click the **right mouse button,** point to (or click) **Pointer Options,** point to (or click) **Pen Color,** then choose (click) a different color. The mouse pointer automatically changes to the pen, and you can annotate the slide in the new color.

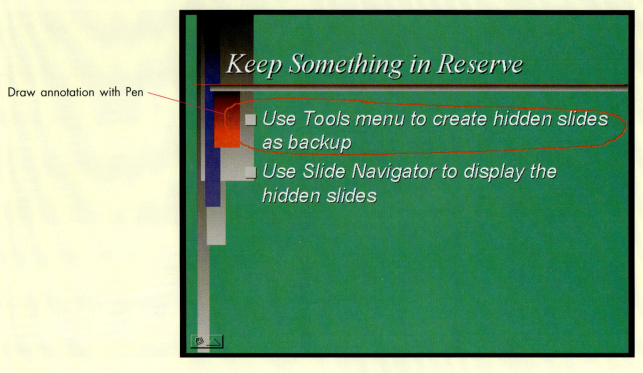

(f) Annotate a Slide (step 6)

FIGURE 1.10   Hands-on Exercise 3 (continued)

THE PEN AND THE ARROW

The shortcut menu can be used to toggle the mouse pointer between the Pen and the arrow, but we find various other shortcuts easier. For example, press Ctrl+P or Ctrl+A at any time to change to the pencil or an arrow, respectively. You can also press the Esc key to return the mouse to a pointer after using it as a Pen. And finally, you can use the keyboard to move to a different slide, which automatically resets the mouse to the pointer.

STEP 7: End the Show

➤ Click the **right mouse button** to display the shortcut menu, then click **End Show** to end the presentation.

➤ Pull down the **File menu.** Click **Print** to produce the Print dialog box. Click the **arrow** in the **Print What** drop-down list box. Click **Handouts (6 slides per page).** Check the boxes for **Frame Slides** and **Print Hidden Slides.**

➤ Check that the **All option button** is selected under Print Range. You will print every slide in the presentation, including the hidden slide and the slide containing the action items. Click **OK.**

➤ Pull down the **File menu** and click **Exit** to leave PowerPoint. Click **Yes** when asked whether to save the changes to the presentation.

SUMMARY

A PowerPoint presentation consists of a series of slides with a consistent design and color scheme. A PowerPoint presentation may be delivered on a computer, via overhead transparencies or 35-mm slides, and/or printed in a variety of formats.

The PowerPoint window contains the basic elements of any Windows application. The benefits of the common user interface are magnified further if you are familiar with other applications in the Microsoft Office such as Word or Excel. PowerPoint is designed for a mouse, but it provides keyboard equivalents for almost every command. Toolbars provide still another way to execute the most frequent operations.

PowerPoint has five different views, each with unique capabilities. The Slide view displays one slide at a time and enables all operations on that slide. The Slide Sorter view displays multiple slides on one screen (each slide is in miniature) and lets you see the overall flow of the presentation. The Outline view shows the presentation text in outline form and is the fastest way to enter or edit text. The Notes Pages view enables you to create speaker's notes for use in giving the presentation. The Slide Show view displays the slides one at a time with transition effects for added interest.

Slides are added to a presentation using one of 24 predefined slide formats known as AutoLayouts. Each AutoLayout contains placeholders for the different objects on the slide. A slide may be deleted from a presentation in any view except the Slide Show view.

PowerPoint includes several slide show tools to help you enliven a presentation. The Rehearse Timings feature enables you to time and/or automate a presentation. The Slide Navigator enables you to branch directly to any slide, including hidden slides. The Pen lets you annotate a slide for added emphasis. The Meeting Minder enables you to create a list of action items.

Although PowerPoint helps to create attractive presentations, you are still the most important element in delivering the presentation. The chapter ended with several hints on how to rehearse and present presentations effectively.

KEY WORDS AND CONCEPTS

Annotating a slide	Menu bar	Slide Layout button
AutoLayout	New Slide button	Slide Navigator
Clip art	Notes Pages view	Slide Show view
Close command	Open command	Slide Sorter view
Common user interface	Outline view	Slide view
Drawing toolbar	Pen	Standard toolbar
Elevator	Placeholders	Status bar
Exit command	Print Command	ToolTip
File menu	Redo command	Transition effects
Formatting toolbar	Rehearse Timings	Undo command
Hidden slide	Save command	View buttons
Meeting Minder	Scroll bar	

Multiple Choice

1. How do you save changes to a PowerPoint presentation?
   (a) Pull down the File menu and click the Save command
   (b) Click the Save button on the Standard toolbar
   (c) Both (a) and (b)
   (d) Neither (a) nor (b)

2. Which toolbars are displayed by default in all views?
   (a) The Standard toolbar
   (b) The Formatting toolbar
   (c) Both (a) and (b)
   (d) Neither (a) nor (b)

3. Which view displays multiple slides on a single screen?
   (a) Outline view
   (b) Slide Sorter view
   (c) Both (a) and (b)
   (d) Neither (a) nor (b)

4. Which view displays multiple slides and also shows the graphical elements in each slide?
   (a) Outline view
   (b) Slide Sorter view
   (c) Both (a) and (b)
   (d) Neither (a) nor (b)

5. Which view lets you delete a slide?
   (a) Outline view
   (b) Slide Sorter view
   (c) Both (a) and (b)
   (d) Neither (a) nor (b)

6. Which of the following can be printed in support of a PowerPoint presentation?
   (a) Audience handouts
   (b) Speaker's notes
   (c) An outline
   (d) All of the above

7. Which menu contains the Undo command?
   (a) File menu
   (b) Edit menu
   (c) Tools menu
   (d) Format menu

8. Ctrl+Home and Ctrl+End are keyboard shortcuts that move to the beginning or end of the presentation in the:
   (a) Outline view
   (b) Slide Sorter view
   (c) Slide view
   (d) All of the above

9. The predefined slide formats in PowerPoint are known as:
   (a) Views
   (b) AutoLayouts
   (c) Audience handouts
   (d) Speaker notes

10. Which menu contains the commands to save the current presentation, or to open a previously saved presentation?
    (a) The Tools menu
    (b) The File menu
    (c) The View menu
    (d) The Edit menu

11. The Open command:
    (a) Brings a presentation from disk into memory
    (b) Brings a presentation from disk into memory, then erases the presentation on disk
    (c) Stores the presentation in memory on disk
    (d) Stores the presentation in memory on disk, then erases the presentation from memory

12. The Save command:
    (a) Brings a presentation from disk into memory
    (b) Brings a presentation from disk into memory, then erases the presentation on disk
    (c) Stores the presentation in memory on disk
    (d) Stores the presentation in memory on disk, then erases the presentation from memory

13. Which of the following is true about hidden slides?
    (a) Hidden slides are invisible in every view
    (b) Hidden slides cannot be accessed during a slide show
    (c) Both (a) and (b)
    (d) Neither (a) nor (b)

14. Which view displays timings for individual slides after the timings have been established by rehearsing the presentation?
    (a) Slide view
    (b) Outline view
    (c) Slide Sorter view
    (d) All of the above

15. Which of the following is true about annotating a slide?
    (a) The annotations are permanent; that is, once entered on a slide, they cannot be erased
    (b) The annotations are entered by using the pen during the slide show
    (c) Both (a) and (b)
    (d) Neither (a) nor (b)

ANSWERS

1. c   3. c   5. c
2. c   4. b   6. d

7. b	10. b	13. d
8. d	11. a	14. c
9. b	12. c	15. b

Exploring Microsoft PowerPoint 7.0

1. Use Figure 1.11 to match each action with its result. A given action may be used more than once or not at all. Some results can be achieved by more than one action.

Action

a. Click at 1
b. Click at 2
c. Click at 3
d. Click at 4
e. Click at 5
f. Click at 6
g. Click at 7
h. Click at 8
i. Click at 9
j. Click at 10

Result

_____ Open an existing presentation
_____ Save the current presentation
_____ Change to the Outline view
_____ Change to the Slide Sorter view
_____ Insert a new slide
_____ Move to slide 2
_____ Print the current presentation
_____ Run (show) the current presentation
_____ Exit PowerPoint
_____ Access online help

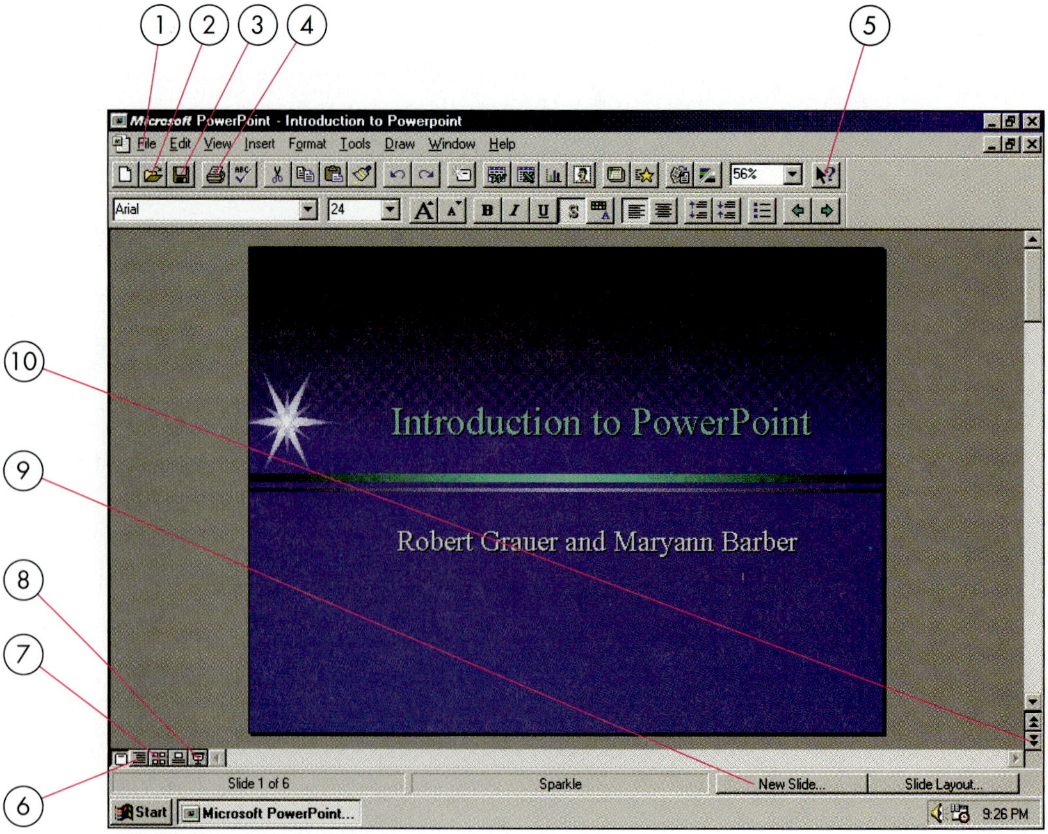

FIGURE 1.11 Screen for Problem 1

2. PowerPoint uses the same commands and follows the same conventions as other applications in Microsoft Office. This means that you can apply what you already know about basic operations in Word or Excel to PowerPoint. Answer the questions below, realizing that in every instance the answer is the same for PowerPoint, Word, and Excel.
   a. Which button on which toolbar saves a PowerPoint presentation? a Word document? an Excel spreadsheet?
   b. How do you print a PowerPoint presentation? a Word document? an Excel spreadsheet?
   c. How do you boldface or italicize existing text?
   d. Which keystroke combination moves immediately to the beginning (end) of a PowerPoint presentation? a Word document? an Excel spreadsheet?
   e. How do you access online help?
   f. What happens if you point to a button on a toolbar? What happens if you click the Help button, then point to a different toolbar button?
3. Answer the following with respect to the presentation shown in Figure 1.12:
   a. What is the name of the presentation?
   b. Are the Standard and Formatting toolbars both visible? How do you display the missing toolbar?
   c. What would be the effect of typing *Quotations,* given the selected text shown on the screen?
   d. How do you save the presentation after making the change in part c?
   e. In which view is the slide displayed? How would you change to the Outline view? to the Slide Sorter view?
   f. Which slide is selected? How would you move to the first slide in the presentation? to the last slide?
   g. How would you add a new slide at the end of the presentation?

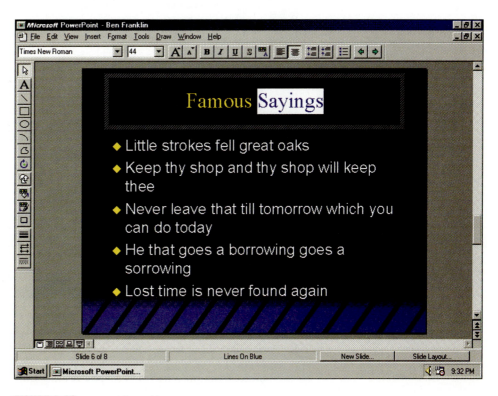

FIGURE 1.12   Screen for Problem 3

4. Online help functions identically in PowerPoint as it does in the other Office applications. Accordingly, use what you know about Microsoft Office, or explore on your own, to answer the following questions with respect to the dialog box in Figure 1.13:
   a. How do you display the dialog box in Figure 1.13?
   b. What is the difference between the Contents and Index tabs? Which tab is currently selected? How do you select a different tab?
   c. Which books are open in the figure? Which books are closed? How do you open a closed book? How do you close an open book?
   d. What is the Answer Wizard?
   e. How is the dialog box in Figure 1.13 similar to the corresponding dialog boxes in other Office applications?

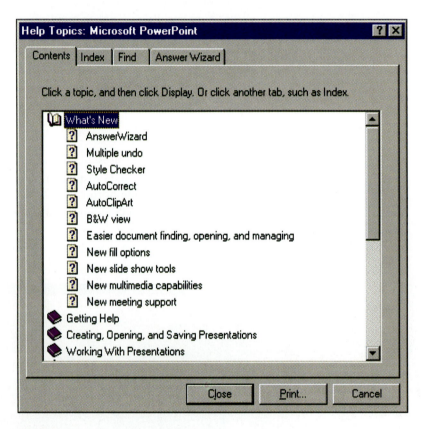

FIGURE 1.13   Screen for Problem 4

Practice with Microsoft PowerPoint 7.0

1. Figure 1.14 displays the Slide Sorter view of a presentation that was created by one of our students in a successful job search. Open the presentation as it exists on the data disk (it is found in the Exploring PowerPoint folder), then modify the presentation to reflect your personal data. Print the revised audience handouts (six per page) and submit them to your instructor.

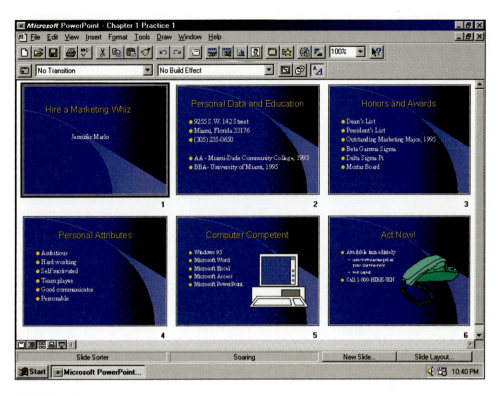

FIGURE 1.14   Screen for Practice Exercise 1

2. Ready-made presentations: The most difficult part of a presentation is getting started. PowerPoint anticipates the problem and provides general outlines on a variety of topics as shown in Figure 1.15.

   a. Pull down the File menu, click New, click the Presentations tab (if necessary), then click the Details button so that your screen matches Figure 1.15.

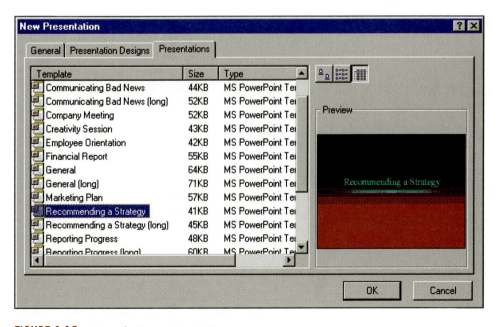

FIGURE 1.15   Screen for Practice Exercise 2

INTRODUCTION TO POWERPOINT

b. Select Recommending a Strategy as shown in Figure 1.15. Click OK to open the presentation.

c. Change to the Outline view so that you can see the text of the overall presentation, which is general in nature and intended for any type of strategy. Modify the presentation to develop a strategy for doing well in this class.

d. Add your name to the title page. Print the presentation in miniature and submit it to your instructor.

3. The PowerPoint Write-Up command imports a presentation into a Word document as shown in Figure 1.16. The command combines audience handouts with speaker notes, enabling you to display several slides on one page with notes for each. It also gives you the option to link the slides to the Word document, so that if a slide changes, the Word document is updated automatically. (The document is not, however, updated to reflect the insertion or deletion of slides.)

a. Do Hands-on Exercises 1 and 2 as described in the chapter, then retrieve the Finished Introduction presentation as the basis of this problem.

b. Pull down the Tools menu and click the Write-Up command to display the Write-Up dialog box. Click the option button for the type of document you want (e.g., Notes Next to Slide so that you will create Figure 1.16 at the end of this exercise).

c. Click the option button to Paste Link the slides to a Word document, then click OK. PowerPoint will create a document similar to the one in Figure 1.16. Be patient, for this step takes time, especially on a non-Pentium machine.

d. Change to the Page Layout view in Word and zoom to Two Pages. Click in the cell next to each slide (the Word document is a table) and enter an appropriate comment.

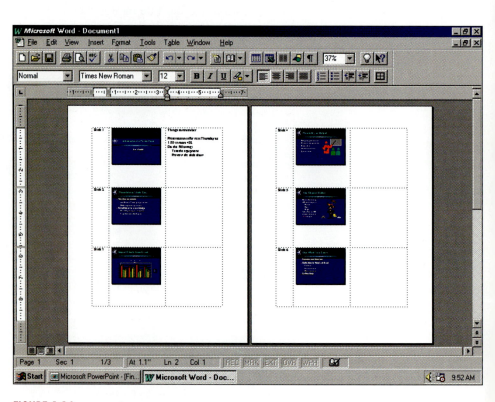

FIGURE 1.16 Screen for Practice Exercise 3

e. Save and print the document just as you would any other Word document. Submit the finished document to your instructor as proof that you did this exercise.

4. Adding Sound: The presentation in Figure 1.17 is one of many presentations included on the CD-ROM version of Microsoft Office. (See the Valuepack case study for additional information.)

a. Start PowerPoint, pull down the File menu, and click Open. Select the CD-ROM drive in the Look In box, then scroll until you can open (double click) the Valuepack folder. Open the Audio folder, open the Network folder, and finally double click the Netmusic presentation.

b. Be sure that you are on the first slide in the presentation, click the Slide Show button, and enjoy the show.

c. Print the audience handouts (six per page) and submit the document to your instructor as proof that you did the exercise.

d. A different sound presentation (from another company) is found in the Cambium folder within the Audio folder. If you enjoyed this exercise, you might be interested in viewing (hearing) that presentation as well.

FIGURE 1.17   Screen for Practice Exercise 4

CASE STUDIES

Planning for Disaster

This case has nothing to do with presentations per se, but it is perhaps the most important case of all, as it deals with the question of backup. Do you have a backup strategy? Do you even know what a backup strategy is? This is a good time to learn, because sooner or later you will need to recover a file. The problem always seems to occur the night before an assignment is due. You accidentally erased a file, are unable to read from a floppy disk, or worse yet, suffer a hardware failure in which you are unable to access the hard drive. The ultimate disaster is the disappearance of your computer, by theft or natural disaster (e.g., Hurricane Andrew, the floods in the Midwest, or the Los Angeles earthquake). Describe in 250 or fewer words the backup strategy you plan to implement in conjunction with your work in this class.

Slides to Go

You have created the perfect presentation and are scheduled for delivery next week. The presentation looks great on your PC, but you have to deliver the presentation without the aid of a computer. How do you create 35-mm slides or overhead transparencies as an alternative to the slide show? It's much easier than you think as PowerPoint provides access to the Genigraphics Corporation through the File menu. Use the Genigraphics Wizard to determine what can be done, then call the company (an 800 number is provided) to determine the exact costs for a 20-slide presentation. Summarize your findings in a one-page report to your instructor.

Clip Art

Clip art—you see it all the time, but where do you get it, and how much does it cost? A limited number of images are installed automatically with PowerPoint, but you will quickly grow tired of this selection. Additional clip art is available on the Valuepack (see the next case study), and we recommend that you install this clip art to your hard drive (assuming you have the space). Scan the computer magazines and find at least two sources for additional clip art. Return to class with specific information on price and the nature of the clip art. You might also research the availability of photographs, as opposed to clip art.

PowerPoint Valuepack

The CD version of Microsoft Office contains a Valuepack with more than 200MB of multimedia files for PowerPoint. You will find clip art, sound bites, photographs, video files, and so on. Microsoft did not create these elements, but instead went to outside vendors, giving each vendor an opportunity to advertise its product. Use the Windows 95 Find command to search on the PPT extension (enter *.PPT) in the Names list box to search for all presentations contained on the CD-ROM. Double click the icon of any presentation that seems interesting to start PowerPoint and load that presentation. Add a slide(s) to the presentation (immediately after the title page) with your impression of that presentation. Print the modified presentation (six slides per page) and submit it to your instructor.

CREATING A PRESENTATION: CONTENT, FORMATTING, AND ANIMATION

OBJECTIVES

After reading this chapter you will be able to:

1. Use the Outline view to create and edit a presentation; display and hide text within the Outline view.
2. Check the spelling in a presentation.
3. Apply a design template to a presentation.
4. Add transition effects to the slides in a presentation; apply build effects to the bullets and graphical objects in a specific slide.
5. Modify the template of an existing presentation by changing its color scheme and/or background shading.
6. Explain the role of masters in formatting a presentation; modify the slide master to include a company name.
7. Use the Style Checker to ensure consistent formatting in a presentation.

OVERVIEW

There are in essence two independent steps to creating a PowerPoint presentation. You must develop the content, and you must format the presentation. PowerPoint lets you do the steps in either order, but we suggest you start with the content. Both steps are iterative in nature, and you are likely to go back and forth many times before you are finished.

We begin the chapter by showing you how to enter the text of a presentation in the Outline view. We show you how to move and copy text within a slide (or from one slide to another) and how to rearrange the order of the slides within the presentation. We illustrate the use of the Spell Check and AutoCorrect features that are common to all Office applications. We also introduce the Style Checker to ensure consistent formatting from one slide to the next.

The chapter also shows you how to format a presentation using one of many professionally designed templates that are supplied with PowerPoint. The templates control every aspect of a presentation, from the formatting of the text to the color scheme of the slides. We describe how to change the template and/or how to vary a color scheme. We show you how to add transition and build effects to individual slides to enhance a presentation as it is given on a computer. The chapter also shows you how to fine-tune a presentation by changing the slide master to include a corporate logo (or other text) on every slide.

> **CRYSTALLIZE YOUR MESSAGE**
>
> Every presentation exists to deliver a message, whether it's to sell a product, present an idea, or provide instruction. Decide on the message you want to deliver, then write the text for the presentation. Edit the text to be sure it is consistent with your objective. Then, and only then, should you think about formatting, but always keep the message foremost in your mind.

CREATING A PRESENTATION

The text of a presentation can be developed in the Slide view or the Outline view or a combination of the two. You can begin in the Outline view, switch to the Slide view to see how a particular slide will look, return to the Outline view to enter the text for additional slides, and so on. We prefer the Outline view because it displays the text for many slides at once. It also enables you to change the order of slides and to move and copy text from one slide to another.

The Outline View

Figure 2.1 displays the outline of the presentation we will develop in this chapter. The outline shows the title of each slide, followed by the text on that slide. (Graphic elements such as clip art and charts are not visible in the Outline view.) Each slide is numbered, and the numbers adjust automatically for the insertion or deletion of slides as you edit the presentation.

A *slide icon* appears between the number and title of the slide. The icon is subtly different, depending on the slide layout. In Figure 2.1, for example, the same icon appears next to slides 1 through 6 and indicates the slides contain only text. A different icon appears next to slide 7 and indicates the presence of a graphic element, such as clip art.

Each slide begins with a title, followed by bulleted items, which are indented one to five levels corresponding to the importance of the item. The main points appear on level one. Subsidiary items are indented below the main point to which they apply. Any item can be *promoted* to a higher level or *demoted* to a lower level, either before or after the text is entered.

Consider, for example, slide 4 in Figure 2.1a. The title of the slide, *Develop the Content*, appears immediately after the slide number and icon. The first bullet, *Use the Outline view,* is indented one level under the title, and it in turn has two subsidiary bullets. The next main bullet, *Review the flow of ideas,* is moved back to level one, and it, too, has two subsidiary bullets.

The outline is (to us) the ideal way to create and edit the presentation. The *insertion point* marks the place where new text is entered; this is established by

```
1   A Guide to Successful Presentations
        Robert Grauer and Maryann Barber
2   Define the Audience
        • Who is in the audience
            – Managers
            – Coworkers
            – Clients
        • What are their expectations
3   Create the Presentation
        • Develop the content
        • Format the presentation
        • Animate the slide show
4   Develop the Content
        • Use the Outline view
            – Demote items (Tab)
            – Promote items (Shift+Tab)
        • Review the flow of ideas
            – Cut, copy, and paste text
            – Drag and drop
5   Format the Presentation
        • Choose a design template
        • Customize the design
            – Change the color scheme
            – Change background shading
        • Modify slide masters
6   Animate the Slide Show
        • Transitions
        • Builds
        • Hidden slides
7   Tips for Delivery
        • Rehearse Timings
        • Arrive early
        • Maintain eye contact
        • Know your audience
```

(a) The Expanded Outline

```
1   A Guide to Successful Presentations
2   Define the Audience
3   Create the Presentation
4   Develop the Content
5   Format the Presentation
6   Animate the Slide Show
7   Tips for Delivery
```

(b) The Collapsed Outline

FIGURE 2.1   The Outline View

clicking anywhere in the outline. (The insertion point is automatically placed at the title of the first slide in a new presentation.) To enter text, click in the outline to establish the insertion point, then start typing. Press enter after typing the title of a slide or after entering the text of a bulleted item, which starts a new slide or bullet, respectively. The new item may then be promoted (by pressing **Shift+Tab**) or demoted (by pressing **Tab**) as necessary.

Editing is accomplished through the same techniques used in other Windows applications. For example, you can use the Cut, Copy, and Paste commands in the Edit menu (or the corresponding buttons on the Standard toolbar) to move and copy selected text, or you can simply drag and drop text from one place to another.

Figure 2.1b displays a collapsed view of the outline, which displays only the title of each slide. The advantage to this view is that you see more slides on the screen at the same time, making it easier to move slides within the presentation. The slides are expanded or collapsed by using the appropriate tool on the Outline toolbar as described in a hands-on exercise. (The ***Outline toolbar*** appears

SPELLING COUNTS

You are in the midst of giving your presentation when all of a sudden someone in the audience points out a misspelling in the title of a crucial slide. Take it from us, nothing takes more away from a presentation than a misspelled word. You've lost your audience, and it didn't have to happen. PowerPoint provides a full-featured spelling checker. Use it!

automatically when you switch to the Outline view. As with the Standard and Formatting toolbars in Chapter 1, a ToolTip will appear when you point to a button to describe its function.)

Text is formatted by using the select-then-do approach common to Word and Excel; that is, you select the text, then you execute the appropriate command or click the appropriate button. The selected text remains highlighted and is affected by all subsequent commands until you click elsewhere in the outline.

The AutoContent Wizard

Outline or not, one of the hardest things about creating a presentation is getting started. You have a general idea of what you want to say, but the words do not come to you. The **AutoContent Wizard** helps you begin. It is accessed through the New command in the File menu and is illustrated in Figure 2.2.

The AutoContent Wizard asks you a series of questions, then uses your answers to create a presentation. The Wizard asks for your name and other information to create the title slide, as shown in Figure 2.2a. It prompts for the type of presentation you intend to give in Figure 2.2b, and for the visual style and duration in Figure 2.2c. The Wizard selects a template for you according to the requested style (e.g., Professional), and it ends by displaying the title slide in Figure 2.2d.

The real benefit of the Wizard, however, is the suggested outline shown in Figure 2.2e, which corresponds to the topic you selected earlier (Selling a Product, Service, or Idea). The outline is very general, as it must be, but it provides the essential topics to include in your presentation. You simply replace the general topic with the specific information unique to your presentation.

You work with the outline provided by the AutoContent Wizard just as you would with any other outline. You can type over existing text, add or delete slides, move slides around, promote or demote items, and so on. In short, you don't use the AutoContent outline exactly as it is presented; instead, you use the outline as a starting point, then modify it to fit the needs of your presentation.

SUGGESTED PRESENTATIONS

PowerPoint provides a total of 21 suggested presentations covering a wide range of topics. You will find a presentation to create a business or a marketing plan as well as a presentation to prepare a financial report. There is a Top Ten Presentation with animation effects built in. There is even a presentation to communicate bad news. All of these presentations can be accessed through the AutoContent Wizard, or alternatively, through the New command in the File menu. (Select the Presentations tab from the New Presentation dialog box.)

TEMPLATES

PowerPoint enables you to concentrate on the content of a presentation without concern for its appearance. You focus on what you are going to say, and trust in PowerPoint to format the presentation attractively. The formatting is implemented automatically by selecting one of the more than 100 templates that are supplied with PowerPoint.

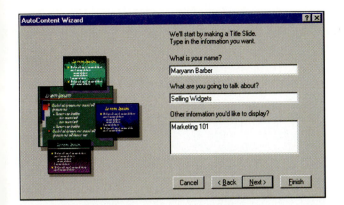
(a) Information for the Title Slide

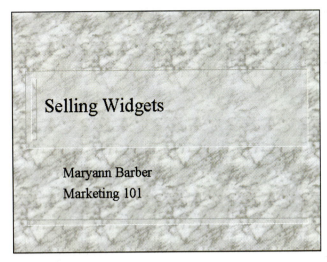
(d) Title Slide

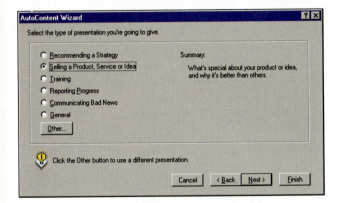
(b) Select the Topic

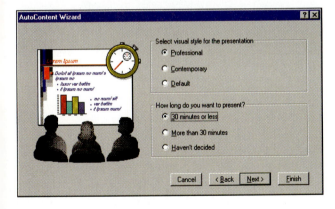
(c) Additional Information

(e) Suggested Outline

FIGURE 2.2   The AutoContent Wizard

A ***template*** is a design specification that controls every element in a presentation. It specifies the color scheme for the slides and the arrangement of the different elements (placeholders) on each slide. It determines the formatting of the text, the fonts that are used, and the design, size, and placement of the bulleted text.

Figure 2.3 displays the title slide of a presentation in four different templates. Just choose the template you like, and PowerPoint formats the entire presentation

CREATING A PRESENTATION   51

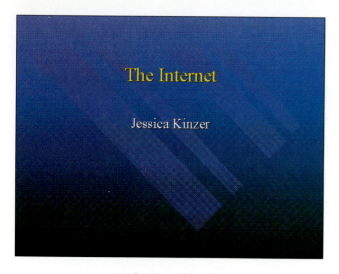
(a) Blue Diagonal Template

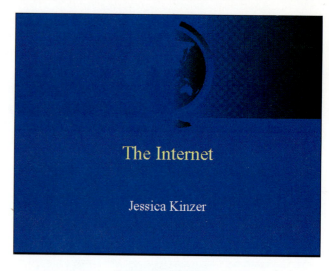
(b) International Template

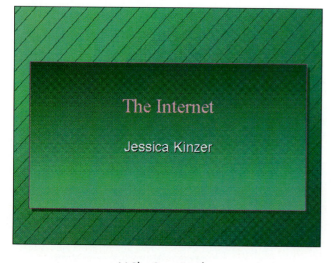
(c) Blue Green Template

(d) Bevel Template

FIGURE 2.3   Templates

according to that template. And don't be afraid to change your mind. You can use the Format menu at any time to select a different template and change the look of your presentation.

CHOOSE AN APPROPRIATE TEMPLATE

A template should enhance a presentation without calling attention to itself. It should be consistent with your message, and as authoritative or informal as the situation demands. Choosing the right template requires common sense and good taste. What works in one instance will not necessarily work in another. You wouldn't, for example, use the same template to proclaim a year-end bonus as you would to announce a fourth-quarter loss and impending layoffs.

HANDS-ON EXERCISE 1

Creating a Presentation

Objective: To create a presentation by entering text in the Outline view; to check a presentation for spelling errors, and to apply a design template to a presentation. Use Figure 2.4 as a guide in the exercise.

STEP 1: Create a New Presentation

➤ Start PowerPoint. Click **OK** to close the Tip of the Day dialog box, which in turn displays the PowerPoint dialog box.

➤ Click the **option button** to create a new presentation using a **Blank Presentation**. Click **OK**. You should see the **New Slide** dialog box in Figure 2.4a with the AutoLayout for the title slide already selected. Click **OK** to create a title slide and simultaneously close the New Slide dialog box.

➤ If necessary, click the **Maximize buttons** in both the application and document windows so that PowerPoint takes the entire desktop and the current presentation is as large as possible. Both Maximize buttons will be replaced with Restore buttons as shown in Figure 2.4a.

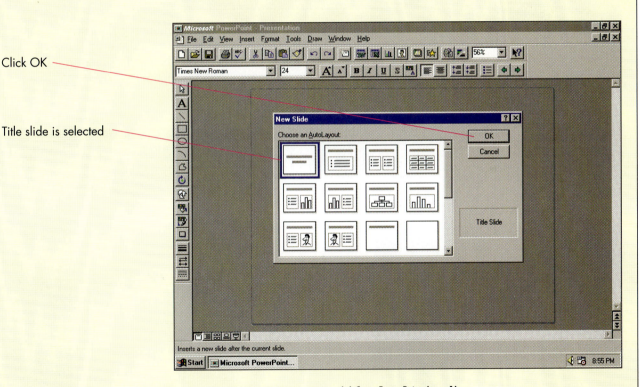

(a) Start PowerPoint (step 1)

FIGURE 2.4 Hands-on Exercise 1

CONTENT, CONTENT, AND CONTENT

It is much more important to focus on the content of the presentation than to worry about how it will look. Start with the AutoContent Wizard or with a blank presentation in the Outline view. Save the formatting for last. Otherwise you will spend too much time changing templates and too little time developing the text.

STEP 2: Create the Title Slide
- Click anywhere in the box containing **Click to add title**, then type the title **A Guide to Successful Presentations** as shown in Figure 2.4b. The title will automatically wrap to a second line.
- Click anywhere in the box containing **Click to add sub-title** and enter your name. Click outside the sub-title area when you have completed your name.

THE DEFAULT PRESENTATION

PowerPoint supplies a default presentation containing the specifications for color, text formatting, and AutoLayouts. The default presentation is selected automatically when you work on a blank presentation, and it remains in effect until you choose a different template.

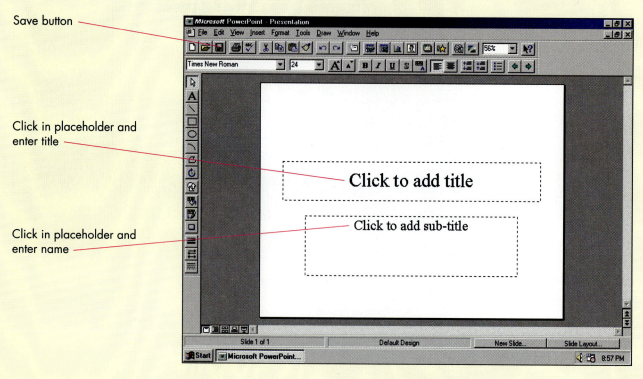

(b) Create the Title Slide (step 2)

FIGURE 2.4 Hands-on Exercise 1 (continued)

STEP 3: Save the Presentation

➤ Pull down the **File menu** and click **Save** (or click the **Save button** on the Standard toolbar). You should see the File Save dialog box in Figure 2.4c. If necessary, click the **List button** so that the display on your monitor more closely matches our figure.

➤ To save the file:
- Click the **drop-down arrow** on the Save In list box.
- Click the appropriate drive, drive C or drive A, depending on whether or not you installed the data disk on your hard drive.
- Double click the **Exploring PowerPoint folder,** to make it the active folder (the folder in which you will save the document).
- Enter **My First Presentation** as the name of the presentation.
- Click **Save** or press the **enter key.** Click **Cancel** or press the **Esc key** if you see the Properties dialog box. The title bar changes to reflect the name of the presentation.

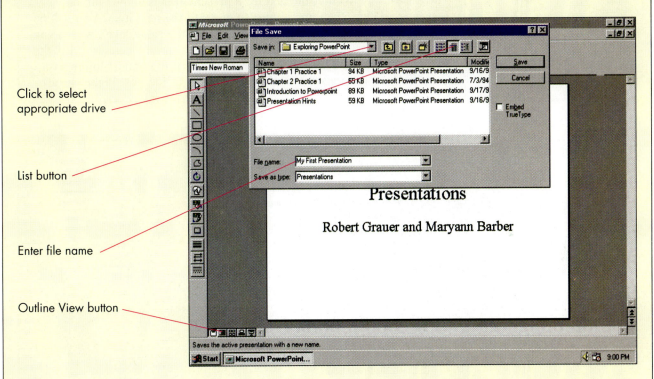

(c) The Save Command (step 3)

FIGURE 2.4 Hands-on Exercise 1 (continued)

STEP 4: Create the Presentation

➤ Click the **Outline view button** above the status bar to change to the Outline view. Your presentation at this point contains only the title slide with your name.

➤ Click the **New Slide button** on the status bar. The icon for slide 2 will appear in the outline. Type **Define the Audience** as the title of the slide and press **enter.**

➤ Press the **Tab key** (or click the **Demote button** on the Outline toolbar) to enter the first bullet. Type **Who is in the audience** and press **enter.**

CREATING A PRESENTATION 55

➤ Press the **Tab key** (or click the **Demote button** on the Outline toolbar) to enter the second-level bullets.
  - Type **Managers.** Press **enter.**
  - Type **Coworkers.** Press **enter.**
  - Type **Clients.** Press **enter.**
➤ Press **Shift+Tab** (or click the **Promote button** on the Outline toolbar) to return to the first-level bullets.
  - Type **What are their expectations.** Press **enter.**
➤ Press **Shift+Tab** to enter the title of the third slide. Type **Tips for Delivery.** Add the remaining text for this slide and for slide 4 as shown in Figure 2.4d.

> **JUST KEEP TYPING**
>
> The easiest way to enter the text for a presentation is in the Outline view. Just type an item, then press enter to move to the next item. You will be automatically positioned at the next item on the same level, where you can type the next entry. Continue to enter text in this manner. Press the Tab key as necessary to demote an item (move it to the next lower level). Press Shift+Tab to promote an item (move it to the next higher level).

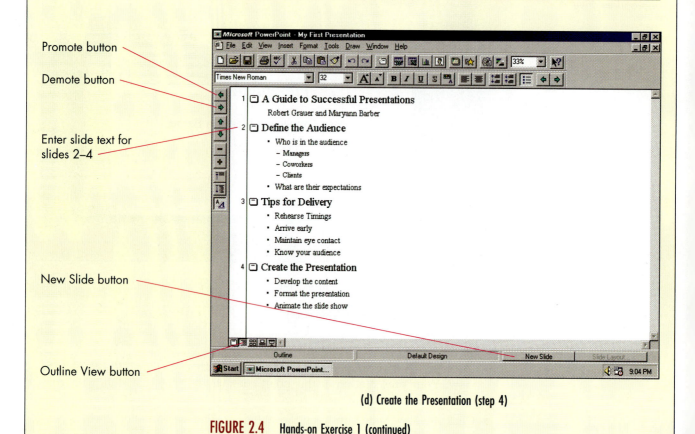

(d) Create the Presentation (step 4)

FIGURE 2.4 Hands-on Exercise 1 (continued)

STEP 5: The Spell Check

➤ Enter the title of the fifth slide as **Develop teh Content** (deliberately misspelling the word "the"). Try to look at the monitor as you type to see the AutoCorrect feature (common to all Office applications) in action. PowerPoint will correct the misspelling and change *teh* to *the*.

➤ If you did not see the correction being made, click the arrow next to the Undo button on the Standard toolbar and undo the last several actions. Click the arrow next to the Redo button and redo the corrections in order to see the error and subsequent auto correction.

➤ Enter the text of the remaining slides as shown in Figure 2.4e. Do *not* press enter after entering the last bullet on the last slide or else you will add a blank slide at the end of your presentation.

➤ Click the **Spelling button** on the Standard toolbar to check the presentation for spelling:

- The result of the Spell Check will depend on how accurately you entered the text of the presentation. We deliberately misspelled the word "Transitions" in the last slide.
- Continue to check the document for spelling errors. Click **OK** when PowerPoint indicates it has checked the entire presentation.

➤ Click the **Save button** on the Standard toolbar to save the presentation.

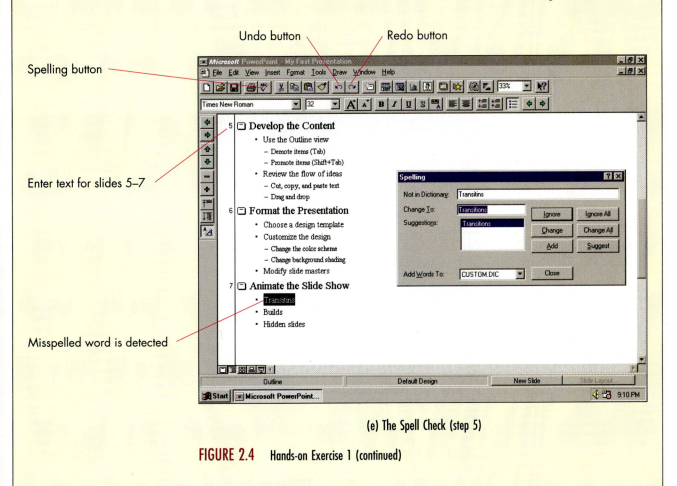

(e) The Spell Check (step 5)

FIGURE 2.4 Hands-on Exercise 1 (continued)

> **CREATE YOUR OWN SHORTHAND**
>
> Use the AutoCorrect feature, which is common to all Office applications, to expand abbreviations such as "usa" for United States of America. Pull down the Tools menu, click AutoCorrect, then type the abbreviation in the Replace text box and the expanded entry in the With text box. Click the Add command button, then click OK to exit the dialog box and return to the document. The next time you type usa in a presentation, it will automatically be expanded to United States of America.

STEP 6: Drag and Drop

➤ Press **Ctrl+Home** to move to the beginning of the presentation. Click the **Show Titles button** on the Outline toolbar to collapse the outline as shown in Figure 2.4f.

➤ Click the **icon** for **slide 3** (Tips for Delivery). The slide is selected and its title is highlighted. Point to the **slide icon** (the mouse pointer changes to a four-headed arrow), then click and drag to move the slide to the end of the presentation. Release the mouse.

➤ All of the slides have been renumbered. The slide titled Tips for Delivery has been moved to the end of the presentation and appears as slide 7. Click the **Show All button** to display the contents of each slide. Click anywhere in the presentation to deselect the last slide.

➤ Click the **Save button** on the Standard toolbar to save the presentation.

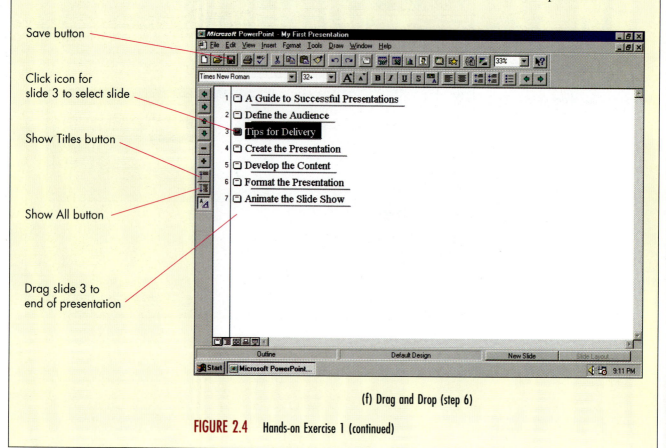

(f) Drag and Drop (step 6)

FIGURE 2.4   Hands-on Exercise 1 (continued)

SELECTING SLIDES IN THE OUTLINE VIEW

Click the slide icon or the slide number next to the slide title to select the slide. PowerPoint will select the entire slide (including its title, text, and any other objects that are not visible in the Outline view). Press and hold the Shift key, then click the beginning and ending slides to select a group of sequential slides. Press Ctrl+A to select the entire outline. You can use these techniques to select multiple slides regardless of whether the outline is collapsed or expanded. The selected slides can be copied, moved, or deleted as a unit.

STEP 7: Choose a Design Template

➤ Pull down the **Format menu.** Click **Apply Design Template** to display the dialog box in Figure 2.4g:

- The **Presentation Designs folder** should appear automatically in the List box. If it doesn't, change to this folder, which is contained within the Templates folder within the MSOffice folder.
- **Presentation Templates** should be selected in the Files of Type list box. If it isn't, click the **drop-down arrow** to change this file type.
- The **Preview view** should be selected. If it isn't, click the **Preview button** so that you can preview the selected template.
- Scroll through the available designs to select (click) the **Double Lines template** as shown in Figure 2.4g. Click **Apply** to apply the template to your presentation and close the dialog box.

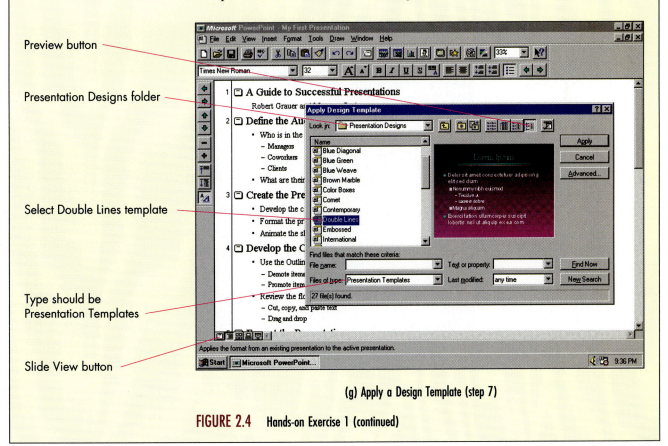

(g) Apply a Design Template (step 7)

FIGURE 2.4 Hands-on Exercise 1 (continued)

CREATING A PRESENTATION 59

➤ You are still in the Outline view, which does not show the selected template. Click the **Slide View button** to change to the Slide view to see that the template has been applied.

➤ Save the presentation.

STEP 8: View the Presentation

➤ Press **Ctrl+Home** to move to the beginning of the presentation. Click the **Slide Show button** on the status bar to view the presentation as shown in Figure 2.4h.

- To move to the next slide: Click the **left mouse button,** type the letter **N,** or press the **PgDn key.**

- To move to the previous slide: Type the letter **P,** or press the **PgUp key.**

➤ Continue to move from one slide to the next until you come to the end of the presentation and are returned to the Slide view.

➤ Pull down the **File menu** and click **Exit** if you do not want to continue with the next exercise at this time.

THE SLIDE NAVIGATOR

The Slide Navigator enables you to branch directly to a specific slide and provides the utmost in flexibility during a presentation. Click the right mouse button at any time to display a shortcut menu, click Go To, click Slide Navigator to display a list of all the slides in the presentation, then double click the desired slide to move directly to that slide.

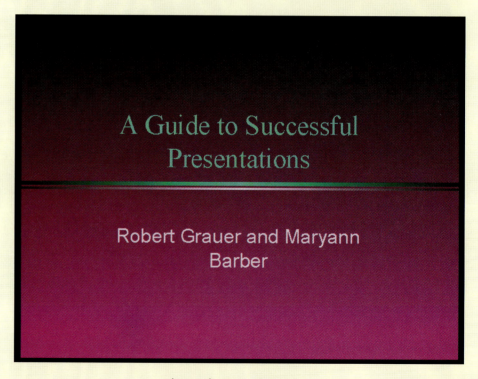

(h) View the Presentation (step 8)

FIGURE 2.4 Hands-on Exercise 1 (continued)

CREATING A SLIDE SHOW

You develop the content of a presentation, then you format it attractively using a PowerPoint template. The most important step is yet to come—the delivery of the presentation to an audience, which is best accomplished through a computerized slide show (as opposed to using overhead transparencies or 35-mm slides). The computer becomes the equivalent of a slide projector, and the presentation is called a slide show.

PowerPoint can help you add interest to the slide show in two ways, transitions and builds. *Transitions* control the way in which one slide moves off the screen and the next slide appears. *Builds* are used to vary the display of the elements on a single slide.

Transitions are created through the Slide Transition command in the Tools menu, which displays the dialog box in Figure 2.5a. The drop-down list box enables you to choose the transition effect. Slides may move on to the screen from the left or right, be uncovered by horizontal or vertical blinds, fade, dissolve, and so on. The dialog box also enables you to set the speed of the transition and/or to preview the effect.

A build displays the bulleted items one at a time with each successive mouse click. It is created through the Build Slide Text command in the Tools menu, which displays the Animation Settings dialog box of Figure 2.5b. Each bullet can appear with its own transition effect. You can make the bullets appear one word or one letter at a time. You can specify that the bullets appear in reverse order (i.e., the bottom bullet first), and you can dim each bullet as the next one appears. You can even add sound and make the bullets appear in conjunction with a round of applause.

Transitions and builds can also be created from the Slide Sorter toolbar as shown in Figure 2.5c. As with the other toolbars, a ToolTip is displayed when you point to a button on the toolbar.

ANIMATE THE OTHER OBJECTS

A build can be applied to any object on a slide although it is used most frequently with bulleted text. You can create a special effect by animating another object, such as a piece of clip art or a chart. Point to the object, click the right mouse button to display a shortcut menu, then click Animation Settings to display a dialog box in which you choose the build effect(s).

AUTOLAYOUTS

Every slide in a presentation is created according to one of 24 predefined slide formats known as AutoLayouts. The AutoLayout determines the objects that will appear on a slide (e.g., text, clip art, a chart, or other object) and specifies the placement for those objects. You can choose the AutoLayout explicitly, or you can have PowerPoint do it for you. Any text entered through the Outline view, for example, is automatically formatted according to the Bullet List AutoLayout.

What if, however, you want to add a graphic element, such as clip art or a chart, to a bulleted slide that was created initially from the Outline view? The easiest way to do this is to change to the Slide view, then change the AutoLayout of the slide from a Bulleted List to one containing text and clip art. This procedure is illustrated in steps 1 and 2 of the next hands-on exercise.

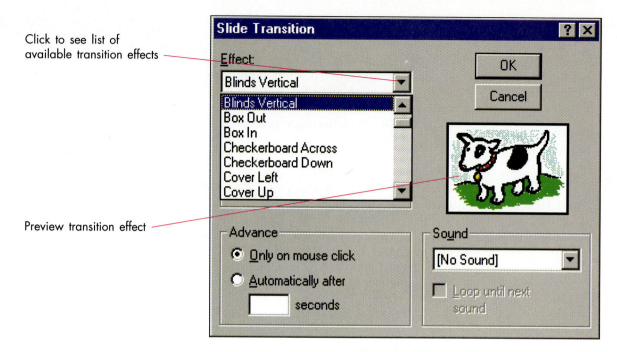

(a) Transitions

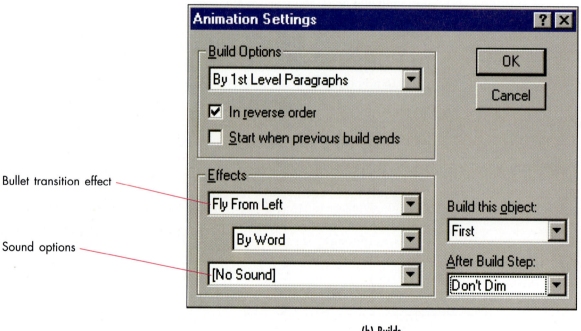

(b) Builds

(c) Slide Sorter Toolbar

FIGURE 2.5 Transitions and Builds

HANDS-ON EXERCISE 2

Animating the Presentation

Objective: To change the layout of an existing slide; to establish transition and build effects. Use Figure 2.6 as a guide in the exercise.

STEP 1: Change the AutoLayout

- Start PowerPoint and open **My First Presentation** from the previous exercise. If necessary, switch to the Slide view, then press **Ctrl+End** to move to the last slide as shown in Figure 2.6a, which is currently a bulleted list.
- Pull down the **Format menu** and click **Slide Layout** (or click the **Slide Layout button** on the status bar).
- Choose the **Text and Clip Art layout** as shown in Figure 2.6a. Click the **Apply command button** to change the slide layout.

> ### ADDING CLIP ART
>
> The easiest way to add clip art to a bulleted list is to change to the Slide view, then change the AutoLayout of the slide. Click the Slide Layout button on the status bar, choose the AutoLayout with Text and Clip Art, and click the Apply command button. Double click the clip art placeholder on the slide, then select the desired image from the ClipArt Gallery in the usual fashion.

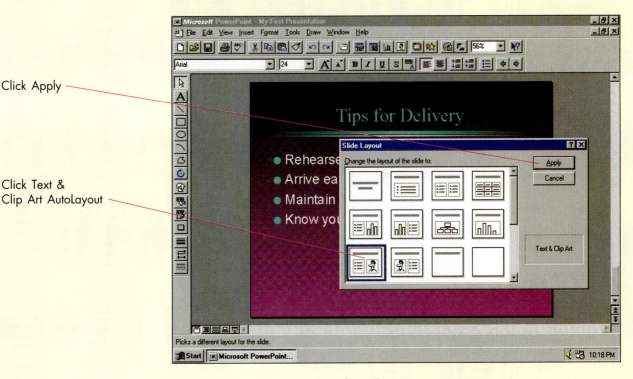

(a) Change the AutoLayout (step 1)

FIGURE 2.6 Hands-on Exercise 2

STEP 2: Add the Clip Art

➤ Double click the **placeholder** on the slide to add clip art. You will see the Microsoft ClipArt Gallery dialog box as shown in Figure 2.6b (although you may not see all of the categories listed in the figure).

➤ Scroll until you can click the **People category**. Click the **down arrow** to scroll through the available images until you can select the **Man at Podium**. Click **Insert** to add the clip art to the slide.

➤ Save the presentation.

> ### FIND THE RIGHT CLIP ART
>
> The Find button within the ClipArt Gallery enables you to search for specific images. Open the ClipArt Gallery, then click the Find button to display the Find Clip Art dialog box. Click in the Description text box, then enter a key word (e.g., woman) that describes the clip art you want. Click the Find Now button, and the ClipArt Gallery will search for images that match the description. Remember to install the additional clip art images from the Valuepack on the Office CD-ROM.

(b) Add the Clip Art (step 2)

FIGURE 2.6   Hands-on Exercise 2

STEP 3: Add Transition Effects

➤ Click the **Slide Sorter View button** to change to the Slide Sorter view as shown in Figure 2.6c. The number of slides you see at one time depends on the resolution of your monitor and the zoom percentage.

➤ Press **Ctrl+Home** to select the first slide. Pull down the **Tools menu,** then click **Slide Transition** to display the dialog box in Figure 2.6c. Click the **down arrow** on the Effect list box, then click the **Blinds Vertical** effect. You will see the effect displayed on the sample slide (dog) in the Transition box. If you miss the effect, click the **dog** (or the **key**) to repeat the effect.

➤ Click **OK** to accept the transition and close the dialog box. A slide icon appears under slide 1, indicating that a transition effect has been implemented. The effect you chose (Blinds Vertical) appears in the Transition Effects list box on the Slide Sorter toolbar.

➤ Point to slide 2, click the **right mouse button** to display a shortcut menu, then click the **Slide Transition command.** Choose **Checkerboard Across** as the effect, click the **Slow option button,** then click **OK** to close the Slide Transition dialog box.

➤ Save the presentation.

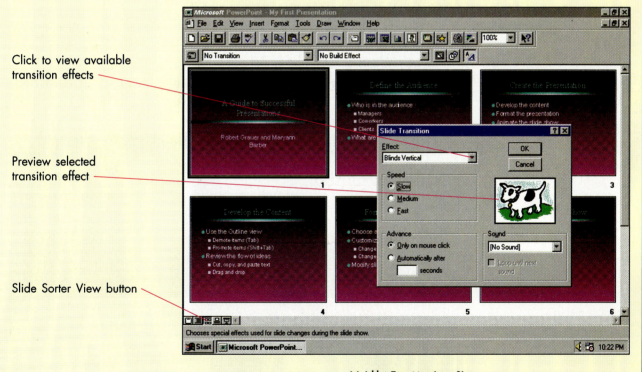

(c) Add a Transition (step 3)

FIGURE 2.6 Hands-on Exercise 2 (continued)

CHANGE THE MAGNIFICATION

Click the down arrow on the Zoom Control box to change the display magnification, which in turn controls the size of individual slides. The higher the magnification, the easier it is to read the text of an individual slide, but the fewer slides you see at one time. Conversely, changing to a smaller magnification decreases the size of the individual slides, but enables you to see more of the presentation. Use whatever magnification appeals to you.

STEP 4: Create a Build

➤ Press **Ctrl+End** to move to the last slide (the slide containing the clip art image). Point to the slide, and click the **right mouse button** to display a shortcut menu as shown in Figure 2.6d.

➤ Click or point to **Build Slide Text,** then click **Fly From Left** as shown in the figure.

➤ Click the **Slide Show button.** You will see the title of the slide as well as the clip art. You will not, however, see any of the bullets.

- Click the **left mouse button** to display the first bullet, which flies in from the left.
- Click the **left mouse button** a second time to see the second bullet.
- Click the **left mouse button** twice more to display the third and fourth (last) bullets.

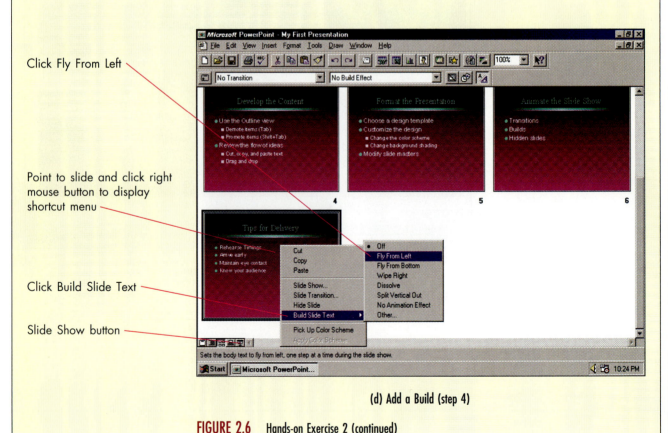

(d) Add a Build (step 4)

FIGURE 2.6 Hands-on Exercise 2 (continued)

➤ Press the **Esc key** to end the show and return to the Slide Sorter view.
➤ Save the presentation.

> ### ANIMATION SETTINGS
>
> Add additional interest to a build by displaying the bullets a letter or a word at a time. Select the slide to which you want to add the build, pull down the Tools menu, click Build Slide Text, then click Other to display the Animation Settings dialog box. Click the down arrow on the Build Options dialog box to choose how you want the build to occur (e.g., by first- or second-level bullets). Click the down arrow on the various list boxes to choose the special effects. Click OK to accept the settings and close the dialog box. Click the Slide Show button on the status bar to view the build effect (click the left mouse button to display each bullet).

STEP 5: Animation Settings (clip art)
➤ Be sure that the last slide is still selected, then change to the Slide view. Point to the clip art object, click the **right mouse button** to display a shortcut menu, then click **Animation Settings** to display the dialog box in Figure 2.6e:
- Click the **down arrow** on the Build Options list box. Click **Build.**
- Click the **down arrow** on the first Effects list box. Click **Fly From Top.**

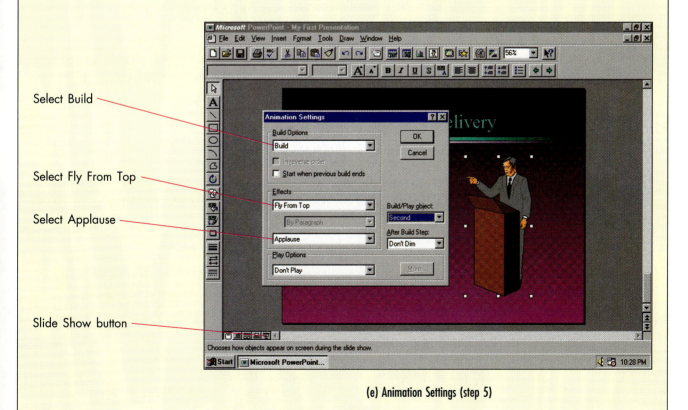

(e) Animation Settings (step 5)

FIGURE 2.6   Hands-on Exercise 2 (continued)

CREATING A PRESENTATION

- Click the **down arrow** on the last Effects list box. Click **Applause** (you need a sound card to hear the effect).
- Click the **down arrow** on the Build/Play object list box to select **Second**.
- Click **OK** to accept the settings and close the dialog box.

➤ Click the **Slide Show button** to view the animation effects for this slide. Click the **mouse** several times to see the bullets fly in from the left. Click the **mouse** one additional time (after the last bullet) to watch the clip art fly in from the top to the sound of applause.

➤ Press **Esc** to leave the show and continue building the presentation.

SELECTING MULTIPLE SLIDES

You can apply the same transition or build effect to multiple slides with a single command. Change to the Slide Sorter view, then press and hold the Shift key as you click multiple slides to select the slides. Use the Tools menu or the Slide Sorter toolbar to select the desired transition or build effect when all the slides have been selected. (You can select every slide by choosing the Select All command in the Edit menu.) Click anywhere in the Slide Sorter view to deselect the slides and continue working.

STEP 6: Change the Template

➤ Pull down the **Format menu** and click **Apply Design Template** or double click the Template area of the status bar. You should see the Apply Design Template dialog box in Figure 2.6f.
- The **Presentation Designs folder** should appear automatically in the List box. If it doesn't, change to this folder, which is contained within the Templates folder within the MSOffice folder.
- **Presentation Templates** should be selected in the Files of Type list box. If it isn't, click the **drop-down arrow** to change this file type.
- The **Preview view** should be selected. If it isn't, click the **Preview button** so that you can preview the selected template.
- Scroll through the available designs to select (click) the **Soaring template** as shown in Figure 2.6f. Click **Apply** to apply the template to your presentation and close the dialog box.

➤ Save the presentation.

CHANGE THE TEMPLATE

You can change the Design Template at any time, either through the Apply Design Template command in the Format menu, or more easily by double clicking the template portion of the status bar, which displays the name of the current template. Either way you will see the Apply Design Template dialog box from which you can select a new template.

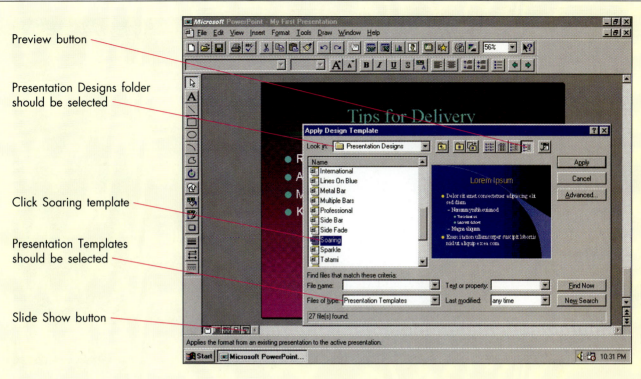

(f) Change the Design Template (step 6)

FIGURE 2.6 Hands-on Exercise 2 (continued)

STEP 7: Show the Presentation

➤ Press **Ctrl+Home** to return to the first slide, then click the **Slide Show button** to view the presentation. You should see the slide in Figure 2.6g.

➤ Click the **left mouse button** (or press the **PgDn key** or the letter **N**) to move to the next slide (or to the next bullet on the current slide when a build is in effect).

➤ Press the **PgUp key** (or the letter **P**) to return to the previous slide (or to the previous bullet on the current slide when a build is in effect).

➤ Continue to view the presentation until you come to the end. Click the left mouse button a final time to return to the Slide view.

THE MEETING MINDER

The Meeting Minder enables you to keep track of action items as they occur and to summarize them at the end of the presentation. Click the right mouse button at any time to display a shortcut menu, click Meeting Minder, then click the Action Items tab in the Meeting Minder dialog box. Enter the action item(s) and click OK to close the dialog box, then continue through the slide show. An Action Items slide will appear at the end of the presentation with the items you added during the show.

CREATING A PRESENTATION 69

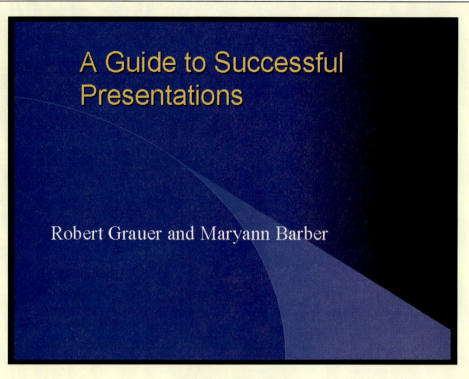

(g) The Completed Presentation

FIGURE 2.6 Hands-on Exercise 2 (continued)

STEP 8: Exit PowerPoint
➤ Exit PowerPoint if you do not want to continue with the next exercise at this time.

FINE-TUNING A PRESENTATION

A template is a design specification that controls every aspect of a presentation. It specifies the formatting of the text, the fonts and colors that are used, and the design, size, and placement of the bullets. You can change the look of a presentation at any time by applying a different template. Changing from the Double Lines to the Soaring template (as you did in the previous exercise) changes the appearance of the presentation in every way.

What if, however, you want to make subtle changes to the template? In other words, you are content with the overall design, but you want to change one or more of its elements. You don't want a radical change, but you want to fine-tune the presentation by modifying its color scheme and/or *background shading.* Or perhaps you want to add a consistent element to every slide, such as a corporate name or logo.

The Color Scheme

A *color scheme* is a set of eight balanced colors that is associated with a template. It consists of a background color, a color for the title of each slide, a color for lines and text, and five additional colors to provide accents to different elements, such as shadows and fill colors. Each template has a default color scheme, which is applied when the template is selected. Each template also has a set of alternate color schemes from which to choose.

Figure 2.7a displays the title slide of our presentation at the end of the second exercise. The Soaring template has just been selected and the default (blue) color scheme is in effect. Figure 2.7b displays the Color Scheme dialog box (which is accessed through the Format menu) with the suggested color schemes for this template. To choose one of the other color schemes (e.g., green), select the color scheme, then click the Apply All command button to apply the new color scheme to the entire presentation.

You have additional flexibility in that you can change any of the individual colors within a color scheme. Select the desired color scheme, click the Custom tab, select the color you wish to change (e.g., the color of the Title Text), then click the Change Color command button as shown in Figure 2.7c. Figure 2.7d

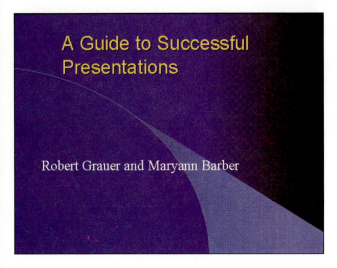

(a) Original Slide

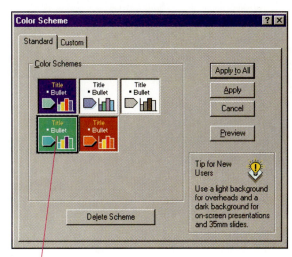

(b) Standard Color Scheme

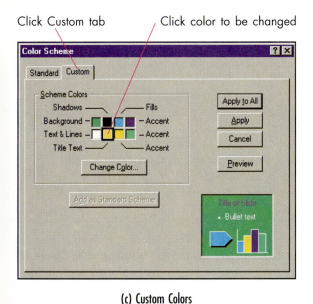

(c) Custom Colors

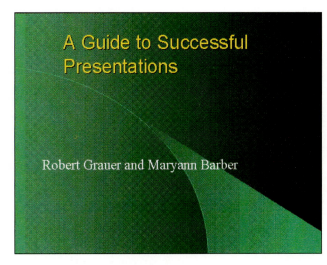

(d) Modified Slide

FIGURE 2.7 Changing the Color Scheme

displays the title slide after the color scheme has been changed to green, then further customized by changing the color of the title text to bright yellow.

> **SLIDES VERSUS TRANSPARENCIES**
>
> Choose the color scheme in conjunction with the means of delivery. Light backgrounds work best for overhead transparencies, whereas dark backgrounds are preferable for computer presentations and 35-mm slides. This suggestion is presented in the Color Scheme dialog box itself (as can be seen in Figure 2.7a). We urge you to look for similar tips as you use other PowerPoint features.

The Background Shading

The ***Custom Background command*** in the Format menu changes the background shading of a slide, enabling you to truly fine-tune a presentation. Figure 2.8a displays the title slide of a presentation using the International template. This design incorporates background shading that goes from blue to black in the top half of the slide. The shading is built into the template according to the Shaded Fill dialog box in Figure 2.8b.

Figure 2.8c changes the parameters within the Shaded Fill dialog box to use a single color (blue) and a horizontal shading pattern. Again, you have additional flexibility in that you can change the variation in color by dragging the scroll box from dark to light. You can also choose from one of four variations of horizontal shading. The modified title slide is shown in Figure 2.8d.

PowerPoint Masters

One of the best ways to customize a presentation is to add a unifying element to each slide, such as a corporate name or logo. You could add the element to every slide, but that would be unnecessarily tedious. It is much easier to use the View menu to add the element to the ***slide master,*** which defines the formatting and other elements that appear on the individual slides. Any change to the slide master is automatically reflected in every slide in the presentation (except for the title slide.)

Consider, for example, the slide master shown in Figure 2.9 on page 74, which contains a placeholder for the title of the slide and a second placeholder for the bulleted text. The slide master also contains additional placeholders at the bottom of the slide for the date, footer, and slide number. Change the position of any of these elements on the master slide, and the corresponding element will be changed throughout the presentation. In similar fashion, any change to the font, point size, or alignment within a placeholder would also carry through to all of the individual slides.

The slide master is modified by using commands from the appropriate menu or toolbar. The easiest way to place a logo on the slide master (such as the small computer in Figure 2.9), is to click the Insert Clip Art button on the Standard toolbar. This in turn displays the Microsoft ClipArt Gallery dialog box, in which you select the desired clip art. Once the clip art has been added to the slide master, you can click and drag its sizing handles to move and size the clip art like any other Windows object. Every slide in the presentation will contain the clip art image that was added to the slide master.

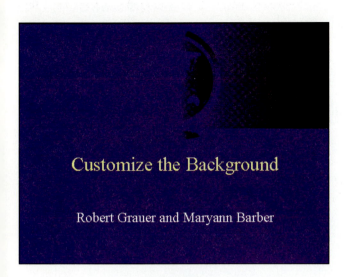
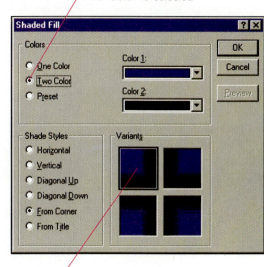
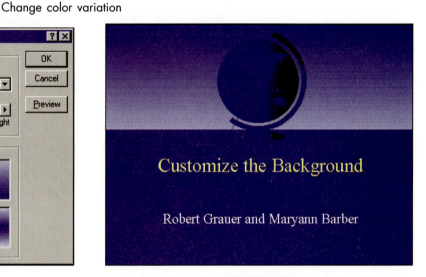

FIGURE 2.8 Customize the Background

Style Checker

Are you conscious of the subtle uses of style that occur when you create a presentation? For example, do you use all uppercase letters for each word in the title of your slides, or do you begin each word with an uppercase letter? Do you place periods at the end of each title or each bullet? Is there a uniform look from one slide to the next with respect to punctuation and capitalization? Perhaps you never thought about the appearance of your slides in such detail, but it takes only a few minutes to ensure uniform style throughout a presentation.

The ***Style Checker*** checks the slides in a presentation for consistency in punctuation and capitalization. It is similar in concept to the ***Spell Check*** and is illustrated in steps 1 and 2 in the following hands-on exercise.

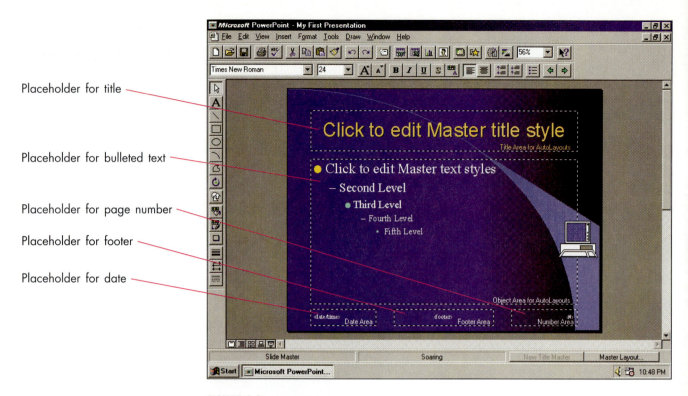

FIGURE 2.9 The Slide Master

SET A TIME LIMIT

We warn you—it's addictive and it can be very time consuming. Yes, it's fun to experiment with different color schemes and backgrounds, but it is all too easy to spend too much time fine-tuning the design by changing its color scheme or background shading. Concentrate on the content of your presentation rather than its appearance. Impose a limit on the amount of time you will spend on formatting. End the session when the limit is reached.

HANDS-ON EXERCISE 3

Fine-Tuning a Presentation

Objective: To use the Style Checker to check for consistency in punctuation and capitalization; to experiment with different color schemes and custom backgrounds. Use Figure 2.10 as a guide in the exercise.

STEP 1: Open the Presentation

➤ Start PowerPoint and open **My First Presentation** from the previous exercise. Change to the **Outline view** as shown in Figure 2.10a.

➤ Change the title of the first slide so that it appears in lowercase. Change the title of the second slide to uppercase. Add a period at the end of both titles.

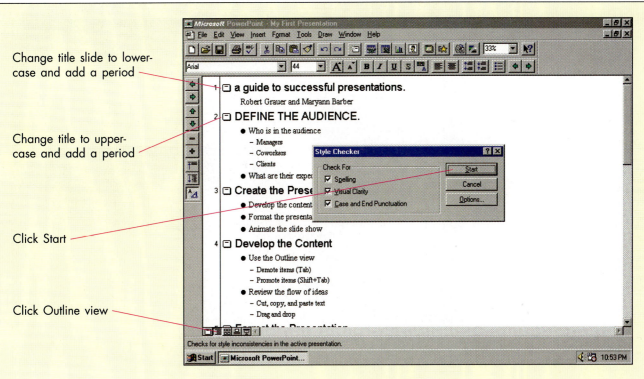

(a) The Style Checker (step 1)

FIGURE 2.10   Hands-on Exercise 3

➤ Press **Ctrl+Home** to return to the beginning of the presentation. Pull down the **Tools menu.** Click **Style Checker** to display the Style Checker dialog box in Figure 2.10a. Click **Start** to begin checking the document.

THE DOCUMENTS SUBMENU

One of the fastest ways to get to a recently used document, regardless of the application, is through the Windows 95 Start menu, which includes a Documents submenu containing the last 15 documents that were opened. Click the Start button, click (or point to) the Documents submenu, then click the document you wish to open (e.g., My First Presentation) if it appears on the submenu.

STEP 2: The Style Checker

➤ The Style Checker goes through the document looking for various errors. Some mistakes are fixed automatically (e.g., a change in case), whereas others require confirmation from you.

➤ Click the **Change button** to remove the period at the end of the title as shown in Figure 2.10b. Click the **Change button** a second time when asked to remove the period at the end of the second slide.

➤ Continue to check the presentation until PowerPoint indicates it has finished, then click **OK** to exit the Style Checker.

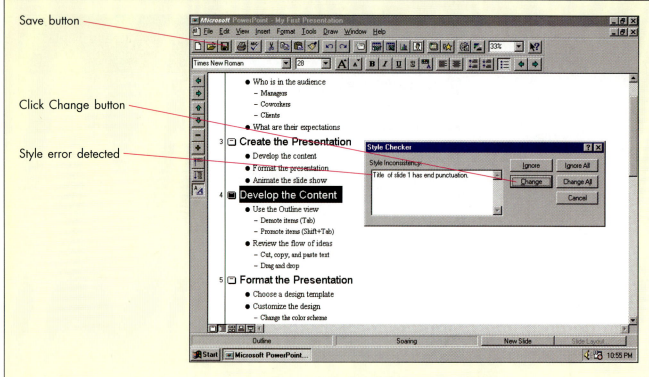

(b) The Style Checker Continued (step 2)

FIGURE 2.10 Hands-on Exercise 3 (continued)

➤ Look carefully at the text of the presentation and note the consistency imposed by the Style Checker:
- The titles for slides 1 and 2 have been restored to title case (from lower- and uppercase, respectively).
- The periods at the end of the titles in slides 1 and 2 have been removed.

➤ Click the **Save button** on the Standard toolbar to save the presentation.

CUSTOMIZE THE STYLE CHECKER

The Style Checker enables you to ensure consistency throughout a presentation with respect to capitalization, punctuation, and formatting. The standards are your own, and you can change the default options to meet your personal preferences. Pull down the Tools menu, click Style Checker, then click the Options command button to display a dialog box in which you customize the Style Checker. Select the desired settings under both the Visual Clarity and Case and End Punctuation tabs, click OK to accept the new settings, then click Start to check the presentation for conformity to your standards.

STEP 3: Change the Slide Master

➤ Pull down the **View menu,** click **Master,** then click **Slide Master** to display the slide master as shown in Figure 2.10c. (The Header and Footer dialog box is not yet visible.)

➤ Click the **dashed lines** surrounding the number area at the bottom right of the slide to select this element. Press the **Del key** to delete this element.

➤ Click the **dashed lines** surrounding the footer area in the center of the slide, then click and drag the footer to the right side of the slide as shown in Figure 2.10c.

➤ Pull down the **View menu.** Click **Header and Footer** to display the Header and Footer dialog box:

- Select the Date and Time check box. Click the **option button** to Update Automatically.
- Select the Footer check box, then enter the name of your school as shown in Figure 2.10c.
- Check the box to suppress the display on the title slide.
- Click the **Apply to All command button** to accept these settings and close the dialog box.

➤ Click the **Slide view button** on the status bar, then press the **PgDn key** once or twice to move from slide to slide. You should see today's date and the name of your school at the bottom of each slide except for the title slide. (Press **Ctrl+Home** to view the title slide.)

➤ Save the presentation.

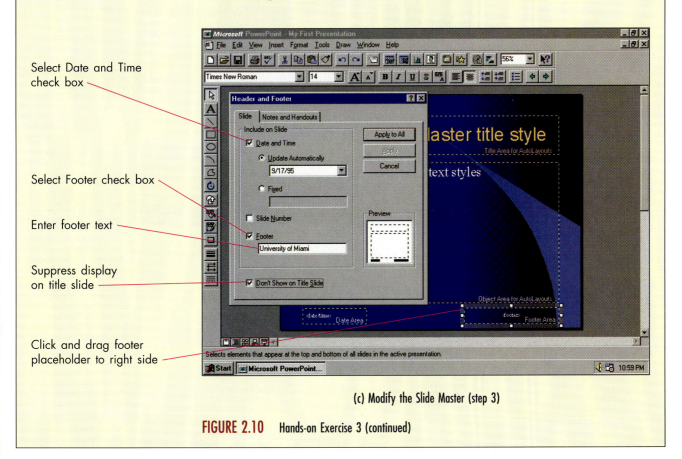

(c) Modify the Slide Master (step 3)

FIGURE 2.10 Hands-on Exercise 3 (continued)

THE VIEW BUTTONS AND THE SHIFT KEY

The Slide View button provides the fastest way to change to the slide master. Select any slide other than the title slide, then press and hold the Shift key as you click the Slide View button above the status bar to display the slide master. You can also press and hold the Shift key as you click the Slide Sorter or Outline View buttons to customize the handouts master for slide miniatures and outline handouts.

STEP 4: Change the Color Scheme

➤ Change to the **Slide Sorter view.** You should see a footer (containing the name of your school) on every slide except the title slide, as shown in Figure 2.10d.

➤ Pull down the **Format menu.** Click **Slide Color Scheme** to display the Color Scheme dialog box. Select a different color scheme (e.g., green), then click the **Apply to All button** to change the color scheme of every slide.

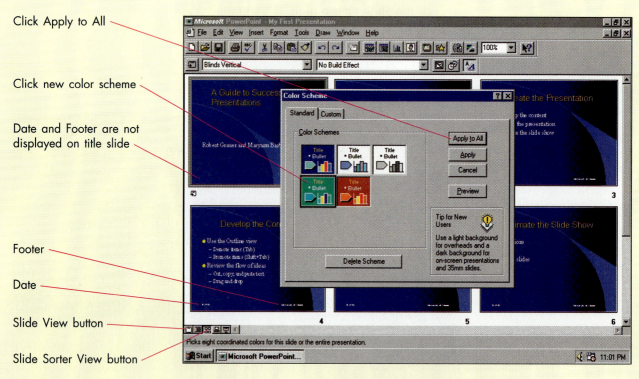

(d) Change the Color Scheme (step 4)

FIGURE 2.10 Hands-on Exercise 3 (continued)

STEP 5: Customize the Background

➤ Pull down the **Format menu.** Click **Custom Background** to display the Custom Background dialog box in Figure 2.10e.

➤ Click the **drop-down arrow** to display the various types of backgrounds (which are not shown in Figure 2.10e). Click **Shaded** to display the Shaded Fill dialog box.

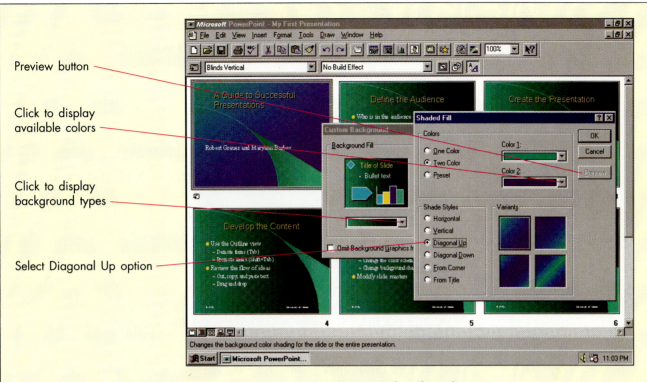

(e) Customize the Background (step 5)

FIGURE 2.10 Hands-on Exercise 3 (continued)

- Click the **drop-down arrow** on the Color 2 list box. Select a different color (e.g., blue). Click the **Diagonal Up option button** as the Shade style.
- Click the **Preview button** to see the effect of these changes on the currently selected slide (slide 1 in Figure 2.10e). Experiment with additional changes, then click **OK** to accept the changes and close the Shaded Fill dialog box.
- Click **Apply to All** to apply the changes to all slides and close the Custom Background dialog box. Use the Undo command to return to the initial design if you are disappointed with your modification.

MULTIPLE LEVEL UNDO COMMAND

The Undo command reverses (undoes) the most recent command. The command is executed from the Edit menu or more easily by clicking the Undo button on the Standard toolbar. Each click of the Undo button reverses one command; that is, click the Undo button and you reverse the last command. Click the Undo button a second time and you reverse the previous command. The Redo button works in reverse and undoes the most recent Undo command (i.e., it redoes the command you just undid). The maximum number of Undo commands (the default is 20) is set through the Tools menu. Pull down the Tools menu, click Options, click the Advanced tab, then enter the desired number.

STEP 6: Print the Audience Handouts

➤ Pull down the **File menu.** Click **Print** to display the Print dialog box in Figure 2.10f. Set the print options to match those in the figure:

- Click the **All option button** as the print range.
- Click the **down arrow** on the Print What list box to select **6 Handouts per page.**
- Check the box to **Frame Slides.**
- Click **OK**.

➤ Submit the audience handouts to your instructor as proof that you did the exercise.

➤ Exit PowerPoint. Congratulations on a job well done.

PRINT THE OUTLINE

You can print the outline of a presentation and distribute it to the audience in the form of a handout. This enables the audience to follow the presentation as it is delivered and gives them an ideal vehicle on which to take notes. Pull down the File menu, click Print, then choose Outline view from the Print What list box. Be sure you know the expected size of the audience so that you will have an adequate number of handouts.

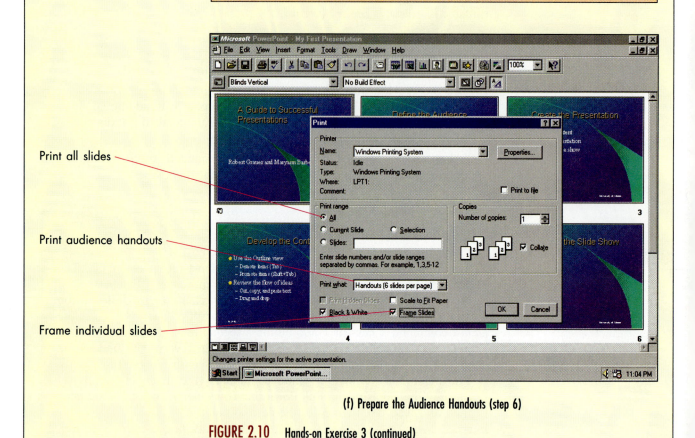

(f) Prepare the Audience Handouts (step 6)

FIGURE 2.10 Hands-on Exercise 3 (continued)

SUMMARY

There are in essence two independent steps to creating a PowerPoint presentation. You must develop the content, and you must format the presentation. Both steps are iterative in nature, and you are likely to go back and forth many times before you are finished.

The text of a presentation can be developed from the Slide view or the Outline view or a combination of the two. The Outline view is easier because it displays the contents of many slides at once, enabling you to see the overall flow of your ideas. You can change the order of the slides and/or move text from one slide to another as necessary. Text can be entered continually in the outline, then promoted or demoted so that it appears on the proper level in the slide.

The AutoContent Wizard asks you questions about the type of presentation you are planning to give, then creates an outline for you. The outline is based on one of many predefined outlines and is a good starting point.

A template is a design specification that controls every aspect of a presentation. It specifies the formatting of the text, the fonts and colors that are used, and the design, size, and placement of the bullets.

Transitions and builds can be added to a presentation for additional interest. Transitions control the way in which one slide moves off the screen and the next slide appears. Builds are used to display the individual elements on a single slide.

The design of a presentation can be customized by modifying its color scheme or background shading. The slide master enables you to add a unifying element to every slide, such as a corporate name or logo.

Every presentation should be checked for spelling. The Style Checker ensures consistency throughout a presentation with respect to capitalization and punctuation.

KEY WORDS AND CONCEPTS

AutoContent Wizard	Demote	Spell Check
AutoCorrect	Insertion point	Style Checker
Background color	Outline toolbar	Template
Background shading	Promote	Transition
Build	Slide icon	
Color scheme	Slide master	
Custom Background command	Slide Sorter toolbar	

MULTIPLE CHOICE

1. Which view displays multiple slides while letting you change the text in a slide?
   (a) Outline view
   (b) Slide Sorter view
   (c) Both (a) and (b)
   (d) Neither (a) nor (b)

2. Where will the insertion point be after you complete the text for a bullet in the Outline view and press the enter key?
   (a) On the next bullet at the same level of indentation
   (b) On the next bullet at a higher level of indentation
   (c) On the next bullet at a lower level of indentation
   (d) Impossible to determine

3. Which of the following is true?
   (a) Shift+Tab promotes an item to the next higher level
   (b) Tab demotes an item to the next lower level
   (c) Both (a) and (b)
   (d) Neither (a) nor (b)

4. Which of the following is true about the Outline view?
   (a) The position of a slide may be changed by dragging its icon
   (b) All slides display the identical icon regardless of content
   (c) Both (a) and (b)
   (d) Neither (a) nor (b)

5. What advantage, if any, is there to collapsing the Outline view so that only the slide titles are visible?
   (a) More slides are displayed at one time, making it easier to rearrange the slides in the presentation
   (b) Transition and build effects can be added
   (c) Graphic objects become visible
   (d) All of the above

6. Which of the following is true regarding transition and build effects?
   (a) Every slide must have the same transition effect
   (b) Every bullet must have the same build effect
   (c) Both (a) and (b)
   (d) Neither (a) nor (b)

7. The AutoContent Wizard provides suggested presentations for:
   (a) Communicating bad news
   (b) Selling a product, service, or idea
   (c) Both (a) and (b)
   (d) Neither (a) nor (b)

8. Which of the following is true?
   (a) Slides can be added to a presentation after a template has been chosen
   (b) The template can be changed after all of the slides have been created
   (c) Both (a) and (b)
   (d) Neither (a) nor (b)

9. What is the easiest way to add a corporate name to every slide (except the title slide) in the presentation?
   (a) Add the information to the handout master
   (b) Add the information to the slide master
   (c) Both (a) and (b)
   (d) Neither (a) nor (b)

10. Which of the following can be changed after a slide has been created?
    (a) Its layout and transition effect
    (b) Its position within the presentation
    (c) Both (a) and (b)
    (d) Neither (a) nor (b)

11. Which view enables you to select multiple slides?
    (a) Outline view
    (b) Slide sorter view
    (c) Both (a) and (b)
    (d) Neither (a) nor (b)

12. Which applications in Microsoft Office support the AutoCorrect feature?
    (a) PowerPoint
    (b) Word
    (c) Excel
    (d) All of the above

13. How do you move to the next slide during a slide show?
    (a) Click the left mouse button
    (b) Type the letter N
    (c) Press the PgDn key
    (d) All of the above

14. Which of the following can be corrected using the Style Checker?
    (a) Inconsistent use of capitalization
    (b) Inconsistent punctuation at the end of bulleted items
    (c) Both (a) and (b)
    (d) Neither (a) nor (b)

15. Which of the following can be changed without changing the template?
    (a) The color scheme and background shading
    (b) The slide master
    (c) Both (a) and (b)
    (d) Neither (a) nor (b)

ANSWERS

1. a	6. d	11. c
2. a	7. c	12. d
3. c	8. c	13. d
4. a	9. b	14. c
5. a	10. c	15. c

EXPLORING MICROSOFT POWERPOINT 7.0

1. Use Figure 2.11 to match each action with its result; a given action may be used more than once or not at all.

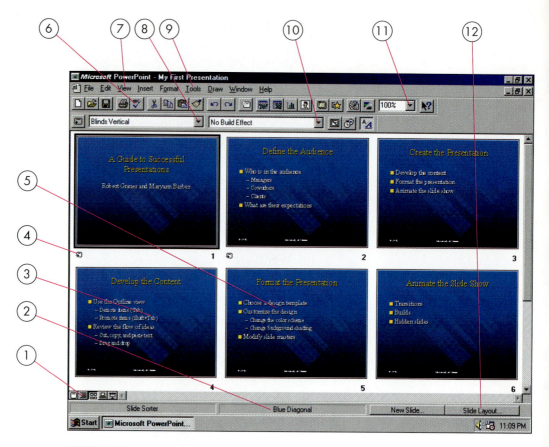

FIGURE 2.11 Screen for Problem 1

Action	**Result**
a. Click at 1	_____ Choose a new template
b. Double click at 2	_____ Spell check the presentation
c. Click at 4	_____ Switch to the Outline view
d. Click at 5, click at 10	_____ Run the Style Checker
e. Click at 3, click at 8	_____ Create a build for slide 5
f. Click at 6	_____ Change the AutoLayout for the current slide
g. Click at 7	
h. Click at 9	_____ Preview the transition for the first slide
i. Click at 11	
j. Click at 12	_____ Create a transition for slide 4
	_____ Modify the slide master
	_____ Change the zoom in effect

2. The Answer Wizard functions identically in PowerPoint as it does in the other Office applications. Accordingly, use what you know about Microsoft Office, or explore on your own, to answer the following with respect to Figure 2.12:

    a. How do you display the dialog box in Figure 2.12? Is this type of help information available in the other Office applications?

    b. What is the difference between the Contents, Index, Find, and Answer Wizard tabs? Which tab is currently selected?

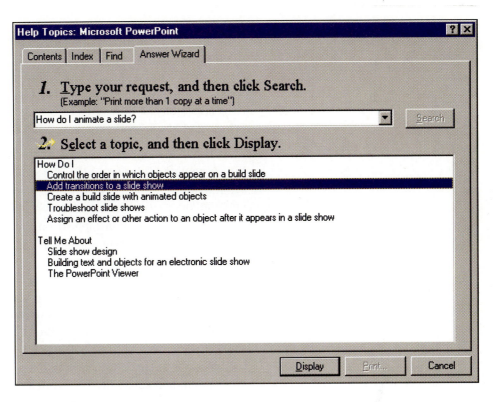

FIGURE 2.12 Screen for Problem 2

c. What did the user enter once the dialog box appeared? What was displayed in response to the user's input?
d. What would be the effect of clicking the Display command button?

3. Answer the following with respect to the dialog box in Figure 2.13:
    a. What command(s) displayed the dialog box?
    b. What is the difference between the Presentation Designs tab and the Presentations tab? Which one is currently selected?

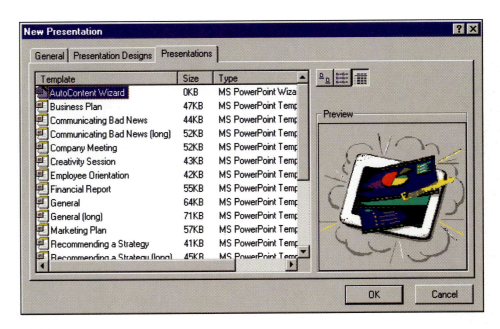

FIGURE 2.13 Screen for Problem 3

CREATING A PRESENTATION

c. What is the function of the three buttons that appear toward the upper right side of the dialog box? Which of these buttons is currently in effect?

d. What additional information would you expect to see if you clicked the down arrow on the vertical scroll bar?

e. What additional information would you expect to see if you clicked the right arrow on the horizontal scroll bar?

f. What would happen if you clicked the OK button? The Cancel button?

4. Answer the following with respect to the dialog boxes in Figure 2.14:

    a. Which command displayed the dialog box in Figure 2.14a?

    b. What date will appear on each slide in the presentation? Will this date be updated automatically in the future?

    c. Will the specified options appear on the title slide?

    d. What footer (if any) will appear on each slide? How do you change the contents of the footer?

    e. Which command produced the dialog box in Figure 2.14b?

    f. What is the difference between Title Case and Sentence case? What are the other options available for capitalization?

    g. Will periods be added to or removed from the slide titles? Will they be added to or removed from bulleted text?

    h. Is it possible to check for punctuation other than periods?

    i. What additional capability is provided through the Visual Clarity tab?

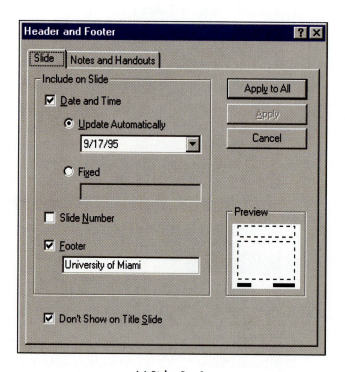

(a) Dialog Box 1

FIGURE 2.14   Screen for Problem 4

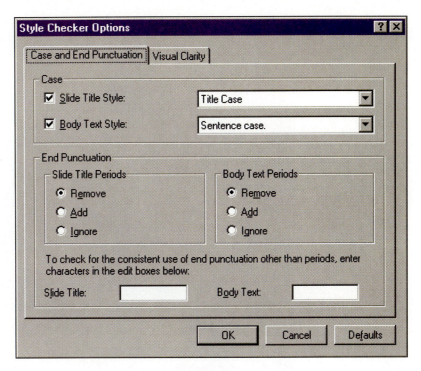

(b) Dialog Box 2

FIGURE 2.14 Screen for Problem 4 (continued)

PRACTICE WITH MICROSOFT POWERPOINT 7.0

1. Figure 2.15 displays the title slide of a presentation that can be found in the Exploring PowerPoint folder on the data disk. Much of the presentation has been created for you, but there are several finishing touches:
   a. Open the existing presentation titled Chapter 2 Practice 1, then save it as Finished Chapter 2 Practice 1 so that you can return to the original presentation if necessary.
   b. Add your name to the title slide.
   c. Move the slide that describes printers after the slide about video.
   d. Delete the slide that describes the bus.
   e. Add a slide at the end of the presentation to consider mail-order purchase. Enter the names and phone numbers of three such companies.
   f. Change the layout of slide 2 to include clip art. Use any image you think is appropriate.
   g. Change the template to Comet.
   h. Print the completed presentation in both outline and handout form. Submit both to your instructor.

2. Figure 2.16 displays a very general outline for a presentation. The outline can be accessed through the AutoContent Wizard or directly through the File New command.
   a. Pull down the File menu, click New to display the New Presentation dialog box, click the Presentations tab, then double click the General presentation.

CREATING A PRESENTATION **87**

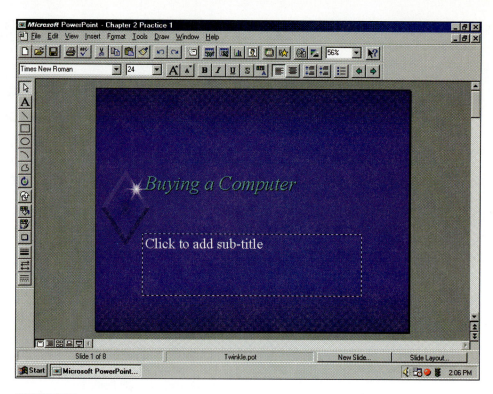

FIGURE 2.15 Screen for Practice Exercise 1

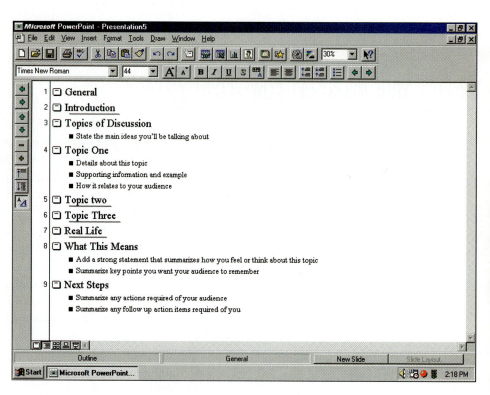

FIGURE 2.16 Screen for Practice Exercise 2

b. Change to the Outline view to display the presentation in Figure 2.16. (Some slides have been collapsed in our outline as can be seen by the underlined slide titles.)

c. Choose any topic you like, then prepare a presentation on that topic using the outline provided. You need not follow the outline exactly, but it should provide a good beginning. The completed presentation should contain from six to ten slides.

d. Apply a new (different) design template to the completed presentation.

e. Use the Style Checker to check for spelling, punctuation, and consistent capitalization throughout the presentation.

f. Print the completed presentation in both outline and miniature slide form. Submit both handouts to your instructor.

3. It began with David Letterman, but today almost everyone has a list of the top ten reasons for something, and PowerPoint is no exception. Use the AutoContent Wizard (or the File New command as described in the previous exercise) to select the Top Ten List template shown in Figure 2.17.

a. Complete the presentation by entering your top 10 list in either the Slide or Outline view.

b. Press Ctrl+Home to return to the first slide, change to the Slide Show view, then sit back and enjoy the show. (The template includes transition and build effects as can be seen by the tiny icons under each slide in the Slide Sorter view of Figure 2.17.)

c. Prove to your instructor that you have done the exercise by providing a hard copy of the completed presentation. Print the presentation in Slide view, but be sure to print the slides without builds so that you conserve paper.

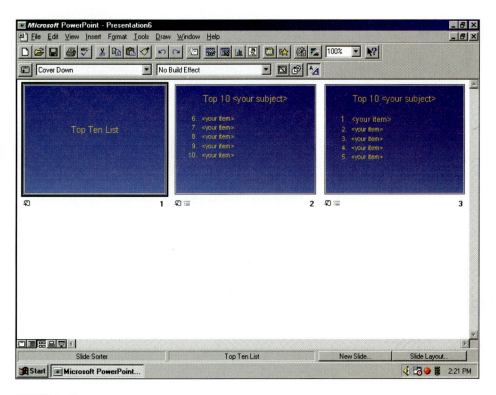

FIGURE 2.17   Screen for Practice Exercise 3

4. Figure 2.18 displays the Slide Sorter view of the Reporting Progress template that is accessed through the AutoContent Wizard or the File New command. (Six of the nine slides are visible.)

   a. Change the title of the presentation to reflect your progress in this course (e.g., CIS120 as shown in Figure 2.18).
   b. Modify the slides to reflect your progress in the class to date. You can add or delete slides as appropriate. You can also change the slide layout and content. Be as accurate and as honest as you can to provide feedback to your instructor on how the course is going.
   c. Use the Header and Footer command in the View menu to print today's date on every slide except the title slide.
   d. Modify the slide master to include a piece of clip art in the lower-right corner of each slide except the title slide.
   e. Use the Style Checker to check for spelling, punctuation, and consistent capitalization throughout the presentation.
   f. Print the completed presentation in miniature slide form and submit the printout to your instructor.

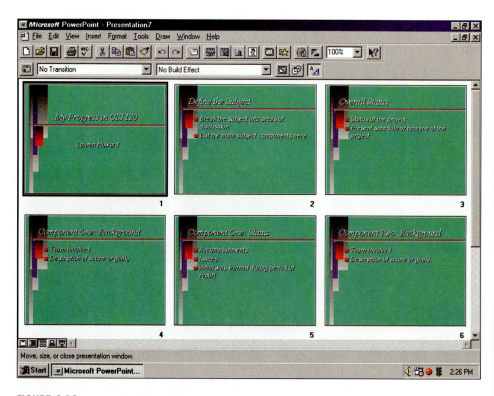

FIGURE 2.18 Screen for Practice Exercise 4

Case Studies

Be Creative

One interesting way of exploring the potential of presentation graphics is to imagine it might have been used by historical figures had it been available. Choose any historical figure or current personality and create at least a six-slide presentation.

You could, for example, show how Columbus might have used PowerPoint to request funding from Queen Isabella, or how Elvis Presley might have pleaded for his first recording contract. The content of your presentation should be reasonable, but you don't have to spend an inordinate amount of time on research. Just be creative and use your imagination. Use clip art as appropriate, but don't overdo it. Place your name on the title slide as technical adviser.

The Annual Report

Corporate America spends a small fortune to produce its annual reports, which are readily available to the public. Choose any company and obtain a copy of its most recent annual report. Use your imagination on how best to obtain the data. You might try a stockbroker, the 800 directory, or even the Internet. Use the information in the annual report as the basis for a PowerPoint presentation. PowerPoint is one step ahead of you and offers a suggested financial report through the AutoContent Wizard.

Director of Marketing

Congratulations on your appointment as Director of Marketing. The company into which you have been hired has 50 sales representatives across the United States. Laptop computers have just been ordered for the entire sales staff and will be delivered at next week's annual sales meeting. Your job is to prepare a PowerPoint presentation that can be used by the sales staff in future sales calls. It's short notice, but it is a critical assignment. Use the Selling a Product template provided by the AutoContent Wizard as the basis for your presentation.

Take it on the Road

Your presentation looks great on the desktop, but you have to deliver it to a crowd of 50, too many people to crowd around your machine. Fortunately, however, you have a notebook computer and a generous budget. What equipment do you need to show the presentation from your notebook computer? How much will the equipment cost to buy? Can you rent the equipment instead, and if so, from whom?

APPENDIX A: TOOLBARS

OVERVIEW

PowerPoint has nine predefined toolbars, which provide access to commonly used commands. The toolbars are displayed in Figure A.1 and are listed here for convenience. They are the Animation Effects, AutoShapes, Drawing, Drawing+, Formatting, Microsoft, Outlining, Slide Sorter, and Standard toolbars. When you first start PowerPoint, the Standard and Formatting toolbars are displayed immediately below the menu bar, and the Drawing toolbar is displayed along the left edge of the window. The Outlining and Slide Sorter toolbars are displayed automatically when you switch to the Outline and Slide Sorter views, respectively. The Animation Effects, AutoShape, Drawing+, and Microsoft toolbars are available for use as needed.

The buttons on the toolbars are intended to be indicative of their functions. Clicking the Print button, for example (the fourth button from the left on the Standard toolbar), executes the Print command. If you are unsure of the purpose of any toolbar button, point to it, and a ToolTip will appear that displays its name.

You can display multiple toolbars at one time, move them to new locations on the screen, customize their appearance, or suppress their display.

- To display or hide a toolbar, pull down the View menu and click the Toolbars command. Select (deselect) the toolbar(s) that you want to display (hide). The selected toolbar(s) will be displayed in the same position as when last displayed. You may also point to any toolbar and click with the right mouse button to bring up a shortcut menu, after which you can select the toolbar to be displayed (hidden).
- To change the size of the buttons, display them in monochrome rather than color, or suppress the display of the ToolTips, pull down the View menu, click Toolbars, and then select (deselect) the appropriate check box. Alternatively, you can click on any toolbar with the right mouse button, select Toolbars, and then select (deselect) the appropriate check box.

- Toolbars may be either docked (along the edge of the window) or left floating (in their own window). A toolbar moved to the edge of the window will dock along that edge. A toolbar moved anywhere else in the window will float in its own window. Docked toolbars are one tool wide (high), whereas floating toolbars can be resized by clicking and dragging a border or corner as you would with any other window.
  - To move a docked toolbar, click anywhere in the gray background area and drag the toolbar to its new location.
  - To move a floating toolbar, drag its title bar to its new location.
- To customize one or more toolbars, display the toolbar(s) on the screen. Then pull down the View menu, click Toolbars, and click the Customize command button. Alternatively, you can click on any toolbar with the right mouse button, and then select Customize from the shortcut menu.
  - To move a button, drag the button to its new location on that toolbar or any other displayed toolbar.
  - To copy a button, press the Ctrl key as you drag the button to its new location on that toolbar or any other displayed toolbar.
  - To delete a button, drag the button off the toolbar and release the mouse button.
  - To add a button, select the category from the Categories list box and then drag the button to the desired location on the toolbar. (To see a description of a tool's function prior to adding it to a toolbar, click the tool in the Customize dialog box and read the displayed description.)
  - To restore a predefined toolbar to its default appearance, pull down the View menu, click Toolbars, select (highlight) the desired toolbar, and click the Reset command button.
- Buttons can also be moved, copied, or deleted without displaying the Customize dialog box.
  - To move a button, press the Alt key as you drag the button to the new location.
  - To copy a button, press the Alt and Ctrl keys as you drag the button to the new location.
  - To delete a button, press the Alt key as you drag the button off the toolbar.
- To create your own toolbar, pull down the View menu, click Toolbar, and click the New command button. Alternatively, you can click on any toolbar with the right mouse button, select Toolbars from the shortcut menu, and then click the New command button.
  - Enter a name for the toolbar in the dialog box that follows. The name can be any length and can contain spaces.
  - The new toolbar will appear at the top left of the screen. Initially it will be big enough to hold only one button. Add, move, and delete buttons following the same procedures as outlined above. The toolbar will automatically size itself as new buttons are added and deleted.
  - To delete a custom toolbar, pull down the View menu, click Toolbars, and make sure that the custom toolbar to be deleted is the only one selected (highlighted). Click the Delete command button. Prior to closing the dialog box, you can undelete the toolbar by clicking the Undelete button. Once you have exited the dialog box, however, the custom toolbar cannot be undeleted. (Note that a predefined toolbar cannot be deleted.)

Animation Effects Toolbar

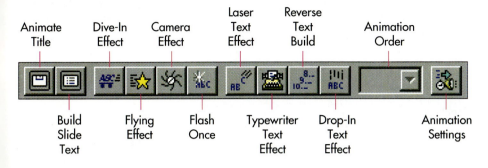

AutoShapes Toolbar

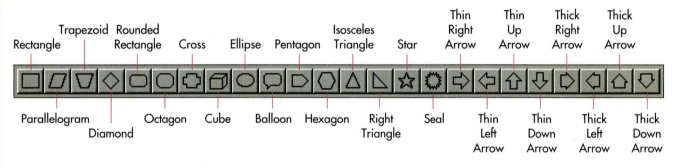

Drawing Toolbar

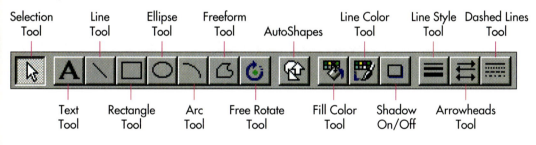

Drawing+ Toolbar

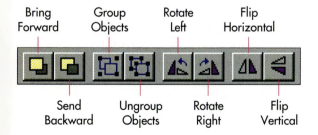

FIGURE A.1 PowerPoint Toolbars

Formatting Toolbar

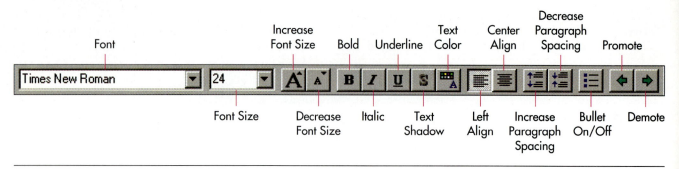

Microsoft Toolbar

Outlining Toolbar

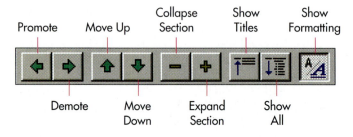

Slide Sorter Toolbar

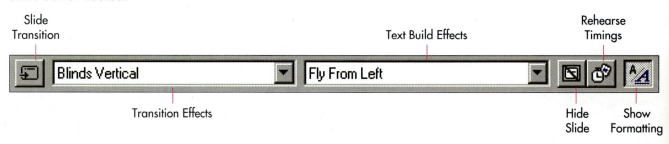

Standard Toolbar

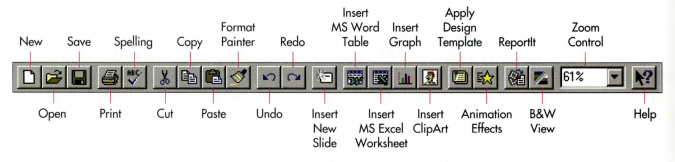

FIGURE A.1 PowerPoint Toolbars (continued)

PREREQUISITES: ESSENTIALS OF WINDOWS 95®

OBJECTIVES

After reading this appendix you will be able to:

1. Describe the objects on the Windows desktop; use the Start button to access the online help.
2. Explain the function of the minimize, maximize, restore, and close buttons; move and size a window.
3. Discuss the function of a dialog box; describe the different types of dialog boxes and the various ways in which information is supplied.
4. Format a floppy disk.
5. Use My Computer to locate a specific file or folder; describe the different views available for My Computer.
6. Describe how folders are used to organize a disk; create a new folder; copy and/or move a file from one folder to another.
7. Delete a file, then recover the deleted file from the Recycle Bin.
8. Describe the document orientation of Windows 95; use the New command to create a document without explicitly opening the associated application.
9. Explain the differences in browsing with My Computer versus browsing with the Windows Explorer.

OVERVIEW

Windows 95 is a computer program (actually many programs) that controls the operation of your computer and its peripherals. One of the most significant benefits of the Windows environment is the common user interface and consistent command structure that are imposed on every Windows application. Once you learn the basic concepts and techniques, you can apply that knowledge to every Windows application. This appendix teaches you those concepts so that you will be able to work productively in the Windows environment. It is written for you, the computer novice, and assumes no previous knowledge about a computer or about Windows. Our goal is to get you "up and running" as quickly as possible so that you can do the work you want to do.

We begin with an introduction to the Windows desktop, the graphical user interface that lets you work in intuitive fashion by pointing at icons and clicking the mouse. We show you how to use the online help facility to look up information when you need it. We identify the basic components of a window and describe how to execute commands and supply information through various types of dialog boxes.

The appendix also shows you how to manage the hundreds (indeed, thousands) of files that are stored on the typical system. We describe the use of My Computer to search the drives on your computer for a specific file or folder. (All files in Windows 95 are stored in folders, which are the electronic equivalent of manila folders in a filing cabinet.) We show you how to create a new folder and how to move or copy a file from one folder to another. We show you how to rename a file, how to delete a file, and how to recover a deleted file from the Recycle Bin.

All file operations are done through My Computer or through the more powerful Windows Explorer. My Computer is intuitive and geared for the novice, as it opens a new window for each folder you open. Explorer, on the other hand, is more sophisticated and provides a hierarchical view of the entire system in a single window. A beginner will prefer My Computer, whereas a more experienced user will most likely opt for the Explorer. This is the same sequence in which we present the material. We start with My Computer, then show you how to accomplish the same result more quickly through the Explorer.

THE DESKTOP

Windows 95 creates a working environment for your computer that parallels the working environment at home or in an office. You work at a desk. Windows operations take place on the ***desktop.***

There are physical objects on a desk such as folders, a dictionary, a calculator, or a phone. The computer equivalent of those objects appear as ***icons*** (pictorial symbols) on the desktop. Each object on a real desk has attributes (properties) such as size, weight, and color. In similar fashion, Windows assigns properties to every object on its desktop. And just as you can move the objects on a real desk, you can rearrange the objects on the Windows desktop.

Figure 1a displays the desktop when Windows is first installed on a new computer. This desktop has only a few objects and is similar to the desk in a new office, just after you move in. Figure 1b displays a different desktop, one with three open windows, and is similar to a desk during the middle of a working day. Do not be concerned if your Windows desktop is different from ours. Your real desk is arranged differently from those of your friends, and so your Windows desktop will also be different.

The simplicity of the desktop in Figure 1a helps you to focus on what's important. The ***Start button,*** as its name suggests, is where you begin. Click the Start button (mouse operations are explained in the next section) and you see a menu that provides access to any program (e.g., Microsoft Word or Microsoft Excel) on your computer. The Start button also gives you access to an online help facility that provides information about every aspect of Windows.

In addition to the Start button, the desktop in Figure 1a contains three objects, each of which has a special purpose. ***My Computer*** enables you to browse the disk drives (and optional CD-ROM drive) that are attached to your computer.

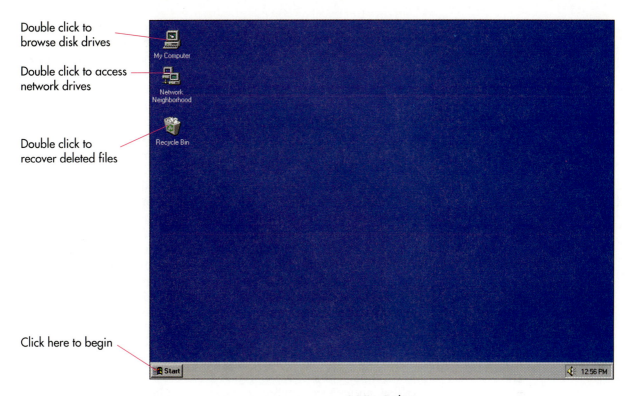

(a) New Desktop

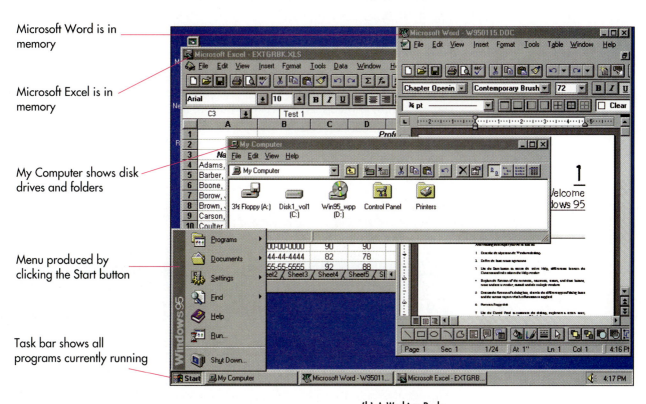

(b) A Working Desk

FIGURE 1 The Windows Desktop

Network Neighborhood extends your view of the computer to include the accessible drives on the network to which your machine is attached, if indeed it is part of a network. (You will not see this icon if you are not connected to a network.) The ***Recycle Bin*** lets you recover a file that was previously deleted and is illustrated in a hands-on exercise later in the appendix (see page 40).

Each object in Figure 1a contains additional objects that are displayed when you open (double click) the object. Double click My Computer in Figure 1a, for example, and you see the objects contained in the My Computer window of Figure 1b. Double click Network Neighborhood, and you will see all of the drives available on your network.

Two additional windows are open on the desktop in Figure 1b and correspond to programs that are currently in use. Each window has a title bar that displays the name of the program and the associated document. (The Start button was used to open each program, Microsoft Word and Microsoft Excel, in Figure 1b.) You can work in any window as long as you want, then switch to a different window. ***Multitasking,*** the ability to run several programs at the same time, is one of the major benefits of the Windows environment. It lets you run a word processor in one window, a spreadsheet in a second window, communicate online in a third window, run a game in a fourth window, and so on.

The ***taskbar*** at the bottom of the desktop shows all of the programs that are currently running (open in memory). It contains a button for each open program and lets you switch back and forth between those programs, by clicking the appropriate button. The taskbar in Figure 1a does not contain any buttons (other than the Start button) since there are no open applications. The taskbar in Figure 1b, however, contains three additional buttons, one for each open window.

ANATOMY OF A WINDOW

Figure 2 displays a typical window and labels its essential elements. Every window has the same components as every other window, which include a title bar, a Minimize button, a Maximize or Restore button, and a Close button. Other elements, that may or may not be present, include a horizontal and/or vertical scroll bar, a menu bar, a status bar, and a toolbar. Every window also contains additional objects (icons) that pertain specifically to the programs(s) or data associated with that window.

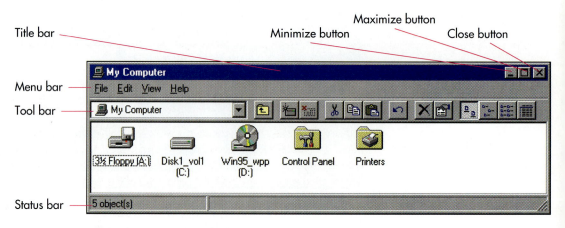

FIGURE 2   Anatomy of a Window

The ***title bar*** appears at the top of the window and displays the name of the window—for example, My Computer in Figure 2. The icon at the extreme left of the title bar provides access to a control menu that lets you select operations relevant to the window. The **Minimize button** shrinks the window to a button on the taskbar. The **Maximize button** enlarges the window so that it takes up the entire desktop. The **Restore button** (which is not shown in Figure 2) appears instead of the Maximize button after a window has been maximized, and restores the window to its previous size. The **Close button** closes the window and removes it from the desktop.

The ***menu bar*** appears immediately below the title bar and provides access to pull-down menus as discussed in the next section. A ***toolbar*** appears below the menu bar and lets you execute a command by clicking an icon, as opposed to pulling down a menu. The ***status bar*** is found at the bottom of the window and displays information about the window as a whole or about a selected object within a window.

A ***vertical (horizontal) scroll bar*** appears at the right (bottom) border of a window when its contents are not completely visible and provides access to the unseen areas. Scroll bars do not appear in Figure 2 since all five objects in the window are visible.

MY COMPUTER

My Computer lets you browse the disk drives (and CD-ROM) on your system. It is present on every desktop, but the contents depend on the specific configuration. Our system, for example, has one floppy drive, one hard disk, and a CD-ROM, each of which is represented by an icon within the My Computer window. My Computer is discussed in greater detail later in this appendix, beginning on page 19.

Moving and Sizing a Window

Any window can be sized or moved on the desktop through appropriate actions with the mouse. To ***size a window,*** point to any border (the mouse pointer changes to a double arrow), then drag the border in the direction you want to go: inward to shrink the window or outward to enlarge it. You can also drag a corner (instead of a border) to change both dimensions at the same time. To ***move a window*** while retaining its current size, click and drag the title bar to a new position on the desktop.

Pull-down Menus

The menu bar provides access to ***pull-down menus*** that enable you to execute commands within an application (program). A pull-down menu is accessed by clicking the menu name or by pressing the Alt key plus the underlined letter in the menu name; for example, press Alt+V to pull down the View menu. Three pull-down menus associated with My Computer are shown in Figure 3.

The commands within a menu are executed by clicking the command once the menu has been pulled down, or by typing the underlined letter (for example, C to execute the Close command in the File menu). Alternatively, you can bypass the menu entirely if you know the equivalent keystrokes shown to the right of the command in the menu (e.g., Ctrl+X, Ctrl+C, or Ctrl+V to cut, copy, or paste as

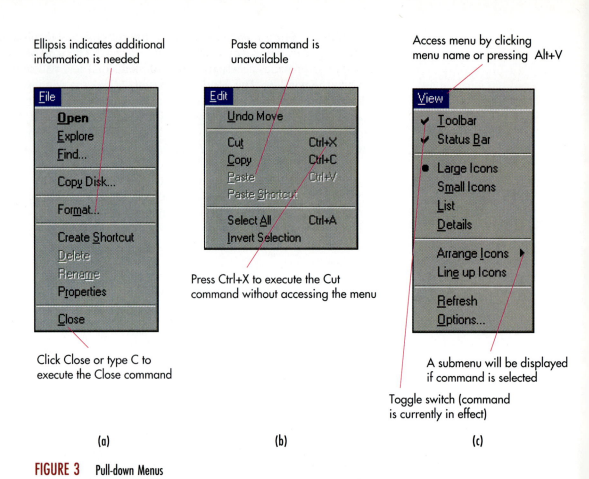

FIGURE 3 Pull-down Menus

shown within the Edit menu). A ***dimmed command*** (e.g., the Paste command in the Edit menu) means the command is not currently executable, and that some additional action has to be taken for the command to become available.

An ***ellipsis*** (. . .) following a command indicates that additional information is required to execute the command; for example, selection of the Format command in the File menu requires the user to specify additional information about the formatting process. This information is entered into a dialog box (discussed in the next section), which appears immediately after the command has been selected.

A check next to a command indicates a toggle switch, whereby the command is either on or off. There is a check next to the Toolbar command in the View menu of Figure 3, which means the command is in effect (and thus the toolbar will be displayed). Click the Toolbar command and the check disappears, which suppresses the display of the toolbar. Click the command a second time, the check reappears, as does the toolbar in the associated window.

An arrowhead after a command (e.g., the Arrange Icons command in the View menu) indicates a ***submenu*** will follow with additional menu options.

Dialog Boxes

A ***dialog box*** appears when additional information is needed to execute a command. The Format command, for example, requires information about which drive to format and the type of formatting desired.

Option (radio) buttons indicate mutually exclusive choices, one of which must be chosen; for example, one of three Format Type options in Figure 4a. Click a button to select an option, which automatically deselects the previously selected option.

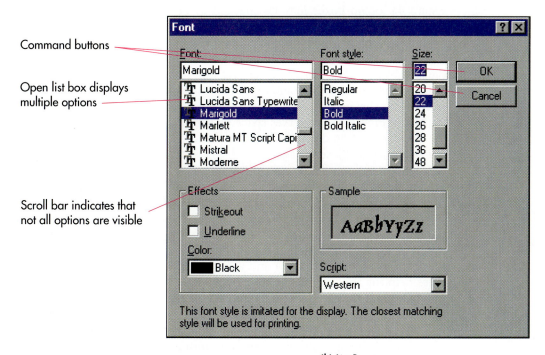

FIGURE 4 Dialog Boxes

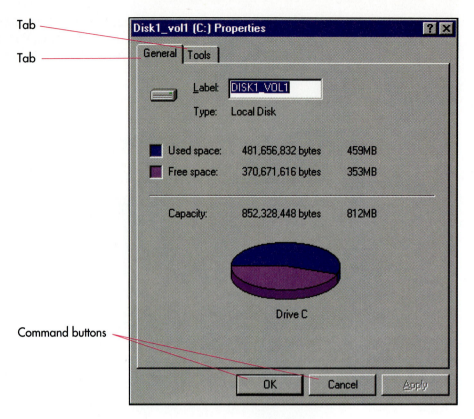

(c) Tabbed Dialog Box

FIGURE 4 Dialog Boxes (continued)

Check boxes are used instead of option buttons if the choices are not mutually exclusive or if an option is not required. Multiple boxes can be checked as in Figure 4a, or no boxes may be checked as in Figure 4b. Individual options are selected (cleared) by clicking on the appropriate check box.

A *text box* is used to enter descriptive information, such as Bob's Disk in Figure 4a. A flashing vertical bar (an I-beam) appears within the text box (when the text box is active) to mark the insertion point for the text you will enter.

A *list box* displays some or all of the available choices, any one of which is selected by clicking the desired item. A *drop-down list box,* such as the Capacity list box in Figure 4a, conserves space by showing only the current selection. Click the arrow of a drop-down list box to produce a list of available options. An *open list box,* such as those in Figure 4b, displays the choices without having to click a down arrow. (A scroll bar appears within an open list box if not all of the choices are visible at one time and provides access to the hidden choices.)

A *tabbed dialog box* provides multiple sets of options. The dialog box in Figure 4c, for example, has two tabs, each with its own set of options. Click either tab (the General tab is currently selected) to display the associated options.

All dialog boxes have a title bar, which contains a What's This button (in the form of a question mark) and a Close button. The ***What's This button*** provides help for any item in the dialog box; click the button, then click the item in the dialog box for which you want additional information. The Close button at the right of the title bar closes the dialog box.

All dialog boxes also contain one or more ***command buttons,*** the function of which is generally apparent from the button's name. The Start button, in Figure 4a, for example, initiates the formatting process. The OK Command button in

Figure 4b accepts the settings and closes the dialog box. The Cancel button does just the opposite, and ignores (cancels) the settings, then closes the dialog box without further action.

ONLINE HELP

Windows 95 has an extensive *online help* facility that contains information about virtually every topic in Windows. We believe that the best time to learn about help is as you begin your study of Windows. Help is available at any time, and is accessed most easily by clicking the *Help command* in the Start menu, which produces the help window in Figure 5.

The *Contents tab* in Figure 5a is similar to the table of contents in an ordinary book. The major topics are represented by books, each of which can be opened to display additional topics. Each open book will eventually display one or more specific topics, which may be viewed and/or printed to provide the indicated information.

The *Index tab* in Figure 5b is analogous to the index of an ordinary book. Type the first several letters of the topic to look up, click the topic when it appears in the window, then click the Display button to view the descriptive information as shown in Figure 5c. The help information is task-specific and describes how to accomplish the desired task.

You can print the contents of the Help windows in Figures 5a and 5b by clicking the Print command button at the bottom of a window. You can also print the contents of the display window in Figure 5c by right clicking in the window, then clicking the Print topic command from the shortcut menu.

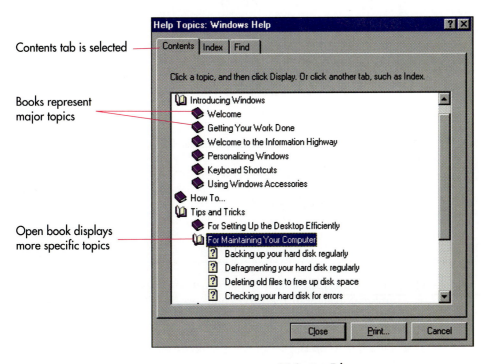

(a) Contents Tab

FIGURE 5   Online Help

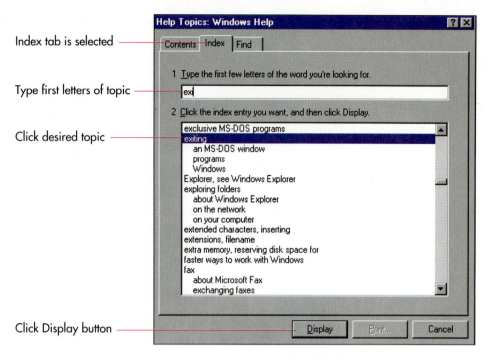

(b) Index Tab

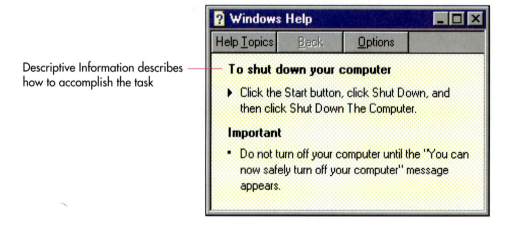

(c) Help Display

FIGURE 5 Online Help (continued)

THE MOUSE

The mouse is indispensable to Windows and is referenced continually in the hands-on exercises throughout the text. There are four basic operations with which you must become familiar:

- To **_point_** to an object, move the mouse pointer onto the object.
- To **_click_** an object, point to it, then press and release the left mouse button; to **_right click_** an object, point to the object, then press and release the right mouse button.

- To **double click** an object, point to it, then quickly click the left button twice in succession.
- To **drag** an object, move the pointer to the object, then press and hold the left button while you move the mouse to a new position.

The mouse is a pointing device—move the mouse on your desk and the **mouse pointer,** typically a small arrowhead, moves on the monitor. The mouse pointer assumes different shapes according to the location of the pointer or the nature of the current action—for example, a double arrow when you change the size of a window, an I-beam to insert text, a hand to jump from one help topic to the next, or a circle with a line through it to indicate that an attempted action is invalid.

The mouse pointer will also change to an hourglass to indicate that Windows is processing your last command, and that no further commands may be issued until the action is completed. The more powerful your computer, the less frequently the hourglass will appear; and conversely, the less powerful your system, the more you see the hourglass.

The Mouse versus the Keyboard

Almost every command in Windows can be executed in different ways, using either the mouse or the keyboard. Most people start with the mouse but add keyboard shortcuts as they become more proficient. There is no right or wrong technique, just different techniques, and the one you choose depends entirely on personal preference in a specific situation. If, for example, your hands are already on the keyboard, it is faster to use the keyboard equivalent. Other times, your hand will be on the mouse and that will be the fastest way. Toolbars provide still other ways to execute common commands.

In the beginning you may wonder why there are so many different ways to do the same thing, but you will eventually recognize the many options as part of Windows' charm. It is not necessary to memorize anything, nor should you even try; just be flexible and willing to experiment. The more you practice, the faster all of this will become second nature to you.

FORMATTING A DISK

All disks have to be formatted before they can hold data. The formatting process divides a disk into concentric circles called tracks, then further divides each track into sectors. You don't have to worry about formatting a hard disk, as that is done at the factory prior to the machine being sold. You do, however, have to format a floppy disk in order for Windows to read from and write to the disk. The procedure to format a floppy disk is described in step 6 of the following exercise.

FORMATTING A DISK

You must format a floppy disk at its rated capacity or else you may be unable to read the disk. There are two types of 3½-inch disks, double-density (720KB) and high-density (1.44MB). The easiest way to determine the type of disk is to look at the disk itself for the labels DD or HD, for double- and high-density, respectively. You can also check the number of square holes in the disk; a double-density disk has one, a high-density has two.

LEARNING BY DOING

Learning is best accomplished by doing, and so we come to the first of four exercises in this appendix. The exercises enable you to apply the concepts you have learned, then extend those concepts to further exploration on your own.

Our first exercise welcomes you to Windows 95, shows you how to open, move, and size a window on the desktop, and how to format a floppy disk.

HANDS-ON EXERCISE 1

Welcome to Windows 95

Objective: To turn on the computer and start Windows 95; to use the help facility and explore the topic "Ten Minutes to Using Windows"; to open, move, and size a window; to format a floppy disk. Use Figure 6 as a guide in the exercise.

STEP 1: Turn the Computer On

➤ The floppy drive should be empty prior to starting your machine. This ensures that the system starts by reading files from the hard disk (which contains the Windows files), as opposed to a floppy disk (which does not).

➤ The number and location of the on/off switches depend on the nature and manufacturer of the devices connected to the computer. The easiest possible setup is when all components of the system are plugged into a surge protector, in which case only a single switch has to be turned on. In any event:

- Turn on the monitor if it has a separate switch.
- Turn on the printer if it has a separate switch.
- Turn on the power switch of the system unit.

➤ Your system will take a minute or so to get started, after which you should see the desktop in Figure 6a (the Start menu is *not* yet visible). Do not be concerned if the appearance of your desktop is different from ours.

➤ You may (or may not) see the Welcome message in Figure 6a. All of the command buttons are interesting and merit further exploration, which we will do at a later time. But for now, we ask that you click the **Close button** if you see the Welcome message.

➤ Click the **Start button** to display the Start menu. Again, do not be concerned if your start menu is different from ours, or if your icons are smaller (or larger) than ours.

➤ Click the **Help command** as shown in Figure 6a.

> **MASTER THE MOUSE**
>
> Moving the mouse pointer is easy, but it takes practice to move it to an exact position on the screen. If you're having trouble, be sure the mouse is perpendicular to the system unit. Move the mouse to the left or right, and the mouse pointer moves left or right on the screen. Move the mouse forward or back, and the pointer moves up or down.

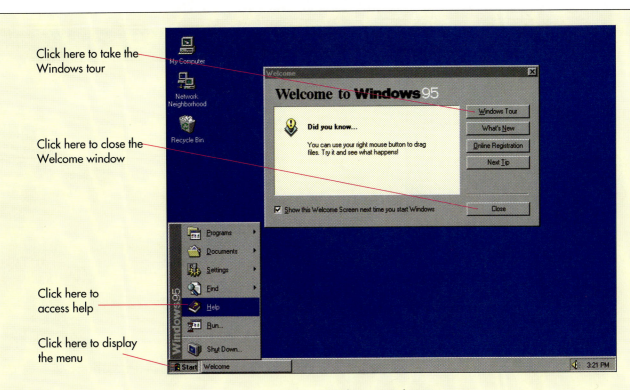

(a) Welcome to Windows 95 (step 1)

FIGURE 6   Hands-on Exercise 1

STEP 2: Ten Minutes to Windows

➤ If necessary, click the **Contents tab** in the Help Topics dialog box. All of the books on your screen will be closed.

➤ Click the topic **Ten Minutes to Using Windows,** then click the **Display button** to begin the Windows tour. (You can double click the topic to avoid having to click the Display button.)

➤ You should see the menu in Figure 6b. Click the **Book icon** next to Using Help to learn about the help facility.

➤ Follow the instructions provided by Windows until you complete the session on help. Click the **Exit button** at the upper right of the screen, then click the **Exit Tour button** to return to the desktop and continue with the exercise.

DOUBLE CLICKING FOR BEGINNERS

If you are having trouble double clicking, it is because you are not clicking quickly enough, or more likely, because you are moving the mouse (however slightly) between clicks. Relax, hold the mouse firmly on your desk, and try again.

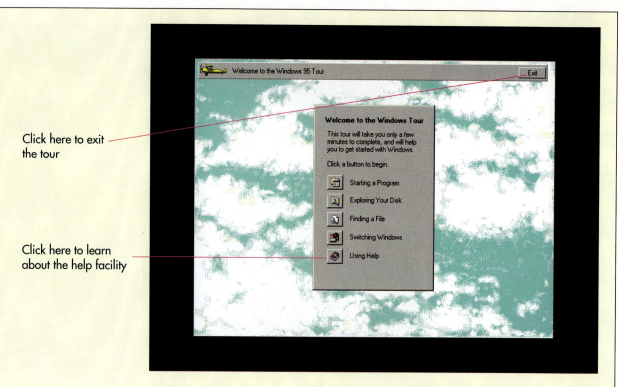

(b) Windows 95 Tour (step 2)

FIGURE 6 Hands-on Exercise 1 (continued)

STEP 3: Open My Computer

➤ Point to the **My Computer icon,** click the **right mouse button,** then click the **Open command** from the shortcut menu. (Alternatively, you can double click the **icon** to open it directly.)

➤ My Computer will open into a window as shown in Figure 6c. (The menus are not yet visible.) Do not be concerned if the contents of your window or its size and position on the desktop are different from ours.

➤ Pull down the **View menu** (point to the menu and click) as shown in Figure 6c. Make or verify the following selections. (You have to pull down the menu each time you choose a different command.)

- The **Toolbar command** should be checked. The Toolbar command functions as a toggle switch. Click the command and the toolbar is displayed; click the command a second time and the toolbar disappears.)

- The **Status Bar command** should be checked. The Status Bar command also functions as a toggle switch.

- **Large Icons** should be selected.

➤ Pull down the **View menu** a final time. Click the **Arrange Icons command** and (if necessary) click the **AutoArrange command** so that a check appears. Click outside the menu (or press the **Esc key**) if the command is already checked.

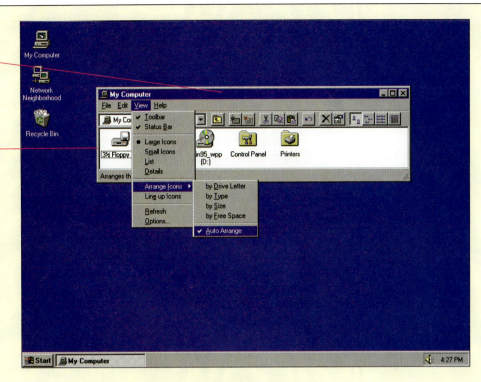

Drag the title bar to move the window (when menu is closed)

Click and drag a border to size the window (when menu is closed)

(c) My Computer (step 3)

FIGURE 6 Hands-on Exercise 1 (continued)

TOOLTIPS

Point to any button on the toolbar, and Windows displays the name of the button, which is indicative of its function. Point to the clock at the extreme right of the taskbar, and you will see a ToolTip with today's date. Point to the Start button, and you will see a ToolTip telling you to click here to begin.

STEP 4: Move and Size the Window

➤ Move and size the My Computer window on your desk to match the display in Figure 6c. (Press **Esc** to close the open menus.)
- Click the **Restore button** (which appears only if the window has been maximized) or else you will not be able to move and size the window.
- To change the width or height of the window, click and drag a border (the mouse pointer changes to a double arrow) in the direction you want to go; drag the border inward to shrink the window or outward to enlarge it.
- To change the width and height at the same time, click and drag a corner rather than a border.
- To change the position of the window, click and drag the title bar.

➤ Click the **Maximize button** so that the window expands to fill the entire screen. Click the **Restore button** (which replaces the Maximize button and is not shown in Figure 6c) to return the window to its previous size.

➤ Click the **Minimize button** to shrink the My Computer window to a button on the taskbar. My Computer is still open and remains active in memory.

➤ Click the **My Computer button** on the taskbar to reopen the window.

STEP 5: Scrolling

➤ Pull down the **View menu** and click **Details** (or click the **Details button** on the toolbar). You are now in the Details view as shown in Figure 6d.

➤ Click and drag the bottom border of the window inward so that you see the vertical scroll bar in Figure 6d. The scroll bar indicates that the contents of the window are not completely visible.

- Click the **down arrow** on the scroll bar. The top line (for drive A) disappears from view, and a new line containing the Control Panel comes into view.

- Click the **down arrow** a second time, which brings the Printers folder into view at the bottom of the window as the icon for drive C scrolls off the screen.

➤ Click the **Small Icons button** on the toolbar. Size the window so that the scroll bar disappears when the contents of the window become completely visible.

➤ Click the **Details button** on the toolbar. The scroll bar returns because you can no longer see the complete contents. Move and/or size the window to your personal preference.

(d) Scrolling (step 5)

FIGURE 6   Hands-on Exercise 1 (continued)

ESSENTIALS OF WINDOWS 95

THE DETAILS VIEW

The Details view provides information about each object in a folder—for example, the capacity (total size) and amount of free space on a disk. To switch to the Details view, pull down the View menu and click Details. You can also click the Details button on the toolbar, provided the toolbar is displayed.

STEP 6: Format a Floppy Disk

➤ Click the **icon** for **drive A.** Pull down the **File menu** and click **Format.**

➤ You will see the dialog box in Figure 6e. Move the dialog box by clicking and dragging its **title bar** so that your screen matches ours.

➤ Click the **What's This button** (the mouse pointer changes to a question mark). Click the **Full option button** (under Format type) for an explanation. Click anywhere in the dialog box to close the popup window.

➤ Set the formatting parameters as shown in Figure 6e:

- Set the **Capacity** to match the floppy disk you purchased (see boxed tip on page 11).
- Click the **Full option button** to choose a full format. This option is well worth the extra time as it ensures the integrity of your disk.

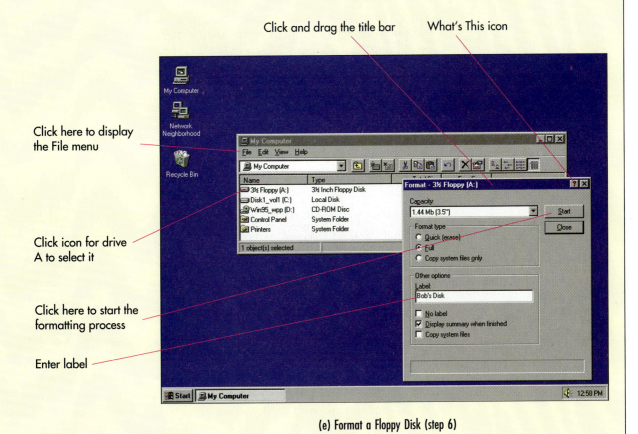

(e) Format a Floppy Disk (step 6)

FIGURE 6   Hands-on Exercise 1 (continued)

ESSENTIALS OF WINDOWS 95   17

- Click the **Label text box** if it's empty, or click and drag over the existing label if there is an entry. Enter a new label such as **Bob's Disk** as shown in Figure 6e.
➤ Click the **Start command button** to begin the formatting operation. This will take about a minute, and you can see the progress of the formatting process at the bottom of the dialog box.
➤ After the formatting process is complete, you will see an informational dialog box with the results of the formatting operation. Read the information, then click the **Close command button** to close the informational dialog box.
➤ Click the **Close button** to close the Format dialog box.

WHAT'S THIS?

The What's This button (a question mark) appears in the title bar of almost every dialog box. Click the question mark, then click the item you want information about, which then appears in a popup window. To print the contents of the popup window, click the right mouse button inside the window, and click Print Topic. Click outside the popup window to close the window and continue working.

STEP 7: Disk Properties
➤ Click the **drive A icon** in the My Computer window, click the **right mouse button** to display a shortcut menu, then click the **Properties command.**
➤ You should see the Properties dialog box in Figure 6f although you may have to move and size the window to match our figure. The pie chart displays the percentage of free and unused space.
➤ Click **OK** to close the Properties dialog box. Click the **Close button** to close My Computer.

PROPERTIES EVERYWHERE

Windows assigns *properties* to every object on the desktop and stores those properties with the object itself. Point to any object on the desktop, including the desktop itself, then click the right mouse button to display the property sheet for that object.

STEP 8: Exit Windows
➤ Click the **Start button,** then click the **Shut Down command.** You will see a dialog box asking whether you're sure that you want to shut down the computer. (The option button to shut down the computer is already selected.)
➤ Click the **Yes command button,** then wait as Windows gets ready to shut down your system. Wait until you see another screen indicating that it is OK to turn off the computer.

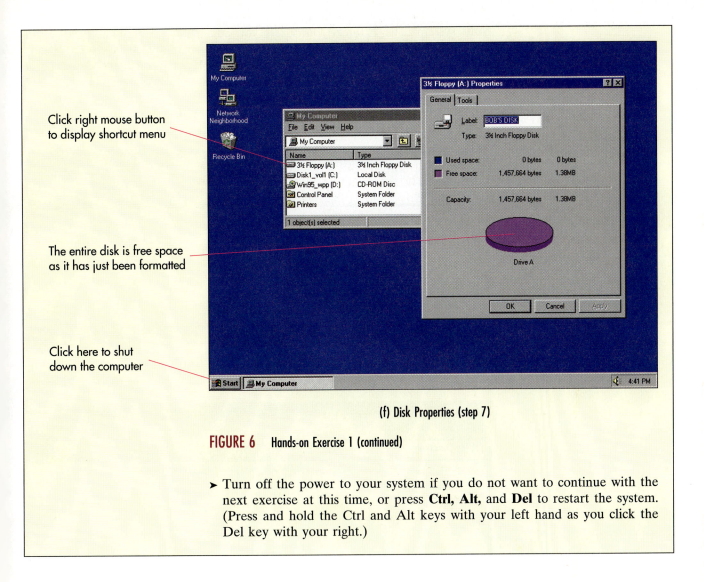

(f) Disk Properties (step 7)

FIGURE 6 Hands-on Exercise 1 (continued)

▶ Turn off the power to your system if you do not want to continue with the next exercise at this time, or press **Ctrl, Alt,** and **Del** to restart the system. (Press and hold the Ctrl and Alt keys with your left hand as you click the Del key with your right.)

MY COMPUTER

My Computer enables you to browse all of the drives (floppy disks, hard disks, and CD-ROM drive) that are attached to your computer. It is present on every desktop, but its contents will vary, depending on the specific configuration. Our system, for example, has one floppy drive, one hard disk, and a CD-ROM as shown in Figure 7. Each drive is represented by an icon and is assigned a letter.

The first (often only) floppy drive is designated as drive A, regardless of whether it is a 3½-inch drive or the older, and now nearly obsolete, 5¼-inch drive. A second floppy drive, if it exists, is drive B. Our system contains a single 3½ floppy drive (note the icon in Figure 7a) and is typical of systems purchased in today's environment.

The first (often only) hard disk on a system is always drive C, whether or not there are one or two floppy drives. A system with one floppy drive and one hard disk (today's most common configuration) will contain icons for drive A and drive C. Additional hard drives (if any) and/or the CD-ROM are labeled from D on.

In addition to an icon for each drive on your system, My Computer contains two other folders. (Folders are discussed in the next section.) The *Control Panel* enables you to configure (set up) all of the devices (mouse, sound, and so on) on

ESSENTIALS OF WINDOWS 95 **19**

your system. The **Printers folder** lets you add a new printer and/or view the progress of a printed document.

The contents of My Computer can be displayed in different views (Large Icons, Small Icons, Details, and List) according to your preference or need. You can switch from one view to the next by choosing the appropriate command from the View menu or by clicking the corresponding button on the toolbar.

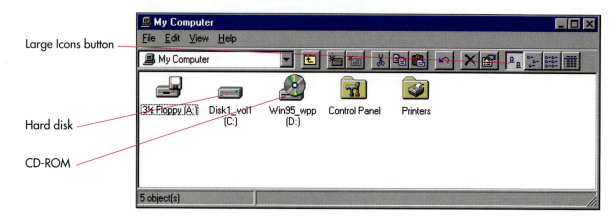

(a) Large Icons

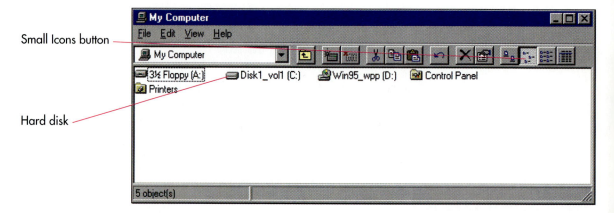

(b) Small Icons

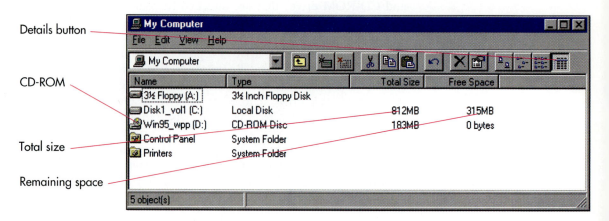

(c) Details View

FIGURE 7   My Computer

The ***Large Icons view*** and ***Small Icons view*** in Figures 7a and 7b, respectively, display each object as a large or small icon. The choice between the two depends on your personal preference. You might, for example, choose large icons if there are only a few objects in the window. Small icons would be preferable if there were many objects and you wanted to see them all. The ***Details view*** in Figure 7c displays additional information about each object. You see the type of object, the total size of the disk, and the remaining space on the disk. (A List view is also available and displays the objects with small icons but without the file details.)

FILES AND FOLDERS

A ***file*** is any data or set of instructions that have been given a name and stored on disk. There are, in general, two types of files, program files and data files. Microsoft Word and Microsoft Excel are program files. The documents and spreadsheets created by these programs are data files. A ***program file*** is executable because it contains instructions that tell the computer what to do. A ***data file*** is not executable and can be used only in conjunction with a specific program.

A file must have a name by which it can be identified. The file name can contain up to 255 characters and may include spaces and other punctuation. (This is very different from the rules that existed under MS-DOS that limited file names to eight characters followed by an optional three-character extension.) Long file names permit descriptive entries such as, *Term Paper for Western Civilization* (as opposed to a more cryptic *TPWCIV* that would be required under MS-DOS).

Files are stored in ***folders*** to better organize the hundreds (often thousands) of files on a hard disk. A Windows folder is similar in concept to a manila folder in a filing cabinet and contains one or more documents (files) that are somehow related to each other. An office worker stores his or her documents in manila folders. In Windows, you store your data files (documents) in electronic folders on disk.

Folders are the key to the Windows storage system. You can create any number of folders to hold your work just as you can place any number of manila folders into a filing cabinet. You can create one folder for your word processing documents and a different folder for your spreadsheets. Alternatively, you can create a folder to hold all of your work for a specific class, which may contain a combination of word processing documents and spreadsheets. The choice is entirely up to you, and you can use any system that makes sense to you. Anything at all can go into a folder—program files, data files, even other folders.

Figure 8 displays two different views of a folder containing six documents. The name of the folder (Homework) appears in the title bar next to the icon of an open folder. The Minimize, Maximize, and Close buttons appear at the right of the title bar. A toolbar appears below the menu bar in each view.

The Details view in Figure 8a displays the name of each file in the folder (note the descriptive file name), the file size, the type of file, and the date and time the file was last modified. Figure 8b shows the Large Icons view, which displays only the file name and an icon representing the application that created the file. The choice between views depends on your personal preference. (A Small Icons view and List view are also available.)

File Type

Every data file has a specific ***file type*** that is determined by the application that created the file initially. One way to recognize the file type is to examine the Type column in the Details view as shown in Figure 8a. The History Term Paper, for

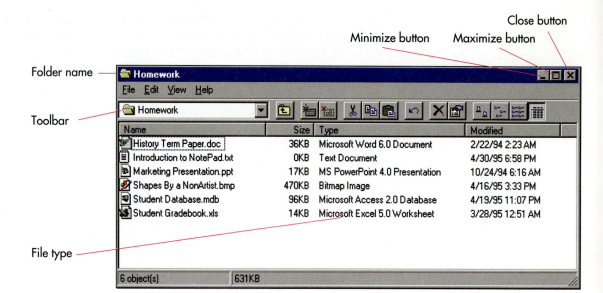

(a) Details View

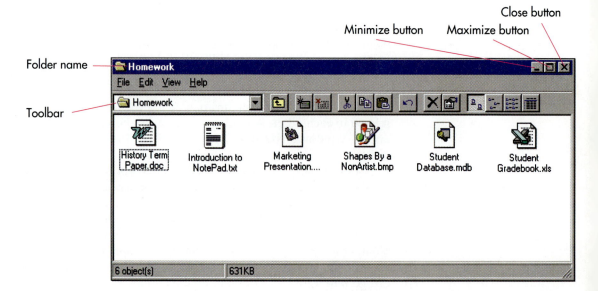

(b) Large Icons View

FIGURE 8 The Homework Folder

example, is a Microsoft Word 6.0 document, and the Student Gradebook is an Excel 5.0 workbook.

You can also determine the file type (or associated application) from any view (not just the Details view) by examining the application icon displayed next to the file name. Look carefully at the icon next to the History Term Paper in Figure 8a, for example, and you will recognize the icon for Microsoft Word. The application icon is recognized more easily in the Large Icons view in Figure 8b.

Still another way to determine the file type is through the three-character extension displayed after the file name. (A period separates the file name from the extension.) Each application has a specific extension, which is automatically assigned to the file name when the file is created. DOC and XLS, for example, are the extensions for Microsoft Word and Excel, respectively. The extension may be suppressed or displayed according to an option in the View menu of My Computer. See step 2 of the hands-on exercise on page 25.

Browsing My Computer

You need to be able to locate a folder and/or its documents quickly so that you can retrieve the documents and go to work. There are several ways to do this, the easiest of which is to browse My Computer. Assume, for example, that you are looking for the Homework folder in Figure 9 in order to work on your term paper for history. Figure 9 shows how easy it is to locate the Homework folder.

You would start by double clicking the My Computer icon on the desktop. This opens the My Computer window and displays all of the drives on your system. Next you would double click the icon for drive C because this is the drive that contains the folder you are looking for. This opens a second window, which displays all of the folders on drive C. And finally you would double click the icon for the Homework folder to open a third window containing the documents in the Homework folder. Once you are in the Homework folder, you would double click the icon of any existing document (which starts the associated application and opens the document), enabling you to begin work.

LEARNING BY DOING

The following exercise has you create a new folder on drive C, then create various files in that folder. The files are created using Notepad and Paint, two accessories that are included in Windows 95. We chose to create the files using these

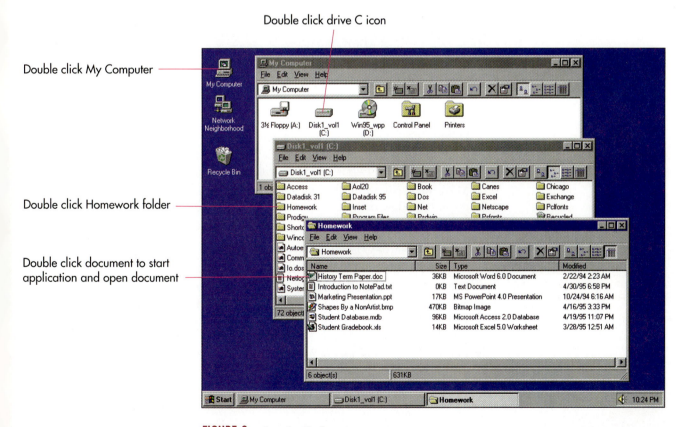

FIGURE 9 Browsing My Computer

simple accessories, rather than more powerful applications such as Word or Excel, because we wanted to create the files quickly and easily. We also wanted to avoid reliance on specific applications that are not part of Windows 95. The emphasis throughout this appendix is the ability to manipulate files within the Windows environment after they have been created.

The exercise also illustrates the document orientation of Windows 95, which enables you to think in terms of the document rather than the application that created it. You simply point to an open folder, click the right mouse button to display a shortcut menu, then select the *New command.* You will be presented with a list of objects (file types) that are recognized by Windows 95 because the associated applications have been previously installed. Choose the file type that you want, and the associated application will be opened automatically. (See step 4 in the following hands-on exercise.)

THE NOTEPAD ACCESSORY

The Notepad accessory is ideal to create "quick and dirty" files that require no formatting and that are smaller than 64K. Notepad opens and saves files in ASCII (text) format only. Use a different editor, e.g., the WordPad accessory or a full-fledged word processor such as Microsoft Word, to create larger files or files that require formatting.

HANDS-ON EXERCISE 2

My Computer

Objective: Open My Computer and create a new folder on drive C. Use the New command to create a Notepad document and a Paint drawing. Use Figure 10 as a guide in the exercise.

STEP 1: Create a Folder

➤ Double click the **My Computer icon** to open My Computer. Double click the **icon** for **drive C** to open a second window as shown in Figure 10a. The size and/or position of your windows will be different from ours.

➤ Make or verify the following selections in each window. (You have to pull down the View menu each time you choose a different command.)
- The **Toolbar command** should be checked.
- The **Status Bar command** should be checked.
- **Large Icons** should be selected.

➤ If necessary, click anywhere within the window for drive C to make it the active window. (The title bar reflects the internal label of your disk, which was assigned when the disk was formatted. Your label will be different from ours.)

➤ Pull down the **File menu,** click (or point to) **New** to display the submenu, then click **Folder** as shown in Figure 10a.

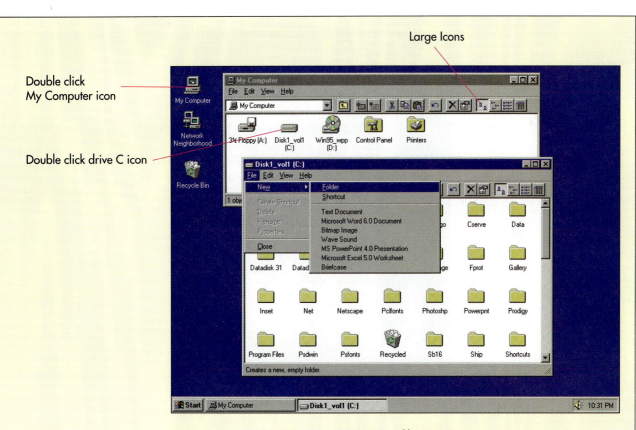

(a) Create a Folder (step 1)

FIGURE 10 Hands-on Exercise 2

ONE WINDOW OR MANY

If opening a window for drive C causes the My Computer window to disappear (and its button to vanish from the taskbar), you need to set an option to open each folder in a separate window. Pull down the View menu, click Options, click the Folder tab, then click the option button to use a separate window for each folder. Click the OK command button to accept this setting and return to the desktop

STEP 2: The View Menu

➤ A new folder has been created within the window for drive C with the name of the folder (New Folder) highlighted. Type **Homework** to change the name of the folder as shown in Figure 10b. Press **enter**.

➤ Pull down the **View menu** and click the **Arrange Icons command.** Click **By Name** to arrange the folders alphabetically within the window for drive C.

➤ Pull down the **View menu** a second time. Click **Options,** then click the **View tab** in the Options dialog box. Check the box (if necessary) to **Hide MS-DOS file extensions.** Click **OK**.

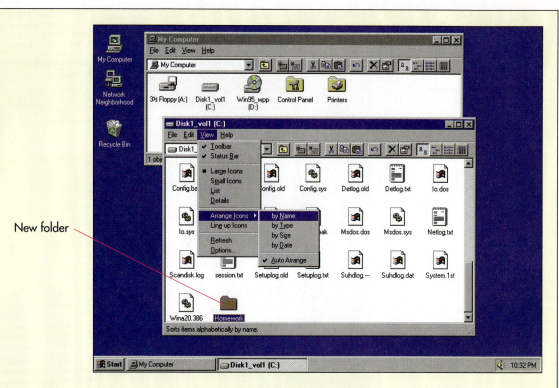

(b) View Menu (step 2)

FIGURE 10 Hands-on Exercise 2 (continued)

RENAME COMMAND

Point to a file or a folder, then click the right mouse button to display a menu with commands pertaining to the object. Click the Rename command. The name of the file or folder will be highlighted with the insertion point (a flashing vertical line) positioned at the end of the name. Type a new name—for example, Homework—to replace the selected name, or click anywhere within the name to change the insertion point and edit the name.

STEP 3: Open the Homework Folder

➤ Click the **Homework folder** to select it. Pull down the **File menu** and click **Open** (or double click the **folder** without pulling down the menu) to open the Homework folder.

➤ The Homework folder opens into a window as shown in Figure 10c. The window is empty because the folder does not contain any documents. If necessary, pull down the **View menu** and check the **Toolbar command** to display the toolbar.

➤ **Right click** a blank position on the taskbar to display the menu in Figure 10c. Click **Tile Vertically** to tile the three open windows.

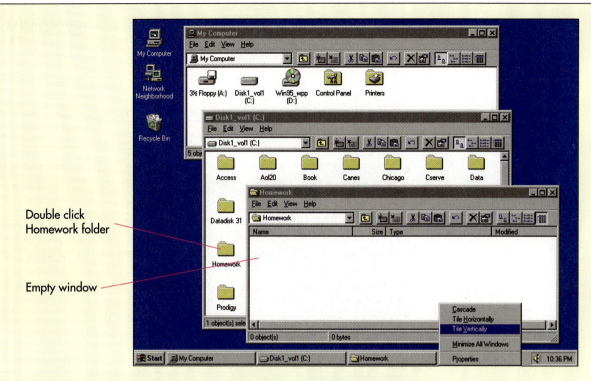

(c) Open the Homework Folder (step 3)

FIGURE 10 Hands-on Exercise 2 (continued)

THE RIGHT MOUSE BUTTON

The right mouse button is the fastest way to change the properties of any object on the desktop or even the desktop itself. Point to a blank area on the desktop, click the right mouse button, then click Properties in the shortcut menu to display the dialog box (property sheet) for the desktop. In similar fashion, you can right click the taskbar to change its properties. You can also right click any icon on the desktop or any icon in a window.

STEP 4: The New Command

➤ The windows on your desktop should be tiled vertically as shown in Figure 10d. Click in the **Homework window.** The title bar for the Homework window should be highlighted, indicating that this is the active window.

➤ Pull down the **File menu** (or point to an empty area in the window and click the right mouse button).

➤ Click (or point to) the **New command** to display a submenu. The document types depend on the installed applications:

  • You may (or may not) see Microsoft Word Document or Microsoft Excel Worksheet, depending on whether or not you have installed these applications.

ESSENTIALS OF WINDOWS 95   27

- You will see Text Document and Bitmap Image, corresponding to the Notepad and Paint accessories that are installed with Windows 95.

➤ Select (click) **Text Document** as the type of file to create as shown below in Figure 10d. The icon for a new document will appear with the name of the document, New Text Document, highlighted.

➤ Type **Files and Folders** to change the name of the document. Press the **enter** key.

THE DOCUMENT, NOT THE APPLICATION

Windows 95 enables you to create a document without first starting the associated application. Select the folder that is to contain the document, pull down the File menu, and click New (or right click an empty space within a folder), then choose the type of document you want to create. Once the document has been created, double click its icon to load the associated application and begin editing the document. In other words, you can think about the document and not the application.

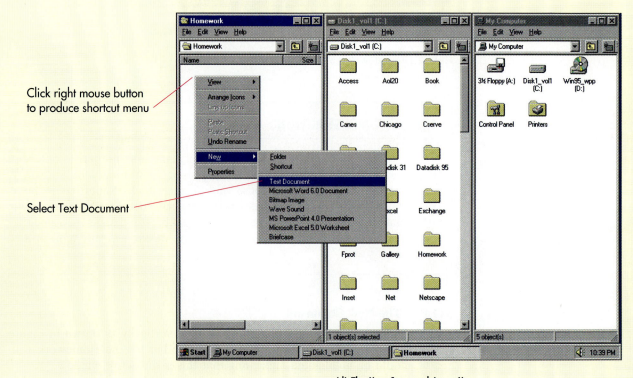

(d) The New Command (step 4)

FIGURE 10 Hands-on Exercise 2 (continued)

STEP 5: Create the Document

➤ If necessary, pull down the **View menu** and change to the **Large Icons view** so that the view in your Homework folder matches the view in Figure 10e.

➤ Select (click) the **Files and Folders document.** Pull down the **File menu.** Click **Open** (or double click the **Files and Folders icon** without pulling down the File menu) to load Notepad and open a Notepad window. The window is empty because the text of the document has not yet been entered.

➤ Pull down the **Edit menu:**

- If there is no check mark next to Word Wrap, click the **Word Wrap** command to enable this feature.
- If there is a check mark next to Word Wrap, click outside the menu to close the menu without changing any settings.

➤ Type the text of the document as shown in Figure 10e. Type just as you would on a regular typewriter with one exception—press the enter key only at the end of a paragraph, not at the end of every line. Since word wrap is in effect, Notepad will automatically start a new line when the word you are typing does not fit at the end of the current line.

➤ Pull down the **File menu** and click **Save** to save the document when you are finished.

➤ Click the **Close button** to close the Notepad accessory.

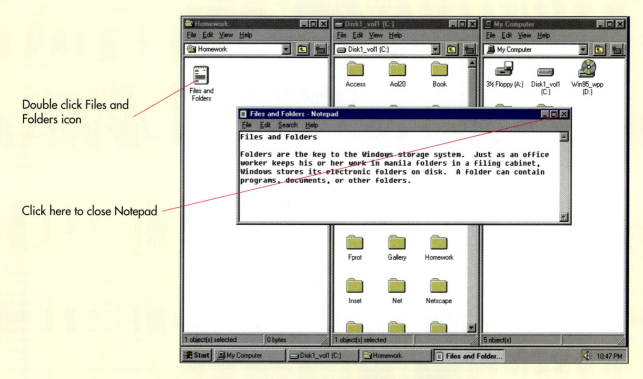

(e) Create the Document (step 5)

FIGURE 10   Hands-on Exercise 2 (continued)

ESSENTIALS OF WINDOWS 95   **29**

FILE EXTENSIONS

Long-time DOS users will recognize a three-character extension at the end of a file name to indicate the file type; for example, TXT to indicate a text (ASCII) file. The extensions are displayed or hidden according to the option you establish through the View menu of My Computer. Open My Computer, pull down the View menu, and click the Options command. Click the View tab, then check (clear) the box to hide (show) MS-DOS file extensions. Click OK.

STEP 6: Create a Drawing

➤ **Right click** within the Homework folder, click the **New command,** then click **Bitmap Image** as the type of file to create. The icon for a new drawing will appear with the name of the drawing (New Bitmap Image) highlighted.

➤ Type **Rectangles** to change the name of the drawing. Press **enter.**

➤ Pull down the **File menu** and click **Open** (or double click the **Rectangles icon** without pulling down the menu) to open a Paint window. The window is empty because the drawing has not yet been created.

➤ Click the **Maximize button** (if necessary) so that the window takes the entire desktop. Create a drawing of various rectangles as shown in Figure 10f.

➤ To draw a rectangle:
  • Select (click) the rectangle tool.

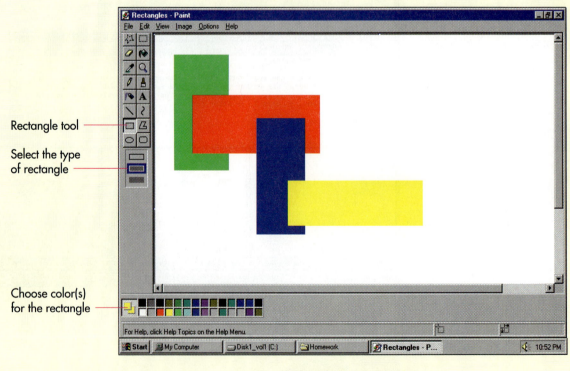

(f) Create the Drawing (step 6)

FIGURE 10   Hands-on Exercise 2 (continued)

- Select (click) the type of rectangle you want (a border only, a filled rectangle with a border, or a filled rectangle with no border).
- Select (click) the colors for the border and fill using the left and right mouse button, respectively.
- Click in the drawing area, then click and drag to create the rectangle.

➤ Pull down the **File menu** and click **Save As** to produce the Save As dialog box. Change the file type to **16-Color Bitmap** (from the default 256-color bitmap) to create a smaller file and conserve space on the floppy disk.

➤ Click **Save.** Click **Yes** to replace the file.

➤ Click the **Close button** to close Paint when you have finished the drawing.

THE PAINT ACCESSORY

The Paint accessory enables you to create simple or (depending on your ability) elaborate drawings. There is a sense of familiarity to the application since it follows the common user interface and consistent command structure common to all Windows applications. The Open, Save, and Print commands, for example, are found in the File menu. The Cut, Copy, Paste, and Undo commands are in the Edit menu. There is also a Help menu, which explains the various Paint commands and which functions identically to the Help menu in all Windows applications.

STEP 7: Edit the Document

➤ Double click the **Files and Folders icon** to reopen the document in a Notepad window. Pull down the **Edit menu** and toggle **Word Wrap on.** Press **Ctrl+End** to move to the end of the document.

➤ Add the additional text as shown in Figure 10g. Do *not* save the document at this time.

➤ Click the **Close button** to exit Notepad. You will see the informational message in Figure 10g, which indicates you have forgotten to save the changes. Click **Yes** to save the changes and exit.

DOS NOTATION

The visually oriented storage system within Windows 95 makes it easy to identify folders and the documents within those folders. DOS, however, was not so simple and used a text-based notation to indicate the drive, folder, and file. For example, C:\HOMEWORK\FILES AND FOLDERS specifies the file FILES AND FOLDERS, in the HOMEWORK folder, on drive C.

STEP 8: Change the View

➤ Right click an empty space on the taskbar, then click the **Tile Horizontally command** to tile the windows as shown in Figure 10h. (The order of your windows may be different from ours.)

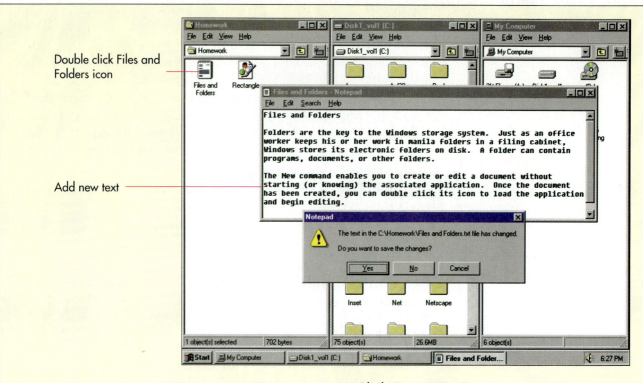

(g) Edit the Document (step 7)

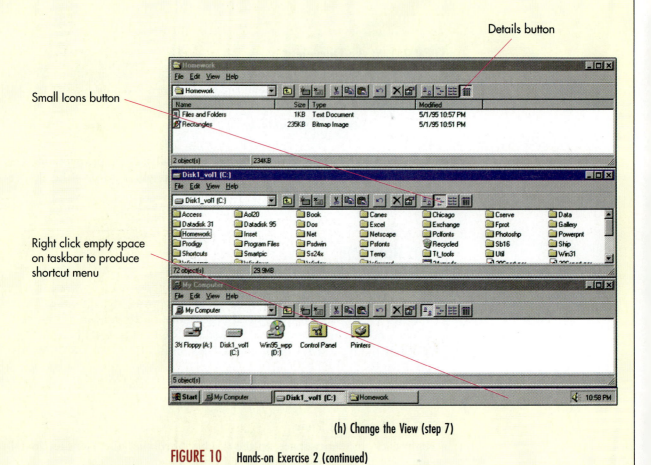

(h) Change the View (step 7)

FIGURE 10 Hands-on Exercise 2 (continued)

> Click in the window for the **Homework folder,** then click the **Details button** on the toolbar to display the details view.
> Press the **F5 key** to refresh the window and update the file properties (the file size, type, and the date and time of the last modification).
> Click in the window for drive C, then click the **List view** or **Small Icons button** on the toolbar to display small icons as shown in Figure 10h.

STEP 9: Exit Windows
> Click the **Close button** in each of the three open windows (My Computer, drive C, and Homework) to close each window.
> Exit Windows if you do not want to continue with the next exercise at this time.

FILE OPERATIONS

The exercise just completed had you create a folder and place documents in that folder. As you continue to work on the computer, you will create additional folders, as well as files within those folders. Learning how to manage those files is one of the most important skills you can acquire. This section describes the different types of file operations that you will perform on a daily basis.

Moving and Copying a File

There are two basic ways to move or copy a file from one location to another. You can use the *Cut, Copy,* and *Paste commands,* or you can simply drag and drop the files from one location to the other. Both techniques require you to open the disk or folder containing the source file (the file you are moving or copying) in order to select the file you will move or copy. This is typically done by opening successive windows through My Computer.

Assume, for example, that you want to copy a file from the Homework folder on drive C to a floppy disk in drive A. You would begin by double clicking the My Computer icon to open the My Computer window. Then you would double click the icon for drive C because that is the drive containing the file you want to copy. And then you would double click the icon for the Homework folder (opening a third window) because that is the folder containing the file to be copied.

To copy the file (after the Homework folder has been opened), select the file by clicking its icon, then drag the icon to the drive A icon in the My Computer window. (Alternatively, you could select the file, pull down the Edit menu, and click the Copy command, then click the icon for drive A, pull down the Edit menu, and click the Paste command.) It sounds complicated, but it's not and you will get a chance to practice in the hands-on exercise.

Backup

It's not a question of if it will happen, but when—hard disks die, files are lost, or viruses may infect a system. It has happened to us and it will happen to you, but you can prepare for the inevitable by creating adequate *backup* before the problem occurs. The essence of a backup strategy is to decide which files to back up, how often to do the backup, and where to keep the backup. Once you decide on a strategy, follow it, and follow it faithfully!

Our strategy is very simple—back up what you can't afford to lose, do so on a daily basis, and store the backup away from your computer. You need not copy every file, every day. Instead copy just the files that changed during the current session. Realize, too, that it is much more important to back up your data files, rather than your program files. You can always reinstall the application from the original disks, or if necessary, go to the vendor for another copy of an application. You, however, are the only one who has a copy of the term paper that is due tomorrow.

Deleting Files

The **Delete command** deletes (removes) a file from a disk. If, however, the file was deleted from a hard disk, it is not really gone, but moved instead to the Recycle Bin from where it can be subsequently recovered.

The **Recycle Bin** is a special folder that contains all of the files that were previously deleted from any hard disk on your system. Think of the Recycle Bin as similar to the wastebasket in your room. You throw out (delete) a report by tossing it into a wastebasket. The report is gone (deleted) from your desk, but you can still get it back by taking it out of the wastebasket as long as the basket wasn't emptied. The Recycle Bin works the same way. Files are not deleted from the hard disk per se, but are moved instead to the Recycle Bin from where they can be recovered. The Recycle Bin should be emptied periodically, however, or else you will run out of space on the disk. Once a file is removed from the Recycle Bin, it can no longer be recovered.

WRITE-PROTECT YOUR BACKUP DISKS

You can write-protect a floppy disk to ensure that its contents are not accidentally altered or erased. A 3½-inch disk is write-protected by sliding the built-in tab so that the write-protect notch is open. The disk is write-enabled when the notch is covered. The procedure is reversed for a 5¼-inch disk; that is, the disk is write-protected when the notch is covered and write-enabled when the notch is open.

HANDS-ON EXERCISE 3

File Operations

Objective: Copy a file from drive C to drive A, and from drive A back to drive C. Delete a file from drive C, then restore the file using the Recycle Bin. Demonstrate the effects of write-protecting a disk. Use Figure 11 as a guide in the exercise.

STEP 1: Open the Homework Folder

▶ Double click the **icon** for **My Computer** to open My Computer. Double click the **icon** for **drive C** to open a second window showing the contents of drive C. Double click the **Homework folder** to open a third window showing the contents of the Homework folder.

➤ Right click the taskbar to tile the windows vertically as shown in Figure 11a. Your windows may appear in a different order from those in the figure.

➤ Make or verify the following selections in each window. (You have to pull down the View menu each time you choose a different command.)

- The **Toolbar command** should be checked.
- The **Status Bar command** should be checked.
- Choose the **Details view** in the Homework window and the **Large Icons view** in the other windows.

➤ Pull down the **View menu** in any open window. Click **Options,** then click the **View tab** in the Options dialog box. Check the box (if necessary) to **Hide MS-DOS file extensions.** Click **OK** to exit the dialog box.

> ### QUICK VIEW
>
> If you forget what is in a particular document, you can use the Quick View command to preview the document without having to open it. Select (click) the file you want to preview, then pull down the File menu and click Quick View (or right click the file and select the Quick View command) to display the file in a preview window. If you decide to edit the file, pull down the File menu and click Open File for Editing; otherwise click the Close button to close the preview window.

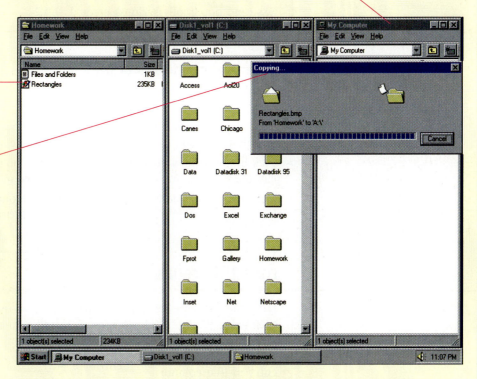

(a) Copy to Drive A (step 1)

FIGURE 11 Hands-on Exercise 3

STEP 2: Backup the Homework Folder

➤ Place a freshly formatted disk in drive A. Be sure that the disk is not write-protected or else you will not be able to copy files to the disk.

➤ Click and drag the icon for the **Rectangles file** from the Homework folder to the icon for **drive A** in the My Computer window.

- You will see the ⊘ symbol as you drag the file until you reach a suitable destination (e.g., until you point to the icon for drive A). The ⊘ symbol will change to a plus sign when the icon for drive A is highlighted, indicating that the file can be copied successfully.

- Release the mouse to complete the copy operation. You will see a popup window as shown in Figure 11a, indicating the progress of the copy operation. This takes several seconds since Rectangles is a large file (235KB).

➤ Click and drag the icon for the **Files and Folders file** from the Homework folder to the icon for drive A. You may or may not see a popup window showing the copy operation since the file is small (1KB) and copies quickly.

USE THE RIGHT MOUSE BUTTON TO MOVE OR COPY A FILE

The result of dragging a file with the left mouse button depends on whether the source and destination folders are on the same or different drives. Dragging a file to a folder on a different drive copies the file. Dragging the file to a folder on the same drive moves the file. If you find this hard to remember, and most people do, click and drag with the right mouse button to produce a shortcut menu asking whether you want to copy or move the file. This simple tip can save you from making a careless (and potentially serious) error. Use it!

STEP 3: View the Contents of Drive A

➤ Double click the **icon** for **drive A** in the My Computer window to open a fourth window.

➤ Right click a blank area on the taskbar. Tile the windows vertically or horizontally (it doesn't matter which) to display the windows as in Figure 11b.

➤ Click in the window for drive A. If necessary, pull down the **View menu,** display the toolbar, and change to the **Details view.**

➤ Compare the file details for each file in the Homework folder and drive A; the details are identical, reflecting the fact that the files have been copied.

CHANGE THE COLUMN WIDTH

Drag the right border of a column heading to the right (left) to increase (decrease) the width of the column in order to see more (less) information in that column. Double click the right border of a column heading to automatically adjust the column width to accommodate the widest entry in that column.

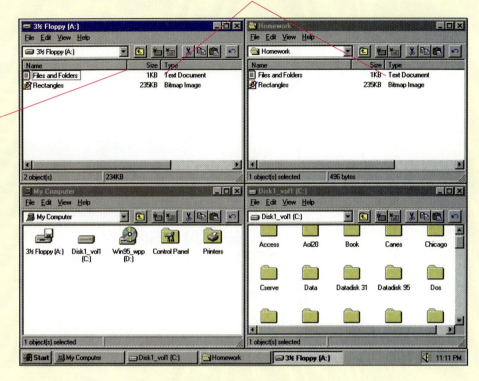

(b) View the Contents of Drive A (step 3)

FIGURE 11 Hands-on Exercise 3 (continued)

STEP 4: Delete a File

➤ Select (click) the **Files and Folders icon** in the Homework folder. Pull down the **File menu.** Click **Delete.**

➤ You will see the dialog box in Figure 11c, asking whether you want to delete the file. Click **Yes** to delete the file.

➤ Right click the **Rectangles icon** in the Homework folder to display a shortcut menu. Click **Delete.**

➤ Click **Yes** when asked whether to delete the Rectangles file. The Homework folder is now empty.

THE UNDO COMMAND

The Undo command pertains not just to application programs such as Notepad or Paint, but to file operations as well. It will, for example, undelete a file if it is executed immediately after the Delete command. Pull down the Edit menu and click Undo to reverse (undo) the last command. Some operations cannot be undone (in which case the command will be dimmed out), but Undo is always worth a try.

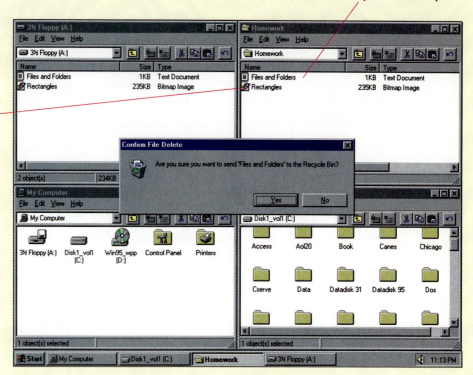

(c) Delete a File (step 4)

FIGURE 11   Hands-on Exercise 3 (continued)

STEP 5: Copy from Drive A to Drive C

➤ The backup you did in step 2 enables you to copy (restore) the Files and Folders file from drive A to drive C. You can do this in one of two ways:

- Select (click) the **Files and Folders icon** in the window for drive A. Pull down the **Edit menu.** Click **Copy.** Click in the **Homework folder.** Pull down the **Edit menu.** Click **Paste** as shown in Figure 11d.
- Click and drag the **icon** for the **Files and Folders file** from drive A to the Homework folder.

➤ Either way, you will see a popup window showing the Files and Folders file being copied from drive A to drive C.

➤ Use whichever technique you prefer to copy the Rectangles file from drive A to drive C.

BACK UP IMPORTANT FILES

We cannot overemphasize the importance of adequate backup and urge you to copy your data files to floppy disks and store those disks away from your computer. It takes only a few minutes, but you will thank us, when (not if) you lose an important file and wish you had another copy.

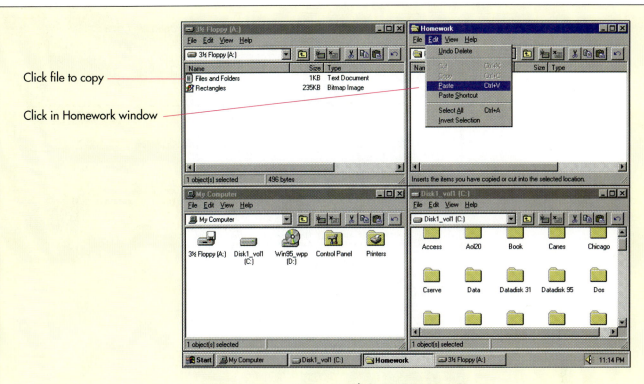

(d) Copy to Drive C (step 5)

FIGURE 11 Hands-on Exercise 3 (continued)

STEP 6: Modify a File

➤ Double click the **Files and Folders icon** in the Homework folder to reopen the file as shown in Figure 11e. Pull down the **Edit menu** and toggle **Word Wrap on.**

➤ Press **Ctrl+End** to move to the end of the document. Add the paragraph shown in Figure 11e.

➤ Pull down the **File menu** and click **Save** to save the modified file. Click the **Close button** to close the file.

➤ The Files and Folders document has been modified and should once again be backed up to drive A. Click and drag the **icon** for **Files and Folders** from the Homework folder to the drive A window.

➤ You will see a message indicating that the folder (drive A) already contains a file called Files and Folders (which was previously copied in step 2) and asking whether you want to replace the existing file with the new file. Click **Yes.**

THE SEND TO COMMAND

The Send To command is an alternative way to copy a file to a floppy disk and has the advantage that the floppy disk icon need not be visible. Select (click) the file to copy, then pull down the File menu (or simply right click the file). Click the Send To command, then select the appropriate floppy drive from the resulting submenu.

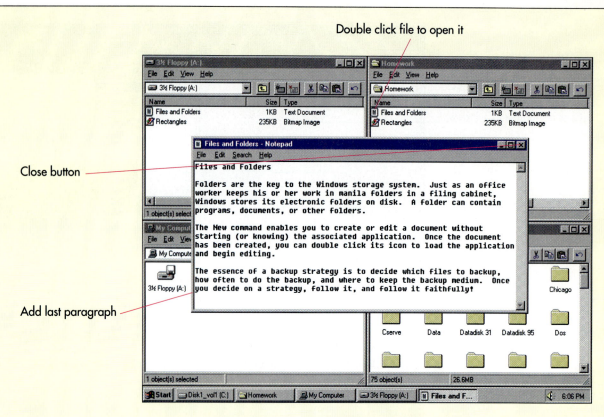

(e) Modify the File (step 6)

FIGURE 11 Hands-on Exercise 3 (continued)

STEP 7: Write-protect a Disk

➤ You can write-protect a floppy disk so that its contents cannot be changed; that is, existing files cannot be modified or erased nor can new files be added.

➤ Remove the floppy disk from drive A and follow the appropriate procedure:
  • To write-protect a 3½ disk, move the built-in tab so that the write-protect notch is open.
  • To write-protect a 5¼ disk, cover the write-protect notch with a piece of opaque tape.

➤ Return the write-protected disk to the floppy drive.

➤ Click the **icon** for the **Rectangles file** on drive A, then press the **Del key** to delete the file.

➤ You will see a warning message asking whether you are sure you want to delete the file. Click **Yes.**

➤ You will see the error message in Figure 11f, indicating that the file cannot be deleted because the disk is write-protected. Click **OK.**

➤ Remove the write-protection by reversing the procedure you followed earlier. Select the **Rectangles file** a second time and delete the file. Click **Yes** in response to the confirmation message, after which the file will be deleted from drive A.

➤ You have just deleted the Rectangles file, but we want it back on drive A for the next exercise. Accordingly, click and drag the **Rectangles icon** in the Homework folder to the icon for **drive A** in the My Computer window.

Click file to delete, press Del key

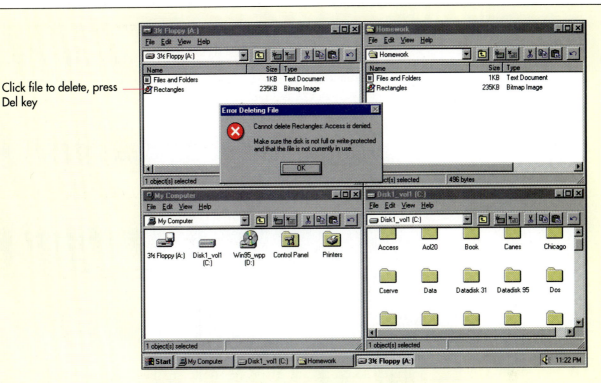

(f) Write-Protect a Disk (step 7)

FIGURE 11   Hands-on Exercise 3 (continued)

➤ Click the **Close button** in the window for drive A.

STEP 8: The Recycle Bin

➤ Select (click) the **Files and Folders icon** in the Homework folder. Pull down the **File menu** and click **Delete.** Click **Yes** in the dialog box asking whether you want to delete the file.

➤ To restore a file, you need to open the Recycle Bin:
  • Double click the **Recycle Bin icon** if you can see the icon on the desktop
  or
  • Double click the **Recycled icon** within the window for drive C. (You may have to scroll in order to see the icon.)

➤ Right click a blank area on the taskbar, then tile the open windows as shown in Figure 11g. The position of your windows may be different from ours. The view in the Recycle Bin may also be different.

➤ Your Recycle Bin contains all files that have been previously deleted from drive C, and hence you may see a different number of files than those displayed in Figure 11g.

➤ Scroll until you can select the (most recent) **Files and Folders icon.** Pull down the **File menu** and click the **Restore command.** The Files and Folders file is returned to the Homework folder.

EMPTY THE RECYCLE BIN

All files that are deleted from a hard drive are automatically moved to the Recycle Bin. This enables you to restore (undelete) a file, but it also prevents you from recovering the space taken up by those files. Accordingly, you should periodically delete files from the Recycle Bin or otherwise you will find yourself running out of space on your hard disk. Be careful, though, because once you delete a file from the Recycle Bin, it is gone for good!

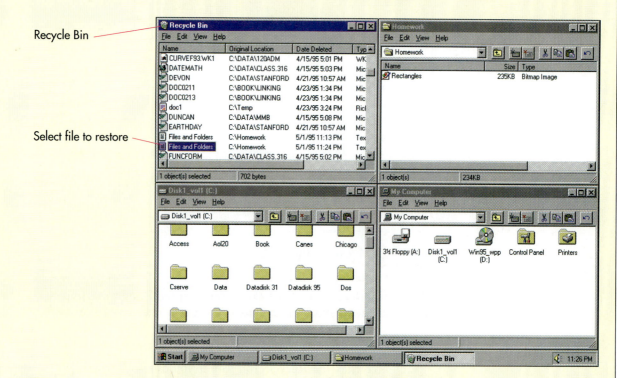

(g) The Recycle Bin (step 8)

FIGURE 11   Hands-on Exercise 3 (continued)

STEP 9: Exit Windows

➤ Click the **Close button** in each of the four open windows (the Recycle Bin, My Computer, drive C, and Homework) to close each window.

➤ Exit Windows if you do not want to continue with the next exercise.

WINDOWS EXPLORER

The *Windows Explorer* enables you to browse through all of the drives, folders, and files on your system. It does not do anything that could not be accomplished through successive windows via My Computer. The Explorer does, however, let you perform a given task more quickly, and for that reason is preferred by more experienced users.

Assume, for example, that you are taking five classes this semester, and that you are using the computer in each course. You've created a separate folder to hold the work for each class and have stored the contents of all five folders on a single floppy disk. Assume further that you need to retrieve your third English assignment so that you can modify the assignment.

You can use My Computer to browse the system as shown in Figure 12a. You would start by opening My Computer, double clicking the icon for drive A to open a second window, then double clicking the icon for the English folder to display its documents. The process is intuitive, but it can quickly lead to a desktop cluttered with open windows. And what if you next needed to work on a paper for Art History? That would require you to open the Art History folder, which produces yet another open window on the desktop.

The Explorer window in Figure 12b offers a more sophisticated way to browse the system as it shows the hierarchy of folders as well as the contents of the selected folder. The Explorer window is divided into two panes. The left pane contains a tree diagram of the entire system, showing all drives and optionally the folders in each drive. One (and only one) object is always selected in the left pane, and its contents are displayed automatically in the right pane.

Look carefully at the tree diagram in Figure 12b and note that the English folder is currently selected. The icon for the selected folder is an open folder to differentiate it from the other folders, which are closed and are not currently selected. The right pane displays the contents of the selected folder (English in Figure 12b) and is seen to contain three documents, Assignments 1, 2, and 3. The right pane is displayed in the Details view, but could just as easily have been displayed in another view (e.g., Large or Small Icons) by clicking the appropriate button on the toolbar.

As indicated, only one folder can be selected (open) at a time in the left pane, and its contents are displayed in the right pane. To see the contents of a different folder (e.g., Accounting), you would select (click) the Accounting folder, which will automatically close the English folder.

The tree diagram in the left pane displays the drives and their folders in hierarchical fashion. The desktop is always at the top of the hierarchy and contains My Computer, which in turn contains various drives, each of which contains folders, which in turn contain documents and/or additional folders. Each object may be expanded or collapsed to display or hide its subordinates.

Look again at the icon next to My Computer in Figure 12b, and you see a minus sign indicating that My Computer has been expanded to show the various drives on the system. There is also a minus sign next to the icon for drive A to indicate that it too has been expanded to show the folders on the disk. Note, however, the plus sign next to drives C and D, indicating that these parts of the tree are currently collapsed and thus their subordinates are not visible.

A folder may contain additional folders, and thus individual folders may also be expanded or collapsed. The minus sign to the left of the Finance folder in Figure 12b, for example, shows that the folder has been expanded and contains two additional folders, for Assignments and Spreadsheets, respectively. The plus sign next to the Accounting folder, however, indicates the opposite; that is, the folder is collapsed and its folders are not currently visible. A folder with neither a plus or minus sign, such as Art History or Marketing, means that the folder does not contain additional folders and cannot be expanded or collapsed.

The advantage of the Windows Explorer over My Computer is the uncluttered screen and ease with which you switch from one folder to the next. If, for example, you wanted to see the contents of the Art History folder, all you would do would be to click its icon in the left pane, which automatically changes the right pane to show the documents in Art History. The Explorer also makes it easy to move or copy a file from one folder or drive to another as you will see in the hands-on exercise that follows shortly.

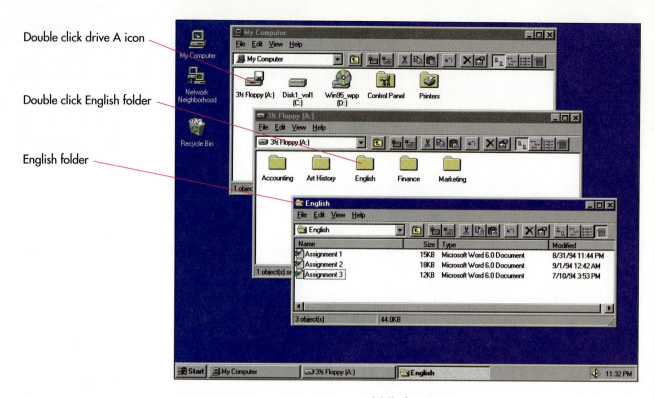

(a) My Computer

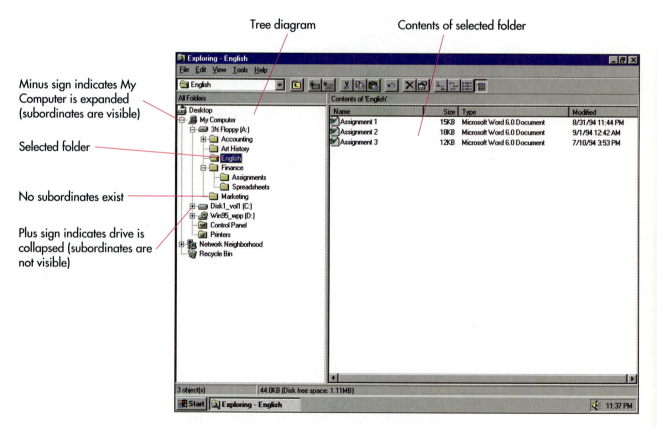

(b) Explorer

FIGURE 12 Browsing a System

ORGANIZE YOUR WORK

A folder may contain anything at all—program files, document files, or even other folders. Organize your folders in ways that make sense to you such as a separate folder for every class you are taking. You can also create folders within a folder; for example, a correspondence folder may contain two folders of its own, one for business correspondence and one for personal letters.

LEARN BY DOING

The Explorer is especially useful for moving or copying files from one folder or drive to another. You simply open the folder that contains the file, use the scroll bar in the left pane (if necessary) so that the destination folder is visible, then drag the file from the right pane to the destination folder. The Explorer is a powerful tool, but it takes practice to master.

The next exercise illustrates the procedure for moving and copying files and uses the floppy disk from the previous exercise. The disk already contains two files—one Notepad document and one Paint drawing. The exercise has you create an additional document of each type so that there are a total of four files on the floppy disk. You then create two folders on the floppy disk, one for drawings and one for documents, and move the respective files into each folder. And finally, you copy the contents of each folder from drive A to a different folder on drive C. By the end of the exercise you will have had considerable practice in both moving and copying files.

HANDS-ON EXERCISE 4

Windows Explorer

Objective: Use the Windows Explorer to copy and move a file from one folder to another. Use Figure 13 as a guide in the exercise.

STEP 1: Open the Windows Explorer

➤ Click the **Start button.** Click (or point to) the **Programs command** to display the Programs menu. Click **Windows Explorer.**

➤ Click the **Maximize button** so that the Explorer takes the entire desktop as shown in Figure 13a. Do not be concerned if your screen is different from ours.

➤ Make or verify the following selections using the **View menu.** (You have to pull down the View menu each time you choose a different command.)
- The **Toolbar command** should be checked.
- The **Status Bar command** should be checked.
- The **Details view** should be selected.

➤ Pull down the **View menu** a second time. Click **Options,** then click the **View tab** in the Options dialog box. Check the box (if necessary) to **Hide MS-DOS file extensions.** Click **OK.**

ESSENTIALS OF WINDOWS 95 **45**

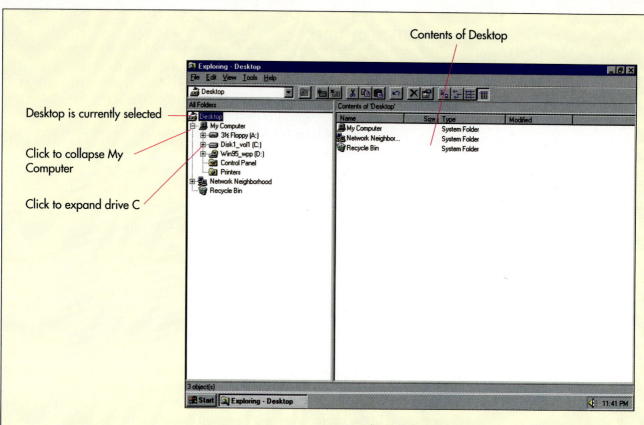

(a) Open the Windows Explorer (step 1)

FIGURE 13 Hands-on Exercise 4

STEP 2: Collapse and Expand My Computer

➤ Click (select) the **Desktop icon** in the left pane to display the contents of the desktop in the right pane. Our desktop contains only the icons for My Computer, Network Neighborhood, and the Recycle Bin. Your desktop may have different icons.

➤ Toggle back and forth between expanding and collapsing My Computer by clicking the plus or minus sign that appears next to the icon for My Computer. Clicking the plus sign expands My Computer, after which a minus sign is displayed. Clicking the minus sign collapses My Computer and changes to a plus sign. End with My Computer expanded and the **minus sign** displayed as shown in Figure 13a.

➤ Place the disk from the previous exercise in drive A. Expand and collapse each drive within My Computer. (Drive A does not have any folders at this time, and hence will have neither a plus nor a minus sign.)

➤ End with a **plus sign** next to drive C so that the hard drive is collapsed as shown in Figure 13a. (The contents of My Computer will depend on your particular configuration.)

STEP 3: Create a Notepad Document

➤ Click the **icon** for **drive A** in the left pane to view the contents of the disk in the right pane. You should see the Files and Folders and Rectangles files that were created in the previous exercise.

➤ Pull down the **File menu.** Click (or point to) **New** to display the submenu. Click **Text Document** as the type of file to create.

➤ The icon for a new document will appear with the name of the document (New Text Document) highlighted. Type **About Explorer** to change the name of the document. Press **enter.** Double click the **file icon** to open the Notepad accessory and create the document.

➤ Move and/or size the Notepad window to your preference. You can also maximize the window so that you have more room in which to work.

➤ Pull down the **Edit menu** and toggle **Word Wrap** on. Enter the text of the document as shown in Figure 13b.

➤ Pull down the **File menu** and click **Save** to save the document when you are finished. Click the **Close button** to close Notepad and return to the Explorer.

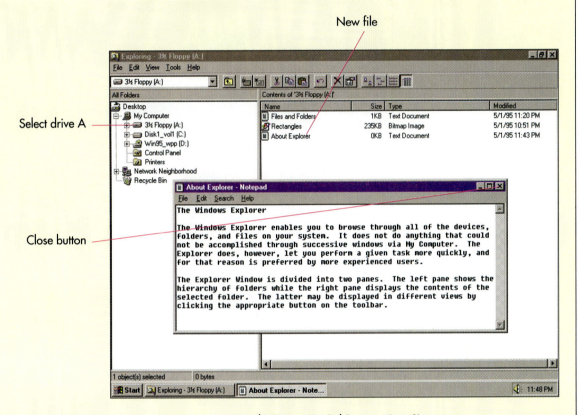

(b) Create a NotePad Document (step 3)

FIGURE 13 Hands-on Exercise 4 (continued)

STEP 4: Create a Paint Drawing

➤ Click the **icon** for **drive A** in the Explorer window, then pull down the **File menu.** (Alternatively, you can click the **right mouse button** in the right pane of the Explorer window when drive A is selected in the left pane.)

➤ Click (or point to) the **New command** to display the submenu. Click **Bitmap Image** as the type of file to create.

➤ The icon for a new drawing will appear with the name of the file (New Bitmap Image) highlighted. Type **Circles** to change the name of the file. Press **enter.** Double click the **file icon** to open the Paint accessory and create the drawing.

➤ Move and/or size the Paint window to your preference. You can also maximize the window so that you have more room in which to work.

➤ Create a simple drawing consisting of various circles and ellipses as shown in Figure 13c.

➤ Pull down the **File menu.** Click **Save As** to produce the Save As dialog box. Change the file type to **16-Color Bitmap** (from the default 256-color bitmap) to create a smaller file and conserve space on the floppy disk. Click **Save.** Click **Yes** to replace the file.

➤ Click the **Close button** to close Paint and return to the Explorer.

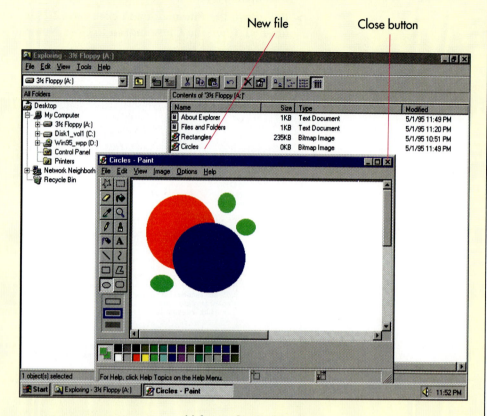

(c) Create a Drawing (step 4)

FIGURE 13 Hands-on Exercise 4 (continued)

STEP 5: Create the Folders

➤ If necessary, click the **icon** for **drive A** in the left pane of the Explorer window. Drive A should contain four files as shown in Figure 13d (the folders have not yet been created).

➤ Pull down the **File menu,** click (or point to) the **New command,** then click **Folder** as the type of object to create.

➤ The icon for a new folder will appear with the name of the folder (New Folder) highlighted. Type **Documents** to change the name of the folder. Press **enter.**

➤ Click the **icon** for **drive A** in the left pane. Pull down the **File menu.** Click (or point to) the **New command.** Click **Folder** as the type of object to create.

➤ The icon for a new folder will appear with the name of the folder (New Folder) highlighted. Type **Drawings** to change the name of the folder. Press **enter.** The right pane should now contain four documents and two folders.

➤ Pull down the **View menu.** Click (or point to) the **Arrange Icons command** to display a submenu, then click the **By Name command.**

➤ Click the **plus sign** next to drive A to expand the drive. Your screen should match Figure 13d:
- The left pane shows the subordinate folders on drive A.
- The right pane displays the contents of drive A (the selected object in the left pane). The folders are shown first and appear in alphabetical order. The document names are displayed after the folders and are also in alphabetical order.

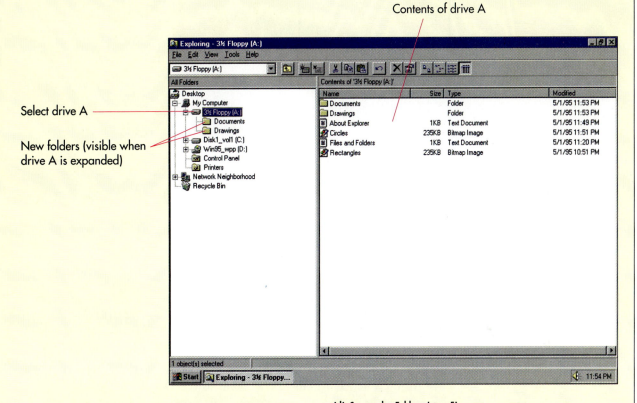

(d) Create the Folders (step 5)

FIGURE 13   Hands-on Exercise 4 (continued)

STEP 6: Move the Files

➤ This step has you move the Notepad documents and Paint drawings to the Documents and Drawings folders, respectively.

➤ To move the About Explorer document:
- Point to the **icon** for **About Explorer** in the right pane. Use the **right mouse button** to click and drag the icon to the Documents folder in the left pane.
- Release the mouse to display the menu shown in Figure 13e. Click **Move Here** to move the file. A popup window will appear briefly as the file is being moved.

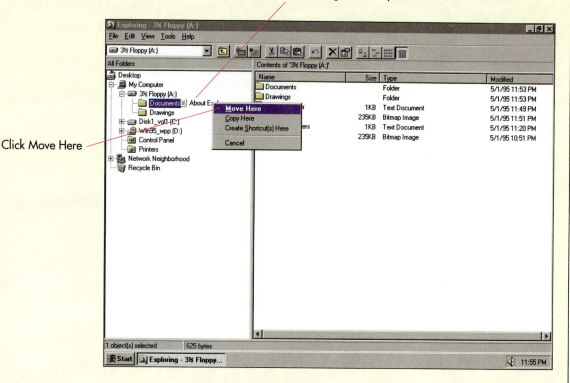

(e) Move the Files (step 6)

FIGURE 13 Hands-on Exercise 4 (continued)

➤ To prove that the file has been moved, you can view the contents of the Documents folder:
  • Click the **Documents folder** in the left pane to select the folder. The icon for the Documents folder changes to an open folder and its contents (About Explorer) are displayed in the right pane.
➤ Move the Files and Folders document to the Documents folder:
  • Click the **icon** for **drive A** to select the drive and display its contents.
  • Point to the **icon** for **Files and Folders.** Use the **right mouse button** to click and drag the icon to the Documents folder in the left pane.
  • Release the mouse to display a menu. Click **Move Here** to move the file.
➤ Use the **right mouse button** to move the Circles and Rectangles files to the Drawings folder.

STEP 7: Copy the Contents of the Documents Folder

➤ This step has you copy the contents of the Documents folder on drive A to the Homework folder on drive C. Click (select) the **Documents folder** on drive A to open the folder and display its contents as shown in Figure 13f.
➤ Click the **plus sign** next to the icon for drive C to expand the drive and display its folders. You should see the Homework folder that was created in the first exercise. Do *not* click the folder on drive C as the Documents folder on drive A is to remain open.

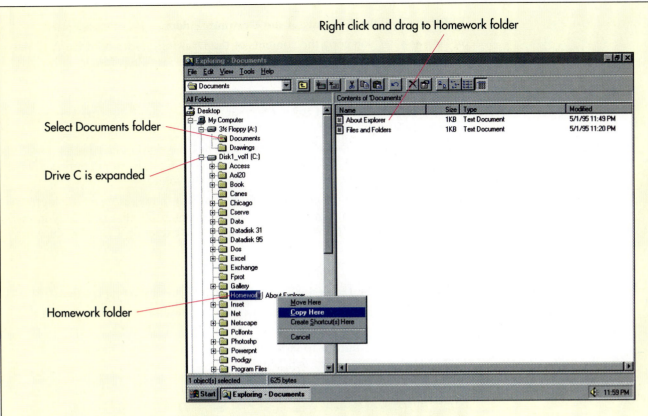

(f) Copy to Drive C (step 7)

FIGURE 13 Hands-on Exercise 4 (continued)

➤ Point to the **About Explorer file** (in the Documents folder on drive A). Use the **right mouse button** to click and drag the icon to the Homework folder on drive C. Release the mouse. Click **Copy Here** to copy the file to the Homework folder.

➤ Point to the **Files and Folders file** (in the Documents folder on drive A). Use the **right mouse button** to click and drag the icon to the Homework folder on drive C. Release the mouse. Click **Copy Here.**

➤ You will see a dialog box asking whether you want to replace the Files and Folders file that is already in the Homework folder (from the previous hands-on exercise). Click **No** since the files are the same.

OPEN FOLDERS QUICKLY

Click in the left pane of the Explorer window, then type any letter to select (open) the first folder whose name begins with that letter. If you type two letters in quick succession—for example, W and O—you will open the first folder beginning with the letters W and O. Pausing between the letters—that is, typing W, then leisurely typing O—will open a folder beginning with W, then open a second folder (while closing the first) whose name begins with O.

STEP 8: Copy the Contents of the Drawings Folder

➤ This step has you copy the contents of the Drawings folder on drive A to the Homework folder on drive C. Click (select) the **Drawings folder** on drive A to open the folder and display its contents. You should see the Circles and Rectangles files that were moved to this folder in the previous step.

➤ Click the **icon** for the **Circles file,** then press and hold the **Ctrl key** as you click the **icon** for the **Rectangles file** to select both files.

➤ Point to either of the selected files, then click the **right mouse button** as you drag both files to the Homework folder on drive C. Release the mouse. Click **Copy Here** to copy the files to the Homework folder.

➤ Explorer will begin to copy both files. You will, however, see a dialog box asking whether you want to replace the Rectangles file that is already in the Homework folder (from the previous hands-on exercise). Click **No** since the files are the same.

STEP 9: Check Your Work

➤ Select (click) the **Homework folder** on drive C to display its contents.

➤ The icon changes to an open folder, and you should see the four files in Figure 13g.

➤ Click the **Close button** to close Explorer. Click the **Start button.** Click the **Shut Down** command to exit Windows.

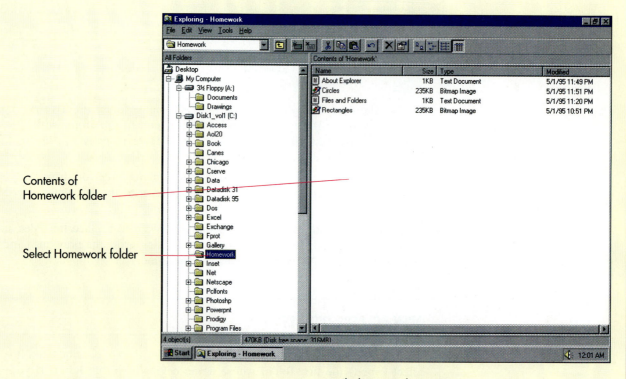

(g) Check Your Work (step 9)

FIGURE 13   Hands-on Exercise 4 (continued)

52   ESSENTIALS OF WINDOWS 95

A PC BUYING GUIDE

OVERVIEW

Are you confused about all the ads for personal computers? You can buy from hundreds of companies, retail or through the mail, with no such thing as a standard configuration. The microprocessor can be one of many 486 or Pentium chips, each of which can be configured with any amount of memory. You can select a desktop, tower, or notebook configuration. You can choose a variety of monitors in different sizes, and can input data from one of many keyboards, a mouse, a trackball, or even a touch screen. Hard disks run up to 1GB or more. There are fax/modem cards, sound cards, tape backup units, and CD-ROM devices.

The personal computer has, in effect, become a commodity where the consumer is able to select the individual elements in the configuration. And, as with the purchase of any other big-ticket item, you must understand what you are buying, so that the decision you make is right for you. This appendix will familiarize you with the components in a computer system so that you can select the machine best suited to your needs and budget.

DON'T FORGET THE SOFTWARE

Any machine you buy will come with Windows 95, but that is only the beginning since you must also purchase the application software you intend to run. Many first-time buyers are surprised that they have to pay extra for software, but you had better allow for software in your budget. A software suite, purchased at an educational discount through the university bookstore, is generally your best bet. The software is at least as important as the hardware, because it is the software that drives the hardware and determines how successful a system will be in meeting your objectives.

THE PERSONAL COMPUTER

The personal computer is a marvel of miniaturization and technology. We take it for granted, but the IBM PC, which jump-started the industry, is just a teenager. IBM announced the PC in 1981 (three years after the Apple II) and broke a long-standing corporate tradition by going to external sources for supporting hardware and software. The *microprocessor* inside the PC was produced by **Intel Corporation.** The operating system was developed by **Microsoft Corporation.**

In terms of today's capabilities, IBM's initial offering was hardly spectacular. A fully loaded system with two floppy disk drives (a hard disk was not available), monochrome monitor, and 80 cps (character per second) dot matrix printer sold for $4425. Software was practically nonexistent. Lotus 1-2-3 had not yet been released, and WordPerfect was a little-known program not yet modified to run on the PC. Yet the PC, with little software and limited hardware, was an instant success for two reasons. The IBM name, and its reputation for quality and service, meant that corporate America could order the machine and be assured that it would perform as promised.

Of equal, or even greater, significance, was the PC's open design, which meant that independent vendors could offer supporting products to enhance performance. This was accomplished through *expansion slots* that held additional circuit boards that added functionality to the basic PC. IBM made public the technical information to create *expansion cards* (also knows as adapters) so that other companies could build peripherals for the PC, thus enhancing its capabilities. Today you can purchase expansion cards that add sound, increase the number of colors, resolution, and speed of the monitor, or add peripheral devices such as CD-ROMs and tape-backup units that did not exist when the PC was introduced.

PC-compatibles, computers based on the same microprocessor and able to run the same software, began to appear as early as 1982 and offered superior performance for less money. Companies and individuals who were once willing to pay a premium for the IBM name began ordering the "same" machine from other vendors. PC has become a generic term for any computer based on Intel-compatible microprocessors and capable of running Microsoft Windows.

Figure 1 illustrates a typical Windows workstation. We view the system from the front (Figure 1a), the rear (Figure 1b), and from inside the system unit (Figure 1c). Your system will be different from ours, but you should be able to recognize the various components as they are discussed in this appendix. Whether you choose a desktop or tower for your system unit, or whether you purchase a laptop or notebook computer, you will have to decide on each component of your system.

LET YOUR FINGERS DO THE WALKING

A single issue of a computer magazine contains advertisements from many vendors, making it possible to comparison shop from multiple mail-order vendors from the convenience of home. Computer magazines are also the source of the latest technical information, and thus a subscription to a magazine is a must for the serious user. Our three favorites (*PC Computing, PC Magazine,* and *Windows Magazine*) are found on most newsstands.

THE MICROPROCESSOR

The capability of a PC depends in large part on the microprocessor on which it is based. Intel microprocessors are currently in their fifth generation, with each

(a) Front View

(b) Rear View

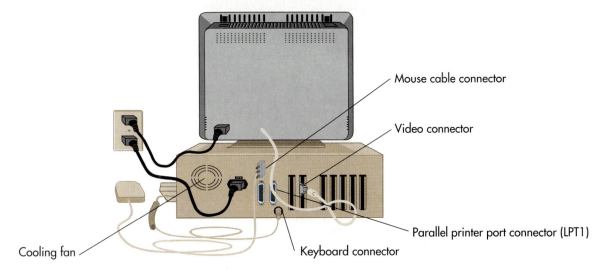

(c) Inside the Computer

FIGURE 1 The Windows Workstation

generation giving rise to increasingly powerful personal computers. All generations are upward compatible; that is, software written for one generation will automatically run on the next. This upward compatibility is crucial because it protects your investment in software when you upgrade to a faster computer.

Today's purchase decision comes down to a fourth or fifth generation microprocessor, either a 486 or a 586 (e.g., a Pentium), as the earlier generations are obsolete. The 486 is manufactured by several companies beside Intel (e.g., AMD or Cyrix). A Pentium, however, is available only from Intel, because Intel has trademarked the Pentium name to differentiate its product from the competition. 586 chips, without the Pentium name, are available from other vendors.

Each generation has multiple microprocessors, which are differentiated by *clock speed,* an indication of how fast instructions are executed. Clock speed is measured in *megahertz (MHz).* The higher the clock speed, the faster the machine. There can also be different versions of a microprocessor at the same clock speed; for example, the SX microprocessor is a less powerful chip than the corresponding DX version.

Intel has also created the DX2 series of chips that double the clock speed of the microprocessor for internal calculations. The DX2/66, for example, is really a 33MHz chip that runs at 66MHz internally, but communicates with other components (e.g., memory) at 33MHz. And finally, Intel has trademarked the DX4 designation to indicate a clock tripling of its 486 chips; for example the DX4/75 is a 25MHz chip that runs internally at 75MHz but communicates with the other components at 25MHz.

Fortunately, however, the technical specifications of the individual microprocessors are not important here. What is important is their relative performance to one another as measured by the *Intel CPU performance index.* The index consists of a single number to indicate the relative performance of a microprocessor: the higher the number, the faster the processor. Figure 2 displays the index values for selected Intel microprocessors (the index does not include Intel-compatible microprocessors manufactured by other vendors). This is the table to use when you are selecting a computer because you want to purchase the fastest machine that you can afford.

Any comparison of one machine to another—for example, an IBM PC to one made by Zeos or Gateway—must be based on the identical microprocessor, or else the comparison will not be valid. Realize, too, that machines based on different microprocessors should reflect a price differential. You would, for example, expect to pay more for a Pentium running at 90 MHz than you would for the same chip running at 66MHz.

CPU	Index Rating
Pentium (133 MHz)	1,110
Pentium (120 MHz)	1,000
Pentium (100 MHz)	815
Pentium (90 MHz)	735
Pentium (75 MHz)	610
Pentium (66 MHz)	567
Pentium (60 MHz)	510
486 DX4 (100 MHz)	435
486 DX4 (75 MHz)	319
486 DX2 (66 MHz)	297
486 DX2 (50 MHz)	231
486 DX (33 MHz)	166
486 SX (33 MHz)	136
486 DX (25 MHz)	122
486 SX (25 MHz)	100
386 DX (33 MHz)	68
386 SX (25 MHz)	49

FIGURE 2 CPU Performance Index

THE MICROPROCESSOR—PAST, PRESENT, AND FUTURE

The IBM PC was based on the 8088 microprocessor, which had the equivalent of 29,000 transistors and was capable of 333,000 instructions per second. Today's Pentium has the equivalent of 3 million transistors and is capable of more than 100,000,000 instructions per second. If the increase in capability continues to hold, and there is every reason to believe that it will, then a 100,000,000 transistor chip, capable of two billion instructions per second, is possible by the year 2000.

MEMORY

The microprocessor is the brain of the PC, but it needs instructions that tell it what to do, data on which to work, and a place to store the results of its calculations. All of this takes place in *memory,* a temporary storage area that holds data, instructions, and results, and passes everything back and forth to the CPU. The amount of memory a system has is important because the larger the memory, the more sophisticated the programs are that the computer is capable of executing, and the more data it can work with.

The *memory* of a computer (also known as *random access memory* or *RAM*) is made up of individual storage locations, each of which holds the same amount of data, one *byte* or one character. In the early days of the PC, memory was measured in *kilobytes (KB).* Today memory is measured in *megabytes (MB).* One KB and one MB are equal to approximately one thousand and one million characters, respectively. (In actuality, 1KB equals 1024 bytes, or 2^{10} bytes, whereas 1MB is 1,048,576 bytes, or 2^{20} bytes.)

A computer's memory is volatile (temporary), and its contents are erased when the power is off. Hence a computer also needs a permanent means of storage that can retain data without power.

DON'T SKIMP ON MEMORY

The more memory a system has, the better its overall performance. Windows and its associated applications are powerful indeed, but they require adequate resources to run efficiently. 8MB of RAM is the minimum you should consider in today's environment, but you should anticipate a future upgrade. Be sure the system you buy can accommodate additional memory easily and inexpensively.

AUXILIARY STORAGE

Unlike memory, magnetic disks are permanent storage devices that retain their contents when the power is off. Disks fall into two categories—*floppy disks* and *hard disks.* A hard disk is also known as a fixed disk because it remains permanently inside the system unit. The floppy disk gets its name because it is made of a flexible Mylar plastic. The hard disk uses rigid metal platters.

A hard disk holds significantly more data than a floppy disk, and it accesses that data much faster. Hard disks are rated by capacity and access time. Capacity is measured in megabytes, and in today's environment you should not purchase any system with less than 350MB of disk space. The *access time* is the time in milliseconds that a disk needs to locate and begin retrieving data. The smaller the access time, the faster the disk, and the more expensive.

The hard disk connects to the motherboard with one of three interfaces: IDE (Integrated Drive Electronics), ESDI (Enhanced Small Device Interface), or SCSI

(Small Computer System Interface). We mention this only because you are likely to see these initials in any advertisement that you read. The IDE technology is the cheapest and most common and more than adequate for the typical Windows user.

A floppy disk (and the corresponding drive) comes in two sizes, 3½ and 5¼ inches. The latter is nearly obsolete and no longer a consideration. The capacity of a 3½ floppy disk is either 720KB or 1.44MB, depending on whether the disk is double density or high density. A **high-density drive** (the only kind you can buy today) can read either a **double-density disk** or a high-density disk. We suggest, however, that you use high-density disks exclusively.

> **MASS STORAGE: BUY MORE THAN YOU NEED**
>
> Windows 95 takes approximately 15 MB of disk space and requires another 20 to 30MB for a swap file. The typical Windows application takes approximately 10 to 15MB of disk space. Multimedia applications require even more. The best advice, therefore, is to buy a bigger disk than you think you need. *A 500 MB disk is a minimum.* You should also check that the system unit has room for a second hard disk that can be added in the future.

VIDEO

The video system consists of the monitor and display adapter (video card). The first consideration is the **resolution** of the monitor, which is defined in terms of **pixels** (the tiny dots or *pic*ture *el*ements that make up a picture). Resolution is stated as the number of pixels across by the number down; for example, **VGA** is 640 across by 480 down. **Super VGA,** another common resolution, is 800 pixels across by 600 pixels down. The higher the resolution, the more of the document (or spreadsheet) you can see at one time.

Any image at a given resolution always contains the same number of pixels; for example, a Windows screen in Super VGA (800 × 600) contains 480,000 pixels regardless of the size of the monitor on which it is displayed. The advantage to the larger monitor is that the individual pixels are bigger and thus the image on the screen is easier to read. The advantage of the higher resolution is that more pixels are displayed and hence you see more on the screen at one time—for example, more columns in a spreadsheet or more pages in a word processing document. Figure 3 lists the available resolutions with the recommended size of the monitor.

The desired resolution and monitor size are selected in conjunction with one another, so that the image displayed on a screen can be easily read. It would be foolish, for example, to display a 1024 × 768 image on a 14-inch screen because the individual pixels would be too small and the display unreadable. Higher resolutions demand bigger monitors, which are significantly more expensive.

The **video (display) adapter** is a separate card that is placed in an expansion slot within the system unit. The video card accepts information from the CPU (central processing unit) and sends it to the monitor, which displays the image. For best performance, the video card should have its own processing capability in the form of an accelerator chip. This enables the CPU to perform other tasks while the image is displayed, thus improving the overall performance of the system. The video card should also have its own memory. A minimum of 1MB is suggested but 2MB is preferable.

Resolution	Number of Pixels	Minimum Screen Size
640 × 480 (VGA)	307,200	14 inches
800 × 600 (Super VGA)	480,000	15 inches
1024 × 768 (Extended VGA)	782,462	17 inches
1280 × 1024	1,310,720	19 inches

FIGURE 3 Resolution and Monitor Size

THE FINER POINTS OF CHOOSING A MONITOR

Do some monitors produce a sharper, crisper picture than others, even at the same resolution? Does the image on one monitor appear to flicker while the image on another remains constant? The differences are due to information that is often buried in the fine print of an advertisement

The ***dot pitch*** is the distance between adjacent pixels. The smaller the dot pitch, the crisper the image; or conversely, the larger the dot pitch, the more grainy the picture. Choose a monitor with a dot pitch of .28 or less.

The ***vertical refresh rate*** determines how frequently the screen is repainted from top to bottom. A rate that is too slow causes the screen to flicker because it is not being redrawn fast enough to fool the eye into seeing a constant pattern. A rate of 70Hz (70 cycles per second) is the minimum you should accept.

A ***noninterlaced monitor*** repaints every line whenever the electron gun moves down the screen. An interlaced monitor scans every other line; all even lines are drawn on the first pass and all odd lines on the next pass. An interlaced monitor is *unacceptable* in today's environment because the pixels have more time to fade and thus flicker is more common.

THE LOCAL BUS

The ***bus*** is the circuitry on the motherboard that provides the path by which data travels from one component to another. (The motherboard, or system board, is the main board within the system unit that holds the microprocessor, memory, and adapter cards.) All peripheral devices—including the hard disk, video display adapter, and printer—transmit data along the same bus. As you might expect, the more data that is traveling within the system, the more crowded the bus, and like any highway, bottlenecks will occur if traffic moves too slowly.

Older PCs used the ***ISA (Industry Standard Architecture)*** bus, which was 16 bits wide and ran at 8MHz. The ISA bus was sufficient in the early days of the PC with low-speed devices and low data requirements, but it proved inadequate in the Windows environment with its high graphic requirements. The constant need to refresh the screen, especially with displays that rendered 256 colors (or more), overwhelmed the ISA bus and slowed the overall system. The problem with the ISA bus is twofold—it runs at 8MHz (regardless of the speed of the microprocessor), and it fails to take advantage of the 32-bit path available with 80386 (and higher) microprocessors.

To solve the problem, the industry created a second bus called the ***video local bus (VLB),*** which is 32 bits wide and runs at the speed of the microprocessor. Equally important, the VLB bus connects the microprocessor directly to the video display adapter, which no longer has to share the ISA bus with other devices.

Think of the new bus as a super highway where traffic goes directly from one place to another, with a higher speed limit (the speed of the microprocessor versus 8MHz), and has twice as many lanes (32 bits versus 16) as previously.

Intel has recently designed the PCI bus in conjunction with the Pentium processor. Either a VLB or PCI bus is standard on today's machines, and you should not consider a system without one or the other. Both designs also support other high-speed devices (e.g., a fixed disk). Look for a system that offers multiple local bus slots on the motherboard.

PRINTERS

Printers vary greatly in terms of design, price, and capability, with dot matrix, ink jet, and laser printers the most common in today's environment. The type of printer you choose depends on your budget and the quality of output you require.

A ***dot matrix printer*** represents the oldest technology and is the least expensive. These printers produce an image on paper by driving a series of small pins against a ribbon. They create letters, numbers, symbols, and/or graphics out of a series of dots, and can print any shape at all depending on the accompanying software. The disadvantage to a dot matrix printer is the less than perfect print quality since its characters are formed as a pattern of dots. The introduction of the 24-pin print head (in place of the 9-pin version used in earlier models) has improved the quality of output but has done nothing to reduce the noise level.

The ***inkjet printer*** offers improved speed and print quality over a dot matrix printer. It is also quiet since the ink is squirted onto the page rather than hammered onto it as with the dot matrix. The purchase price is slightly higher than a dot matrix printer, but it is well worth the investment.

Laser printers are the top-of-the-line devices, and have created new expectations in terms of print quality, speed, and quietness of operation. They produce consistently dense characters and graphics, suitable for both reports and presentations. The resolution of a laser printer is measured in dots per inch (dpi). Laser printer speed is measured in pages per minute (ppm). Entry-level laser printers at 600 dpi and 4 ppm are available for approximately $600 in today's environment.

FAX/MODEM

A ***modem*** connects your computer to the outside world, be it an information service such as Prodigy or CompuServe, or your friend two blocks away. All means of data communications process data in its most elementary form, as a series of electronic pulses represented numerically as ***bits*** (***bi***nary digi***ts***). Every message transmitted by a computer, be it words, numbers, or pictures, is broken down into a series of 1s and 0s, which are sent over the transmission medium. The telephone uses an analog signal, whereas a computer uses a digital signal and thus some type of conversion is necessary.

Modulation is the process of converting a digital signal to an analog one; demodulation is the reverse process. A modem (derived from the combination of modulate and demodulate) performs both functions. On the transmitting end, a modem converts binary signals (1s and 0s) produced by the computer to analog signals, which can be sent over the telephone system. On the receiving end, the modem converts the analog signal from the telephone back to a digital signal, which is forwarded to the computer or peripheral device.

The speed of a modem—that is, the maximum rate at which it can transmit or receive data—is measured in ***bits per second (bps).*** A 14,400 bps modem is standard in today's environment. A 28,800 bps modem is more expensive but will return savings in the form of lower communications costs as you will be transmitting for shorter periods of time. A *fax/modem* combines the functions of a modem and a fax machine into a single card and is our recommendation for you.

CD-ROM

The data on a compact disk can be read, but it cannot be erased, hence the name ***CD-ROM,*** for Compact Disk/Read Only Memory. A single CD-ROM holds approximately 650MB of data, making it an ideal medium for the mass distribution of data and absolutely essential for multimedia applications.

The performance of a CD-ROM is measured by two parameters, access time and transfer rate. ***Access time*** is the average time to find a specific item (the smaller, the better). ***Transfer rate*** is the amount of data that is read every second (the higher, the better).

The first CD-ROM drives for the PC had access times of approximately 600 milliseconds (ms) and transfer rates of approximately 150KB per second. As with all technology, both parameters have improved significantly, giving rise to double-speed and quadruple-speed devices. A double-speed drive (300 ms access time and 300KB/sec transfer rate) is standard in today's environment. Quadruple-speed devices (150 ms access time and 600 KB/second transfer rate) are becoming increasingly common.

AUDIO

The standard PC comes with a simple speaker that is capable of little more than a beep, which you hear when you press the wrong key. True sound requires the installation of a sound card and the availability of speakers. A microphone is necessary if you want to record your own sound.

A ***sound card*** has two basic functions—to play a previously recorded sound and to record a new sound. Thus every sound card contains (a minimum of) two chips. One chip converts the sound from a microphone to a digital form the PC can store on disk. The second chip works in reverse and translates a digital file into sound. More sophisticated (and more expensive) ***audio cards*** include additional capabilities, such as voice recognition, that enable you to talk to your computer and have it respond to your commands.

If you intend to run multimedia applications, look for a sound card that supports wave table synthesis (as opposed to older cards that used a technique known as FM synthesis). A wave table produces higher-quality musical notes because it stores samples of actual instruments, then uses those samples to reproduce the music. And don't forget the speakers. No matter how good your sound card, you will be disappointed if you don't have a correspondingly good pair of speakers.

RESOLUTION AND SAMPLING RATE

The specifications of a sound card include its resolution and maximum sampling rate. The resolution is the number of bits (binary digits) used to store each sample. The more bits, the better. Eight-bit cards are obsolete, making 16-bit sound today's standard. The sampling rate is the number of samples per second and is measured in KHz (thousands of samples a second). The higher the sampling rate, the better. CD-quality recording and playback requires a sampling rate of 44KHz.

A GUIDE TO SMART SHOPPING

The purchase of a computer should be approached in much the same way as any other big-ticket item and requires similar research and planning. First and foremost, do not walk into a computer store without some idea of your hardware requirements, or you will spend too much or buy the wrong system. Know the technical specifications in advance, in order to ask intelligent questions about the various brands and systems. Stick to your requirements and don't be swayed to a different item if the vendor is out of stock. You've waited this long to buy a computer and another week or two won't matter.

The best place to start is often the university's computer center, which may allow a local vendor or manufacturer(s) to maintain a store on the premises. The university will use its buying power to secure a favorable price or educational discount, and the promise of additional business guarantees continuing service and support. In addition, people you know will purchase similar equipment, which means additional sources of help later on. Alternatively, you may consider the retail store (be it local or part of a national chain) or mail order. Either or both may be appropriate, and you may avail yourself of both sources, at different times and for different equipment.

> **CHECK OUT A NOTEBOOK BEFORE YOU BUY**
>
> The purchase of a notebook computer has additional considerations beyond those of a desktop configuration—weight, size, battery life, keyboard, and screen. Is the computer light enough so that you won't leave it behind when you travel? Is the life of the battery sufficient to accomplish what you need to do? Can you type comfortably on the keyboard over long periods of time? Is the screen readable in different levels of light? Is the hard disk large enough to accommodate all of your applications? Does it have a modem so that you can communicate when you take the machine on the road? Be sure to see the machine and test it before you buy so that you won't be disappointed later.

Mail order will almost always offer better prices than a retail establishment, but price should not be the sole consideration. Local service and support are also important, especially if you are a nontechnical new user. A little research, however, and you can purchase through the mail with confidence, and save yourself money in the process. A good way to choose a vendor, mail-order or retail, is to ask your friends where they purchased their systems, because a satisfied customer is always the best recommendation.

If you buy by mail, confirm all orders in writing, stating exactly what you are expecting to receive and when. Include the specific brands and/or model numbers and the agreed-upon price, including shipping and handling, to have documentation in the event of a dispute. State that the seller is not to deviate from the terms in your letter without prior written agreement.

Look for a steady advertising history by the mail-order firm, searching back issues of the magazine to see if the company has been in business over time. Avoid companies that appear to be in financial difficulty; for example, a company that previously ran four-page full-color ads and now runs a half-page, black-and-white advertisement. Check out service in advance, by calling the toll-free technical support number to determine the level of service you can expect. You might also inquire about the cost of on-site service. If you buy locally, try to choose a vendor with an on-site facility.

Pay with a credit card that offers a buyer protection plan to double the manufacturer's warranty (up to an additional year). The use of a credit card also gives you additional leverage if you are dissatisfied with an item. If you are purchasing by mail, make sure the charge is not entered until you receive the merchandise. Do not buy from anyone, retail store or mail order, that insists all sales are final, that offers a store credit in lieu of a refund, or that charges a restocking fee on returned items. Settle for nothing less than a no-strings-attached, 30-day, money-back guarantee, and be sure the vendor guarantees in writing a rebate if the price goes down within 30 days.

Make bundling (unbundling) work for you by obtaining credit for substituted items—for example, a name-brand monitor in place of the vendor's off-brand monitor, which often sacrifices quality for price. Software bundling may or may not be a good deal; for example, Windows should be included, but you may not need the application software; ask for credit if you don't take it. Conversely, bundled software may be a good deal if you don't already have the application.

Our experience has been that the vast majority of dealers, both retail and mail order, are reputable; but as with any purchase, *caveat emptor*. Good luck and good shopping.

BE KIND TO YOURSELF

Are you the type of person who will spend thousands on a new computer, only to set it up on your regular desk and sit on a $10 bridge chair? Don't. A conventional desk (or the dining room table) is 30 inches high, but the recommended typing height is 27 inches. The difference accounts for the stiff neck, tight shoulders, and aching backs reported by many people who sit at a computer over an extended period of time. Be kind to yourself and include a computer table with lots of room as well as a comfortable chair in your budget. Proper lighting is essential.

SUMMARY

The open design of the PC enabled companies other than IBM to build a functionally equivalent PC-compatible; IBM today has only ten percent of the market it was so instrumental in creating. Intel and Microsoft, IBM's original partners, continue to dominate their respective areas.

The capability of a PC is determined by the microprocessor on which it is based. The relative performances of the various Intel microprocessors are provided in Figure 2.

The more memory in a system, the better its overall performance; we recommend a minimum of 8MB. The best advice regarding a hard disk is to buy one larger than you think you need; a 350 MB hard disk is our suggested minimum, but larger disks are well worth the investment.

The resolution of a system is the number of pixels displayed on the monitor; the higher the resolution, the greater the detail and the larger the supporting monitor should be. The performance of the video adapter can be improved significantly with an accelerator card.

The ISA (Industry Standard Architecture) bus is 16 bits wide, runs at 8MHz, and is shared by all peripheral devices. The video local bus (VLB) is 32 bits wide, runs at the speed of the microprocessor, and is dedicated to the video display adapter.

The purchase of a computer should be approached in much the same way as any other "big-ticket" item. Mail order will almost always offer better prices than a retail establishment, but local service and support may outweigh price considerations for first-time buyers.

The price of software must be included in the budget for a computer system. A software suite, purchased at an educational discount through the university bookstore, is generally your best bet.

The purchase of a laptop computer has additional considerations beyond those of a desktop configuration: weight, size, battery life, keyboard, and screen.

OUR RECOMMENDATION

As technology continues to advance, yesterday's top-of-the-line system has become today's entry-level computer. We recommend, therefore, that you settle for nothing less than an entry-level Pentium processor with 8MB of RAM, a 500MB hard disk, quad-speed CD-ROM with 16-bit sound card, a 15-inch monitor with .28 dot pitch, and a 14,400 bps modem. If your budget can stand it, go beyond this configuration to buy a faster CPU, more memory, and a larger disk drive.

KEY WORDS AND CONCEPTS

- Access time
- Audio card
- Bit
- Bits per second (bps)
- Bus
- Byte
- CD-ROM
- Clock speed
- Dot matrix printer
- Dot pitch
- Double-density disk
- Expansion card
- Expansion slot
- Fax/modem card
- Floppy disk
- Hard disk
- High-density drive
- Inkjet printer
- Intel Corporation
- Intel CPU performance index
- ISA (Industry Standard Architecture)
- Kilobyte (KB)
- Laser printer
- Local bus
- Megabyte (MB)
- Megahertz (MHz)
- Memory
- Microprocessor
- Microsoft Corporation
- Modem
- Noninterlaced monitor
- PC-compatible
- Pixel
- Random access memory (RAM)
- RAM
- Resolution
- Sound card
- Super VGA
- Transfer rate
- Vertical refresh rate
- VGA
- Video adapter

A PC BUYING GUIDE

THE INTERNET AND WORLD WIDE WEB

OVERVIEW

The Internet. You read about it in magazines such as *Time* or *Newsweek*. Television programs provide their Internet addresses so they can be contacted by viewers. You use e-mail to communicate with your friends at other universities. The media make continual references to the Information Highway. But what exactly is the Internet and how does a message or file get from one computer to another?

This appendix provides basic information about the Internet, what it is, and how it works. It describes the World Wide Web and the underlying concept of hypertext and hypermedia. The appendix also includes an introduction to Mosaic and Netscape, the powerful Windows-based tools that brought ease-of-use to the Internet and, more than any other piece of software, are responsible for the explosion of interest in the Internet and World Wide Web.

E-MAIL AND THE INTERNET

E-mail is indeed a powerful means of communication, but it is only one of many services provided through the Internet. If you have never used e-mail, ask your instructor about using e-mail in conjunction with this class. If you are already familiar with e-mail, but do not use the Internet in any other way, you are in for a treat as you move through this appendix.

THE INTERNET

The *Internet* is a network of networks that connects computers across the country and around the world. It grew out of a government project that began in 1969 to test the feasibility of a network where scientists and military personnel could share messages and data no matter where they were. The government imposed the additional requirement that the experimental network be able to function with partial outages in times of national emergency, when one or more computers were down.

The proposed solution was to create a network with no central authority. Each node would be equal to all other nodes, with the ability to originate, pass, and receive messages. The path that a particular message took in getting to its destination would be insignificant. Only the final result was important as the message would be passed from node to node until it arrived at its destination.

The experiment was (to say the least) successful. Known originally as the **ARPAnet** (Advanced Research Projects Agency), the original network of four computers grew exponentially to include thousands of computers at virtually every major university and government agency, and an ever-increasing number of private corporations. To say that the Internet is large is a gross understatement, but by its very nature, it's impossible to say just how large the Internet really is. (One commonly accepted estimate is 25 million users.) The Internet is not a single network, but a collection of networks. How many networks there are, and how many users are connected to those networks, is of no importance as long as you yourself have access.

Unlike an ordinary network, such as the LAN you may be connected to at school, there is no single computer (or server) that controls the Internet. There is, however, a requirement that any computer connected to the Internet follow a uniform **protocol** (set of rules) that specifies how data is to be sent. That agreement, and the adoption of the Transmission Control Protocol/Internet Protocol (or TCP/IP), has led to the global network of interconnected computers we know as the Internet.

Each institution that maintains a node on the Internet is responsible for supporting and administering that node. The National Science Foundation, however, maintains the backbone of the Internet, which consists of a series of super computers that provide long distance communications links across the country.

THE INTERNET IS NOT FREE

The fact that there is no "Internet Incorporated" to collect a usage fee has given many people the mistaken idea that the Internet is free. The Internet is not free, although you may be lucky enough to have free access through your school or university, which has elected not to pass the cost on to you. The computers that make up the Internet cost money, and each node (e.g., your university) must pay its own way by funding its own network connection. The US taxpayer also funds the backbone of the Internet through the NSFNet (National Science Foundation Network) that provides the long distance communication links.

How It Works

The postal system provides a good analogy of how (but certainly not how fast) information travels across the Internet.[1] (E-mail is infinitely faster than "snail-mail.") When you mail a letter, you drop it in a mailbox, where it is picked up with a lot of other letters and delivered to the local post office. The letters are sorted and sent on their way to a larger post office or substation, where the letters are sorted again, until eventually each letter reaches the post office closest to

---

[1]Krol, Ed, *The Whole Internet,* O'Reilly and Associates, Inc., Sebastopol, CA, 1992, pages 24, 26.

its destination. The local mail carrier at the receiving post office then delivers each letter to its final destination.

There is no direct connection between the origin and destination because it is impossible to connect every pair of cities within the United States. If you were to send a letter from Coral Springs, Florida, to Englewood Cliffs, New Jersey, the post office would not charter a plane from Coral Springs to Englewood Cliffs. Instead it would route the letter from one substation to the next, making a new decision at each substation—for example, from Coral Springs, to Miami, to Newark, to Englewood Cliffs.

Each postal substation considers all of the routes it has available to the next substation and makes the best possible decision according to the prevailing conditions. This means that the next time you mail a letter from Coral Springs, Florida, to Englewood Cliffs, New Jersey, the letter may travel a completely different path. If the mail truck from Coral Springs to Miami had already left or was full to capacity, the letter could be routed through Fort Lauderdale to New York City and then to Englewood Cliffs. It really doesn't matter because your only concern is that the letter arrive at its final destination.

The Internet works the same way, as data travels across the Internet through several levels of networks until it gets to its destination. E-mail messages arrive at the local post office (the host computer) from a remote PC (connected by modem), or from a node on a local area network. The messages then leave the local post office and pass through a more powerful computer (known as a router) that connects the networks on the Internet to one another.

A message may pass through several networks to get to its destination. Each network has its own router that determines how best to move the message closer to its destination, taking into account the traffic on the network. A message passes from one network to the next, until it arrives at the local area network on the other end, from where it can be sent to its final destination. The process is depicted graphically in Figure 1.

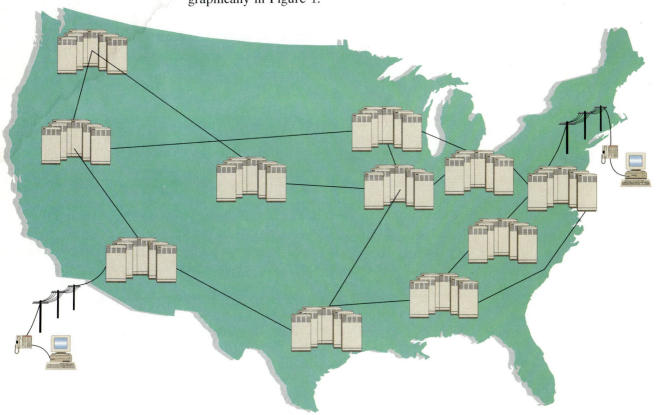

FIGURE 1   The Internet

The TCP/IP Protocol

Let's pretend for a moment that the Post Office no longer accepted packages and that you wanted to send a book to your friend across the country. Your only alternative would be to rip the pages out of the book, put each page in its own envelope, mail the individual envelopes, then trust in your friend to open the envelopes and put the book back together. That may sound awkward, but that is a truer picture of how the Internet works.

Information is sent across the Internet in *packets,* with each packet limited in size. The rules for creating and sending the packets are specified by the *TCP/IP protocol* (Transmission Control Protocol/Internet Protocol) that governs the flow of data across the Internet. The TCP portion divides the file that you want to send into pieces, then numbers each piece so that the message can be reconstructed at the other end. The IP portion addresses each packet by specifying the address of the sending and receiving computer so that the routers will be able to do their job.

Why, you might ask, are files divided into packets rather than being sent in their entirety? The answer has to do with ensuring that data is transmitted correctly. Static or noise on a telephone line is merely annoying to people having a conversation, but devastating when a file (especially a computer program) is transmitted and a byte or two is garbled. The larger the file being sent, the greater the chance that noise will be introduced and that the file will be corrupted. Sending the data in smaller pieces (packets), and verifying that the packets were received correctly, helps ensure the integrity of the data.

The Internet is built in layers that revolve around the TCP/IP protocol. At the sending computer, the application layer creates the message and passes it to the TCP layer, where the message is divided into packets. The packets are addressed at the IP layer, then sent across the Internet over the hardware layer (the various levels of networks through which the data must travel to get to its destination). The process is reversed at the receiving computer. The IP layer receives the individual packets, then passes the packets up to the TCP layer, where they are reassembled and sent to the application layer to display the message.

Connecting to the Internet

The way in which you are connected to the Internet is of little concern as long as you can do what you want to do. There are, however, different ways to connect, and the distinction becomes important when you are connecting for the first time—for example, when you are setting up a home computer.

A full (dedicated) *TCP/IP connection* connects directly to the Internet over a high-speed transmission line 24 hours a day. This is the most powerful (and by far the most expensive) type of connection and is suitable only for universities and large corporations. A TCP/IP connection makes the site a node on the Internet and provides each workstation at that site with full Internet access. Anything that can happen between networked computers can occur at any workstation. You can run client/server software such as Mosaic or Netscape, and you can download files directly onto your workstation.

The best way to access the Internet at home is through a *SLIP* or *PPP connection,* which is obtained through a local service provider. This type of connection provides direct access to all Internet services over a high-speed modem (14,400 bps or higher), but is significantly slower than a full TCP/IP connection. It does, however, enable you to download files directly onto your computer, and to run graphic client/server software such as Mosaic or Netscape.

A simple dial-up account is less expensive than a SLIP or PPP connection. It is also a more limited type of connection in that your PC functions as a "dumb terminal" of the host computer, which prevents you from running client/server software. Nor can you download a file directly to your computer since your computer is not known to the Internet. Instead, the file is saved first on the host computer. Then you must go through the extra step of downloading from the host to your computer. Nevertheless, you have access to basic Internet services (e.g., e-mail), and hence it might be all you need.

> **CONNECTING TO THE INTERNET**
>
> Your school or university probably has an Internet connection, in which case all you have to do is ask your instructor for information on how to access the connection. You can also obtain Internet access through the Microsoft Network or through other services such as America Online, Prodigy, or CompuServe.

THE DOMAIN NAME SYSTEM

Most people are introduced to the Internet through e-mail. You can send e-mail to anyone, anywhere in the world, as long as you have access to the Internet and you know the recipient's Internet address. The latter is developed through the **Domain Name System (DNS),** which ensures that every Internet address is unique.

The Internet divides its component networks into a series of domains that enable e-mail (and other files) to be sent across the network. Universities, for example, belong to the EDU domain. Government agencies are in the GOV domain. Commercial organizations (companies) are in the COM domain. Large domains are in turn divided into smaller domains, with each domain responsible for maintaining unique addresses in the next lower-level domain.

An *Internet address* consists of the username, the host computer, and the domain (or domains) by which the computer is connected to the Internet. President Clinton's e-mail address is PRESIDENT@WHITEHOUSE.GOV, where President is the username, Whitehouse is the host computer, and GOV is the domain. Vice President Gore may be reached at VICE-PRESIDENT@WHITEHOUSE.GOV. The President's domain and host computer are the same as the Vice President's. The only difference between the two addresses is the username, President and Vice-President, respectively.

THE WORLD WIDE WEB

The original language of the Internet was uninviting, to say the least. You needed a variety of esoteric programs (e.g., Telnet, FTP, Archie, and Gopher), which were derived from the UNIX operating system. You had to know the precise syntax of those programs. And even if you were able to get what you wanted, everything was communicated in plain text (graphics and sound were not available).

The *World Wide Web* was created in 1991 and introduced a new way to connect the resources on the Internet to one another. The Web is based on the technology of **hypertext** and **hypermedia,** which link computer-based documents in nonlinear fashion. Unlike a traditional document, that is read sequentially from top to bottom, a hypertext document includes links to other documents, which can be viewed (or not) at the reader's discretion. Hypermedia is similar in concept except that it provides links to graphic and video files in addition to text files.

Assume, for example, that you're reading a hypertext or hypermedia document about the American Revolution. You come to a reference to the Declaration of Independence, and rather than finishing the descriptive text, you can click a hypertext reference and be linked to the actual document. That in turn may contain a link to Thomas Jefferson or Benjamin Franklin, and those links may contain other links to other topics. You can choose to explore the link about Jefferson or you can go back to reading about the Revolution.

To explore the Web, you need a program called a **browser,** which requests files from various nodes on the Internet, then displays the hypertext (or hypermedia) documents on your computer. The first browsers were restricted to text, but were able to follow links from one document to another, even if the documents were on different computers. As users began to create other document types (images, sound, and video), the text browsers evolved naturally into a more powerful GUI tool.

Mosaic was the first Windows-based browser and it introduced point-and-click navigation to the Web. Today there are many different browsers from which to choose, but all browsers offer the same basic capabilities. We have chosen to focus on **Netscape,** a newer and more powerful browser than Mosaic. The discussion is sufficiently general to apply to other programs.

Netscape

A Windows browser, such as Netscape, is easy to use because it shares the common user interface and consistent command structure present in every Windows application. You already know several things about Netscape because of your basic understanding of Windows.

Consider, for example, Figure 2, which displays the Netscape home page. (The **home page** is the first document you see at a web site.) You should recognize several familiar elements, such as the title bar and the Minimize, Maximize (or Restore), and Close buttons. As with any other Windows application, commands are executed from pull-down menus or from command buttons that appear under the menu bar. A vertical and/or horizontal scroll bar appears if the entire document is not visible at one time.

The title bar displays the name of the document (Welcome to Netscape in Figure 2.). The document itself contains **hyperlinks** (graphic icons or underlined items) that point to other documents. The Netscape home page, for example, contains several hyperlinks (Escapes, Company & Products, and so on). Click any link and you are automatically presented with another document that displays the requested information. That document may contain links to other documents, which may take you to still other documents, at other sites anywhere on the Internet.

The location (or address) of a document appears in the location text box and is known as a **Uniform Resource Locator (URL).** The URL is the primary means of navigating the Web and indicates the **Web site** (computer) on which you are working. Change the URL (we describe how in the next section) and you change the document.

A URL address consists of several parts: the method of access, the computer (web site) where the document is located, the path (if any) to that document, and the file name. For example:

http://home.mcom.com/home/welcome.html

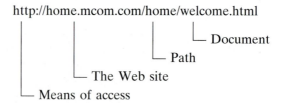

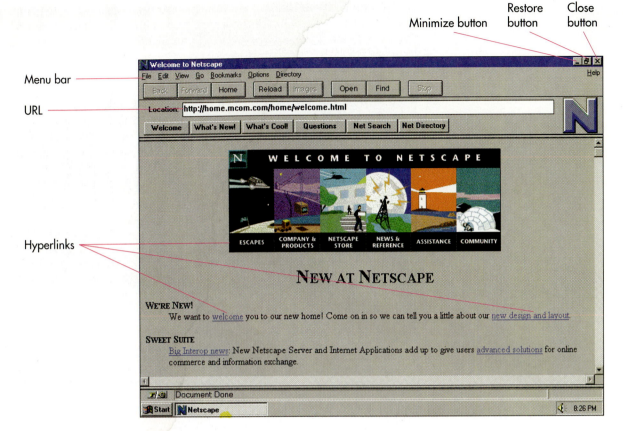

FIGURE 2 The Netscape Home Page

Most URL address begins with the letters ***http*** to indicate the HyperText Transfer Protocol that specifies the way web documents are requested and retrieved. Two slashes separate the means of access from the Web site (the address of the computer) on which the document is located. The information following the web site indicates the path on the computer to get to the document (e.g., home), and finally the document name (e.g., welcome.html).

To go to a particular site, enter its URL address through the Open URL command in the File menu. (You can also type the address directly in the Location text box.) Just enter the address and off you go.

WHAT IS HTML?

All Web documents are written in ***HTML*** (HyperText Markup Language). An HTML document consists of tags that describe how to display the text, hyperlinks, and multimedia elements within a document. The letters HTML appear at the end of many URL addresses to indicate this type of document.

Hypertext and Hypermedia

A web document contains hyperlinks to other documents that appear as underlined items or as graphic icons. Consider, for example, the hypermedia document in Figure 3. We began by choosing a Web site and entering its URL address (http://underground.net/oscarnet) in Figure 3a. (Yes, it helps to know various sites on the Web, and we suggest several sites in Table 1 on page 10.) Most of the time,

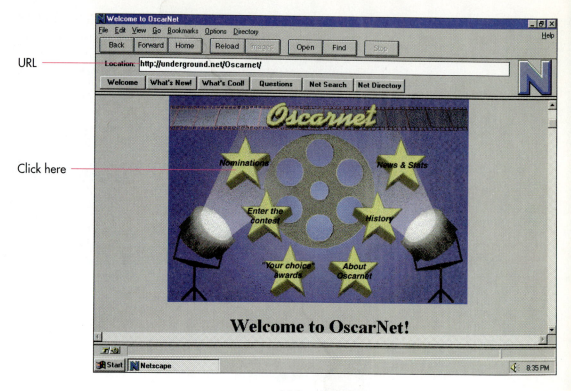

(a) Oscar Home Page

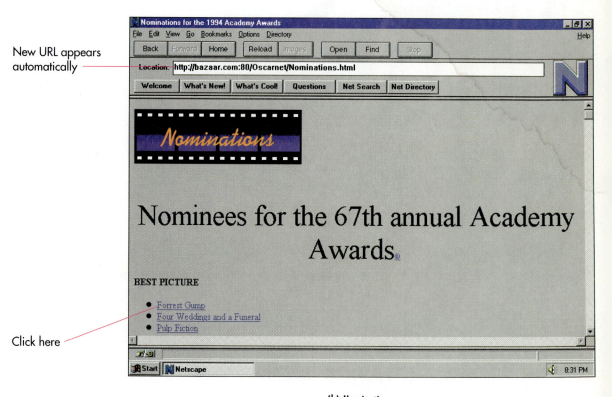

(b) Nominations

FIGURE 3   A Hypermedia Document

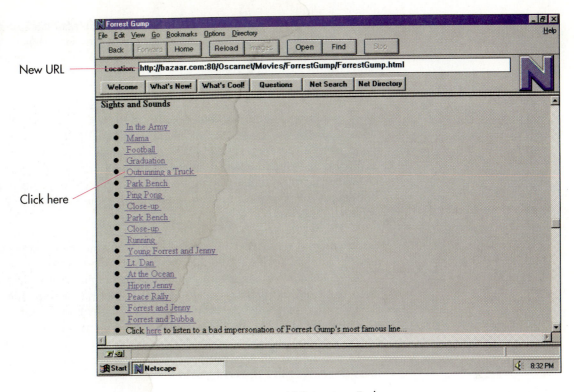

(c) Outrunning a Truck

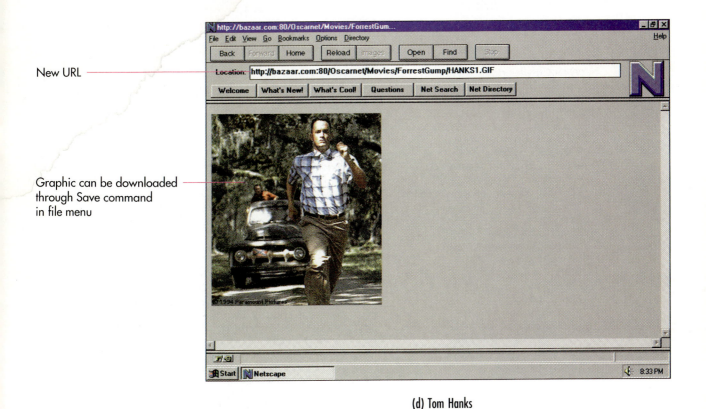

(d) Tom Hanks

FIGURE 3   A Hypermedia Document (continued)

however, you don't even have to enter the URL address, because Netscape is constantly suggesting sites to explore. And those sites may suggest other sites. The Oscarnet was in fact a "cool site" of the day (see Table 1) in March 1995, just prior to the Academy Awards.

The first document at a web site is known as a home page. Once you arrive at a home page (e.g., Figure 3a), click any link that interests you. We clicked on Nominations in Figure 3a, which took us to the document in Figure 3b. (The URL address in the location text box changes automatically to reflect the new document.) From there we clicked on Forrest Gump, which took us to the document in Figure 3c, which led to the picture in Figure 3d. There is no beginning (other than the starting point or home page) and no end. You simply read a hypermedia document in any way that makes sense to you, stopping to explore whatever topic you want to see next.

The World Wide Web is a "living document" that is constantly changing. The information at many sites is updated daily, and you never know just what you will find. We doubt, for example, that you will be able to retrieve the exact screens in Figure 3 because a new set of movies will be nominated for next year's Academy Awards. It doesn't matter, because you will always find something of interest.

Your exploration of the World Wide Web is limited only by your imagination. The What's Cool button suggests several interesting sites and is an excellent place to begin your exploration. Alternatively, you may begin with any of the sites listed in Table 1. Be sure you look at Bob Grauer's **home page** to download the data disks from the *Exploring Windows* series.

TABLE 1 Exploring the World Wide Web

Site	URL
Bob Grauer's Home Page	http://www.bus.miami.edu/~rgrauer
US Bureau of Census	http://www.census.gov
Web Crawler Home Page	http://webcrawler.cs.washington.edu/WebCrawler/WebQuery.html
Prentice Hall Home Page	http://www.prenhall.com
Microsoft Home Page	http://www.microsoft.com
Star Trek Home Page	http://voyager.paramount.com
Australian National University Art	http://rubens/anu.edu.au/
Map Viewer Home Page	http://pubweb.parc.xerox.com/map
Buena Vista Movie Plex	http://bvp.wdp.com/BVPM/MooVPlex.html
The Whole Internet Home Page	http://nearnet.gnn.com/gnn/wic/newrescat.toc.html
Movies and Television	http://alpha.acast.nova.edu/movies.html
Economy Markets and Investments	http://www.yahoo.com/Economy/Markets_and_Investments
Dow Jones Quote Server	http://www.secapl.com/cgi-bin/qs
JobWeb	http://www.risetime.com/risetime/preview.html
Planet Earth Home Page	http://white.nosc.mil/info_modern.html
Yahoo (Guide to the Web)	http://www.yahoo.com
White House	http://www.whitehouse.gov
Library of Congress	http://lcweb.loc.gov/homepage/lchp.html
Galaxy	http://www.einet.net/galaxy.html
Sports Schedules	http://www.cs.rochester.edu/u/ferguson/schedules/
Internet Movie Database	http://www.cm.cf.au.uk/Movies/Oscars.html
Underground Music Archive	http://sunsittee.unc.edu/IUMA
Travel and Tourist Information	http://www.digimark.net/rec-travel
Best of the Web Awards	http://wings.buffalo.edu/contest
GNN Best of the Net	http://nearnet.gnn.com/gnn/wic/best.toc.html
Cool Site of the Day	http://www.infi.net/cool.html
The Simpsons	http://www.digimark.net/TheSimpsons
Wide Web of Sports	http://tnswww.lcs.mit.edu/cgibin/sports
Ultimate TV List	http://cinenet.net.UTVL/utvl.html
Chocolate Lover's Page	http://www.ios.com/~mb/chocolate
Natural History	coast.http://ucmp1.berkeley.edu/welcome.html
Internet Business Center	http://www.tig.com/IBC/index.html

Index

A = Access   E = Excel   P = PowerPoint   W = Word

#NAME error, E122
#REF error, E108

A

Absolute reference, E44, E70, E97
  conversion to, E120
Accounting format, E56
Action items, P28–P30
Active cell, E7, E14–E15
Adding a record, A11–A12
Adding slides, P19
Agenda Wizard, W122–W123, W127–W128
Alignment, E57, W76–W77
Allow Zero Length property, A45
Alt+Tab shortcut, E179
AND condition, A108
Animating a presentation, P63–P70
Annotating a slide, P35–P36
Answer Wizard, E15, W24
Arial, W63, W64
Arrow tool, E157–E158
Ascending sequence. *See* Sort row
Assumptions, isolation of, E70, E72, E97
Asterisk, as record selector symbol, A5
Audience handouts, printing of, P36, P80
AutoComplete, E27
AutoContent Wizard, P50–P51
AutoCorrect, A12, P58, W28–W29, W35, W110, W147, W150
AutoFill command, E114, E116
AutoFormat, W110, W147, W150
AutoLayout, P18–P19, P20, P61
  changing of, P63
Automatic formatting, E63
Automatic replacement, W50
AutoNumber field, A43

AVERAGE function, E5, E107–E108
Avg function, A119
Award Wizard, W122–W123

B

Backup, A13, P34, W30, W32, W57
Background color, P72, P74, P78–P79
Background shading, P72
Bar chart, E143–E144
Best fit column width, E102
Between function, A110
Border property, A130
Border tab, E59
Borders and Shading command, W82–W83, W87
Borders toolbar, W87
Bound control, A55, A96
Breakpoint, E111
Build, P61–P62, P66
Bullet, indentation of, P21

C

Calculated control, A55, A63, A96, A120–A121
Calculated field, A42
Calendar Wizard, W122–W123
Caps Lock key, W3
  correction of, W28
Caption property, A45
Case insensitive replacement, W50
Case sensitive replacement, A14, W50
Category label, E140, E146
Cell, E4
Cell formulas, E7
  printing of, E28
Cell range, E43

noncontiguous, E65
Center across columns, E105
Chart, E139–E185
Chart sheet, E146
   moving and copying, E168
   renaming of, E164–E165
Chart toolbar, E150
Chart type, E140–E146, E148, E166
ChartWizard, E148–E149, E151–E152
Check box, on a form, A70
Clear command, E101
Client application, E171
Clip art, P21–P22, P63–P64, W129
Clipboard, E44, W49, W59
Close button, W5, W6
Close command, A13, E9, E17, P5
Collapsed outline, P48
Color, E65
Color scheme, P70–P72, P78
Column chart, E143–E146
Column command, E55
Column headings, E4–E5
   printing of, E21, E22
Column width, A122, E55, E62
   best fit, E102
Columnar report, A92
Combination chart, E182
Command button, on a form, A70, A74
Common user interface, A23, P4
Compacting a database, A130
Compound document, E171, W129
Constant, E5
Control, A55–A56
   aligning, A66, A75
   moving, A60, A64
   selecting, A59–A60, A126
   sizing, A60, A64
Copy command, E43–E44, E50–E52, E97, W49, W59
   shortcut for, W60
Count function, A119
COUNT function, E108
COUNTA function, E108
Counter field. *See* AutoNumber field
Courier New, W63, W64
Criteria row, A107–A110
   flexibility in, A113
Currency field, A43
Currency format, E56
Current record, A5
Custom dictionary, W26
   deletion from, W115
Custom format, E57
Custom series, creation of, E117
Cut command, E46, W49
   shortcut for, W60

D

Data, versus information, A92
Data disk, A6, A8, E13, P9, P10, W11
Data point, E140
Data series, E140
   formatting of, E159
   multiple, E160–E170
Data type, A43, A50
   effect on query criteria, A107
Data validation, A15, A21, A54
Database, A2
   compacting of, A130
   properties of, A117
Database window, A3–A4
Datasheet view, A4, A44
Date format, E56
Date function, A68
Date/Time field, A43
Default chart, E164
Default file location, E60
Default folder, changing of, A46, P31, W31
Default presentation, P54
Default value property, A45, A52
Delete command, A20, E18–E19, E24
Deleting text, W5, W22
   caution with, W49
Demote, within an outline, P48–P49, P56
Descending sequence. *See* Sort row
Description property, A104
Deselecting text, W5, W22
Design view
   form, A55–A56
   table, A4, A44
Destination range, E43
Detail section
   in a form, A57
   in a report, A94, A117
Dialog box, shortcuts for, W74
Docked toolbar, E154
Documents submenu, in Windows 95, A18, P75
Double clicking, W14
Drag and drop, W61
   in Outline view, P58
   in Slide Sorter view, P23–P24
Drawing toolbar, E8, E157–E158, P16
Drop cap, W140
Drop shadow, E59, W83, W140
Drop-down list box, on a form, A70
Dynaset, A105–A106, A124

E

Embedded chart, E146–E147, E153, E156
Embedded object, E172
ENIAC computer, W101

Envelopes and Labels command, W111, W118
Exit command, A13, E9, P5, P15
Expanded outline, P48
Exploded pie chart, E141, E143

F

Fax Cover Sheet Wizard, W122–W123
Field, A2, W110
Field code, W113
Field name, A4, A43
Field result, W113
Field row, A107
Field size property, A45, A52
Field width, changing of, A53
File location, default, E60
File menu, E9–E10, P5, P7, W8
File name, rules for, E9, P5, W8
File properties, P13
Fill handle, E98, E104
Find command, A14–A15, A19, W50, W59
   with formatting, W71
First line indent, W78
Floating toolbar, E154
Font, E58, W65
Footer, E21, E22, E29
Form, A4, A16
   opening of, A21
   properties of, A57
Form Design View, A55–A56
Form header, A67
Form View, A55–A56
Form Wizard, A57–A58, A60–A61
Formatting, E53–E59
Format Cells command, E55–E59
Format Font command, W65–W67
Format Frame command, E180, W131, W137
Format Object command, E154
Format painter, E64, W72, W73
Format Paragraph command, W80–W82
Format property, A45, A52
Formatting toolbar, A67, E7–E8, E74, P5–P6, W5, W7
Formula bar, E7, E14–E15
Fraction format, E56
Frame, W127
Freezing panes, E112–E114
Functions, A101
Function Wizard, E98–E99, E103
Function, E5, E106–E112
   versus formula, E108–E109

G

General format, E55–E56
GIGO (garbage in, garbage out), A15
Goal Seek command, E90–E91, E93–E94
Grammar check, W104, W106–W107
   customization of, W116–W117
Gridlines, printing of, E21, E22
Group footer, A94, A118, A127
Group header, A94, A117
Grouping records, A117–A130

H

Hanging indent, W78
Hard page break, W68
Hard return, W2, W13, W20
Header, E21, E22, E29
Help, W24
Help button, E73, P14
Hidden slide, P29, P31–P32
Horizontal ruler, W6
Horizontal scroll bar, E170

I

IF function, E109–E111, E119–E120
Illegal cell reference, E108
Indents, W76, W78, W86–W87
   increasing and decreasing, W88
Indexed property, A45
Information, versus data, A92
Inheritance, A72, A97
Initial conditions, isolation of, E70
In-place editing, W139
Input mask property, A45, A51
Input Mask Wizard, A51
Insert command, E18–E19, E25, E27
Insert Date and Time command, W110
Insert Frame command, W136
Insert mode, W4, W57
Insert Object command, W129–W133
Insert Symbol command, W110–W111
Insertion point, A5, P48–P49, W2

L

Label tool, A101–A102
Landscape orientation, E20, E29, W67
Landscape printing, A12–A13, A55
Leader character, W79
Left indent, W76

Legend, with multiple data series, E162
Line chart, E181, E182
Line spacing, W79
   shortcut for, W86
Linked object, E172
Long filenames, E48
Lookup Wizard, A70

M

Magnification. *See* Zoom control box
Many-to-many relationship, A28
Margins, changing of, E20, E22, W73
Max function, A119, E107–E108
Maximize button, W5, W6, W12
Meeting Minder, P28, P33, P69
Memo field, A43
Menu bar, P4
Microsoft ClipArt Gallery, W129–W131, W134–W137
Microsoft Fax Accessory, W126
Microsoft toolbar, E173
Microsoft WordArt, W131–W133, W138–W139
Min function, A119, E107–E108
Minimize button, W5, W6
Mixed reference, E44
   conversion to, E120
Module, A4
Monospaced typeface, W65
Move operation, E44–E46
Multiple data series, E160–E170
Multitasking, E172

N

Name box, E7
New Record button, A11
New Slide button, P4
Noncontiguous range, selecting of, E65
Normal view, W16–W17, W53
NOT function, A110
Notes Pages view, P16–P17, P27
Number field, A43
Number format, E56

O

Object linking and embedding (OLE), E171–E180, W133
Object, E171, W129
Objects, names for, A121
OLE field, A43
One-to-many relationship, A26
Open command, E9–E10, E13–E14, P5, P7, P10–P11, W8–W9, W18–W19
   shortcuts for, P20, P31
Option group, on a form, A70, A72–A73
OR condition, A108
Outline, printing of, P80
Outline toolbar, P49, P56
Outline view, P16–P17, P24–P25, P48–P50
Overtype mode, W4, W57

P

Page break, W67–W68
Page footer, A94, A118
Page header, A94, A117
Page Layout view, W16–W17, W53–W54
Page Setup command, A55, A77, E20–E22, E29, E67, W67–W68, W73
Paper, selection of, W101
Paragraph formatting, W76–W90
Paste command, E44, E46, E177, W49, W59
   shortcut for, W60
Paste Link command, E174, E177
Paste Special command, E174, E177
Patterns tab, E59
Pen tool. *See* Annotating a slide
Pencil, as record selector symbol, A5
Percentage format, E56
Pie chart, E141–E143
Placeholders, P18–P19
PMT function, E89–E90, E92, E95–E97
Point size, W65
Pointing, E98
Portrait orientation, E20, W67
Primary key, A4, A43–A44
   changing of, A50
Print command, E9, E17, P5, P15, W15
Print preview, A100, A102, E22, E30
Promote, within an outline, P48–P49, P56
Property sheet, A57–A58, A64–A65
Proportional typeface, W65

Q

QBE grid, A108–A109
Query, A4, A17, A105–A116
   running of, A24
Query by example, A105
Query window, A105–A107

R

Range. *See* Cell range
Record, A2
   adding of, A11–A12
   saving of, A11
Record selector symbol, A5, A20
Redo command, P24, W49, W60
Rehearse Timings, P28–P29, P32
Relational database, A25–A28
Relational operators, A109, E110
Relative reference, E44, E70, E97
   conversion to, E120
Replace command, A14–A15, A23, W50, W58–W59
   with formatting, W71
Report, A4, A17, A92–A104, A114–A117
   properties of, A129
   sections in, A94
Report footer, A94, A118, A128
Report header, A94, A117
Report Wizard, A94–A95, A98–A99
Required property, A45, A52
Restore button, W5
Résumé Wizard, W120–W121
Right indent, W76
Row command, E55
Row headings, E4–E5
   printing of, E21, E22
Row height, E55, E62
Ruler, W6

S

Sans serif typeface, W63
Save As command, E11, E23, P8, P12, W28–W29, W32
Save command, E9–E10, P5, P7, W8–W9, W13–W14
Scenario Manager, E114, E122–E125
Scientific format, E56
Scroll bar, E116, P4
Scrolling, E112–E113, W51–W53
   mouse versus keyboard, W57, W58
Select query, A105
Selecting text, with F8 key, W84
Selection bar, W69
Selection criteria, A108–A110
Selective replacement, W50
Select-then-do, E55, P22–P23, W48
Serif typeface, W63
Server application, E171
Shading, E59
Shortcut menu, E28, E164, W48, W70
Show row, A107, A112–A113
Show/Hide ¶ button, W13
Simple Query Wizard, A110
Sizing handle, E146, W131, W137
Slide elevator, P25
Slide Layout button, P4
Slide master, P72, P74, P77
Slide Navigator, P30, P34–P35, P60
Slide show, creation of, P61–P70
Slide Show view, P14, P26
Slide Sorter toolbar, P62
Slide Sorter view, P16–P17, P24–P25
Slide view, P16–P17, P25
Soft page break, W68
Soft return, W2
Sort row, A107, A112–A113
   with multiple fields, A120
Sorting and Grouping command, A102, A126–A127
Source range, E43
Special format, E57
   for social security number, E66, E117
Spell check, E91, E100–E101, P57, W26–W28, W32, W34
   customization of, W113
Stacked columns, E160, E161
   improper use of, E184–E185
Standard format, A107
Standard toolbar, E7–E8, P5–P6, W5, W7
Statistical functions, E107–E108, E122
Status bar, E7, P4, W6
Style checker, P73, P75–P76
Sum function, A119, E108–E109
Summary information, W25
System info command button, A12, E17

T

Tab order, A76
Table, A2, A4–A6
   creation of, A45–A55
   design of, A40–A42
   moving in, A9–A11
   opening of, A9
   printing of, A12
Table Design view, A4
Table Wizard, A43, A47–A49
Tabs, W79–W80
Tabular report, A92
Taskbar, E174
Tech support, A12
Technical support, E17
Template, E88, P50–P52, P59, P68, W120
Text box, creation of, E150
Text box tool, A127
Text field, A43
Text format, E56
Thesaurus, W104, W105, W115
Time format, E56

Times New Roman, W63, W64
Tip of the Day, P10, W17, W20
TipWizard, E6, E46, E53, E101
  resetting of, E47, W17–W18, W20
Toggle switch, W3
Toolbar, E7–E8, E25, W5, W7, W17, W19
  customization of, W119
  fixed versus floating, A61
  missing, A74, A102
Toolbox toolbar, A102
ToolTip, A25, E7, P50, W21
Top Values property, A123
Transition effects, P61–P62, P65
Transparencies, template for, P72
Triangle, as record selector symbol, A5
Type size, W65
Type style, W65
Typeface, W63–W64
Typography, W63–W67

U

Unbound control, A55, A96
Undo command, A20, A63, E16, E25, P24, W23, W49, W60

V

Validation rule property, A45, A52
Validation text property, A45, A52
Valuepack, on CD-ROM, P22
Vertical ruler, W6
View buttons, P4

View menu, W17, W19, W53–W54, W56
Views, P16–P17
VLOOKUP function, E111–E112, E120

W

Whole word replacement, W50
Widows and orphans, W81–W82
Wild card, A110
Windows 95, introduction to, A7
Windows 95, tour of, W10
Windows 95, Welcome to, E12–E13, P8–P9
Wizard, W120–W129
Word wrap, W2
WordPerfect, conversion from, W17
Workbook, E6, E7
Worksheet, E6
Worksheet tab, renaming of, E164–E165

Y

Yes/No field, A43

Z

Zoom command, W53–W54
Zoom control box, P66